THE NEW ATLAS OF WORLD HISTORY

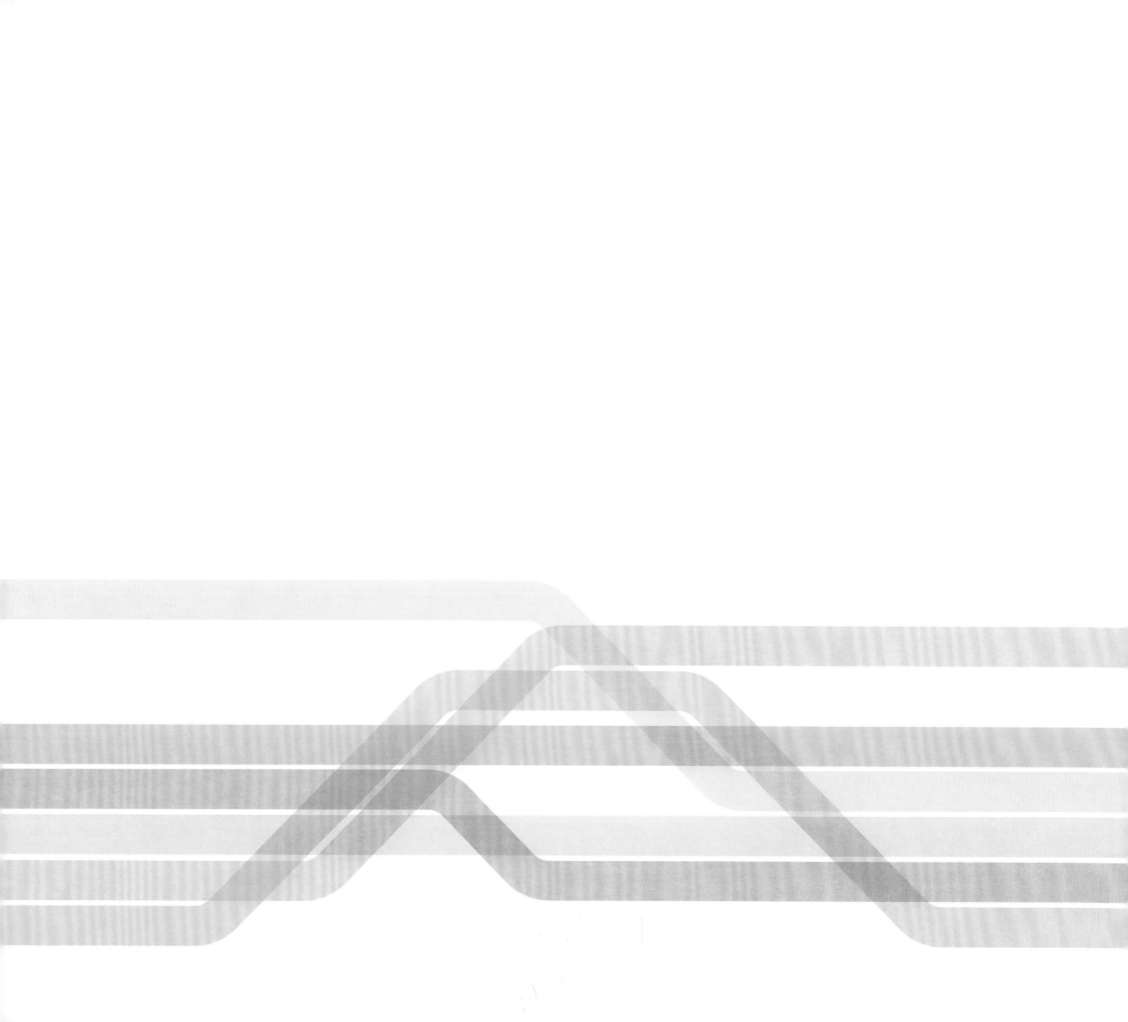

THE NEW ATLAS OF
WORLD HISTORY

Global Events at a Glance

JOHN HAYWOOD

With 433 illustrations and 56 maps

Thames & Hudson

Contents

How to Use this Book

The atlas consists of 49 chronologically organized political maps, each followed by a timeline, together with six more specialized maps displaying world religions, writing systems, trade routes or migrations at a particular date. All maps are somewhat stylized to give graphic emphasis to salient features. For any given year the reader may like to study the political map with its introductory text, noting for instance how the geographical extent of more complex societies has increased from the previous map. The timeline on the following two pages then yields information on the specific events and developments in the world's cultural evolution during the years, decades or centuries leading up to the highlighted year in question. Each timeline is illustrated with works of art and monuments from that era. Further background information about particular peoples, cultures and nations shown on the maps or mentioned in the introductory texts and timelines can be found in the reference section at the end of the book.

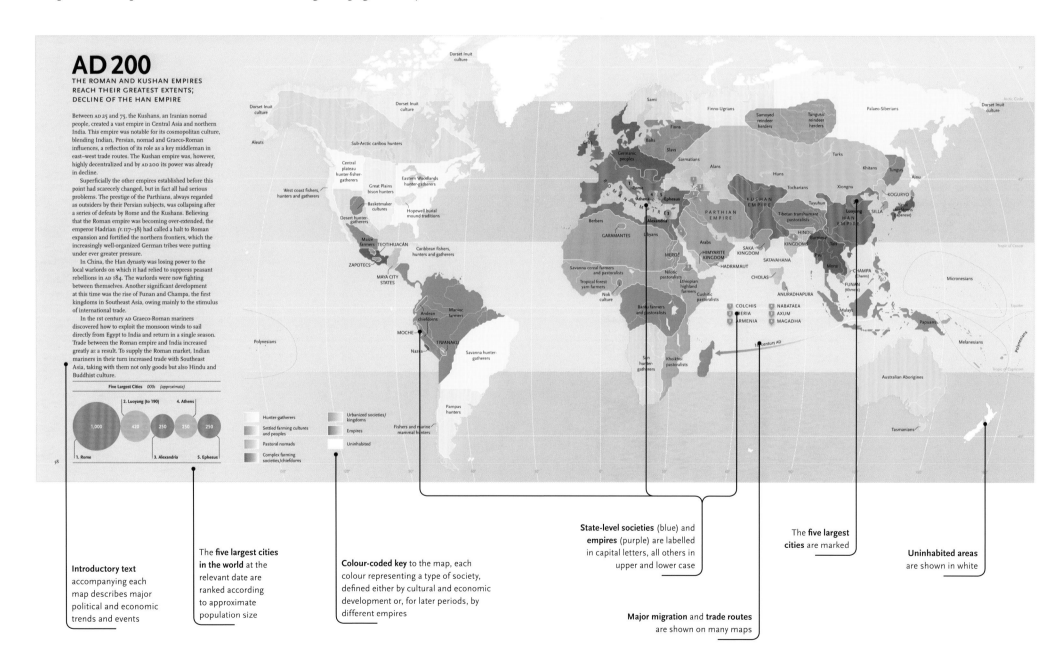

AD 200

THE ROMAN AND KUSHAN EMPIRES
REACH THEIR GREATEST EXTENTS;
DECLINE OF THE HAN EMPIRE

Between AD 25 and 75, the Kushans, an Iranian nomad people, created a vast empire in Central Asia and northern India. This empire was notable for its cosmopolitan culture, blending Indian, Persian, nomad and Graeco-Roman influences, a reflection of its role as a key middleman in east–west trade routes. The Kushan empire was, however, highly decentralized and by AD 200 its power was already in decline.

Superficially the other empires established before this point had scarcely changed, but in fact all had serious problems. The prestige of the Parthians, always regarded as outsiders by their Persian subjects, was collapsing after a series of defeats by Rome and the Kushans. Believing that the Roman empire was becoming over-extended, the emperor Hadrian (r. 117–38) had called a halt to Roman expansion and fortified the northern frontiers, which the increasingly well-organized German tribes were putting under ever greater pressure.

In China, the Han dynasty was losing power to the local warlords on which it had relied to suppress peasant rebellions in AD 184. The warlords were now fighting between themselves. Another significant development at this time was the rise of Funan and Champa, the first kingdoms in Southeast Asia, owing mainly to the stimulus of international trade.

In the 1st century AD Graeco-Roman mariners discovered how to exploit the monsoon winds to sail directly from Egypt to India and return in a single season. Trade between the Roman empire and India increased greatly as a result. To supply the Roman market, Indian mariners in their turn increased trade with Southeast Asia, taking with them not only goods but also Hindu and Buddhist culture.

Introductory text accompanying each map describes major political and economic trends and events

The **five largest cities in the world** at the relevant date are ranked according to approximate population size

Colour-coded key to the map, each colour representing a type of society, defined either by cultural and economic development or, for later periods, by different empires

State-level societies (blue) and **empires** (purple) are labelled in capital letters, all others in upper and lower case

Major migration and **trade routes** are shown on many maps

The **five largest cities** are marked

Uninhabited areas are shown in white

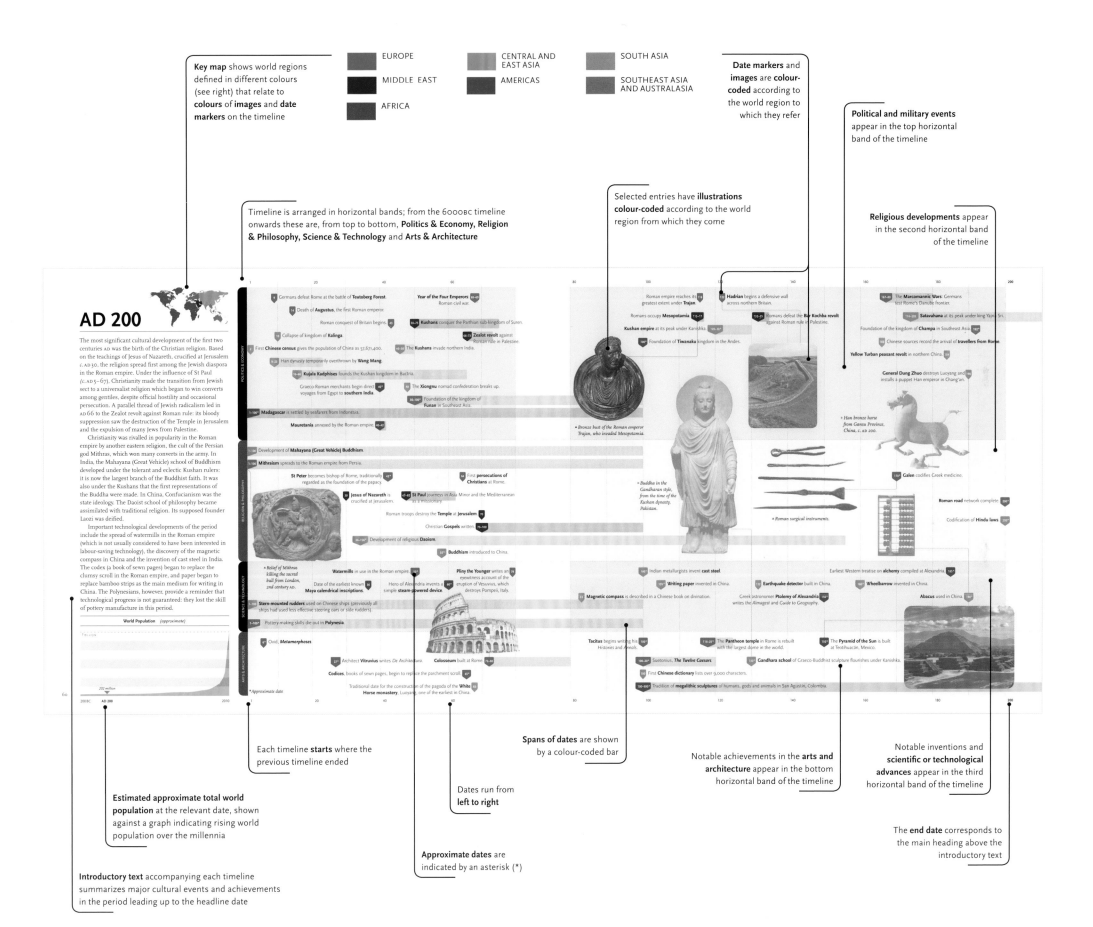

Key map shows world regions defined in different colours (see right) that relate to **colours** of **images** and **date markers** on the timeline

EUROPE

MIDDLE EAST

AFRICA

CENTRAL AND EAST ASIA

AMERICAS

SOUTH ASIA

SOUTHEAST ASIA AND AUSTRALASIA

Date markers and **images** are **colour-coded** according to the world region to which they refer

Political and military events appear in the top horizontal band of the timeline

Religious developments appear in the second horizontal band of the timeline

Timeline is arranged in horizontal bands; from the 6000BC timeline onwards these are, from top to bottom, **Politics & Economy, Religion & Philosophy, Science & Technology** and **Arts & Architecture**

Selected entries have **illustrations colour-coded** according to the world region from which they come

AD 200

The most significant cultural development of the first two centuries AD was the birth of the Christian religion. Based on the teachings of Jesus of Nazareth, crucified at Jerusalem c. AD 30, the religion spread first among the Jewish diaspora in the Roman empire. Under the influence of St Paul (c. AD 5–67), Christianity made the transition from Jewish sect to a universalist religion which began to win converts among gentiles, despite official hostility and occasional persecution. A parallel thread of Jewish radicalism led in AD 66 to the Zealot revolt against Roman rule: its bloody suppression saw the destruction of the Temple in Jerusalem and the expulsion of many Jews from Palestine.

Christianity was rivalled in popularity in the Roman empire by another eastern religion, the cult of the Persian god Mithras, which won many converts in the army. In India, the Mahayana (Great Vehicle) school of Buddhism developed under the tolerant and eclectic Kushan rulers: it is now the largest branch of the Buddhist faith. It was also under the Kushans that the first representations of the Buddha were made. In China, Confucianism was the state ideology. The Daoist school of philosophy became assimilated with traditional religion. Its supposed founder Laozi was deified.

Important technological developments of the period include the spread of watermills in the Roman empire (which is not usually considered to have been interested in labour-saving technology), the discovery of the magnetic compass in China and the invention of cast steel in India. The codex (a book of sewn pages) began to replace the clumsy scroll in the Roman empire, and paper began to replace bamboo strips as the main medium for writing in China. The Polynesians, however, provide a reminder that technological progress is not guaranteed: they lost the skill of pottery manufacture in this period.

World Population (approximate)

1 billion

202 million

60

200 BC   AD 200   2010

Politics & Economy

Germans defeat Rome at the battle of **Teutoberg Forest**.

Death of **Augustus**, the first Roman emperor.

Roman conquest of Britain begins. 43

Collapse of kingdom of **Kalinga**.

First **Chinese census** gives the population of China as 57,671,400.

Han dynasty temporarily overthrown by Wang Mang.

Kujala Kadphises founds the Kushan kingdom in Bactria.

Graeco-Roman merchants begin direct voyages from Egypt to **southern India**.

1–100* **Madagascar** is settled by seafarers from Indonesia.

Mauretania annexed by the Roman empire. 40–43

Roman civil war.

Year of the Four Emperors: 68–69

50–75 **Kushans** conquer the Parthian sub-kingdom of Suren.

66–70 **Zealot revolt** against Roman rule in Palestine.

48–50 The **Kushans** invade northern India.

The **Xiongnu** nomad confederation breaks up.

38–50* Foundation of the kingdom of **Funan** in Southeast Asia.

Roman empire reaches its greatest extent under **Trajan**. 116

Romans occupy **Mesopotamia** 115–17

Kushan empire at its peak under **Kanishka**. 120–35*

100* Foundation of **Tiwanaku** kingdom in the Andes.

115 **Hadrian** begins a defensive wall across northern Britain.

132–35 Romans defeat the **Bar Kochba** revolt against Roman rule in Palestine.

167–80 The **Marcomannic Wars**: Germans test Rome's Danube frontier.

170–200 **Satavahana** at its peak under king Yajñi Śri.

Foundation of the kingdom of **Champa** in Southeast Asia. 192*

166 Chinese sources record the arrival of **travellers from Rome**.

Yellow Turban peasant revolt in northern China.

General Dung Zhuo destroys Luoyang and installs a puppet Han emperor in Chang'an.

Religion & Philosophy

1–100 Development of **Mahayana (Great Vehicle) Buddhism**.

1–100 **Mithraism** spreads to the Roman empire from Persia.

St Peter becomes bishop of Rome, traditionally regarded as the foundation of the papacy. 42*

30 **Jesus of Nazareth** is crucified at Jerusalem.

47–60 **St Paul** journeys in Asia Minor and the Mediterranean as a missionary.

First **persecutions of Christians** at Rome.

Roman troops destroy the **Temple** at Jerusalem. 70

Christian **Gospels** written. 75–100

14–156* Development of religious **Daoism**.

65* **Buddhism** introduced to China.

100* Indian metallurgists invent **cast steel**.

175* **Galen** codifies Greek medicine.

Codification of **Hindu laws**.

Science & Technology

Watermills in use in the Roman empire. 14*

Date of the earliest known **Maya calendrical inscriptions**. 36

Hero of Alexandria invents a simple steam-powered device. 60*

79 Pliny the Younger writes an eyewitness account of the eruption of Vesuvius, which destroys Pompeii, Italy.

Stern-mounted rudders used on Chinese ships (previously all ships had used less effective steering oars or side rudders).

1–100* Pottery-making skills die out in **Polynesia**.

83 **Magnetic compass** is described in a Chinese book on divination.

105* **Writing paper** invented in China.

132 **Earthquake detector** built in China.

Greek astronomer **Ptolemy of Alexandria** writes the Almagest and Guide to Geography. 150*

Earliest Western treatise on **alchemy** compiled at Alexandria. 165*

Roman road network complete. 200*

Wheelbarrow invented in China.

Abacus used in China. 190*

Arts & Architecture

Ovid, Metamorphoses.

27* Architect **Vitruvius** writes De Architectura.

Codices, books of sewn pages, begin to replace the parchment scroll. 45*

Traditional date for the construction of the pagoda of the **White Horse monastery**, Luoyang, one of the earliest in China. 68

Colosseum built at Rome. 72–80

100–20* Suetonius, **The Twelve Caesars**.

First **Chinese dictionary** lists over 9,000 characters.

100–200* Tradition of **megalithic sculptures** of humans, gods and animals in San Agustín, Colombia.

Tacitus begins writing his Histories and Annals. 100*

118–25 The **Pantheon temple** in Rome is rebuilt with the largest dome in the world.

150* The **Pyramid of the Sun** is built at Teotihuacán, Mexico.

120* **Gandhara school** of Graeco-Buddhist sculpture flourishes under Kanishka.

* Approximate date

Bronze bust of the Roman emperor Trajan, who invaded Mesopotamia.

Buddha in the Gandharan style, from the time of the Kushan dynasty, Pakistan.

Roman surgical instruments.

Relief of Mithras killing the sacred bull from London, 2nd century AD.

Han bronze horse from Gansu Province, China, c. AD 200.

Political and military events appear in the top horizontal band of the timeline

Estimated approximate total world population at the relevant date, shown against a graph indicating rising world population over the millennia

Introductory text accompanying each timeline summarizes major cultural events and achievements in the period leading up to the headline date

Each timeline **starts** where the previous timeline ended

Approximate dates are indicated by an asterisk (*)

Dates run from **left to right**

Spans of dates are shown by a colour-coded bar

Notable achievements in the **arts and architecture** appear in the bottom horizontal band of the timeline

Notable inventions and **scientific or technological advances** appear in the third horizontal band of the timeline

The **end date** corresponds to the main heading above the introductory text

Introduction: World History in Overview

Does history have a trajectory? This is not the same as asking if history has a purpose, the working out of a divinely ordained plan, for instance, or the inevitable triumph of a particular political or socio-economic system. The continuous rise and fall of nations and empires, cultures, ideologies and religions demonstrates that history has neither purpose nor inevitability. However, beneath the distracting film of events human history has followed a clear and scarcely interrupted trajectory.

Since the end of the last Ice Age around 10,000 years ago, there has been an accelerating trend of global population, urban and economic growth; increasing contacts between cultures and civilizations; and a rarely interrupted development of greater social and economic complexity. It is this grand sweep of global history that *The New Atlas of World History* presents in an immediately accessible format using maps, text, timelines and graphics.

Human history has been marked by a number of step-changes in productivity that have fuelled social, cultural and political change and caused, or enabled, mass movements of peoples that have constantly reshaped the world. For the vast majority of prehistory, all humans lived by hunting wild animals and gathering wild plant foods. Their numbers were constrained, like those of any other animal, by the natural productivity of the environment. As the Ice Age came to an end, groups in different parts of the world independently took up farming as a way to secure their food supplies. It was no accident that the earliest farming societies arose in the Middle East: this was the part of the world with the greatest number of plants and animals suitable for domestication. This development was the first step-change in human history, as it made possible an enormous increase in the human population. The fertility of the soil has limits, but predictions that the human population would exceed the capacity of the land to feed it have not yet been fulfilled. The development of higher-yielding crops and domestic animals by selective breeding and genetic engineering, irrigation, mechanized farming and synthetic fertilizers have so far allowed agricultural productivity to keep ahead of rising numbers. Famines and plagues have proved no more than temporary setbacks to population growth.

The capacity of farmers to grow more food than they needed for subsistence led to a second step-change in human history. Surplus food was the first form of wealth: those who controlled it acquired power over their fellows, leading to the development of hierarchical societies and political centralization. Surplus food also meant that it was not necessary for everyone to be a farmer. Some people, at first a very small minority, could now devote themselves full time to craft production, trade, military training, administration or religion. These social and economic changes led to the growth of cities, states and civilizations, beginning in those areas, mostly in the temperate latitudes, that were environmentally most favourable to intensive agriculture. The first civilizations developed in isolation but as their influence spread they became connected through trade, diplomacy, war and migration. These connections encouraged the spread of ideas and

8

technological innovations. Individual civilizations may have collapsed, but there has never been a global collapse of civilization: the trajectory of history has always been towards ever more complex and interconnected civilizations.

From the beginning, cities were the main centres of civilization, but the vast majority of people continued to live in the countryside working on the land. The proportion of people living in cities grew only slowly until the beginning of the Industrial Revolution in the 18th century. This was a third step-change in human history, turning manufacturing and services, rather than agriculture, into the primary source of wealth. This change was underpinned by improvements in agricultural efficiency, which released labour from the land to work in urban factories. Beginning in Britain, labour migrated from the countryside to the towns in search of work, leading to explosive urban growth. In the 19th century the Industrial Revolution spread to Europe and North America, and in the 20th century to South America and Asia. Only Africa has yet to feel the full impact of industrialization, but even here the drift to the towns is in full flood. By 2005 more than half the human population lived in cities, while hunting and gathering,

humanity's ancestral way of life, was all but extinct.

Because of the increasing specialization of modern scholarship, and the resulting narrowing of school and university curricula, this underlying global trajectory of history is too often obscured. The wider context of events has gone missing. *The New Atlas of World History* provides that missing global context. Unlike conventional atlases of world history, which all to a greater or lesser extent compartmentalize the world into distinct regions, this new atlas is based entirely on a sequence of more than 50 maps of the whole world at different times in history. The maps chart the evolution and migrations of early humans, the spread of agriculture and the development of cultures, states and empires. Thematic maps explore the development of the world religions, writing systems, migrations and

global trade. Graphics displaying statistics on world population and the five largest cities at any period emphasize the overarching trajectories of world history, while the timelines with their carefully selected illustrations chart developments in politics, religion, technology, the arts and architecture in each time period. Together, all the elements of *The New Atlas of World History* combine to create an unrivalled overview of human history in its entirety.

From the Stone Age to the Computer Age:

1 The Venus figurine from Brassempouy, France, *c.* 25,000 years ago.
2 Triad showing King Menkaure flanked by two goddesses from Giza, Egypt, *c.* 2490–2472 BC.
3 The temple at Borobudur with a statue of the Buddha, Java, Indonesia, *c.* AD 900.
4 The Blue Mosque, Istanbul, built for Sultan Ahmed I, 1609–18.
5 The Hindu temple at Virupaksha, Hampi, India, 14th century AD.
6 *The Qianlong Emperor in Ceremonial Armour on Horseback* by Giuseppe Castiglione, mid-18th century.
7 *The Ambassadors*, Hans Holbein the Younger, England, 1533.
8 The iPad, a tablet computer designed by Apple, 2010 model.

6,000,000–100,000 years ago
THE ORIGINS AND DISTRIBUTION OF EARLY HUMAN SPECIES

Human history began between 8 and 6 million years ago in East Africa. At this time, according to the evidence of our DNA, humans began their separate evolution from the great apes. Between 6 and 4 million years ago, the ardipithecines evolved. Like modern apes, ardipithecines were forest dwellers and good climbers. On the ground, however, they walked upright, albeit inefficiently. It is thought that their range was limited to East Africa. The ardipithecines were succeeded *c.* 4 million years ago by the australopithecines, efficient omnivorous bipeds who lived in open woodland and savanna across a wide area of Africa. Over half a dozen species of australopithecines are known but the exact evolutionary relationship between them, and with modern humans, is still uncertain.

Australopithecines possessed brains about the same size as modern apes. The evolution of the large brains characteristic of modern humans began *c.* 2.3 million years ago with the appearance of the first hominin species judged to be human, *Homo habilis*. Anatomically, *H. habilis* closely resembled the australopithecines but possessed a brain that was 50 per cent larger. *Homo erectus*, which appeared *c.* 1.8 million years ago, was in most respects more human and possessed a brain up to two-thirds the size of a modern human's. *H. erectus* became the first human species to live outside Africa, migrating into Europe and as far east as China and Indonesia, where it survived until some 50,000 years ago. In Africa and Eurasia, *H. erectus* evolved seamlessly into the still larger-brained *Homo heidelbergensis* (often called *Homo rhodesiensis* in Africa). In Europe, *H. heidelbergensis* evolved into the Neanderthals, who were physically adapted to a colder climate, while in Africa it evolved directly into anatomically fully modern humans, *Homo sapiens, c.* 200,000 years ago.

The formation of the East African Rift Valley system was probably a major influence on early human evolution. Hot rocks from the mantle raised and stretched the earth's crust, cutting East Africa off from moist westerly winds, creating a drier and more open landscape in which the energy efficiency of bipedalism gave early hominins a competitive advantage. Bipedalism, crucially, freed human hands to do other things. Similarly, the climatic instability of the Ice Age, which saw conditions oscillate between cold glacial periods and warm inter-glacial periods, favoured flexible and adaptive behaviour, so acting as a spur to the evolution of larger brains and greater intelligence.

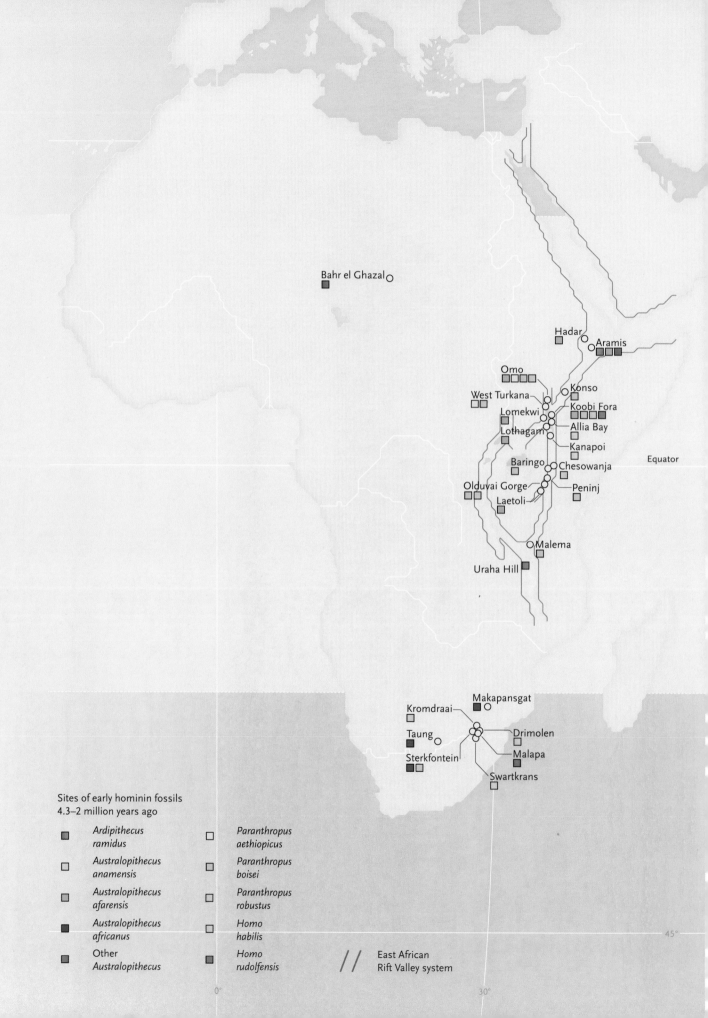

Sites of early hominin fossils
4.3–2 million years ago

■ *Ardipithecus ramidus*	□ *Paranthropus aethiopicus*
□ *Australopithecus anamensis*	□ *Paranthropus boisei*
■ *Australopithecus afarensis*	□ *Paranthropus robustus*
■ *Australopithecus africanus*	□ *Homo habilis*
■ *Other Australopithecus*	■ *Homo rudolfensis*

// East African Rift Valley system

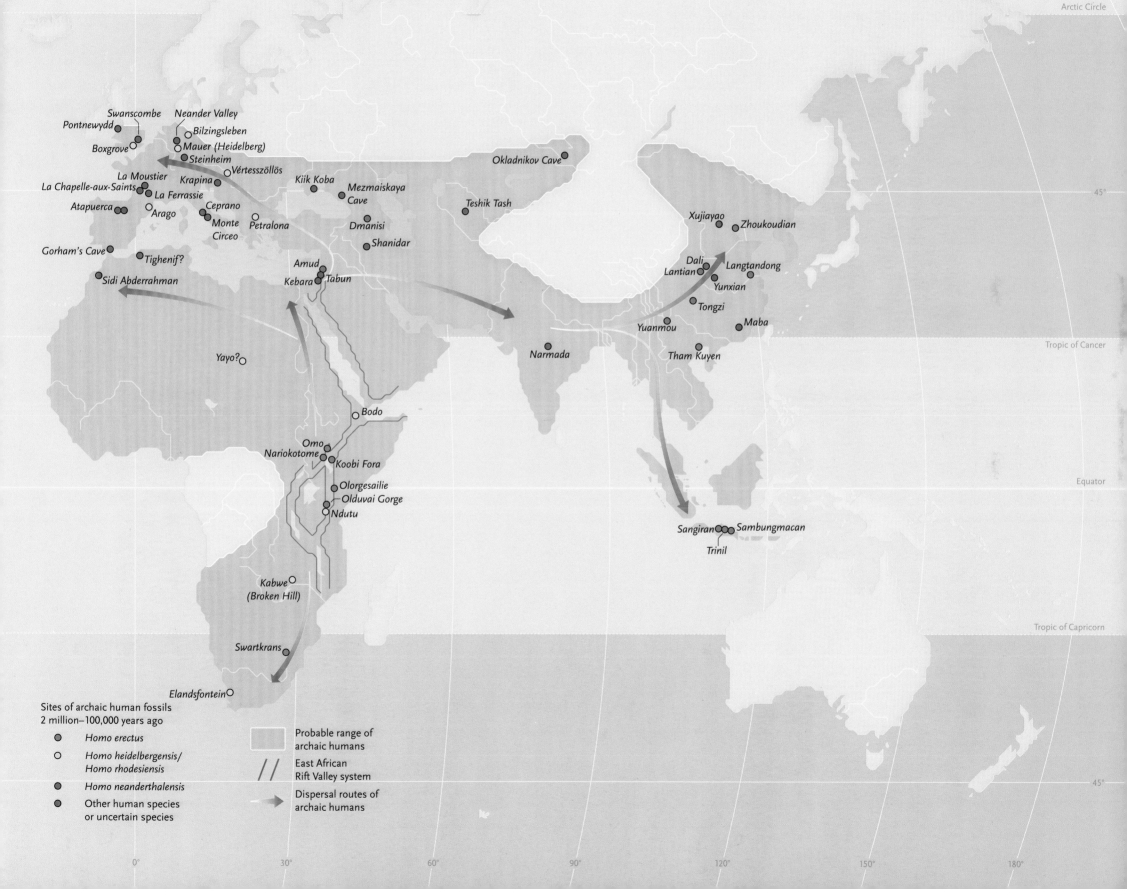

Swanscombe   Neander Valley
Pontnewydd
Boxgrove   Bilzingsleben
                            Mauer (Heidelberg)
                            Steinheim
                        Vértesszöllös
La Moustier   Krapina   Kiik Koba   Okladnikov Cave
La Chapelle-aux-Saints
                La Ferrassie   Mezmaiskaya
Atapuerca   Arago   Cave
                    Ceprano   Teshik Tash
                    Monte   Petralona   Xujiayao
                    Circeo   Dmanisi   Zhoukoudian
Gorham's Cave   Shanidar   Dali   Langtandong
        Tighenif?   Lantian
                            Amud   Yunxian
Sidi Abderrahman   Kebara   Tabun   Tongzi
                                                                                                               Maba
                                                                            Yuanmou
                                                                                            Tham Kuyen
        Yayo?   Narmada

                            Bodo

                    Omo
            Nariokotome
                        Koobi Fora
                        Olorgesailie   Sangiran   Sambungmacan
                        Olduvai Gorge   Trinil
                        Ndutu

                Kabwe
                (Broken Hill)

        Swartkrans

    Elandsfontein

Sites of archaic human fossils
2 million–100,000 years ago

● Homo erectus   Probable range of
                                        archaic humans
○ Homo heidelbergensis/
  Homo rhodesiensis   // East African
                                        Rift Valley system
● Homo neanderthalensis
                                     ➜ Dispersal routes of
● Other human species   archaic humans
  or uncertain species

6,000,000–100,000 years ago

The evolution of behavioural modernity – toolmaking, language and a capacity for abstract and symbolic thought – was a gradual process which took place alongside the evolution of anatomical modernity. Toolmaking is the aspect of modern behaviour for which there is the earliest evidence. Chimpanzees are known to use naturally occurring objects, often twigs and pebbles, as simple tools. Early hominins may, therefore, have had a long history of similar tool use before the earliest manufactured tools of the Oldowan industry appeared *c.* 2.6 million years ago.

Probably originating with the australopithecines, Oldowan tools – typically choppers and scrapers made by flaking river cobbles to create a sharp edge – were used for butchering animals. However, it is unknown whether early hominins actively hunted or simply scavenged the kills of other predators. It is not until *c.* 500,000–400,000 years ago that there is unambiguous evidence, such as hunting spears, that early hominins actively hunted.

Oldowan tools continued to be made by later human species for more than 1 million years alongside more complex tools. Following the evolution of the large-brained *Homo erectus* a new tool type, the hand axe (actually a leaf-shaped butchery knife), appeared. Both Neanderthals and early anatomically modern humans used a wider range of tools than earlier human species. Evidence suggests that hominins mastered the use of fire at least 800,000 years ago and had begun to cook food by *c.* 500,000 years ago.

Language is central to the modern human capacity for abstract and symbolic thought, but its origins are poorly understood. *H. erectus* was the first species with the physical capacity to speak with a recognizably human voice and it is generally assumed that *H. heidelbergensis* and the Neanderthals had some capacity for language.

The earliest evidence for behavioural modernity, however, comes from sites in Africa and the Levant occupied by early anatomically modern humans between 190,000 and 75,000 years ago. The occupants exploited a wide range of terrestrial and marine food resources, possessed sophisticated toolmaking skills and engaged in symbolic behaviour, such as wearing necklaces of shells, using pigments and creating geometrical designs. These were people we would have recognized as being like ourselves.

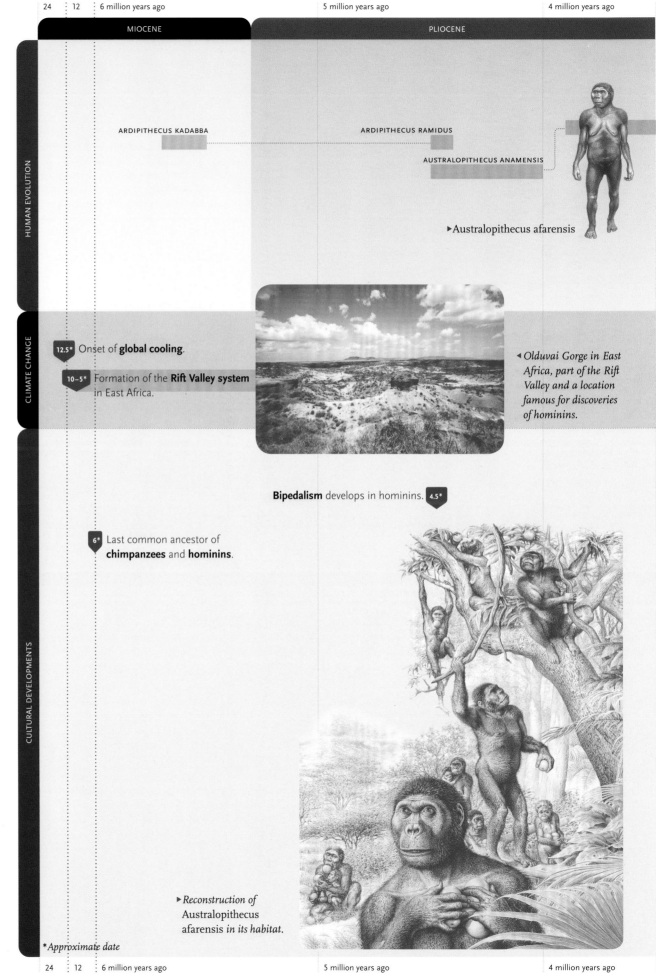

MIOCENE

PLIOCENE

HUMAN EVOLUTION

ARDIPITHECUS KADABBA

ARDIPITHECUS RAMIDUS

AUSTRALOPITHECUS ANAMENSIS

▶Australopithecus afarensis

CLIMATE CHANGE

12.5* Onset of **global cooling**.

10–5* Formation of the **Rift Valley system** in East Africa.

◀ *Olduvai Gorge in East Africa, part of the Rift Valley and a location famous for discoveries of hominins.*

Bipedalism develops in hominins. **4.5***

6* Last common ancestor of **chimpanzees** and **hominins**.

CULTURAL DEVELOPMENTS

▶*Reconstruction of* Australopithecus afarensis *in its habitat.*

*Approximate date

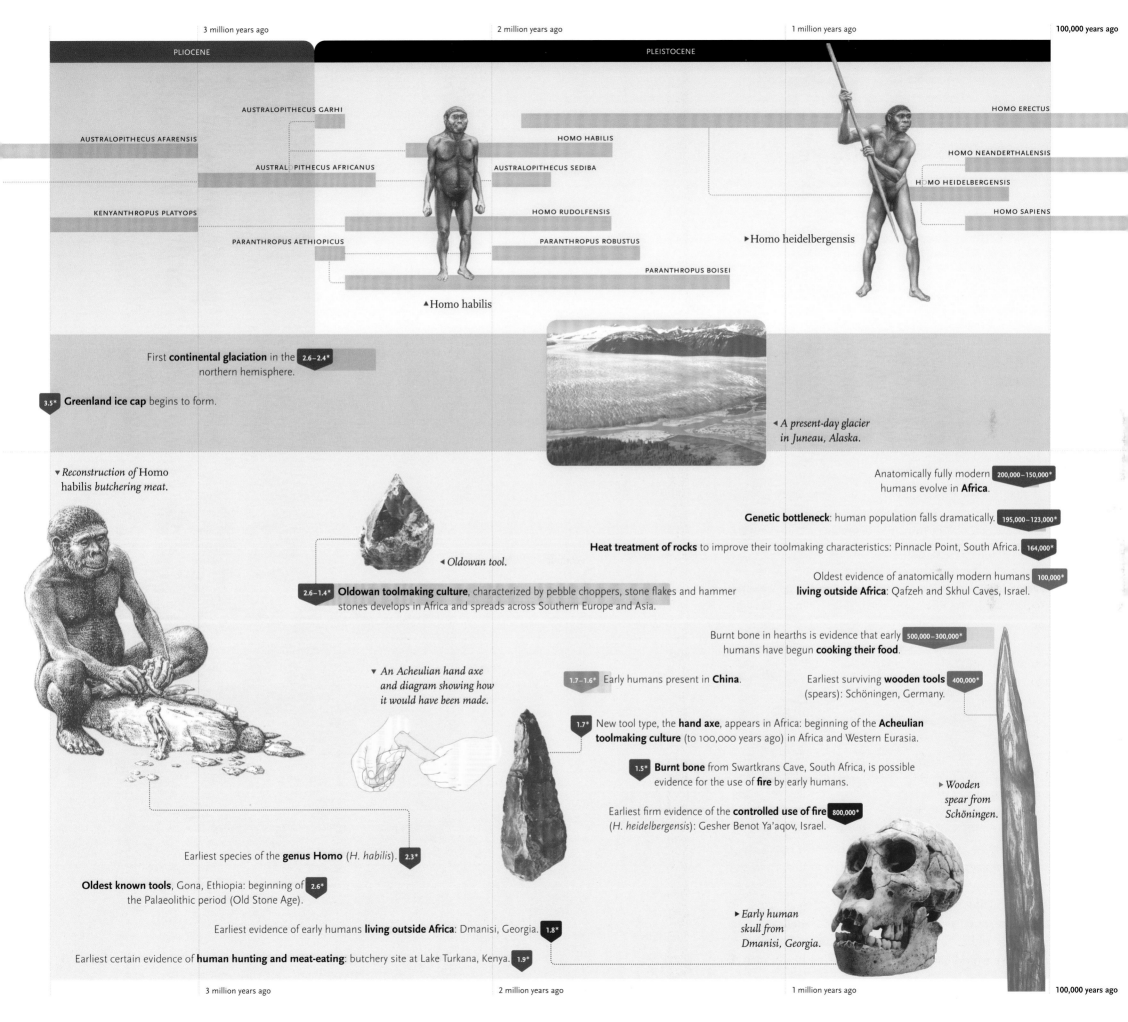

PLIOCENE

PLEISTOCENE

AUSTRALOPITHECUS GARHI

AUSTRALOPITHECUS AFARENSIS

HOMO HABILIS

HOMO ERECTUS

AUSTRALOPITHECUS AFRICANUS

AUSTRALOPITHECUS SEDIBA

HOMO NEANDERTHALENSIS

HOMO HEIDELBERGENSIS

KENYANTHROPUS PLATYOPS

HOMO RUDOLFENSIS

HOMO SAPIENS

PARANTHROPUS AETHIOPICUS

PARANTHROPUS ROBUSTUS

▶ Homo heidelbergensis

PARANTHROPUS BOISEI

▲ Homo habilis

◀ A present-day glacier in Juneau, Alaska.

First **continental glaciation** in the `2.6–2.4*` northern hemisphere.

`3.5*` **Greenland ice cap** begins to form.

▼ *Reconstruction of* Homo habilis *butchering meat.*

Anatomically fully modern `200,000–150,000*` humans evolve in **Africa**.

Genetic bottleneck: human population falls dramatically. `195,000–123,000*`

Heat treatment of rocks to improve their toolmaking characteristics: Pinnacle Point, South Africa. `164,000*`

Oldest evidence of anatomically modern humans `100,000*` **living outside Africa**: Qafzeh and Skhul Caves, Israel.

◀ *Oldowan tool.*

`2.6–1.4*` **Oldowan toolmaking culture**, characterized by pebble choppers, stone flakes and hammer stones develops in Africa and spreads across Southern Europe and Asia.

Burnt bone in hearths is evidence that early `500,000–300,000*` humans have begun **cooking their food**.

▼ *An Acheulian hand axe and diagram showing how it would have been made.*

`1.7–1.6*` Early humans present in **China**.

Earliest surviving **wooden tools** `400,000*` (spears): Schöningen, Germany.

`1.7*` New tool type, the **hand axe**, appears in Africa: beginning of the **Acheulian toolmaking culture** (to 100,000 years ago) in Africa and Western Eurasia.

`1.5*` **Burnt bone** from Swartkrans Cave, South Africa, is possible evidence for the use of **fire** by early humans.

Earliest firm evidence of the **controlled use of fire** `800,000*` (*H. heidelbergensis*): Gesher Benot Ya'aqov, Israel.

▶ *Wooden spear from Schöningen.*

Earliest species of the **genus Homo** (*H. habilis*). `2.3*`

Oldest known tools, Gona, Ethiopia: beginning of `2.6*` the Palaeolithic period (Old Stone Age).

Earliest evidence of early humans **living outside Africa**: Dmanisi, Georgia. `1.8*`

Earliest certain evidence of **human hunting and meat-eating**: butchery site at Lake Turkana, Kenya. `1.9*`

▶ *Early human skull from Dmanisi, Georgia.*

100,000–11,000 years ago
THE SPREAD OF MODERN HUMANS AROUND THE WORLD DURING THE ICE AGE

All modern humans are descended from populations of *Homo sapiens* that lived in Africa *c.* 200,000 years ago. Around 70,000 years ago a small group of humans left Africa and over the next 50,000 years its descendants colonized all the world's other continents except Antarctica, in the process replacing all other human species. These migrations were aided by low sea levels during glaciations, which created land bridges linking islands and continents: humans were able to reach most parts of the world on foot. It was in this period of initial colonization of the globe that modern racial characteristics evolved.

Modern humans had first migrated out of Africa *c.* 100,000 years ago, probably following the Nile valley and crossing the isthmus of Suez into the Levant. For unknown reasons, the descendants of these pioneers died out within a few thousand years, leaving the area to the Neanderthals. Some 30,000 years later, another small group of modern humans migrated out of Africa, perhaps crossing the Red Sea from the Horn of Africa to Arabia. In the Middle East, they encountered Neanderthals. All non-African modern humans carry small traces of Neanderthal DNA so relations between the two were not necessarily hostile.

From the Middle East, modern humans quickly spread east to India and Southeast Asia, replacing the indigenous populations. By 50,000 years ago, humans had reached Australia and New Guinea, which at that time formed a single continent. At no point did sea levels ever fall low enough to link Australia to Southeast Asia, so for this migration some form of seafaring technology was required. Around this time also, the first modern humans arrived in China, reaching Japan *c.* 30,000 years ago. Perhaps because of the harsh glacial conditions, modern humans did not begin colonizing Europe until *c.* 45,000 years ago. Modern humans gradually replaced indigenous Neanderthals, who became extinct *c.* 30,000 years ago.

The last continents to be colonized by humans were the Americas. Alaska was reached *c.* 16,000 years ago from Northeast Asia via the Bering Sea land bridge, but further progress was barred until the continental ice sheets began to retreat *c.* 14,000 years ago. By this time, other groups had already bypassed the ice sheets by migrating along the Pacific coast, reaching South America by 14,500 years ago.

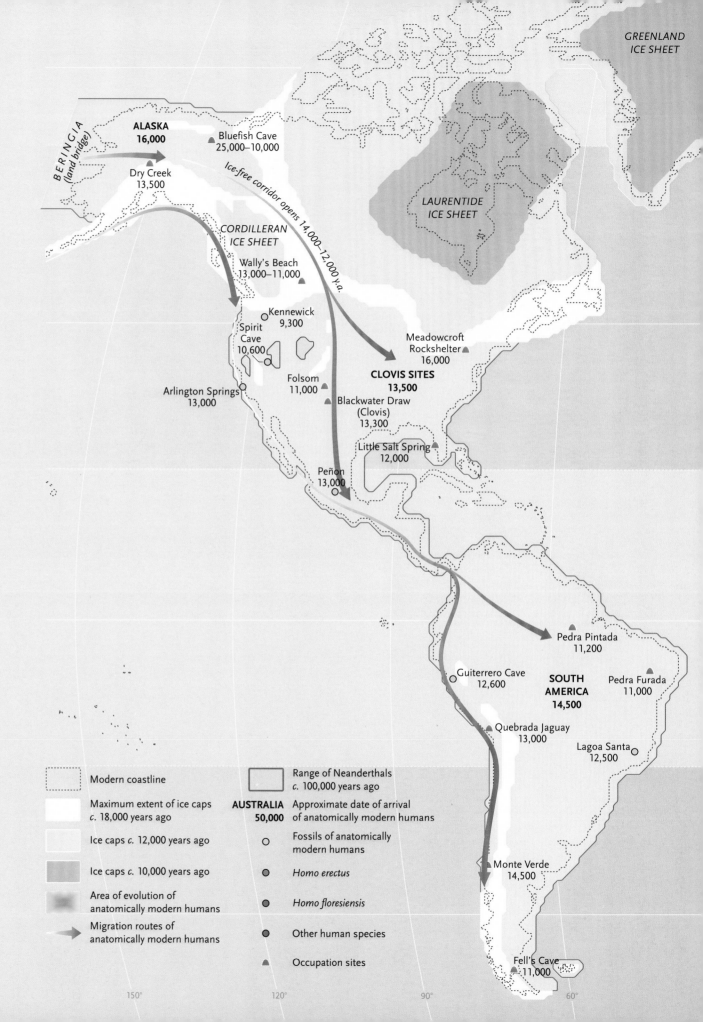

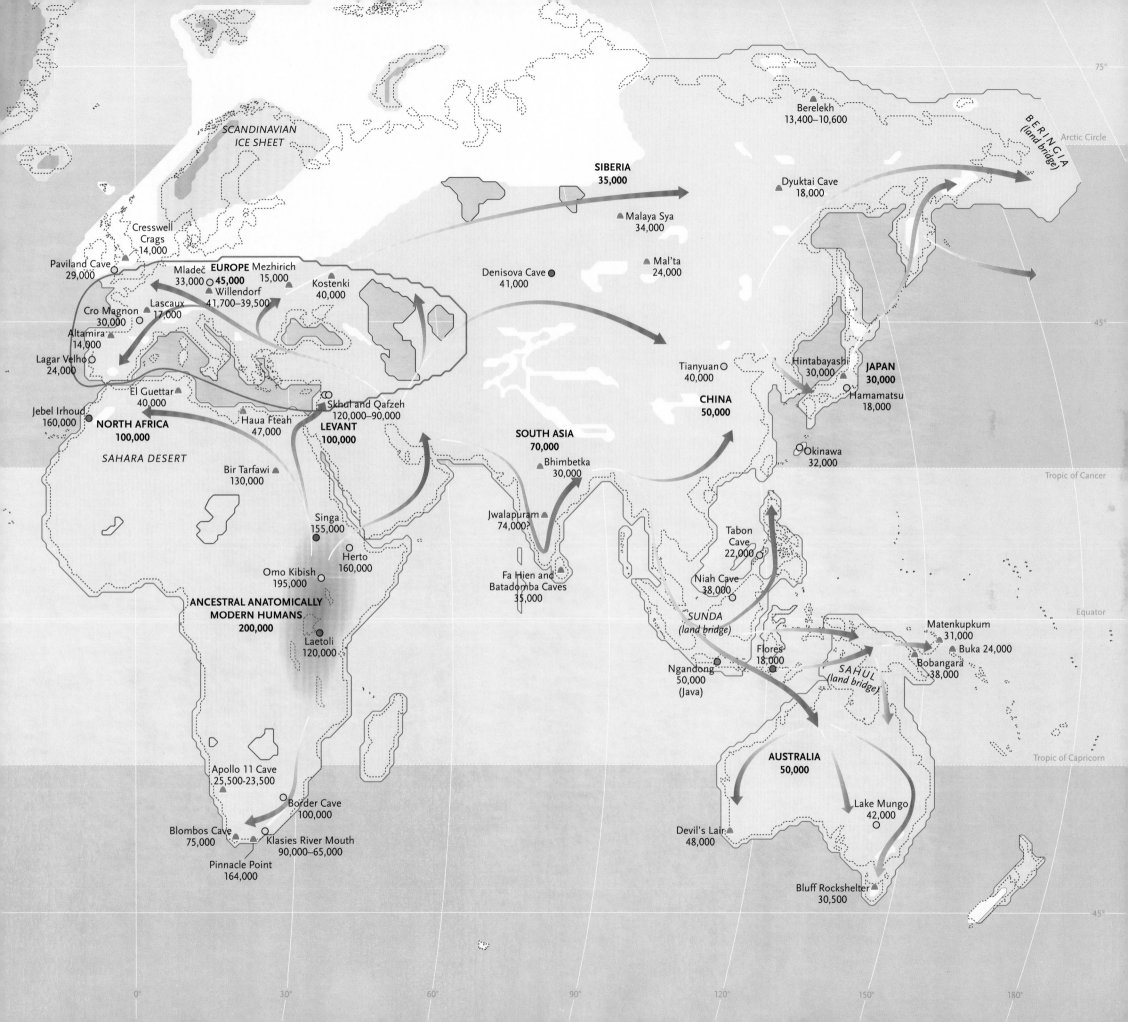

BERINGIA
(land bridge)

Berelekh
13,400–10,600

SCANDINAVIAN
ICE SHEET

SIBERIA
35,000

Dyuktai Cave
18,000

Malaya Sya
34,000

Cresswell
Crags
14,000

Mal'ta
24,000

Paviland Cave
29,000

Mladeč   EUROPE Mezhirich
33,000   45,000   15,000

Denisova Cave
41,000

Hintabayashi
30,000

JAPAN
30,000

Kostenki
40,000

Willendorf
41,700–39,500

Lascaux
17,000

Cro Magnon
30,000

Tianyuan
40,000

Hamamatsu
18,000

Altamira
14,000

CHINA
50,000

Lagar Velho
24,000

Okinawa
32,000

El Guettar
40,000

Skhul and Qafzeh
120,000–90,000

Jebel Irhoud
160,000

NORTH AFRICA
100,000

Haua Fteah
47,000

LEVANT
100,000

SOUTH ASIA
70,000

Bhimbetka
30,000

SAHARA DESERT

Tropic of Cancer

Bir Tarfawi
130,000

Jwalapuram
74,000?

Tabon
Cave
22,000

Singa
155,000

Matenkupkum
31,000

Herto
160,000

Fa Hien and
Batadomba Caves
35,000

Niah Cave
38,000

Buka 24,000

Omo Kibish
195,000

Equator

Bobangara
38,000

ANCESTRAL ANATOMICALLY
MODERN HUMANS
200,000

SUNDA
(land bridge)

Flores
18,000

SAHUL
(land bridge)

Laetoli
120,000

Ngandong
50,000
(Java)

Apollo 11 Cave
25,500–23,500

AUSTRALIA
50,000

Tropic of Capricorn

Border Cave
100,000

Lake Mungo
42,000

Blombos Cave
75,000

Devil's Lair
48,000

Klasies River Mouth
90,000–65,000

Pinnacle Point
164,000

Bluff Rockshelter
30,500

100,000–11,000 years ago

Early human migrations around the world brought about a proliferation of different cultures as different groups split from one another and adapted to different environments.

Throughout the last Ice Age, all humans lived by hunting wild animals, fishing, and gathering wild plant foods and shellfish, as dictated by local availability. Hunter-gatherers generally lived in bands of no more than 20–30 people, migrating seasonally to make the most efficient use of the territory's resources. This mobility placed practical limits on cultural and technological development because hunter-gatherers' possessions needed to be easily portable. The growth of the human population was also strictly limited by the natural productivity of the environment.

With so much water locked up in ice sheets, the Ice Age world was drier as well as cooler. Forests retreated and there were vast areas of savanna, open steppe and tundra supporting herds of large herbivores. Big-game hunting cultures developed in many parts of the world, most notably in Europe, where spectacular cave paintings of Ice Age wildlife were made, and in North America. In most parts of the Old World new toolmaking technologies were adopted, using microliths (tiny stone blades) to make composite hunting weapons such as spears, arrows and harpoons.

As the Ice Age began to draw to an end c. 14,000 years ago, hunter-gatherers in some highly productive environments adopted strategies that allowed them to become semi-sedentary. The Jomon in Japan probably did this by exploiting abundant marine resources. Freed from a need to move regularly, they were among the earliest people to use pottery. The Natufians in the Levant built villages of permanent huts, developing a new technology of sickles and grindstones for harvesting and processing wild cereals.

Although global population was still only c. 4 million, humans had already had a considerable impact on the environment by the end of the last Ice Age. Their arrival in Australia and the Americas was quickly followed by mass extinctions of local megafauna ('large animals' such as the woolly mammoth) either because of hunting or indirectly as a result of environmental changes caused by human activities such as lighting bush fires. In historical times, similar mass extinctions followed the arrival of humans on Madagascar, New Zealand and many other islands.

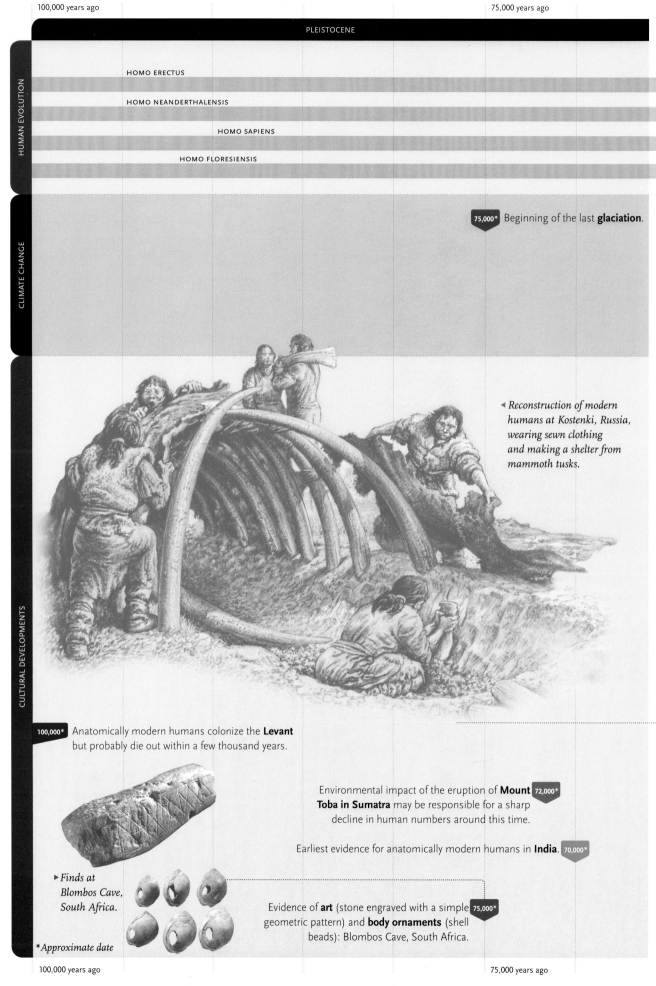

PLEISTOCENE

HUMAN EVOLUTION

HOMO ERECTUS

HOMO NEANDERTHALENSIS

HOMO SAPIENS

HOMO FLORESIENSIS

CLIMATE CHANGE

75,000* Beginning of the last **glaciation**.

◄ *Reconstruction of modern humans at Kostenki, Russia, wearing sewn clothing and making a shelter from mammoth tusks.*

CULTURAL DEVELOPMENTS

100,000* Anatomically modern humans colonize the **Levant** but probably die out within a few thousand years.

Environmental impact of the eruption of **Mount** **72,000*** **Toba in Sumatra** may be responsible for a sharp decline in human numbers around this time.

Earliest evidence for anatomically modern humans in **India**. **70,000***

►*Finds at Blombos Cave, South Africa.*

Evidence of **art** (stone engraved with a simple **75,000*** geometric pattern) and **body ornaments** (shell beads): Blombos Cave, South Africa.

*Approximate date

▶Homo floresiensis

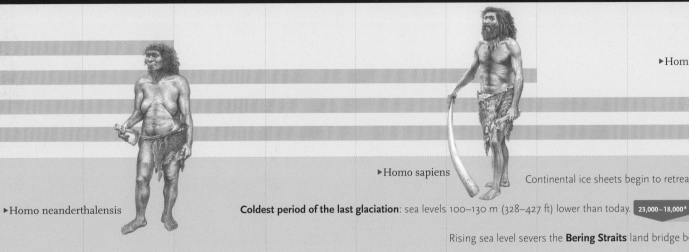
▶Homo sapiens

Continental ice sheets begin to retreat as **global warming** sets in. `14,000*`

▶Homo neanderthalensis

Coldest period of the last glaciation: sea levels 100–130 m (328–427 ft) lower than today. `23,000–18,000*`

Rising sea level severs the **Bering Straits** land bridge between Siberia and Alaska. `13,500–11,000*`

Melt-water interrupts the **Gulf Stream**, causing a return to glacial conditions in Europe and North America. `12,800*`

End of the last glaciation marks the end of the **Pleistocene** (geological) and **Palaeolithic** (cultural) **periods**. `11,500*`

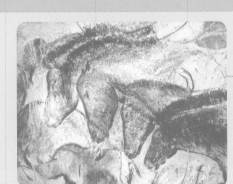
◀ *Wall paintings from Chauvet Cave, France.*

`35,000–14,000*` Period of **cave art traditions** in Europe.

Gravettian culture develops microlithic tool technology. `28,000–23,000*`

Earliest known ceramic objects: **Venus figurines** from Central Europe. `29,000–25,000*`

Humans certainly `16,000*` present in **Alaska**.

`25,000–23,000*` **Cave paintings** in Apollo 11 cave, Namibia.

Extensive settlement of the **Sahara** by hunter-fisher-gatherers is made possible by the beginning of a **period of higher rainfall**. `12,500*`

Natufian hunter-gatherers harvest wild cereals in the Levant and live in **permanent settlements**. `12,500*`

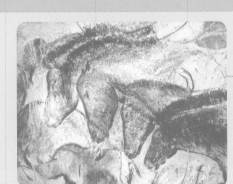
▶ *The Venus of Willendorf, Austria.*

Anatomically modern humans reach Japan from **Korea**. `30,000*`

Beginnings of **cereal cultivation** in the Middle East. `12,500*`

The probable extinction of *Homo floresiensis* leaves **Homo sapiens** as the only surviving hominin species. `12,000*`

Earliest **Aboriginal rock art** in Australia. `40,000*`

Oldest known **pottery vessels**: Yuchanyan Cave, China. `18,300–17,500*`

Extinction of *Homo erectus* in **Southeast Asia**. `50,000*`

`45,000*` Anatomically modern humans begin to colonize **Europe**.

`28,000*` **Solomon Islands** are settled.

Earliest evidence of **sewn clothing**: bone needles and awls at Kostenki, Russia. `40,000*`

Pottery vessels in common use for storage and cooking by the **Jomon hunter-gatherers** of Japan. `14,000*`

`60,000*` Modern humans return to the **Middle East**.

Neanderthals become extinct in Europe. `30,000*`

As the ice sheets retreat, modern humans colonize **Britain**. `12,000*`

`60,000–50,000*` Main **dispersal around the world** of anatomically modern humans begins.

Earliest firm evidence for the **domestic dog**: Kesserloch Cave, Switzerland. `14,600–14,100*`

`60,000*` Neanderthal burials at **Shanidar**, Iraq.

Cave paintings at **Lascaux**, France, are made. `17,000*`

Modern humans reach **Australia**. `50,000*`

▶ *Stone spear points from the Clovis culture.*

Emergence of **Mesolithic** intensive hunter-gatherer cultures. `11,600*`

Mass extinction of **marsupial megafauna** in Australia. `47,000–20,000*`

Human occupation at **Monte Verde**, Chile. `14,500*`

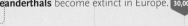

Anatomically modern humans reach **China**. `40,000*`

Clovis culture spreads across the Great Plains of North America. `13,500*`

`61,000*` Earliest evidence for the use of **bow and arrow** (probable arrow heads): Sibudu Cave, South Africa.

Oldest known musical instrument, a simple **bone flute** from Divje Babe, Slovenia. `35,000*`

Mass extinction of **American megafauna**. `11,500*`

Ancestors of the **Na-Dene-speaking peoples** (Athabaskans, Navajo and Apache) migrate to North America from Siberia. `11,000*`

6000 BC

AFTER THE ICE: HUMAN ADAPTATIONS TO A WARMER WORLD AND THE BEGINNING OF AGRICULTURE

The end of the last glaciation brought far-reaching environmental changes to most parts of the world. The vast amount of water locked up in the continental ice sheets returned to the seas, inundating coastal lowlands and severing land bridges before the sea level stabilized around 6000 BC. Large areas of the northern hemisphere that had lain under permanent ice became habitable. The cold steppes and game-rich tundras retreated as forests spread north, while changing rainfall patterns caused the greening of the Sahara, desertification in Australia and the spread of equatorial rainforests.

In many parts of the world, humans adapted to the changing conditions by intensifying their exploitation of small game, wildfowl, fish, shellfish and plant foods. Areas of great ecological diversity, such as Northwest Europe, were able to support relatively dense populations of hunter-gatherers. In other areas, humans adapted by taking up farming. The first stage was planting the seeds of favoured wild food plants near regular campsites to ensure a convenient supply. The next step was the domestication of wild food plants by selective breeding for desirable qualities. Cereals, such as wheat, barley, rice and millet, were among the earliest plants to be domesticated because their seeds are rich in carbohydrates and easy to store. Most animal species to be domesticated were herd animals, whose 'follow-the-leader' instincts made them easy to manage.

The first farming societies emerged around 8000 BC, in the so-called Fertile Crescent in the Middle East, an area exceptionally rich in plants and animals that were suitable for domestication. The transition from hunting and gathering to full dependence on farming took two or three centuries. Farming spread from the Middle East to North Africa and Southeast Europe by around 6500 BC, and to South Asia around 6000 BC. Farming developed independently in China and New Guinea by around 7000 BC. Cultivation of wild plants began in the Americas at much the same time as it did in the Old World, but the transition there to full dependence on farming took several thousand years. Few animals in the Americas were suitable for domestication and, outside the Andes, pastoralism remained unimportant until European contact.

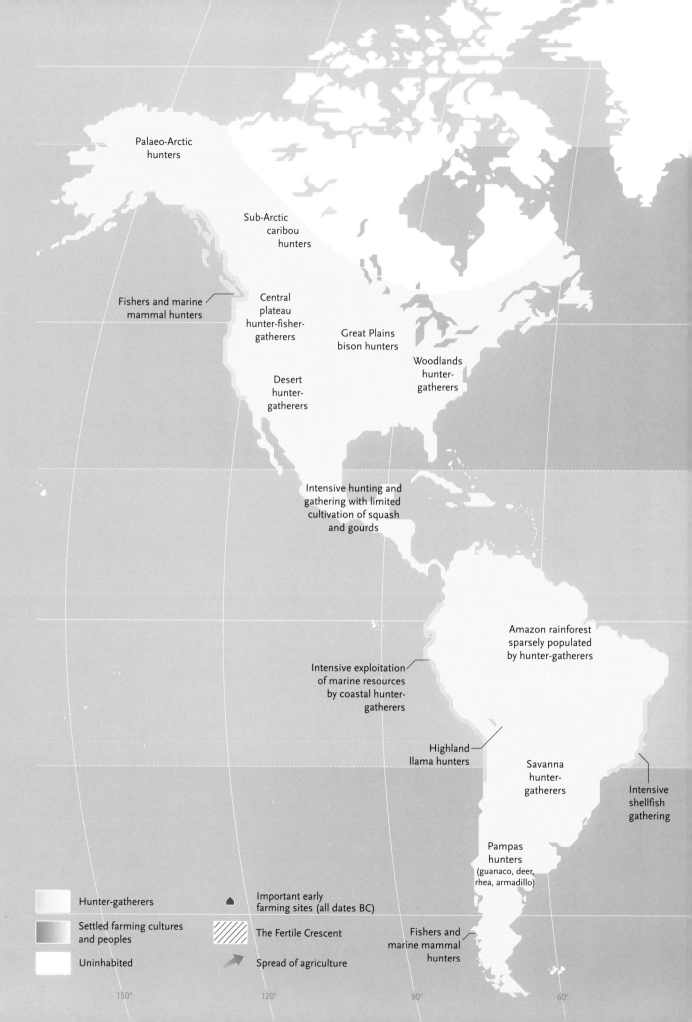

Palaeo-Arctic hunters

Sub-Arctic caribou hunters

Fishers and marine mammal hunters

Central plateau hunter-fisher-gatherers

Great Plains bison hunters

Woodlands hunter-gatherers

Desert hunter-gatherers

Intensive hunting and gathering with limited cultivation of squash and gourds

Amazon rainforest sparsely populated by hunter-gatherers

Intensive exploitation of marine resources by coastal hunter-gatherers

Highland llama hunters

Savanna hunter-gatherers

Intensive shellfish gathering

Pampas hunters (guanaco, deer, rhea, armadillo)

Fishers and marine mammal hunters

Hunter-gatherers	Important early farming sites (all dates BC)
Settled farming cultures and peoples	The Fertile Crescent
Uninhabited	Spread of agriculture

Palaeo-Siberian taiga hunter-gatherers

Palaeo-Asiatic
hunter-gatherers

Mesolithic intensive
hunter-gatherers
and fishers

SOUTHWEST ASIA AND SOUTHEAST EUROPE
Wheat and barley cultivation,
goat, sheep and cattle rearing

*Çatalhöyük
7300*

*Hacılar
7000*

Nea Nikomedia 6500

Argissa 6500

Çayönü Tepesi 7200

Knossos 7000

Ganj Dareh 8000

Jericho 9600

Ali Kosh 8000

Mehrgarh 6500

YELLOW RIVER REGION
Millet cultivation

Palaeo-Asiatic
hunter-gatherers

Dadiwan 6000

Cishan 6000

Peiligang 6000

Jiahu 6500

Jomon intensive
hunter-gatherers
and fishers

Bashidang 7000

Pengtoushan 7000

YANGTZE RIVER REGION
Rice cultivation

Saharan wild
cattle hunters
and wild cereal
gatherers

*'Ain Ghazal
7250*

*Abu Hureyra
11,000–
9000*

*Nabta Playa
7000 (disputed)*

Tropical forest hunter-gatherers,
limited cultivation of yams

Tropical
forest
hunter-
gatherers

NEW GUINEA HIGHLANDS
Early cultivation of
taro and sugar cane

Equatorial
rainforest sparsely
populated by
hunter-gatherers

Pre-Austronesian
hunter-gatherers
intensively exploiting
marine resources

Kuk 7000–5000

Khoisan
hunter-
gatherers

Australian Aboriginal
hunter-gatherers
exploit river and
coastal habitats

Tasmanian
hunter-gatherers

Arctic Circle

Tropic of Cancer

Equator

Tropic of Capricorn

75°

45°

45°

6000 BC

The emergence of farming was the first great change in human history, enabling a huge increase in the population. The numbers of hunter-gatherers were always strictly constrained by the natural productivity of the environment: if the population rose to an unsustainable level, starvation quickly restored balance. In historical times, hunter-gatherers practised infanticide and other methods to limit their numbers. Even in favourable environments, hunting and gathering can support a population density of only about one person to 25 square kilometres. In contrast, even the simple techniques employed by the first farmers could support around 500 people on the same area of land.

In farming there is a close relationship between productivity and the amount of work put into the land. Thus, for farmers, a high birthrate was positively desirable: extra hands could be put to work intensifying cultivation or clearing new fields to increase food production even more. Famines resulting from crop failures struck mainly at the very young or very old and did little to restrain long-term population growth. Thanks to their numerical advantage, farmers were able steadily to encroach on the territories of neighbouring hunter-gatherers, who were forced either to adopt farming themselves or starve.

Farming led to many technological and social changes as settled farmers were not limited to what was portable. New tools, such as polished stone axes, hoes, sickles and grindstones appeared. Looms were invented for weaving textiles and pottery came into widespread use for storage and cooking. In many areas, the kilns used for firing pottery also enabled another technological breakthrough: the smelting and casting of copper and gold. It was worthwhile for farmers to invest time and effort in building durable houses and they could accumulate possessions, ultimately leading to the emergence of social distinctions.

World Population (very approximate)

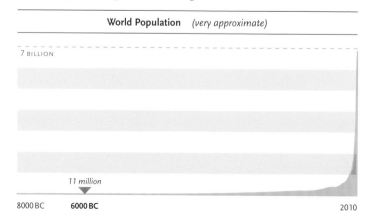

7 BILLION

11 million

8000 BC   **6000 BC**   2010

20

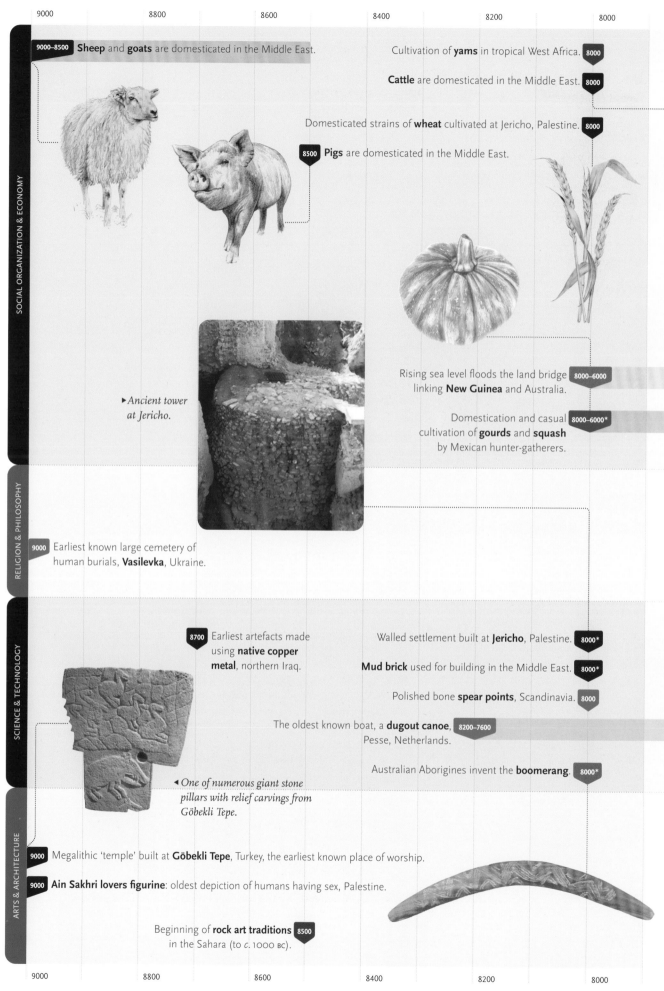

SOCIAL ORGANIZATION & ECONOMY

9000–8500 **Sheep** and **goats** are domesticated in the Middle East.

Cultivation of **yams** in tropical West Africa. **8000**

Cattle are domesticated in the Middle East. **8000**

Domesticated strains of **wheat** cultivated at Jericho, Palestine. **8000**

8500 **Pigs** are domesticated in the Middle East.

Rising sea level floods the land bridge **8000–6000** linking **New Guinea** and Australia.

Domestication and casual **8000–6000*** cultivation of **gourds** and **squash** by Mexican hunter-gatherers.

▶ *Ancient tower at Jericho.*

RELIGION & PHILOSOPHY

9000 Earliest known large cemetery of human burials, **Vasilevka**, Ukraine.

SCIENCE & TECHNOLOGY

8700 Earliest artefacts made using **native copper metal**, northern Iraq.

Walled settlement built at **Jericho**, Palestine. **8000***

Mud brick used for building in the Middle East. **8000***

Polished bone **spear points**, Scandinavia. **8000**

The oldest known boat, a **dugout canoe**, **8200–7600** Pesse, Netherlands.

Australian Aborigines invent the **boomerang**. **8000***

◀ *One of numerous giant stone pillars with relief carvings from Göbekli Tepe.*

ARTS & ARCHITECTURE

9000 Megalithic 'temple' built at **Göbekli Tepe**, Turkey, the earliest known place of worship.

9000 **Ain Sakhri lovers figurine**: oldest depiction of humans having sex, Palestine.

Beginning of **rock art traditions** **8500** in the Sahara (to *c.* 1000 BC).

9000   8800   8600   8400   8200   8000

The **cat** is domesticated, according to genetic evidence, probably in Cyprus. 7000

6500 **Farming** begins in Southeast Europe.

7500 Domestication of **chick peas**, **lentils** and **peas**, Middle East.

Britain becomes an island due to rising post-glacial sea levels. **6000**

Farming spreads to **Italy**. 6000

Farming villages develop in the mountains of **Baluchistan**. 6000

Millet farming in the Yellow river region, China. 6000

6500 Possible beginning of **cattle** domestication and **cereal** cultivation in the Sahara.

7000 **Rice** cultivation in the Yangtze river region, China.   **6500** Earliest **domestic dog** in the Americas, Danger Cave, Utah.

Gourds cultivated in eastern North America, probably for use as fishing-net floats. 6000

Tasmania becomes an island: Tasmanian Aborigines remain isolated from all outside contacts until AD 1772. 6000

7000–5000 Beginning of cultivation of taro and sugar cane in the **New Guinea highlands**.

◄ *Figurine showing a seated 'mother goddess' from Çatalhöyük; her head and the animal head on her left are not original.*

7500–5700 Clay figurines of a **'mother goddess'** made at Çatalhöyük, Turkey.

6800* Plastered and painted **human skulls** at Jericho and other sites: possible evidence of an ancestor cult.

7000–6000* **Skis** are used in northwest Russia.

7500 Earliest known **basketry**, Hinds Cave, Texas.

6500 **Pottery** is in widespread use in the Middle East.

Lead smelting, **basketry** and **textile** **6200** production at Çatalhöyük, Turkey.

Warp-weighted loom used in Southeast Europe. **6000***

Copper smelting in the Middle East. **6000***

► *Running or dancing figure painted in red on the wall of a house, Çatalhöyük.*

6500–5500 Sculptures of **anthropomorphic figures with fish heads** at the Mesolithic settlement of Lepenski Vir, Serbia.

7500–5700 Buildings at **Çatalhöyük**, Turkey, decorated inside and out with murals.

6500 Earliest evidence of **board games**, Jordan, Syria and Iran.

*Approximate date

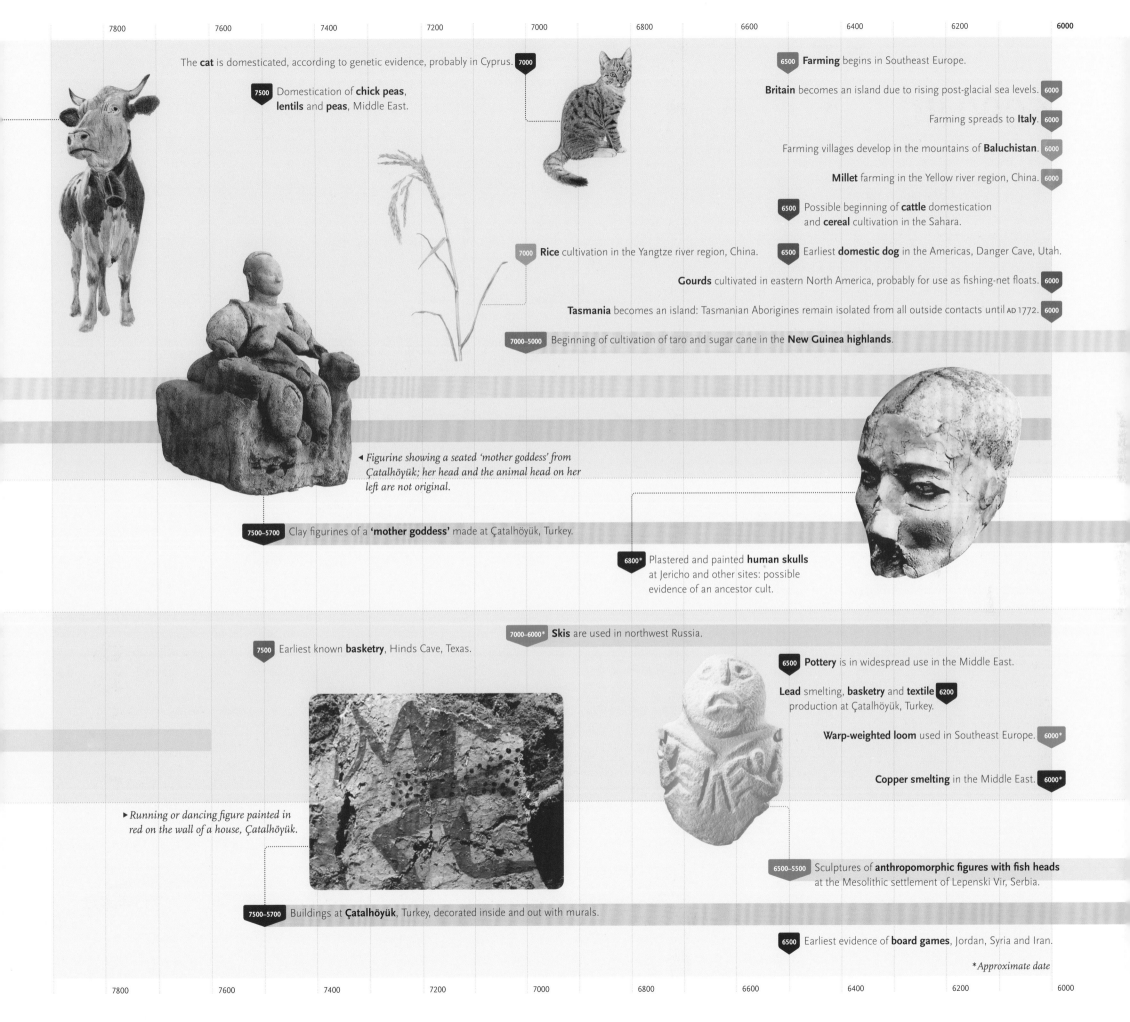

4000 BC

THE SPREAD OF FARMING SOCIETIES IN THE OLD WORLD

Between 6000 and 4000 BC the farming way of life spread across the Middle East to the Indus river valley, into Western Europe and North Africa and across most of East Asia. In the most densely populated parts of the Middle East, hierarchical societies developed, which by 4000 BC were in the early stages of urbanization.

Farming spread most readily to locations where environmental conditions bore the closest resemblance to those in the areas where it first originated. The Mediterranean, the Sahara (then experiencing a 'wet' phase) and the Indus valley, for example, had climates naturally suited to the cultivation of Middle Eastern crops like wheat and barley. Farming first left this natural comfort zone when it spread to Central and Western Europe, a move which was made possible by the gradual development of crop strains that could tolerate shorter growing seasons and cooler, wetter summers, and also by greater reliance on stock rearing. By 4000 BC farming was also spreading onto the Eurasian steppes. An increasing body of genetic evidence indicates that farming was spread through Europe mainly by migrants who assimilated or replaced the indigenous hunter-gatherers.

In the Middle East, technological innovations, such as the plough and irrigation, allowed farmers to increase their productivity greatly and to colonize areas like the fertile Mesopotamian flood plain which did not have enough rainfall to support farming. By 4000 BC Mesopotamia was probably the most densely populated part of the world. Small towns dotted the plains, and temple complexes hint that a ruling class had emerged which combined religious and political authority.

In the Americas, distinct regional variations on the hunter-gatherer way of life developed, each specifically adapted to local environmental conditions. With its rich marine resources, the Pacific coast became relatively densely populated. Farming was not established anywhere in the Americas, but in many areas hunter-gatherers cultivated wild food plants as supplementary foods, unconsciously beginning the process of domestication that would eventually make farming possible. These plants included future staples such as potatoes in the Andes and maize in Mesoamerica. In a similar way, hunter-gatherers in the West African forests cultivated wild yams as a supplementary food.

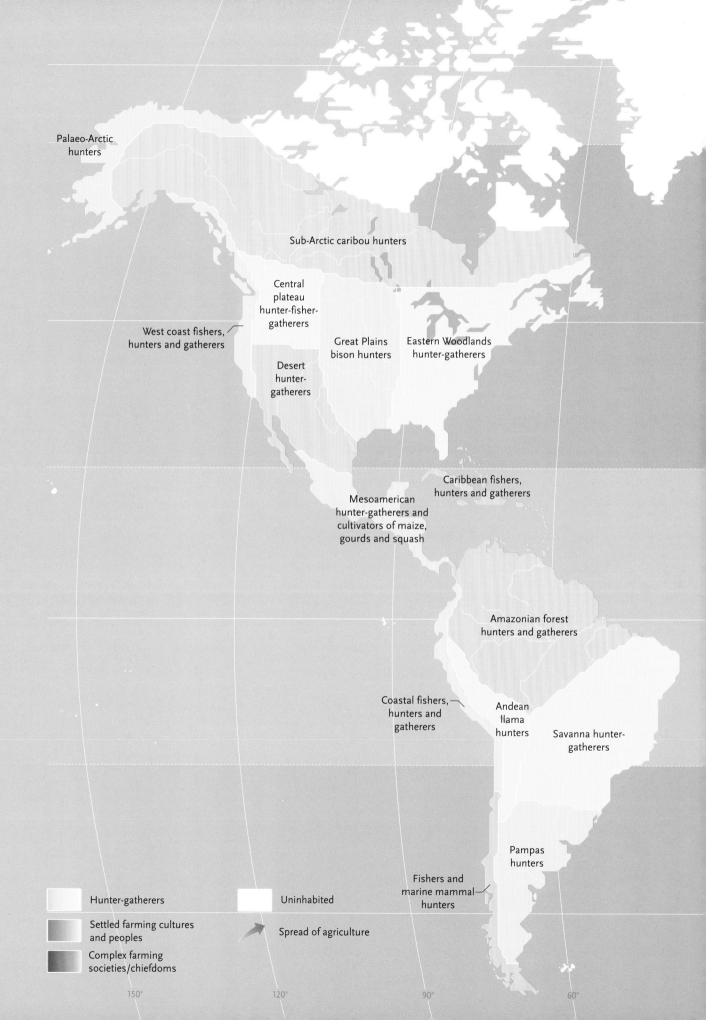

Palaeo-Arctic hunters

Sub-Arctic caribou hunters

Central plateau hunter-fisher-gatherers

West coast fishers, hunters and gatherers

Great Plains bison hunters

Eastern Woodlands hunter-gatherers

Desert hunter-gatherers

Caribbean fishers, hunters and gatherers

Mesoamerican hunter-gatherers and cultivators of maize, gourds and squash

Amazonian forest hunters and gatherers

Coastal fishers, hunters and gatherers

Andean llama hunters

Savanna hunter-gatherers

Pampas hunters

Fishers and marine mammal hunters

Hunter-gatherers

Uninhabited

Settled farming cultures and peoples

Spread of agriculture

Complex farming societies/chiefdoms

150°   120°   90°   60°

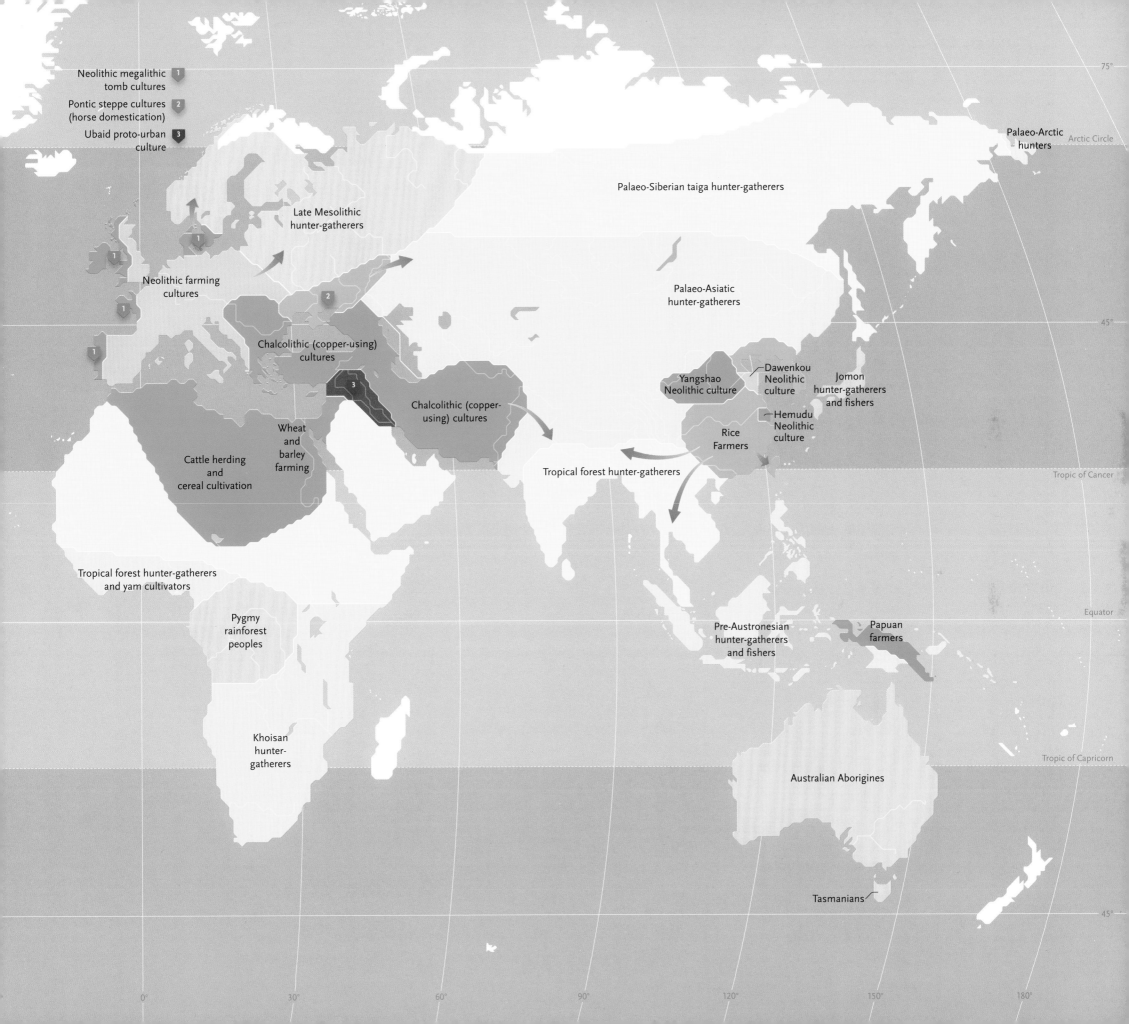

Neolithic megalithic tomb cultures `1`
Pontic steppe cultures (horse domestication) `2`
Ubaid proto-urban culture `3`

Palaeo-Arctic hunters

Palaeo-Siberian taiga hunter-gatherers

Late Mesolithic hunter-gatherers

Neolithic farming cultures

Palaeo-Asiatic hunter-gatherers

Jomon hunter-gatherers and fishers

Chalcolithic (copper-using) cultures

Dawenkou Neolithic culture

Yangshao Neolithic culture

Hemudu Neolithic culture

Chalcolithic (copper-using) cultures

Wheat and barley farming

Rice Farmers

Cattle herding and cereal cultivation

Tropical forest hunter-gatherers

Tropical forest hunter-gatherers and yam cultivators

Pygmy rainforest peoples

Pre-Austronesian hunter-gatherers and fishers

Papuan farmers

Khoisan hunter-gatherers

Australian Aborigines

Tasmanians

Arctic Circle

Tropic of Cancer

Equator

Tropic of Capricorn

75°

45°

0°   30°   60°   90°   120°   150°   180°

4000 BC

By 4000 BC the long-term social and cultural consequences of the adoption of agriculture were becoming clearer. Population growth was much accelerated: in the 200,000 years up to the time of the first farming communities *c.* 8000 BC, human numbers grew from a few thousand to an estimated 5 million. By 6000 BC, the global population had doubled and by 4000 BC it had more than doubled again. Hunter-gatherers were already greatly outnumbered by farmers.

Farming also had the power to transform society. Even subsistence farmers are able to produce more food than they need in most years. This surplus food was the first form of wealth. Cereal crops such as wheat and rice were particularly useful because they can easily be stored against shortages or for later exchange. Farmers more successful at accumulating surpluses acquired power because they could afford exotic goods and control their distribution, or force other farmers into dependent relationships during food shortages. Distinctions of rank and status began to develop. More intensive agriculture enabled greater surpluses and a more hierarchical society. Surpluses also fuelled an increase in technological and cultural innovation because specialist workers could be supported in non-agricultural occupations. In 4000 BC this process was most evident on the fertile plains of Mesopotamia.

In other parts of the world, farming societies were still relatively egalitarian, as shown by the communal megalithic tombs of early farmers along Europe's Atlantic coast. Also significant is the Pontic steppe culture, centred on Ukraine, which domesticated the horse. Horses would revolutionize transport and warfare, but they were initially seen only as sources of meat and milk. In East Asia, the widespread and diverse farming cultures laid the foundations for Chinese cultural development.

World Population *(very approximate)*

7 BILLION

28 million

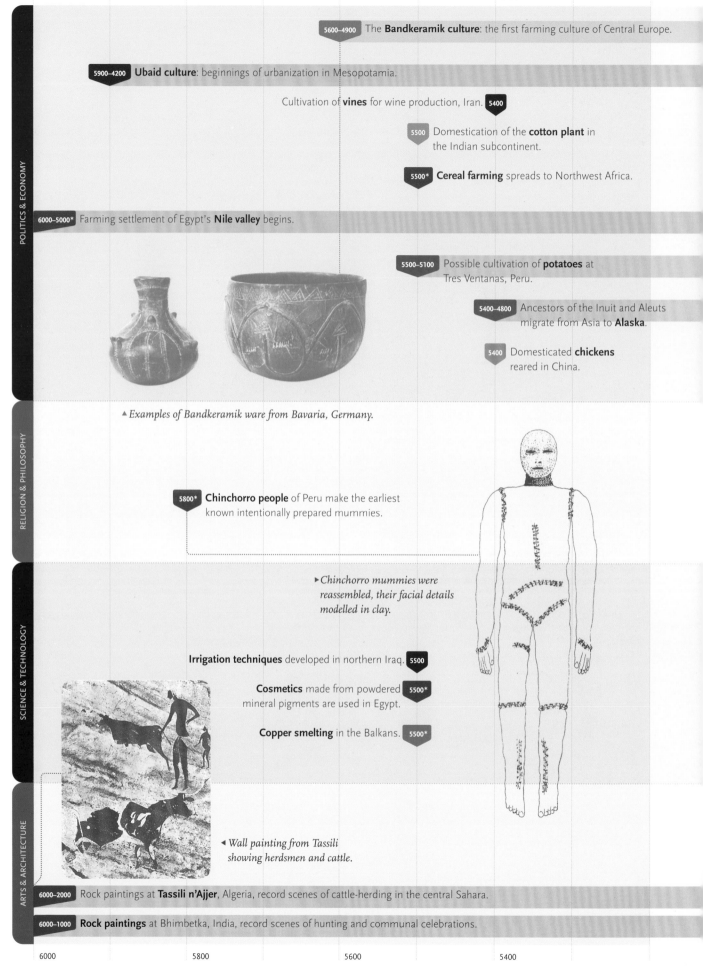

6000   5800   5600   5400

POLITICS & ECONOMY

5600–4900 The **Bandkeramik culture**: the first farming culture of Central Europe.

5900–4200 **Ubaid culture**: beginnings of urbanization in Mesopotamia.

Cultivation of **vines** for wine production, Iran. **5400**

5500 Domestication of the **cotton plant** in the Indian subcontinent.

5500* **Cereal farming** spreads to Northwest Africa.

6000–5000* Farming settlement of Egypt's **Nile valley** begins.

5500–5100 Possible cultivation of **potatoes** at Tres Ventanas, Peru.

5400–4800 Ancestors of the Inuit and Aleuts migrate from Asia to **Alaska**.

5400 Domesticated **chickens** reared in China.

▲ *Examples of Bandkeramik ware from Bavaria, Germany.*

RELIGION & PHILOSOPHY

5800* **Chinchorro people** of Peru make the earliest known intentionally prepared mummies.

▶ *Chinchorro mummies were reassembled, their facial details modelled in clay.*

SCIENCE & TECHNOLOGY

Irrigation techniques developed in northern Iraq. **5500**

Cosmetics made from powdered **5500*** mineral pigments are used in Egypt.

Copper smelting in the Balkans. **5500***

ARTS & ARCHITECTURE

◀ *Wall painting from Tassili showing herdsmen and cattle.*

6000–2000 Rock paintings at **Tassili n'Ajjer**, Algeria, record scenes of cattle-herding in the central Sahara.

6000–1000 **Rock paintings** at Bhimbetka, India, record scenes of hunting and communal celebrations.

6000   5800   5600   5400

Expansion of **pastoralists** across `4500*` the Eurasian steppes begins.

The **horse** is domesticated on the western `4000` Eurasian steppes, initially for its meat and milk.

`5000` Cultivation of **olives** in the Middle East.

Farming is introduced to Britain and southern Scandinavia. `4000`

`5000*` Desertification of the **Sahara** begins.

The **Uruk period** sees the growth `4200–3100` of the first cities in Mesopotamia.

Domestication of the **zebu** (Asian ox) in South Asia. `4000`

Farmers begin to settle on the **Indus river flood plain**. `4000`

`4300` **Maize** domestication at Guilá Naquitz, Mexico.

▲ *Impression from an Uruk-period seal showing a priest and acolyte.*

`5000–3200*` Early Chinese **Yangshao culture** flourishes in Yangtze river region.

The **first megalithic tombs** are built, Brittany, France. `4500`

`5000` The earliest known **Mesopotamian temple complex** is built at Eridu: it is probably dedicated to the water god Enki.

▲ *Chamber tomb from the early Neolithic tomb at Barnenez, Brittany.*

`4500–4200` Earliest intentionally prepared **Egyptian mummies** (full development of the technique *c.* 2600 BC).

Copper used in the Indus river valley region. `4000`

Opium poppy domesticated in the western Mediterranean. `4200`

◄ *Hammered gold appliqué in the shape of an animal, from Varna, Bulgaria.*

`4500` The **plough** is in use in Southeast Europe.

`4500` The **plough** and the **sail** are used in Mesopotamia.

`5000` Earliest known **goldworking**, Bulgaria.

`5000` **Incised clay tablets** from Tartaria, Romania, show that a simple system of **notation** is used in Southeast Europe.

*Approximate date

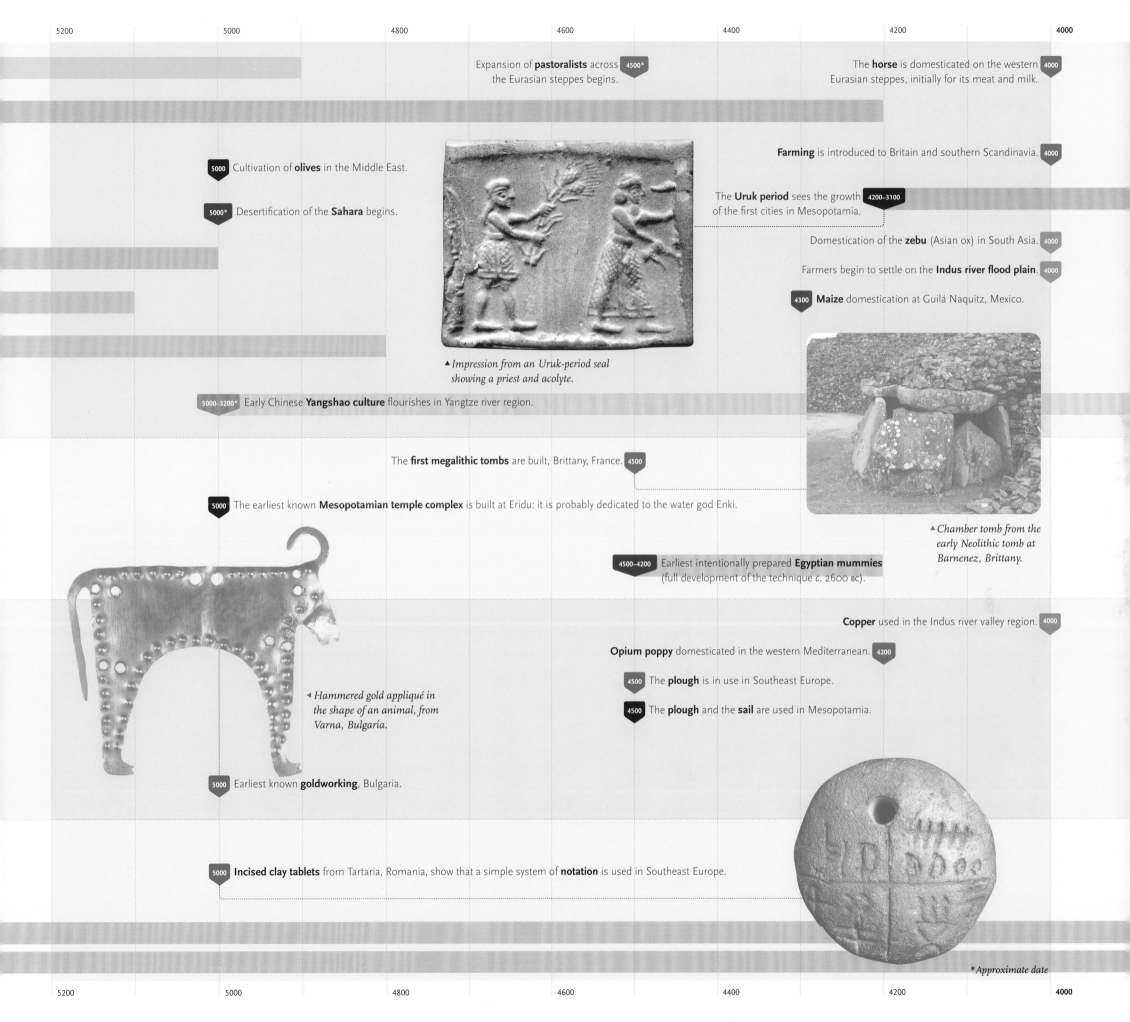

2000 BC

BIRTH OF THE FIRST CIVILIZATIONS IN SUMER AND EGYPT; EARLY FARMING SOCIETIES IN THE NEW WORLD

Civilizations – complex societies with cities and state organization through formal governments – first arose during the 4th and 3rd millennia BC. The first, the Sumerian civilization, emerged *c.* 3500 BC in southern Mesopotamia. Independent city states grew up, each focused on a temple complex that acted as a centre for the collection and redistribution of food surpluses, craft production and trade goods. Rulers combined political and religious authority and wars between cities were common. Around 2334 BC Sargon the Great, ruler of Akkad, conquered all of Mesopotamia, creating the first known empire. After the fall of this Akkadian empire *c.* 2193 BC, the city of Ur rose to dominate the region until its empire was overthrown in 2004 BC.

Local kingdoms developed in Egypt's fertile Nile valley towards the end of the 4th millennium BC. United by Narmer *c.* 3000 BC, Egypt developed a tradition of divine monarchy whose enormous pyramid tombs are testimony to its power and organization during the Old Kingdom period. The political organization of the Indus Valley civilization, which arose *c.* 2600 BC, is poorly understood. The Minoan Palace civilization of Crete, which emerged *c.* 2000 BC, was ruled from palaces which functioned in a similar way to Mesopotamian temple complexes.

In China, the advanced Neolithic Longshan culture developed growing social stratification with powerful rulers and skilled artisans. This may have resulted from rapid population growth following the beginning of intensive rice farming in the Yellow river region. Also significant was the spread of pastoralist cultures across the steppes as far east as the Altai Mountains. In the Americas, the first farming societies emerged, while marine-mammal hunters began the colonization of the high Arctic.

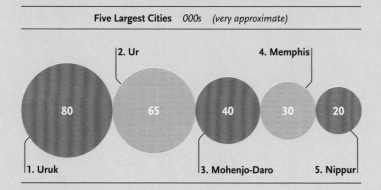

Five Largest Cities   *000s*   *(very approximate)*

2. Ur — 65
4. Memphis — 30
1. Uruk — 80
3. Mohenjo-Daro — 40
5. Nippur — 20

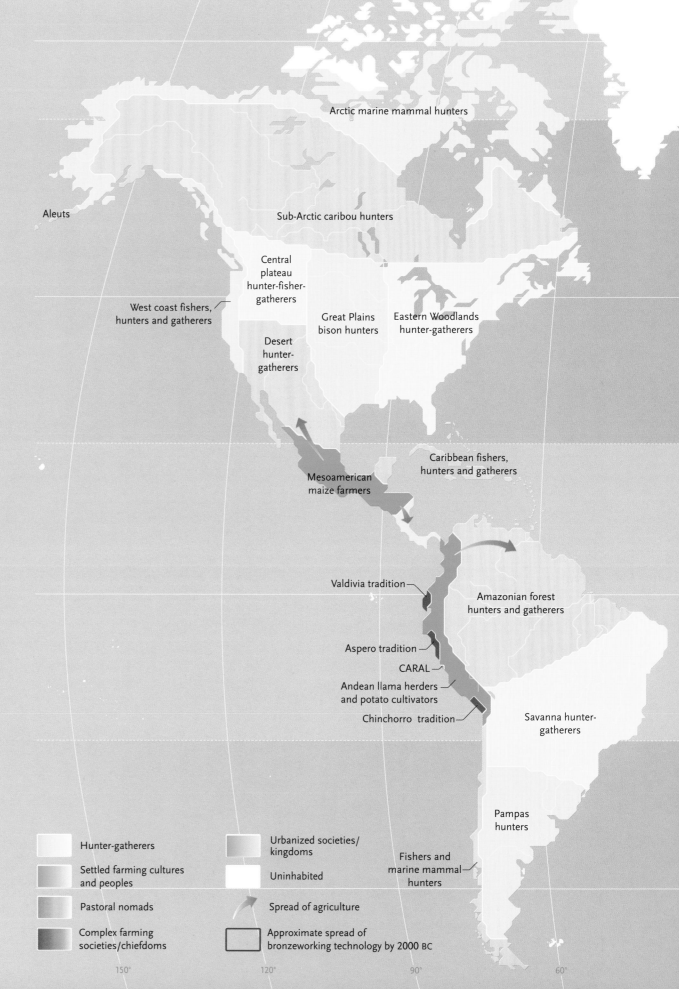

Arctic marine mammal hunters

Aleuts

Sub-Arctic caribou hunters

Central plateau hunter-fisher-gatherers

West coast fishers, hunters and gatherers

Great Plains bison hunters

Eastern Woodlands hunter-gatherers

Desert hunter-gatherers

Caribbean fishers, hunters and gatherers

Mesoamerican maize farmers

Valdivia tradition

Amazonian forest hunters and gatherers

Aspero tradition

CARAL

Andean llama herders and potato cultivators

Chinchorro tradition

Savanna hunter-gatherers

Pampas hunters

Fishers and marine mammal hunters

Hunter-gatherers

Urbanized societies/kingdoms

Settled farming cultures and peoples

Uninhabited

Pastoral nomads

Spread of agriculture

Complex farming societies/chiefdoms

Approximate spread of bronzeworking technology by 2000 BC

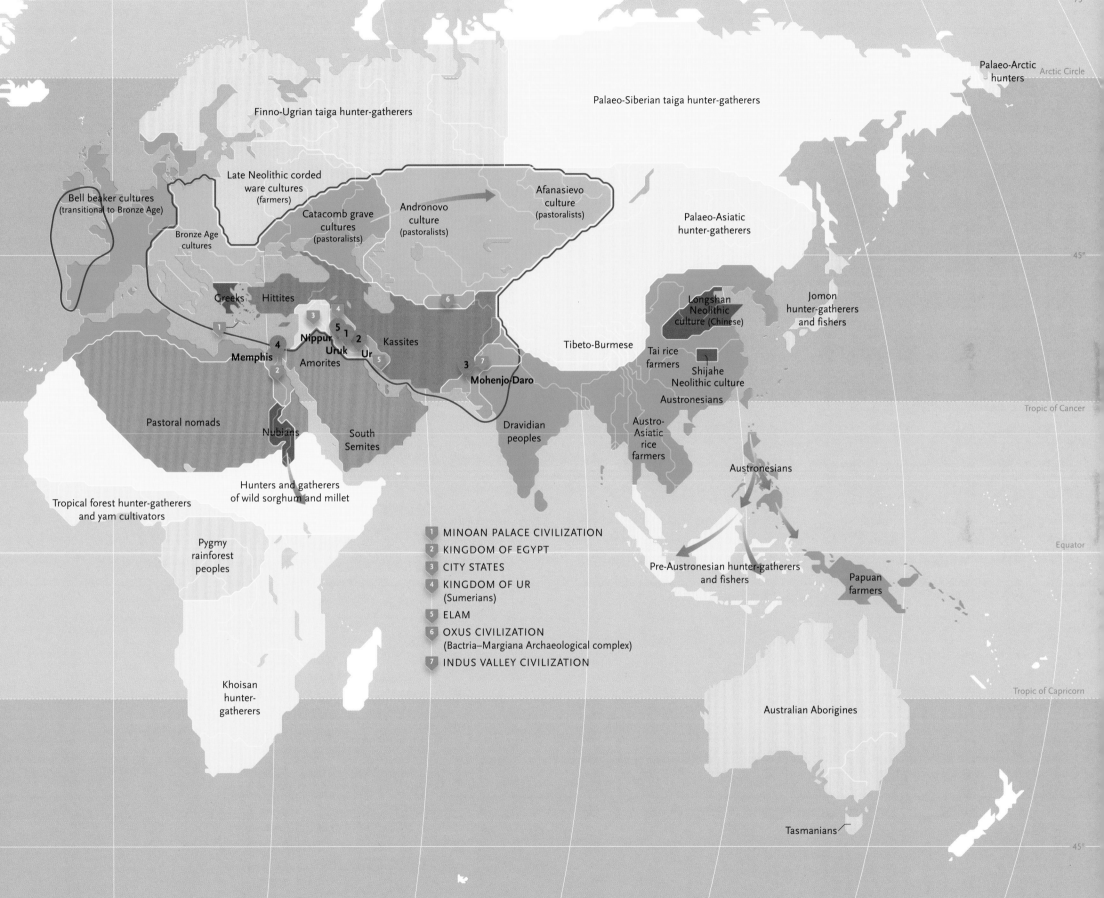

Palaeo-Arctic hunters

Arctic Circle

Finno-Ugrian taiga hunter-gatherers

Palaeo-Siberian taiga hunter-gatherers

Late Neolithic corded ware cultures (farmers)

Bell beaker cultures (transitional to Bronze Age)

Bronze Age cultures

Catacomb grave cultures (pastoralists)

Andronovo culture (pastoralists)

Afanasievo culture (pastoralists)

Palaeo-Asiatic hunter-gatherers

Greeks   Hittites

3

5 1 2

Nippur
Uruk   Ur

4   Memphis

2

Amorites

Kassites

5

Longshan Neolithic culture (Chinese)

Jomon hunter-gatherers and fishers

Tibeto-Burmese

Tai rice farmers

Shijahe Neolithic culture

3   7

Mohenjo-Daro

Austronesians

Nubians

Pastoral nomads

South Semites

Dravidian peoples

Austro-Asiatic rice farmers

Hunters and gatherers of wild sorghum and millet

Austronesians

Tropical forest hunter-gatherers and yam cultivators

Equator

Pygmy rainforest peoples

Pre-Austronesian hunter-gatherers and fishers

Papuan farmers

1 MINOAN PALACE CIVILIZATION

2 KINGDOM OF EGYPT

3 CITY STATES

4 KINGDOM OF UR (Sumerians)

5 ELAM

6 OXUS CIVILIZATION (Bactria–Margiana Archaeological complex)

7 INDUS VALLEY CIVILIZATION

Khoisan hunter-gatherers

Tropic of Capricorn

Australian Aborigines

Tasmanians

Tropic of Cancer

0°   30°   60°   90°   120°   150°   180°

75°

45°

6

45°

2000 BC

The most important cultural development of the 4th and 3rd millennia BC was the invention of writing, an advance which effectively marks the beginning of the end of human prehistory. Writing was most probably invented as an aid to administration in societies that had grown so large and complex that human memory alone could not hold all the information for their efficient government.

The earliest writing system, the Sumerian pictographic script, which appeared c. 3400 BC, was probably a development of a widely used clay-token system. In the early 3rd millennium BC, Sumerian pictographic evolved into the more versatile cuneiform writing system. Hieroglyphic writing systems evolved independently in Egypt and the Indus valley. By 2000 BC a hieroglyphic script was also used by the Minoans on Crete, possibly as a result of trade contacts with Egypt.

Equally important was the invention, c. 3800 BC, of bronze, probably in Iran. For millennia, copper (and later gold) had been widely used in the Middle East and Europe to make ornaments, jewelry, and small tools, but it was far too soft to supplant stone tools in everyday use. Bronze, an alloy of copper and arsenic or tin, was much harder than copper, kept an edge better and, unlike stone tools, when worn out could be melted down and recast. As the technology spread, bronze tools gradually replaced stone ones for most purposes.

Unlike stone, the raw materials of bronze are relatively rare. A side effect of the invention of bronze was, therefore, an increase in long-distance trade that, in its turn, promoted contacts between cultures. The invention, also in the 4th millennium BC, of the lost-wax method of metal casting allowed increasingly complex objects to be made of bronze, copper and gold. Another seminal invention of the period was the wheel, used for both transport and making pottery.

World Population (very approximate)

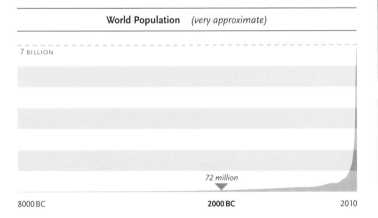

7 BILLION

72 million

8000 BC   2000 BC   2010

28

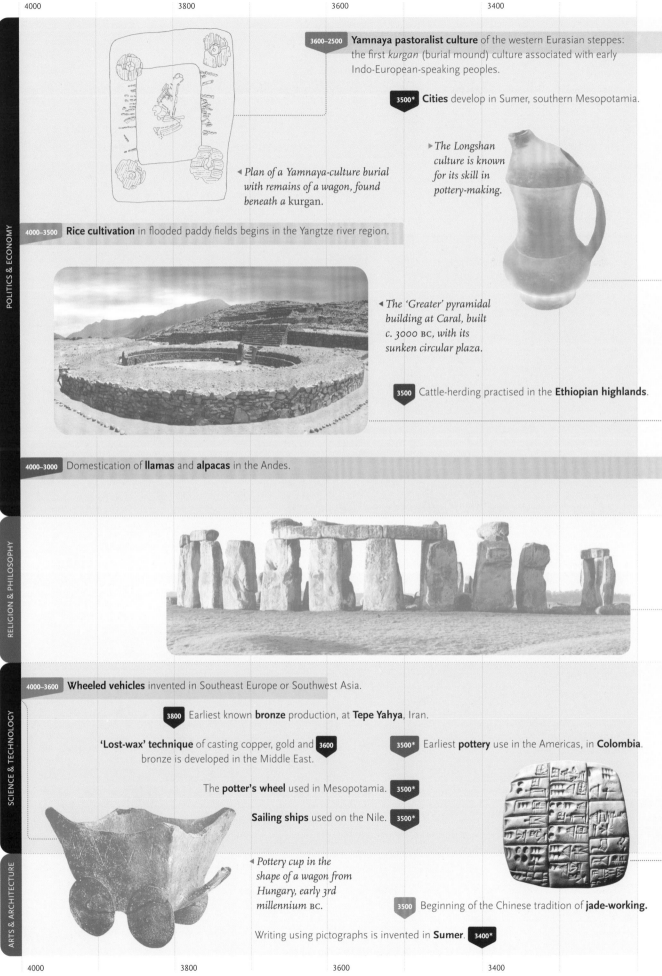

POLITICS & ECONOMY

3600–2500 **Yamnaya pastoralist culture** of the western Eurasian steppes: the first *kurgan* (burial mound) culture associated with early Indo-European-speaking peoples.

3500* **Cities** develop in Sumer, southern Mesopotamia.

◄ *Plan of a Yamnaya-culture burial with remains of a wagon, found beneath a kurgan.*

► *The Longshan culture is known for its skill in pottery-making.*

4000–3500 **Rice cultivation** in flooded paddy fields begins in the Yangtze river region.

◄ *The 'Greater' pyramidal building at Caral, built c. 3000 BC, with its sunken circular plaza.*

3500 Cattle-herding practised in the **Ethiopian highlands**.

4000–3000 Domestication of **llamas** and **alpacas** in the Andes.

RELIGION & PHILOSOPHY

SCIENCE & TECHNOLOGY

4000–3600 **Wheeled vehicles** invented in Southeast Europe or Southwest Asia.

3800 Earliest known **bronze** production, at **Tepe Yahya**, Iran.

'Lost-wax' technique of casting copper, gold and 3600 bronze is developed in the Middle East.

3500* Earliest **pottery** use in the Americas, in **Colombia**.

The **potter's wheel** used in Mesopotamia. 3500*

Sailing ships used on the Nile. 3500*

ARTS & ARCHITECTURE

◄ *Pottery cup in the shape of a wagon from Hungary, early 3rd millennium BC.*

3500 Beginning of the Chinese tradition of **jade-working**.

Writing using pictographs is invented in **Sumer**. 3400*

4000   3800   3600   3400

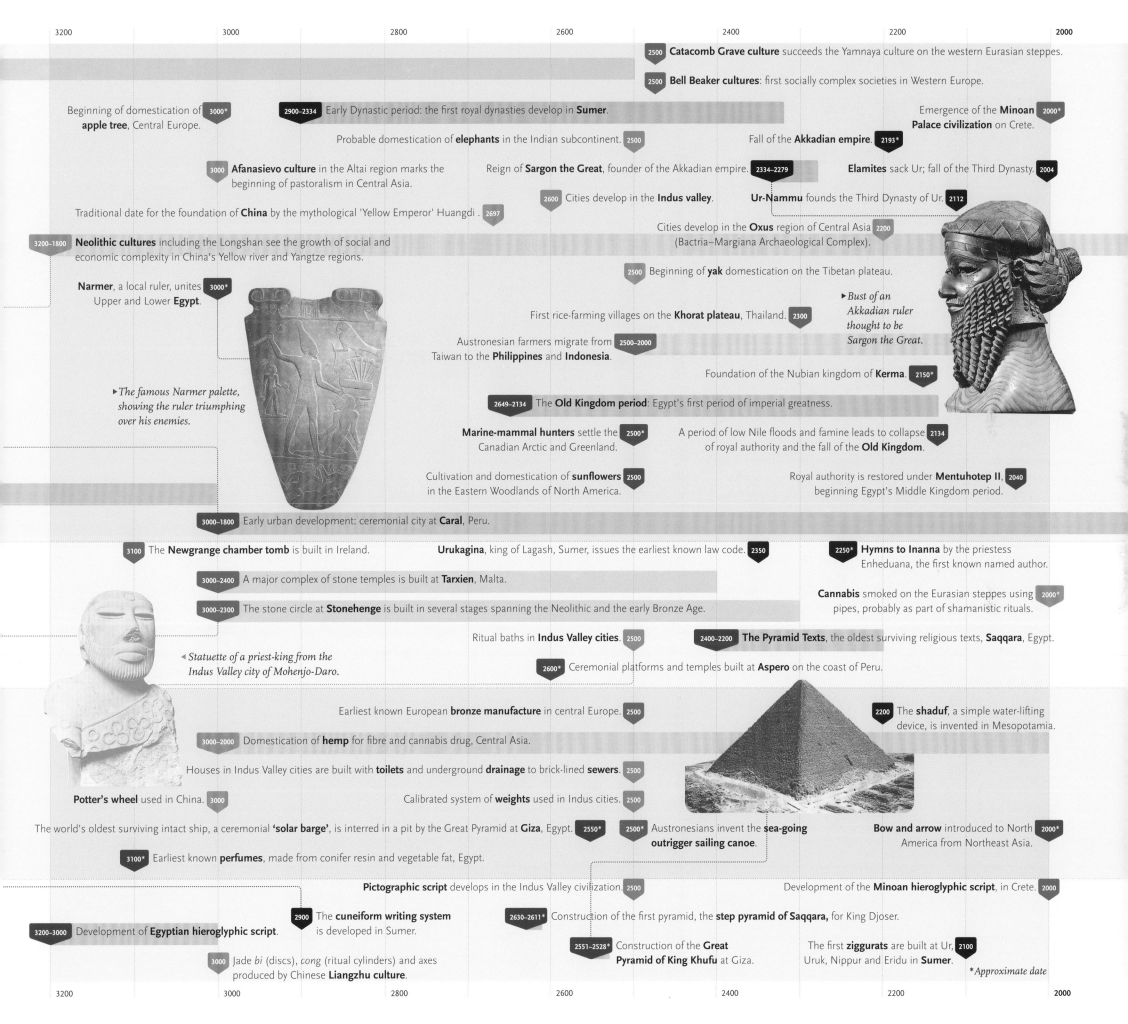

3200 3000 2800 2600 2400 2200 **2000**

2500 **Catacomb Grave culture** succeeds the Yamnaya culture on the western Eurasian steppes.

2500 **Bell Beaker cultures**: first socially complex societies in Western Europe.

Beginning of domestication of **3000*** **apple tree**, Central Europe.

2900–2334 Early Dynastic period: the first royal dynasties develop in **Sumer**.

Emergence of the **Minoan** **2000*** **Palace civilization** on Crete.

Probable domestication of **elephants** in the Indian subcontinent. **2500**

Fall of the **Akkadian empire**. **2193***

3000 **Afanasievo culture** in the Altai region marks the beginning of pastoralism in Central Asia.

Reign of **Sargon the Great**, founder of the Akkadian empire. **2334–2279**

Elamites sack Ur; fall of the Third Dynasty. **2004**

2600 Cities develop in the **Indus valley**.

Ur-Nammu founds the Third Dynasty of Ur. **2112**

Traditional date for the foundation of **China** by the mythological 'Yellow Emperor' Huangdi . **2697**

Cities develop in the **Oxus** region of Central Asia **2200** (Bactria–Margiana Archaeological Complex).

3200–1800 **Neolithic cultures** including the Longshan see the growth of social and economic complexity in China's Yellow river and Yangtze regions.

2500 Beginning of **yak** domestication on the Tibetan plateau.

Narmer, a local ruler, unites **3000*** Upper and Lower **Egypt**.

First rice-farming villages on the **Khorat plateau**, Thailand. **2300**

▶ *Bust of an Akkadian ruler thought to be Sargon the Great.*

Austronesian farmers migrate from **2500–2000** Taiwan to the **Philippines** and **Indonesia**.

Foundation of the Nubian kingdom of **Kerma**. **2150***

▶ *The famous Narmer palette, showing the ruler triumphing over his enemies.*

2649–2134 The **Old Kingdom period**: Egypt's first period of imperial greatness.

Marine-mammal hunters settle the **2500*** Canadian Arctic and Greenland.

A period of low Nile floods and famine leads to collapse **2134** of royal authority and the fall of the **Old Kingdom**.

Cultivation and domestication of **sunflowers** **2500** in the Eastern Woodlands of North America.

Royal authority is restored under **Mentuhotep II**, **2040** beginning Egypt's Middle Kingdom period.

3000–1800 Early urban development: ceremonial city at **Caral**, Peru.

3100 The **Newgrange chamber tomb** is built in Ireland.

Urukagina, king of Lagash, Sumer, issues the earliest known law code. **2350**

2250* **Hymns to Inanna** by the priestess Enheduana, the first known named author.

3000–2400 A major complex of stone temples is built at **Tarxien**, Malta.

Cannabis smoked on the Eurasian steppes using **2000*** pipes, probably as part of shamanistic rituals.

3000–2300 The stone circle at **Stonehenge** is built in several stages spanning the Neolithic and the early Bronze Age.

Ritual baths in **Indus Valley cities**. **2500**

2400–2200 **The Pyramid Texts**, the oldest surviving religious texts, **Saqqara**, Egypt.

◀ *Statuette of a priest-king from the Indus Valley city of Mohenjo-Daro.*

2600* Ceremonial platforms and temples built at **Aspero** on the coast of Peru.

Earliest known European **bronze manufacture** in central Europe. **2500**

2200 The **shaduf**, a simple water-lifting device, is invented in Mesopotamia.

3000–2000 Domestication of **hemp** for fibre and cannabis drug, Central Asia.

Houses in Indus Valley cities are built with **toilets** and underground **drainage** to brick-lined **sewers**. **2500**

Potter's wheel used in China. **3000**

Calibrated system of **weights** used in Indus cities. **2500**

The world's oldest surviving intact ship, a ceremonial **'solar barge'**, is interred in a pit by the Great Pyramid at **Giza**, Egypt. **2550***

2500* Austronesians invent the **sea-going outrigger sailing canoe**.

Bow and arrow introduced to North **2000*** America from Northeast Asia.

3100* Earliest known **perfumes**, made from conifer resin and vegetable fat, Egypt.

Pictographic script develops in the Indus Valley civilization. **2500**

Development of the **Minoan hieroglyphic script**, in Crete. **2000**

2900 The **cuneiform writing system** is developed in Sumer.

2630–2611* Construction of the first pyramid, the **step pyramid of Saqqara,** for King Djoser.

3200–3000 Development of **Egyptian hieroglyphic script**.

2551–2528* Construction of the **Great Pyramid of King Khufu** at Giza.

The first **ziggurats** are built at Ur, **2100** Uruk, Nippur and Eridu in **Sumer**.

*Approximate date

3000 Jade *bi* (discs), *cong* (ritual cylinders) and axes produced by Chinese **Liangzhu culture**.

3200 3000 2800 2600 2400 2200 **2000**

1300 BC

THE BRONZE AGE EMPIRES OF EGYPT, THE MEDITERRANEAN, MESOPOTAMIA AND CHINA

The early 2nd millennium BC brought the first sign that civilizations can fall as well as rise. The Indus Valley civilization, in terms of area the world's most widespread in 2000 BC, abruptly collapsed some time around 1900 BC. Changes to the course of the Indus and its tributaries are the most likely culprits, reducing agricultural productivity so much that the cities' dense populations could no longer be sustained.

The Minoan Palace civilization of Crete has also vanished. This was conquered c. 1450 BC by the Mycenaean Greeks, whose own civilization had arisen in the Peloponnese about 200 years earlier. The period also saw the growth of Chinese civilization in the Yellow river region under the Shang dynasty of kings. By 1300 BC other centres of civilization had developed in the Yangtze river region, outside the Shang world.

In the first half of the 2nd millennium BC, Mesopotamia came to be dominated by Assyria and its rival, the city of Babylon. However, in 1300 BC both were overshadowed by the Hittite empire of Anatolia, which arose c. 1600 BC. The Hittites vied for control of the Levant with Egypt, then at the height of its power under the New Kingdom rulers. This period saw the onset of state formation in Nubia, but it was brought to an end when the Egyptians conquered the region c. 1500 BC.

Around 1500 BC Austronesians of the Lapita culture took a great leap into the unknown when they began voyaging out into the Pacific Ocean in search of new islands to colonize. This development shows the result of the earlier invention of the stable and seaworthy outrigger canoe. The emergence, also around this time, of chiefdoms among the Olmecs and Zapotecs, marks the beginning of state formation in Mesoamerica.

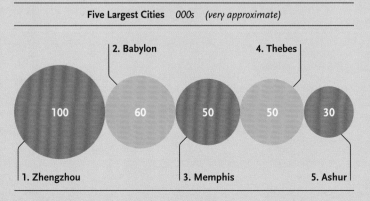

Five Largest Cities *000s* *(very approximate)*

2. Babylon — 4. Thebes

100 | 60 | 50 | 50 | 30

1. Zhengzhou — 3. Memphis — 5. Ashur

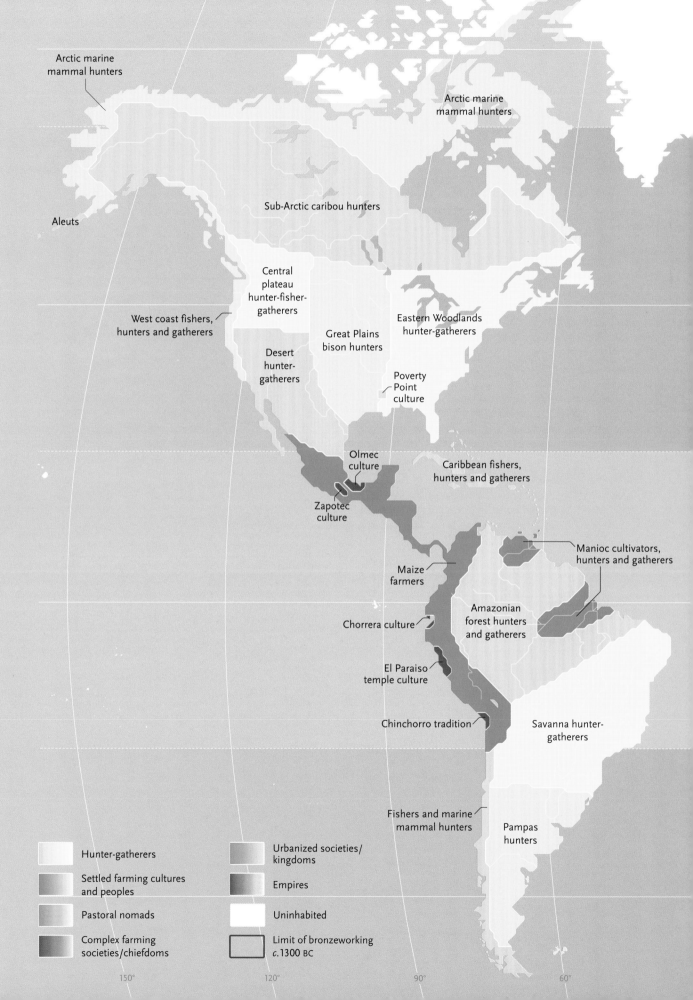

Arctic marine mammal hunters

Arctic marine mammal hunters

Sub-Arctic caribou hunters

Aleuts

Central plateau hunter-fisher-gatherers

West coast fishers, hunters and gatherers

Desert hunter-gatherers

Great Plains bison hunters

Eastern Woodlands hunter-gatherers

Poverty Point culture

Olmec culture

Zapotec culture

Caribbean fishers, hunters and gatherers

Maize farmers

Manioc cultivators, hunters and gatherers

Chorrera culture

Amazonian forest hunters and gatherers

El Paraiso temple culture

Chinchorro tradition

Savanna hunter-gatherers

Fishers and marine mammal hunters

Pampas hunters

Hunter-gatherers

Settled farming cultures and peoples

Pastoral nomads

Complex farming societies/chiefdoms

Urbanized societies/kingdoms

Empires

Uninhabited

Limit of bronzeworking c.1300 BC

150°   120°   90°   60°

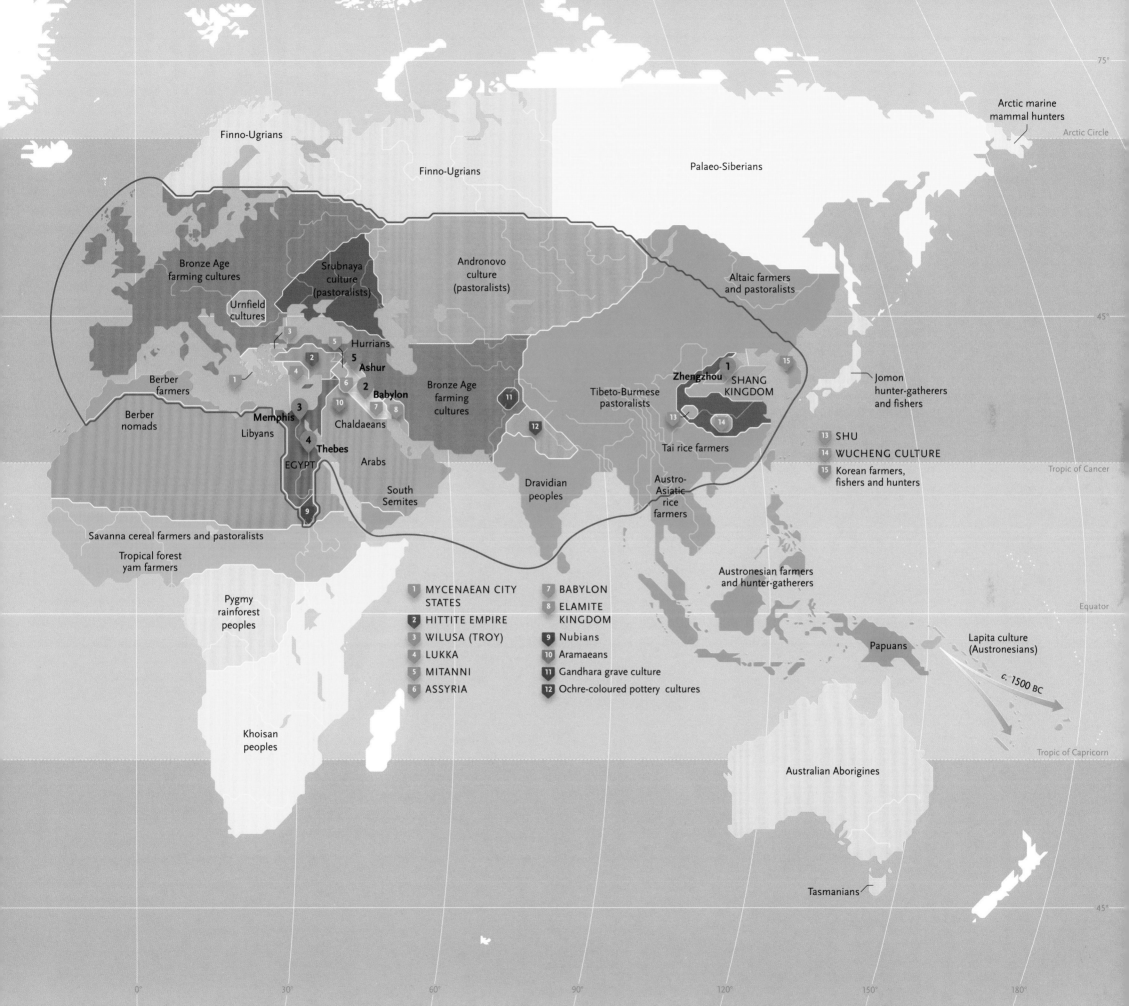

Arctic marine
mammal hunters

Finno-Ugrians

Palaeo-Siberians

Finno-Ugrians

Bronze Age
farming cultures

Srubnaya
culture
(pastoralists)

Andronovo
culture
(pastoralists)

Altaic farmers
and pastoralists

Urnfield
cultures

Hurrians

Jomon
hunter-gatherers
and fishers

5 **Ashur**

1

15

Berber
farmers

2 **Babylon**

Bronze Age
farming cultures

Zhengzhou

SHANG
KINGDOM

Memphis

3

Chaldaeans

Tibeto-Burmese
pastoralists

13

14

13 SHU

Berber
nomads

Libyans

4 **Thebes**

10

11

12

14 WUCHENG CULTURE

EGYPT

Arabs

Tai rice farmers

15 Korean farmers,
fishers and hunters

South
Semites

Dravidian
peoples

Austro-
Asiatic
rice
farmers

9

Savanna cereal farmers and pastoralists

Tropical forest
yam farmers

Pygmy
rainforest
peoples

Austronesian farmers
and hunter-gatherers

Papuans

Lapita culture
(Austronesians)

1	MYCENAEAN CITY STATES	**7**	BABYLON
2	HITTITE EMPIRE	**8**	ELAMITE KINGDOM
3	WILUSA (TROY)	**9**	Nubians
4	LUKKA	**10**	Aramaeans
5	MITANNI	**11**	Gandhara grave culture
6	ASSYRIA	**12**	Ochre-coloured pottery cultures

c. 1500 BC

Khoisan
peoples

Australian Aborigines

Tasmanians

1300 BC

In 2000 BC, the cultural links between the world's civilizations were still tenuous. By 1300 BC, the civilizations of the Middle East, Egypt and the eastern Mediterranean had developed close contacts through trade, diplomacy and war. The effects were most profound in Egypt, which had still not fully entered the Bronze Age when it was invaded in 1640 BC by the Hyksos, a Semitic people from the Levant. By the time they drove the Hyksos out in 1532 BC, the Egyptians had acquired the latest technology of the Middle East, including the horse-drawn chariot. Invented somewhere in Western Asia *c.* 1700 BC, the chariot revolutionized warfare by introducing a new element of rapid mobility to the battlefield. Another revolutionary development of the period was the invention of iron smelting, probably in Anatolia.

During this period the highly mobile pastoralist peoples of the Eurasian steppes first emerged as cultural intermediaries between east and west. For much of subsequent history, the steppe peoples carried the products of Chinese technology to the West, but initially the flow of ideas and technology went exclusively in the other direction. It was from the steppe peoples that the fledgling Chinese civilization acquired its knowledge of bronze and wheeled vehicles, including the chariot. Chinese bronze-casters developed astonishing skills, creating intricately detailed vessels using complex piece-moulds.

Early civilizations were still primarily oral cultures which used writing only for those things which could not easily be committed to memory, such as lists of stored goods, tax returns and laws. It was only slowly that writing came to be used to record poetry, stories, religious beliefs and history: the first substantial body of 'popular', non-funerary literature to survive was produced in Egypt during the Middle Kingdom period (2040–1640 BC).

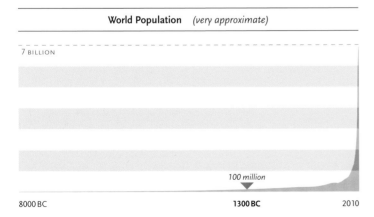

World Population *(very approximate)*

7 BILLION

100 million

8000 BC   **1300 BC**   2010

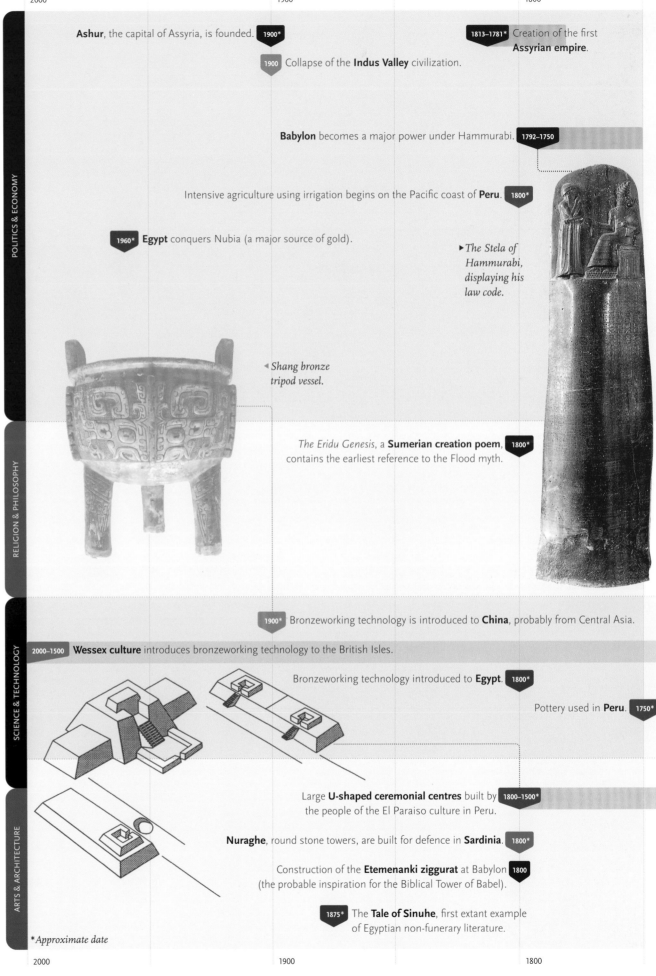

2000   1900   1800

POLITICS & ECONOMY

Ashur, the capital of Assyria, is founded. `1900*`

`1813–1781*` Creation of the first **Assyrian empire.**

`1900` Collapse of the **Indus Valley** civilization.

Babylon becomes a major power under Hammurabi. `1792–1750`

Intensive agriculture using irrigation begins on the Pacific coast of **Peru.** `1800*`

`1960*` **Egypt** conquers Nubia (a major source of gold).

▶ *The Stela of Hammurabi, displaying his law code.*

RELIGION & PHILOSOPHY

◀ *Shang bronze tripod vessel.*

The Eridu Genesis, a **Sumerian creation poem**, `1800*` contains the earliest reference to the Flood myth.

SCIENCE & TECHNOLOGY

`1900*` Bronzeworking technology is introduced to **China**, probably from Central Asia.

`2000–1500` **Wessex culture** introduces bronzeworking technology to the British Isles.

Bronzeworking technology introduced to **Egypt.** `1800*`

Pottery used in **Peru.** `1750*`

ARTS & ARCHITECTURE

Large **U-shaped ceremonial centres** built by `1800–1500*` the people of the El Paraiso culture in Peru.

Nuraghe, round stone towers, are built for defence in **Sardinia.** `1800*`

Construction of the **Etemenanki ziggurat** at Babylon `1800` (the probable inspiration for the Biblical Tower of Babel).

`1875*` The **Tale of Sinuhe**, first extant example of Egyptian non-funerary literature.

*Approximate date

2000   1900   1800

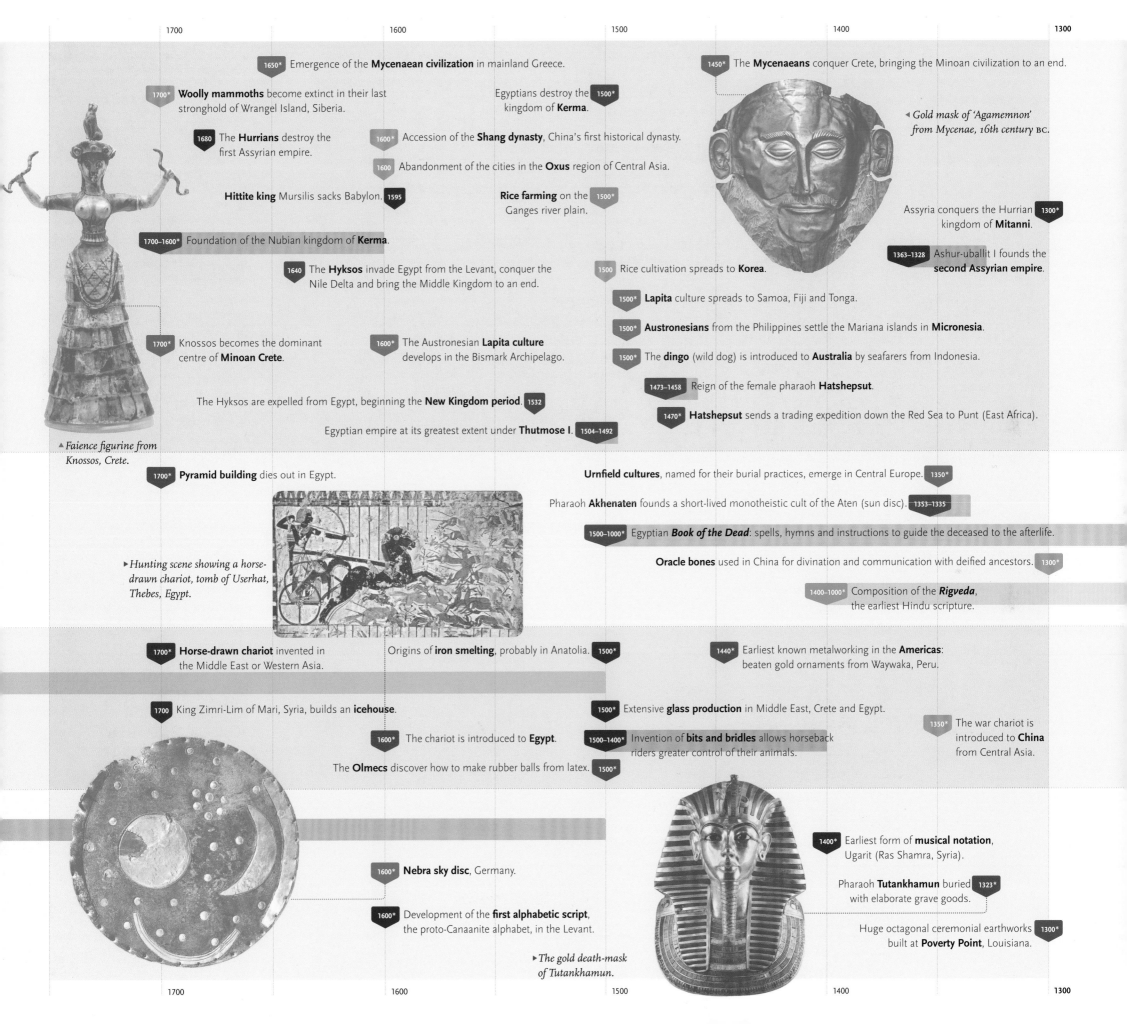

1650* Emergence of the **Mycenaean civilization** in mainland Greece.

1450* The **Mycenaeans** conquer Crete, bringing the Minoan civilization to an end.

1700* **Woolly mammoths** become extinct in their last stronghold of Wrangel Island, Siberia.

1500* Egyptians destroy the kingdom of **Kerma**.

1680 The **Hurrians** destroy the first Assyrian empire.

1600* Accession of the **Shang dynasty**, China's first historical dynasty.

1600 Abandonment of the cities in the **Oxus** region of Central Asia.

Gold mask of 'Agamemnon' from Mycenae, 16th century BC.

Hittite king Mursilis sacks Babylon. **1595**

1500* **Rice farming** on the Ganges river plain.

1300* Assyria conquers the Hurrian kingdom of **Mitanni**.

1700–1600 Foundation of the Nubian kingdom of **Kerma**.

1363–1328 Ashur-uballit I founds the **second Assyrian empire**.

1640 The **Hyksos** invade Egypt from the Levant, conquer the Nile Delta and bring the Middle Kingdom to an end.

1500 Rice cultivation spreads to **Korea**.

1500* **Lapita** culture spreads to Samoa, Fiji and Tonga.

1500* **Austronesians** from the Philippines settle the Mariana islands in **Micronesia**.

1700* Knossos becomes the dominant centre of **Minoan Crete**.

1600* The Austronesian **Lapita culture** develops in the Bismark Archipelago.

1500* The **dingo** (wild dog) is introduced to **Australia** by seafarers from Indonesia.

1473–1458 Reign of the female pharaoh **Hatshepsut**.

The Hyksos are expelled from Egypt, beginning the **New Kingdom period**. **1532**

1470* **Hatshepsut** sends a trading expedition down the Red Sea to Punt (East Africa).

Egyptian empire at its greatest extent under **Thutmose I**. **1504–1492**

Faience figurine from Knossos, Crete.

1700* **Pyramid building** dies out in Egypt.

Urnfield cultures, named for their burial practices, emerge in Central Europe. **1350***

Pharaoh **Akhenaten** founds a short-lived monotheistic cult of the Aten (sun disc). **1353–1335**

1500–1000* Egyptian *Book of the Dead*: spells, hymns and instructions to guide the deceased to the afterlife.

Oracle bones used in China for divination and communication with deified ancestors. **1300***

Hunting scene showing a horse-drawn chariot, tomb of Userhat, Thebes, Egypt.

1400–1000* Composition of the *Rigveda*, the earliest Hindu scripture.

1700* **Horse-drawn chariot** invented in the Middle East or Western Asia.

Origins of **iron smelting**, probably in Anatolia. **1500***

1440* Earliest known metalworking in the **Americas**: beaten gold ornaments from Waywaka, Peru.

1700 King Zimri-Lim of Mari, Syria, builds an **icehouse**.

1500* Extensive **glass production** in Middle East, Crete and Egypt.

1350* The war chariot is introduced to **China** from Central Asia.

1600* The chariot is introduced to **Egypt**.

1500–1400* Invention of **bits and bridles** allows horseback riders greater control of their animals.

The **Olmecs** discover how to make rubber balls from latex. **1500***

1400* Earliest form of **musical notation**, Ugarit (Ras Shamra, Syria).

Pharaoh **Tutankhamun** buried **1323*** with elaborate grave goods.

1600* **Nebra sky disc**, Germany.

1600* Development of the **first alphabetic script**, the proto-Canaanite alphabet, in the Levant.

Huge octagonal ceremonial earthworks built at **Poverty Point**, Louisiana. **1300***

The gold death-mask of Tutankhamun.

1000 BC

THE AEGEAN AND MESOPOTAMIAN DARK AGES; RISE OF THE ZHOU IN CHINA

The late 2nd millennium BC was a time of severe political instability in the Middle East and the eastern Mediterranean. The main casualties were the Mycenaean Greek kingdoms and the Hittite empire. New city walls are evidence that the Mycenaeans of the 13th century BC felt threatened. Their efforts were to no avail: around 1200 BC all of their cities were destroyed by unknown invaders and abandoned. Writing fell out of use and Greece entered a 'dark age'. At almost exactly the same time, the powerful Hittite empire of Anatolia collapsed equally abruptly, destroyed probably by Phrygian invaders from Southeast Europe.

Mesopotamia also suffered invasions, by the Aramaean and Chaldaean nomads of the Arabian desert. Assyria and Babylon were reduced to local powers. Egypt was invaded *c.*1180 BC by a coalition of Mediterranean peoples called (by modern historians) the Sea Peoples. Though they were beaten off, royal authority was progressively undermined by an over-mighty priesthood and by 1070 BC Egypt's New Kingdom had collapsed. The decline of the region's great powers favoured the foundation of small kingdoms in the Levant, the most influential of which would be the Hebrew kingdom founded *c.*1020 BC. Also influential were the Phoenicians, a seafaring people, who began to create a Mediterranean trading network in this period.

In China, the ruling Shang dynasty was overthrown in 1046 BC by its vassals, led by the Zhou. The Shang claimed legitimacy by divine descent. The Zhou justified their seizure of power by claiming that Heaven had transferred its 'Mandate' to them because the Shang had become corrupt and unjust. All later Chinese dynasties claimed legitimacy by the same doctrine. The first civilization of the Americas arose among the Olmec people of Mexico's Gulf coast *c.*1200 BC.

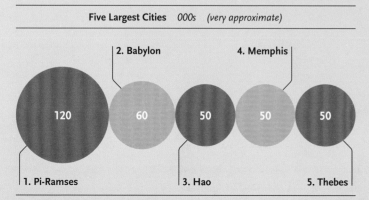

Five Largest Cities *000s* *(very approximate)*

1. Pi-Ramses	2. Babylon	3. Hao	4. Memphis	5. Thebes
120	60	50	50	50

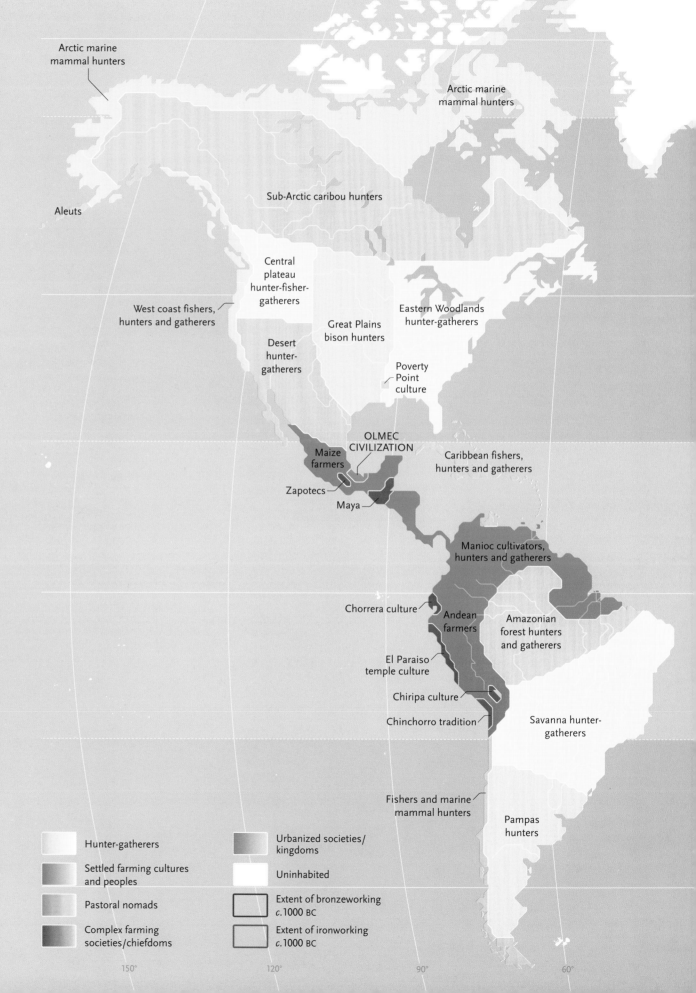

Arctic marine mammal hunters

Arctic marine mammal hunters

Aleuts

Sub-Arctic caribou hunters

Central plateau hunter-fisher-gatherers

West coast fishers, hunters and gatherers

Great Plains bison hunters

Eastern Woodlands hunter-gatherers

Desert hunter-gatherers

Poverty Point culture

Maize farmers

OLMEC CIVILIZATION

Caribbean fishers, hunters and gatherers

Zapotecs

Maya

Manioc cultivators, hunters and gatherers

Chorrera culture

Andean farmers

Amazonian forest hunters and gatherers

El Paraiso temple culture

Chiripa culture

Chinchorro tradition

Savanna hunter-gatherers

Fishers and marine mammal hunters

Pampas hunters

Hunter-gatherers		Urbanized societies/kingdoms
Settled farming cultures and peoples		Uninhabited
Pastoral nomads		Extent of bronzeworking *c.*1000 BC
Complex farming societies/chiefdoms		Extent of ironworking *c.*1000 BC

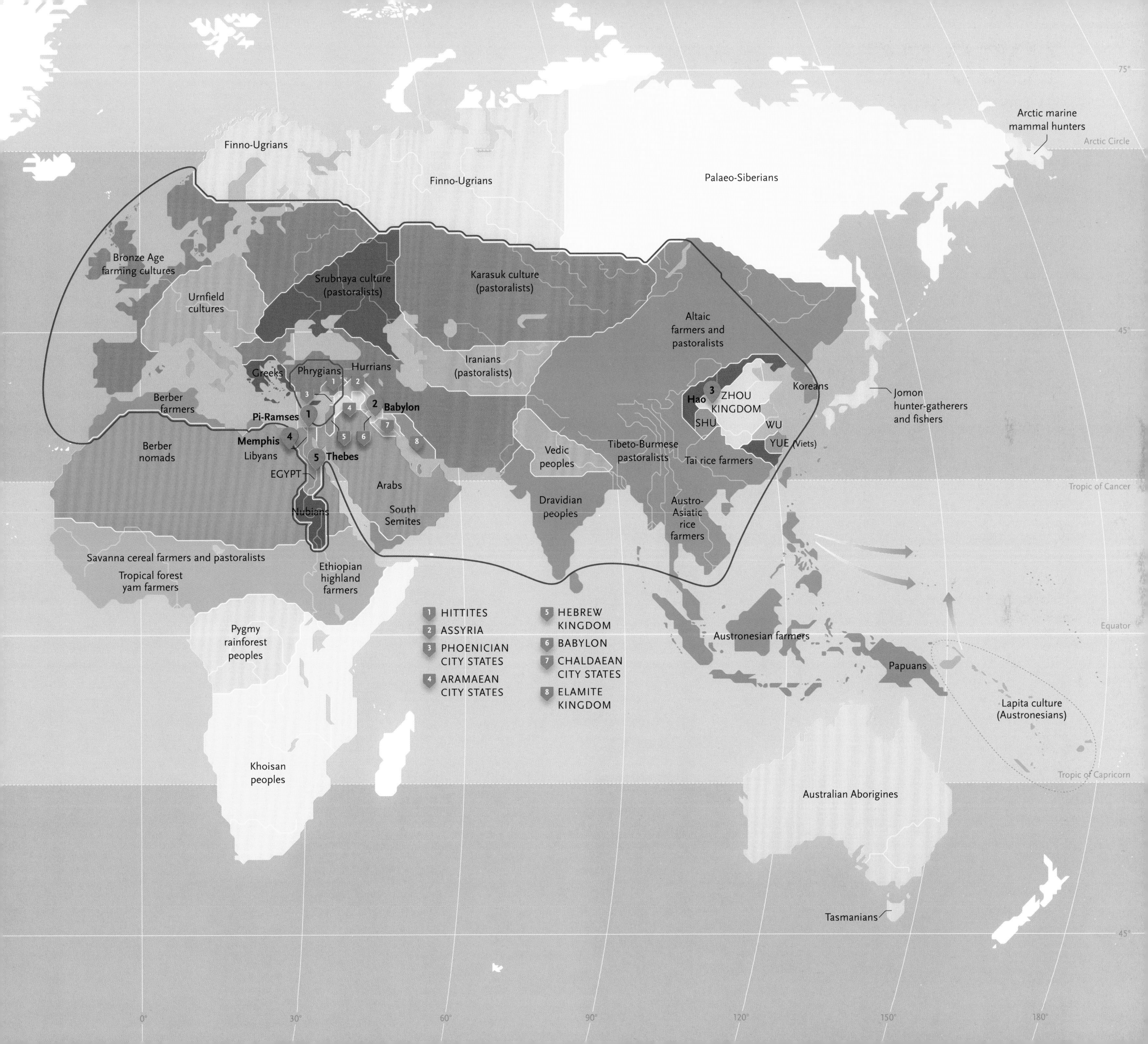

Finno-Ugrians
Finno-Ugrians
Palaeo-Siberians
Arctic marine mammal hunters
Arctic Circle
75°
Bronze Age farming cultures
Urnfield cultures
Srubnaya culture (pastoralists)
Karasuk culture (pastoralists)
Altaic farmers and pastoralists
45°
Iranians (pastoralists)
Greeks
Phrygians
Hurrians
Berber farmers
Pi-Ramses
Babylon
Memphis
Thebes
Berber nomads
Libyans
EGYPT
Arabs
Nubians
South Semites
Hao
ZHOU KINGDOM
SHU
WU
YUE (Viets)
Koreans
Jomon hunter-gatherers and fishers
Vedic peoples
Tibeto-Burmese pastoralists
Tai rice farmers
Dravidian peoples
Austro-Asiatic rice farmers
Tropic of Cancer
Savanna cereal farmers and pastoralists
Tropical forest yam farmers
Ethiopian highland farmers
Pygmy rainforest peoples
Austronesian farmers
Equator
Papuans
Lapita culture (Austronesians)
Khoisan peoples
Australian Aborigines
Tropic of Capricorn
Tasmanians
45°
0°
30°
60°
90°
120°
150°
180°
1 HITTITES
2 ASSYRIA
3 PHOENICIAN CITY STATES
4 ARAMAEAN CITY STATES
5 HEBREW KINGDOM
6 BABYLON
7 CHALDAEAN CITY STATES
8 ELAMITE KINGDOM

1000 BC

The foundation of the Hebrew kingdom went unnoticed by the troubled great powers of the region, yet it was an event of fundamental importance to the development of the Jewish, Christian and Islamic religions. By making Jerusalem his capital, the Hebrew king David ensured its lasting importance as a holy site for all three faiths.

The Hebrews were closely related to the Canaanites, the first people to write using an alphabetic script. Around 1100 BC, their neighbours the Phoenicians devised their own alphabet based on the Canaanite original. Thanks to their seafaring activities, the Phoenicians gradually disseminated their script around the Mediterranean. A writing system based on pictographs came into use in Shang China around 1200 BC. Though much modified over the centuries, this script is the direct ancestor of the modern Chinese logographic script.

As well as inventing their own hieroglyphic script, the Olmec civilization established many of the features common to later Mesoamerican civilizations, including temple pyramids and a sacred ball game. They may also have been the first to make drinking chocolate and learn how to cure rubber.

The technology of iron smelting, invented in Anatolia *c.* 1500 BC, had yet to make much impact: by 1000 BC it was still confined only to Anatolia, Cyprus and the Levant. The enormous potential that bronze still possessed was spectacularly demonstrated by Shang metalworkers who cast ritual vessels of amazing decorative complexity.

Two documents of the period stand out. One is the earliest known peace treaty, agreed between the Egyptians and the Hittites in 1256 BC. Remarkably, both the Egyptian and Hittite copies of the treaty survive. The other is the definitive version of what was already an ancient Mesopotamian tale, *The Epic of Gilgamesh.*

World Population *(very approximate)*

7 BILLION

115 million

8000 BC   1000 BC   2010

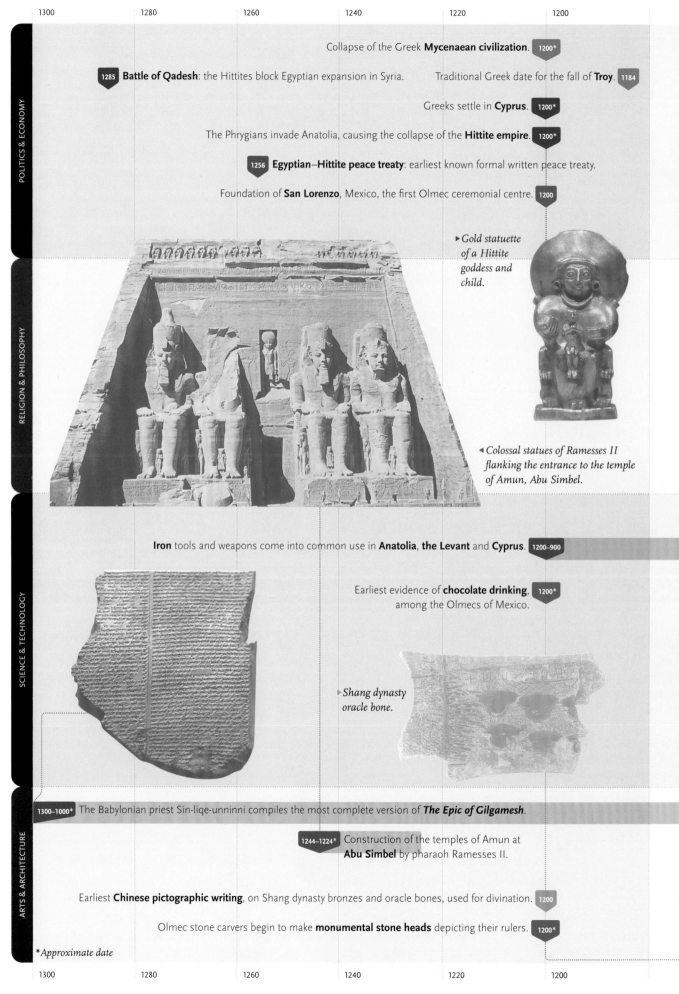

POLITICS & ECONOMY

Collapse of the Greek **Mycenaean civilization.** `1200*`

`1285` **Battle of Qadesh**: the Hittites block Egyptian expansion in Syria.   Traditional Greek date for the fall of **Troy.** `1184`

Greeks settle in **Cyprus.** `1200*`

The Phrygians invade Anatolia, causing the collapse of the **Hittite empire.** `1200*`

`1256` **Egyptian–Hittite peace treaty**: earliest known formal written peace treaty.

Foundation of **San Lorenzo**, Mexico, the first Olmec ceremonial centre. `1200`

▶ *Gold statuette of a Hittite goddess and child.*

RELIGION & PHILOSOPHY

◀ *Colossal statues of Ramesses II flanking the entrance to the temple of Amun, Abu Simbel.*

SCIENCE & TECHNOLOGY

Iron tools and weapons come into common use in **Anatolia**, **the Levant** and **Cyprus.** `1200–900`

Earliest evidence of **chocolate drinking**, `1200*` among the Olmecs of Mexico.

▶ *Shang dynasty oracle bone.*

ARTS & ARCHITECTURE

`1300–1000*` The Babylonian priest Sin-liqe-unninni compiles the most complete version of **The Epic of Gilgamesh**.

`1244–1224*` Construction of the temples of Amun at **Abu Simbel** by pharaoh Ramesses II.

Earliest **Chinese pictographic writing**, on Shang dynasty bronzes and oracle bones, used for divination. `1200`

Olmec stone carvers begin to make **monumental stone heads** depicting their rulers. `1200*`

*Approximate date

Dromedary camel domesticated in southeast Arabia. `1100*`

In China, the Shang dynasty is overthrown by the **Zhou** `1046` **dynasty** (according to some estimates 1122 BC).

Urnfield cultures spread to Western Europe. `1000`

`1180` Pharaoh Ramesses III defeats an invasion by the **Sea Peoples**, a coalition of Mediterranean peoples.

Fall of the 21st dynasty marks the end of Egypt's **New Kingdom period.** `1070`

The **Chaldaeans** occupy southern Mesopotamia; `1000*`
Aramaean invasions cause the decline of Assyrian power.

The **Phoenicians** found a trading colony at **Kition**, Cyprus. `1000*`

San Lorenzo is ritually destroyed and replaced by a new ceremonial centre at **La Venta**, Mexico. `1000`

Saul founds the Hebrew monarchy. `1020*`

King David captures Jerusalem from the Canaanites and makes it capital of the **Hebrew kingdom.** `1000*`

`1100` **Trundholm sun chariot,** Denmark, evidence of a solar cult.

▲ *Depiction of a relief at Medinet Habu, Thebes, showing a battle between Egyptians and the Sea Peoples.*

`1114–1076*` Assyrian king **Tiglath-pileser I** creates a botanical garden.

◄ *Olmec colossal basalt head from San Lorenzo, Mexico.*

▶ *The early hillfort of Mam Tor, Derbyshire, England.*

`1100*` Beginning of **hillfort** construction in Western Europe.

`1100` Origins of the influential **Phoenician alphabet** (a development of the earlier Canaanite alphabet).

Cupellation process to separate silver from `1000*` lead ore is developed, Middle East.

Earliest **bronze** made in the Americas, in the Peruvian Andes. `1000*`

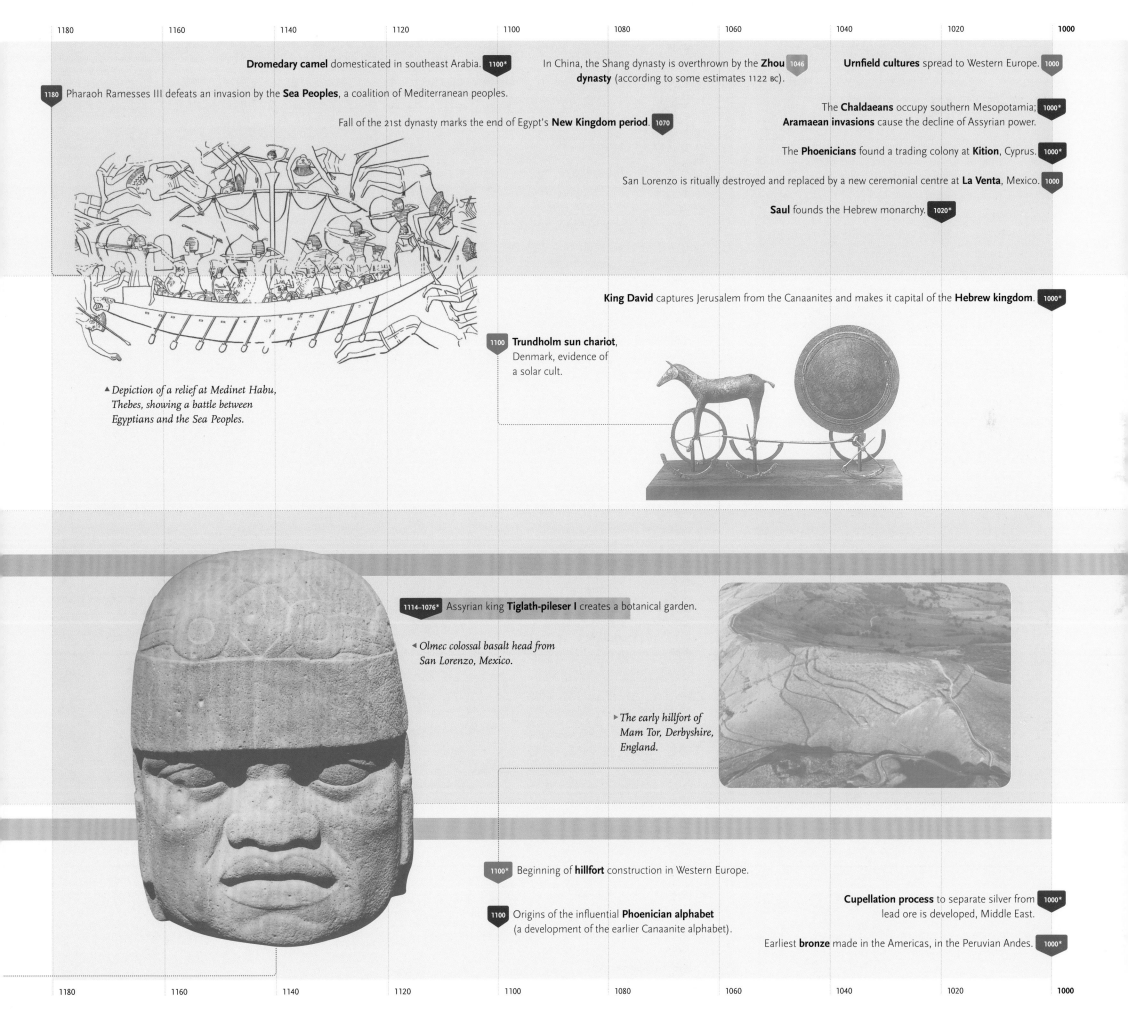

800 BC

DOMINANT ASSYRIA AND EXPANSIONIST ZHOU; COLONIZING PHOENICIANS

In the later 10th century BC, Assyrian power began to revive under a succession of able militaristic kings. Babylon became a satellite of Assyria in the 9th century BC, but remained Mesopotamia's leading cultural centre. Assyria's growing wealth, and its demands for metals, timber, precious stones, ivory and other commodities, stimulated an economic recovery throughout the Middle East and Mediterranean after the 'dark ages'. In Greece, city life, which had completely died out after the fall of the Mycenaeans, began to revive strongly in the 9th century BC.

The Phoenicians were well placed to take advantage of the economic recovery and by 800 BC they were the dominant trading power of the Mediterranean. Phoenician cities were independent states, many of which founded trading colonies around the Mediterranean. The most successful of these cities was Tyre, whose colonies included Gadir (Cadiz) in metal-rich southwest Spain and Carthage in North Africa. It was through Phoenician colonies that the influence of the Middle Eastern civilizations began to be felt in the western Mediterranean.

Very little is known about the 1000 years of Indian history following the fall of the Indus Valley civilization *c.* 1900 BC. In the early 1st millennium BC a new Indian civilization began to develop on the Ganges river plain with the emergence of around 25 tribal kingdoms and republics known as *janapadas* (realms). The Chinese Zhou kingdom was expansionist, extending its power south from the Shang heartlands around the Yellow river region into the Yangtze river basin.

The fall of the New Kingdom in 1070 BC had allowed the Nubians to break free of Egyptian rule. Around 900 BC they founded the kingdom of Kush, the first great kingdom of Black Africa. In the Peruvian Andes, the cult centre of Chavín was established *c.* 850 BC.

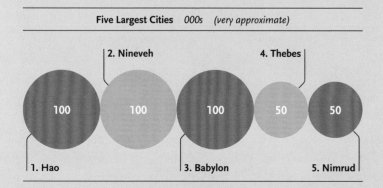

Five Largest Cities   *000s*   *(very approximate)*

| 2. Nineveh | 4. Thebes |
| 100 | 50 |

1. Hao	100
3. Babylon	100
5. Nimrud	50

Dorset Inuit culture

Dorset Inuit culture

Aleuts

Sub-Arctic caribou hunters

Central plateau hunter-fisher-gatherers

West coast fishers, hunters and gatherers

Great Plains bison hunters

Eastern Woodlands hunter-gatherers

Desert hunter-gatherers

OLMEC CIVILIZATION

Maize farmers

Caribbean fishers, hunters and gatherers

Zapotecs

Maya

Manioc farmers

Chorrera culture

Amazonian forest hunters and gatherers

Chavín culture

Chiripa culture

Chinchorro tradition

Savanna hunter-gatherers

Fishers and marine mammal hunters

Pampas hunters

Hunter-gatherers

Settled farming cultures and peoples

Pastoral nomads

Complex farming societies/chiefdoms

Urbanized societies/kingdoms

Uninhabited

Extent of bronzeworking technology *c.* 800 BC

Extent of ironworking technology *c.* 800 BC

150°   120°   90°   60°

Dorset Inuit
culture

Arctic Circle

Sami reindeer hunters
(Finno-Ugrians)

Finno-Ugrians

Palaeo-Siberians

Proto-Germans

Cimmerians
(Iranians)

Iranian pastoral
nomads

Altaic
reindeer
herders

Celts

Altaic
farmers and
pastoralists

75°

45°

Iberians

Etruscans

Illyrians

Thracians

Italics

GREEK
CITY
STATES

1

2 **5**

Nineveh **Nimrud**

Medes
Persians

2

3

7

Babylon

4

5

Iranian pastoral
nomads

Koreans

Jomon
hunter-gatherers
and fishers

1
Hao ZHOU
KINGDOM

Berber
farmers

Tibetans

YUE

Berber
nomads

Libu

EGYPT

6

Aramaeans

8

9

HINDU
KINGDOMS

Burmese

Tais

Tropic of Cancer

4
Thebes

Arabs

KUSH
(Nubians)

Dravidians

Austro-
Asiatics

Savanna cereal farmers and pastoralists

10

Austronesians

Micronesians

Tropical forest
yam farmers

Bantu
farmers

Ethiopian
highland
farmers

Pygmy
rainforest
peoples

Austronesians

Equator

Khoisan
peoples

Papuans

Lapita culture
(Austronesians)

1 PHRYGIA		**6** JUDAH	
2 URARTU		**7** BABYLON	
3 ASSYRIA		**8** CHALDAEAN CITY STATES	
4 PHOENICIAN CITY STATES		**9** ELAMITE KINGDOM	
5 ISRAEL		**10** SABA (South Semites)	

Khoisan
peoples

Tropic of Capricorn

Australian Aborigines

Tasmanians

0°   30°   60°   90°   120°   150°   180°

800 BC

The early steppe pastoralist peoples built permanent settlements but probably practised a form of transhumance, a way of life which involves seasonal migrations to move herds and flocks to fresh grazing land. Ox carts allowed the pastoralists to move their belongings and helped them expand into new territories. Around the beginning of the 1st millennium BC Iranian steppe pastoralists, such as the Cimmerians, adopted a fully nomadic way of life. The cause of this is thought to have been the adoption of horseback riding – this allowed pastoralists to manage much larger herds which needed to be moved on regularly to avoid overgrazing. The consequences of this development were far-reaching, as the speed and mobility of horseback riding were as useful in war as in stock management. The first recorded cavalry regiment was raised in Assyria in 890–884 BC and war chariots began to fall out of use.

Their mobility gave the nomads a great military advantage over the settled peoples around the steppes, whom they frequently raided. Providing security for its northern frontier would be a constant headache for China's rulers after it experienced its first nomad raids *c.* 400 BC. Nomad invasions frequently had drastic and destructive consequences for the Old World civilizations for the next 2500 years.

While the religious beliefs of the Indus Valley peoples are not known, the inhabitants of the *janapadas* of the Ganges plain practised an early form of Hinduism based on the *Rigveda*, a collection of hymns and liturgies that were probably composed late in the 2nd millennium BC. In the four *varnas* (classes) of the *Rigveda* can be seen the beginnings of the Hindu caste system. The *Rigveda* was composed in Sanskrit, an Indo-European language ancestral to some of the most widely spoken South Asian languages, such as Hindi and Urdu.

World Population *(very approximate)*

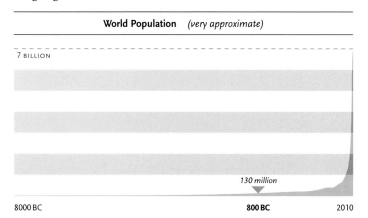

7 BILLION

130 million

8000 BC   **800 BC**   2010

40

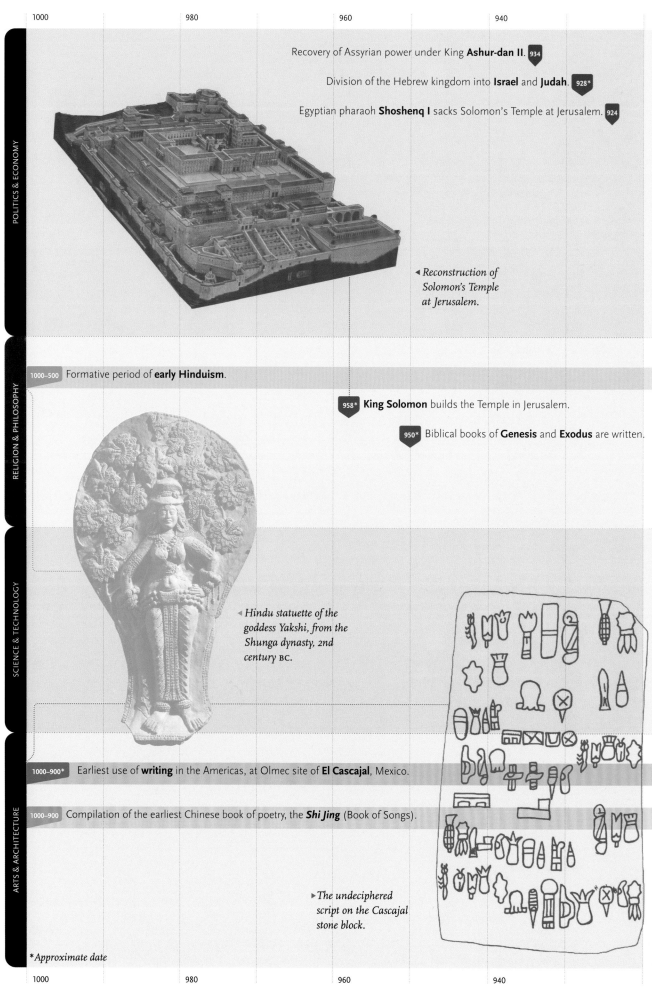

1000	980	960	940

POLITICS & ECONOMY

Recovery of Assyrian power under King **Ashur-dan II**. `934`

Division of the Hebrew kingdom into **Israel** and **Judah**. `928*`

Egyptian pharaoh **Shoshenq I** sacks Solomon's Temple at Jerusalem. `924`

◀ *Reconstruction of Solomon's Temple at Jerusalem.*

RELIGION & PHILOSOPHY

1000–500   Formative period of **early Hinduism**.

`958*` **King Solomon** builds the Temple in Jerusalem.

`950*` Biblical books of **Genesis** and **Exodus** are written.

SCIENCE & TECHNOLOGY

◀ *Hindu statuette of the goddess Yakshi, from the Shunga dynasty, 2nd century BC.*

1000–900*   Earliest use of **writing** in the Americas, at Olmec site of **El Cascajal**, Mexico.

ARTS & ARCHITECTURE

1000–900   Compilation of the earliest Chinese book of poetry, the **Shi Jing** (Book of Songs).

▶ *The undeciphered script on the Cascajal stone block.*

*Approximate date

1000	980	960	940

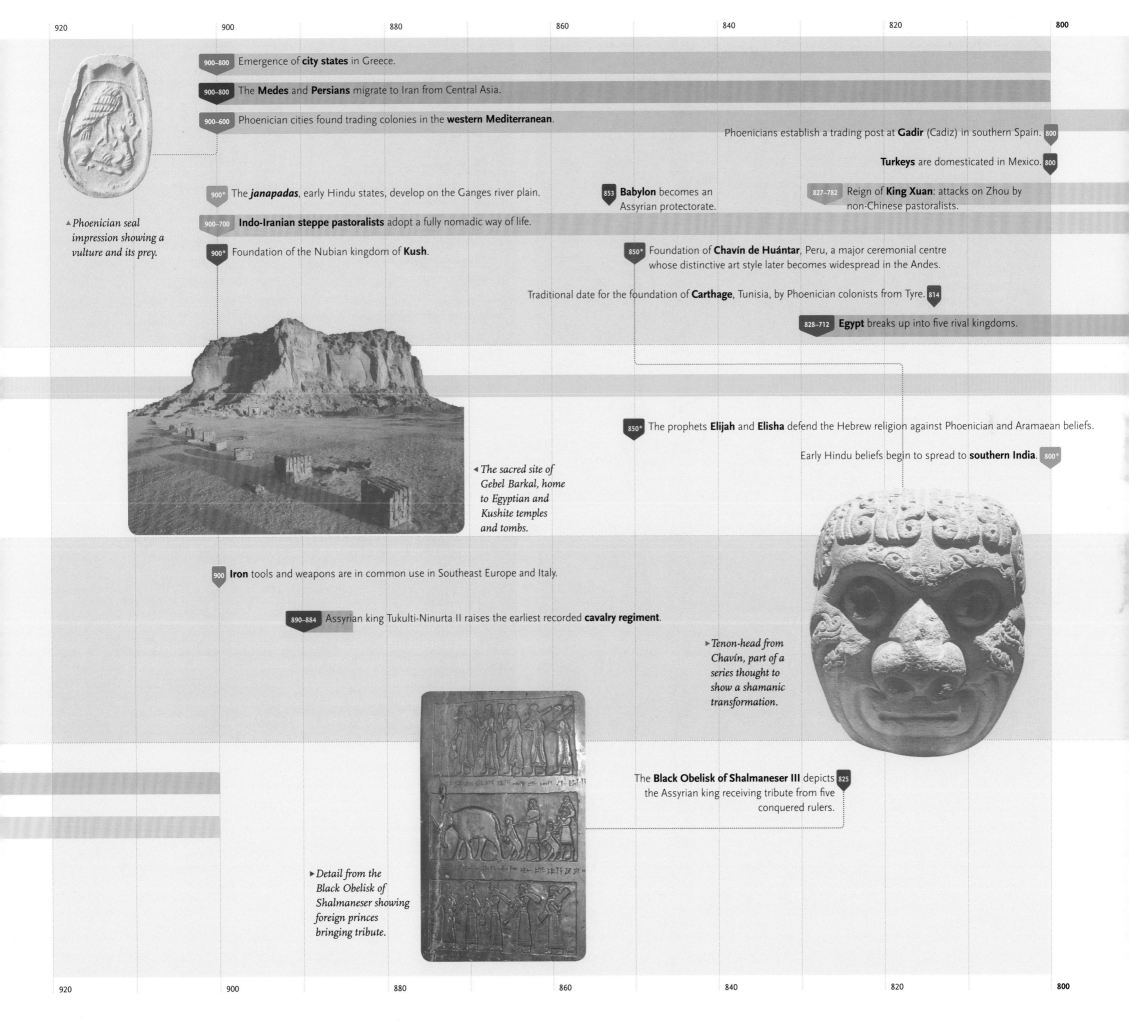

900–800 Emergence of **city states** in Greece.

900–800 The **Medes** and **Persians** migrate to Iran from Central Asia.

900–600 Phoenician cities found trading colonies in the **western Mediterranean**.

Phoenicians establish a trading post at **Gadir** (Cadiz) in southern Spain. 800

Turkeys are domesticated in Mexico. 800

900* The *janapadas*, early Hindu states, develop on the Ganges river plain.

853 **Babylon** becomes an Assyrian protectorate.

827–782 Reign of **King Xuan**: attacks on Zhou by non-Chinese pastoralists.

900–700 **Indo-Iranian steppe pastoralists** adopt a fully nomadic way of life.

900* Foundation of the Nubian kingdom of **Kush**.

850* Foundation of **Chavín de Huántar**, Peru, a major ceremonial centre whose distinctive art style later becomes widespread in the Andes.

Traditional date for the foundation of **Carthage**, Tunisia, by Phoenician colonists from Tyre. 814

828–712 **Egypt** breaks up into five rival kingdoms.

▲ *Phoenician seal impression showing a vulture and its prey.*

850* The prophets **Elijah** and **Elisha** defend the Hebrew religion against Phoenician and Aramaean beliefs.

Early Hindu beliefs begin to spread to **southern India**. 800*

◄ *The sacred site of Gebel Barkal, home to Egyptian and Kushite temples and tombs.*

900 **Iron** tools and weapons are in common use in Southeast Europe and Italy.

890–884 Assyrian king Tukulti-Ninurta II raises the earliest recorded **cavalry regiment**.

► *Tenon-head from Chavín, part of a series thought to show a shamanic transformation.*

The **Black Obelisk of Shalmaneser III** depicts 825 the Assyrian king receiving tribute from five conquered rulers.

► *Detail from the Black Obelisk of Shalmaneser showing foreign princes bringing tribute.*

500 BC

ASSYRIA, BABYLON AND THE RISE OF PERSIA; FALL OF THE ZHOU KINGDOM

Early Mesopotamian empires expanded and contracted according to the military abilities of their rulers. This was because they were based on tributary relationships. If a weak ruler came to the throne of the imperial power, its vassals easily reasserted their independence.

The Assyrian empire under Tiglath-pileser III (r. 742–727 BC) embarked upon a new chapter in imperialism when it began to impose centrally appointed provincial governments on conquered areas, underpinned by a standing army. Assyria enjoyed a century of unparalleled dominance but the empire became overextended and quickly collapsed after Babylon rebelled in 626 BC. Magnificently rebuilt by Nebuchadnezzar (r. 604–562 BC), Babylon dazzled contemporaries, but this was the last time a Mesopotamian power dominated the Middle East.

In 539 BC the Persian king Cyrus the Great (r. 559–530 BC) conquered the Babylonian empire. The Persians were former steppe nomads who had settled in southern Iran in the 9th century BC. Under Cyrus, the Persians had already conquered their neighbours the Medes (another former nomad people) and the wealthy Anatolian kingdom of Lydia. By the end of the 6th century BC, Cyrus's successors had conquered Egypt (which had already experienced periods of Nubian and Assyrian rule), the Indus valley and a large part of Central Asia, creating the world's first superpower.

China's Zhou kingdom had broken up into a patchwork of feudal states by 500 BC. Attacks by non-Chinese peoples forced the Zhou to leave their traditional heartland in 771 BC and transfer their capital to Luoyang. The transplanted dynasty was unable to re-establish its authority. Now able to defy the kings, the feudal aristocrats who governed the provinces asserted their independence, starting the break-up of the kingdom.

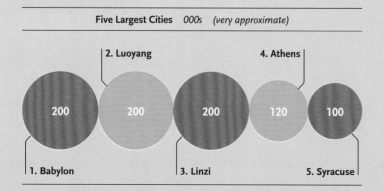

Five Largest Cities *000s* *(very approximate)*

2. Luoyang		4. Athens	
200	**200**	**200**	**120**	**100**
1. Babylon		3. Linzi		5. Syracuse

Dorset Inuit culture

Dorset Inuit culture

Sub-Arctic caribou hunters

Aleuts

Central plateau hunter-fisher-gatherers

West coast fishers, hunters and gatherers

Great Plains bison hunters

Eastern Woodlands hunter-gatherers

Desert hunter-gatherers

OLMEC CIVILIZATION

Maize farmers

Caribbean fishers, hunters and gatherers

Zapotecs

MAYA CITY STATES

Manioc farmers

Chorrera culture

Chavín culture

Pucara culture

Paracas culture

Chiripa culture

Chinchorro tradition

Savanna hunter-gatherers

Fishers and marine mammal hunters

Pampas hunters

Hunter-gatherers

Settled farming cultures and peoples

Pastoral nomads

Complex farming societies/chiefdoms

Urbanized societies/ kingdoms

Empires

Uninhabited

Extent of ironworking technology *c.* 500 BC

Greek city states

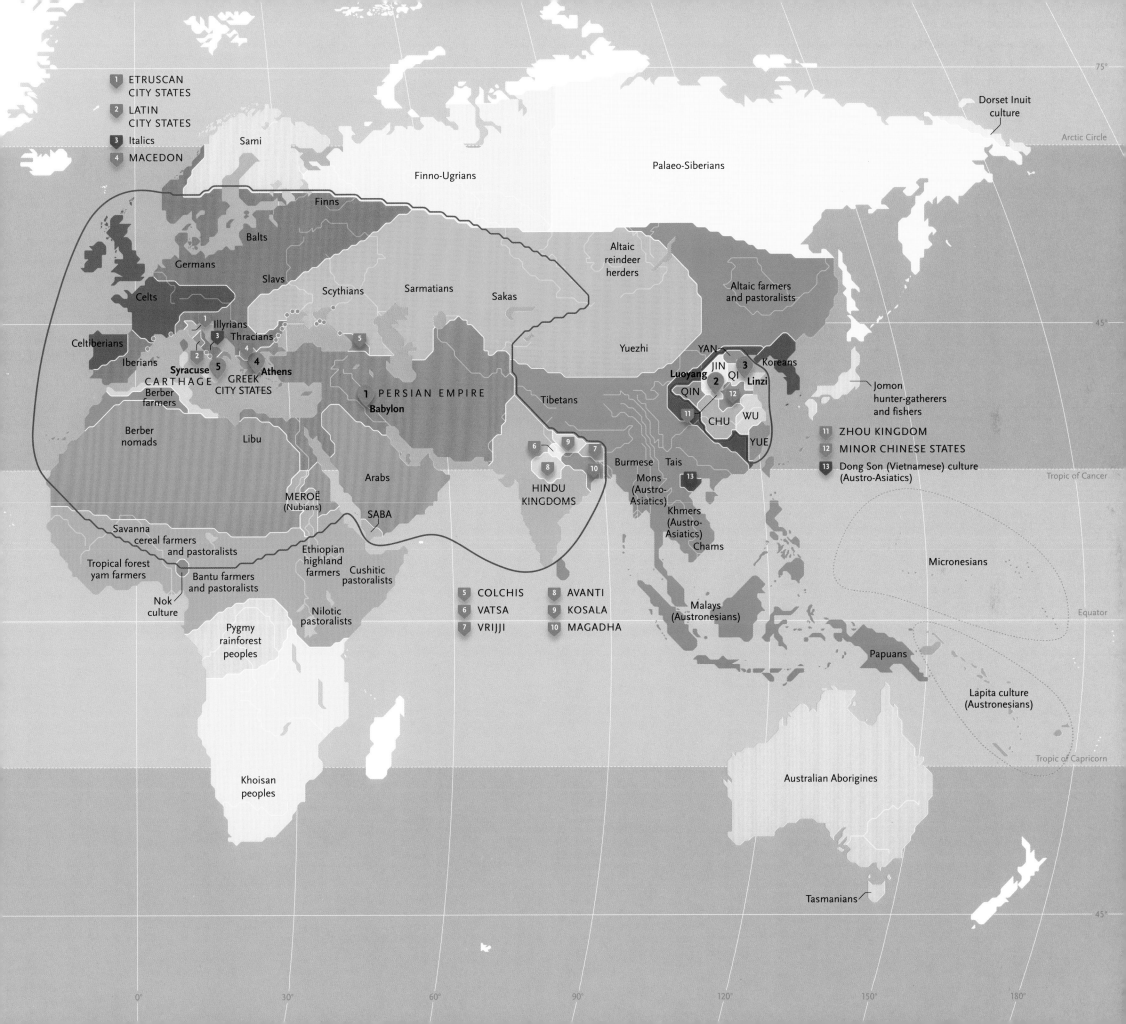

ETRUSCAN CITY STATES
1

LATIN CITY STATES
2

Italics
3

MACEDON
4

Dorset Inuit culture

Sami

Finno-Ugrians

Palaeo-Siberians

Finns

Balts

Germans

Slavs

Scythians

Sarmatians

Sakas

Altaic reindeer herders

Altaic farmers and pastoralists

Celts

Illyrians

Thracians

YAN

Koreans

Celtiberians

3

4

4

Luoyang

JIN

QI

Linzi

Iberians

2

5

Athens

QIN

QI

Syracuse

GREEK CITY STATES

1 PERSIAN EMPIRE

Yuezhi

Tibetans

12

Jomon hunter-gatherers and fishers

CARTHAGE

Berber farmers

Babylon

ZHOU KINGDOM
11

MINOR CHINESE STATES
12

Dong Son (Vietnamese) culture (Austro-Asiatics)
13

Berber nomads

Libu

6

9

7

Burmese

Tais

Arabs

8

10

Mons (Austro-Asiatics)

MEROË (Nubians)

HINDU KINGDOMS

13

SABA

Khmers (Austro-Asiatics)

Savanna cereal farmers and pastoralists

Ethiopian highland farmers

Cushitic pastoralists

Chams

Tropical forest yam farmers

Micronesians

Bantu farmers and pastoralists

Nilotic pastoralists

COLCHIS
5

AVANTI
8

Nok culture

VATSA
6

KOSALA
9

Pygmy rainforest peoples

VRIJJI
7

MAGADHA
10

Malays (Austronesians)

Papuans

Khoisan peoples

Lapita culture (Austronesians)

Australian Aborigines

Tasmanians

500 BC

The 7th and 6th centuries BC were among the most important ever in the history of religion and ideas. In the 8th and 7th centuries BC the Hebrew kingdoms had been conquered first by Assyria and then by Babylon. Large numbers of Jews (as Hebrews were beginning to be called) were deported to Mesopotamia. Among these Jewish exiles, the main books of the Old Testament were written in approximately their present form and Judaism emerged as a definitively monotheistic religion. The Old Testament shows an understanding of Mesopotamian mythology and it was probably also influenced by the Iranian prophet Zoroaster's espousal of monotheism and cosmic dualism.

In India the composition of the philosophical *Upanishads* was a major step in the development of classical Hinduism. At the same time, the ritualistic nature of Hinduism was challenged by the religious ascetic Mahavira, founder of the Jain religion, and Siddhartha Gautama, the founder of Buddhism. In China, the same period saw the life of the sage Confucius. A response to troubled times, his emphasis on respect for legitimate authority, social order, the family, ancestors, tradition and education became fundamental to Chinese thought. In later times, it was thought that Laozi, the mythical founder of Daoism, lived during this period.

The 6th century BC saw the beginning of the Greek scientific tradition in the works of the mathematicians Thales of Miletos and Pythagoras of Samos. The foundation of a drama festival in honour of the god Dionysus at Athens was an important moment in the development of Western theatre. Greek culture spread widely around the Mediterranean and Black Sea through colonies founded by the growing Greek city states. When Athens attempted to deal with its social tensions by introducing a form of democracy in 509 BC, it gave birth to one of history's most potent political ideas.

World Population *(very approximate)*

7 BILLION

150 million

44

8000 BC   500 BC   2010

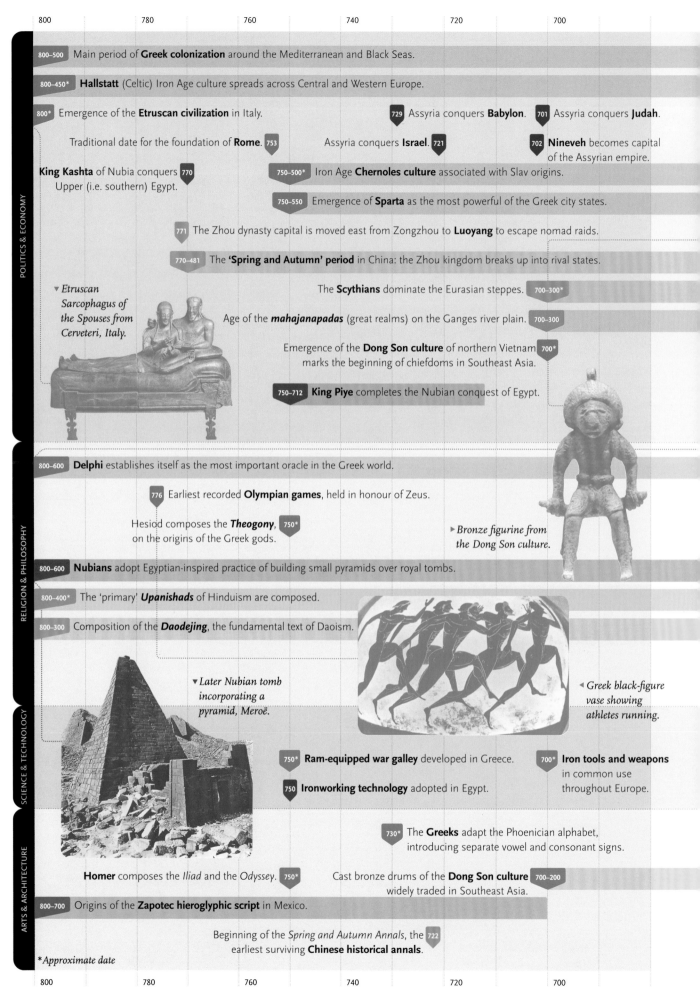

POLITICS & ECONOMY

800–500 Main period of **Greek colonization** around the Mediterranean and Black Seas.

800–450* **Hallstatt** (Celtic) Iron Age culture spreads across Central and Western Europe.

800* Emergence of the **Etruscan civilization** in Italy.

729 Assyria conquers **Babylon**.　701 Assyria conquers **Judah**.

Traditional date for the foundation of **Rome**. 753

Assyria conquers **Israel**. 721

702 **Nineveh** becomes capital of the Assyrian empire.

King Kashta of Nubia conquers 770 Upper (i.e. southern) Egypt.

750–500* Iron Age **Chernoles culture** associated with Slav origins.

750–550 Emergence of **Sparta** as the most powerful of the Greek city states.

771 The Zhou dynasty capital is moved east from Zongzhou to **Luoyang** to escape nomad raids.

770–481 The **'Spring and Autumn' period** in China: the Zhou kingdom breaks up into rival states.

▼ *Etruscan Sarcophagus of the Spouses from Cerveteri, Italy.*

The **Scythians** dominate the Eurasian steppes. 700–300*

Age of the ***mahajanapadas*** (great realms) on the Ganges river plain. 700–300

Emergence of the **Dong Son culture** of northern Vietnam 700* marks the beginning of chiefdoms in Southeast Asia.

750–712 **King Piye** completes the Nubian conquest of Egypt.

RELIGION & PHILOSOPHY

800–600 **Delphi** establishes itself as the most important oracle in the Greek world.

776 Earliest recorded **Olympian games**, held in honour of Zeus.

Hesiod composes the ***Theogony***, 750* on the origins of the Greek gods.

▶ *Bronze figurine from the Dong Son culture.*

800–600 **Nubians** adopt Egyptian-inspired practice of building small pyramids over royal tombs.

800–400* The 'primary' **Upanishads** of Hinduism are composed.

800–300 Composition of the **Daodejing**, the fundamental text of Daoism.

SCIENCE & TECHNOLOGY

▼ *Later Nubian tomb incorporating a pyramid, Meroë.*

◀ *Greek black-figure vase showing athletes running.*

750* **Ram-equipped war galley** developed in Greece.

700* **Iron tools and weapons** in common use throughout Europe.

750 **Ironworking technology** adopted in Egypt.

ARTS & ARCHITECTURE

730* The **Greeks** adapt the Phoenician alphabet, introducing separate vowel and consonant signs.

Homer composes the *Iliad* and the *Odyssey*. 750*

Cast bronze drums of the **Dong Son culture** 700–200 widely traded in Southeast Asia.

800–700 Origins of the **Zapotec hieroglyphic script** in Mexico.

Beginning of the *Spring and Autumn Annals*, the 722 earliest surviving **Chinese historical annals**.

*Approximate date

800   780   760   740   720   700

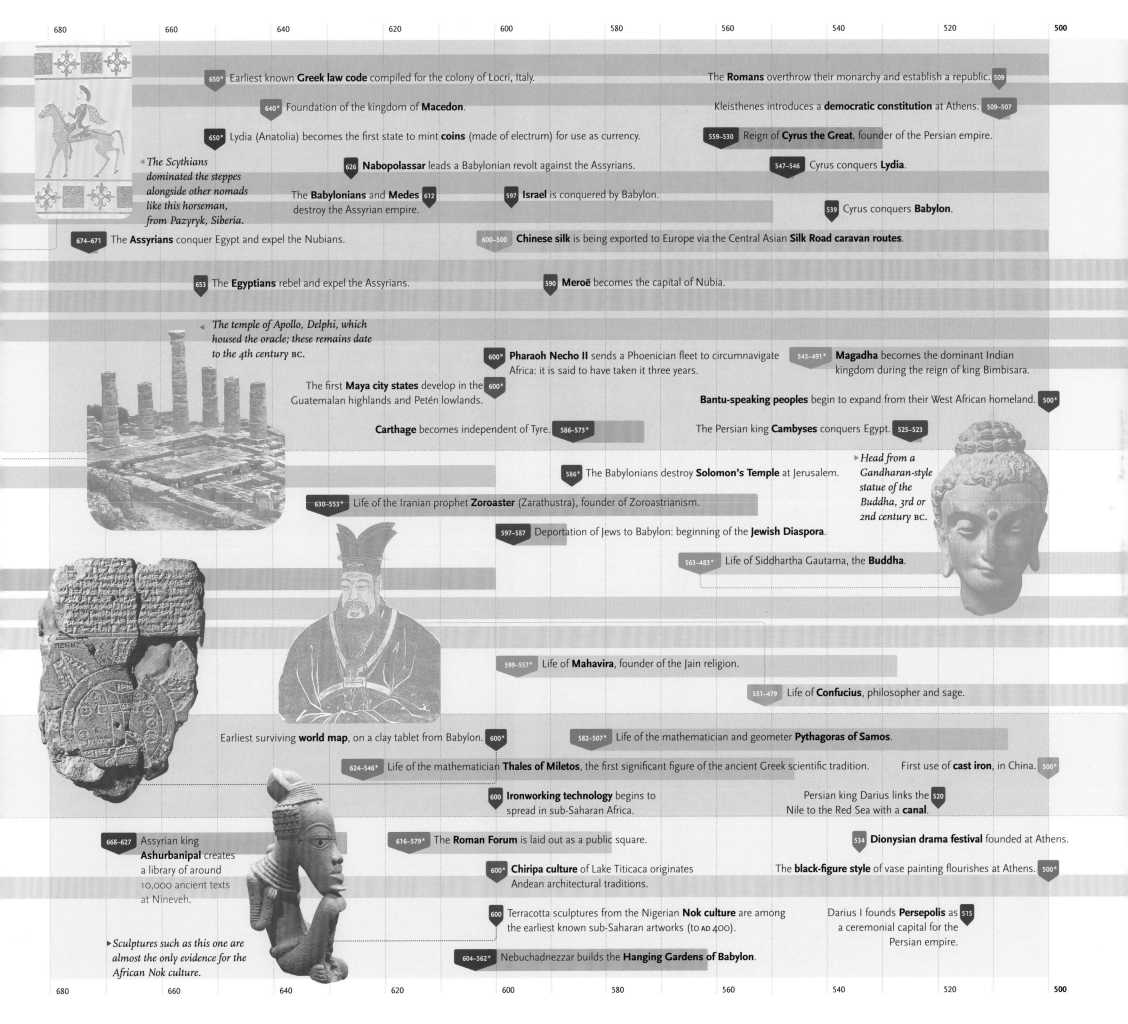

650* Earliest known **Greek law code** compiled for the colony of Locri, Italy.

The **Romans** overthrow their monarchy and establish a republic. **509**

640* Foundation of the kingdom of **Macedon**.

Kleisthenes introduces a **democratic constitution** at Athens. **509–507**

650* Lydia (Anatolia) becomes the first state to mint **coins** (made of electrum) for use as currency.

559–530 Reign of **Cyrus the Great**, founder of the Persian empire.

◄ *The Scythians dominated the steppes alongside other nomads like this horseman, from Pazyryk, Siberia.*

626 **Nabopolassar** leads a Babylonian revolt against the Assyrians.

547–546 Cyrus conquers **Lydia**.

The **Babylonians** and **Medes** **612** destroy the Assyrian empire.

597 **Israel** is conquered by Babylon.

539 Cyrus conquers **Babylon**.

674–671 The **Assyrians** conquer Egypt and expel the Nubians.

600–500 **Chinese silk** is being exported to Europe via the Central Asian **Silk Road caravan routes**.

653 The **Egyptians** rebel and expel the Assyrians.

590 **Meroë** becomes the capital of Nubia.

◄ *The temple of Apollo, Delphi, which housed the oracle; these remains date to the 4th century* BC.

600* **Pharaoh Necho II** sends a Phoenician fleet to circumnavigate Africa: it is said to have taken it three years.

543–491* **Magadha** becomes the dominant Indian kingdom during the reign of king Bimbisara.

The first **Maya city states** develop in the **600*** Guatemalan highlands and Petén lowlands.

Bantu-speaking peoples begin to expand from their West African homeland. **500***

Carthage becomes independent of Tyre. **586–573***

The Persian king **Cambyses** conquers Egypt. **525–523**

▶ *Head from a Gandharan-style statue of the Buddha, 3rd or 2nd century* BC.

586* The Babylonians destroy **Solomon's Temple** at Jerusalem.

630–553* Life of the Iranian prophet **Zoroaster** (Zarathustra), founder of Zoroastrianism.

597–587 Deportation of Jews to Babylon: beginning of the **Jewish Diaspora**.

563–483* Life of Siddhartha Gautama, the **Buddha**.

599–557* Life of **Mahavira**, founder of the Jain religion.

551–479 Life of **Confucius**, philosopher and sage.

Earliest surviving **world map**, on a clay tablet from Babylon. **600***

582–507* Life of the mathematician and geometer **Pythagoras of Samos**.

624–546* Life of the mathematician **Thales of Miletos**, the first significant figure of the ancient Greek scientific tradition.

First use of **cast iron**, in China. **500***

600 **Ironworking technology** begins to spread in sub-Saharan Africa.

Persian king Darius links the **520** Nile to the Red Sea with a **canal**.

668–627 Assyrian king **Ashurbanipal** creates a library of around 10,000 ancient texts at Nineveh.

616–579* The **Roman Forum** is laid out as a public square.

534 **Dionysian drama festival** founded at Athens.

600* **Chiripa culture** of Lake Titicaca originates Andean architectural traditions.

The **black-figure style** of vase painting flourishes at Athens. **500***

600 Terracotta sculptures from the Nigerian **Nok culture** are among the earliest known sub-Saharan artworks (to AD 400).

Darius I founds **Persepolis** as **515** a ceremonial capital for the Persian empire.

▶ *Sculptures such as this one are almost the only evidence for the African Nok culture.*

604–562* Nebuchadnezzar builds the **Hanging Gardens of Babylon**.

323 BC

ALEXANDER THE GREAT, CARTHAGE AND CHINA'S WARRING STATES PERIOD

The expansion of the Persian empire came to a halt in the early 5th century BC, stopped in its tracks by the quarrelsome Greek city states. Faced with a common enemy, the Greeks united for just long enough to inflict exemplary defeats on the Persians at Salamis (480 BC) and Plataea (479 BC) before renewing their traditional rivalries. Most Greek cities were forced to take sides with either Athens or Sparta as they vied for the leadership of Greece in the two Peloponnesian Wars (457–445 BC and 431–404 BC).

Ultimately, no Greek state could achieve a lasting dominance and, worn out by their struggles, they were conquered by Philip II of Macedon in 338 BC. Hoping to unite the Greeks behind him, Philip's son Alexander the Great invaded the Persian empire in 334 BC. A prodigious military genius, Alexander conquered the Persian empire in only five years. His death at Babylon in 323 BC, without a viable heir, left the future of his empire in doubt.

At the time of his death, Alexander was planning the conquest of the western Mediterranean. Here the main power was the Phoenician trading city of Carthage, which had become independent. Its ally, the Roman republic, was just establishing itself as the most powerful state in Italy. Meanwhile, much of Western and Central Europe was dominated by the Celts.

In the Warring States period (5th–3rd centuries BC), China's great powers controlled their people through bureaucratic structures and mobilized them for total war against each other. In India, the *janapadas* of the early 1st millennium BC had coalesced into a smaller number of *mahajanapadas* (great realms) by 500 BC, the most powerful of which by 323 BC was Magadha. In Mesoamerica, the Olmec civilization was declining but the younger Zapotec and Maya civilizations were beginning to flourish.

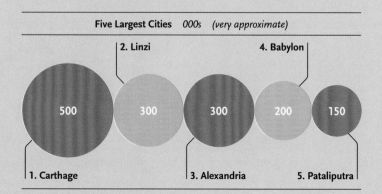

Five Largest Cities *000s* *(very approximate)*

	2. Linzi		4. Babylon	
500	**300**	**300**	**200**	**150**
1. Carthage		**3. Alexandria**		**5. Pataliputra**

Dorset Inuit culture

Dorset Inuit culture

Aleuts

Sub-Arctic caribou hunters

West coast fishers, hunters and gatherers

Central plateau hunter-fisher-gatherers

Great Plains bison hunters

Eastern Woodlands hunter-gatherers

Desert hunter-gatherers

Adena complex

Maize farmers

OLMEC CIVILIZATION

Valley of Mexico chiefdoms

Caribbean fishers, hunters and gatherers

ZAPOTECS

MAYA CITY STATES

Manioc farmers

Chorrera culture

Chavín culture

Pucara culture

Paracas culture

Chiripa culture

Chinchorro tradition

Savanna hunter-gatherers

Fishers and marine mammal hunters

Pampas hunters

Hunter-gatherers	Urbanized societies/ kingdoms
Settled farming cultures and peoples	Empires
Pastoral nomads	Uninhabited
Complex farming societies/chiefdoms	

150°   120°   90°   60°

1 ETRUSCAN CITY STATES
2 ROMAN REPUBLIC
3 GREEK CITY STATES
4 Italics
5 KINGDOM OF BOSPOROS

6 COLCHIS
7 CAPPADOCIA
8 ARMENIA
9 ATROPATENE
10 DAMOT

11 MINOR CHINESE KINGDOMS
12 Dong Son (Vietnamese) culture

Dorset Inuit culture

Sami

Finno-Ugrians

Palaeo-Siberians

Finns

Balts

Germans

Slavs

Scythians

Sarmatians

Sakas

Tungusic reindeer herders (Altaics)

Altaic nomads

Tungusic farmers and pastoralists (Altaics)

Celts

Celtiberians
Iberians

Illyrians

1 4
2 3
1

CARTHAGE

Carthage

5

6

7
8
9

Alexandria 3

4 Babylon

EMPIRE OF ALEXANDER THE GREAT

Yuezhi

ZHAO

YAN

2

Linzi QI

Koreans

Jomon hunter-gatherers and fishers

QIN

CHU

YUE

Tibetans

MAGADHA

5 Pataliputra

Viets

Berber farmers

Berber nomads

Garamantes (Berbers)

Libu

Arabs

HINDU KINGDOMS

Burmese

Tais

Savanna cereal farmers and pastoralists

MEROË

SABA

HADRAMAUT
QATABAN

Mons

Khmers

Chams

Tropical forest yam farmers

10

Ethiopian highland farmers

Cushitic pastoralists

Nok culture

Bantu farmers and pastoralists

Nilotic pastoralists

Micronesians

Pygmy rainforest peoples

Khoisan pastoralists

Malays (Austronesians)

Papuans

Melanesians

Polynesians

Khoisan peoples

Australian Aborigines

Tasmanians

Arctic Circle

Tropic of Cancer

Equator

Tropic of Capricorn

75°

45°

0°   30°   60°   90°   120°   150°   180°

323 BC

The Classical civilization of 5th- and 4th-century Greece was one of the most inventive and influential in world history. The philosophical thought of Socrates and the works of Plato and Aristotle laid the foundations of Western philosophy. Aristotle's thought was also fundamental to the development of scientific method, and in Hippocrates the Greeks produced one of the first physicians to eschew supernatural causes and cures for diseases. The works of Herodotus and Thucydides show the beginning of a critical analytical approach to history.

Athens was Greece's greatest cultural centre, producing some of the finest art and architecture of the Classical age, while the first great plays were staged at its Dionysian drama festival. As a result of Alexander's conquests, the influence of Greek civilization extended as far east as India. Alexander founded new cities, most of them named Alexandria after himself, throughout his empire and populated them with Greek and Macedonian settlers. The most successful was the Alexandria he founded in Egypt: strategically sited close to the mouth of the Nile it grew rapidly into a great trade centre.

Interstate conflict in China led to competition between rival theorists of politics and warfare. Sun Tzu wrote the military classic, *The Art of War*, and the dominant Legalist school advocated total state power over society. The vast Hindu epic, the *Mahabharata*, began to take shape in this period, but did not reach its final form until *c.* AD 400. It popularized worship of the new deity Krishna.

The Mesoamerican civilizations shared the use of a 52-year ritual calendar cycle: this was first used at the Zapotec site of Monte Albán. In the Peruvian Andes an art style first developed at the ceremonial centre of Chavín was adopted over a wide area, probably as a result of the spread of a religious cult rather than conquest.

World Population *(very approximate)*

7 BILLION

165 million

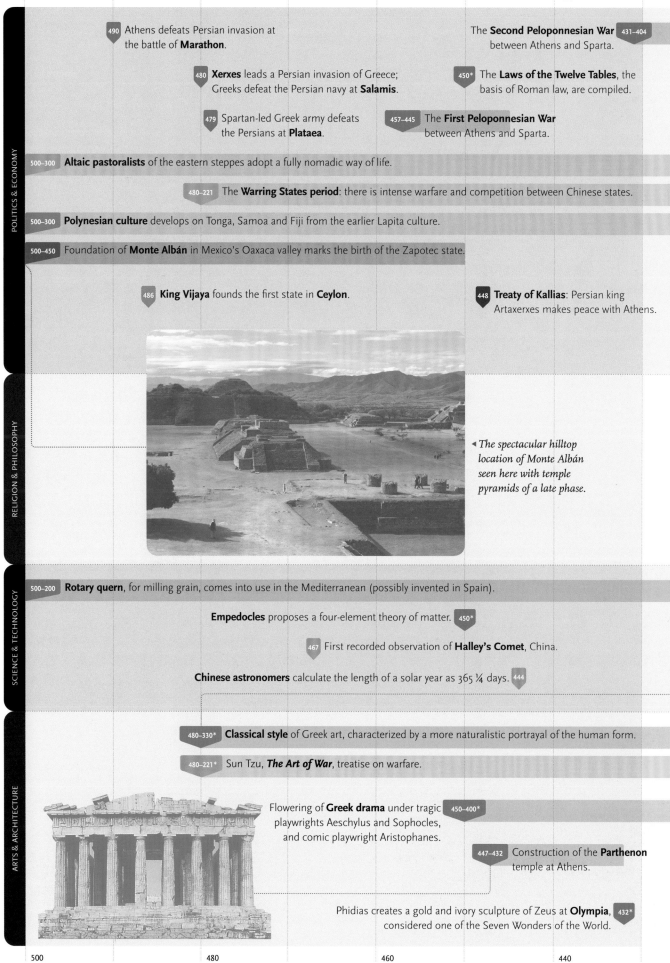

POLITICS & ECONOMY

490 Athens defeats Persian invasion at the battle of **Marathon**.

The **Second Peloponnesian War** **431–404** between Athens and Sparta.

480 **Xerxes** leads a Persian invasion of Greece; Greeks defeat the Persian navy at **Salamis**.

450* The **Laws of the Twelve Tables**, the basis of Roman law, are compiled.

479 Spartan-led Greek army defeats the Persians at **Plataea**.

457–445 The **First Peloponnesian War** between Athens and Sparta.

500–300 **Altaic pastoralists** of the eastern steppes adopt a fully nomadic way of life.

480–221 The **Warring States period**: there is intense warfare and competition between Chinese states.

500–300 **Polynesian culture** develops on Tonga, Samoa and Fiji from the earlier Lapita culture.

500–450 Foundation of **Monte Albán** in Mexico's Oaxaca valley marks the birth of the Zapotec state.

486 **King Vijaya** founds the first state in **Ceylon**.

448 **Treaty of Kallias**: Persian king Artaxerxes makes peace with Athens.

RELIGION & PHILOSOPHY

◄ *The spectacular hilltop location of Monte Albán seen here with temple pyramids of a late phase.*

SCIENCE & TECHNOLOGY

500–200 **Rotary quern**, for milling grain, comes into use in the Mediterranean (possibly invented in Spain).

Empedocles proposes a four-element theory of matter. **450***

467 First recorded observation of **Halley's Comet**, China.

Chinese astronomers calculate the length of a solar year as 365 ¼ days. **444**

480–330* **Classical style** of Greek art, characterized by a more naturalistic portrayal of the human form.

480–221 Sun Tzu, **The Art of War**, treatise on warfare.

ARTS & ARCHITECTURE

Flowering of **Greek drama** under tragic **450–400*** playwrights Aeschylus and Sophocles, and comic playwright Aristophanes.

447–432 Construction of the **Parthenon** temple at Athens.

Phidias creates a gold and ivory sculpture of Zeus at **Olympia**, **432*** considered one of the Seven Wonders of the World.

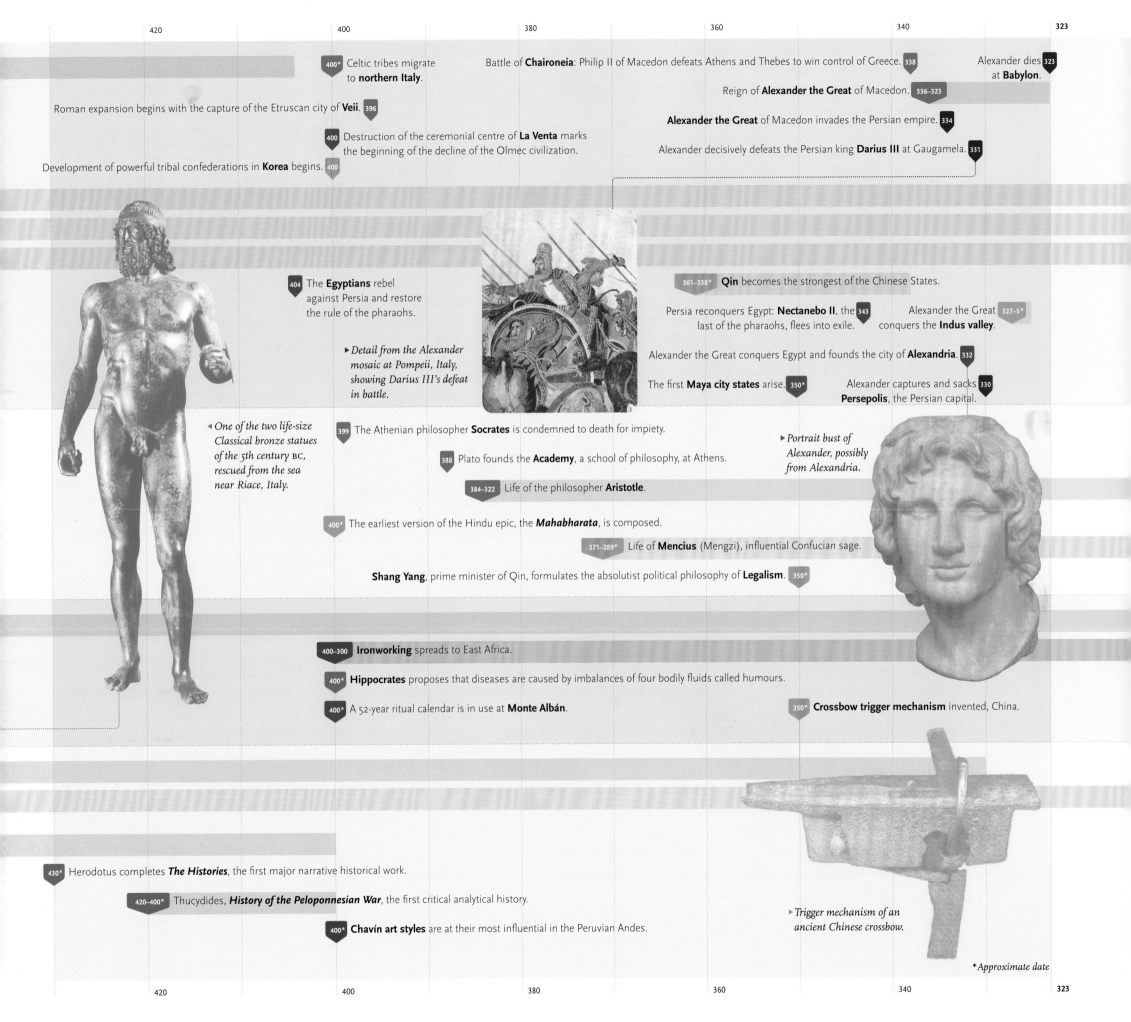

400* Celtic tribes migrate to **northern Italy**.

Battle of **Chaironeia**: Philip II of Macedon defeats Athens and Thebes to win control of Greece. **338**

Alexander dies **323** at **Babylon**.

Roman expansion begins with the capture of the Etruscan city of **Veii**. **396**

Reign of **Alexander the Great** of Macedon. **336–323**

400 Destruction of the ceremonial centre of **La Venta** marks the beginning of the decline of the Olmec civilization.

Alexander the Great of Macedon invades the Persian empire. **334**

Development of powerful tribal confederations in **Korea** begins. **400**

Alexander decisively defeats the Persian king **Darius III** at Gaugamela. **331**

404 The **Egyptians** rebel against Persia and restore the rule of the pharaohs.

361–338* **Qin** becomes the strongest of the Chinese States.

Persia reconquers Egypt: **Nectanebo II**, the **343** last of the pharaohs, flees into exile.

Alexander the Great **327–5*** conquers the **Indus valley**.

▶ *Detail from the Alexander mosaic at Pompeii, Italy, showing Darius III's defeat in battle.*

Alexander the Great conquers Egypt and founds the city of **Alexandria**. **332**

The first **Maya city states** arise. **350***

Alexander captures and sacks **330** **Persepolis**, the Persian capital.

◀ *One of the two life-size Classical bronze statues of the 5th century BC, rescued from the sea near Riace, Italy.*

399 The Athenian philosopher **Socrates** is condemned to death for impiety.

388 Plato founds the **Academy**, a school of philosophy, at Athens.

▶ *Portrait bust of Alexander, possibly from Alexandria.*

384–322 Life of the philosopher **Aristotle**.

400* The earliest version of the Hindu epic, the **Mahabharata**, is composed.

371–289* Life of **Mencius** (Mengzi), influential Confucian sage.

Shang Yang, prime minister of Qin, formulates the absolutist political philosophy of **Legalism**. **350***

400–300 **Ironworking** spreads to East Africa.

400* **Hippocrates** proposes that diseases are caused by imbalances of four bodily fluids called humours.

400* A 52-year ritual calendar is in use at **Monte Albán**.

350* **Crossbow trigger mechanism** invented, China.

430* Herodotus completes **The Histories**, the first major narrative historical work.

420–400* Thucydides, **History of the Peloponnesian War**, the first critical analytical history.

400* **Chavín art styles** are at their most influential in the Peruvian Andes.

▶ *Trigger mechanism of an ancient Chinese crossbow.*

*Approximate date

200 BC

THE UNIFICATION OF CHINA, BREAK-UP OF ALEXANDER'S EMPIRE AND THE RISE OF ROME

China's Warring States period reached its climactic conclusion during the 3rd century BC. Qin, the strongest of the states, destroyed the last remnant of the Zhou kingdom in 256 BC. In nine years of brutal campaigning, King Zheng (r. 246–210 BC) of Qin conquered the remaining states, completing the unification of China in 221 BC. Zheng marked his achievement by adopting the ruling name Shi Huangdi (First Emperor).

Shi Huangdi destroyed all vestiges of the old states, banned all challenges to Qin power and imposed cultural and economic uniformity; he ruled through professional, non-hereditary, local and central bureaucracies. Oppressive Qin rule was hated and, after Shi Huangdi's death, rebellions across the former states overthrew Qin. The Han dynasty (206 BC–AD 220) gradually re-established central power, keeping much of the Qin legal and administrative structure but ruling with a lighter hand at first.

The 3rd century BC saw most of India united under the Mauryan dynasty of Magadha. The empire reached its height under Asoka, but it lacked internal unity and went into decline immediately after his death. The memory of a pan-Indian empire remained influential, however.

Alexander's empire broke up immediately after his death in 323 BC as his generals carved out kingdoms for themselves. The most important were those of Seleucos, based in Babylon, and Ptolemy, based in Egypt. The sprawling Seleucid kingdom immediately began to fray at the edges and was in decline by 200 BC. In contrast, the Ptolemies won acceptance from their Egyptian subjects by adopting the trappings of pharaonic rule. Rome and Carthage fell out over spheres of influence in Sicily. Two bitter wars broke Carthage's power and left Rome dominating the western Mediterranean.

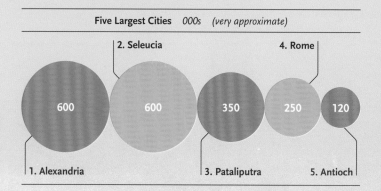

Five Largest Cities *000s* *(very approximate)*

2. Seleucia		4. Rome	
600	600	350	250	120
1. Alexandria		3. Pataliputra	5. Antioch

Dorset Inuit culture

Dorset Inuit culture

Aleuts

Sub-Arctic caribou hunters

Central plateau hunter-fisher-gatherers

West coast fishers, hunters and gatherers

Desert hunter-gatherers

Great Plains bison hunters

Eastern Woodlands hunter-gatherers

Adena complex

Maize farmers

OLMEC CIVILIZATION

Valley of Mexico chiefdoms

Caribbean fishers, hunters and gatherers

ZAPOTECS

MAYA CITY STATES

Andean chiefdoms

Manioc farmers

Andean chiefdoms

Polynesians

Paracas culture

Pucara culture

Savanna hunter-gatherers

Fishers and marine mammal hunters

Pampas hunters

Hunter-gatherers

Settled farming cultures and peoples

Pastoral nomads

Complex farming societies/chiefdoms

Urbanized societies/kingdoms

Empires

Uninhabited

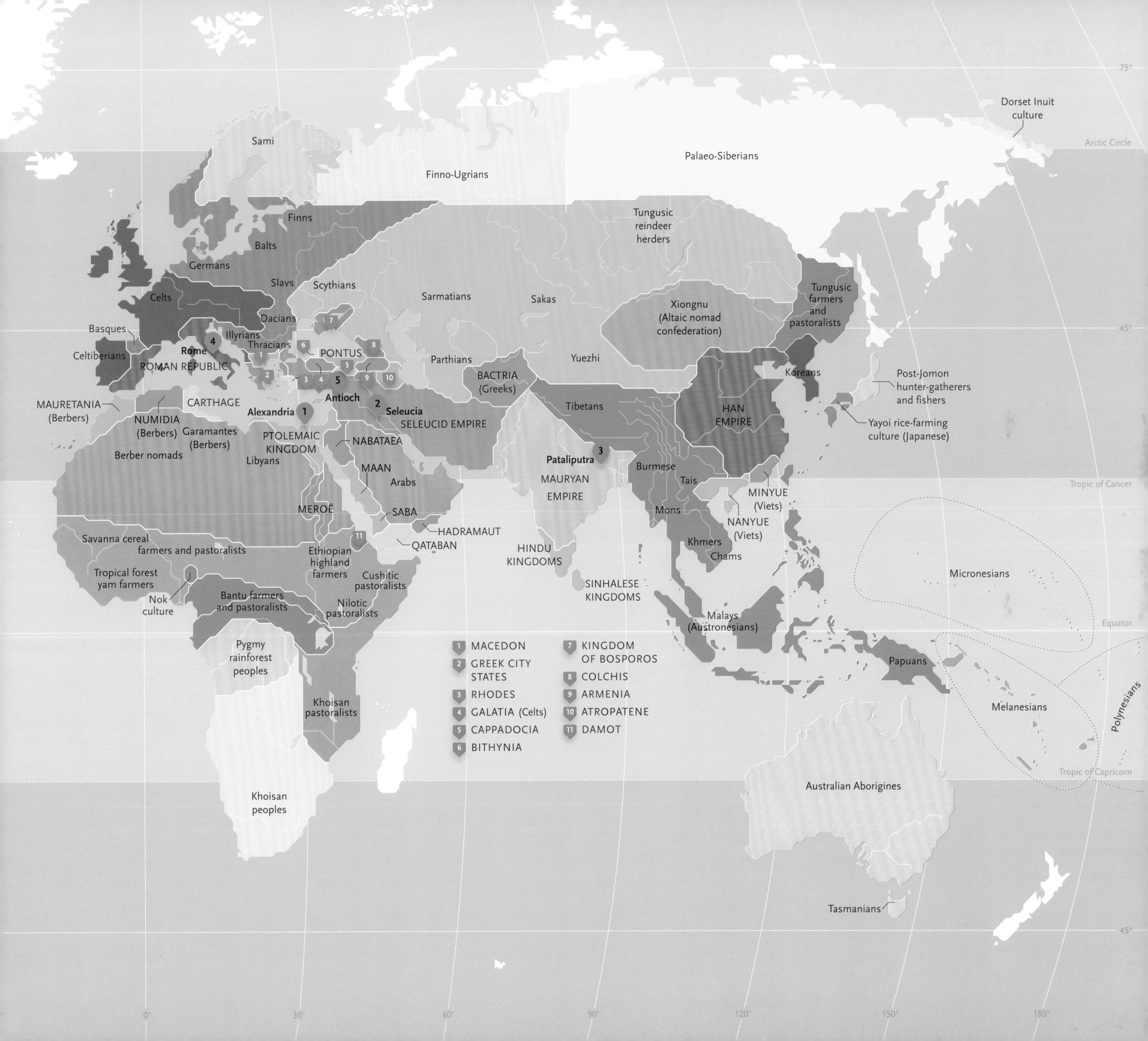

Dorset Inuit culture

Sami

Palaeo-Siberians

Finno-Ugrians

Finns

Tungusic reindeer herders

Balts

Germans

Slavs

Scythians

Celts

Dacians

Basques

Illyrians

Thracians

Celtiberians

Rome

ROMAN REPUBLIC

Sarmatians

Sakas

Tungusic farmers and pastoralists

4

PONTUS

Xiongnu (Altaic nomad confederation)

Yuezhi

Koreans

Post-Jomon hunter-gatherers and fishers

7

6

8

Parthians

MAURETANIA (Berbers)

CARTHAGE

1

2

3 **4** **5**

9 **10**

BACTRIA (Greeks)

HAN EMPIRE

Yayoi rice-farming culture (Japanese)

Antioch

NUMIDIA (Berbers)

Alexandria **1**

2 **Seleucia**

SELEUCID EMPIRE

Tibetans

Garamantes (Berbers)

PTOLEMAIC KINGDOM

NABATAEA

Berber nomads

Libyans

MAAN

Arabs

Pataliputra **3**

Burmese

MINYUE (Viets)

MEROË

SABA

MAURYAN EMPIRE

Tais

NANYUE (Viets)

HADRAMAUT

Mons

Savanna cereal farmers and pastoralists

11

QATABAN

HINDU KINGDOMS

Khmers

Chams

Tropical forest yam farmers

Ethiopian highland farmers

Cushitic pastoralists

SINHALESE KINGDOMS

Malays (Austronesians)

Micronesians

Nok culture

Bantu farmers and pastoralists

Nilotic pastoralists

Papuans

Pygmy rainforest peoples

Melanesians

Khoisan pastoralists

	MACEDON		KINGDOM OF BOSPOROS
1	MACEDON	**7**	KINGDOM OF BOSPOROS
2	GREEK CITY STATES	**8**	COLCHIS
3	RHODES	**9**	ARMENIA
4	GALATIA (Celts)	**10**	ATROPATENE
5	CAPPADOCIA	**11**	DAMOT
6	BITHYNIA		

Khoisan peoples

Australian Aborigines

Tasmanians

Polynesians

200 BC

Alexander's conquests placed Greece itself almost at the margin of the Greek world and his successors continued his policy of founding new cities and encouraging Greek colonization. Greek became the common language of trade, diplomacy and culture across the whole Middle East. The region became a vast melting pot in which Egyptians, Jews, Persians, Parthians and Indians borrowed and adapted Greek culture, creating a new international Hellenistic civilization. Even the remote Greek kingdom of Bactria in Central Asia remained part of the Greek cultural mainstream. Alexandria and Pergamon overshadowed Athens as cultural centres, though it retained primacy as a centre for philosophical study. Greek cultural leadership was manifest even in areas never conquered by Alexander, such as the growing Roman empire, where Greek literary forms were freely adapted by Latin poets and playwrights.

Supposedly horrified by the suffering caused by one of his military campaigns, the Indian emperor Asoka converted to Buddhism. Asoka actively promoted Buddhism in India and supported Buddhist missions abroad, doing much to turn it into a major world religion. Asoka may have seen Buddhism as a means to unite a population divided by caste and cultural diversity. In this he failed: Hinduism remained the majority religion in India. It was probably during Asoka's reign that the first stupas were built. These distinctive Buddhist monuments house relics of the Buddha and his disciples.

The invention of stirrups in this period, possibly in India, allowed a horse rider to sit more securely in the saddle, greatly improving the effectiveness of cavalry. The innovation first became widespread among the steppe nomads two or three centuries later. The invention by the Polynesians of the ocean-going double-hulled canoe opened up the furthest reaches of the Pacific to human settlement.

World Population *(very approximate)*

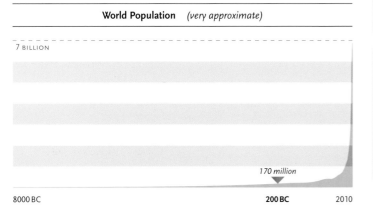

7 BILLION

170 million

8000 BC   **200 BC**   2010

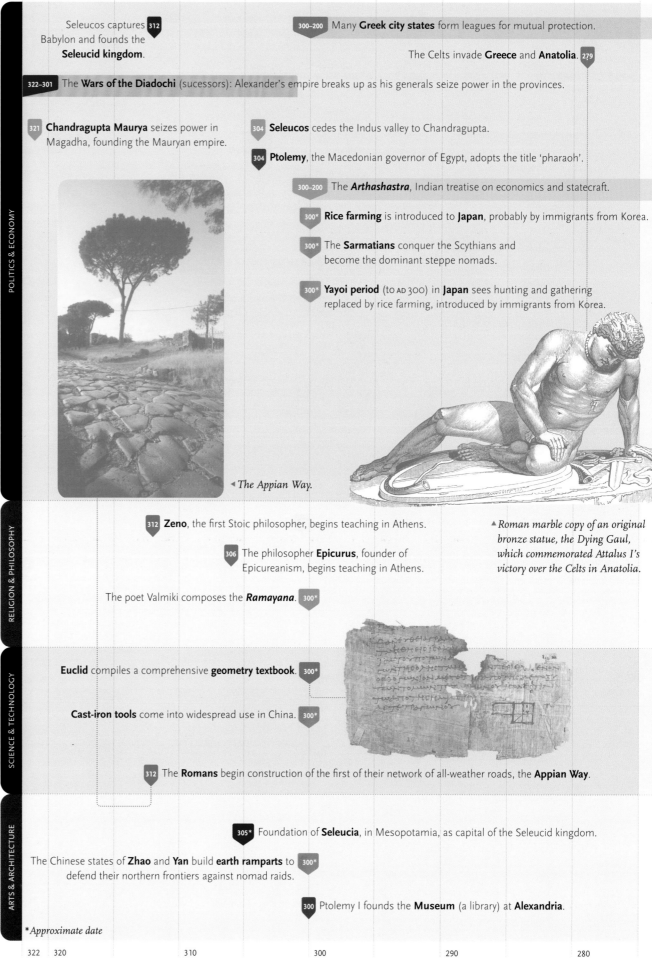

322   320   310   300   290   280

POLITICS & ECONOMY

312 Seleucos captures Babylon and founds the **Seleucid kingdom**.

300–200 Many **Greek city states** form leagues for mutual protection.

The Celts invade **Greece** and **Anatolia**. **279**

322–301 The **Wars of the Diadochi** (sucessors): Alexander's empire breaks up as his generals seize power in the provinces.

321 **Chandragupta Maurya** seizes power in Magadha, founding the Mauryan empire.

304 **Seleucos** cedes the Indus valley to Chandragupta.

304 **Ptolemy**, the Macedonian governor of Egypt, adopts the title 'pharaoh'.

300–200 The **Arthashastra**, Indian treatise on economics and statecraft.

300 **Rice farming** is introduced to **Japan**, probably by immigrants from Korea.

300 The **Sarmatians** conquer the Scythians and become the dominant steppe nomads.

300* **Yayoi period** (to AD 300) in **Japan** sees hunting and gathering replaced by rice farming, introduced by immigrants from Korea.

◄ *The Appian Way.*

▲ *Roman marble copy of an original bronze statue, the Dying Gaul, which commemorated Attalus I's victory over the Celts in Anatolia.*

RELIGION & PHILOSOPHY

312 **Zeno**, the first Stoic philosopher, begins teaching in Athens.

306 The philosopher **Epicurus**, founder of Epicureanism, begins teaching in Athens.

The poet Valmiki composes the **Ramayana**. **300***

SCIENCE & TECHNOLOGY

Euclid compiles a comprehensive **geometry textbook**. **300***

Cast-iron tools come into widespread use in China. **300***

312 The **Romans** begin construction of the first of their network of all-weather roads, the **Appian Way**.

ARTS & ARCHITECTURE

305* Foundation of **Seleucia**, in Mesopotamia, as capital of the Seleucid kingdom.

The Chinese states of **Zhao** and **Yan** build **earth ramparts** to **300*** defend their northern frontiers against nomad raids.

300 Ptolemy I founds the **Museum** (a library) at **Alexandria**.

*Approximate date

322   320   310   300   290   280

272 **Rome** completes the conquest of peninsular Italy.

264–241 Rome defeats Carthage in the **First Punic War**.

239 **Bactria** becomes independent of the Seleucid kingdom under a Greek dynasty.

238 **Parthia** becomes independent of the Seleucid kingdom under Arsaces I.

218–202 **Rome** becomes the dominant power of the western Mediterranean after defeating Carthage in the **Second Punic War**.

The last king of the Zhou dynasty is overthrown by **Qin**. **256**

Foundation Vietnamese kingdom of **Au Lac**. **258**

237–218 **Carthage** conquers southern Spain.

268–233 Reign of **Asoka**, Mauryan empire at its peak.

230–221 **King Zheng of Qin** (r. 246–210) unifies China, ending the Warring States period.

221 King Zheng adopts the title **Shi Huangdi**, the 'First Emperor' of China.

Death of **Shi Huangdi**: he is buried in a city-sized tomb complex at **Lintong**. **210**

Civil war in China, during which the Qin dynasty is overthrown. **209–203**

Xiongnu dominate the eastern steppes under Modun. **209–174**

Emperor Gaodi (r. 206–195) founds the **Han dynasty**. **206**

Au Lac conquered by China. **214**

Vietnamese kingdom of **Nanyue** (Nam Viet) conquered by Chinese general Zhao Tuo. **203**

Polynesians settle **Tahiti** and the **Marquesas Islands**. **200***

Berber kingdoms of **Mauretania** and **Numidia** emerge in North Africa. **200***

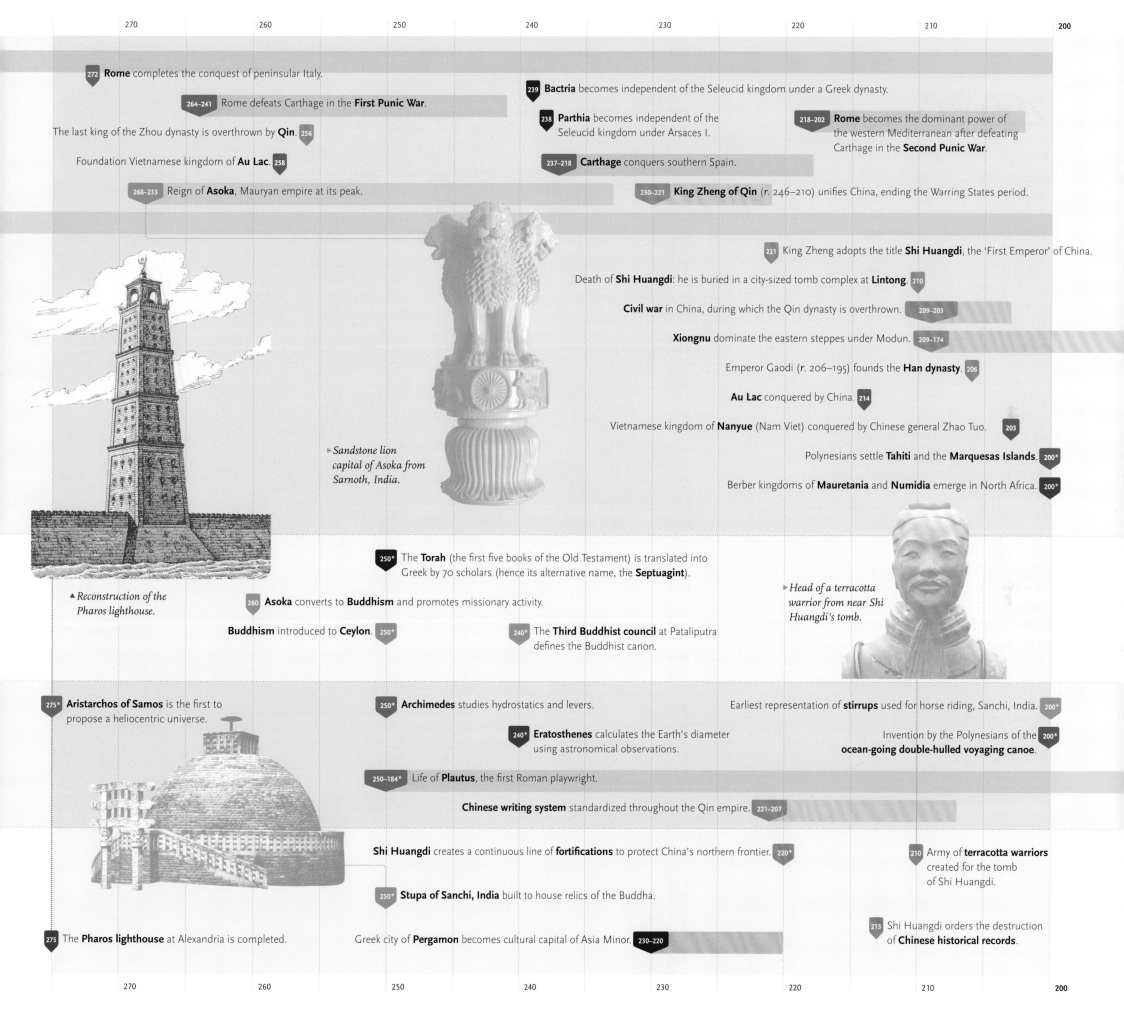

▶ *Sandstone lion capital of Asoka from Sarnoth, India.*

▲ *Reconstruction of the Pharos lighthouse.*

250* The **Torah** (the first five books of the Old Testament) is translated into Greek by 70 scholars (hence its alternative name, the **Septuagint**).

260 **Asoka** converts to **Buddhism** and promotes missionary activity.

Buddhism introduced to **Ceylon**. **250***

240* The **Third Buddhist council** at Pataliputra defines the Buddhist canon.

▶ *Head of a terracotta warrior from near Shi Huangdi's tomb.*

275* **Aristarchos of Samos** is the first to propose a heliocentric universe.

250* **Archimedes** studies hydrostatics and levers.

Earliest representation of **stirrups** used for horse riding, Sanchi, India. **200***

240* **Eratosthenes** calculates the Earth's diameter using astronomical observations.

Invention by the Polynesians of the **200*** **ocean-going double-hulled voyaging canoe**.

250–184* Life of **Plautus**, the first Roman playwright.

Chinese writing system standardized throughout the Qin empire. **221–207**

Shi Huangdi creates a continuous line of **fortifications** to protect China's northern frontier. **220***

210 Army of **terracotta warriors** created for the tomb of Shi Huangdi.

250* **Stupa of Sanchi, India** built to house relics of the Buddha.

275 The **Pharos lighthouse** at Alexandria is completed.

Greek city of **Pergamon** becomes cultural capital of Asia Minor. **230–220**

213 Shi Huangdi orders the destruction of **Chinese historical records**.

1BC
CHINA'S HAN DYNASTY EMPIRE AT ITS GREATEST EXTENT

Following its victories over Carthage in the 3rd century BC, Rome continued to expand for more than 200 years. Neither the warlike Celts of Western Europe nor the wealthy Hellenistic kingdoms of the eastern Mediterranean proved capable of resisting Rome's disciplined armies of legionary infantry. As plunder and slaves flooded into Rome, social divisions were exacerbated. Following a civil war, the general Julius Caesar declared himself dictator for life, effectively destroying the republic. His murder in 44 BC provoked further civil wars. The eventual winner, Caesar's nephew Octavian, introduced imperial government, adopting the ruling name Augustus (revered one). With the bloodless annexation of Egypt in 30 BC, Rome's mastery of the entire Mediterranean world was complete.

The main foreign rival to the Han dynasty in China was the Xiongnu nomad confederation, with both sides launching attacks on each other. The Han extended the Qin border wall system westwards and tried to outflank the Xiongnu in Central Asia. It also expanded into parts of Korea and Vietnam. The Xiongnu began to break up in 36 BC after a succession of defeats by the Han. The collapse of the Mauryan empire of India was complete c. 185 BC. India was divided into competing dynastic states, which rose and fell according to the abilities of their rulers. Like China, India suffered nomad invasions during the 2nd century BC: the Sakas, an Indo-Iranian people, established a kingdom of their own c. 94 BC.

This period saw the emergence of the Moche kingdom in the coastal valleys of Peru, the first state to develop in South America. In Mesoamerica the city of Teotihuacán became a dominant regional power. In North America, the adoption of maize cultivation by the Basketmaker cultures around the end of the millennium began a gradual transition to dependence on farming.

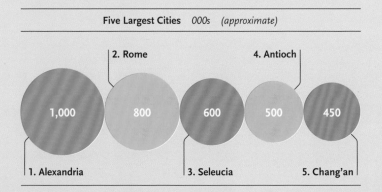

Five Largest Cities *000s* *(approximate)*

1. Alexandria — 1,000
2. Rome — 800
3. Seleucia — 600
4. Antioch — 500
5. Chang'an — 450

Dorset Inuit culture

Dorset Inuit culture

Aleuts

Sub-Arctic caribou hunters

Central plateau hunter-fisher-gatherers

West coast fishers, hunters and gatherers

Desert hunter-gatherers

Great Plains bison hunters

Eastern Woodlands hunter-gatherers

Basketmaker cultures (maize cultivators and hunter-gatherers)

Hopewell burial mound traditions

Maize farmers

OLMEC CIVILIZATION

TEOTIHUACÁN

ZAPOTECS

MAYA CITY STATES

Caribbean fishers, hunters and gatherers

Manioc farmers

Andean chiefdoms

MOCHE

Nazca culture

Pucara culture

Savanna hunter-gatherers

Polynesians

Fishers and marine mammal hunters

Pampas hunters

Hunter-gatherers

Settled farming cultures and peoples

Pastoral nomads

Complex farming societies/chiefdoms

Urbanized societies/kingdoms

Empires

Uninhabited

Sami

Finno-Ugrians

Palaeo-Siberians

Dorset Inuit culture

Finns

Tungusic reindeer herders

Balts

Celts

Slavs

Germans

Sarmatians

Tungusic farmers and pastoralists

Ainu

Dacians

Alans

Wusun

Xiongnu

KOGURYO (Koreans)

2 Rome

1

2

Yayoi rice farmers (Japanese)

ROMAN EMPIRE

4 Antioch

3

Kushans

5 Chang'an

SILLA (Koreans)

1 Alexandria

3 Seleucia

Tibetans

HAN EMPIRE

Berbers

PARTHIA

HINDU KINGDOMS

GARAMANTES

Libyans

Arabs

SUREN KINGDOM

SAKA KINGDOM

Burmese

Tais

MEROË

SATAVAHANA KALINGA

Pyu (Tibeto-Burmese)

Micronesians

5

HADRAMAUT

Mons

Savanna cereal farmers and pastoralists

Nilotic pastoralists

Ethiopian highland farmers

4

Khmers

Malays

Tropical forest yam farmers

Cushitic pastoralists

HINDU KINGDOMS

Chams

Nok culture

ANURADHAPURA

Malays

Papuans

Bantu farmers and pastoralists

1 COLCHIS

Malays

Pygmy peoples

2 IBERIA

3 ARMENIA

Melanesians

Khoisan pastoralists

4 AXUM

5 HIMYARITE KINGDOM

Polynesians

Khoisan peoples

Australian Aborigines

Tasmanians

1 BC

Systematic timekeeping is important in most civilizations, for administrative purposes, for the recording of major events and to ensure the regular performance of important religious rituals. The 1st century BC saw the introduction of two important calendars. In the Roman empire the Julian calendar introduced a regular year of 365 days divided into 12 months, with a leap day added to every fourth year. From c. 400 BC the Mesoamericans used a ritual calendar that repeated itself every 52 years. This did not allow for accurate historical dating. To solve the problem, a Long Count calendar based on a cycle of 5,125 years was devised, probably by the Olmecs.

Even after their conquest by Rome, Greeks continued to be the cultural leaders in the Mediterranean world. However, the turbulent last years of the Roman republic and the early years of the empire saw the flourishing of Latin literature. Much of this literature celebrated Rome's achievements, none more so than Virgil's epic poem, *The Aeneid*, which recounted the adventures of the Trojan prince Aeneas, the legendary ancestor of the Romans.

Differential gearing, watermills and glass-blowing were important technological developments in the eastern Mediterranean region during this period. The abandonment of Babylon c. 140 BC marks the effective extinction of the ancient Mesopotamian tradition of civilization after centuries of foreign rule.

Though it was not impossible to cross, the Sahara desert was a major obstacle to trade and other cultural contacts between West Africa and the Mediterranean world. With the introduction of the dromedary camel to the Sahara c. 100 BC, this began slowly to change. Long used for desert transport in the Middle East, camels made travel in the Sahara easier and led to the opening of regular caravan routes to West Africa.

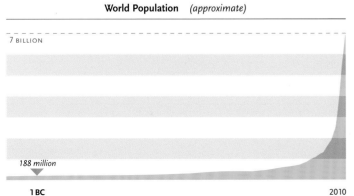

World Population *(approximate)*

7 BILLION

188 million

1 BC   2010

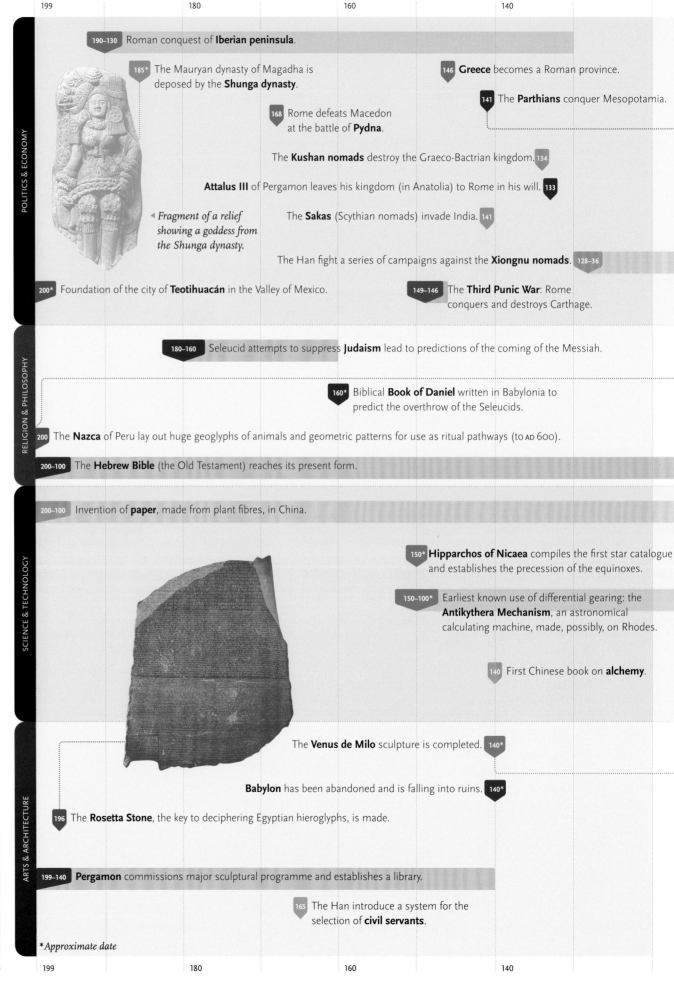

199   180   160   140

POLITICS & ECONOMY

190–130 Roman conquest of **Iberian peninsula**.

185* The Mauryan dynasty of Magadha is deposed by the **Shunga dynasty**.

146 **Greece** becomes a Roman province.

141 The **Parthians** conquer Mesopotamia.

168 Rome defeats Macedon at the battle of **Pydna**.

The **Kushan nomads** destroy the Graeco-Bactrian kingdom. **134**

Attalus III of Pergamon leaves his kingdom (in Anatolia) to Rome in his will. **133**

◄ *Fragment of a relief showing a goddess from the Shunga dynasty.*

The **Sakas** (Scythian nomads) invade India. **141**

The Han fight a series of campaigns against the **Xiongnu nomads**. **128–36**

200* Foundation of the city of **Teotihuacán** in the Valley of Mexico.

149–146 The **Third Punic War**: Rome conquers and destroys Carthage.

RELIGION & PHILOSOPHY

180–160 Seleucid attempts to suppress **Judaism** lead to predictions of the coming of the Messiah.

160* Biblical **Book of Daniel** written in Babylonia to predict the overthrow of the Seleucids.

200 The **Nazca** of Peru lay out huge geoglyphs of animals and geometric patterns for use as ritual pathways (to AD 600).

200–100 The **Hebrew Bible** (the Old Testament) reaches its present form.

SCIENCE & TECHNOLOGY

200–100 Invention of **paper**, made from plant fibres, in China.

150* **Hipparchos of Nicaea** compiles the first star catalogue and establishes the precession of the equinoxes.

150–100* Earliest known use of differential gearing: the **Antikythera Mechanism**, an astronomical calculating machine, made, possibly, on Rhodes.

140 First Chinese book on **alchemy**.

ARTS & ARCHITECTURE

The **Venus de Milo** sculpture is completed. **140***

Babylon has been abandoned and is falling into ruins. **140***

196 The **Rosetta Stone**, the key to deciphering Egyptian hieroglyphs, is made.

199–140 **Pergamon** commissions major sculptural programme and establishes a library.

165 The Han introduce a system for the selection of **civil servants**.

*Approximate date

199   180   160   140

111 Vietnamese **Nanyue kingdom** conquered by China.

Collapse of the **Seleucid kingdom**. **83**

100* The **dromedary camel** is introduced to the Sahara desert.

The Parthians defeat a Roman invasion at the battle of **Carrhae**. **53**

With the fall of the Shunga dynasty, **Magadha** becomes a minor kingdom. **73**

94* The **Sakas** establish a kingdom in northwest India.

100* The **Moche state** is founded in the coastal valleys of Peru.

117–59 Han expansion into Central Asia to counter the **Xiongnu**.

58–51 **Julius Caesar** conquers Gaul.

Murder of **Julius Caesar** leads to Roman civil war. **44**

64–63 **Syria** and **Palestine** become part of the Roman empire.

Octavian adopts the title **Augustus** **27** and introduces imperial rule.

Battle of Actium: Octavian wins control of the Roman empire. **31**

57 Traditional date for the foundation of **Silla**, the first Korean state.

Roman frontier advanced **20–15** to the **Danube**.

30 **Egypt** is annexed by the Roman empire.

Cleopatra, last Ptolemaic ruler **31** of Egypt, commits suicide.

Emergence of **Basketmaker II culture** marks the **1*** beginning of farming in North America.

Roman occupation of **Germany**. **12**

◄ *Gold crown from the later Silla state.*

► *Giant geoglyphs of a bird and a monkey created by the Nazca of Peru.*

► *The Prima Porta marble statue of Augustus from Rome.*

45 In **On the Nature of the Gods**, Cicero questions the literal existence of the pagan Roman gods.

Jesus is born at Bethlehem. **6***

46 Caesar introduces the **Julian calendar**.

65* Earliest known **watermills**, in Anatolia.

50* **Glass-blowing technique** invented, probably by the Phoenicians.

Systematic recording of sun spots by **Chinese astronomers**. **28**

Earliest known inscription using the **Mesoamerican Long Count** calendar, at the Olmec site of Tres Zapotes. **32**

105* A **school of technology** is founded at Alexandria.

100* **Sima Qian** writes a history of China from its beginnings to his own times.

30* **Livy** begins his monumental history of Rome.

84–10* Major Latin love poets, **Catullus**, **Propertius** and **Tibullus**.

30–19* Virgil writes his epic poem **The Aeneid**.

20 King Herod rebuilds the **Temple at Jerusalem**.

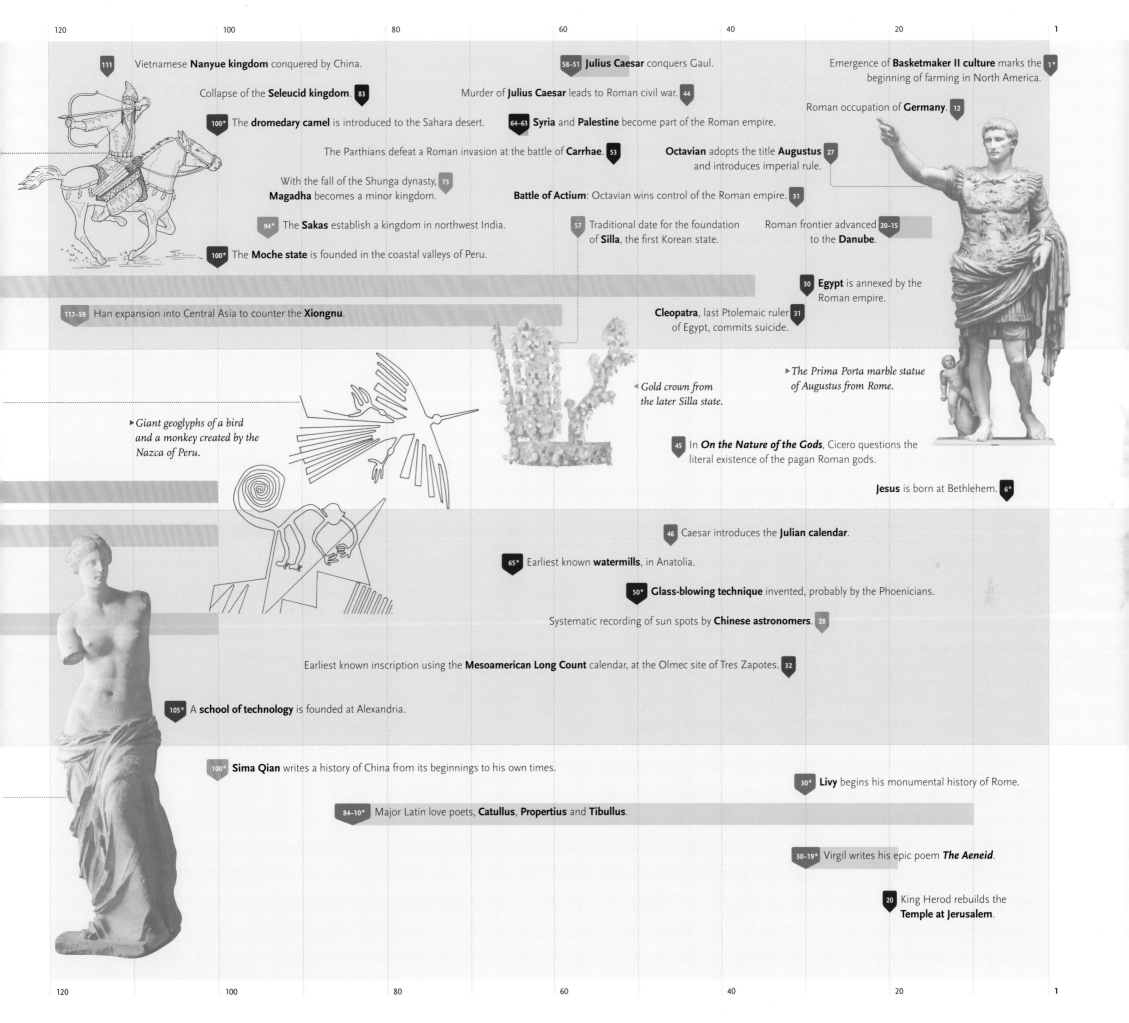

AD 200

THE ROMAN AND KUSHAN EMPIRES REACH THEIR GREATEST EXTENTS; DECLINE OF THE HAN EMPIRE

Between AD 25 and 75, the Kushans, an Iranian nomad people, created a vast empire in Central Asia and northern India. This empire was notable for its cosmopolitan culture, blending Indian, Persian, nomad and Graeco-Roman influences, a reflection of its role as a key middleman in east–west trade routes. The Kushan empire was, however, highly decentralized and by AD 200 its power was already in decline.

Superficially the other empires established before this point had scarcely changed, but in fact all had serious problems. The prestige of the Parthians, always regarded as outsiders by their Persian subjects, was collapsing after a series of defeats by Rome and the Kushans. Believing that the Roman empire was becoming over-extended, the emperor Hadrian (r. 117–38) had called a halt to Roman expansion and fortified the northern frontiers, which the increasingly well-organized German tribes were putting under ever greater pressure.

In China, the Han dynasty was losing power to the local warlords on which it had relied to suppress peasant rebellions in AD 184. The warlords were now fighting between themselves. Another significant development at this time was the rise of Funan and Champa, the first kingdoms in Southeast Asia, owing mainly to the stimulus of international trade.

In the 1st century AD Graeco-Roman mariners discovered how to exploit the monsoon winds to sail directly from Egypt to India and return in a single season. Trade between the Roman empire and India increased greatly as a result. To supply the Roman market, Indian mariners in their turn increased trade with Southeast Asia, taking with them not only goods but also Hindu and Buddhist culture.

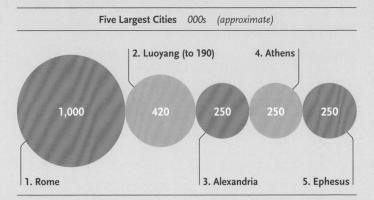

Five Largest Cities *000s* *(approximate)*

1. Rome	2. Luoyang (to 190)	3. Alexandria	4. Athens	5. Ephesus
1,000	420	250	250	250

Dorset Inuit culture

Dorset Inuit culture

Dorset Inuit culture

Aleuts

Sub-Arctic caribou hunters

Central plateau hunter-fisher-gatherers

West coast fishers, hunters and gatherers

Great Plains bison hunters

Eastern Woodlands hunter-gatherers

Basketmaker cultures

Hopewell burial mound traditions

Desert hunter-gatherers

Maize farmers   TEOTIHUACÁN

Caribbean fishers, hunters and gatherers

ZAPOTECS

MAYA CITY STATES

Polynesians

Andean chiefdoms

Manioc farmers

MOCHE

TIWANAKU

Nazca

Savanna hunter-gatherers

Pampas hunters

Fishers and marine mammal hunters

Legend

- Hunter-gatherers
- Settled farming cultures and peoples
- Pastoral nomads
- Complex farming societies/chiefdoms
- Urbanized societies/kingdoms
- Empires
- Uninhabited

Sami

Finno-Ugrians

Palaeo-Siberians

Dorset Inuit
culture

Samoyed
reindeer
herders

Tungusic
reindeer
herders

Finns

Balts

Slavs

Sarmatians

Alans

Turks

Khitans

Tungus

Celts

Germanic
peoples

Huns

Tocharians

Xiongnu

Ainu

1

ROMAN EMPIRE

1

Rome

2

3

4   5

Athens   Ephesus

3

Alexandria

PARTHIAN
EMPIRE

KUSHAN
EMPIRE

Tibetan transhumant
pastoralists

Tuyuhun

2

Luoyang

H A N
E M P I R E

KOGURYO

SILLA

Yayoi
chiefdoms
(Japanese)

Berbers

GARAMANTES

Libyans

4

Arabs

HINDU

6   Burmese

KINGDOMS

Tais

MEROË

HIMYARITE
KINGDOM

SAKA
KINGDOM

Pyu

Savanna cereal farmers
and pastoralists

Tropical forest
yam farmers

Nok
culture

Nilotic
pastoralists

Ethiopian
highland
farmers

Cushitic
pastoralists

HADRAMAUT

5

SATAVAHANA

CHOLAS

Mons

CHAMPA
(Chams)

FUNAN
(Khmers)

Micronesians

ANURADHAPURA

1   COLCHIS   4   NABATAEA

2   IBERIA   5   AXUM

3   ARMENIA   6   MAGADHA

Malays

Papuans

Bantu farmers
and pastoralists

Melanesians

1st century AD

San
hunter-
gatherers

Khoikhoi
pastoralists

Australian Aborigines

Tasmanians

AD 200

The most significant cultural development of the first two centuries AD was the birth of the Christian religion. Based on the teachings of Jesus of Nazareth, crucified at Jerusalem *c.* AD 30, the religion spread first among the Jewish diaspora in the Roman empire. Under the influence of St Paul (*c.* AD 5–67), Christianity made the transition from Jewish sect to a universalist religion which began to win converts among gentiles, despite official hostility and occasional persecution. A parallel thread of Jewish radicalism led in AD 66 to the Zealot revolt against Roman rule: its bloody suppression saw the destruction of the Temple in Jerusalem and the expulsion of many Jews from Palestine.

Christianity was rivalled in popularity in the Roman empire by another eastern religion, the cult of the Persian god Mithras, which won many converts in the army. In India, the Mahayana (Great Vehicle) school of Buddhism developed under the tolerant and eclectic Kushan rulers: it is now the largest branch of the Buddhist faith. It was also under the Kushans that the first representations of the Buddha were made. In China, Confucianism was the state ideology. The Daoist school of philosophy became assimilated with traditional religion. Its supposed founder Laozi was deified.

Important technological developments of the period include the spread of watermills in the Roman empire (which is not usually considered to have been interested in labour-saving technology), the discovery of the magnetic compass in China and the invention of cast steel in India. The codex (a book of sewn pages) began to replace the clumsy scroll in the Roman empire, and paper began to replace bamboo strips as the main medium for writing in China. The Polynesians, however, provide a reminder that technological progress is not guaranteed: they lost the skill of pottery manufacture in this period.

World Population (*approximate*)

7 BILLION

202 million

200 BC **AD 200** 2010

60

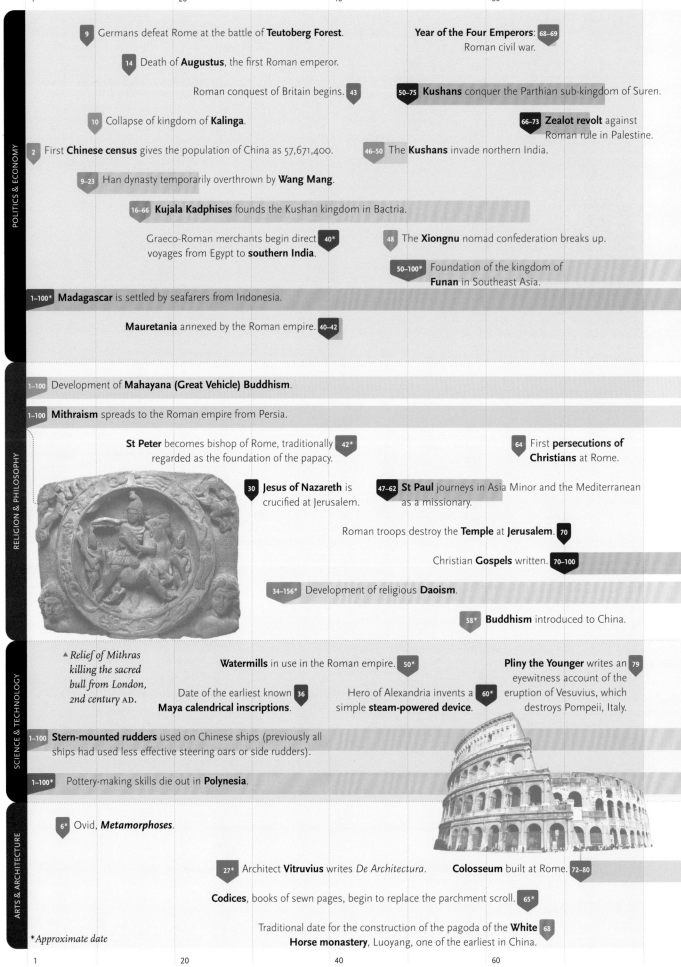

POLITICS & ECONOMY

9 Germans defeat Rome at the battle of **Teutoberg Forest**.

Year of the Four Emperors: 68–69 Roman civil war.

14 Death of **Augustus**, the first Roman emperor.

Roman conquest of Britain begins. **43**

50–75 Kushans conquer the Parthian sub-kingdom of Suren.

10 Collapse of kingdom of **Kalinga**.

66–73 Zealot revolt against Roman rule in Palestine.

2 First **Chinese census** gives the population of China as 57,671,400.

46–50 The **Kushans** invade northern India.

9–23 Han dynasty temporarily overthrown by **Wang Mang**.

16–66 Kujala Kadphises founds the Kushan kingdom in Bactria.

Graeco-Roman merchants begin direct **40*** voyages from Egypt to **southern India**.

48 The **Xiongnu** nomad confederation breaks up.

50–100* Foundation of the kingdom of **Funan** in Southeast Asia.

1–100* Madagascar is settled by seafarers from Indonesia.

Mauretania annexed by the Roman empire. **40–42**

RELIGION & PHILOSOPHY

1–100 Development of **Mahayana (Great Vehicle) Buddhism**.

1–100 Mithraism spreads to the Roman empire from Persia.

St Peter becomes bishop of Rome, traditionally **42*** regarded as the foundation of the papacy.

64 First **persecutions of Christians** at Rome.

30 Jesus of Nazareth is crucified at Jerusalem.

47–62 St Paul journeys in Asia Minor and the Mediterranean as a missionary.

Roman troops destroy the **Temple** at **Jerusalem**. **70**

Christian **Gospels** written. **70–100**

34–156* Development of religious **Daoism**.

58* Buddhism introduced to China.

SCIENCE & TECHNOLOGY

▲ *Relief of Mithras killing the sacred bull from London, 2nd century* AD.

Watermills in use in the Roman empire. **50***

Date of the earliest known **36 Maya calendrical inscriptions**.

Hero of Alexandria invents a **60*** simple **steam-powered device**.

Pliny the Younger writes an **79** eyewitness account of the eruption of Vesuvius, which destroys Pompeii, Italy.

1–100 Stern-mounted rudders used on Chinese ships (previously all ships had used less effective steering oars or side rudders).

1–100* Pottery-making skills die out in **Polynesia**.

ARTS & ARCHITECTURE

6* Ovid, *Metamorphoses*.

27* Architect **Vitruvius** writes *De Architectura*.

Colosseum built at Rome. **72–80**

Codices, books of sewn pages, begin to replace the parchment scroll. **65***

*Approximate date

Traditional date for the construction of the pagoda of the **White 68 Horse monastery**, Luoyang, one of the earliest in China.

Roman empire reaches its **116** greatest extent under **Trajan**.

122 **Hadrian** begins a defensive wall across northern Britain.

167–80 The **Marcomannic Wars**: Germans test Rome's Danube frontier.

Romans occupy **Mesopotamia**. **115–17**

132–35 Romans defeat the **Bar Kochba revolt** against Roman rule in Palestine.

174–203 **Satavahana** at its peak under king Yajna Sri.

Kushan empire at its peak under Kanishka. **120–30***

Foundation of the kingdom of **Champa** in Southeast Asia. **192***

100* Foundation of **Tiwanaku** kingdom in the Andes.

166 Chinese sources record the arrival of **travellers from Rome**.

Yellow Turban peasant revolt in northern China. **184**

General Dung Zhuo destroys Luoyang and **190** installs a puppet Han emperor in Chang'an.

▲ *Bronze bust of the Roman emperor Trajan, who invaded Mesopotamia.*

▶ *Han bronze horse from Gansu Province, China, c. AD 200.*

▶ *Buddha in the Gandharan style, from the time of the Kushan dynasty, Pakistan.*

170* **Galen** codifies Greek medicine.

Roman road network complete. **200***

Codification of **Hindu laws**. **200***

▲ *Roman surgical instruments.*

100* Indian metallurgists invent **cast steel**.

Earliest Western treatise on **alchemy** compiled at Alexandria. **185***

105* **Writing paper** invented in China.

132 **Earthquake detector** built in China.

160* **Wheelbarrow** invented in China.

83 **Magnetic compass** is described in a Chinese book on divination.

Greek astronomer **Ptolemy of Alexandria** **150*** writes the *Almagest* and *Guide to Geography*.

Abacus used in China. **190***

Tacitus begins writing his **100*** *Histories* and *Annals*.

118–25* The **Pantheon temple** in Rome is rebuilt with the largest dome in the world.

150* The **Pyramid of the Sun** is built at Teotihuacán, Mexico.

100–20* Suetonius, ***The Twelve Caesars***.

130* **Gandhara school** of Graeco-Buddhist sculpture flourishes under Kanishka.

100 First **Chinese dictionary** lists over 9,000 characters.

100–800* Tradition of **megalithic sculptures** of humans, gods and animals in San Agustín, Colombia.

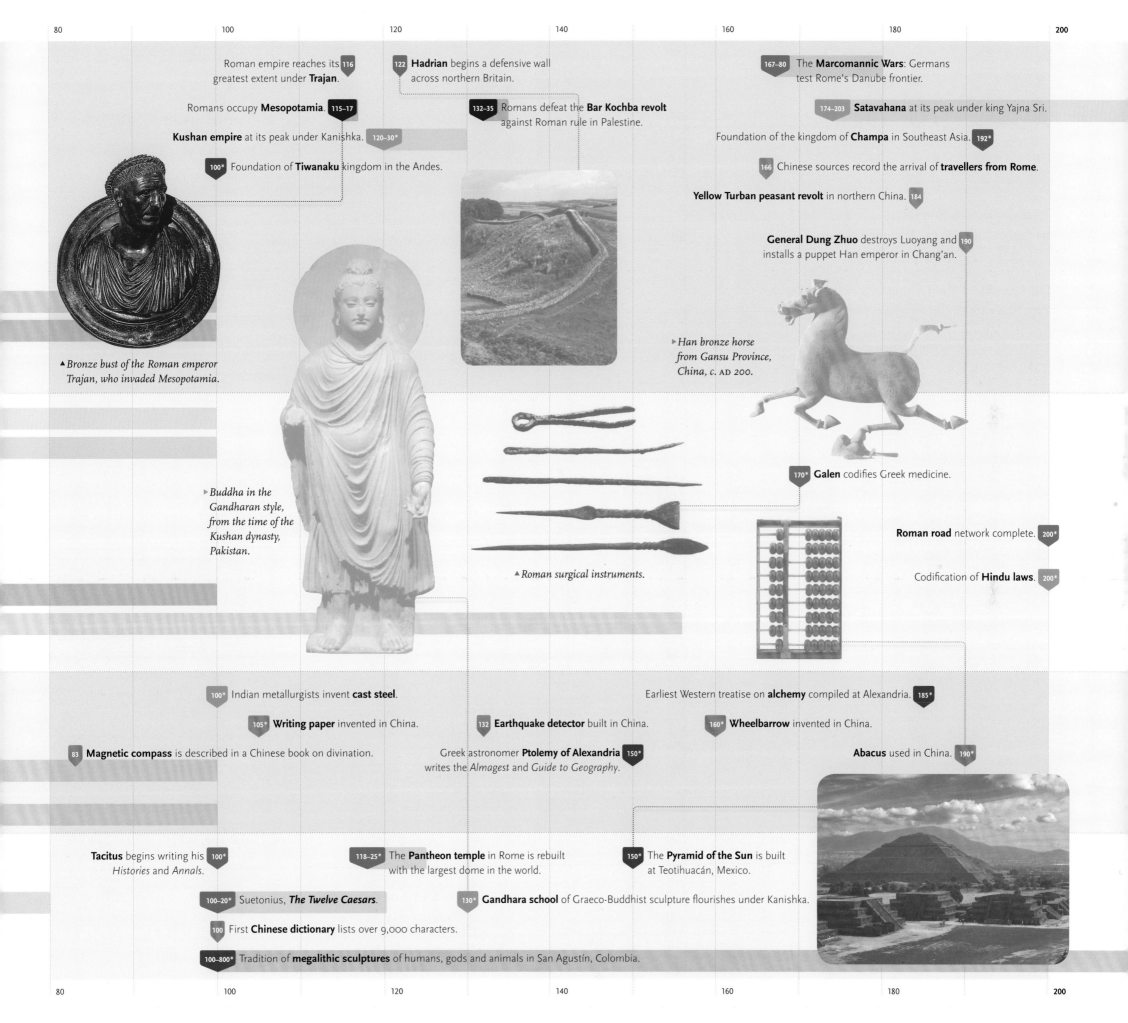

400

ROMAN EMPIRE AND CHINA DIVIDED; THE RISE OF SASANIAN PERSIA AND GUPTA INDIA; THE CLASSIC MAYA CIVILIZATION

Persia, under foreign rule since Alexander the Great, made a strong resurgence in the 3rd century when the Parthians were overthrown by the native Sasanian dynasty in 224–26. The Sasanians were set on restoring Persia's ancient glory and they became a formidable threat to the Roman empire, which was already struggling with political instability, inflation and Germanic invasions. The Roman empire survived the crisis and, under the emperor Diocletian, was divided into eastern and western halves, each with its own emperor. Constantine the Great founded Constantinople in 324 as the capital of the eastern half of the empire, and Rome decreased in importance. By 400 the Romans were again struggling. The nomadic Huns had invaded Eastern Europe, completely destabilizing the German tribes. The Romans admitted the Goths as refugees but they soon rebelled and in 400 had still not been pacified.

Apart from a brief period of unity between 280 and 291, China was divided into rival states after the late 180s. From 304, non-Chinese nomad leaders fought for control of the north while the south stayed under Chinese rule. In contrast, India gained in unity when the kingdom of Magadha made a strong revival under the Gupta dynasty. By 400 all of northern India was under Gupta rule. The construction of enormous earth burial mounds *c.*300 in the Yamato region of Japan marks the foundation of the Japanese state.

In Mesoamerica the Maya civilization entered its most brilliant period *c.*300 and in South America the Tiwanaku state began *c.*375 to create what would be the first great Andean empire. During this time the East African kingdom of Axum became the dominant trading power of the Red Sea and the first cities began to develop in West Africa.

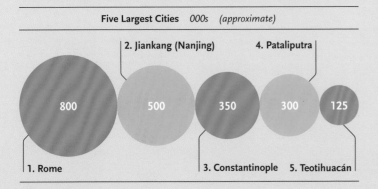

Five Largest Cities *000s* (approximate)

2. Jiankang (Nanjing)   4. Pataliputra

800   500   350   300   125

1. Rome   3. Constantinople   5. Teotihuacán

Dorset Inuit culture

Dorset Inuit culture

Dorset Inuit culture

Aleuts

Sub-Arctic caribou hunters

Central plateau hunter-fisher-gatherers

Great Plains bison hunters

Eastern Woodlands hunter-gatherers

West coast fishers, hunters and gatherers

Basketmaker cultures

Hopewell burial mound traditions

Hohokam culture

Mogollon culture

Desert hunter-gatherers

Maize farmers

VERACRUZ CIVILIZATION

Teotihuacán

5

Caribbean fishers, hunters and gatherers

Hawaiian Islands

TEOTIHUACÁN

ZAPOTECS

MAYA CITY STATES

c. AD 400

Amazonian chiefdoms

Andean chiefdoms

Manioc farmers

MOCHE

Polynesians

TIWANAKU

Nazca

Savanna hunter-gatherers

Andean chiefdoms

Pampas hunters

Fishers and marine mammal hunters

Hunter-gatherers

Urbanized societies/kingdoms

Settled farming cultures and peoples

Empires

Pastoral nomads

Uninhabited

Complex farming societies/chiefdoms

150°   120°   90°   60°

Sami

Finno-Ugrians

Samoyed
reindeer
herders

Tungusic
reindeer
herders

Palaeo-Siberians

Dorset Inuit
culture

Finns

Balts

Germans

Celts

Slavs

Huns

Alans

Turks

Rouran
(Altaic nomad
confederation)

Tungus

Ainu

1
2

3

WESTERN
ROMAN
EMPIRE

1 Rome

3
Constantinople

Ephthalites
(Huns)

Tuyuhun

Nomad warlord
states

KOGURYO
SILLA

4

EASTERN
ROMAN
EMPIRE

SASANIAN
EMPIRE
(Persians)

7

Tibetans

NEPAL

2
Jiankang
(Nanjing)

PAEKCHE

JAPAN

Berbers

GARAMANTES

Libyans

Arabs

GUPTA
EMPIRE
(Magadha)

4
Pataliputra

Burmese

JIN
EMPIRE
(Chinese)

5

VAKATAKA
KINGDOM

Pyu

Tais
Mons

Savanna cereal
farmers and pastoralists

6

AXUM

HIMYARITE
KINGDOM

HINDU
KINGDOMS

FUNAN

CHAMPA

Micronesians

Tropical forest
yam farmers

Nok
culture

Nilotic
pastoralists

Cushitic
pastoralists

ANURADHAPURA

Malays

Malay
chiefdoms

Papuans

1 ABASGIA

2 LAZICA

3 IBERIA

4 ARMENIA

5 NOBATIA (Nubians)

6 MAKURIA (Nubians)

7 KUSHAN
PRINCIPALITIES

Bantu farmers
and pastoralists

Melanesians

Malagasy
(Malays)

San
hunter-
gatherers

Australian Aborigines

Khoikhoi
pastoralists

Tasmanians

400

In the 4th century, the culture of the Roman empire was transformed by the spread of Christianity. When the century began, Christians were a persecuted minority. This changed dramatically in 312 when the emperor Constantine, ascribing his victory in a civil war to the Christian god, converted and legalized Christianity. Under Constantine's patronage, Christianity began to win converts in the ruling classes and the first great Christian architecture was commissioned. In 325 Constantine convened the Council of Nicaea, which agreed the first uniform Christian doctrine.

An attempt by the emperor Julian to revive paganism in 360–63 failed completely: in 391 Christianity became the empire's official religion and paganism was proscribed. Despite this, knowledge of pagan myth and literature continued to command respect as a sign of good education and there was a creative interaction between Christian theologians and pagan Neoplatonist philosophers. Christianity was strongest in the eastern empire and it was in Egypt that the Christian monastic tradition developed. It was also from Egypt that Christianity reached Axum, originating the Ethiopian church.

In Persia, the Sasanians made Zoroastrianism the state religion. An offshoot, Manichaeism, won converts despite official persecution and spread widely across the Roman empire as a rival to Christianity. The Gupta dynasty was a generous patron of Hinduism and Buddhism, whose influence was growing in China, Tibet and Korea. It was at some time during the Gupta period that the playwright Kalidasa founded Indian theatre traditions. Buddhism brought books, art, medicine, music and ideas from India and Central Asia to China, effecting the biggest pre-19th-century cultural changes there. Also at this time, tea drinking first became an important part of Chinese culture.

World Population (approximate)

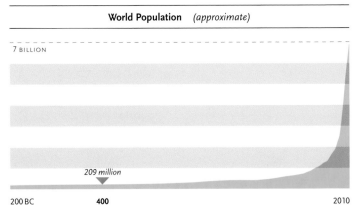

7 BILLION

209 million

200 BC   400   2010

201   220   240   260

Ardashir I of the Persian Sasanian dynasty overthrows the Parthian kingdom. `224–26`

`235–84` The **Roman empire** comes close to collapse due to civil wars, invasions, inflation and other economic problems.

`220` Fall of the **Han dynasty**: China splits into three rival states.

`260` **Shapur I** captures the Roman emperor Valerian at Edessa.

`240–72*` The **Kushan empire** loses its western territories to the Sasanians.

`200–400*` The **Moche state** of Peru is at its peak.

▶ *Cameo showing the victory of Shapur I over Valerian.*

◀ *A stirrup-spout vessel in the shape of a human head, Moche culture, Peru.*

Ardashir I makes **Zoroastrianism** the Persian state religion. `224–40*`

`244` **Plotinus**, founder of Neoplatonism, begins teaching in Rome.

The Persian mystic **Mani**, the founder of Manichaeism, `276` dies in prison after he is accused of heresy.

`200–300` Codification of **Hindu laws**.

Life of **Ge Hong**, Daoist philosopher who advocated `253–333` alchemy as a way to achieve immortality.

Life of the theologian **Arius of Alexandria**: `250–336` originator of Arian Christianity.

The Chinese physician **Huang Fu** writes a treatise on acupuncture. `260`

Diophantus of Alexandria writes a treatise on equations. `250*`

▲ *Colossal head of the Roman emperor Constantine, from Rome.*

Monumental reliefs at **Naqsh-i Rustam**, `260` Iran, commemorate Shapur I's victories over the Romans.

`200–400` Erection of **multi-storeyed monolithic stelae** at Axum: the largest is 33 m (108 ft) tall and weighs 520 tonnes.

POLITICS & ECONOMY

RELIGION & PHILOSOPHY

SCIENCE & TECHNOLOGY

ARTS & ARCHITECTURE

201   220   240   260

286 **Diocletian** divides the Roman empire into eastern and western halves.

372 The **Huns** conquer the steppes of Eastern Europe.

300–30 Re-establishment of fiscal and monetary stability in the **Roman empire**.

Gothic refugees fleeing the Huns are **376** admitted into the Roman empire.

300* The **Vakatakas** replace the Satavahaniharas as the dominant dynasty in southern India.

The Goths rebel, defeating and killing the eastern **378** Roman emperor Valens at the battle of **Adrianople**.

280 China reunified by the state of **Jin**.

300* Emergence of the early Japanese **Yamato kingdom**.

335–80 **Samudragupta**, king of Magadha, conquers northern and eastern India, including the Kushan and Saka kingdoms.

300* Beginning of the **Classic Period** of Maya civilization.

Sack of **Luoyang** by rebel nomad mercenaries marks **311** the end of Chinese rule in northern China.

Axum overthrows the Nubian kingdom of Meroë. **350***

363 Roman emperor **Julian** is killed invading the Sasanian empire.

291–306 **Rebellion of the Eight Princes**: northern China breaks away from Jin control.

Armenia is partitioned between the Roman and Sasanian empires. **378**

Nomadic Xianbei establish the **Northern** **386–97** **Wei state** in northern China.

Chandragupta, founder of the Gupta dynasty, becomes king of Magadha. **320**

The **Rouran** (or Juan-juan) nomad confederation dominates the eastern steppes. **400***

Polynesians from the Marquesas Islands settle **Hawaii**. **400***

◀ *Gold coin of Chandragupta.*

Jenne-jeno, Mali, becomes the earliest known city in West Africa. **400***

The **Tiwanaku state** begins a **375*** **378** The Maya city of **Tikal** becomes subject period of imperial expansion. to a Mexican dynasty from Teotihuacán.

▲ *Reconstruction of the central pyramid of the Mundo Perdido complex at Tikal.*

303–11 Persecution of Christians by **Diocletian**.

340–48 Ulfilas converts the **Goths** to Arian Christianity.

Theodosius I proscribes paganism in the Roman empire. **391**

313 Edict of Milan: **Constantine** grants toleration for Christians.

360–63 **Julian** attempts to restore pagan religion and values.

Earliest Christian **400*** missions to **Ireland**.

325 **First Council of Nicaea** (Iznik, Turkey) held to agree Christian doctrine.

360–400* Cappadocian fathers **Basil** and **Gregory** establish tradition of Greek theology.

300* **Armenia** becomes the first country to adopt Christianity as its state religion.

350* **King Ezana of Axum** converts to Christianity: origins of the Ethiopian church.

Vatsayara writes the **Kamasutra**. **400***

Christian hermits form communities **320–30*** in the Egyptian desert, beginning the monastic movement.

First Buddhist missions to **Tibet**. **367*** **372*** Buddhism is introduced to **Korea**.

Hinduism is introduced to Southeast Asia by Indian merchants and seafarers. **400***

▶*Constantine at the Council of Nicaea in a 15th-century depiction.*

366–375* An anonymous Roman inventor produces a design for a **paddle-wheeled ship** powered by oxen.

350 Earliest account of the cultivation and use of **tea**, China.

Constantine initiates construction of churches **312–30** of St Peter and St John Lateran at Rome.

St Hilary of Poitiers composes a book of hymns. **360***

▶*Chinese shanshui painting: an 11th-century example.*

324 Constantine founds **Constantinople** (Istanbul) as a new eastern capital for the Roman empire on the site of Byzantium.

Corbelled arches and vaults 300* appear in Maya architecture.

300–470* Origins of Indian theatre traditions, influenced by the Sanskrit playwright **Kalidasa** (dates very uncertain).

306–65 Life of **Wang Xizhi** who raised Chinese calligraphy to a fine art.

300–500 Origins of the Chinese **shanshui** (mountain-water) school of landscape painting.

*Approximate date

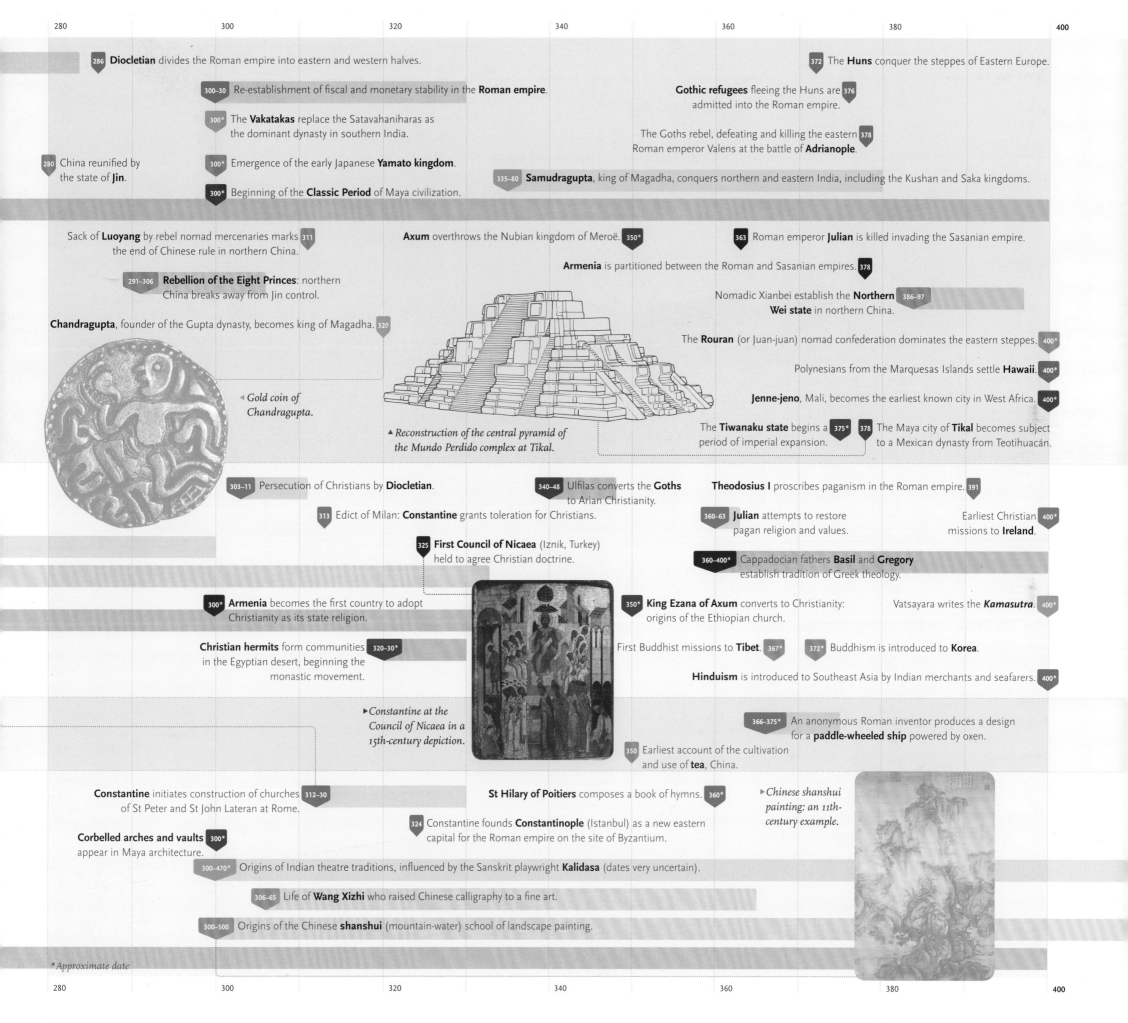

500

THE FALL OF ROME AND THE RISE OF THE FIRST EMPIRES OF THE ANDES

Rome's German problem took a turn for the worse in the early 5th century. In 406 a coalition of Germanic tribes crossed the Rhine and invaded the western empire. In 410 a Visigothic army sacked Rome, making the empire's declining power shockingly obvious. Poorer and less populated than the east, the western empire struggled to contain the invaders and by 476 it had dissolved, its territory partitioned between different Germanic peoples.

In 500 the big winners seemed to be the Goths, who had founded two kingdoms, in Spain and Italy, but the Franks under their king Clovis were a rising power. Anglo-Saxon tribes from northern Germany had by this time established a number of small kingdoms in eastern Britain. Though it bore the brunt of attacks by Attila the Hun, the eastern Roman empire survived the 5th century with its territory intact. It probably helped that the Sasanians had their own problems with the powerful Ephthalite branch of the Huns. The Sasanians repelled the Ephthalites but the Gupta empire was less fortunate, losing its northwestern territories to them c. 475.

After Attila's death in 453 the Huns broke up. In the aftermath, the Slavs emerged as the dominant peoples of eastern Europe, occupying much of the territory inhabited by Germans before the Hun invasions. In Africa, the millennium-long Bantu migration was nearing an end: they now dominated most of Central and Southern Africa. The first towns in tropical West Africa were beginning to develop in the fertile inland delta of the river Niger. In South America, the central Andes were now divided by two powerful empires, the Tiwanaku empire to the south and the Wari empire to the north. The power of the Mexican city of Teotihuacán was at its height, extending throughout Mesoamerica. Even the most powerful Maya city, Tikal, was ruled by a Teotihuacán dynasty.

Five Largest Cities   000s   (approximate)

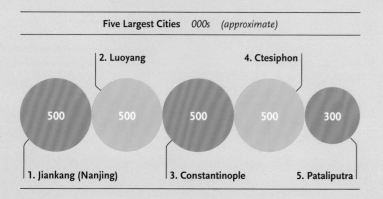

2. Luoyang

4. Ctesiphon

500 · 500 · 500 · 500 · 300

1. Jiankang (Nanjing)   3. Constantinople   5. Pataliputra

Dorset Inuit culture

Dorset Inuit culture

Dorset Inuit culture

Aleuts

Sub-Arctic caribou hunters

Central plateau hunter-fisher-gatherers

Great Plains bison hunters

Eastern Woodlands hunter-gatherers

West coast fishers, hunters and gatherers

Hopewell burial mound traditions

Basketmaker cultures

Hohokam culture

Mogollon culture

Desert hunter-gatherers

VERACRUZ CIVILIZATION

TEOTIHUACÁN

ZAPOTECS

MAYA CITY STATES

North Andean chiefdoms

Amazonian chiefdoms

Manioc farmers

MOCHE

WARI EMPIRE

Polynesians

TIWANAKU EMPIRE

Savanna hunter-gatherers

Pampas hunters

Fishers and marine mammal hunters

Hunter-gatherers

Settled farming cultures and peoples

Pastoral nomads

Complex farming societies/chiefdoms

Urbanized societies/kingdoms

Empires

Uninhabited

150°   120°   90°   60°

BASQUES **1**
SUEVIC KINGDOM **2**
BURGUNDIAN KINGDOM **3**
OSTROGOTHIC KINGDOM **4**
LOMBARD KINGDOM **5**
GEPID KINGDOM **6**

Sami
Finno-Ugrians
Samoyed reindeer herders
Tungusic reindeer herders
Palaeo-Siberians
Dorset Inuit culture

Scandinavians
Finns
Anglo-Saxons
Balts
Slavs
CELTIC KINGDOMS
Germans
Turks
Khitans
Tungus
FRANKISH KINGDOM
Huns
Alans
Avars
Ainu
5
3
4
6
7
8
1
2
Rouran confederation
KOGURYO
SILLA
3 Constantinople
Ephthalites
NORTHERN WEI
2 Luoyang
JAPAN
VISIGOTHIC KINGDOM
VANDAL KINGDOM
EASTERN ROMAN EMPIRE
4 Ctesiphon
SASANIAN EMPIRE
HUNAS (Ephthalites)
Tuyuhun
Tibetan chiefdoms
1
Jiankang (Nanjing)
QI EMPIRE
PAEKCHE
Berbers
Berber nomads
Libyans
Arabs
HINDU KINGDOMS
NEPAL
GUPTA EMPIRE
5 Pataliputra
Burmese
Tais
Trading towns
Savanna cereal farmers and pastoralists
Tropical forest yam farmers
9
10
11
AXUM
Nilotic pastoralists
Cushitic pastoralists
HIMYARITE KINGDOM
VAKATAKA KINGDOM
KADAMBAS
HINDU KINGDOMS
PYU CITY STATES
Mons
CHENLA
CHAMPA
FUNAN
Micronesians
7 ABASGIA
8 IBERIA
9 NOBATIA
10 MAKURIA
11 ALODIA (Nubians)
ANURADHAPURA
Malay chiefdoms
Malays
Papuans
San hunter-gatherers
Bantu farmers and pastoralists
Malagasy
SMALL MALAY KINGDOMS
Melanesians
Khoikhoi pastoralists
Australian Aborigines
Tasmanians

500

Christianity continued to transform the culture of the Roman world in the 5th century. Theological speculation was dominated by disputes about the nature of the relationship between Christ and God. Orthodox teaching on the Trinity (accepted by modern Roman Catholic, Orthodox and Protestant churches) was challenged by the monophysite (one nature) doctrine which had many followers in Egypt and Syria. Unable to find agreement, the church split after the Council of Chalcedon in 451, monophysite beliefs influencing to varying degrees the Coptic and other Oriental Orthodox churches.

Monophysites frequently suffered persecution by the imperial authorities, who sought to impose doctrinal uniformity. In the West, orthodox teaching on the Trinity was challenged by Arianism, which became widespread among the Germanic peoples, notably the Goths and Vandals. This became a serious obstacle to their acceptance by their Roman subjects, who regarded them as heretics.

The Germans were not hostile to the Romans and ultimately the two cultures would assimilate. In the short term, however, the Germanic invasions caused major economic disruption to Western Europe and there was a corresponding decline in cultural activity. The church became the main patron of art, architecture and book production. Roman culture remained most vibrant in the Ostrogothic kingdom of Italy. In the eastern empire, growing intolerance of pagan culture resulted in the neglect of the works of Classical philosophers and scientists.

Buddhism steadily increased in importance in China, aided by the translation of major Buddhist texts into Chinese. Buddhism remained vibrant in India, with the foundation by the Guptas of a Buddhist university at Nalanda and the execution of some of the finest Buddhist frescoes at Ajanta.

World Population (approximate)

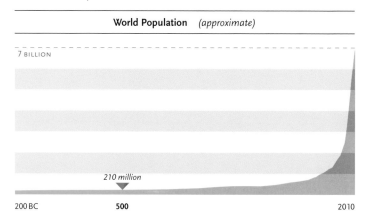

7 BILLION

210 million

200 BC   500   2010

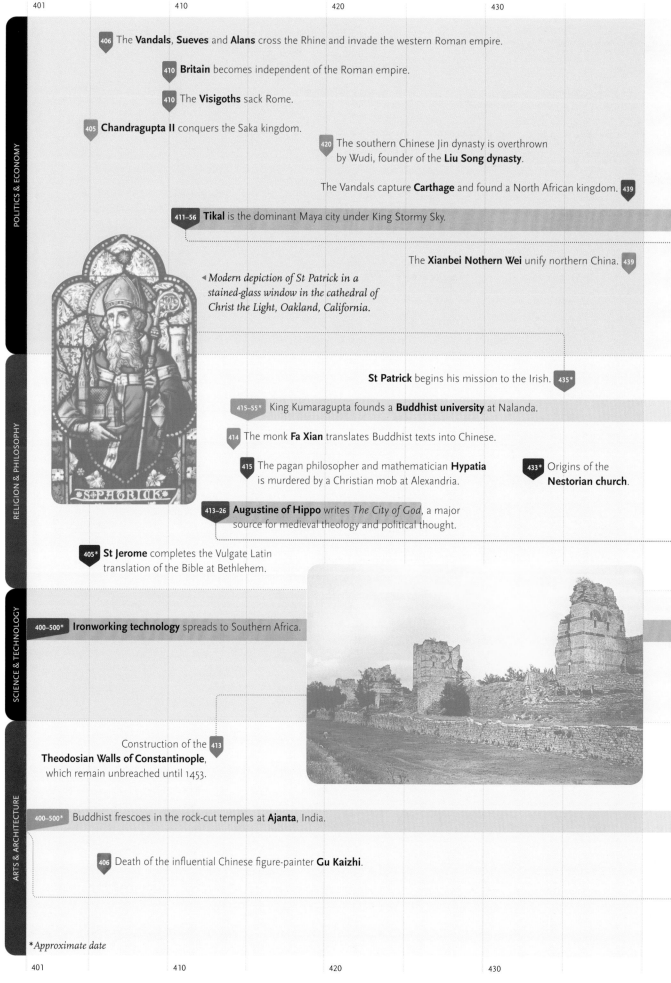

401   410   420   430

POLITICS & ECONOMY

406 The **Vandals**, **Sueves** and **Alans** cross the Rhine and invade the western Roman empire.

410 **Britain** becomes independent of the Roman empire.

410 The **Visigoths** sack Rome.

405 **Chandragupta II** conquers the Saka kingdom.

420 The southern Chinese Jin dynasty is overthrown by Wudi, founder of the **Liu Song dynasty**.

The Vandals capture **Carthage** and found a North African kingdom. **439**

411–56 **Tikal** is the dominant Maya city under King Stormy Sky.

The **Xianbei Nothern Wei** unify northern China. **439**

◄ *Modern depiction of St Patrick in a stained-glass window in the cathedral of Christ the Light, Oakland, California.*

RELIGION & PHILOSOPHY

St Patrick begins his mission to the Irish. **435***

415–55* King Kumaragupta founds a **Buddhist university** at Nalanda.

414 The monk **Fa Xian** translates Buddhist texts into Chinese.

415 The pagan philosopher and mathematician **Hypatia** is murdered by a Christian mob at Alexandria.

433* Origins of the **Nestorian church**.

413–26 **Augustine of Hippo** writes *The City of God*, a major source for medieval theology and political thought.

405* **St Jerome** completes the Vulgate Latin translation of the Bible at Bethlehem.

SCIENCE & TECHNOLOGY

400–500* **Ironworking technology** spreads to Southern Africa.

ARTS & ARCHITECTURE

Construction of the **413** **Theodosian Walls of Constantinople**, which remain unbreached until 1453.

400–500* Buddhist frescoes in the rock-cut temples at **Ajanta**, India.

406 Death of the influential Chinese figure-painter **Gu Kaizhi**.

*Approximate date

401   410   420   430

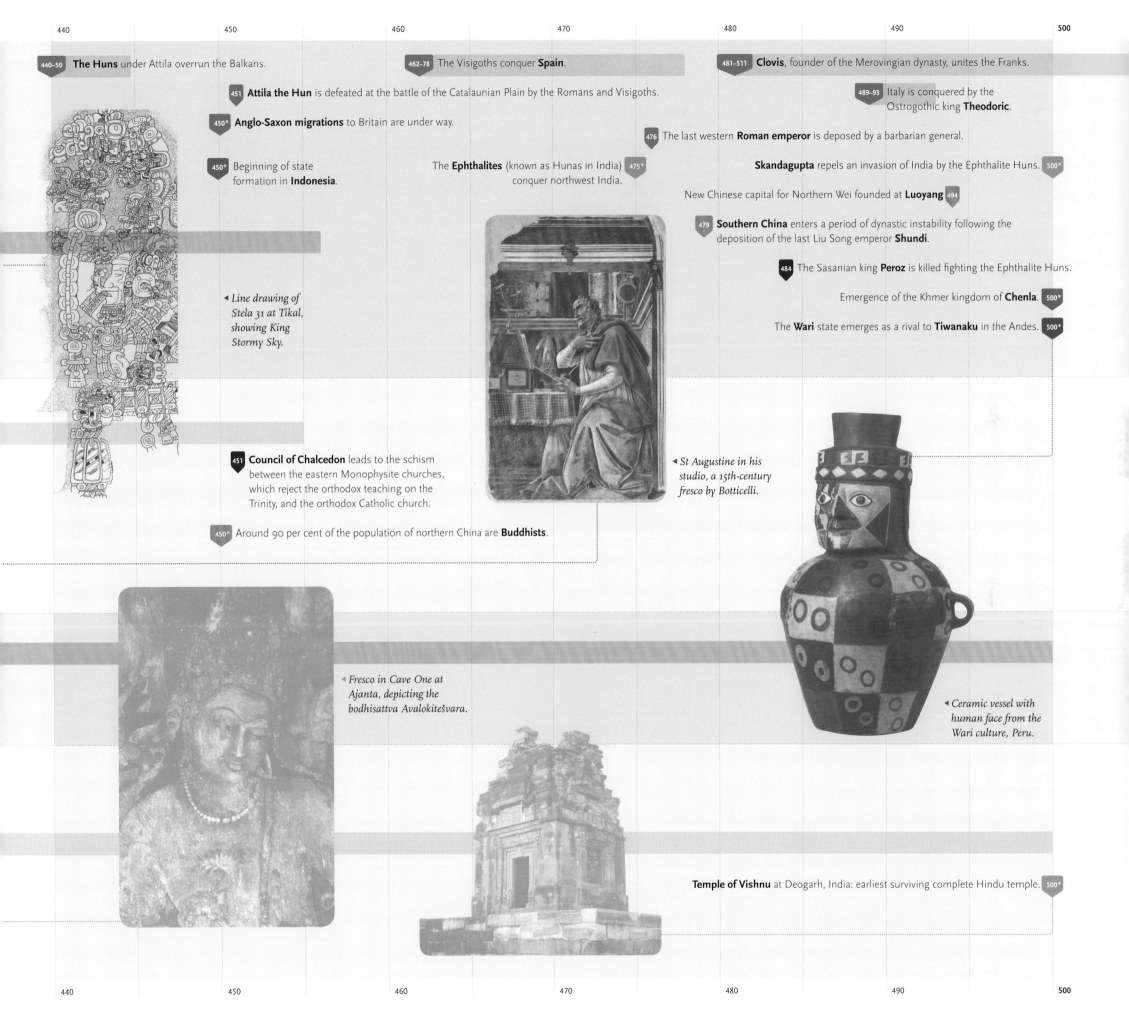

440–50 **The Huns** under Attila overrun the Balkans.

462–78 The Visigoths conquer **Spain**.

481–511 **Clovis**, founder of the Merovingian dynasty, unites the Franks.

451 **Attila the Hun** is defeated at the battle of the Catalaunian Plain by the Romans and Visigoths.

489–93 Italy is conquered by the Ostrogothic king **Theodoric**.

450* **Anglo-Saxon migrations** to Britain are under way.

476 The last western **Roman emperor** is deposed by a barbarian general.

450* Beginning of state formation in **Indonesia**.

The **Ephthalites** (known as Hunas in India) conquer northwest India. **475***

Skandagupta repels an invasion of India by the Ephthalite Huns. **500***

New Chinese capital for Northern Wei founded at **Luoyang** **494**

479 **Southern China** enters a period of dynastic instability following the deposition of the last Liu Song emperor **Shundi**.

484 The Sasanian king **Peroz** is killed fighting the Ephthalite Huns.

◀ *Line drawing of Stela 31 at Tikal, showing King Stormy Sky.*

Emergence of the Khmer kingdom of **Chenla**. **500***

The **Wari** state emerges as a rival to **Tiwanaku** in the Andes. **500***

◀ *St Augustine in his studio, a 15th-century fresco by Botticelli.*

451 **Council of Chalcedon** leads to the schism between the eastern Monophysite churches, which reject the orthodox teaching on the Trinity, and the orthodox Catholic church.

450* Around 90 per cent of the population of northern China are **Buddhists**.

◀ *Fresco in Cave One at Ajanta, depicting the bodhisattva Avalokiteśvara.*

◀ *Ceramic vessel with human face from the Wari culture, Peru.*

Temple of Vishnu at Deogarh, India: earliest surviving complete Hindu temple. **500***

650

THE ISLAMIC ERA BEGINS; CHINA'S TANG DYNASTY EMPIRE REACHES ITS PEAK; DESTRUCTION OF TEOTIHUACÁN

In the 530s, the eastern Roman empire reconquered much of the former western Roman empire. By the end of the 6th century, however, the empire was on the defensive against attacks from the Lombards, Slavs, Avar nomads and the Sasanians. After defeating the Sasanians in 622–27, the emperor Heraclius reformed the empire and made Greek its official language. Because of this, the eastern Roman empire is known as the Byzantine empire from this time on. By the 7th century, the Franks were the main power in the West, while in Britain the Anglo-Saxons had occupied most of what would become known as England.

While the Byzantines and Sasanians fought, the Arabs were being united in the name of Islam by Muhammad. A widespread rebellion after Muhammad's death in 632 showed that Arab unity was fragile. To consolidate Arab unity, Muhammad's successors, the caliphs, invaded the weakened Byzantine and Sasanian empires. The Sasanian empire collapsed rapidly and by 650 the Byzantines had lost Syria, Palestine and Egypt.

Defeat by the Ephthalites in the 5th century broke the power of the Gupta empire and by 550 it had collapsed. Harsha, the king of Kannauj, reunited northern India in the first half of the 7th century but his empire did not long survive his death in 647. Around 550 the Chalukya dynasty replaced the Uakatakas as the main power of the south. After centuries of division and dynastic instability, China was reunited by the Sui dynasty in 589. Under the able Tang dynasty, which succeeded in 618, China expanded far into Central Asia. Japan emerged fully from prehistory in this period, following prince Shotoku's introduction of a Chinese-style imperial government. In Mesoamerica, the great city of Teotihuacán was violently destroyed and abandoned c. 650, leaving a yawning power vacuum.

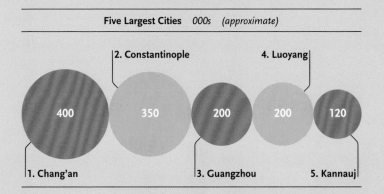

Five Largest Cities *000s* *(approximate)*

2. Constantinople   4. Luoyang

400   350   200   200   120

1. Chang'an   3. Guangzhou   5. Kannauj

Dorset Inuit culture

Dorset Inuit culture

Aleuts

Sub-Arctic caribou hunters

Central plateau hunter-fisher-gatherers

Great Plains bison hunters

Eastern Woodlands hunter-gatherers and maize cultivators

West coast fishers, hunters and gatherers

Desert hunter-gatherers

Basketmaker cultures

Hopewell burial mound traditions

Hohokam culture

Mogollon culture

VERACRUZ CIVILIZATION

ZAPOTECS

MAYA CITY STATES

North Andean chiefdoms

Amazonian manioc farmers

Polynesians

Amazonian chiefdoms

MOCHE

WARI EMPIRE

TIWANAKU EMPIRE

Savanna hunter-gatherers

Pampas hunter-gatherers

Fishers and marine mammal hunters

Hunter-gatherers

Urbanized societies/kingdoms

Settled farming cultures and peoples

Empires

Pastoral nomads

Uninhabited

Complex farming societies/chiefdoms

150°   120°   90°   60°

CELTIC KINGDOMS [1]
ANGLO-SAXON KINGDOMS [2]
BASQUES [3]
LOMBARD KINGDOM [4]
LOMBARD DUCHIES [5]

Danube Bulgars [6]
ABASGIA [7]
IBERIA [8]
ARMENIA [9]
TABARISTAN [10]

Sami
Finno-Ugrians
Samoyed reindeer herders
Tungusic reindeer herders
Palaeo-Siberians
Dorset Inuit culture

Scandinavians
Finns
Balts
Germans
Slavs
Volga Bulgars
Khazar Khanate
Kyrgyz
Jürchen (Tungus)
Ainu

FRANKISH KINGDOM
Avar Khanate
Slavs
Western Turk Khanate
Eastern Turk Khanate
KOGURYO
SILLA

Constantinople
BYZANTINE EMPIRE (EASTERN ROMAN EMPIRE)

VISIGOTHIC KINGDOM

Berbers
Berber nomads

ARAB CALIPHATE

Tuyuhun
TIBET
Chang'an [1]
Luoyang [4]
TANG EMPIRE
PAEKCHE
JAPAN

Kannauj [5]
EMPIRE OF HARSHA
Guangzhou [3]

MAKURIA
ALODIA

West African chiefdoms and towns
Tropical forest yam farmers

AXUM
Nilotic pastoralists
Cushitic pastoralists

CHALUKYA KINGDOM
PALLAVA KINGDOM
Burmese
Mons
PYU CITY STATES
CHAMPA
Malays

ANURADHAPURA
CHENLA
SMALL MALAY KINGDOMS

Micronesians

Bantu farmers and herders

SMALL BUDDHIST KINGDOMS [11]
NEPAL [12]
SMALL HINDU KINGDOMS [13]

DVARAVATI (Mons) [14]
TAI KINGDOMS [15]

Papuans

Melanesians

Polynesians

Malagasy

San hunter-gatherers

Khoikhoi pastoralists

Australian Aborigines

Tasmanians

Arctic Circle
Tropic of Cancer
Equator
Tropic of Capricorn

75°
45°
0°
30°
60°
90°
120°
150°
180°

650

The *hijra*, Muhammad's migration to Medina in 622 to escape persecution for his religious teaching at Mecca, marks the beginning of the Muslim era. Most pre-Islamic Arabs were polytheists but many were Jews, Christians, Zoroastrians and Hanifs (Arab monotheists), and all these faiths may have influenced the development of Muhammad's religious ideas. Muhammad did not see himself as the founder of a new faith so much as the restorer of the original religion of Abraham, which Jews and Christians had misunderstood. At Medina, Muhammad established a theocratic Muslim state in which he exercised both religious and political authority. On Muhammad's death, his father-in-law Abu Bakr was elected as the first caliph (successor). It was intended that the institution of the caliphate would continue to unite all Muslims in a single community.

Though it lost territory to Islam, Christianity began to expand in Northern Europe with the conversion of the pagan Franks and Anglo-Saxons. It also expanded in Africa, with the conversion of the Nubians. Nestorian Christians began to win converts in China. Buddhist influence began to decline in India in the face of the Bakhti Hindu revival movement. In 552 Korean monks introduced Chinese schools of Buddhism to Japan. This was just part of a surge in Sinification of Japanese culture in this period, which also saw the adoption of the Chinese script and calendar, Chinese literary and legal forms, and Chinese crafts.

While Byzantine mosaicists produced dazzling Christian art, major engineering achievements of the period include the vast dome of Hagia Sophia cathedral at Constantinople and the construction of the 1,770 km (1,100 mile) Grand Canal in China. The heavy two-wheeled plough, which was to revolutionize European agriculture by greatly increasing crop yields, was probably introduced in this period also.

World Population *(approximate)*

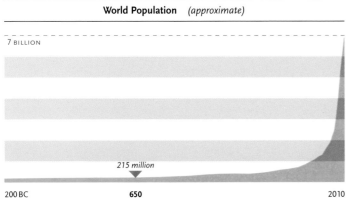

7 BILLION

215 million

200 BC   **650**   2010

---

501   520   540

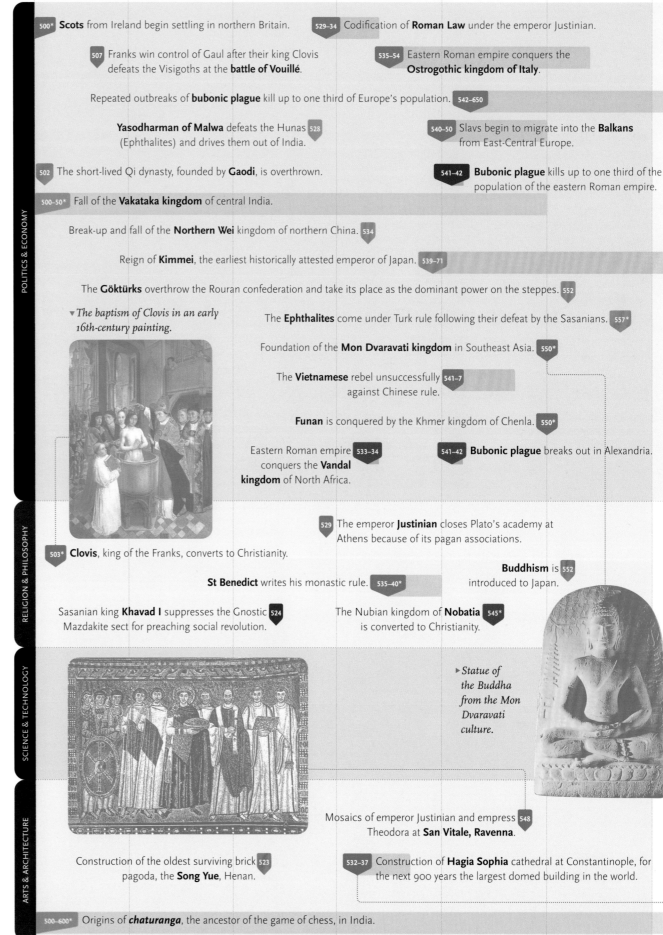

POLITICS & ECONOMY

500* **Scots** from Ireland begin settling in northern Britain.

529–34 Codification of **Roman Law** under the emperor Justinian.

507 **Franks** win control of Gaul after their king Clovis defeats the Visigoths at the **battle of Vouillé**.

535–54 Eastern Roman empire conquers the **Ostrogothic kingdom of Italy**.

Repeated outbreaks of **bubonic plague** kill up to one third of Europe's population. **542–650**

Yasodharman of Malwa defeats the Hunas **528** (Ephthalites) and drives them out of India.

540–50 Slavs begin to migrate into the **Balkans** from East-Central Europe.

502 The short-lived Qi dynasty, founded by **Gaodi**, is overthrown.

541–42 **Bubonic plague** kills up to one third of the population of the eastern Roman empire.

500–50* Fall of the **Vakataka kingdom** of central India.

Break-up and fall of the **Northern Wei** kingdom of northern China. **534**

Reign of **Kimmei**, the earliest historically attested emperor of Japan. **539–71**

The **Göktürks** overthrow the Rouran confederation and take its place as the dominant power on the steppes. **552**

The **Ephthalites** come under Turk rule following their defeat by the Sasanians. **557***

▼ *The baptism of Clovis in an early 16th-century painting.*

Foundation of the **Mon Dvaravati kingdom** in Southeast Asia. **550***

The **Vietnamese** rebel unsuccessfully **541–7** against Chinese rule.

Funan is conquered by the Khmer kingdom of Chenla. **550***

Eastern Roman empire **533–34** conquers the **Vandal kingdom** of North Africa.

541–42 **Bubonic plague** breaks out in Alexandria.

RELIGION & PHILOSOPHY

529 The emperor **Justinian** closes Plato's academy at Athens because of its pagan associations.

503* **Clovis**, king of the Franks, converts to Christianity.

Buddhism is **552** introduced to Japan.

St Benedict writes his monastic rule. **535–40***

Sasanian king **Khavad I** suppresses the Gnostic **524** Mazdakite sect for preaching social revolution.

The Nubian kingdom of **Nobatia** **545*** is converted to Christianity.

SCIENCE & TECHNOLOGY

▶ *Statue of the Buddha from the Mon Dvaravati culture.*

ARTS & ARCHITECTURE

Mosaics of emperor Justinian and empress **548** Theodora at **San Vitale, Ravenna**.

Construction of the oldest surviving brick **523** pagoda, the **Song Yue**, Henan.

532–37 Construction of **Hagia Sophia** cathedral at Constantinople, for the next 900 years the largest domed building in the world.

500–600* Origins of **chaturanga**, the ancestor of the game of chess, in India.

501   520   540

600–30 Slavs and Avars overrun most of the Balkans.

568–82 The **Lombards** conquer northern Italy.

622–27 **Emperor Heraclius** defeats the Sasanians in a long campaign.

The **Sasanians** invade the eastern Roman empire, occupying Anatolia, Syria and Egypt. **603–22**

The Arabs capture **Jerusalem**. **638**

562 **Calakmul** replaces Tikal as the dominant Maya city.

589 **Sui Wendi**, founder of the Sui dynasty, reunites China.

610–22 Heraclius reforms the eastern Roman empire and makes Greek the official language, creating what we now call the **Byzantine empire**.

Muhammad's migration (*hijra*) from Mecca to Medina marks the beginning of **the Muslim era**. **622**

632–34 **Abu Bakr** becomes caliph (successor) after the death of Muhammad.

584* The Göktürk khanate splits into eastern and western **Turk khanates**.

Reign of the caliph **Umar** sees the beginning of Arab expansion. **633–44**

Nubian kingdom of **Makuria** **600*** absorbs Nobatia.

606–47 Harsha, king of **Kannauj**, conquers much of northern India.

593–622 **Prince Shotoku** creates a centralized Japanese state based on Chinese government institutions.

Arabs occupy **Mesopotamia** after **637** defeating the Sasanians at Qadisiya.

640–2 The Arabs conquer **Egypt**.

The Sasanian empire collapses after its defeat by the Arabs at **Nehavend**. **642**

Gaozu overthrows the Sui dynasty and **618** becomes first emperor of the **Tang dynasty**.

633 The **Chalukyas** defeat Harsha's attempt to conquer southern India.

▲ *Reconstruction drawing of Structure 2 at Calakmul as it would have looked in the Late Classic period.*

618–50* **Songtsän Gampo** creates a unified Tibetan kingdom.

Trade links established between East Africa and China. **620***

626–49 Reign of **Taizong**: Chinese expansion into Central Asia.

▶ *Prince Shotoku with his son and brother at his sides: an 8th-century depiction.*

Taika reforms bring all land under the ownership of the Japanese crown. **646**

Teotihuacán is destroyed by unknown invaders and abandoned. **650***

596–97 **Pope Gregory the Great** sends a mission to convert the Anglo-Saxons.

631 **Nestorian Christians** from Persia introduce Christianity to China.

569* The Nubian kingdoms of **Makuria** and **Alodia** are converted to Christianity.

600–700 Beginning of the **Bakhti revival of Hinduism** in India.

Chinese monk **Xuanzang** walks to India, studies Buddhism and brings scriptures back to China **627–645**

570–632* Life of **Muhammad**, founder of the Islamic religion.

580* Avars introduce the **stirrup** to Europe.

600* **Porcelain** invented in China.

575* Indian mathematicians devise the **decimal system of numerals** (known as 'Arabic' numerals in the West) and the concept of zero.

▶ *The name Muhammad written using traditional calligraphy.*

Earliest reference to the use of the **heavy two-wheeled plough** in Western Europe. **643**

627–49 Earliest texts reproduced by **woodblock printing**, China.

591 Gregory of Tours completes his ***History of the Franks***.

◀ *Hagia Sophia cathedral, with its minarets added later by the Ottomans.*

600* **Suspension bridges**, hung from iron chains, built in China.

606–9 Construction of the 1,770 km (1,100 mile) **Grand Canal**, linking Beijing to Yue.

*Approximate date

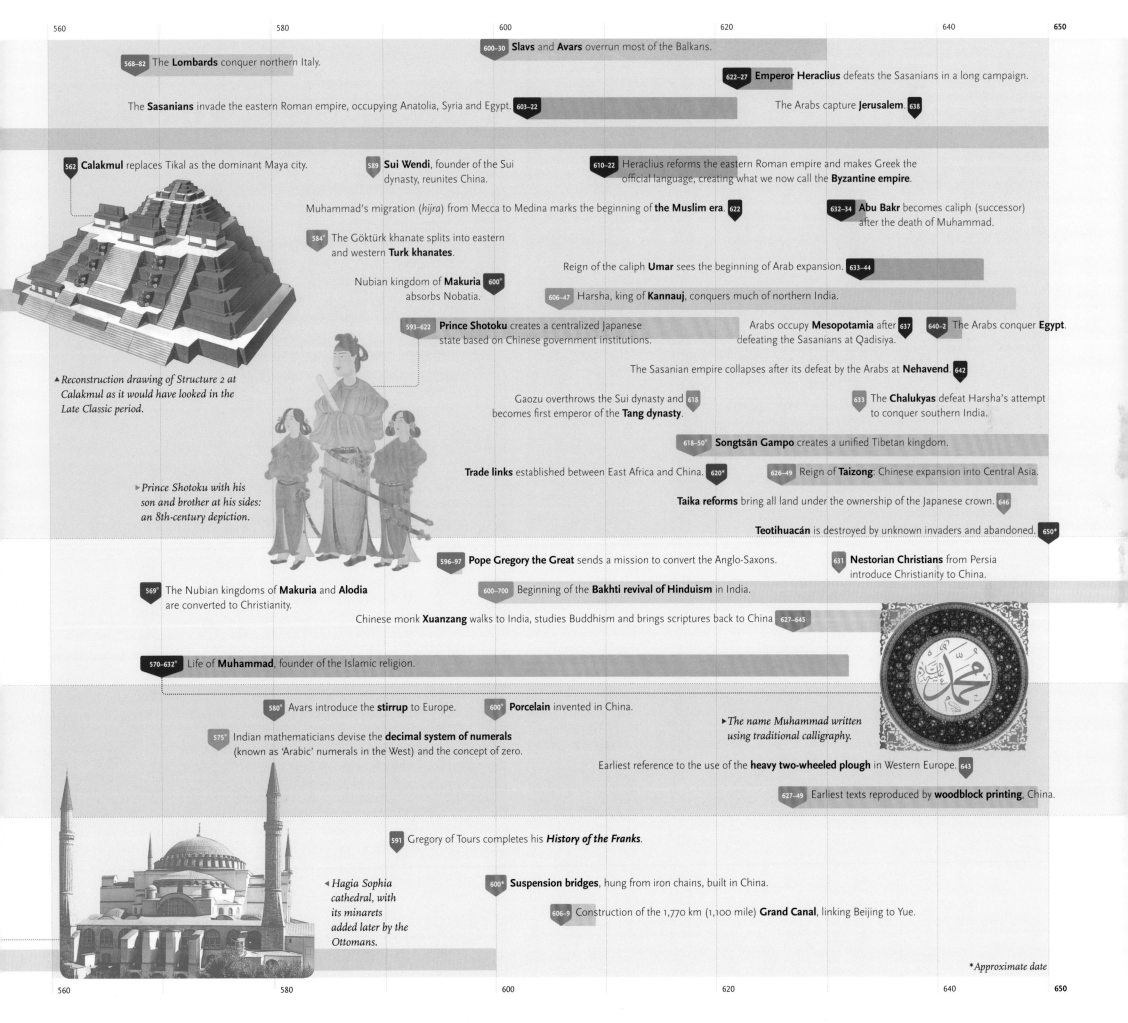

650

THE SPREAD OF HINDUISM, BUDDHISM, ZOROASTRIANISM, JUDAISM, CHRISTIANITY AND ISLAM TO AD 650

The period from 1000 BC to AD 650 saw the birth of all of the major world religions (a world religion being one that has endured having influenced many civilizations and cultures).

Hinduism was arguably the earliest to take shape. Early Hinduism was based on the *Vedas*, the oldest of which, the *Rigveda*, may have been composed as early as 1400 BC. However, the belief in karma and rebirth that are central to modern Hinduism evolved only around the 7th or 6th century BC. In the early centuries AD, Indian merchants introduced Hinduism to Southeast Asia but the caste system never became established there.

India was also the birthplace of Buddhism, based on the teachings of Gautama the Buddha (*c.* 563–483 BC). Gautama offered release from the endless cycle of rebirth. Buddhism developed a strong missionary tradition, spreading to Anuradhapura, Central Asia, Southeast Asia, China, Korea and, by the 6th century AD, Japan. Buddhism was influenced by the indigenous beliefs of many regions, such as Daoism in China and Shintoism in Japan.

The most widespread of the modern world religions, Christianity and Islam, share roots with Judaism. Like Hinduism, Judaism's origins lie in the 2nd millennium BC but its emergence as a definitively monotheistic religion dates only to the 7th or 6th century BC. As a result of voluntary migrations and forcible expulsions, Jewish communities known as the Diaspora became widely scattered across the Mediterranean and Middle East.

Christianity, a religion based on the life and teachings of Jesus of Nazareth, began as a Jewish messianic cult: it was the teachings of St Paul (*c.* AD 5–67) which defined it as a separate religion. Christianity remained a minority, mainly urban, religion until its acceptance by the Roman emperors in the 4th century AD.

Founded in Arabia by Muhammad (*c.* 570–632), Islam was the last of the world religions to appear. In 650 Islam was just beginning to spread beyond Arabia in the wake of the Arab conquests.

Zoroastrianism, the Persian state religion under the Sasanians, declined rapidly following the Arab conquest. However, its monotheism and cosmic dualism were important influences on the development of Judaism, Christianity and Islam.

ZAPOTECS

MAYA CITY STATES

MOCHE

WARI EMPIRE

TIWANAKU EMPIRE

Islam

Buddhism

Hinduism

Major area of Jewish settlement

Other area of Jewish settlement

Christianity

Zoroastrianism

Confucianism and Daoism

Shintoism

150°   120°   90°   60°

CELTIC KINGDOMS **1**
ANGLO-SAXON KINGDOMS **2**
BASQUES **3**
LOMBARD KINGDOM **4**
LOMBARD DUCHIES **5**

1 **2**

FRANKISH KINGDOM

Avar Khanate

Khazar Khanate

Eastern Turk Khanate

3 **4**

Western Turk Khanate

VISIGOTHIC KINGDOM

5

6

7

8

9

KOGURYO
SILLA

BYZANTINE EMPIRE

PAEKCHE
JAPAN

10

TIBET

NEPAL

TANG EMPIRE

ARAB CALIPHATE

11

EMPIRE OF HARSHA

13

MAKURIA

PYU CITY STATES

ALODIA

CHALUKYA KINGDOM

PALLAVA KINGDOM

12

CHAMPA

AXUM

CHENLA

11

ANURADHAPURA

SMALL MALAY KINGDOMS

6 ABASGIA
7 IBERIA
8 ARMENIA
9 TABARISTAN

10 SMALL BUDDHIST KINGDOMS
11 SMALL HINDU KINGDOMS
12 DVARAVATI
13 TAI KINGDOMS

Arctic Circle
75°
45°
Tropic of Cancer
Equator
Tropic of Capricorn
45°

0°   30°   60°   90°   120°   150°   180°

712

THE GREAT ARAB CONQUESTS REACH THE ATLANTIC AND THE INDUS

In 656 the third caliph, Uthman, was murdered. When Muhammad's son-in-law Ali was chosen as caliph, civil war broke out between his supporters and those of Muawiya, a member of Uthman's Umayyad family. Muawiya finally became caliph in 661, following Ali's murder, and was the first of the Umayyad dynasty of caliphs. Under Muawiya, the Arabs suffered their first serious setback when the Byzantines defeated their attack on Constantinople using Greek Fire incendiaries.

On Muawiya's death in 680, Ali's son Husain claimed the caliphate, causing another civil war with the Umayyads: his death in battle at Karbala led to the schism of Islam into majority Sunni and minority Shi'a (from *shi'atu Ali*, 'party of Ali') branches. As political stability returned to the caliphate, Arab expansion resumed, with the conquest of Byzantine North Africa, the Berbers, the Indus valley, Samarkand and Bukhara in Central Asia, and the Visigothic kingdom of Spain. By 712 the Umayyad caliphate was the largest empire the world had so far seen.

The Chinese Tang empire reached its peak in the later 7th century with the conquest of the West Turk khanate and the Korean kingdom of Koguryo. These conquests overextended the empire and were soon lost. By 712 the Tang had strong neighbours in Korea and Tibet and the expanding Umayyad caliphate, but remained the world's wealthiest and most urbanized state. In Indonesia, the Malay kingdom of Srivijaya created the first of a succession of maritime trading empires that dominated the region one after the other until the 16th century. Increased trans-Saharan trade contributed to the emergence of Ghana, the first kingdom of West Africa. Around 700, Polynesians from Tahiti discovered and settled Easter Island: it remained the world's most remote inhabited place until the 19th century.

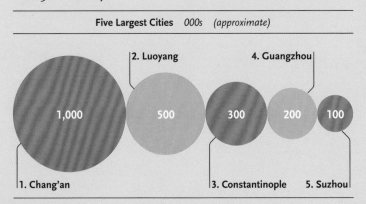

Five Largest Cities *000s* *(approximate)*

2. Luoyang — 500
4. Guangzhou — 300
1,000
200
100
1. Chang'an
3. Constantinople
5. Suzhou

Dorset Inuit culture

Dorset Inuit culture

Aleuts

Sub-Arctic caribou hunters

Central plateau hunter-fisher-gatherers

Great Plains bison hunters

Eastern Woodlands hunter-gatherers and maize cultivators

West coast fishers, hunters and gatherers

Desert hunter-gatherers

Ancestral Puebloan culture

Hopewell burial mound traditions

Hohokam culture

Mogollon culture

VERACRUZ CIVILIZATION

MEXICAN CITY STATES

ZAPOTECS

MAYA CITY STATES

North Andean chiefdoms

Arawak manioc farmers

Polynesians

Amazonian chiefdoms

WARI EMPIRE

TIWANAKU EMPIRE

Savanna hunter-gatherers

Easter Island

Pampas hunter-gatherers

Fishers and marine mammal hunters

Hunter-gatherers

Urbanized societies/ kingdoms

Settled farming cultures and peoples

Empires

Pastoral nomads

Uninhabited

Complex farming societies/chiefdoms

CELTIC KINGDOMS [1]
ANGLO-SAXON KINGDOMS [2]
ASTURIAS [3]
BASQUES [4]
LOMBARD KINGDOM [5]

Sami

Finno-Ugrians

Samoyed reindeer herders

Tungusic reindeer herders

Palaeo-Siberians

Dorset Inuit culture

Scandinavians

Finns

LOMBARD DUCHIES [6]

AVAR KHANATE [7]

BULGAR KHANATE [8]

ABASGIA [9]

LAZICA [10]

Balts

Saxons

Slavs

FRANKISH KINGDOM

Magyars (Ugrians)

Volga Bulgars

Kimek Turks

Kyrgyz

Tatars

Khitans

Jürchen

Khazar Khanate

Oguz Turks

Karluk Turks

Eastern Turk Khanate

PARHAE

Ainu

Slavs

Constantinople

B Y Z A N T I N E   E M P I R E

Chang'an [1]

Luoyang [2]

SILLA

JAPAN

TIBET

Suzhou [5]

U M A Y Y A D   C A L I P H A T E

TANG EMPIRE

[11]

Berber nomads

[12]

MAGADHA

[16]

Guangzhou [4]

Tropic of Cancer

MAKURIA

[13]

Burmese

Tais

MALAKURIA

GURJARA-PRATIHARAS

PYU CITY STATES

GHANA

ALODIA

CHALUKYA KINGDOM

[14]

CHAMPA

West African chiefdoms and towns

AXUM

PALLAVA KINGDOM

[15]

Nilotic pastoralists

Cushitic pastoralists

CHENLA

Micronesians

[13]

ANURADHAPURA

SRIVIJAYA

Malays

Bantu farmers and pastoralists

Papuans

KASHMIR [11]   MON STATES [14]

KANNAUJ [12]   DVARAVATI [15]

SMALL HINDU KINGDOMS [13]   TAI KINGDOMS [16]

SMALL MALAY STATES

Melanesians

Polynesians

Equator

Malagasy

San hunter-gatherers

Australian Aborigines

Tropic of Capricorn

Khoikhoi pastoralists

Tasmanians

712

The Arab conquests completely transformed the culture of the Middle East and North Africa through Islamization and Arabization. Though many Arabs did emigrate to the conquered territories, the main agent of Arabization was Islam. The Arabs did not impose Islam by force, but unbelievers were subject to the *jizya* (tribute) and other disadvantages, providing a strong incentive to convert.

Conversion began the process of Arabization. Because translation of the *Qur'an*, Islam's holy book, was forbidden, converts learned Arabic, useful also for commerce and government employment. Islam is as much a way of life as a religion so conversion also began the acculturation of conquered populations to Arab ways and identity. Mesopotamia, Syria, Palestine, Egypt and most of North Africa eventually became completely Arab in language, culture and identity.

The Arabs were in turn influenced by the culture of the peoples they had conquered, especially Persian art and literature, and Greek science and philosophy. While the Persians accepted Islam, they resisted complete Arabization. In former Byzantine territories, the elite were able to flee to unconquered areas. The complete collapse of the Sasanian state left the Persian elite nowhere to go. By reaching an accommodation with the new rulers, they retained substantial cultural and political influence.

Arab conquest also affected the early Christian church: though previously accorded special respect as patriarchs (along with the bishops of Rome and Constantinople), the bishops of Antioch, Alexandria and Jerusalem now saw their influence diminish, while the bishops, or popes, of Rome asserted their own claims to exercise supreme authority over the church as God's viceregents on earth. While papal claims came to be accepted in Western Europe, they caused increasing friction with the Greek church.

World Population *(approximate)*

7 BILLION

225 million

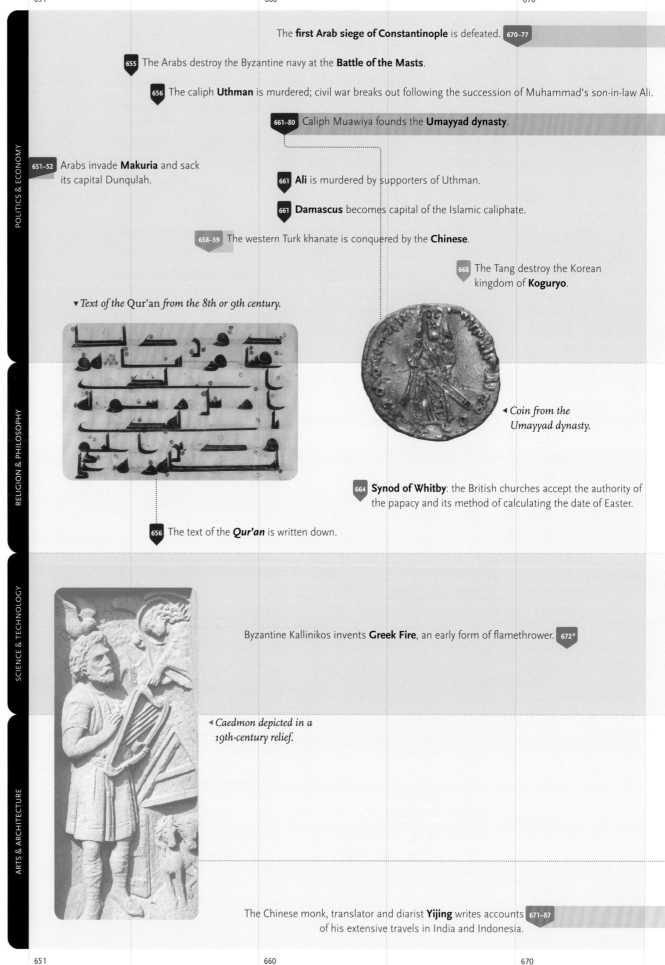

POLITICS & ECONOMY

The **first Arab siege of Constantinople** is defeated. `670–77`

`655` The Arabs destroy the Byzantine navy at the **Battle of the Masts**.

`656` The caliph **Uthman** is murdered; civil war breaks out following the succession of Muhammad's son-in-law Ali.

`661–80` Caliph Muawiya founds the **Umayyad dynasty**.

`651–52` Arabs invade **Makuria** and sack its capital Dunqulah.

`661` **Ali** is murdered by supporters of Uthman.

`661` **Damascus** becomes capital of the Islamic caliphate.

`658–59` The western Turk khanate is conquered by the **Chinese**.

`668` The Tang destroy the Korean kingdom of **Koguryo**.

RELIGION & PHILOSOPHY

▼ *Text of the Qur'an from the 8th or 9th century.*

◄ *Coin from the Umayyad dynasty.*

`664` **Synod of Whitby**: the British churches accept the authority of the papacy and its method of calculating the date of Easter.

`656` The text of the ***Qur'an*** is written down.

SCIENCE & TECHNOLOGY

Byzantine Kallinikos invents **Greek Fire**, an early form of flamethrower. `672*`

◄ *Caedmon depicted in a 19th-century relief.*

ARTS & ARCHITECTURE

The Chinese monk, translator and diarist **Yijing** writes accounts `671–87` of his extensive travels in India and Indonesia.

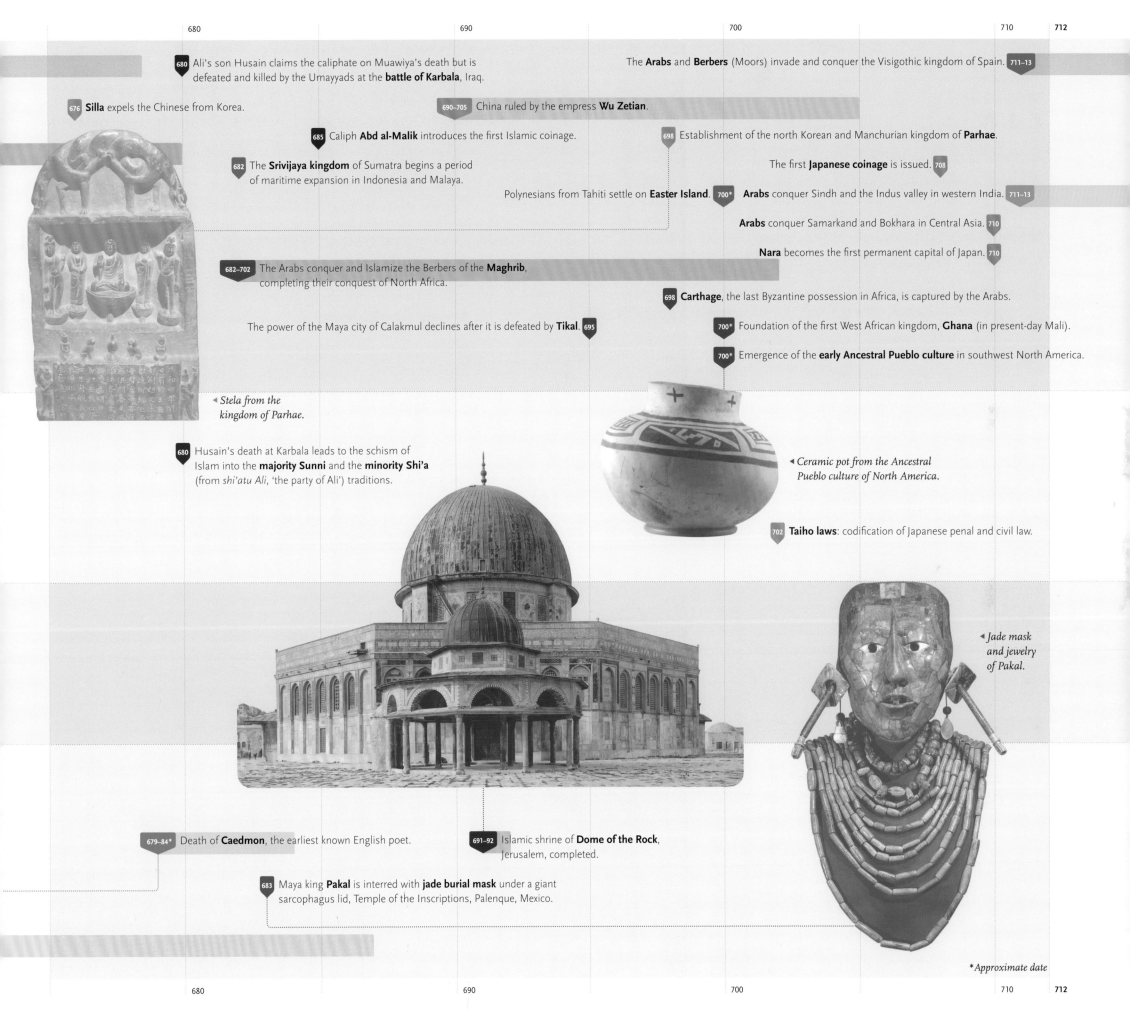

680 Ali's son Husain claims the caliphate on Muawiya's death but is defeated and killed by the Umayyads at the **battle of Karbala**, Iraq.

The **Arabs** and **Berbers** (Moors) invade and conquer the Visigothic kingdom of Spain. 711–13

676 **Silla** expels the Chinese from Korea.

690–705 China ruled by the empress **Wu Zetian**.

685 Caliph **Abd al-Malik** introduces the first Islamic coinage.

698 Establishment of the north Korean and Manchurian kingdom of **Parhae**.

682 The **Srivijaya kingdom** of Sumatra begins a period of maritime expansion in Indonesia and Malaya.

The first **Japanese coinage** is issued. 708

Polynesians from Tahiti settle on **Easter Island**. 700* **Arabs** conquer Sindh and the Indus valley in western India. 711–13

Arabs conquer Samarkand and Bokhara in Central Asia. 710

Nara becomes the first permanent capital of Japan. 710

682–702 The Arabs conquer and Islamize the Berbers of the **Maghrib**, completing their conquest of North Africa.

698 **Carthage**, the last Byzantine possession in Africa, is captured by the Arabs.

The power of the Maya city of Calakmul declines after it is defeated by **Tikal**. 695

700* Foundation of the first West African kingdom, **Ghana** (in present-day Mali).

700* Emergence of the **early Ancestral Pueblo culture** in southwest North America.

◄ *Stela from the kingdom of Parhae.*

680 Husain's death at Karbala leads to the schism of Islam into the **majority Sunni** and the **minority Shi'a** (from *shi'atu Ali*, 'the party of Ali') traditions.

◄ *Ceramic pot from the Ancestral Pueblo culture of North America.*

702 **Taiho laws**: codification of Japanese penal and civil law.

◄ *Jade mask and jewelry of Pakal.*

679–84* Death of **Caedmon**, the earliest known English poet.

691–92 Islamic shrine of **Dome of the Rock**, Jerusalem, completed.

683 Maya king **Pakal** is interred with **jade burial mask** under a giant sarcophagus lid, Temple of the Inscriptions, Palenque, Mexico.

*Approximate date

800

THE ABBASID CALIPHATE, THE CAROLINGIAN EMPIRE AND EARLY IMPERIAL JAPAN

Decisive victories by the Byzantines (716–17), Franks (732) and the Gurjara-Pratiharas (738) brought the years of runaway Arab conquests to an end in the early 8th century. The ideal of Muslim unity in a single community under the religious and political authority of the caliph did not long survive these reverses. The Arabs treated the caliphate as their own private empire, causing increasing resentment towards the Umayyads among new converts who believed that the caliphate existed to spread Islam, not to further Arab interests.

Umayyad authority was also being undermined by the simmering Sunni–Shi'ite split and by the renewal of feuding among the Arab tribes. In 747 a rebellion broke out in Persia and quickly spread. The rebels proclaimed Abu al-Abbas caliph in 749, and in 750 he defeated the Umayyads at the battle of Zab and captured Damascus. Only one significant member of the Umayyad family survived the bloodbath that followed. This was Abd al-Rahman, who escaped from the Abbasids to Spain and founded a breakaway state. By 800 the Abbasid caliphs had also lost control over most of North Africa.

By 800 the Chinese Tang empire was in decline as a result of military rebellions and attacks by the Uighur nomads and the briefly powerful Tibetan empire. The beginning of the classical Heian age of Japanese civilization was marked in 794 by the removal of the court to Kyoto. The Maya civilization of Mesoamerica reached its peak during the 8th century, with rulers commissioning ever more ambitious buildings and commemorative stelae. Under the domination of the Frankish emperor Charlemagne and his Carolingian empire, Western Europe enjoyed greater peace and prosperity than at any time since the fall of the western Roman empire, but the appearance of Viking pirates from Scandinavia along its coasts in the 790s began to pose a threat.

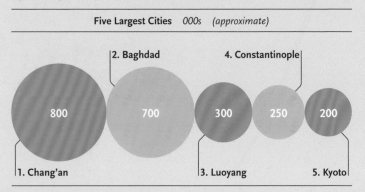

Five Largest Cities *000s* *(approximate)*

2. Baghdad

4. Constantinople

800 700 300 250 200

1. Chang'an   3. Luoyang   5. Kyoto

80

Dorset Inuit culture

Dorset Inuit culture

Aleuts

Sub-Arctic caribou hunters

Central plateau hunter-fisher-gatherers

Great Plains bison hunters

Woodlands hunter-gatherers

West coast fishers, hunters and gatherers

Woodland farmers

Desert hunter-gatherers

Ancestral Pueblo culture

Mississippian temple mound cultures

Hohokam culture

Mogollon culture

Maize farmers

Arawak

MEXICAN CITY STATES

ZAPOTECS

MAYA CITY STATES

North Andean chiefdoms

Arawak

Polynesians

Amazonian chiefdoms

Tupi

WARI EMPIRE

TIWANAKU EMPIRE

Savanna hunter-gatherers

Guarani

Araucanians

Pampas hunters

Fishers and marine mammal hunters

Hunter-gatherers

Urbanized societies/ kingdoms

Settled farming cultures and peoples

Empires

Pastoral nomads

Uninhabited

Complex farming societies/chiefdoms

CELTIC KINGDOMS **1**
ANGLO-SAXON KINGDOMS **2**
ASTURIAS **3**
BASQUES **4**
AVAR KHANATE **5**
BULGAR KHANATE **6**
ABASGIA **7**

Sami

Samoyed reindeer herders

Tungusic and Yakut reindeer herders

Palaeo-Siberians

Dorset Inuit culture

Scandinavians

Finns

Balts

Slavs

Magyars

Volga Bulgars

Kimek Turks

Kyrgyz

Tatars

Khitans

Jürchen

CAROLINGIAN (Frankish) EMPIRE

Khazar Khanate

Oguz Turks

Karluk Turks

Uighur Khanate

Ainu

PARHAE

1
3

SILLA

JAPAN **5**

Kyoto

4
Constantinople

7

UMAYYAD EMIRATE

BYZANTINE EMPIRE

TIBETAN EMPIRE

Chang'an Luoyang

IDRISID CALIPHATE

AGHLABID CALIPHATE

2 Baghdad

ABBASID CALIPHATE

8

TANG EMPIRE

Berbers

PALAS

8

11

NANZHAO

Touaregs

MAKURIA

GURJARA-PRATIHARAS

8

PYU CITY STATES

Tais

Tropic of Cancer

GHANA

GAO

ALODIA

RASHTRAKUTAS

9

CHAMPA

West African chiefdoms

AXUM

PALLAVAS

10

Malays

Micronesians

Nilotic pastoralists

PANDYAS

CHENLA

Cushitic pastoralists

ANURADHAPURA

SRIVIJAYA

Malays

Papuans

Bantu farmers and pastoralists

8 SMALL HINDU KINGDOMS

10 DVARAVATI

11 Burmese

9 MON STATES

MATARAM

Melanesians

Malagasy

Equator

San

Australian Aborigines

Tropic of Capricorn

Khoikhoi pastoralists

Tasmanians

Arctic Circle

75°

45°

0°   30°   60°   90°   120°   150°   180°

800

Despite declining political authority, the Abbasid caliphate remained in 800 the world's wealthiest state. Under Harun al-Rashid (786–809), the caliphate's rapidly growing new capital at Baghdad became the world's leading cultural centre, where the influences of Persian literature and Greek science and philosophy were assimilated to Islamic beliefs. Harun's opulent court became the stuff of legends and the setting for the stories of *The Thousand and One Nights*.

The Umayyads had seen Islam primarily as a symbol of Arab racial superiority, so they treated non-Arab converts as inferiors and excluded them from government office. Under the Abbasids, however, non-Arab converts enjoyed greater equality, thus removing the remaining barriers between the Arabs and their subjects, and also sharpening the distinction between Muslims and non-Muslims. Part of the reaction against the Umayyads was the development of the mystical Sufi tradition.

In 726 the Byzantine emperor Leo III abolished all religious images, bitterly dividing the Greek church and causing a breach with the papacy that lasted until iconoclasm was formally renounced in 842. It was a sign of the papacy's increasing spiritual authority in the West that Pippin III, who had held a senior palace position among the Franks as their Mayor, sought papal blessing for his seizure of the throne from the Merovingian dynasty. Monasteries were the West's main cultural centres; being rich and undefended, they proved attractive targets for Viking raiders.

Though exquisitely refined, the classical Heian culture in Japan remained focused on Buddhist monasteries and on the court, where the emperors became increasingly isolated from their subjects. Buddhism's dominant influence on the culture of Tibet was assured in 791 when it was adopted as the state religion.

World Population *(approximate)*

7 BILLION

240 million

200 BC · 800 · 2010

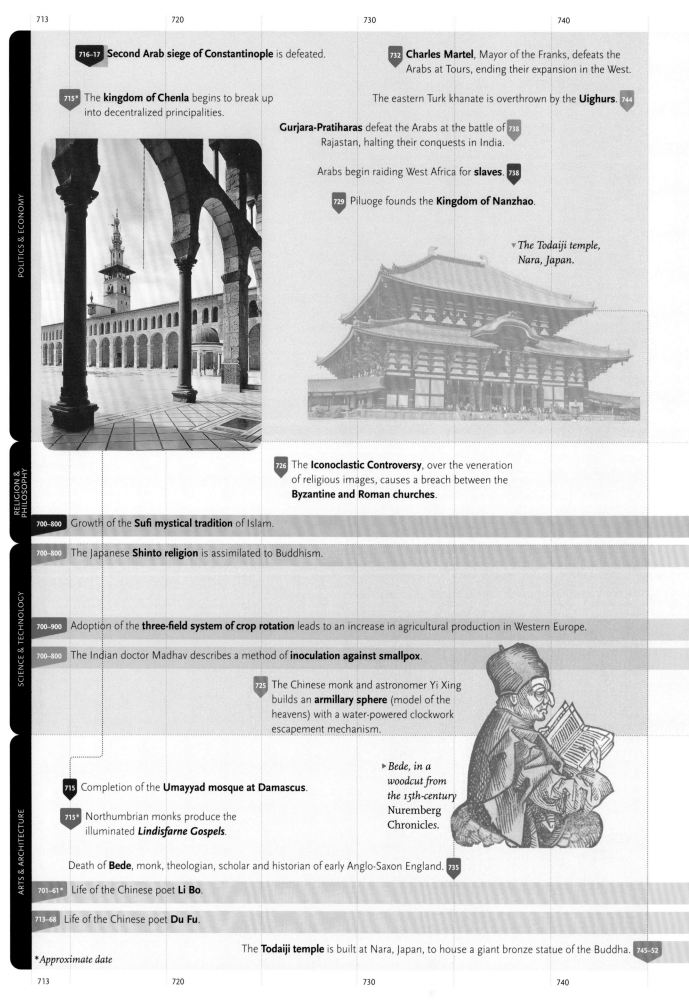

POLITICS & ECONOMY

716–17 **Second Arab siege of Constantinople** is defeated.

715* The **kingdom of Chenla** begins to break up into decentralized principalities.

732 **Charles Martel**, Mayor of the Franks, defeats the Arabs at Tours, ending their expansion in the West.

The eastern Turk khanate is overthrown by the **Uighurs**. **744**

Gurjara-Pratiharas defeat the Arabs at the battle of **738** Rajastan, halting their conquests in India.

Arabs begin raiding West Africa for **slaves**. **738**

729 Piluoge founds the **Kingdom of Nanzhao**.

▼ *The Todaiji temple, Nara, Japan.*

RELIGION & PHILOSOPHY

726 The **Iconoclastic Controversy**, over the veneration of religious images, causes a breach between the **Byzantine and Roman churches**.

700–800 Growth of the **Sufi mystical tradition** of Islam.

700–800 The Japanese **Shinto religion** is assimilated to Buddhism.

SCIENCE & TECHNOLOGY

700–900 Adoption of the **three-field system of crop rotation** leads to an increase in agricultural production in Western Europe.

700–800 The Indian doctor Madhav describes a method of **inoculation against smallpox**.

725 The Chinese monk and astronomer Yi Xing builds an **armillary sphere** (model of the heavens) with a water-powered clockwork escapement mechanism.

ARTS & ARCHITECTURE

715 Completion of the **Umayyad mosque at Damascus**.

715* Northumbrian monks produce the illuminated **Lindisfarne Gospels**.

▶ *Bede, in a woodcut from the 15th-century Nuremberg Chronicles.*

Death of **Bede**, monk, theologian, scholar and historian of early Anglo-Saxon England. **735**

701–61* Life of the Chinese poet **Li Bo**.

713–68 Life of the Chinese poet **Du Fu**.

The **Todaiji temple** is built at Nara, Japan, to house a giant bronze statue of the Buddha. **745–52**

*Approximate date

Al-Mansur makes Baghdad the capital of the Islamic caliphate. **763**

750 **Battle of the Zab**: the Abbasids seize control of the Islamic caliphate from the Umayyad dynasty.

Political break-up of the **Islamic caliphate** **756** begins with the establishment of an independent Umayyad emirate in Spain by Abd al-Rahman.

The **Rashtrakuta dynasty** becomes the **756** dominant power of central India.

751 **Pope Zacharias** authorizes the deposition of the last Merovingian king by the Carolingian Pippin III.

750–800* The **Toltecs** migrate into the Valley of Mexico.

751 The Arabs halt Chinese expansion in Central Asia at the **battle of the Talas river**.

755–63 **An Lushan rebellion** begins the decline of China's Tang dynasty.

▼ *Detail from a Viking picture stone, Gotland, Sweden.*

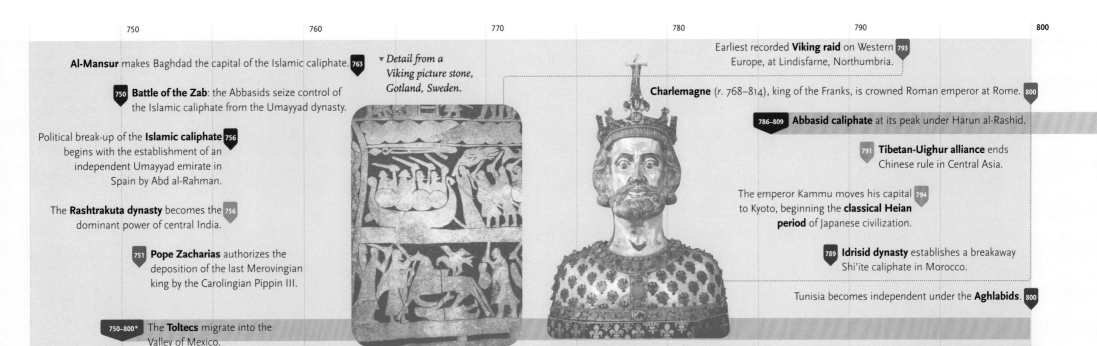

▲ *Golden reliquary of Charlemagne, housed in his cathedral at Aachen, Germany.*

Earliest recorded **Viking raid** on Western **793** Europe, at Lindisfarne, Northumbria.

Charlemagne (r. 768–814), king of the Franks, is crowned Roman emperor at Rome. **800**

786–809 **Abbasid caliphate** at its peak under Harun al-Rashid.

791 **Tibetan-Uighur alliance** ends Chinese rule in Central Asia.

The emperor Kammu moves his capital **794** to Kyoto, beginning the **classical Heian period** of Japanese civilization.

789 **Idrisid dynasty** establishes a breakaway Shi'ite caliphate in Morocco.

Tunisia becomes independent under the **Aghlabids**. **800**

Farming becomes the predominant way of life in the **Eastern Woodlands** in **800*** North America following the introduction of hardy strains of maize and beans.

Beginning of the **decline of the Maya city states**. **800***

Emergence of the **Mississippian temple-mound cultures** in North America. **800***

Uighur nomads adopt the **Manichaean religion**. **762**

Adi Shankara, founder of the Advaita Vedanta school of Hindu philosophy. **788–820**

Buddhism becomes the state religion in Tibet. **791**

Arabs adopt the **Hindu numeral system** (known **760*** as 'Arabic' numerals in Europe).

◄ *Procession of musicians in a mural at Bonampak, Mexico.*

►*This page from the Book of Kells shows the four evangelists – St Matthew, St Mark, St Luke and St John.*

◄ *The Buddhist temple at Borobodur, Java, with its domes and a buddha.*

Murals at the Maya city of **Bonampak**, **792** Mexico, commemorate a battle.

The Book of Kells (illuminated gospels) produced at Iona, Scotland. **800***

785* Construction of the **Great Mosque of Córdoba** begins.

Beginning of the construction of the **Borobodur temple in Java**, **800*** a giant model of the Buddhist path to enlightenment.

780 Lu You's *The Classic of Tea* describes the production and use of tea.

756–814* Life of **Abu Nuwaz**, major classical Arabic poet.

907

DEMISE OF THE TANG AND THE MAYA CITY STATES; THE AGE OF THE VIKINGS

Under frequent attack from Tibet, the Tais of Nanzhao and steppe nomads, China's Tang empire continued its decline in the 9th century. Foreign religions, including Christianity and Buddhism, faced official persecution. Peasant rebellions undermined the last of the dynasty's authority, allowing warlords to seize power in the provinces. In 907 the Tang were finally overthrown and China broke up into several independent kingdoms. In the early 9th century the Khmer empire emerged as the great power of Southeast Asia. Later in the century the first Burmese kingdom was founded at Bagan. The authority of the Japanese emperors entered a long-term decline as power passed to the Fujiwara family of hereditary regents.

During the 9th century, dynastic disputes led to the break-up of Charlemagne's empire. Out of this emerged the kingdoms of Germany and France. Viking raids were to reach all but a few parts of Western Europe in this period – they even penetrated to the Mediterranean. Viking colonies were founded in Ireland, Scotland and Normandy. England escaped total conquest only because of the military leadership of Alfred the Great of Wessex. Vikings became the first inhabitants of Iceland and the Faroe Islands. Swedish Vikings, known as Rus, penetrated Russia's river system, forging trade routes to the Byzantine empire and the Abbasid caliphate. On the way they founded the first Russian state at Kiev, which preyed on the surrounding Slavs for tribute and slaves.

In the course of the 9th century, the Maya city states collapsed one after another, most probably because of an ecological crisis brought on by deforestation and soil exhaustion. Maya civilization survived in northern Yucatán in a somewhat reduced form. The power vacuum in Mexico created by the fall of Teotihuacán was finally filled by the rising Toltec state.

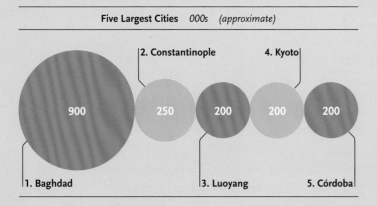

Five Largest Cities 000s *(approximate)*

- 1. Baghdad — 900
- 2. Constantinople — 250
- 3. Luoyang — 200
- 4. Kyoto — 200
- 5. Córdoba — 200

Dorset Inuit culture

Dorset Inuit culture

Aleuts

Sub-Arctic caribou hunters

Central plateau hunter-fisher-gatherers

Great Plains bison hunters

Woodlands hunter-gatherers

West coast fishers, hunters and gatherers

Woodland farmers

Desert hunter-gatherers

Ancestral Pueblo culture

Mississippian temple mound cultures

Hohokam culture

Mogollon culture

MAYA CITY STATES

MEXICAN CITY STATES

Arawak

TOLTECS
ZAPOTECS

North Andean chiefdoms

Arawak

Polynesians

Amazonian chiefdoms

Tupi

WARI EMPIRE

TIWANAKU EMPIRE

Savanna hunter-gatherers

Guarani

Araucanians

Pampas hunters

Fishers and marine mammal hunters

Legend

- Hunter-gatherers
- Settled farming cultures and peoples
- Pastoral nomads
- Complex farming societies/chiefdoms
- Urbanized societies/kingdoms
- Empires
- Uninhabited

IRISH KINGDOMS **1**
WELSH KINGDOMS **2**
WESSEX **3**
SCOTLAND **4**
NORTHUMBRIA **5**
SMALL DANISH KINGDOMS **6**

ASTURIAS **7**
PAMPLONA **8**
COUNTY OF BARCELONA **9**
BURGUNDY **10**
PROVENCE **11**
LOMBARD DUCHIES **12**
BULGAR KHANATE **13**

Norse

Sami

Tungusic and Yakut reindeer herders

Samoyed reindeer herders

Palaeo-Siberians

Dorset Inuit culture

Arctic Circle

c. 870

NORWAY

Swedes

Finns

RUS (Swedes)

DENMARK

Balts

Volga Bulgars

Slavs

Kimek Turks

Kyrgyz

Mongols

Tatars

Jürchen

BOHEMIA

GERMANY (Slavs)

Slavs

Pechenegs

Magyars

FRANCE

10

1

Slavs

ITALY

11

9

12

13

5 Córdoba

UMAYYAD EMIRATE

2 Constantinople

BYZANTINE EMPIRE

14 **15**

Khazar Khanate

Oguz Turks

Uighurs

Karluk Turks

Khitans

PARHAE

Ainu

23 SILLA
24 SOUTHERN HAN

3 Luoyang

JIN YAN

LATER LIANG

4 JAPAN

Kyoto

16

ABBASID CALIPHATE

1 Baghdad

SAMANID EMIRATE

Tanguts

QIN

EARLY SHU

23

AGHLABID CALIPHATE

IDRISID CALIPHATE

Berbers

SAFFARID EMIRATE

ALAVID EMIRATE

SINDH

18 **19**

17

Nepal

TIBET

DALI (NANZHAO)

CHU

WU

WUYUE

MIN

SMALL KINGDOMS

GHANA

SONGHAY

KANEM

MALI

West African chiefdoms

Touaregs

MAKURIA

ALODIA

AXUM

YEMEN

QARMATIANS

GURJARA-PRATIHARA EMPIRE

RASHTRAKUTAS

18

ARAKAN

20

21

22

24

DAI VIET

CHAMPA

KHMER

Malays

Nilotic pastoralists

Cushitic pastoralists

CHOLAS

PANDYAS

18

ANURADHAPURA

SRIVIJAYA

Malays

Micronesians

Tropic of Cancer

Equator

Bantu farmers and pastoralists

Malagasy

MATARAM

Papuans

14 ABASGIA
15 ARMENIA
16 ALAVID EMIRATE
17 MULTAN
18 SMALL HINDU STATES

19 KASHMIR
20 BAGAN (Burmese)
21 MON STATES
22 DVARAVATI

Melanesians

Polynesians

San

Khoikhoi pastoralists

Australian Aborigines

Tropic of Capricorn

Tasmanians

907

The political fragmentation of the Muslim world continued apace in the 9th century: the Persians began to throw off Arab domination and found independent emirates under the Samanid and Saffarid dynasties. Despite its political decline, the 9th-century Abbasid caliphate presided over a golden age of Islamic culture.

Baghdad's House of Wisdom became a centre for translating Greek, Persian and Hindu works into Arabic. Many works of Classical Greek science and philosophy, neglected by the Byzantines because of their pagan associations, were preserved in this way: when such texts were rediscovered in Western Europe in the 12th century, this was often through Arabic translations originally made in Baghdad. The study of astronomy and mathematics also flourished. Influenced by Greek philosophy, the Mutazilist school of theologians attempted to reconcile faith and reason but could not overcome the opposition of *hadith* scholars, who believed it was not for humans to question God's will or explore it intellectually.

In Western Europe, the destruction of monasteries in raids by Viking and Muslim pirates and Magyar nomads brought cultural life to a low ebb in the 9th century. However, it was from the end of this period that the first examples of polyphonic music are known. The dynastic disputes and civil wars that brought about the break-up of the Frankish empire, together with its rulers' failure to prevent Viking raids, led to a decline in royal authority. Control of the kingdoms that emerged was highly decentralized, with weak monarchies and powerful feudal aristocracies.

In China, the Daoist search for an elixir of immortality created a strong interest in alchemy, a dangerous by-product of which was the invention of gunpowder, probably around the middle of the 9th century.

World Population *(approximate)*

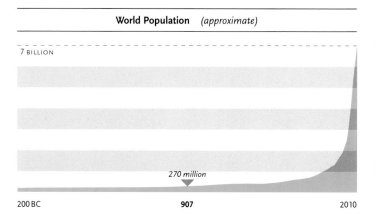

7 BILLION

270 million

200 BC   **907**   2010

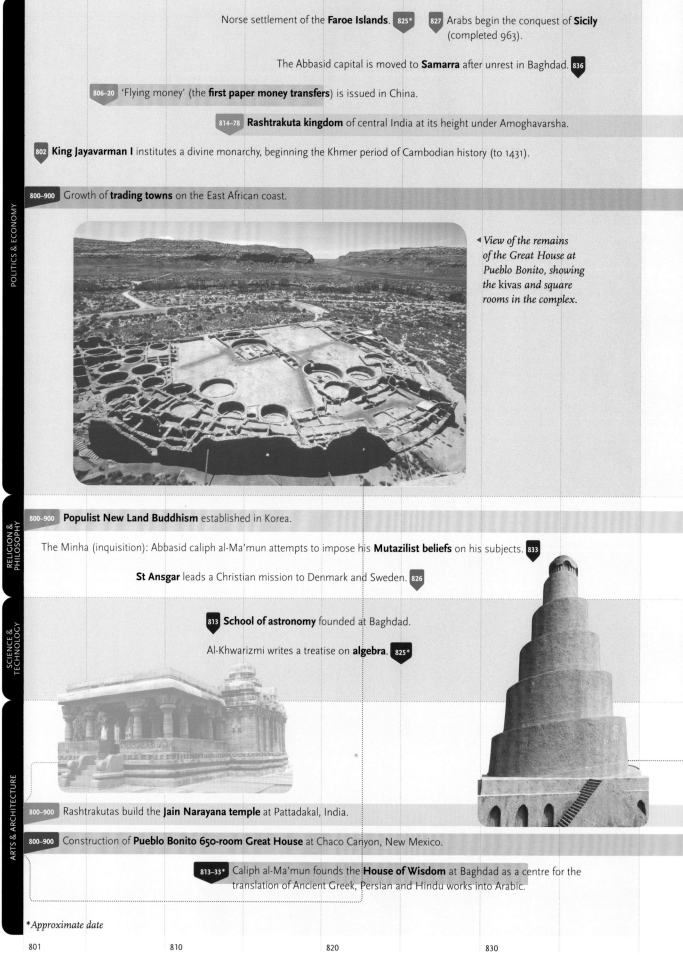

POLITICS & ECONOMY

Norse settlement of the **Faroe Islands**. 825* | 827 Arabs begin the conquest of **Sicily** (completed 963).

The Abbasid capital is moved to **Samarra** after unrest in Baghdad. 836

806–20 'Flying money' (the **first paper money transfers**) is issued in China.

814–78 **Rashtrakuta kingdom** of central India at its height under Amoghavarsha.

802 **King Jayavarman I** institutes a divine monarchy, beginning the Khmer period of Cambodian history (to 1431).

800–900 Growth of **trading towns** on the East African coast.

◄ *View of the remains of the Great House at Pueblo Bonito, showing the kivas and square rooms in the complex.*

RELIGION & PHILOSOPHY

800–900 **Populist New Land Buddhism** established in Korea.

The Minha (inquisition): Abbasid caliph al-Ma'mun attempts to impose his **Mutazilist beliefs** on his subjects. 833

St Ansgar leads a Christian mission to Denmark and Sweden. 826

SCIENCE & TECHNOLOGY

813 **School of astronomy** founded at Baghdad.

Al-Khwarizmi writes a treatise on **algebra**. 825*

ARTS & ARCHITECTURE

800–900 Rashtrakutas build the **Jain Narayana temple** at Pattadakal, India.

800–900 Construction of **Pueblo Bonito 650-room Great House** at Chaco Canyon, New Mexico.

813–33* Caliph al-Ma'mun founds the **House of Wisdom** at Baghdad as a centre for the translation of Ancient Greek, Persian and Hindu works into Arabic.

*Approximate date

801   810   820   830

843 **Treaty of Verdun**: the Frankish empire is divided in three between Charlemagne's grandsons.

865–902* Worst period of **Viking raiding** in Western Europe.

871–99 **Alfred the Great of Wessex** assumes leadership of the Anglo-Saxons against the Vikings.

Authority of the Japanese emperors declines after the aristocratic **Fujiwara family** seizes control of the government. **858**

Kiev becomes capital of the first Russian state. **882***   **885–87** The Frankish empire is reunited by **Charles the Fat**.

The **Frankish empire breaks up into five kingdoms**: France, Germany, Italy, Burgundy and Provence. **889**

896–907 The **Magyar nomads** invade Europe and settle on the Hungarian plain.

846 **Muslim pirates** raid Rome.

Norse settlement of **Iceland**. **870**

874 The Persian Samanid emirate of **Central Asia and Khorasan** becomes independent of the Abbasids.

892 The Abbasid capital is returned to **Baghdad**.

◄ *This statue of Alfred the Great stands in his capital, Winchester.*

Provincial warlords seize power as peasant rebellions **874–84** undermine the authority of the **Tang dynasty**.

886 **Armenia** gains independence from the Abbasids.

Radical **Shi'ite Qarmatian movement** seizes control of Arabia. **899**

Bagan (Pagan) becomes capital of the first Burmese kingdom. **874**

The Persian Saffarid emirate of **Seistan** gains independence from the Abbasids. **903**

Egypt and Palestine become independent of the Abbasid caliphate under the **Tulunids**. **868**

Fall of the Tang dynasty: China breaks up into rival states, beginning the **Five Dynasties and Ten Kingdoms period**. **907**

889 Yasovarman I founds **Angkor** as a new capital for the Khmer empire.

850* The **Tamil Chola dynasty** becomes the dominant power of southern India.

The **Abbasids** regain control of Egypt and Palestine. **905**

The Toltecs found a kingdom in central Mexico with its capital at **Tula**. **900***

▶ *View of the ruins of the city of Bagan, Burma.*

840 **Pyu city states** fall under Burmese control.

Irrigation-based farming practised by the **Hohokam culture** in southwest North America. **900***

850–900 The Itzá Maya found **Chichén Itzá** in Yucatán.

842–45 **Tang dynasty** orders the persecution of non-Chinese religions, including Buddhism and Christianity.

860–900* The **hadith**, the basis of Islamic jurisprudence, are collected in their final form.

◄ *The Persian doctor Razi treats a patient in an illuminated manuscript from the 13th century.*

Possible earliest use of **gunpowder**, China. **850***

858–929* Life of the influential Arab astronomer **al-Battani**.

865–925 Life of the **Persian physician and alchemist Razi** (Rhases), discoverer of kerosene and alcohol.

The **lost-wax method** of gold casting is introduced to Mesoamerica from South America. **900***

847 The spiral minaret of the **Great Mosque of Samarra**.

880–90 Compilation of the **Anglo-Saxon Chronicle** begins.

Byzantine emperor Leo VI writes the **Tactica** on military theory. **900***

▶ *Page from the wood-block printed Chinese copy of the* Diamond Sutra.

Musical treatise *Musica enchiriadis* contains the earliest examples of **polyphonic music**. **900***

850* *Kavirajamarga*, a work on rhetoric and grammar by King Amoghavarsha: the oldest surviving literary work in the Kannada language.

Prambanan Hindu temple completed, Java. **856***

868 The **oldest surviving dated printed book**, a Chinese copy of the Buddhist *Diamond Sutra*.

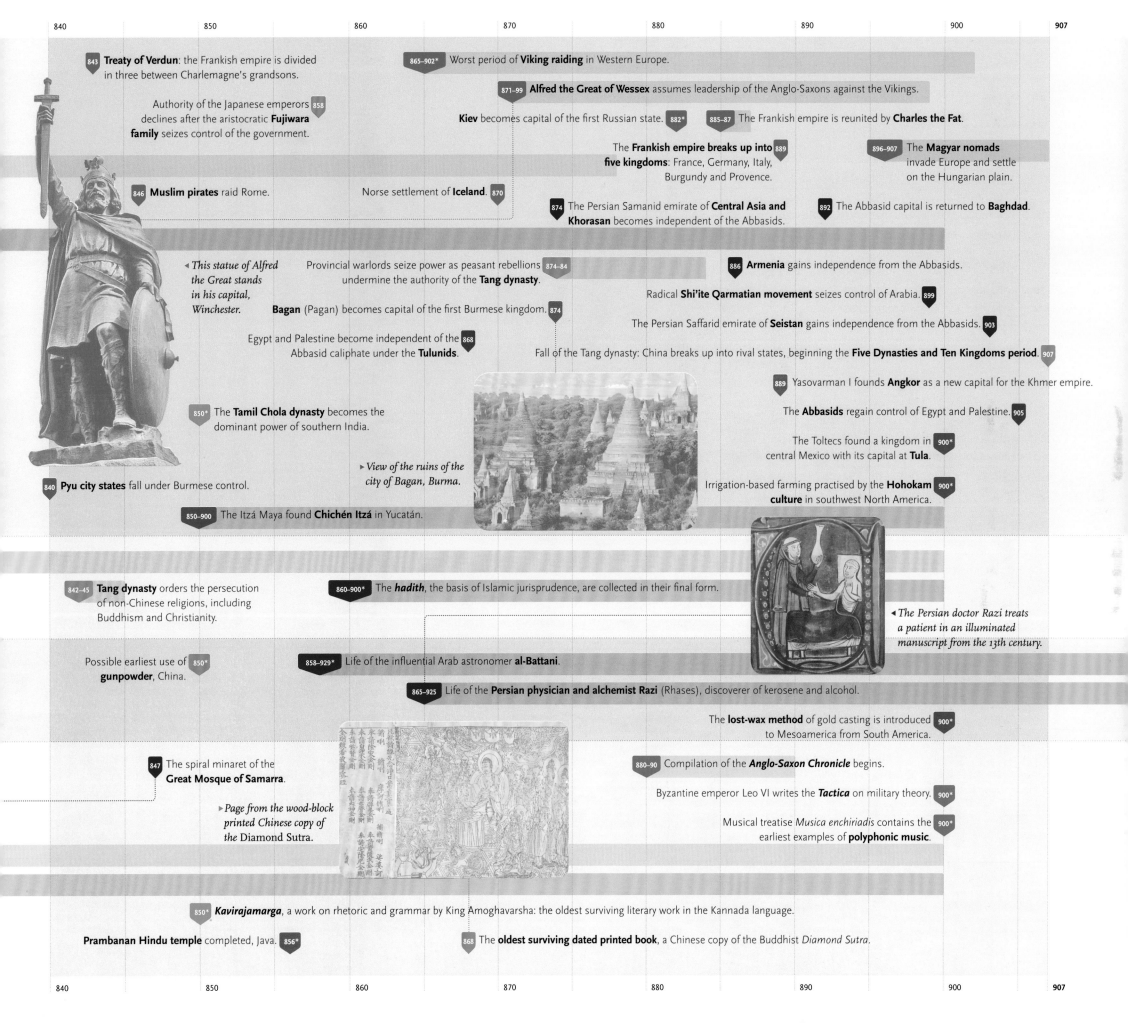

1000

FALL OF THE ABBASIDS; VIKING RAIDS IN EUROPE; UNIFICATION OF KOREA

The Abbasid caliphate's long decline as a political power came to an end in 945, when the Persian Buwayhid dynasty captured Baghdad. The Buwayhids were Shi'ites, but they permitted the Abbasid caliphs to continue as religious figureheads. The religious authority of the Abbasids was more explicitly rejected by the powerful Shi'ite Fatimid dynasty, which came to power in Tunisia in 909. In 941 the Fatimids conquered Egypt and made Cairo the capital of a rival Shi'ite caliphate. Abd al-Rahman III, the Umayyad ruler of Spain, also rejected Abbasid religious authority, reclaiming the title of caliph for his dynasty in 929.

Western Europe became a less turbulent place in the 10th century. Viking raids declined and stable kingdoms developed in Scandinavia. The Viking settlements in Normandy were brought under nominal French sovereignty and the successors of Alfred the Great conquered the Viking settlements in England, bringing the whole country under a single crown. The German king Otto I celebrated his victories over the Magyars and his annexation of Italy with an imperial coronation in Rome in 962: his Holy Roman empire rather ambitiously saw itself as the legal successor to both Charlemagne's empire and the Roman empire. Under Basil II, the Byzantine empire, the real successor of the Roman empire, emerged from centuries of territorial decline.

In 960 the Song dynasty reunited most of China but, hemmed in by powerful states and nomad peoples, its rulers were unable to expand beyond areas of ethnic Chinese settlement. In this period too, Korea emerged as a unified kingdom under the Koryo dynasty from which the country gets its modern name, and the Vietnamese threw off Chinese rule. Around 1000, the Andean Tiwanaku and Wari empires collapsed, beginning a long period of political fragmentation in the Andes: drought caused by a succession of El Niño events is thought to have been the main culprit.

Five Largest Cities *000s* *(approximate)*

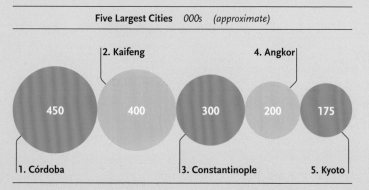

2. Kaifeng — 400
4. Angkor — 200
1. Córdoba — 450
3. Constantinople — 300
5. Kyoto — 175

Dorset Inuit culture

Dorset Inuit culture

Norse

Aleuts

Sub-Arctic caribou hunters

Central plateau hunter-fisher-gatherers

Great Plains bison hunters

Woodlands hunter-gatherers

Woodland farmers

West coast fishers, hunters and gatherers

Desert hunter-gatherers

Ancestral Pueblo culture

Mississippian temple mound cultures

Hohokam culture

Mogollon culture

MAYA CITY STATES

TOLTEC EMPIRE

Arawak

ZAPOTECS

North Andean chiefdoms

Arawak

Tupi

Polynesians

Amazonian chiefdoms

SMALL ANDEAN KINGDOMS AND CITY STATES

Savanna hunter-gatherers

Guarani

Araucanians

Pampas hunters

Fishers and marine mammal hunters

Hunter-gatherers

Urbanized societies/ kingdoms

Settled farming cultures and peoples

Empires

Pastoral nomads

Uninhabited

Complex farming societies/chiefdoms

150°   120°   90°   60°

IRISH KINGDOMS **1**
WELSH KINGDOMS **2**
EARLDOM OF ORKNEY **3**
SCOTLAND **4**
ENGLAND **5**

ICELANDIC COMMONWEALTH

Sami reindeer herders

Samoyed reindeer herders

Tungusic and Yakut reindeer herders

Palaeo-Siberians

Dorset Inuit culture

NORWAY

3

Finns

SWEDEN

NAVARRE **6**
COUNTY OF BARCELONA **7**
BURGUNDY **8**
LOMBARD DUCHIES **9**
Serbs and Croats (Slavs) **10**
ZIRID EMIRATE **11**

4

DENMARK

1

8

9

5

2

Balts

PRINCIPALITY OF KIEV

Volga Bulgars

Kimek Turks

Kyrgyz

Tatars

Mongols

HOLY ROMAN EMPIRE

POLAND

Pechenegs

Jürchen

Ainu

FRANCE

8

HUNGARY (Magyars)

10

12

Khazar Khanate

13

Oguz Turks

LIAO (Khitans)

6

10

7

14 **15**

LEÓN

1

3

Constantinople BYZANTINE EMPIRE

KARAKHANID KHANATE (Karluk Turks)

KARA-KHOJA KHANATES (Uighurs)

Tanguts

2

KOREA

5 JAPAN

Córdoba

11

Kaifeng

Kyoto

UMAYYAD CALIPHATE

ZIRID EMIRATE (Berbers)

BUWAYHID EMIRATES

GHAZNAVID EMIRATE

16

TIBET

SONG EMPIRE

FATIMID CALIPHATE

QARMATIANS

17

GURJARA-PRATIHARAS

HINDU KINGDOMS

DALI

Touaregs

SMALL MUSLIM STATES

18

SMALL KINGDOMS

MAKURIA

WEST CHALUKYA KINGDOM

ARAKAN

DAI VIET

TAKRUR

SONGHAY

KANEM

YEMEN

EAST CHALUKYA KINGDOM

19

CHAMPA

GHANA

ALODIA

HINDU KINGDOMS

20

4

Malays

MALI

Zaghawa

CHOLAS

Angkor

West African chiefdoms

Nilotic pastoralists

ETHIOPIA

KHMER

SMALL MALAY STATES

Micronesians

Cushitic pastoralists

HINDU KINGDOMS

Bantu farmers and pastoralists

SWAHILI CITY STATES

SRIVIJAYA

Malays

Papuans

12 BULGAR KHANATE	**16** KASHMIR
13 GEORGIA	**17** SINDH
14 ARMENIA	**18** BAGAN
15 SMALL EMIRATES	**19** MON STATES
	20 DVARAVATI

MATARAM

Melanesians

Polynesians

San

Malagasy

Australian Aborigines

Khoikhoi pastoralists

Tasmanians

75°
Arctic Circle
45°
Tropic of Cancer
Equator
Tropic of Capricorn
45°

0°   30°   60°   90°   120°   150°   180°

1000

In the 10th century, Christianity began a major expansion into Northern and Eastern Europe. Roman Catholic and Greek Orthodox missionaries competed for influence. Scandinavia, Poland, Bohemia and Hungary were converted by Roman Catholic missionaries, and accepted the authority of the papacy and use of the Roman alphabet. Serbia, Bulgaria and Kievan Russia were converted by Greek missionaries and accepted the traditions of the Greek Orthodox church; they also developed alphabets derived from the Greek alphabet. A major fault line, which still exists, was created through Europe in the process.

An influential monastic reform movement took place in Western Europe during the 10th century, dedicated to faithful observance of the 6th-century Rule of St Benedict. The movement was supported by the German monarchy, which cultivated the church as a counterbalance to the feudal aristocracy and relied on bishops and abbots to fill the highest offices of state. Europe's most important cultural centre, and its largest and wealthiest city, was Córdoba, the capital of Islamic Spain. The library of the caliph al-Hakim at Córdoba was, with over 400,000 volumes, probably the largest in the world at the time.

Islam began to spread among the Turkic peoples of Central Asia following the conversion of the Oguz Turks around 970. By the end of the century, Arab merchants had begun to establish Islam in the trading towns of West Africa and the East African coast.

Although the Song dynasty's empire was the smallest of the Chinese empires, it is remembered as one of the most humane Chinese dynasties and it ushered in a period of extraordinary prosperity and inventiveness: early innovations included the chamber lock and the first known gunpowder weapons. The scale and sophistication of Chinese commerce were unmatched in the world.

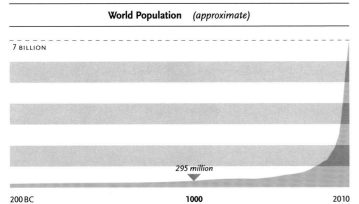

World Population (approximate)

7 BILLION

295 million

200 BC   1000   2010

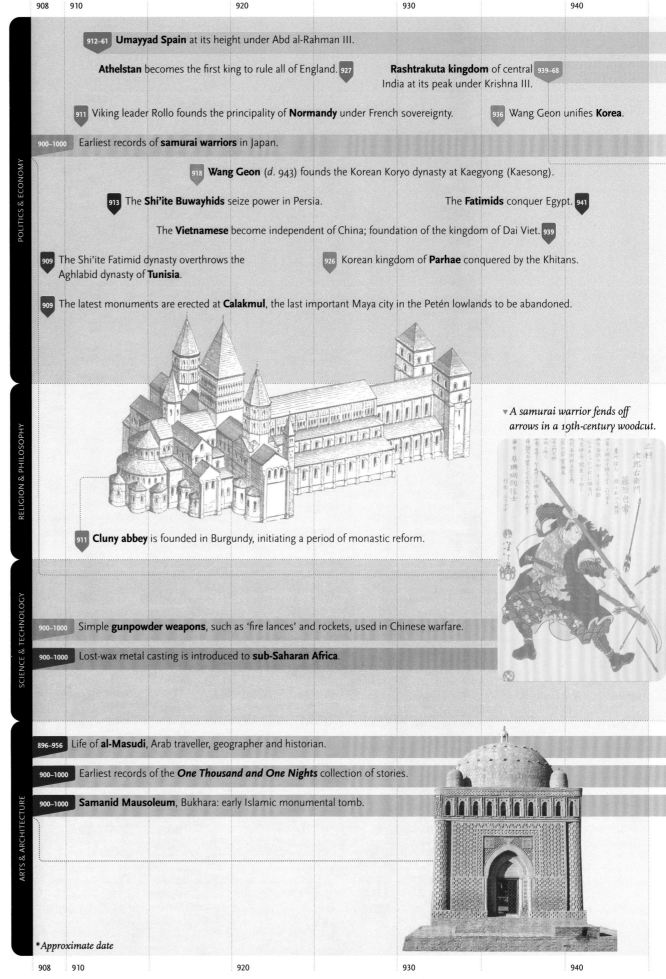

POLITICS & ECONOMY

912–61 **Umayyad Spain** at its height under Abd al-Rahman III.

Athelstan becomes the first king to rule all of England. **927**   **Rashtrakuta kingdom** of central **939–68** India at its peak under Krishna III.

911 Viking leader Rollo founds the principality of **Normandy** under French sovereignty.   **936** Wang Geon unifies **Korea**.

900–1000 Earliest records of **samurai warriors** in Japan.

918 **Wang Geon** (d. 943) founds the Korean Koryo dynasty at Kaegyong (Kaesong).

913 The **Shi'ite Buwayhids** seize power in Persia.   The **Fatimids** conquer Egypt. **941**

The **Vietnamese** become independent of China; foundation of the kingdom of Dai Viet. **939**

909 The Shi'ite Fatimid dynasty overthrows the Aghlabid dynasty of **Tunisia**.   **926** Korean kingdom of **Parhae** conquered by the Khitans.

909 The latest monuments are erected at **Calakmul**, the last important Maya city in the Petén lowlands to be abandoned.

▼ A samurai warrior fends off arrows in a 19th-century woodcut.

RELIGION & PHILOSOPHY

911 **Cluny abbey** is founded in Burgundy, initiating a period of monastic reform.

SCIENCE & TECHNOLOGY

900–1000 Simple **gunpowder weapons**, such as 'fire lances' and rockets, used in Chinese warfare.

900–1000 Lost-wax metal casting is introduced to **sub-Saharan Africa**.

ARTS & ARCHITECTURE

896–956 Life of **al-Masudi**, Arab traveller, geographer and historian.

900–1000 Earliest records of the ***One Thousand and One Nights*** collection of stories.

900–1000 **Samanid Mausoleum**, Bukhara: early Islamic monumental tomb.

*Approximate date

908   910   920   930   940

962 German king Otto I is crowned emperor in Rome, founding the **Holy Roman empire**.

986 **Erik the Red** founds the Norse Greenland colony.

976–1025 **Basil II** reverses the territorial decline of the Byzantine empire by conquests in Syria, Mesopotamia, Armenia, Bulgaria and the Balkans.

945 The Buwayhids capture **Baghdad**, ending the Abbasid caliphate's political power.

Mahmud of Ghazni (Afghanistan) rebels against the Samanids, **997** founding the Ghaznavid emirate.

947 The Khitans conquer northern China, founding the **Liao kingdom**.

◄ *Erik the Red in a 17th-century drawing.*

982 **Indra IV**, the last king of the Rashtrakuta dynasty, fasts to death after his kingdom suffers a series of defeats.

Song Taizu becomes emperor of the **Five Dynasties state**. **960**

Mahmud of Ghazni launches the first of 17 invasions of India. **1000**

979 Song Taizong reunifies most of China, beginning the **Song Dynasty period** (to 1279).

975 The kingdom of **Axum** is destroyed by pagan invaders.

According to later traditions, the **Toltec Kukulcán** conquers the Maya city of Chichén Itzá. **987**

The **Cholas** conquer Ceylon. **1000***

Cairo becomes capital of **969** the Fatimid caliphate.

Collapse of the **Wari** and **Tiwanaku empires**, thought to be due to climate change. **1000***

Leif Eriksson's voyage to Vinland: first European landing on the American continent. **1000***

▲ *Caves at Ellora, constructed under the Rashtrakuta dynasty as shrines for Buddhists, Jains and Hindus.*

Vladimir, Grand Prince of Kiev, converts to Greek Orthodox Christianity. **988**

The first Orthodox monasteries built on **Mount Athos**, Greece. **963**

King Olaf Tryggvason begins to convert Norway to Christianity by force. **995**

965 **King Harald Bluetooth** of Denmark converts to Christianity.

Pilgrimage becomes an important **1000*** part of Hindu devotions.

Al-Azhar Islamic University founded at Cairo. **989**

▶ *The Khajuraho temple, India.*

970* The **Oguz Turks** convert to Islam.

Islam is spread to West Africa and to the Swahili **1000*** coast of East Africa by Arab traders.

Chamber locks built on Chinese canals. **984**

970 Completion of the **al-Azhar mosque**, Cairo.

948–52 ***De Administrando Imperio*** by the Byzantine emperor Constantine VII: a treatise on statecraft and foreign policy.

Rise of the Song school of **landscape painting**. **1000***

950–1000* First **stone castles** built in France.

950–1150* Construction of the **Khajuraho temple complex** in India.

980–1000 Illuminated ***Gospels of Otto III*** made at Reichenau, Germany.

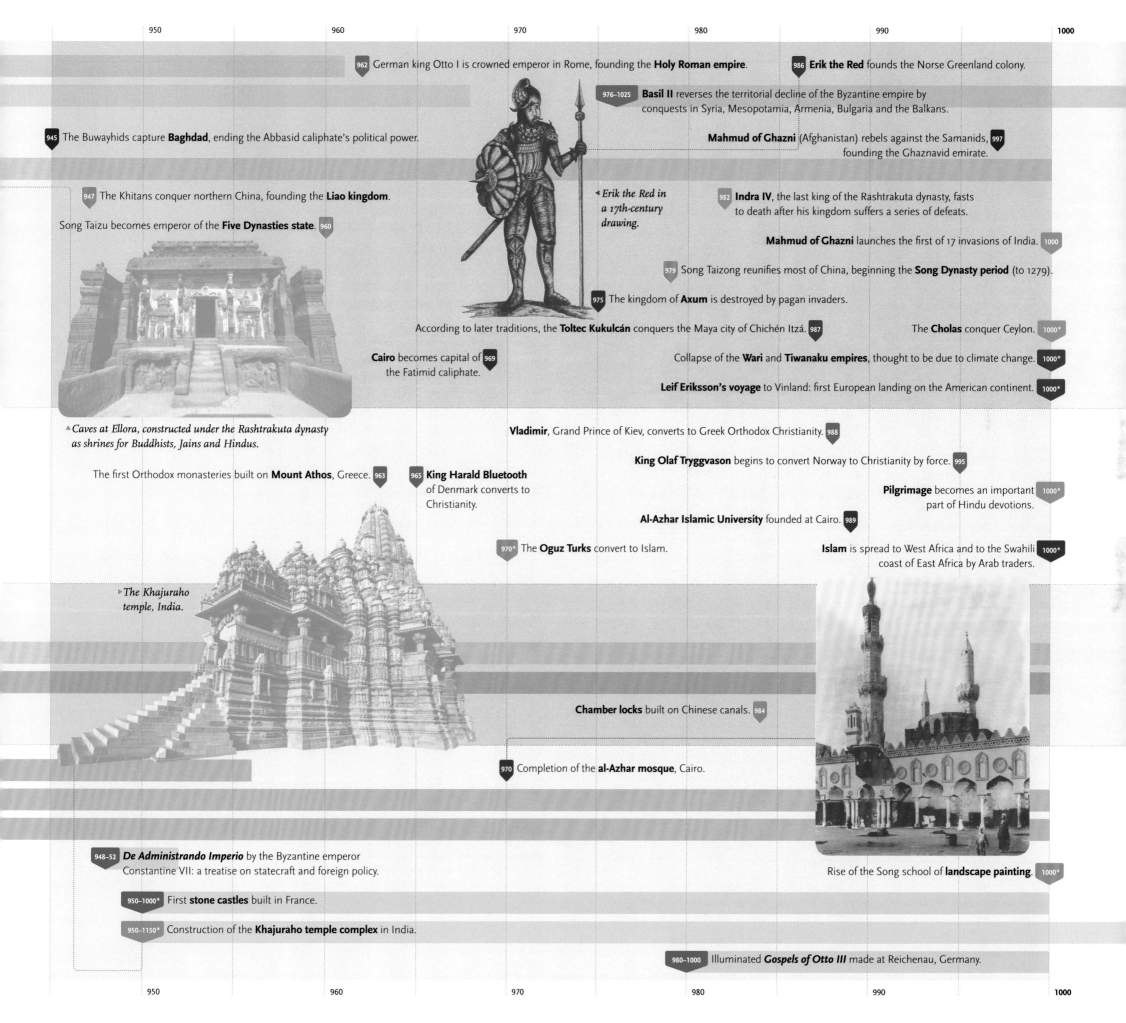

1100

THE TURKISH CONQUEST OF THE MIDDLE EAST; THE FIRST CRUSADE; THE FIRST TOWNS IN NORTH AMERICA

Before the 11th century, the Turks were known in the Middle East mainly as a source of mamluks (slave soldiers). One such was Mahmud of Ghazni, who had overthrown his master and created his own emirate in Afghanistan in 997. A militant Muslim, Mahmud spent his reign (997–1030) sacking the Hindu temples of northern India and conquering Punjab. Between 1037 and 1086 the Seljuk Turks, a branch of the nomadic Oguz Turks, invaded and conquered almost all of the Middle East. The Seljuk sultanate broke up into rival emirates in 1092. The lasting legacy of the Seljuk invasion was that Greek-speaking Anatolia, seized from the Byzantines in 1071–80, became culturally and linguistically Turkish. The loss of manpower seriously weakened the Byzantine empire.

The Seljuk conquests provoked a military response from Catholic Western Europe: the First Crusade, which captured Jerusalem in 1099 and established small Christian states in Syria and Palestine. The crusade's success owed much to Muslim disunity and was an important sign of growing prosperity and confidence within the Catholic West. The Normans, descendants of Viking settlers in France, conquered Muslim and Byzantine lands in southern Italy and Sicily, conquered England and joined the crusades.

Around 1000, the Thule Inuit began to spread east from the Bering Straits towards Greenland: one of the most sophisticated hunter-gatherer cultures, it was superbly adapted to the Arctic environment. Around the same time, Vikings became the first Europeans to reach the Americas, but their attempts to settle failed. By 1100 North America's first towns were developing in the Mississippi basin. In Southeast Asia, Tai peoples began migrating south into present-day Thailand, while, in the first half of the 11th century, the region was raided by the powerful Cholas of south India.

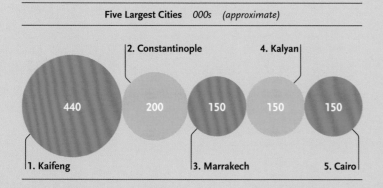

Five Largest Cities *000s (approximate)*

1. Kaifeng — 440
2. Constantinople — 200
3. Marrakech — 150
4. Kalyan — 150
5. Cairo — 150

Thule Inuit culture

Thule Inuit culture

Norse

Aleuts

Sub-Arctic caribou hunters

Central plateau hunter-fisher-gatherers

Great Plains bison hunters

Eastern Woodlands hunter-gatherers

West coast fishers, hunters and gatherers

Woodland farmers

Desert hunter-gatherers

Ancestral Pueblo culture

Mississippian temple mound cultures

Hohokam culture

Mogollon culture

Maize farmers

MAYA CITY STATES

TOLTEC EMPIRE

Arawak

ZAPOTECS

North Andean chiefdoms

Arawak

Polynesians

Amazonian chiefdoms

Tupi

SMALL ANDEAN KINGDOMS AND CITY STATES

Savanna hunter-gatherers

Guarani

Araucanians

Pampas hunters

Fishers and marine mammal hunters

Legend:
- Hunter-gatherers
- Settled farming cultures and peoples
- Pastoral nomads
- Complex farming societies/chiefdoms
- Urbanized societies/kingdoms
- Empires
- Uninhabited

150° 120° 90° 60°

IRISH KINGDOMS 1
WELSH KINGDOMS 2
EARLDOM OF ORKNEY 3
SCOTLAND 4
ENGLAND 5
ICELANDIC COMMONWEALTH

Sami
Samoyeds
Yakuts
Tungus
Palaeo-Siberians
Thule Inuit culture

NORWAY
SWEDEN
Finns
NOVGOROD
ROSTOV-SUZDAL
Volga Bulgars
Kimek Turks
Kyrgyz
Mongols
Tatars
LIAO
Jürchen
Ainu

DENMARK
Balts
POLAND
KIEV
CHERNIGOV
Kipchak-Cuman Confederation (Turks)
Pechenegs
Oguz Turks
KARAKHANID KHANATE
KARA-KHOJA KHANATES
XIXIA (Tanguts)
KOREA
JAPAN

HOLY ROMAN EMPIRE
FRANCE
HUNGARY
Alans
2 Constantinople
BYZANTINE EMPIRE
SMALL SELJUK EMIRATES
GREAT SELJUK TURK SULTANATE
KASHMIR
TIBET
1 Kaifeng
SONG EMPIRE

LEÓN AND CASTILE
ZIRID EMIRATE
5 Cairo
CRUSADER STATES
GHAZNAVID EMPIRE
PALAS
DALI

3 Marrakech
HAMMADID EMIRATE
FATIMID CALIPHATE
SINDH
HINDU KINGDOMS
19 Tais
20

ALMORAVID EMPIRE (Berbers)
Touaregs
MAKURIA
Bedouin Arabs
4 Kalyan
CHALUKYAS
ARAKAN
DAI VIET

TAKRUR
SMALL KINGDOMS
Zaghawa
KANEM
ALODIA
YEMEN
CHOLAS
KHMER
CHAMPA

MALI
SONGHAY
West African chiefdoms
Nilotic pastoralists
ETHIOPIA
Cushitic pastoralists
PANDYAS
POLONNARUWA
SRIVIJAYA
Malays
Micronesians

NAVARRE 6
SMALL CHRISTIAN STATES 7
VENICE 8
NORMAN PRINCIPALITIES 9
SERBIA 10
POLOTSK 11
GALICH-VOLHYNIA 12
SMOLENSK 13
PEREYASLAVL 14

GEORGIA 15
SHIRVAN 16
SELJUK SULTANATE OF RUM 17
DANISHMEND EMIRATE 18
BAGAN 19
HARIPUNJAYA (Mons) 20

SWAHILI CITY STATES
Bantu farmers and pastoralists
Mapungubwe
Malagasy
SMALL MALAY STATES
Papuans
Melanesians
Polynesians

San
Khoikhoi pastoralists
Australian Aborigines
Tasmanians

1100

In the 11th century, China's Song dynasty was forced to pay tribute to its powerful Khitan and Tangut neighbours in return for peace. This China was easily able to afford: the introduction of new strains of rice from Vietnam made growing two crops a year possible, greatly increasing the prosperity of the countryside and allowing peasant farmers to support larger families. Chinese technology was the most sophisticated in the world and can claim the first use of the magnetic compass for navigation, the invention of water-powered mechanical clocks, and the earliest movable-type printing (using clay type). The thousands of characters needed to print the Chinese script meant, however, that nearly all books were printed from carved plates.

This was the era of the crusades, primarily led by the papacy. The popular response to its call for an expedition to free the Holy Land from Muslim control was a sign of its unchallenged spiritual leadership in Catholic Europe. Its power was the result of reforms begun in 1046 aimed at freeing the church from lay control. Pope Gregory VII's decree abolishing lay investiture of bishops led to an open conflict, the Investiture Contest, with the Holy Roman emperor Henry IV, whose government depended on control of the church. The dispute caused a civil war that severely damaged the emperor's authority and began the empire's development into a loose confederation of princely states. The newly assertive papacy had already caused a permanent schism between the Roman Catholic church and the Greek Orthodox church in 1054.

The completion in 1008 by Firdawsi of the *Shahnameh* (*The Book of Kings*) was a landmark in the revival of Persian cultural identity. Written in a pure Persian, excluding Arabic influences that had crept into the language, Firdawsi's legendary history of the kings of Persia quickly established itself as the national epic.

World Population *(approximate)*

7 BILLION

350 million

200 BC   **1100**   2010

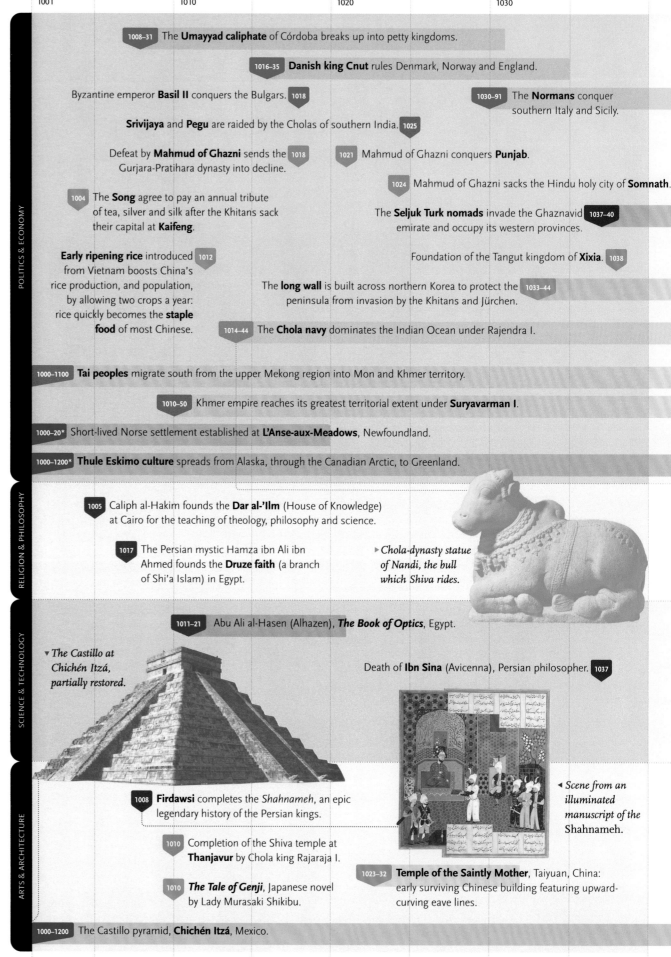

1001   1010   1020   1030

POLITICS & ECONOMY

1008–31 The **Umayyad caliphate** of Córdoba breaks up into petty kingdoms.

1016–35 **Danish king Cnut** rules Denmark, Norway and England.

Byzantine emperor **Basil II** conquers the Bulgars. **1018**

1030–91 The **Normans** conquer southern Italy and Sicily.

Srivijaya and **Pegu** are raided by the Cholas of southern India. **1025**

Defeat by **Mahmud of Ghazni** sends the **1018** Gurjara-Pratihara dynasty into decline.

1021 Mahmud of Ghazni conquers **Punjab**.

1024 Mahmud of Ghazni sacks the Hindu holy city of **Somnath**.

1004 The **Song** agree to pay an annual tribute of tea, silver and silk after the Khitans sack their capital at **Kaifeng**.

The **Seljuk Turk nomads** invade the Ghaznavid **1037–40** emirate and occupy its western provinces.

Early ripening rice introduced **1012** from Vietnam boosts China's rice production, and population, by allowing two crops a year: rice quickly becomes the **staple food** of most Chinese.

Foundation of the Tangut kingdom of **Xixia**. **1038**

The **long wall** is built across northern Korea to protect the **1033–44** peninsula from invasion by the Khitans and Jürchen.

1014–44 The **Chola navy** dominates the Indian Ocean under Rajendra I.

1000–1100 **Tai peoples** migrate south from the upper Mekong region into Mon and Khmer territory.

1010–50 Khmer empire reaches its greatest territorial extent under **Suryavarman I**.

1000–20* Short-lived Norse settlement established at **L'Anse-aux-Meadows**, Newfoundland.

1000–1200* **Thule Eskimo culture** spreads from Alaska, through the Canadian Arctic, to Greenland.

RELIGION & PHILOSOPHY

1005 Caliph al-Hakim founds the **Dar al-'Ilm** (House of Knowledge) at Cairo for the teaching of theology, philosophy and science.

1017 The Persian mystic Hamza ibn Ali ibn Ahmed founds the **Druze faith** (a branch of Shi'a Islam) in Egypt.

▶ *Chola-dynasty statue of Nandi, the bull which Shiva rides.*

SCIENCE & TECHNOLOGY

1011–21 Abu Ali al-Hasen (Alhazen), *The Book of Optics*, Egypt.

Death of **Ibn Sina** (Avicenna), Persian philosopher. **1037**

▼ *The Castillo at Chichén Itzá, partially restored.*

ARTS & ARCHITECTURE

1008 **Firdawsi** completes the *Shahnameh*, an epic legendary history of the Persian kings.

1010 Completion of the Shiva temple at **Thanjavur** by Chola king Rajaraja I.

1010 *The Tale of Genji*, Japanese novel by Lady Murasaki Shikibu.

1023–32 **Temple of the Saintly Mother**, Taiyuan, China: early surviving Chinese building featuring upward-curving eave lines.

◀ *Scene from an illuminated manuscript of the Shahnameh.*

1000–1200 The Castillo pyramid, **Chichén Itzá**, Mexico.

1001   1010   1020   1030

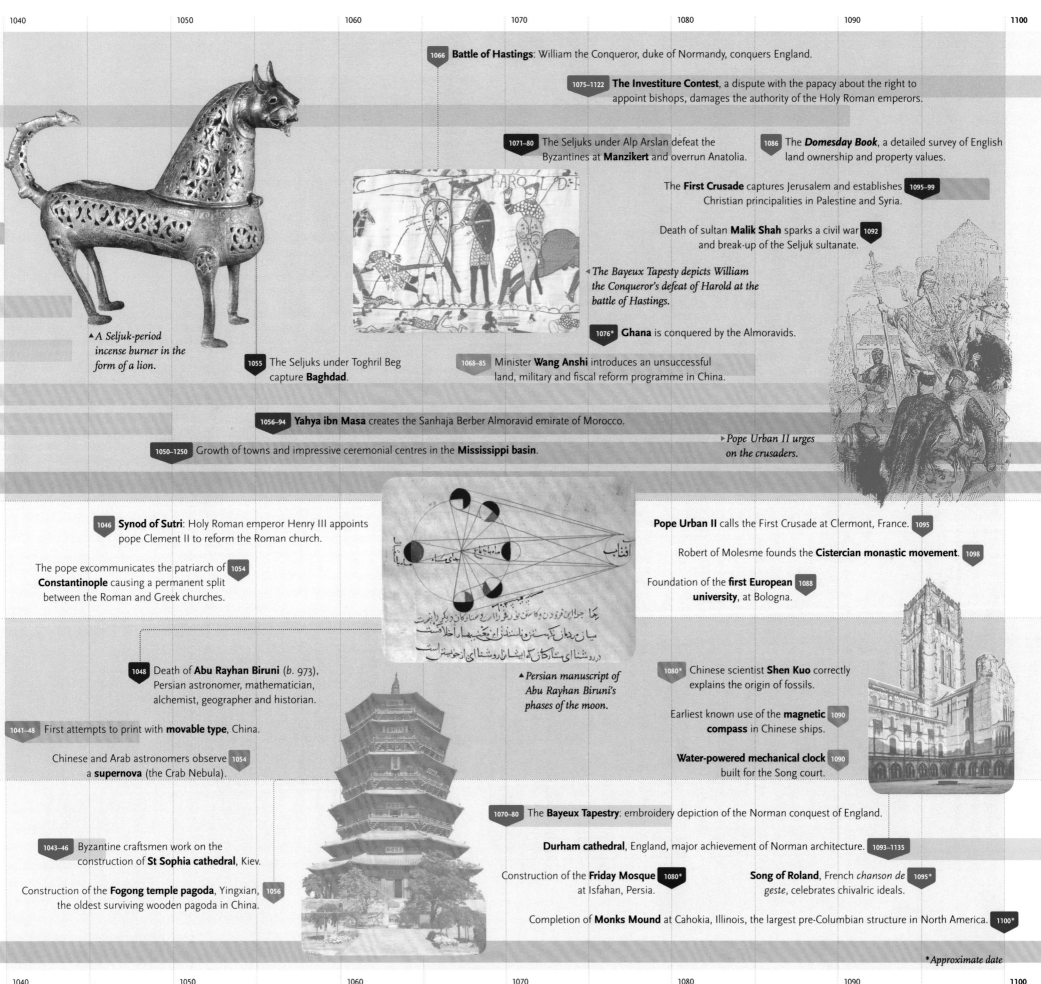

1066 **Battle of Hastings**: William the Conqueror, duke of Normandy, conquers England.

1075–1122 **The Investiture Contest**, a dispute with the papacy about the right to appoint bishops, damages the authority of the Holy Roman emperors.

1071–80 The Seljuks under Alp Arslan defeat the Byzantines at **Manzikert** and overrun Anatolia.

1086 The **Domesday Book**, a detailed survey of English land ownership and property values.

The **First Crusade** captures Jerusalem and establishes Christian principalities in Palestine and Syria. **1095–99**

Death of sultan **Malik Shah** sparks a civil war and break-up of the Seljuk sultanate. **1092**

◄ *The Bayeux Tapesty depicts William the Conqueror's defeat of Harold at the battle of Hastings.*

▲ *A Seljuk-period incense burner in the form of a lion.*

1076* **Ghana** is conquered by the Almoravids.

1055 The Seljuks under Toghril Beg capture **Baghdad**.

1068–85 Minister **Wang Anshi** introduces an unsuccessful land, military and fiscal reform programme in China.

1056–94 **Yahya ibn Masa** creates the Sanhaja Berber Almoravid emirate of Morocco.

1050–1250 Growth of towns and impressive ceremonial centres in the **Mississippi basin**.

▶ *Pope Urban II urges on the crusaders.*

1046 **Synod of Sutri**: Holy Roman emperor Henry III appoints pope Clement II to reform the Roman church.

The pope excommunicates the patriarch of **1054** **Constantinople** causing a permanent split between the Roman and Greek churches.

Pope **Urban II** calls the First Crusade at Clermont, France. **1095**

Robert of Molesme founds the **Cistercian monastic movement**. **1098**

Foundation of the **first European university**, at Bologna. **1088**

1048 Death of **Abu Rayhan Biruni** (*b.* 973), Persian astronomer, mathematician, alchemist, geographer and historian.

1041–48 First attempts to print with **movable type**, China.

Chinese and Arab astronomers observe **1054** a **supernova** (the Crab Nebula).

▲ *Persian manuscript of Abu Rayhan Biruni's phases of the moon.*

1080* Chinese scientist **Shen Kuo** correctly explains the origin of fossils.

Earliest known use of the **magnetic compass** in Chinese ships. **1090**

Water-powered mechanical clock **1090** built for the Song court.

The **Bayeux Tapestry**: embroidery depiction of the Norman conquest of England. **1070–80**

Durham cathedral, England, major achievement of Norman architecture. **1093–1135**

1043–46 Byzantine craftsmen work on the construction of **St Sophia cathedral**, Kiev.

Construction of the **Fogong temple pagoda**, Yingxian, **1056** the oldest surviving wooden pagoda in China.

Construction of the **Friday Mosque** **1080*** at Isfahan, Persia.

Song of Roland, French *chanson de* **1095*** *geste*, celebrates chivalric ideals.

Completion of **Monks Mound** at Cahokia, Illinois, the largest pre-Columbian structure in North America. **1100***

*Approximate date

1206

CHINGGIS KHAN UNITES THE MONGOL TRIBES; INDIA COMES UNDER MUSLIM DOMINION; FALL OF THE TOLTECS

In 11th- and 12th-century Japan, samurai clans competed for control over weak emperors. In 1185 the Minamoto clan destroyed its main rival, the Taira, to emerge supreme. The clan's leader, Minamoto Yoritomo, established a *bakufu* (military government) at Kamakura in 1192. The emperor, now merely the nominal ruler, granted Yoritomo the title shogun (generalissimo), beginning a period of military government that lasted until 1868. In 1125, the recently formed Jürchen state of Jin conquered the Khitan kingdom of Liao, before turning on the Song, taking their capital at Kaifeng. The end of the period saw the emergence of a new nomad confederation on the eastern steppes. In 1204–6, Temujin united the Mongol tribes under his leadership and adopted the title Chinggis (Genghis) Khan (universal ruler).

The crusader states were thrown on the defensive when Zengi, emir of Mosul, began to restore Muslim unity in the 1120s. Saladin, the ruler of Egypt and Syria, recaptured Jerusalem in 1187 and reduced the crusader states to precarious coastal enclaves. The crusades did nothing to improve relations between the Catholic West and the Byzantine empire: the latter's power was broken when in 1204 crusaders captured Constantinople. At the end of the 12th century, most of northern India came under Muslim dominion after its conquest by Muhammad of Ghur (in Afghanistan). After Muhammad's murder in 1206, his Turkish slave-general Qutb-ud-Din seized power, founding a sultanate at Delhi.

The fall of the Toltec empire in 1168 created another longlasting power vacuum in Mexico. Around 1200 the Chimú state of the coastal lowlands of Peru emerged as the first extra-regional power since the fall of the Tiwanaku and Wari empires. At much the same time, New Zealand, the last large uninhabited land mass (except Antarctica), was settled by Polynesians from Tahiti.

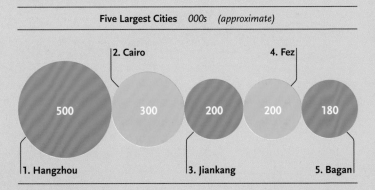

Five Largest Cities   000s *(approximate)*

1. Hangzhou	2. Cairo	3. Jiankang	4. Fez	5. Bagan
500	300	200	200	180

Hunter-gatherers

Settled farming cultures and peoples

Pastoral nomads

Complex farming societies/chiefdoms

Urbanized societies/ kingdoms

Empires

Uninhabited

IRISH **1** KINGDOMS
SCOTLAND **2**
WELSH **3** KINGDOMS
NAVARRE **4**
CASTILE **5**
ARAGON **6**

ICELANDIC COMMONWEALTH

Sami

NORWAY
SWEDEN
Finns
DENMARK
2 ENGLAND
1
3
HOLY ROMAN EMPIRE
FRANCE
POLAND
9
10
RUSSIAN PRINCIPALITIES
NOVGOROD
VLADIMIR-SUZDAL
Balts
KIEV
HUNGARY
Kipchak-Cuman Confederation
Alans
Volga Bulgars

Samoyeds
Yakuts
Tungus
Palaeo-Siberians
Thule Inuit culture

Arctic Circle

LEÓN
PORTUGAL
4
5 **6**
7 **11**
12
16
Oguz Turks
GEORGIA
8
14
15 **17**
13
18
to Venice
20
2 Cairo
AYYUBID SULTANATE
4 Fez
ALMOHAD EMIRATE
19
KHWAREZM SHAHDOM
ABBASID CALIPHATE

Kyrgyz
MONGOL KHANATE

KARAKHITAI KHANATE
KARA-KHOJA KHANATES
KASHMIR
XIXIA
TIBET
JIN (Jürchen)
Ainu
KOREA
JAPAN

Touaregs
MAKURIA
TAKRUR
DIAFUNU
SOSSO SONGHAY
KANEM
ALODIA
Zaghawa
YEMEN
ETHIOPIA
Bedouin Arabs
OMAN
SULTANATE OF DELHI
NEPAL
HINDU KINGDOMS
YADAVAS
KAKATIYAS
DALI
ARAKAN
5 Bagan
22
23
3 Jiankang
SONG EMPIRE
1 Hangzhou
DAI VIET
CHAMPA

Tropic of Cancer

21 MALI
Yoruba
HAUSA STATES
21
IFE
Nilotic pastoralists
Cushitic pastoralists
21
HOYSALAS
HINDU KINGDOMS
SINHALESE KINGDOMS
KHMER
Malays
Micronesians

VENICE **7**
KINGDOM OF **8** SICILY (Norman)
POLOTSK **9**
SMOLENSK **10**
SERBIA **11**
BULGARIA **12**
DESPOTATE OF **13** EPIRUS (Byzantines)
LATIN EMPIRE **14** (Crusaders)
EMPIRE OF **15** NICAEA (Byzantines)
EMPIRE OF **16** TREBIZOND (Byzantines)

SELJUK SULTANATE **17** OF RUM
LESSER ARMENIA **18**
SMALL EMIRATES **19**
CRUSADER STATES **20**

SMALL **21** KINGDOMS
BAGAN **22**
HARIPUNJAYA **23**

SWAHILI CITY STATES
Bantu farmers and pastoralists
Mapungubwe
Malagasy
SRIVIJAYA
SMALL MALAY STATES
Papuans
Melanesians

Equator

San
Khoikhoi pastoralists

Australian Aborigines

Tropic of Capricorn

Polynesians

c. 1200

Tasmanians

Maoris (Polynesians)

0°
30°
60°
90°
120°
150°
180°
75°
45°
45°

1206

Song China continued to demonstrate outstanding inventiveness during the 12th century, devising the earliest cannon and constructing ships with watertight bulkheads and even paddlewheels. By around 1200 the Chinese were also using water-powered machinery for textile production, 500 years before its use in Britain's Industrial Revolution. The commercial economy was huge, with much local and longer-distance trade. Merchants ran their own business affairs, but the state kept strict political control and did not allow cities to govern themselves. The division of property in each generation meant that few families stayed wealthy.

The 12th century saw a strong resurgence of cultural life in Western Europe. One consequence of the Investiture Contest of 1075–1122 was to draw scholars' attention to the contradictions and inconsistencies in scripture and in both secular and church law. This led to renewed interest in the works of Classical Greek philosophers, especially Aristotle, and the application of their methods to the study of theology and law. Most of Aristotle's works were translated into Latin from Arabic versions obtained in Muslim Spain, which still maintained a flourishing cultural life despite its political decline. Increased demand for education led to the foundation of cathedral schools across Europe, some of which developed into universities. Secular literature flourished: chivalric romances idealized the military aristocracy. Western European architecture produced its first truly original style, Gothic, characterized by pointed arches and soaring vaults.

In North America, the years around 1200 saw the development of the Southeastern Ceremonial Complex among the semi-urbanized Mississippian cultures. The complex was characterized by common cosmological motifs and the exchange of exotic materials and symbolic objects associated with rulership and war.

World Population (approximate)

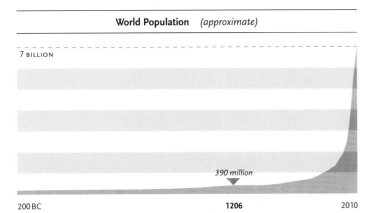

7 BILLION

390 million

200 BC   1206   2010

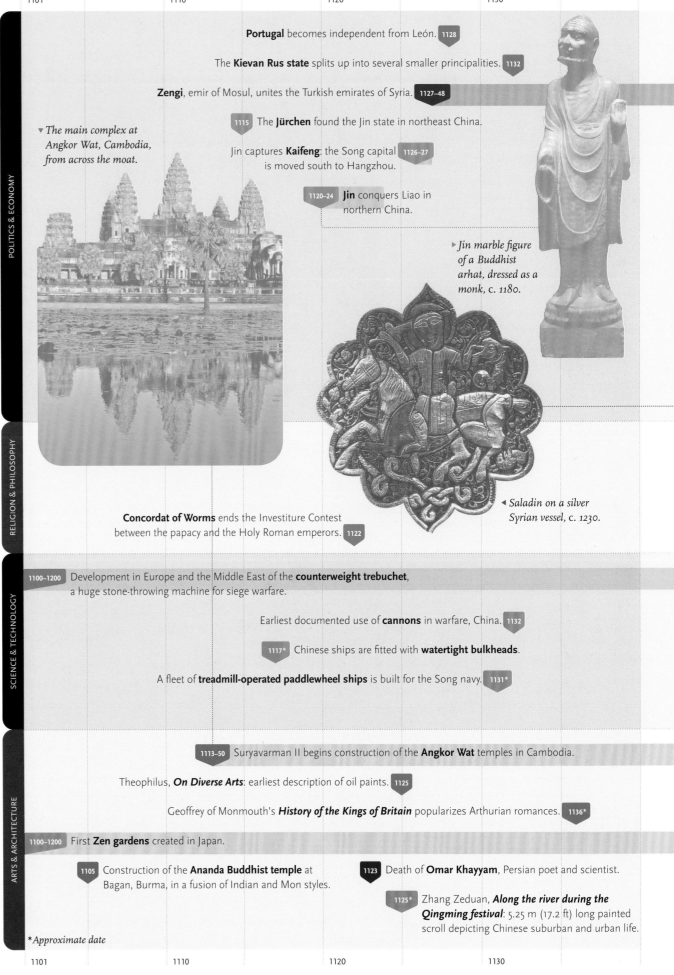

1101   1110   1120   1130

POLITICS & ECONOMY

Portugal becomes independent from León. `1128`

The **Kievan Rus state** splits up into several smaller principalities. `1132`

Zengi, emir of Mosul, unites the Turkish emirates of Syria. `1127–48`

`1115` The **Jürchen** found the Jin state in northeast China.

Jin captures **Kaifeng**: the Song capital `1126–27` is moved south to Hangzhou.

`1120–24` **Jin** conquers Liao in northern China.

▼ *The main complex at Angkor Wat, Cambodia, from across the moat.*

▶ *Jin marble figure of a Buddhist arhat, dressed as a monk, c. 1180.*

RELIGION & PHILOSOPHY

◀ *Saladin on a silver Syrian vessel, c. 1230.*

Concordat of Worms ends the Investiture Contest between the papacy and the Holy Roman emperors. `1122`

SCIENCE & TECHNOLOGY

`1100–1200` Development in Europe and the Middle East of the **counterweight trebuchet**, a huge stone-throwing machine for siege warfare.

Earliest documented use of **cannons** in warfare, China. `1132`

`1117*` Chinese ships are fitted with **watertight bulkheads**.

A fleet of **treadmill-operated paddlewheel ships** is built for the Song navy. `1131*`

ARTS & ARCHITECTURE

`1113–50` Suryavarman II begins construction of the **Angkor Wat** temples in Cambodia.

Theophilus, ***On Diverse Arts***: earliest description of oil paints. `1125`

Geoffrey of Monmouth's ***History of the Kings of Britain*** popularizes Arthurian romances. `1136*`

`1100–1200` First **Zen gardens** created in Japan.

`1105` Construction of the **Ananda Buddhist temple** at Bagan, Burma, in a fusion of Indian and Mon styles.

`1123` Death of **Omar Khayyam**, Persian poet and scientist.

`1125*` Zhang Zeduan, ***Along the river during the Qingming festival***: 5.25 m (17.2 ft) long painted scroll depicting Chinese suburban and urban life.

*Approximate date

1101   1110   1120   1130

1145–48 The **Second Crusade** ends in failure to capture Damascus.

1180 **Serbia** gains independence from the Byzantine empire.

1180–1223 France gains power and prestige under **Philip Augustus**.

1151 The **Ghaznavid emirate** is overthrown by the governor of Ghur.

The **Third Crusade** saves the crusader states from **1189–91** extinction but fails to recapture Jerusalem.

The **Fourth Crusade** captures **1204** Constantinople and founds the Latin empire there.

The **Taira samurai clan** win **1156** control of the Japanese emperor.

Saladin defeats the crusaders at **1187** Hattin and recaptures Jerusalem.

1147 The **Almohads** overthrow the Almoravid emirate of Morocco.

▶ *Siege of Acre from a 14th-century French manuscript.*

1187–91 The **Yadava dynasty** under Bhillama becomes the dominant power in the Deccan, India.

Destruction of **Tula** and collapse of the Toltec state in Mexico. **1168**

1175–1200 **Muhammad of Ghur** (in Afghanistan) conquers northern India: India remains under Muslim dominance until the 18th century.

Muhammad of Ghur is murdered: **Qutb-ud-Din** seizes power and founds a sultanate at Delhi; his **Mamluk** (slave) dynasty rules until 1290. **1206**

The Taira are destroyed by the **Minamoto samurai clan** at the sea battle of Dan-no-ura. **1185**

Temujin unites the Mongols and **1204–6** takes the title **Chinggis Khan**.

Samurai leader **Minamoto Yoritomo** becomes the first shogun (military governor) of Japan: military government continues until 1868. **1192**

◀ *Column in the form of a Toltec warrior from the site of Tula, Mexico.*

Cham naval expedition sacks **Angkor**. **1177**

Polynesians from Tahiti settle **New Zealand**. **1200***

Saladin conquers Egypt for the Zangid emirate. **1169–71**

Beginning of **Chimú expansion** in the coastal lowlands of Peru. **1200***

1174–77 Saladin rebels against the Zangid emirate and seizes power in Egypt and Syria, founding the **Ayyubid sultanate**.

Foundation of the **University of Paris**. **1170**

Muin ud-Din Chishti introduces **Sufism** to India. **1190***

1193 The Buddhist university at **Nalanda** is destroyed by a Muslim army.

1140 Gratian's ***Decretum*** applies dialectic (logic) to the study of law.

1163 A **synagogue** is built in Kaifeng, China.

1191 **Zen Buddhism** introduced to Japan.

1141 The philosopher **Peter Abelard** is condemned for heresy for his rationalist approach to the scriptures.

Development of the **Southeastern Ceremonial Complex** in the Mississippian cultures. **1200***

▶ *Chinggis Khan fights in a battle; a 14th-century scene.*

Death of **Ibn Rushd** (Averröes), Spanish Muslim philosopher and scientist. **1198**

Earliest recorded **European windmills** operating in England. **1191**

1154 Al-Idrisi presents **Roger II of Sicily** with a world map that brings together Western and Islamic knowledge.

Al-Jazari, ***The Book of Knowledge of Ingenious Mechanical Devices***, describes over **1206** 50 machines utilizing camshafts, crankshafts, pistons and escapement mechanisms.

Water-powered textile machinery is used in China. **1200***

Construction of **Nan Madol ceremonial** **1200*** **centre** on Pohnpei, Micronesia.

▶ *Engraved stone palette on which a rattlesnake encircles a hand with an eye, from Moundville, Alabama.*

Rock-cut churches at Lalibela, Ethiopia. **1200***

1193 **Qubbat-ul-Islam mosque** begun at Delhi.

1140* Abbey church of St Denis, near Paris, considered the **first building in the Gothic style**.

Construction of temple mounds and **1200*** plaza at **Moundville**, Alabama.

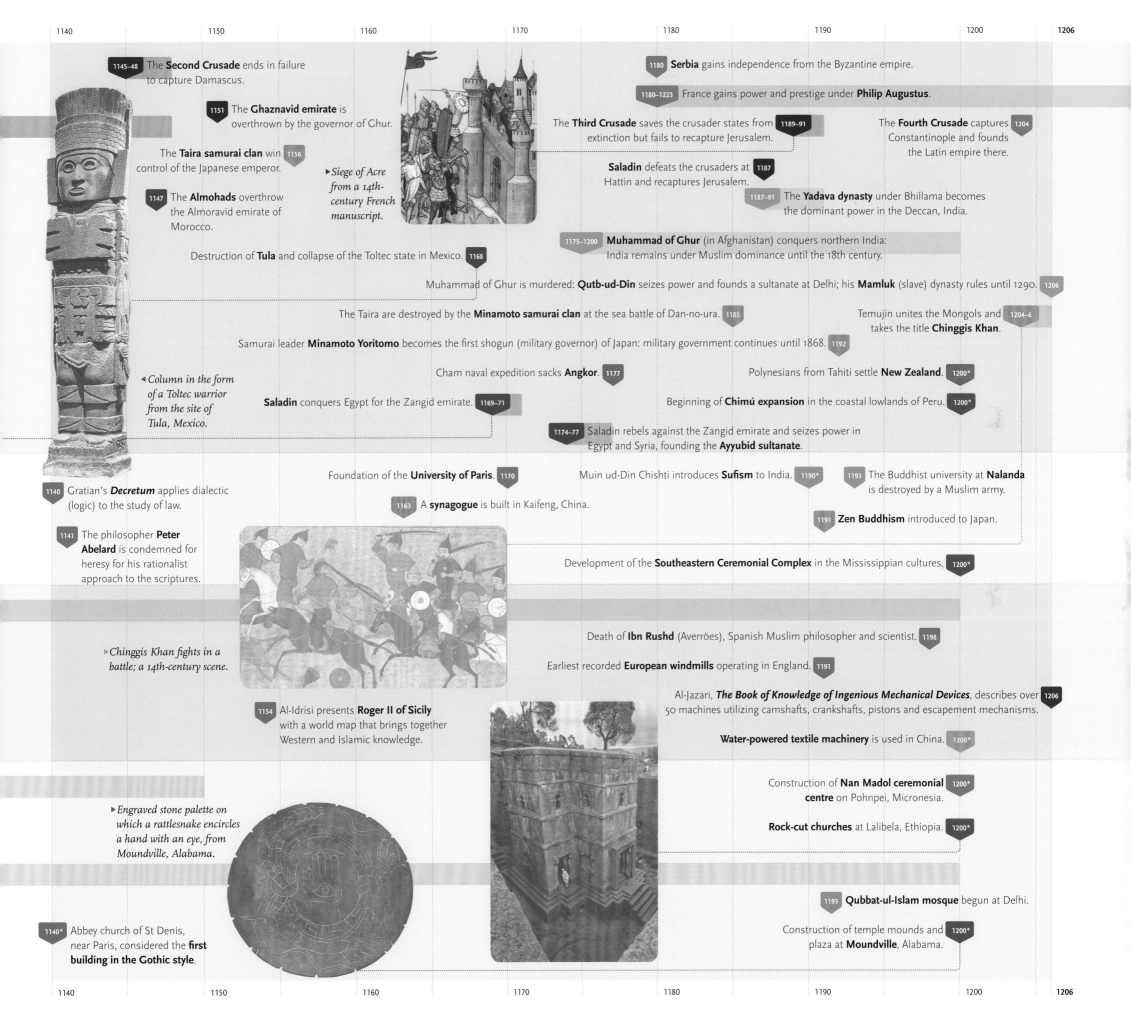

1300

DOMINATION AND FRAGMENTATION OF THE MONGOL EMPIRE; THE RISE OF MALI AND GREAT ZIMBABWE IN AFRICA

The 13th century was the century of the nomads. To consolidate the unity of the Mongols, Chinggis Khan needed success in war. In 1209 he began 70 years of Mongol conquests with raids on Xixia and the Uighurs. By the time of his death in 1227, Chinggis Khan's empire stretched from Manchuria to the Caspian Sea. The speed, manoeuvrability and firepower of his armies of disciplined cavalry archers overwhelmed all opposition.

The Mongols systematically committed horrific atrocities, persuading many of their enemies to submit quickly and enrolling their forces into the Mongol armies, fuelling further conquests. Mongol attacks continued in East Asia, the Middle East and Russia under Chinggis Khan's son Ögedei and his grandsons Güyük and Möngke. By 1259 the Mongols ruled the greatest contiguous land empire in world history, exceeded in area only by the future British empire.

In 1260 Khubilai Khan became Great Khan. The last major Mongol conquest was his conquest of the Song empire, completed in 1279. Khubilai's later campaigns to extend Mongol rule to Japan and Southeast Asia were failures, however. The sultanate of Delhi and the Mamluk sultanate of Egypt also successfully repelled Mongol invasions. The Mongol empire was too vast to be ruled by one man, and so subordinate khanates were created to govern the western conquests. After the accession of Khubilai as Great Khan, the western khanates effectively became independent.

West Africa came to be dominated in this period by the Mali empire, which prospered by controlling the region's gold mines – the Old World's most important source of gold before the European discovery of the Americas. Southern Africa saw the rise of its first major kingdom at Great Zimbabwe.

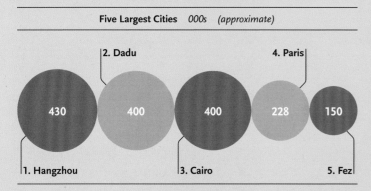

Five Largest Cities *000s (approximate)*

- 2. Dadu — 400
- 4. Paris — 228
- 1. Hangzhou — 430
- 3. Cairo — 400
- 5. Fez — 150

Thule Inuit culture

Thule Inuit culture

Aleuts

Sub-Arctic caribou hunters

West coast fishers, hunters and gatherers

Central plateau hunter-fisher-gatherers

Great Plains bison hunters

Woodlands hunter-gatherers

Woodlands farmers

Desert hunter-gatherers

Ancestral Pueblo culture

Mississippian temple mound cultures

Hohokam culture

Mogollon culture

Maize farmers

MAYA CITY STATES

MEXICAN CITY STATES

Arawak

MIXTECS

ZAPOTECS

Caribs

North Andean chiefdoms

Arawak

Polynesians

CHIMÚ

Amazonian chiefdoms

Tupi

SMALL ANDEAN KINGDOMS AND CITY STATES

AYMARA KINGDOMS

Savanna hunter-gatherers

Guarani

Araucanians

Pampas hunters

Fishers and marine mammal hunters

Hunter-gatherers

Urbanized societies/kingdoms

Settled farming cultures and peoples

Empires

Pastoral nomads

Uninhabited

Complex farming societies/chiefdoms

Mongol empire and vassal states

150°   120°   90°   60°

IRISH
KINGDOMS **1**
SCOTLAND **2**
NAVARRE **3**
EMIRATE OF **4**
GRANADA
VENICE **5**
PAPAL **6**
STATES

KINGDOM OF **7**
NAPLES
TEUTONIC KNIGHTS **8**
(Crusaders)
To DENMARK **9**
POLISH **10**
PRINCIPALITIES
LITHUANIA **11**
SERBIA **12**
BULGARIA **13**
MINOR CHRISTIAN **14**
STATES
TO VENICE **15**

16 EMPIRE OF
TREBIZOND
17 SELJUK SULTANATE
OF RUM
18 MAKURIA
19 SMALL STATES

20 BURMESE
KINGDOMS
21 LANNATHAI
(Thais)
22 SUKHOTHAI
(Thais)

Sami

Samoyeds

Yakuts

Tungus

Palaeo-Siberians

Thule
Inuit
culture

NORWAY   SWEDEN
2
DENMARK   **8**   **9**

NOVGOROD

RUSSIAN
PRINCIPALITIES

KHANATE OF THE
GOLDEN HORDE

Ainu

1
ENGLAND   HOLY
10   ROMAN
EMPIRE

4
Paris
FRANCE

11

HUNGARY

GEORGIA

CHAGATAI
KHANATE

GREAT
KHANATE

2
Dadu

JAPAN

CASTILE   **3**
5
PORTUGAL   ARAGON   **6**   **7**
4   **12**
13
BYZANTINE
EMPIRE
16
17

1
Hangzhou

5
Fez
MARINID
CALIPHATE   HAFSID
CALIPHATE   **14**
15
CYPRUS
3
Cairo

ILKHANATE

KASHMIR

TIBET

ZAYYANID
EMIRATE

MAMLUK
SULTANATE

SULTANATE
OF DELHI

Touaregs

Bedouin
Arabs   OMAN

RAJPUTS

HINDU
KINGDOMS

20

21

DAI VIET

YADAVAS   **22**   CHAMPA

18
DARFUR   ALODIA
YEMEN
MALI   KANEM   ETHIOPIA
HAUSA
STATES
Yoruba   **19**   IFAT
IFE   BENIN   Nilotic   Cushitic
pastoralists   pastoralists

HADRAMAUT

ARAKAN
GANGAS
KAKATIYAS   PEGU

KHMER

Malays

Micronesians

HOYSALAS   PANDYAS

MAJAPAHIT

SMALL
MALAY
STATES

Papuans

Bantu
farmers and
pastoralists

SWAHILI
CITY
STATES

Melanesians

GREAT
ZIMBABWE

Malagasy

San

Australian Aborigines

Khoikhoi
pastoralists

Tasmanians

Maoris

Arctic Circle

Tropic of Cancer

Equator

Tropic of Capricorn

0°   30°   60°   90°   120°   150°   180°

75°

45°

45°

1300

Mongol conquests were savage and destructive. Worst affected were the Middle East and northern China. The Mongol sack of Baghdad in 1258 saw the destruction not only of the Abbasid caliphate but also of the city's great libraries, whose scholars were massacred. Mongol campaigns depopulated northern China, shifting the demographic and economic balance of the country to the south for the first time. Mongol rule eventually brought peace and security to a vast area of Eurasia, greatly increasing trade and cultural contacts between China and the West. Europeans travelled to China and took home the first eye-witness accounts of Chinese civilization.

By the end of the 13th century, the Mongols were beginning to be assimilated by the peoples they had conquered. The khanate of the Golden Horde officially adopted the language of its mainly Turkish subjects and in the 14th century, along with the Mongols of the Ilkhanate of Persia, it adopted Islam, stoking the bitter hostility of its Christian Russian tributaries. Khubilai Khan adopted the Chinese dynastic name Yuan and the whole apparatus of Chinese government. Culturally, the Great khanate became increasingly Sinicized. Traditional Mongol culture survived only on the steppes, where the Mongols could continue to lead their nomadic way of life.

The cultural revival of Western Europe continued in the 13th century, with major technological developments in timekeeping and optics. The invention of double-entry book-keeping in Italy was a sign of Europe's increasingly complex economy. A consequence of wider literacy was the rise of popular heretical movements challenging church authority on doctrine: the church suppressed them with the Inquisition and the crusades. Crusaders enjoyed success against Europe's last pagans in the Baltic but were expelled from the Holy Land and Byzantine empire.

World Population *(approximate)*

7 BILLION

400 million

200 BC   **1300**   2010

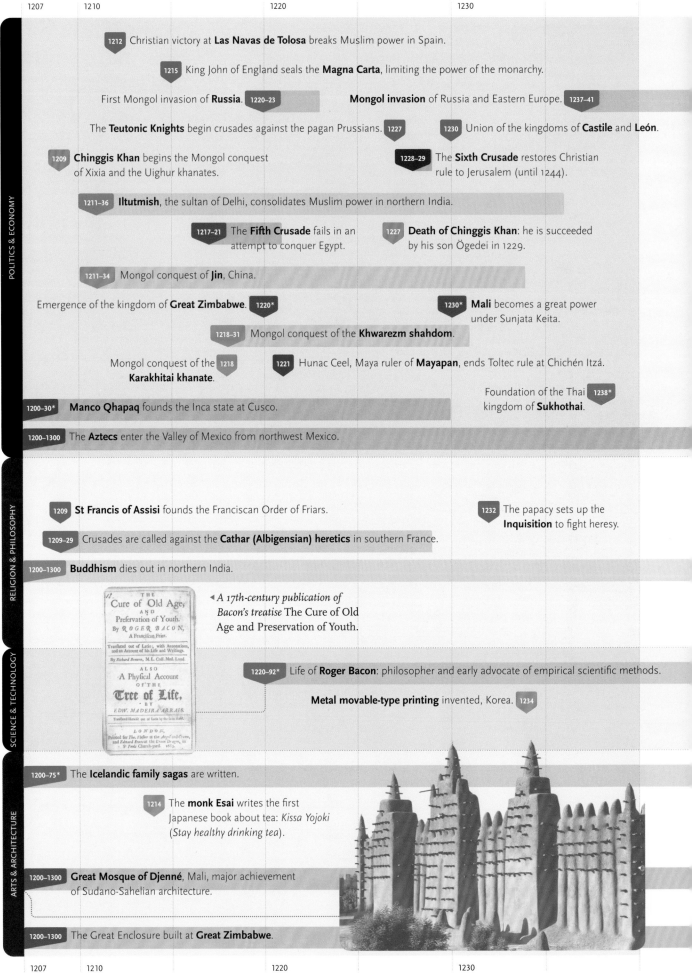

POLITICS & ECONOMY

1212 Christian victory at **Las Navas de Tolosa** breaks Muslim power in Spain.

1215 King John of England seals the **Magna Carta**, limiting the power of the monarchy.

First Mongol invasion of **Russia**. **1220–23**

Mongol invasion of Russia and Eastern Europe. **1237–41**

The **Teutonic Knights** begin crusades against the pagan Prussians. **1227**

1230 Union of the kingdoms of **Castile** and **León**.

1209 **Chinggis Khan** begins the Mongol conquest of Xixia and the Uighur khanates.

1228–29 The **Sixth Crusade** restores Christian rule to Jerusalem (until 1244).

1211–36 **Iltutmish**, the sultan of Delhi, consolidates Muslim power in northern India.

1217–21 The **Fifth Crusade** fails in an attempt to conquer Egypt.

1227 **Death of Chinggis Khan**: he is succeeded by his son Ögedei in 1229.

1211–34 Mongol conquest of **Jin**, China.

Emergence of the kingdom of **Great Zimbabwe**. **1220***

1230* **Mali** becomes a great power under Sunjata Keita.

1218–31 Mongol conquest of the **Khwarezm shahdom**.

Mongol conquest of the **1218** Karakhitai khanate.

1221 Hunac Ceel, Maya ruler of **Mayapan**, ends Toltec rule at Chichén Itzá.

Foundation of the Thai **1238*** kingdom of **Sukhothai**.

1200–30* **Manco Qhapaq** founds the Inca state at Cusco.

1200–1300 The **Aztecs** enter the Valley of Mexico from northwest Mexico.

RELIGION & PHILOSOPHY

1209 **St Francis of Assisi** founds the Franciscan Order of Friars.

1232 The papacy sets up the **Inquisition** to fight heresy.

1209–29 Crusades are called against the **Cathar (Albigensian) heretics** in southern France.

1200–1300 **Buddhism** dies out in northern India.

SCIENCE & TECHNOLOGY

◀ *A 17th-century publication of Bacon's treatise* The Cure of Old Age and Preservation of Youth.

1220–92* Life of **Roger Bacon**: philosopher and early advocate of empirical scientific methods.

Metal movable-type printing invented, Korea. **1234**

ARTS & ARCHITECTURE

1200–75* The **Icelandic family sagas** are written.

1214 The **monk Esai** writes the first Japanese book about tea: *Kissa Yojoki* (*Stay healthy drinking tea*).

1200–1300 **Great Mosque of Djenné**, Mali, major achievement of Sudano-Sahelian architecture.

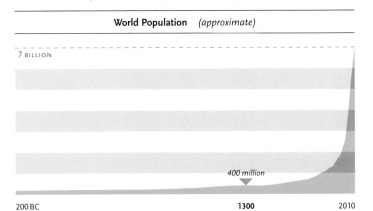

1200–1300 The Great Enclosure built at **Great Zimbabwe**.

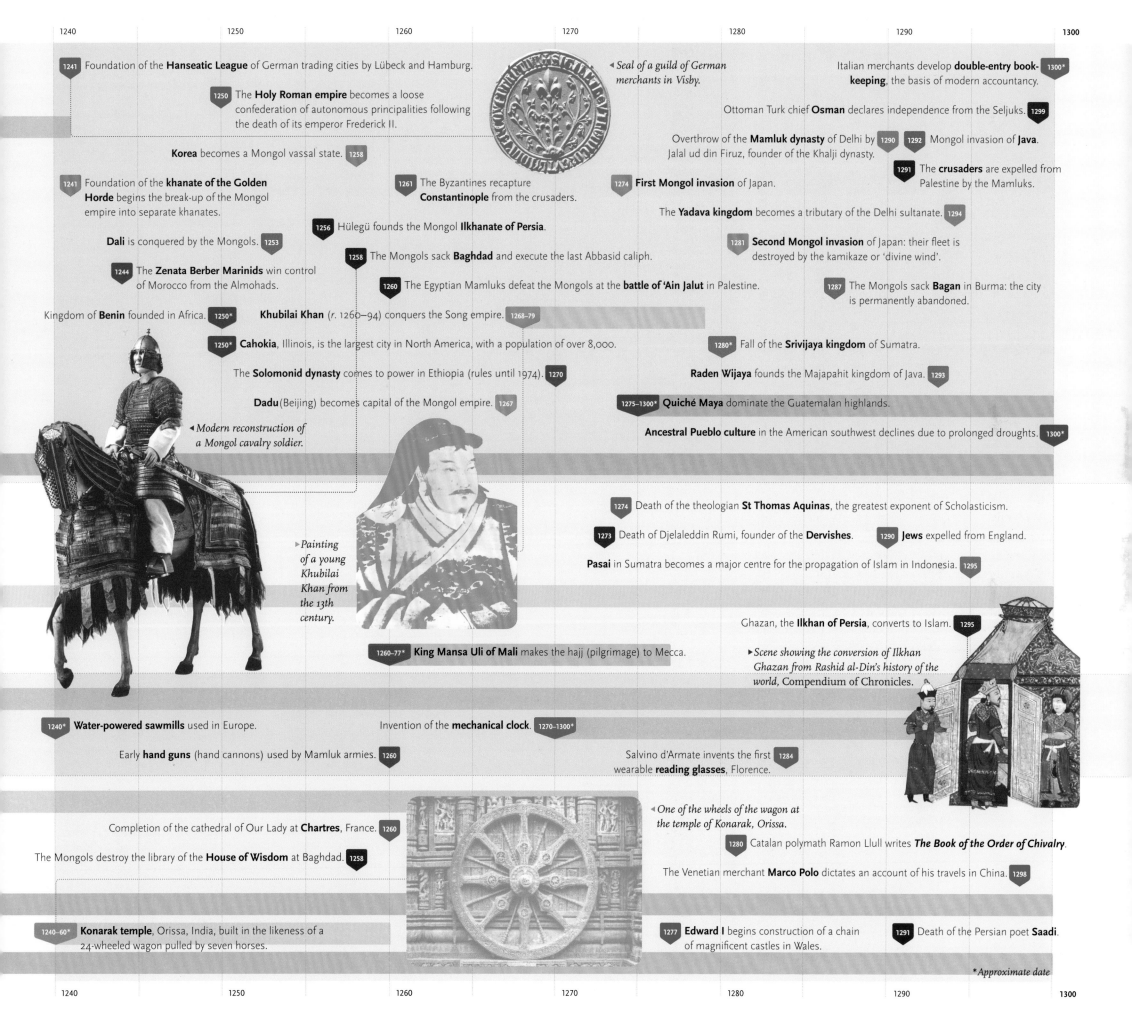

1241 Foundation of the **Hanseatic League** of German trading cities by Lübeck and Hamburg.

◀ *Seal of a guild of German merchants in Visby.*

Italian merchants develop **double-entry book-keeping**, the basis of modern accountancy. **1300***

1250 The **Holy Roman empire** becomes a loose confederation of autonomous principalities following the death of its emperor Frederick II.

Ottoman Turk chief **Osman** declares independence from the Seljuks. **1299**

Korea becomes a Mongol vassal state. **1258**

Overthrow of the **Mamluk dynasty** of Delhi by **1290** **1292** Mongol invasion of **Java**. Jalal ud din Firuz, founder of the Khalji dynasty.

1241 Foundation of the **khanate of the Golden Horde** begins the break-up of the Mongol empire into separate khanates.

1261 The Byzantines recapture **Constantinople** from the crusaders.

1274 **First Mongol invasion** of Japan.

1291 The **crusaders** are expelled from Palestine by the Mamluks.

The **Yadava kingdom** becomes a tributary of the Delhi sultanate. **1294**

Dali is conquered by the Mongols. **1253**

1256 Hülegü founds the Mongol **Ilkhanate of Persia**.

1281 **Second Mongol invasion** of Japan: their fleet is destroyed by the kamikaze or 'divine wind'.

1244 The **Zenata Berber Marinids** win control of Morocco from the Almohads.

1258 The Mongols sack **Baghdad** and execute the last Abbasid caliph.

1287 The Mongols sack **Bagan** in Burma: the city is permanently abandoned.

Kingdom of **Benin** founded in Africa. **1250***

1260 The Egyptian Mamluks defeat the Mongols at the **battle of 'Ain Jalut** in Palestine.

Khubilai Khan (*r*. 1260–94) conquers the Song empire. **1268–79**

1250* **Cahokia**, Illinois, is the largest city in North America, with a population of over 8,000.

1280* Fall of the **Srivijaya kingdom** of Sumatra.

The **Solomonid dynasty** comes to power in Ethiopia (rules until 1974). **1270**

Raden Wijaya founds the Majapahit kingdom of Java. **1293**

Dadu (Beijing) becomes capital of the Mongol empire. **1267**

1275–1300* **Quiché Maya** dominate the Guatemalan highlands.

◀ *Modern reconstruction of a Mongol cavalry soldier.*

Ancestral Pueblo culture in the American southwest declines due to prolonged droughts. **1300***

▶ *Painting of a young Khubilai Khan from the 13th century.*

1274 Death of the theologian **St Thomas Aquinas**, the greatest exponent of Scholasticism.

1273 Death of Djelaleddin Rumi, founder of the **Dervishes**.   **1290** **Jews** expelled from England.

Pasai in Sumatra becomes a major centre for the propagation of Islam in Indonesia. **1295**

Ghazan, the **Ilkhan of Persia**, converts to Islam. **1295**

1260–77* King **Mansa Uli of Mali** makes the hajj (pilgrimage) to Mecca.

▶ *Scene showing the conversion of Ilkhan Ghazan from Rashid al-Din's history of the world,* Compendium of Chronicles.

1240* **Water-powered sawmills** used in Europe.

Invention of the **mechanical clock**. **1270–1300***

Early **hand guns** (hand cannons) used by Mamluk armies. **1260**

Salvino d'Armate invents the first **1284** wearable **reading glasses**, Florence.

◀ *One of the wheels of the wagon at the temple of Konarak, Orissa.*

Completion of the cathedral of Our Lady at **Chartres**, France. **1260**

1280 Catalan polymath Ramon Llull writes ***The Book of the Order of Chivalry***.

The Mongols destroy the library of the **House of Wisdom** at Baghdad. **1258**

The Venetian merchant **Marco Polo** dictates an account of his travels in China. **1298**

1240–60* **Konarak temple**, Orissa, India, built in the likeness of a 24-wheeled wagon pulled by seven horses.

1277 **Edward I** begins construction of a chain of magnificent castles in Wales.

1291 Death of the Persian poet **Saadi**.

*Approximate date

1400

MING DYNASTY CHINA; TIMUR THE LAME;
THE GROWTH OF OTTOMAN POWER

Mongol power faded after the death of Khubilai Khan in 1294. In 1351 the peasant Red Turban rebellion broke out in China, and in 1368 the rebel leader Zhu Yuanzhang expelled the Mongols and proclaimed himself first emperor of the Ming dynasty. The Ming revived Chinese imperial traditions and restored the agricultural economy after years of neglect under the Mongols. The experience of Mongol rule left a legacy of xenophobia and the Ming dynasty was more inward-looking than previous Chinese dynasties.

Mongol rule in the Middle East ended with the break-up of the Ilkhanate in 1335. The Golden Horde continued to dominate Russia, but it was now, effectively, a Tatar (Turk) state. The last conqueror in the Mongol tradition was Timur the Lame (Tamberlaine), who claimed descent from Chinggis Khan but was linguistically and culturally a Turk. Timur, emir of the Silk Road city Samarkand (r. 1361–1405), reconquered the former Ilkhanate lands and almost destroyed the Chagatai khanate.

Timur's campaigns temporarily set back the growth of the Ottoman Turk sultanate, which had been founded in Anatolia around the beginning of the 14th century. The Ottomans invaded Europe in 1354, making extensive conquests in the Balkans. Around 1330 the Delhi sultanate began to extend Muslim power into central India. Much of the newly conquered territory soon broke away under the Bahmani dynasty to form an independent Muslim-ruled state. Muslim advance into the south was checked by the rise of the Vijayanagara kingdom, a champion of Hinduism. In Southeast Asia, the kingdom of Siam, from which the modern kingdom of Thailand is directly descended, was founded in 1351. Indonesia at this time came under the commercial domination of the maritime Majapahit kingdom of Java, the last major Hindu power of the region. In North America, prolonged drought destroyed the Ancestral Pueblo culture.

Five Largest Cities 000s (approximate)

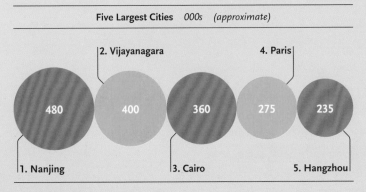

2. Vijayanagara — 400
4. Paris — 275
1. Nanjing — 480
3. Cairo — 360
5. Hangzhou — 235

104

IRISH KINGDOMS [1]
SCOTLAND [2]
NAVARRE [3]
EMIRATE OF GRANADA [4]
VENICE [5]
GENOA [6]

Sami

SWEDEN (in union with Denmark)

NOVGOROD

NORWAY (in union with Denmark)

Yakuts

Tungus

Samoyeds

Palaeo-Siberians

Thule Inuit culture

Arctic Circle
75°

DENMARK

[2]

MOSCOW

[10] [11]
[9] [12]
[13]

KHANATE OF THE GOLDEN HORDE (Tatars)

Kyrgyz

OIRAT KHANATE (Mongols)

Jürchen

Ainu

[1]
ENGLAND

POLAND-LITHUANIA

HOLY ROMAN EMPIRE

45°

Paris [4]
FRANCE

HUNGARY

[15] [16]

GEORGIA

CHAGATAI KHANATE

KOREA

JAPAN

CASTILE

[3]

[5]
[14]

OTTOMAN SULTANATE

[18]

KASHMIR

Nanjing [1]

[5]
Hangzhou

PORTUGAL

[6]
[4]

ARAGON

[7] [8]

[17]

[18]

CYPRUS

[19]

EMPIRE OF TIMUR THE LAME

TIBET

MING EMPIRE (Chinese)

MARINID CALIPHATE

HAFSID CALIPHATE

[3]
Cairo

SULTANATE OF DELHI

Tropic of Cancer

ZAYYANID EMIRATE

MAMLUK SULTANATE

Bedouin Arabs

OMAN

[21]
[22]

[21]

[24]

DAI VIET

Touaregs

SMALL KINGDOMS

SONGHAY

DARFUR

ALODIA

YEMEN

BAHMANI SULTANATE

[21]

ARAKAN

GANGAS

[23]

[25]

[26]
[27]

SIAM

CHAMPA

MALI

BORNU

ETHIOPIA

IFAT

[2]
Vijayanagara

VIJAYANAGARA KINGDOM

PEGU

KHMER

Malays

MOSSI STATES

HAUSA STATES

[20]

Yoruba

IFE

BENIN

Nilotic pastoralists

Cushitic pastoralists

SINHALESE KINGDOMS

SMALL MALAY STATES

Micronesians

Equator

PAPAL STATES [7]

Bantu farmers and pastoralists

SWAHILI CITY STATES

BYZANTINE EMPIRE [18]
TREBIZOND [19]
SMALL STATES [20]
HINDU KINGDOMS [21]
BENGAL [22]

BURMESE KINGDOMS [23]
SHAN STATES [24]
LANNATHAI (Thais) [25]
LAOS [26]
SUKHOTHAI [27]

Papuans

KINGDOM OF NAPLES [8]
TEUTONIC KNIGHTS [9]
PSKOV [10]
TVER [11]
SMOLENSK [12]
RYAZAN [13]
WALLACHIA [14]
MOLDAVIA [15]
GENOESE POSSESSIONS [16]
MINOR CHRISTIAN PRINCIPALITIES [17]

GREAT ZIMBABWE

Malagasy

MAJAPAHIT

Melanesians

San

Australian Aborigines

Tropic of Capricorn

Khoikhoi pastoralists

Maoris

Tasmanians

45°

0°   30°   60°   90°   120°   150°   180°

1400

Arguably the most important event of the 14th century was the Black Death, a pandemic of bubonic or pneumonic plague that broke out on the eastern steppes in 1347 and spread along trade routes to Europe, the Middle East, North Africa, India and China, before burning itself out around 1356. The total mortality can only be guessed at: in Europe at least a third of the population is thought to have died, creating a serious labour shortage.

A result of the plague was that wages and living standards increased for most working people, but the income of the landowning aristocracy declined. Attempts by the aristocracy to hold down wages and impose new burdens on tenants caused peasant revolts across Europe. All were violently suppressed with contrasting consequences in Eastern and Western Europe. In the east, a largely free peasantry was forced into serfdom. In France, serfs gained hereditary rights over their farms, while in England serfdom began to die out altogether. In China, the plague contributed to the peasant unrest that ended Mongol rule. Plague remained endemic for centuries, slowing population growth in many parts of the Old World.

In Italy, the work of artists such as Giotto and of the humanist poets Petrarch and Boccaccio marked the beginning of the Renaissance, a movement that would transform the arts and outlook of Western Europe over the next two centuries. Europeans also developed gunpowder weapons at this time. In Japan, the 14th century saw the development of classical Noh musical theatre, which features masked characters and men playing female roles. Thanks to the generous patronage of its rulers, Vijayanagara became a major centre of Hindu literature, art and architecture. The city's many hundreds of temples were built in a distinctive and eclectic style, incorporating features from many earlier Hindu architectural styles.

World Population (approximate)

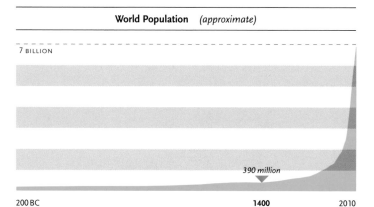

7 BILLION

390 million

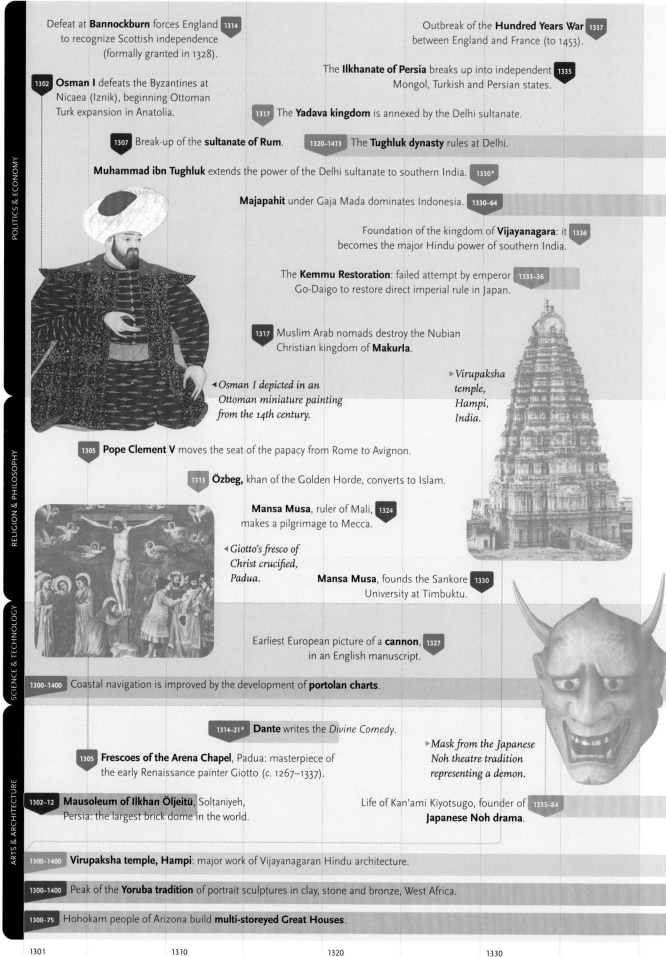

POLITICS & ECONOMY

Defeat at **Bannockburn** forces England to recognize Scottish independence (formally granted in 1328). `1314`

Outbreak of the **Hundred Years War** between England and France (to 1453). `1337`

`1302` **Osman I** defeats the Byzantines at Nicaea (Iznik), beginning Ottoman Turk expansion in Anatolia.

The **Ilkhanate of Persia** breaks up into independent Mongol, Turkish and Persian states. `1335`

`1317` The **Yadava kingdom** is annexed by the Delhi sultanate.

`1307` Break-up of the **sultanate of Rum**.   `1320–1413` The **Tughluk dynasty** rules at Delhi.

Muhammad ibn Tughluk extends the power of the Delhi sultanate to southern India. `1330*`

Majapahit under Gaja Mada dominates Indonesia. `1330–64`

Foundation of the kingdom of **Vijayanagara**: it becomes the major Hindu power of southern India. `1336`

The **Kemmu Restoration**: failed attempt by emperor Go-Daigo to restore direct imperial rule in Japan. `1333–36`

`1317` Muslim Arab nomads destroy the Nubian Christian kingdom of **Makurla**.

◀ *Osman I depicted in an Ottoman miniature painting from the 14th century.*

▶ *Virupaksha temple, Hampi, India.*

RELIGION & PHILOSOPHY

`1305` **Pope Clement V** moves the seat of the papacy from Rome to Avignon.

`1313` **Özbeg,** khan of the Golden Horde, converts to Islam.

Mansa Musa, ruler of Mali, `1324` makes a pilgrimage to Mecca.

◀ *Giotto's fresco of Christ crucified, Padua.*

Mansa Musa, founds the Sankore University at Timbuktu. `1330`

SCIENCE & TECHNOLOGY

Earliest European picture of a **cannon**, `1327` in an English manuscript.

`1300–1400` Coastal navigation is improved by the development of **portolan charts**.

ARTS & ARCHITECTURE

`1314–21*` **Dante** writes the *Divine Comedy*.

`1305` **Frescoes of the Arena Chapel**, Padua: masterpiece of the early Renaissance painter Giotto (c. 1267–1337).

▶ *Mask from the Japanese Noh theatre tradition representing a demon.*

`1302–12` **Mausoleum of Ilkhan Öljeitü**, Soltaniyeh, Persia: the largest brick dome in the world.

Life of Kan'ami Kiyotsugo, founder of **Japanese Noh drama**. `1333–84`

`1300–1400` **Virupaksha temple, Hampi**: major work of Vijayanagaran Hindu architecture.

`1300–1400` Peak of the **Yoruba tradition** of portrait sculptures in clay, stone and bronze, West Africa.

`1300–75` Hohokam people of Arizona build **multi-storeyed Great Houses**.

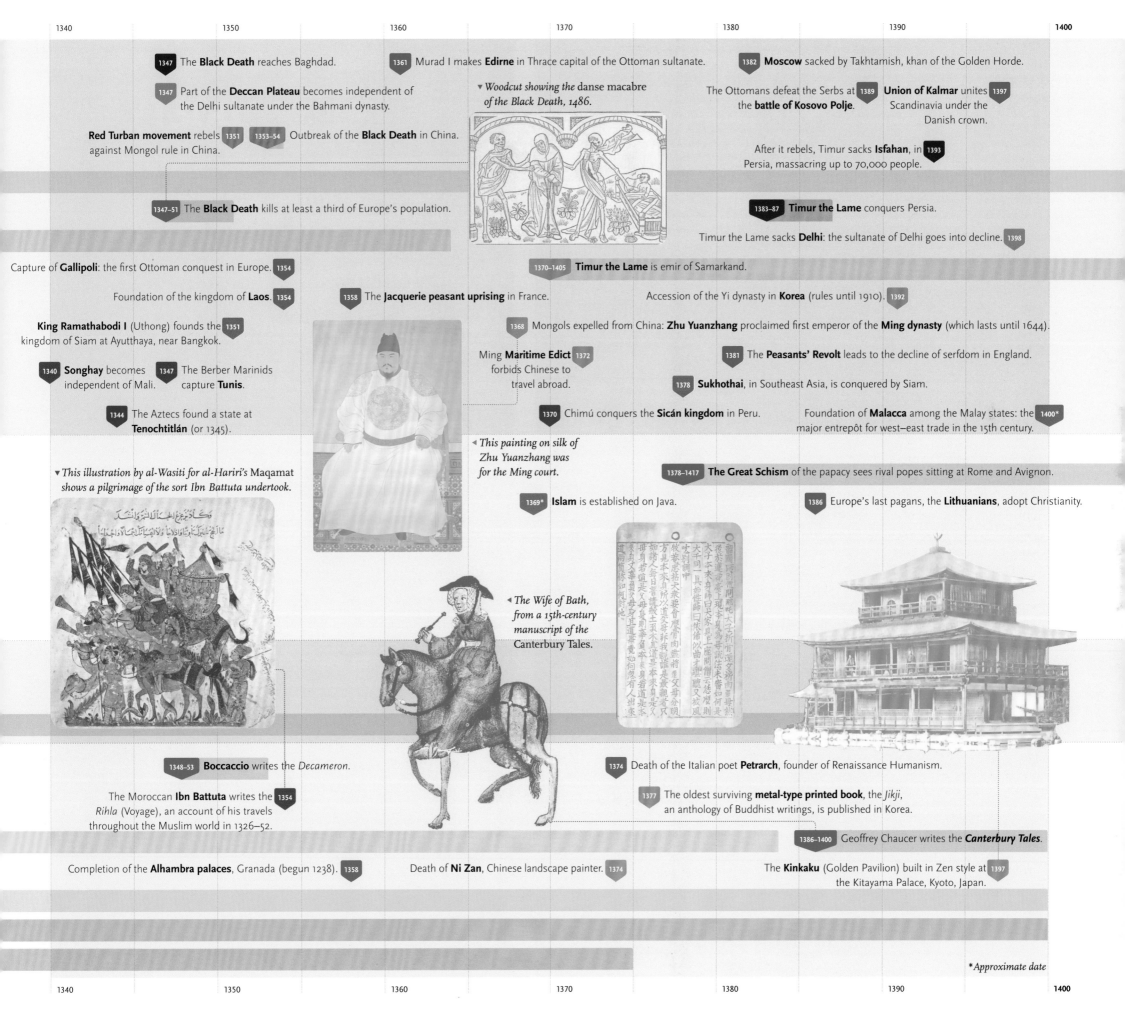

1347 The **Black Death** reaches Baghdad.

1361 Murad I makes **Edirne** in Thrace capital of the Ottoman sultanate.

1382 **Moscow** sacked by Takhtamish, khan of the Golden Horde.

1347 Part of the **Deccan Plateau** becomes independent of the Delhi sultanate under the Bahmani dynasty.

▼ *Woodcut showing the danse macabre of the Black Death, 1486.*

The Ottomans defeat the Serbs at **1389** **Union of Kalmar** unites **1397** the **battle of Kosovo Polje**. Scandinavia under the Danish crown.

Red Turban movement rebels **1351** **1353–54** Outbreak of the **Black Death** in China. against Mongol rule in China.

After it rebels, Timur sacks **Isfahan**, in **1393** Persia, massacring up to 70,000 people.

1347–51 The **Black Death** kills at least a third of Europe's population.

1383–87 **Timur the Lame** conquers Persia.

Timur the Lame sacks **Delhi**: the sultanate of Delhi goes into decline. **1398**

Capture of **Gallipoli**: the first Ottoman conquest in Europe. **1354**

1370–1405 **Timur the Lame** is emir of Samarkand.

Foundation of the kingdom of **Laos**. **1354**

1358 The **Jacquerie peasant uprising** in France.

Accession of the Yi dynasty in **Korea** (rules until 1910). **1392**

King Ramathabodi I (Uthong) founds the **1351** kingdom of Siam at Ayutthaya, near Bangkok.

1368 Mongols expelled from China: **Zhu Yuanzhang** proclaimed first emperor of the **Ming dynasty** (which lasts until 1644).

Ming **Maritime Edict** **1372** forbids Chinese to travel abroad.

1381 The **Peasants' Revolt** leads to the decline of serfdom in England.

1340 **Songhay** becomes independent of Mali. **1347** The Berber Marinids capture **Tunis**.

1378 **Sukhothai**, in Southeast Asia, is conquered by Siam.

1344 The Aztecs found a state at **Tenochtitlán** (or 1345).

1370 Chimú conquers the **Sicán kingdom** in Peru.

Foundation of **Malacca** among the Malay states: the **1400*** major entrepôt for west–east trade in the 15th century.

◄ *This painting on silk of Zhu Yuanzhang was for the Ming court.*

1378–1417 **The Great Schism** of the papacy sees rival popes sitting at Rome and Avignon.

▼ *This illustration by al-Wasiti for al-Hariri's* Maqamat *shows a pilgrimage of the sort Ibn Battuta undertook.*

1369* **Islam** is established on Java.

1386 Europe's last pagans, the **Lithuanians**, adopt Christianity.

◄ *The Wife of Bath, from a 15th-century manuscript of the Canterbury Tales.*

1348–53 **Boccaccio** writes the *Decameron*.

1374 Death of the Italian poet **Petrarch**, founder of Renaissance Humanism.

The Moroccan **Ibn Battuta** writes the **1354** *Rihla* (Voyage), an account of his travels throughout the Muslim world in 1326–52.

1377 The oldest surviving **metal-type printed book**, the *Jikji*, an anthology of Buddhist writings, is published in Korea.

1386–1400 Geoffrey Chaucer writes the **Canterbury Tales**.

Completion of the **Alhambra palaces**, Granada (begun 1238). **1358**

Death of **Ni Zan**, Chinese landscape painter. **1374**

The **Kinkaku** (Golden Pavilion) built in Zen style at **1397** the Kitayama Palace, Kyoto, Japan.

*Approximate date

1400

PATTERNS OF WORLD TRADE ON THE EVE OF EUROPEAN EXPANSION

By AD 1400 all of the Old World civilizations were connected by a network of long-distance trade routes that converged on the Middle East. The wealth generated by its role as global middleman contributed greatly to the cultural and political pre-eminence of the Muslim world.

The most important of these overland routes was the Silk Road, a network of routes which connected China with South and Western Asia, and had developed from shorter trade routes established by steppe nomads in Bronze Age times. The route was named for the luxury fabric silk, China's most famous and valuable product. Very few people ever travelled the complete length of the road: trade was normally conducted through a succession of intermediaries, with the goods becoming more expensive with each exchange along the way.

Graeco-Roman mariners established a second major west–east route, from Egypt across the Indian Ocean to India and Southeast Asia, in the 1st century AD. Sometimes known as the Spice Route after its most valuable commodity, spices from Indonesia, this route came under Arab control following the rise of Islam. Trade between the Mediterranean and sub-Saharan Africa was severely limited before the introduction of camels to the Sahara *c.* 100 BC made desert traffic easier. Until the discovery of the Americas, sub-Saharan Africa was the Old World's main source of gold.

Since ancient times, the Mediterranean linked rather than divided the civilizations around its shores. This remained substantially true even after the Arab conquests, despite the mutual antagonism of the Christian and Muslim worlds. From the 11th century, the Mediterranean trade routes were dominated by the Italian city states of Venice and Genoa. The Hanseatic League of German cities dominated trade in Northern Europe, strictly controlling access to the Baltic Sea.

Long-distance trade in the Americas was much less developed in 1400 than it was in the Old World, but there were sufficient contacts for the transfer of crops and technology between civilizations. The lack of pack animals (except llamas, which were restricted to the Andes) prevented long-distance overland trade in bulky commodities, while the dense, mountainous rainforest of the Isthmus of Panama was an effective barrier to regular north–south overland travel. The lack of developed seafaring technology also limited maritime trade.

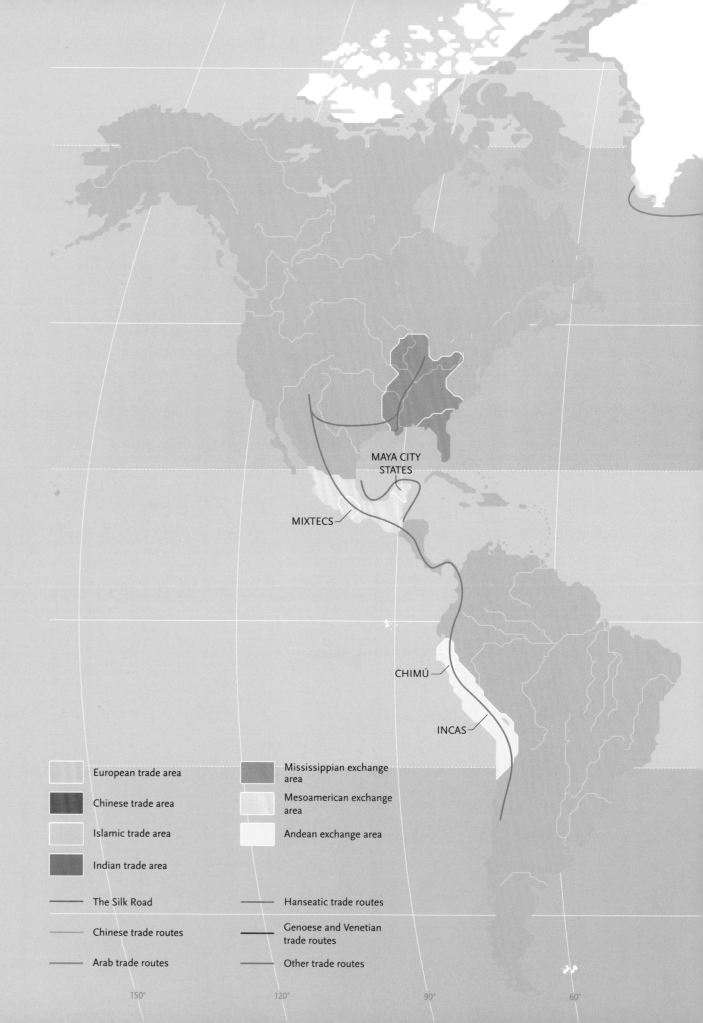

MAYA CITY STATES

MIXTECS

CHIMÚ

INCAS

European trade area

Chinese trade area

Islamic trade area

Indian trade area

Mississippian exchange area

Mesoamerican exchange area

Andean exchange area

The Silk Road

Chinese trade routes

Arab trade routes

Hanseatic trade routes

Genoese and Venetian trade routes

Other trade routes

150°   120°   90°   60°

IRISH
KINGDOMS 1
SCOTLAND 2
EMIRATE OF 3
GRANADA
PAPAL 4
STATES
KINGDOM OF 5
NAPLES

TEUTONIC 6
KNIGHTS
PSKOV 7
SMOLENSK 8
RYAZAN 9
WALLACHIA 10
MOLDAVIA 11
BYZANTINE 12
EMPIRE
HAFSID 13
CALIPHATE

14 TREBIZOND
15 GENOESE
POSSESSIONS
16 BENGAL
17 BURMESE
KINGDOMS

18 SHAN STATES
19 LANNATHAI
(Thais)
20 LAOS
21 SUKHOTHAI
22 KHMER

SWEDEN
(in union with
Denmark)
NOVGOROD
NORWAY
(in union with
Denmark)
Novgorod
MOSCOW
DENMARK
Lübeck
Moscow
POLAND-
LITHUANIA
KHANATE OF THE
GOLDEN HORDE
ENGLAND
London
Antwerp
HOLY
ROMAN
EMPIRE
Kiev
Paris
FRANCE
HUNGARY
New
Sarai
OIRAT KHANATE
CASTILE
Venice
Genoa
GEORGIA
Caffa
PORTUGAL
ARAGON
OTTOMAN
Tashkent
CHAGATAI
KHANATE
Beijing
Lisbon
Constantinople
SULTANATE
Bukhara
Kashgar
KOREA
Tangier
Tunis
Khotan
Xi'an
JAPAN
MARINID
Algiers
Tripoli
Aleppo
Rayy
(Tehran)
Merv
Samarkand
KASHMIR
Nanjing
Nagasaki
CALIPHATE
CYPRUS
Baghdad
EMPIRE OF
TIMUR THE LAME
TIBET
MING
EMPIRE
Hangzhou
ZAYYANID
EMIRATE
Cairo
MAMLUK
SULTANATE
Delhi
SULTANATE
OF DELHI
OMAN
Muscat
BAHMANI
SULTANATE
ARAKAN
GANGAS
DAI VIET
Timbuktu
SONGHAY
DARFUR
ALODIA
YEMEN
VIJAYANAGARA
KINGDOM
Vijayanagara
PEGU
SIAM
CHAMPA
MALI
BORNU
Aden
Calicut
Angkor
MOSSI STATES
HAUSA
STATES
ETHIOPIA
IFAT
SINHALESE
KINGDOMS
IFE
BENIN
Mombasa
SWAHILI
CITY
STATES
Malacca
SMALL MALAY
STATES
Moluccas
(Spice Islands)
MAJAPAHIT
GREAT
ZIMBABWE

Arctic Circle

Tropic of Cancer

Equator

Tropic of Capricorn

0°   30°   60°   90°   120°   150°   180°

75°

45°

45°

1492

THE WORLD ON THE BRINK OF EUROPEAN EXPANSION; THE AZTEC AND INCA EMPIRES AT THEIR PEAK

The European discovery of the Americas by Christopher Columbus in 1492 was one of the major turning points of world history, an event that began Europe's progress from its situation at the margins of the known world to a position of global dominance. The significance of the discovery did not become evident for several decades, however.

Columbus's voyage across the Atlantic, in the service of Castile, and the parallel voyages of exploration along the African coast by the Portuguese were the product of a European sense of vulnerability and exclusion. Europeans resented having to buy eastern spices and Chinese silks through Muslim middlemen at great cost. Europeans were also alarmed by the resurgence of Muslim power represented by the Ottoman Turk empire, which in 1453 extinguished the sad remnants of the Byzantine empire by conquering Constantinople.

The Portuguese hoped to trade directly with the east, and gain allies against the Muslims, by finding a route around Africa. This was achieved by Bartolomeu Dias in 1487–88. Columbus believed he could do the same by sailing west across the Atlantic: it was soon realized that he had actually discovered an unsuspected 'New World'. The Aztec and Inca empires, the greatest states that the Americas had so far seen, were equally unaware of the existence of the Old World.

China, in 1492 the world's richest and most technologically advanced state, had turned inwards. Earlier in the 15th century the Ming emperors had sent a series of great naval expeditions to Southeast Asia, India and East Africa to announce to the known world that China was a great power again after the years of Mongol occupation. But a resurgence of Mongol power forced the Ming to abandon their maritime enterprises and concentrate on fortifying their northern frontier.

Five Largest Cities *000s* (approximate)

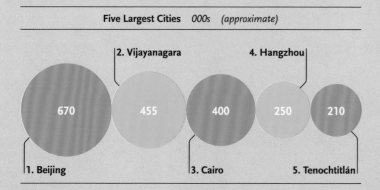

2. Vijayanagara		4. Hangzhou	
670	455	400	250	210
1. Beijing		3. Cairo		5. Tenochtitlán

Inuit

Inuit

Aleuts

Sub-Arctic caribou hunters

West coast fishers, hunters and gatherers

Central plateau hunter-fisher-gatherers

Great Plains bison hunters

Woodlands hunter-gatherers

Woodlands and plains farmers

Desert hunter-gatherers

Mississippian temple mound builders

Puebloans

Maize farmers

Tenochtitlán

5

Arawak

AZTEC EMPIRE

MIXTECS

Carib chiefdoms

MAYA CITY STATES

North Andean chiefdoms

Arawak

Polynesians

Amazonian chiefdoms

Tupi

INCA EMPIRE

Savanna hunter-gatherers

Guarani

Pampas hunters

Fishers and marine mammal hunters

Legend:

Hunter-gatherers

Settled farming cultures and peoples

Pastoral nomads

Complex farming societies/chiefdoms

Urbanized societies/ kingdoms

Empires

Uninhabited

Portuguese possessions

▶▶▶ Dias 1487-88

▶▶▶ Columbus 1492

150°   120°   90°   60°

VENICE **1**
VENETIAN POSSESSIONS **2**
PAPAL STATES **3**
MOLDAVIA **4**
TEUTONIC KNIGHTS **5**
PSKOV **6**
RYAZAN **7**

ICELAND
(to Denmark)

Sami

Yakuts

Palaeo-Siberians

Arctic Circle

75°

NORWAY
(in union with
Denmark)

SWEDEN
(in union with
Denmark)

MOSCOW

Khanate of Sibir

Samoyeds

Tungus

SCOTLAND

DENMARK

5   **6**

POLAND-
LITHUANIA

Khanate
of
Kazan

ENGLAND

HOLY
ROMAN
EMPIRE

HUNGARY   **4**

7

Khanate of the
Golden Horde
(Tatars)

OIRAT KHANATE
(Mongols)

Ainu

Jürchen

45°

FRANCE

1

NAVARRE

CASTILE

PORTUGAL

ARAGON

OTTOMAN TURK
EMPIRE

Khanate of
Astrakhan

Kazakhs

Kyrgyz

Uzbeks

CHAGATAI
KHANATE

Beijing   **1**

KOREA

Azores
(to Portugal)

8   **9**

HAFSID
CALIPHATE

2

GEORGIA

AK KOYUNLU
(White sheep
Turk)
EMIRATE

KASHMIR

TIMURID
EMIRATES

TIBET

NEPAL

MING
EMPIRE

4
Hangzhou

JAPAN

Madeira
(to Portugal)

3
Cairo

SULTANATE
OF
DELHI

ASSAM

Canary
Islands
(to Castile)

Touaregs

MAMLUK
SULTANATE

Bedouin
Arabs

Bedouin
Arabs

OMAN

15   **16**

15

BENGAL

18

Tropic of Cancer

Arguin
(to Portugal)

ÄIR

DARFUR

JIZAN

GUJARAT

ARAKAN

17   **19**

LAOS

WOLOF   TAKRUR

SONGHAY

BORNU

12

YEMEN

HADRAMAUT

ORISSA

DAI VIET

Cape
Verde
Islands
(to
Portugal)

MALI

10   **11**

FUNJ

BAHMANI
SULTANATE

2
Vijayanagara

PEGU

SIAM

CHAMPA

SMALL
MALAY
STATES

Micronesians

BORGU KINGDOMS

ADAL

VIJAYANAGARA
KINGDOM

20

13

IFE

14   BENIN

ETHIOPIA

SINHALESE
KINGDOMS

SULTANATE
OF
MALACCA

21

Cacheu
(to Portugal)

Elmina
(to Portugal)

SULTANATE
OF ACEH

SMALL
MALAY
STATES

Equator

Fernando Póo (to Portugal)

SWAHILI CITY
STATES

15 SMALL INDIAN STATES

Príncipe (to Portugal)

KONGO

SMALL
KINGDOMS

16 RAJPUTS

MAJAPAHIT

22

Papuans

São Tomé
(to Portugal)

17 BURMESE KINGDOMS

Bantu farmers and
pastoralists

18 SHAN KINGDOMS

19 LANNATHAI

WATTASID CALIPHATE **8**

MUTAPA

20 CAMBODIA

Melanesians

ZAYYANID CALIPHATE **9**

BUTUA

21 SULTANATE OF BRUNEI

MOSSI KINGDOMS **10**

Malagasy

22 SULTANATE OF TERNATE

HAUSA CITY STATES **11**

SWAHILI
CITY
STATES

Tropic of Capricorn

ALODIA **12**

Australian Aborigines

AKAN KINGDOMS **13**

San

OYO **14**

Khoikhoi
pastoralists

Polynesians

Tasmanians

Maoris

45°

0°   30°   60°   90°   120°   150°   180°

1492

The beginning of European expansion was made possible by advances in shipbuilding and navigation in the 15th century, in which the Portuguese took the lead. Feudalism declined as rulers curtailed the independence of the aristocracy and created strong centralized governments. At the same time, the cultural transformation of the Renaissance began to spread outside Italy. A major advance was the development of movable-type printing by Johannes Gutenberg, who opened the first European printing press at Mainz, Germany, c. 1455. Printing reduced the costs and increased the speed of book production, making books available to a much wider public: by 1492 the technology had spread throughout Catholic Europe.

The Roman Catholic church reasserted its authority after a split (1378–1417) that saw rival popes sitting at Rome and Avignon. The church began to expand outside Europe: the king of Kongo in Africa was converted by the Portuguese in 1490. Granada, the last Muslim enclave in Spain, was conquered by Castile in 1492 and the Spanish Inquisition supervised the conversion or expulsion of Spanish Muslims and Jews. Following the fall of the Byzantine empire in 1453, Moscow took over leadership of the Orthodox church. When Prince Ivan II adopted the title Tsar (Caesar) in 1472, he consciously appropriated the Byzantine tradition and Moscow became 'the third Rome'.

Despite the Ottoman conquest, Islam did not make great headway in Greece and the Balkans, where the majority of the population remained loyal to Orthodoxy. Islam continued to win converts in Africa and, especially, Indonesia. The political and military resurrection of China under the Ming since they came to power in 1368 was mirrored in intellectual life with a huge state-sponsored effort to edit and consolidate the canon of Chinese literature and learning in vast encyclopaedic works.

World Population (approximate)

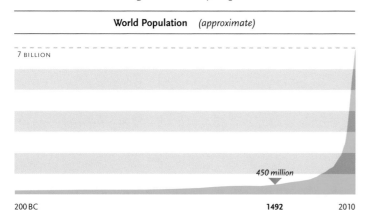

7 BILLION

450 million

200 BC   1492   2010

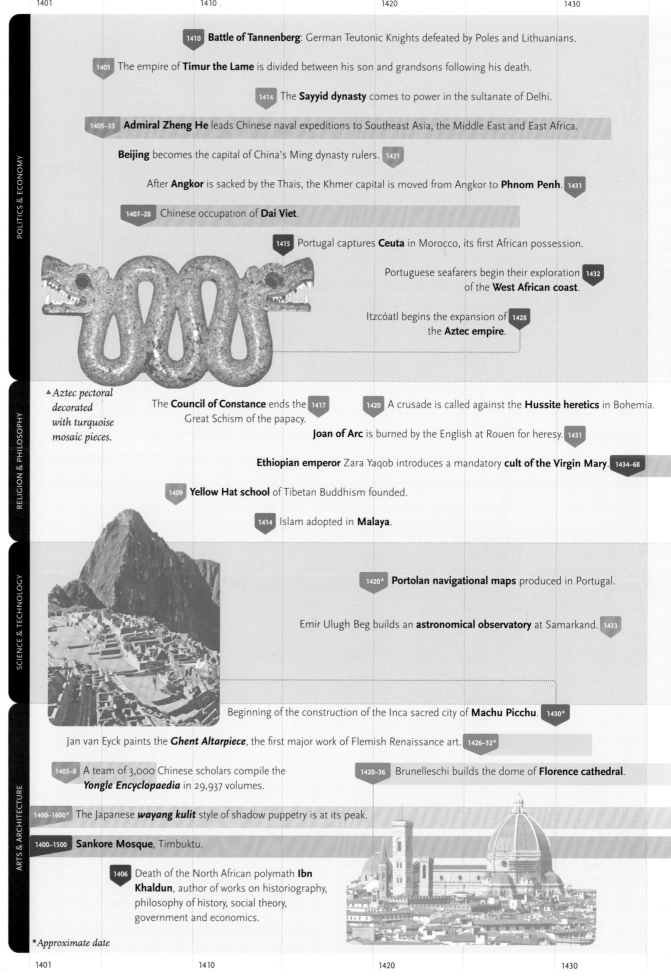

1401   1410   1420   1430

POLITICS & ECONOMY

1410 **Battle of Tannenberg**: German Teutonic Knights defeated by Poles and Lithuanians.

1405 The empire of **Timur the Lame** is divided between his son and grandsons following his death.

1414 The **Sayyid dynasty** comes to power in the sultanate of Delhi.

1405–33 **Admiral Zheng He** leads Chinese naval expeditions to Southeast Asia, the Middle East and East Africa.

Beijing becomes the capital of China's Ming dynasty rulers. **1421**

After **Angkor** is sacked by the Thais, the Khmer capital is moved from Angkor to **Phnom Penh**. **1431**

1407–28 Chinese occupation of **Dai Viet**.

1415 Portugal captures **Ceuta** in Morocco, its first African possession.

Portuguese seafarers begin their exploration **1432** of the **West African coast**.

Itzcóatl begins the expansion of **1428** the **Aztec empire**.

▲ *Aztec pectoral decorated with turquoise mosaic pieces.*

RELIGION & PHILOSOPHY

The **Council of Constance** ends the **1417** Great Schism of the papacy.

1420 A crusade is called against the **Hussite heretics** in Bohemia.

Joan of Arc is burned by the English at Rouen for heresy. **1431**

Ethiopian emperor Zara Yaqob introduces a mandatory **cult of the Virgin Mary**. **1434–68**

1409 **Yellow Hat school** of Tibetan Buddhism founded.

1414 Islam adopted in **Malaya**.

SCIENCE & TECHNOLOGY

1420* **Portolan navigational maps** produced in Portugal.

Emir Ulugh Beg builds an **astronomical observatory** at Samarkand. **1433**

Beginning of the construction of the Inca sacred city of **Machu Picchu**. **1430***

ARTS & ARCHITECTURE

Jan van Eyck paints the ***Ghent Altarpiece***, the first major work of Flemish Renaissance art. **1426–32***

1403–8 A team of 3,000 Chinese scholars compile the ***Yongle Encyclopaedia*** in 29,937 volumes.

1420–36 Brunelleschi builds the dome of **Florence cathedral**.

1400–1600* The Japanese ***wayang kulit*** style of shadow puppetry is at its peak.

1400–1500 **Sankore Mosque**, Timbuktu.

1406 Death of the North African polymath **Ibn Khaldun**, author of works on historiography, philosophy of history, social theory, government and economics.

*Approximate date

1401   1410   1420   1430

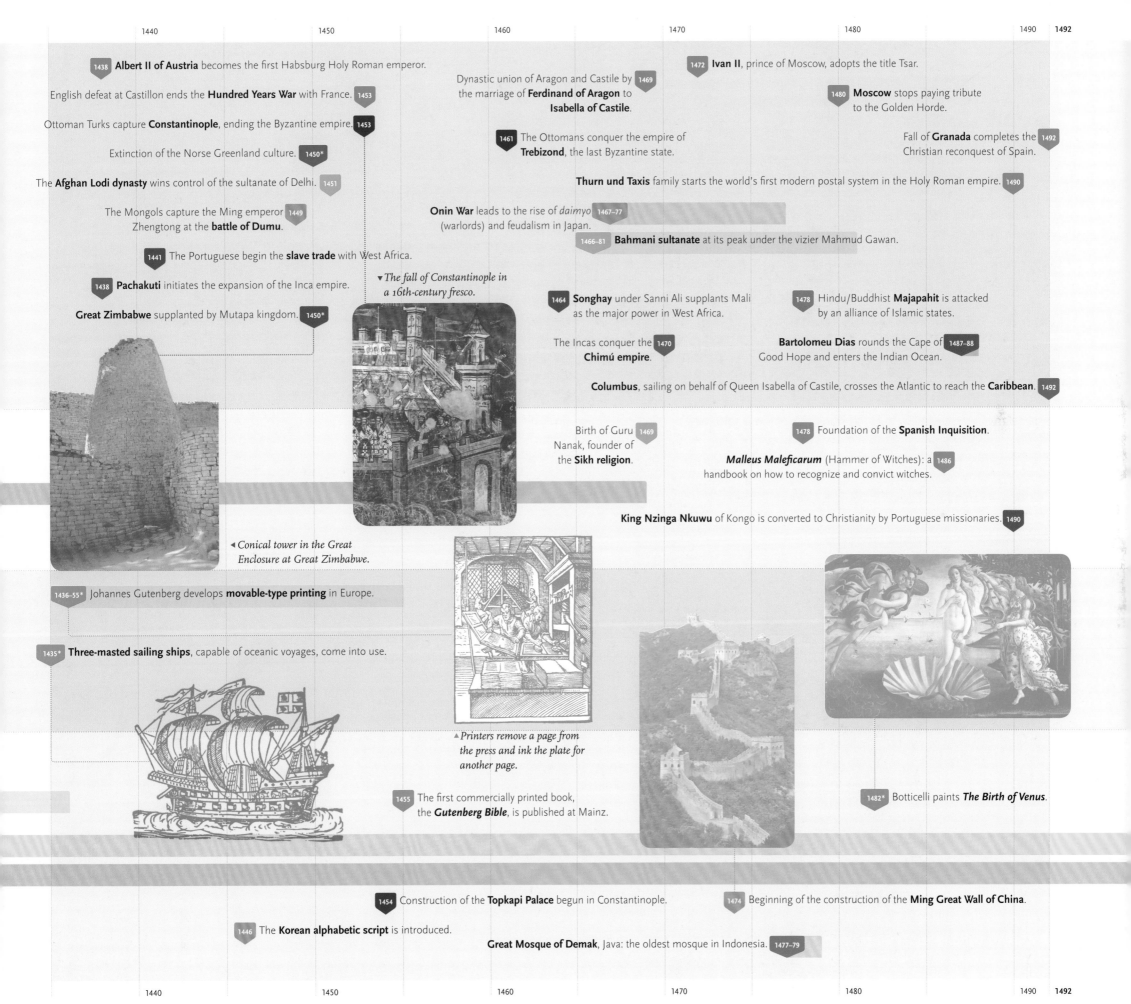

1438 **Albert II of Austria** becomes the first Habsburg Holy Roman emperor.

English defeat at Castillon ends the **Hundred Years War** with France. **1453**

Ottoman Turks capture **Constantinople**, ending the Byzantine empire. **1453**

Extinction of the Norse Greenland culture. **1450***

The **Afghan Lodi dynasty** wins control of the sultanate of Delhi. **1451**

The Mongols capture the Ming emperor **1449** Zhengtong at the **battle of Dumu**.

1441 The Portuguese begin the **slave trade** with West Africa.

1438 **Pachakuti** initiates the expansion of the Inca empire.

Great Zimbabwe supplanted by Mutapa kingdom. **1450***

▼ *The fall of Constantinople in a 16th-century fresco.*

◄ *Conical tower in the Great Enclosure at Great Zimbabwe.*

Dynastic union of Aragon and Castile by **1469** the marriage of **Ferdinand of Aragon** to **Isabella of Castile**.

1461 The Ottomans conquer the empire of **Trebizond**, the last Byzantine state.

Thurn und Taxis family starts the world's first modern postal system in the Holy Roman empire. **1490**

Onin War leads to the rise of *daimyo* **1467–77** (warlords) and feudalism in Japan.

1466–81 **Bahmani sultanate** at its peak under the vizier Mahmud Gawan.

1464 **Songhay** under Sanni Ali supplants Mali as the major power in West Africa.

The Incas conquer the **1470** **Chimú empire**.

1478 Hindu/Buddhist **Majapahit** is attacked by an alliance of Islamic states.

Bartolomeu Dias rounds the Cape of **1487–88** Good Hope and enters the Indian Ocean.

Columbus, sailing on behalf of Queen Isabella of Castile, crosses the Atlantic to reach the **Caribbean**. **1492**

Birth of Guru **1469** Nanak, founder of the **Sikh religion**.

1478 Foundation of the **Spanish Inquisition**.

Malleus Maleficarum (Hammer of Witches): a **1486** handbook on how to recognize and convict witches.

King Nzinga Nkuwu of Kongo is converted to Christianity by Portuguese missionaries. **1490**

1472 **Ivan II**, prince of Moscow, adopts the title Tsar.

1480 **Moscow** stops paying tribute to the Golden Horde.

Fall of **Granada** completes the **1492** Christian reconquest of Spain.

1436–55* Johannes Gutenberg develops **movable-type printing** in Europe.

1435* **Three-masted sailing ships**, capable of oceanic voyages, come into use.

▲ *Printers remove a page from the press and ink the plate for another page.*

1455 The first commercially printed book, the **Gutenberg Bible**, is published at Mainz.

1482* Botticelli paints *The Birth of Venus*.

1454 Construction of the **Topkapi Palace** begun in Constantinople.

1474 Beginning of the construction of the **Ming Great Wall of China**.

1446 The **Korean alphabetic script** is introduced.

Great Mosque of Demak, Java: the oldest mosque in Indonesia. **1477–79**

THE SPREAD OF THE WORLD'S MAJOR WRITING SYSTEMS TO 1492

The adoption of writing marks the end of a society's prehistory. Writing has been invented independently many times during world history and is a natural expression of the human capacity for abstract and symbolic thought. Writing was a response to growing social and economic complexity and as such it is often considered one of the defining characteristics of civilization.

The earliest known writing system was the Sumerian pictographic script which developed *c.* 3400 BC. In the 3rd millennium the pictographs were gradually refined and simplified, developing into the cuneiform script. The Sumerian scripts were adopted widely. Sumerian pictographic was adopted by the Elamites and perhaps inspired the Indus valley pictographic script. Cuneiform was adopted by the Assyrians, Babylonians, Elamites Hittites and Persians among others.

Despite its superficial similarity, the Egyptian hieroglyphic script, which developed *c.* 3100 BC, was probably invented independently of Sumerian pictographic. Its influence was limited to Nubia, Minoan Crete and the Hittite empire. Mesoamerican writing was also based on hieroglyphs, though only the Maya script could represent all aspects of spoken language. The earliest Chinese writing, which appeared *c.* 1200 BC was a pictographic script. Continually refined, this developed in the first millennium BC into a logographic script which is directly ancestral to the modern Chinese script. The only script to develop in the Pacific region, the undeciphered 18th-century Rongorongo script of Easter Island, was also based on pictographs.

The hieroglyphic and cuneiform scripts have thousands of characters and are difficult to learn. This limited literacy to a small elite of professional scribes. In the 16th century BC, the Canaanites invented the much simpler alphabet with only 22 characters representing consonants. All modern alphabets, except possibly the Korean, ultimately derive from the Canaanite alphabet. Western alphabets include characters for vowels as well as consonants, a refinement introduced by the ancient Greeks.

Of major civilizations, only the Andean did not develop a system of writing. In this region information was encoded in knots on devices made from coloured strings known as quipus. The earliest evidence for the use of quipus, from Caral in Peru, dates to around 3000 BC.

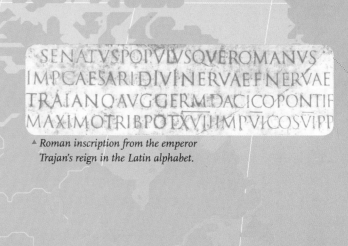

▲ Roman inscription from the emperor Trajan's reign in the Latin alphabet.

▲ Maya hieroglyphs in a page from the 11th- or 12th-century AD Dresden Codex.

Olmec
Epi-Olmec
Mixtec
Zapotec
Maya

▲ Egyptian hieroglyphic inscription from the 4th century BC.

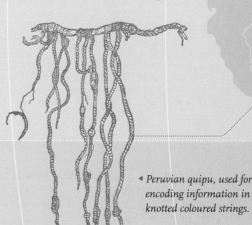

◄ Peruvian quipu, used for encoding information in knotted coloured strings.

Spread of writing by:

3000 BC		500 BC
2000 BC		AD 500
1250 BC		AD 1492

150°   120°   90°   60°

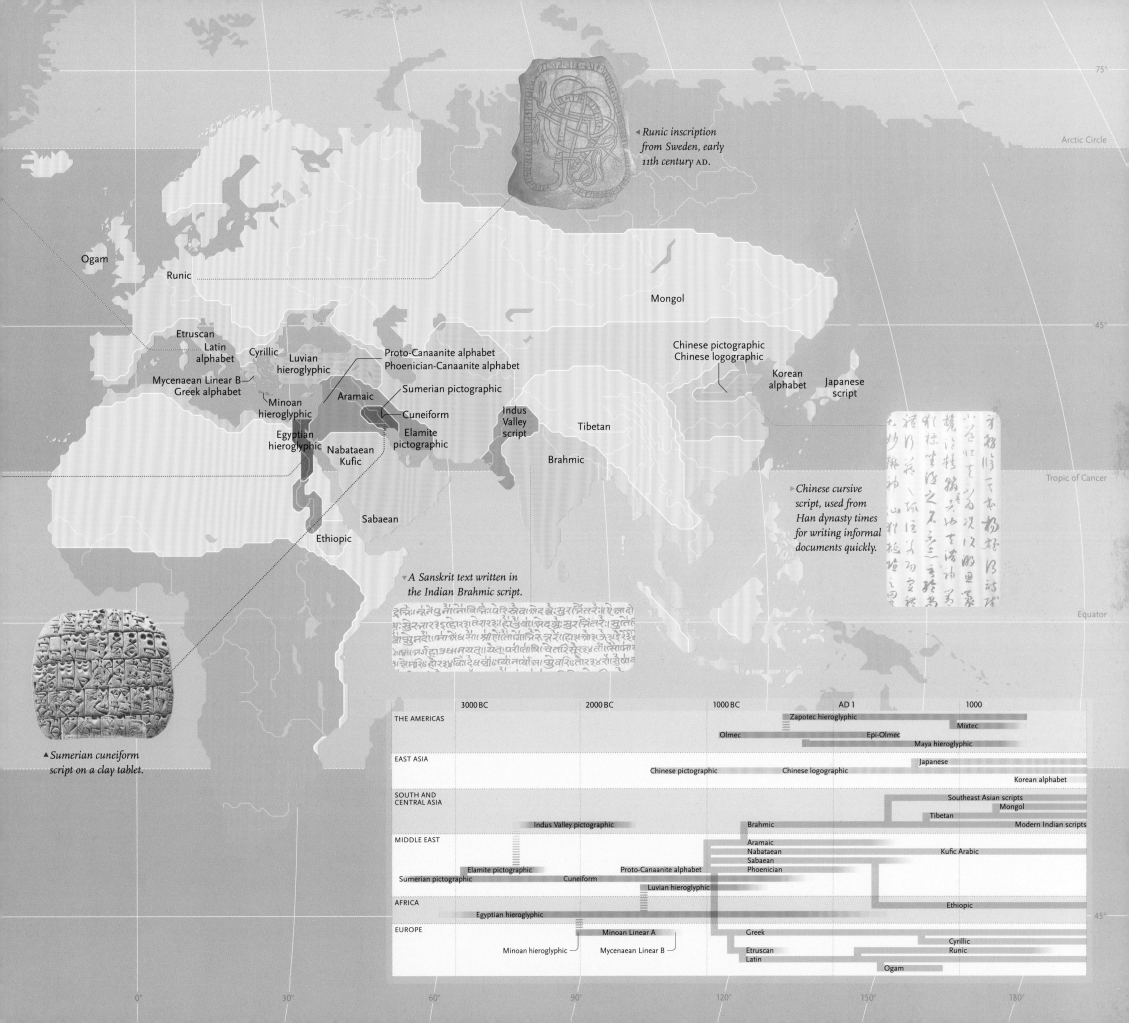

1530

SPAIN AND PORTUGAL DIVIDE THE WORLD BETWEEN THEM; THE OTTOMAN EMPIRE AT ITS PEAK; MUGHAL CONQUESTS IN INDIA

To prevent conflict over the newly discovered lands of the Americas, the papacy negotiated the Treaty of Tordesillas in 1494, dividing the world into Portuguese and Spanish spheres of interest. As the Portuguese seized control of the lucrative East Indian spice trade from the Muslims and founded the first European colonies in India, it seemed that they had the better side of the deal.

Then, in 1519–21, Cortés and his tiny band of conquistadors discovered and conquered the Aztec empire of Mexico. Huge amounts of plundered gold and silver flooded into Spain. Epidemics of European diseases, accidentally introduced by the conquistadors, claimed vast numbers of native Americans and left the survivors demoralized. Spain's ruler, Charles V of Habsburg (r.1516–56 and elected Holy Roman emperor Charles V in 1519), who also ruled Austria, Bohemia, the Netherlands and parts of Italy, became Europe's most powerful ruler.

Charles's power was threatened from within, by the Protestant Reformation, and from outside by France, which fought against encirclement by Habsburg lands, and the Ottoman empire. The Ottomans crushed the Hungarians in 1526, and in 1529 laid siege to the Austrian capital, Vienna. The siege failed but Hungary remained mostly under Ottoman rule. Earlier in the century, the Ottomans had conquered Syria, Palestine and Egypt, and taken northern Mesopotamia from Persia, recently re-established as a territorial state by the Safavid dynasty. In 1504 the Mughal leader Babur, a descendant of Timur and Genghis Khan, established a state around Kabul. In 1526 he invaded India and captured Delhi, establishing the Mughal empire.

In the 1520s the Inca empire reached its height under Wayna Qhapaq but his unexpected death in a smallpox epidemic, which had spread south from a Spanish colony at Panama, threw the empire into civil war.

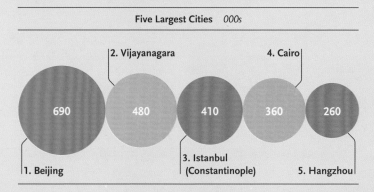

Five Largest Cities   *000s*

2. Vijayanagara — 480
4. Cairo — 360
690 — 1. Beijing
410 — 3. Istanbul (Constantinople)
260 — 5. Hangzhou

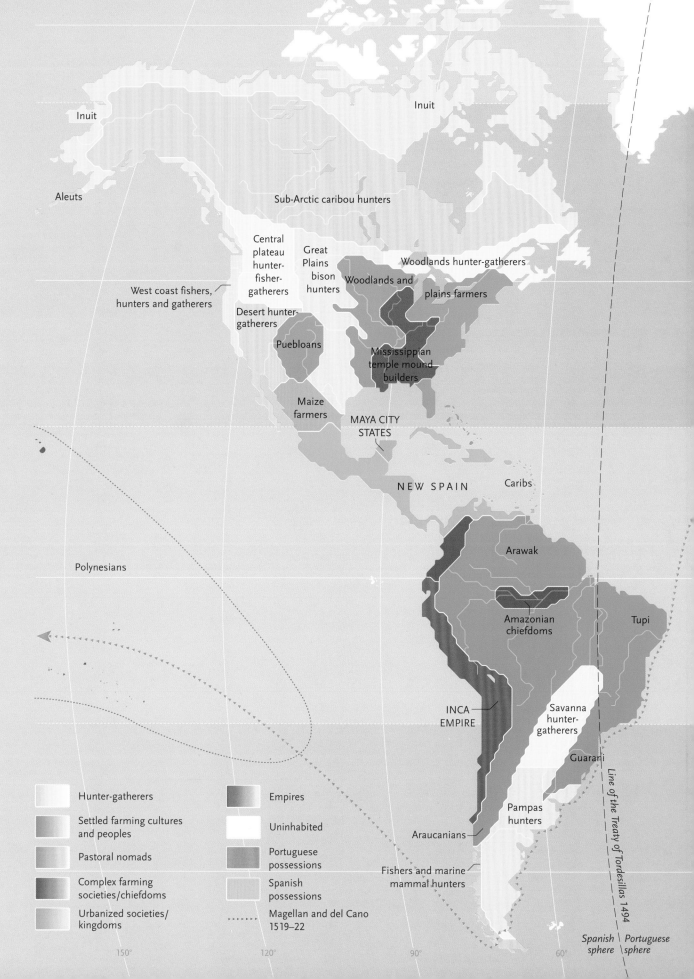

Inuit

Inuit

Aleuts

Sub-Arctic caribou hunters

Central plateau hunter-fisher-gatherers

Great Plains bison hunters

Woodlands hunter-gatherers

West coast fishers, hunters and gatherers

Woodlands and plains farmers

Desert hunter-gatherers

Puebloans

Mississippian temple mound builders

Maize farmers

MAYA CITY STATES

NEW SPAIN

Caribs

Polynesians

Arawak

Amazonian chiefdoms

Tupi

INCA EMPIRE

Savanna hunter-gatherers

Guarani

Araucanians

Pampas hunters

Fishers and marine mammal hunters

Line of the Treaty of Tordesillas 1494

Spanish sphere \ *Portuguese sphere*

Legend

Hunter-gatherers

Settled farming cultures and peoples

Pastoral nomads

Complex farming societies/chiefdoms

Urbanized societies/kingdoms

Empires

Uninhabited

Portuguese possessions

Spanish possessions

Magellan and del Cano 1519–22

150°   120°   90°   60°

SWISS CONFEDERACY 1
VENICE 2
VENETIAN POSSESSIONS 3
PAPAL STATES 4
LIVONIA 5

ICELAND (to Denmark)

Sami

Yakuts

Palaeo-Siberians

Arctic Circle

75°

DENMARK-NORWAY
SWEDEN
MOSCOW
Samoyeds
Tungus

SCOTLAND

Khanate of Sibir

ENGLAND

Khanate of Kazan
Nogai Tatars

HOLY ROMAN EMPIRE
POLAND-LITHUANIA
Khanate of Astrakhan
Kazakhs
Kyrgyz
Mongols
Ainu

FRANCE
HUNGARY
Turkmen
Kalmyks (Oirats)
Jürchen

NAVARRE
KHANATE OF BUKHARA (Uzbeks)
CHAGATAI KHANATE
45°

PORTUGAL
15
GEORGIA 3
KOREA

SPAIN
Istanbul
Beijing 1
JAPAN

HAFSID CALIPHATE
8 6
OTTOMAN TURK EMPIRE
SAFAVID EMPIRE (Persians)
MUGHAL EMPIRE
TIBET
MING EMPIRE

7
3
Cairo 4
Hangzhou 5

Touaregs
Bedouin Arabs
ASSAM

16
Tropic of Cancer

BORNU
DARFUR
FUNJ
OMAN
MUSLIM AND HINDU STATES
ARAKAN
20

SONGHAY
GHARRA
18
ORISSA
19
DAI VIET

MAHRA
Arakan
PEGU
21
SIAM

YEMEN
HADRAMAUT
ADAL
Goa (to Portugal)
2
Vijayanagara
22
CHAMPA

WADAI
ETHIOPIA
VIJAYANAGARA KINGDOM
19
SMALL MALAY SULTANATES
Micronesians

9 11
MALI
10
NUPE
12 IGBO
13
Colombo (to Portugal)
SINHALESE KINGDOMS
23

WOLOF
AKAN KINGDOMS
SULTANATE OF ACEH
24
SULTANATE OF JOHOR

KONGO
Mombasa (to Portugal)
KHANATE OF KHIVA (Uzbeks) 15
Malacca (to Portugal)
SULTANATE OF TERNATE
Equator

Bantu farmers and pastoralists
SWAHILI CITY STATES
RAJPUTS 16
BANTAM
Papuans

BIJAPUR 17
DEMAK
TIMOR (to Portugal)

MALTA (Knights Hospitaller) 6
Mozambique (to Portugal)
BENGAL 18
Melanesians

WATTASID CALIPHATE 7
MUTAPA
BURMESE KINGDOMS 19

ZAYYANID CALIPHATE 8
Malagasy
SHAN KINGDOMS 20

MOSSI KINGDOMS 9
BUTUA
LANNATHAI 21

BORGU 10
San
LAOS 22
Tropic of Capricorn

HAUSA CITY STATES 11
CAMBODIA 23
Australian Aborigines

OYO 12
BRUNEI 24

BENIN 13
Khoikhoi pastoralists

OROMO STATES 14

Polynesians

45°

Maoris

Tasmanians

0°   30°   60°   90°   120°   150°   180°

1530

The political and cultural life of 16th-century Europe was dominated by the Protestant Reformation, which rejected the spiritual authority of the papacy and founded a new major branch of Christianity alongside Roman Catholicism and Orthodoxy. The Reformation was begun by the German monk Martin Luther in 1517, when he attacked spiritual and financial abuses in the Catholic church.

Earlier challenges to the authority of the papacy had failed because they lacked support among the ruling classes, but conditions in the early 16th century were more favourable. The wealth of which reformers complained was much in evidence in Rome, thanks to the papacy's lavish patronage of artists like Michelangelo and its ambitious plans for the construction of St Peter's basilica. Although Luther was condemned as a heretic, he found powerful protectors in the north German princes, who converted to Protestantism for political reasons (to assert their independence against their official overlord Charles V) and, because Luther's theology justified the seizure of church lands, to enrich themselves at the church's expense.

Print technology, now well established, allowed religious tracts to be produced cheaply and in large numbers, so Luther's ideas spread quickly and widely. Nevertheless, the reform movement began to split almost immediately, owing to disagreements about doctrine: the Swiss reformer Huldrych Zwingli, for example, advocated a more extreme form of Protestantism than Luther.

After centuries of division and foreign rule, the Safavids worked to create a cohesive identity that would unite Persians in loyalty to the state. They did this by imposing Shi'a Islam as the state religion, thus deliberately sowing dissension between the Persians and the Sunni Ottomans and Arabs. The Safavids were generous patrons of the arts, promoting distinctive Persian schools in the decorative arts.

World Population

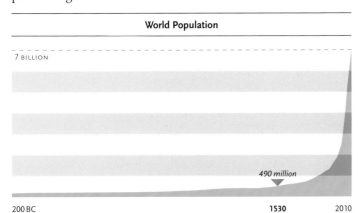

7 BILLION

490 million

200 BC   1530   2010

POLITICS & ECONOMY

1494 The **Treaty of Tordesillas** divides the world between Portugal and Spain.

1494 Beginning of the **Habsburg-Valois (French) wars** for control of Italy (almost continuous to 1559).

1501 **Shah Ismail** establishes the Safavid dynasty in Persia.

Expelled from Bukhara, the **Mughals** under Babur conquer Kabul. **1504**

1497 John Cabot claims **Newfoundland** for England.   **1502** Final collapse of the **Golden Horde**.

1497 The Spanish capture **Melilla**, Morocco, beginning a campaign to capture ports in North Africa.

1497–98 **Vasco da Gama** establishes direct sea route between Portugal and India.

1499 **Swabian War**: Swiss Confederacy becomes independant of the Holy Roman empire.

1499 Amerigo Vespucci explores the coast of **Brazil**.

1500 Portugal claims **Brazil** (first colonies founded 1534).

▲ *The battle between Shah Ismail and Abul-khayr Khan from a 1688 book Tarikh-i Alam-Aray-i.*

◄ *A 17th-century Mexican imagining of the battle for Tenochtitlán during Cortés's conquest of the Aztecs.*

RELIGION & PHILOSOPHY

Shah Ismail makes Shi'a Islam the state religion of Persia. **1501–24**

1497 **Jews** expelled from Portugal.

◄ *The Japanese tea ceremony in a late 18th- or early 19th-century depiction.*

SCIENCE & TECHNOLOGY

1500* **Four-wheeled horse-drawn coaches** with steering and comfortable suspension are first built, Hungary.

ARTS & ARCHITECTURE

1503* Leonardo da Vinci, **Mona Lisa** (painting).

1500–1600 Origins of the **Japanese tea ceremony**.

1501–4 Michelangelo, **David** (sculpture).

*Approximate date

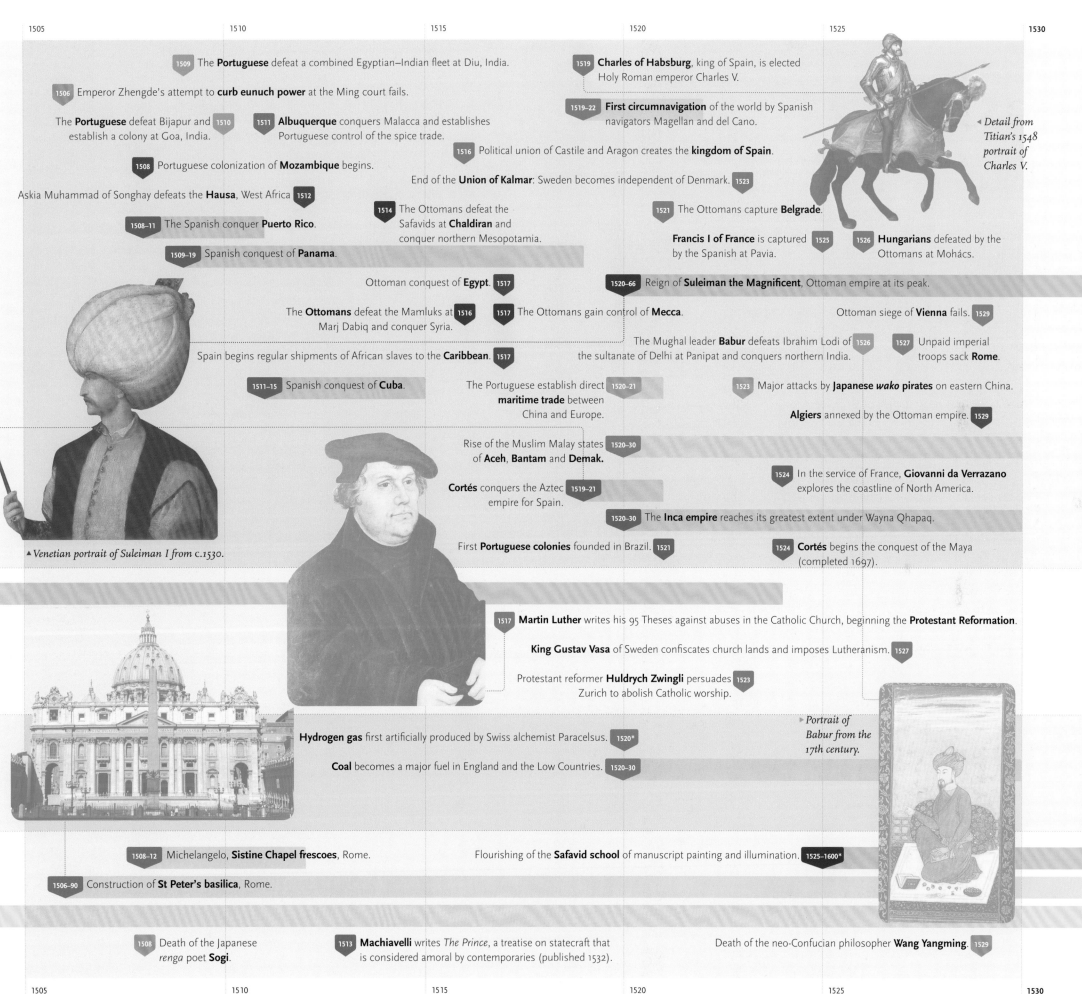

1509 The **Portuguese** defeat a combined Egyptian–Indian fleet at Diu, India.

1519 **Charles of Habsburg**, king of Spain, is elected Holy Roman emperor Charles V.

1506 Emperor Zhengde's attempt to **curb eunuch power** at the Ming court fails.

1519–22 **First circumnavigation** of the world by Spanish navigators Magellan and del Cano.

The **Portuguese** defeat Bijapur and **1510** establish a colony at Goa, India.

1511 **Albuquerque** conquers Malacca and establishes Portuguese control of the spice trade.

◄ *Detail from Titian's 1548 portrait of Charles V.*

1516 Political union of Castile and Aragon creates the **kingdom of Spain**.

1508 Portuguese colonization of **Mozambique** begins.

End of the **Union of Kalmar**: Sweden becomes independent of Denmark. **1523**

Askia Muhammad of Songhay defeats the **Hausa**, West Africa **1512**

1521 The Ottomans capture **Belgrade**.

1508–11 The Spanish conquer **Puerto Rico**.

1514 The Ottomans defeat the Safavids at **Chaldiran** and conquer northern Mesopotamia.

Francis I of France is captured **1525** by the Spanish at Pavia.

1526 **Hungarians** defeated by the Ottomans at Mohács.

1509–19 Spanish conquest of **Panama**.

Ottoman conquest of **Egypt**. **1517**

1520–66 Reign of **Suleiman the Magnificent**, Ottoman empire at its peak.

The **Ottomans** defeat the Mamluks at **1516** Marj Dabiq and conquer Syria.

1517 The Ottomans gain control of **Mecca**.

Ottoman siege of **Vienna** fails. **1529**

The Mughal leader **Babur** defeats Ibrahim Lodi of **1526** the sultanate of Delhi at Panipat and conquers northern India.

1527 Unpaid imperial troops sack **Rome**.

Spain begins regular shipments of African slaves to the **Caribbean**. **1517**

1511–15 Spanish conquest of **Cuba**.

The Portuguese establish direct **1520–21** **maritime trade** between China and Europe.

1523 Major attacks by **Japanese *wako* pirates** on eastern China.

Algiers annexed by the Ottoman empire. **1529**

▲ *Venetian portrait of Suleiman I from c.1530.*

Rise of the Muslim Malay states of **Aceh**, **Bantam** and **Demak. 1520–30**

1524 In the service of France, **Giovanni da Verrazano** explores the coastline of North America.

Cortés conquers the Aztec **1519–21** empire for Spain.

1520–30 The **Inca empire** reaches its greatest extent under Wayna Qhapaq.

First **Portuguese colonies** founded in Brazil. **1521**

1524 **Cortés** begins the conquest of the Maya (completed 1697).

1517 **Martin Luther** writes his 95 Theses against abuses in the Catholic Church, beginning the **Protestant Reformation**.

King Gustav Vasa of Sweden confiscates church lands and imposes Lutheranism. **1527**

Protestant reformer **Huldrych Zwingli** persuades **1523** Zurich to abolish Catholic worship.

▶ *Portrait of Babur from the 17th century.*

Hydrogen gas first artificially produced by Swiss alchemist Paracelsus. **1520***

Coal becomes a major fuel in England and the Low Countries. **1520–30**

1508–12 Michelangelo, **Sistine Chapel frescoes**, Rome.

Flourishing of the **Safavid school** of manuscript painting and illumination. **1525–1600***

1506–90 Construction of **St Peter's basilica**, Rome.

1508 Death of the Japanese *renga* poet **Sogi**.

1513 **Machiavelli** writes *The Prince*, a treatise on statecraft that is considered amoral by contemporaries (published 1532).

Death of the neo-Confucian philosopher **Wang Yangming**. **1529**

1600

CONTINUED SPANISH CONQUEST OF THE
AMERICAS; THE MUGHAL EMPIRE AT ITS PEAK

The European impact on the Americas was already
considerable by 1600. Even areas that had yet to see a
European had suffered devastating depopulation and
social dislocation from European epidemic diseases. In
1531 the Spanish conquistador Francisco Pizarro invaded
and conquered the Inca empire. The conquest brought
Spain fabulous quantities of gold and control of the world's
richest silver mines. Much of this silver made its way across
the world to China and India, having been used to pay for
eastern luxuries.

This period also saw the beginning of Portuguese
colonization of Brazil and the first, unsuccessful, attempts
by the English and French to colonize North America. In
Mesoamerica, the rapid decline of the native American
population led the Portuguese and Spanish to rely
increasingly on imported African slave labour to work their
sugar plantations in Brazil and the Caribbean.

The Ottoman empire consolidated its position as the
leading Muslim power with further conquests in North
Africa, Arabia, Mesopotamia and the Caucasus. Its defeat
in the naval battle of Lepanto by the Spanish-led Holy
League in 1571 showed Europeans that the empire was not
invincible. The Mughal empire's hold on northern India
was shaken by the Suri rebellion of 1539–56, but under
Akbar the Great (r. 1556–1605) the empire recovered,
conquering the Rajputs, Gujarat and the wealthy region of
Bengal, to become one of the world's most powerful states.

Following a civil war in the late 15th century, Japan broke
up into hundreds of autonomous feudal principalities and
the authority of the shogunate collapsed. In the last two
decades of the 16th century a succession of able warlords
reunified Japan, a process that culminated in 1600 with
the foundation of the Tokugawa shogunate, which ruled
Japan until 1868. Late Ming China was a time of cultural
brilliance and political weakness.

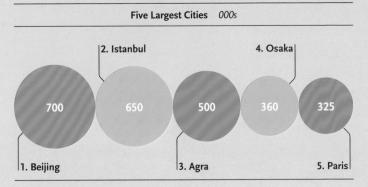

Five Largest Cities *000s*

2. Istanbul   4. Osaka

700   650   500   360   325

1. Beijing   3. Agra   5. Paris

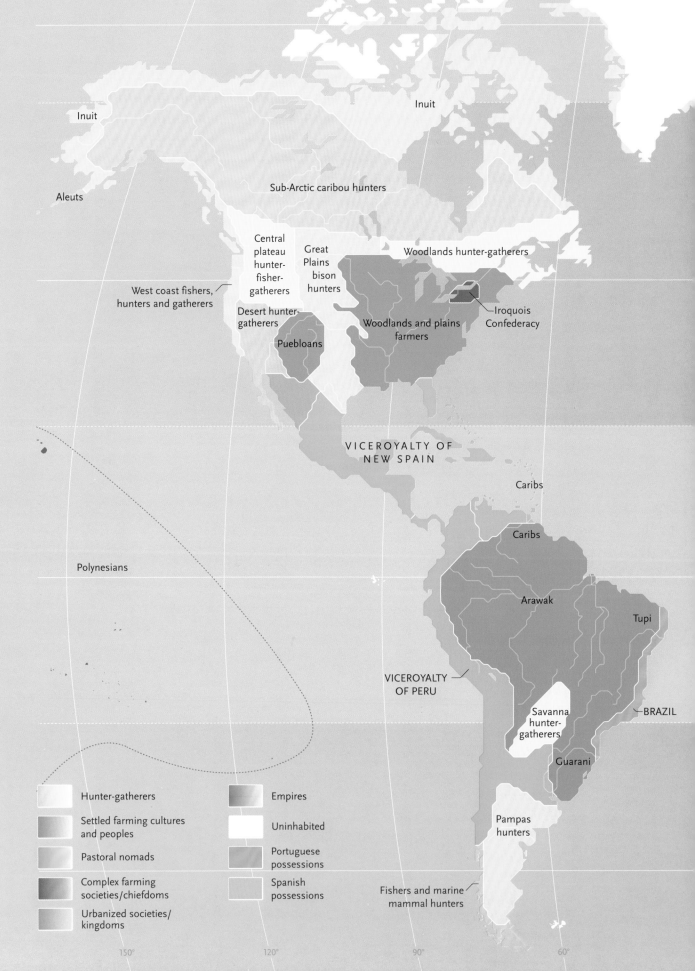

Inuit

Inuit

Aleuts

Sub-Arctic caribou hunters

West coast fishers,
hunters and gatherers

Central
plateau
hunter-
fisher-
gatherers

Great
Plains
bison
hunters

Woodlands hunter-gatherers

Desert hunter-
gatherers

Woodlands and plains
farmers

Iroquois
Confederacy

Puebloans

VICEROYALTY OF
NEW SPAIN

Caribs

Caribs

Polynesians

Arawak

Tupi

VICEROYALTY
OF PERU

BRAZIL

Savanna
hunter-
gatherers

Guarani

Pampas
hunters

Fishers and marine
mammal hunters

Hunter-gatherers

Settled farming cultures
and peoples

Pastoral nomads

Complex farming
societies/chiefdoms

Urbanized societies/
kingdoms

Empires

Uninhabited

Portuguese
possessions

Spanish
possessions

SPANISH NETHERLANDS **1**
NETHERLANDS **2**
SWISS CONFEDERACY **3**
PAPAL STATES **4**
VENICE **5**
HUNGARY **6**

ICELAND (to Denmark)

SCOTLAND

ENGLAND

PORTUGAL (in union with Spain)

MOROCCO

GREAT FULO

SMALL STATES

MOSSI KINGDOMS **7**
HAUSA CITY STATES **8**
BENIN **9**
OROMO STATES **10**
AUSSA **11**
HARAR **12**
SMALL STATES **13**

DENMARK-NORWAY

SWEDEN

HOLY ROMAN EMPIRE

POLAND

5 Paris
FRANCE

SPAIN

MALTA

FEZZAN

Touaregs

ÄIR

SONGHAY

DARFUR

FUNJ

MALI

OYO

NUPE

IGBO

AKAN STATES

BORNU

WADAI

ETHIOPIA

ADAL

KONGO

NDONGO

ANGOLA

Bantu farmers and pastoralists

MUTAPA

BUTUA

San

Khoikhoi pastoralists

Mombasa

SWAHILI CITY STATES

Mozambique

Malagasy

Quelimane

Delagoa Bay

RUSSIAN EMPIRE

Samoyeds

Yakuts

Tungus

Palaeo-Siberians

Kazakhs

Buryats

Kazan Tatars

Nogai Tatars

Mongols

Ainu

Jürchen (Manchus)

Turkmen

Kyrgyz

Kalmyks

KHANATE OF BUKHARA

CHAGATAI KHANATE

1 Beijing

2 Istanbul

OTTOMAN EMPIRE

SAFAVID EMPIRE

Hormuz

NEPALESE STATES

TIBET

BHUTAN

MING EMPIRE

KOREA

4 JAPAN

Osaka

Bedouin Arabs

MUGHAL EMPIRE

3 Agra

Macao

Muscat

OMAN

GHARRA

MAHRA

HADRAMAUT

Diu

15

Bombay

Goa

16

17

18

19

ARAKAN

BURMA

20

21

22

SHAN STATES

SIAM

DAI VIET

PHILIPPINES

Micronesians

CHAMPA

23

BRUNEI

SINHALESE KINGDOMS

SULTANATE OF ACEH

Malacca

JOHOR

SMALL MALAY SULTANATES

BANTAM

MATARAM

Amboina

Papuans

SURABAYA

TIMOR

Melanesians

14 KHANATE OF KHIVA
15 AHMADNAGAR
16 GONDWANA
17 GOLCONDA
18 BIJAPUR
19 VIJAYANARA KINGDOM
20 ASSAM
21 SHAN STATES
22 LAOS
23 CAMBODIA

Australian Aborigines

Polynesians

Maoris

Tasmanians

14

11

12

10

8

7

9

13

13

13

1600

The papacy responded to the Reformation by launching the Counter-Reformation to re-emphasize the tenets of the Catholic faith. In this it relied heavily on the intellectual Jesuit Order to educate Catholics in the faith and to counter Protestant arguments. Two major new Protestant movements had emerged: the French reformer John Calvin's uncompromising version of Protestantism spread to Switzerland, France, the Netherlands and Scotland; while in England Anglicanism remained doctrinally closer to Catholicism than Lutheranism.

The doctrinal conflicts plunged Europe into a century of wars. The Holy Roman empire was divided by civil war when the Protestant princes formed the Schmalkaldic League to defy the emperor Charles V's attempt to enforce Catholic supremacy. The conflict ended in 1555 with the Peace of Augsburg, which allowed princes to decide the religion of their subjects. His failure to suppress Protestantism led to Charles V's abdication in 1556 and the division of the Habsburg dynasty into Spanish and Austrian branches: both remained strong supporters of Catholicism.

Spain's attempt to eradicate Protestantism in the Netherlands provoked a long war of independence. The Spanish king Philip II's attempt to invade England in 1588 and overthrow its Protestant queen Elizabeth I was defeated at sea. France, too, suffered wars of religion, ended by the Edict of Nantes in 1598, which granted toleration to Protestantism. Despite these upheavals, there were important cultural developments in Europe in astronomy, cartography, architecture and drama.

This period also saw the creation of magnificent Ottoman architecture – the mosques at Istanbul and Edirne built by Mimar Sinan for sultans Suleiman the Magnificent and Selim. The Sikh faith's most important monument, the Golden Temple at Amritsar, was also begun at this time.

World Population

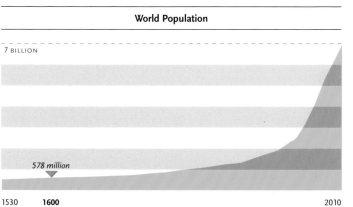

7 BILLION

578 million

POLITICS & ECONOMY

1531 Protestant German princes form the **Schmalkaldic League** to defend their territories against the Catholic Holy Roman emperor Charles V.

1546 The Ottomans capture **Basra**: all of Mesopotamia is now under their control.

1534 The Ottomans capture **Baghdad** from the Safavids.

1547 **Ivan IV 'the Terrible'** is crowned first tsar of Russia.

1535 **Tunis** captured by Spain.

1538 **Yemen** comes under Ottoman control.

1539 The **Suri dynasty** of Bihar rebels against the Mughals.

1534–41 **Jacques Cartier** leads unsuccessful French attempts to colonize the St Lawrence River.

1543 The **Ethiopians** defeat an invasion by Ahmed Gran of Adal with Portuguese support.

1535–92 **Dai Viet** divided into two kingdoms during a civil war.

1531–35 **Pizarro** conquers the Inca empire for Spain.

1542 **Spain abolishes native slavery** in its American empire, leading to a large increase in imports of African slaves.

1539–40 **Tabinshweti** unifies Burma and conquers Pegu.

1542 The Portuguese begin trading with **Japan**.

1538 Spanish conquest of **New Granada** (Colombia).

1545 The world's largest **silver mines** open at **Potosí**, Bolivia.

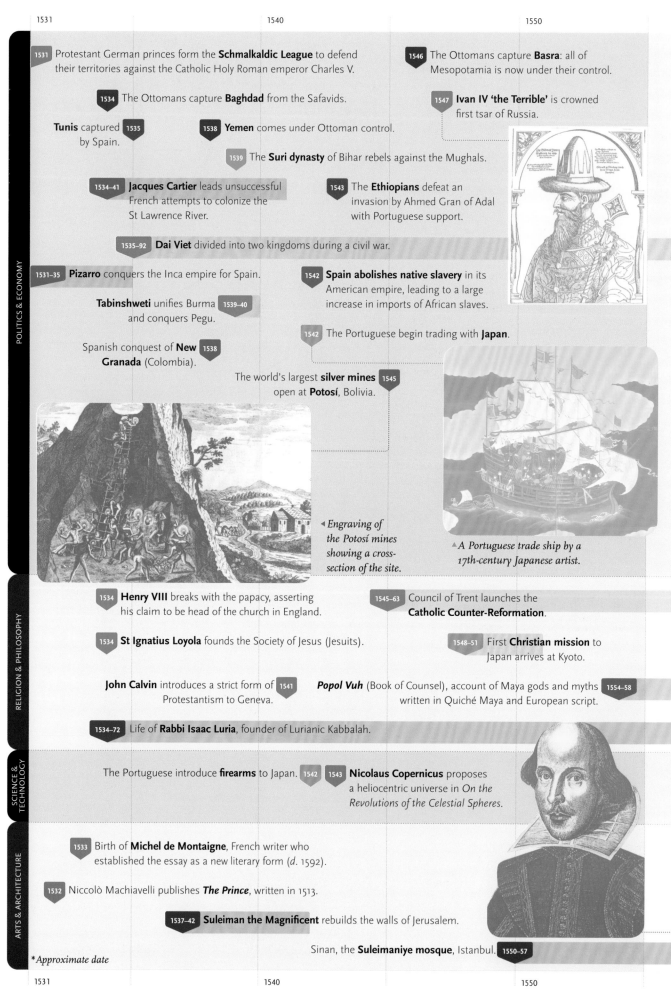

◄ *Engraving of the Potosí mines showing a cross-section of the site.*

▲ *A Portuguese trade ship by a 17th-century Japanese artist.*

RELIGION & PHILOSOPHY

1534 **Henry VIII** breaks with the papacy, asserting his claim to be head of the church in England.

1545–63 Council of Trent launches the **Catholic Counter-Reformation**.

1534 **St Ignatius Loyola** founds the Society of Jesus (Jesuits).

1548–51 First **Christian mission** to Japan arrives at Kyoto.

1541 **John Calvin** introduces a strict form of Protestantism to Geneva.

1554–58 **Popol Vuh** (Book of Counsel), account of Maya gods and myths written in Quiché Maya and European script.

1534–72 Life of **Rabbi Isaac Luria**, founder of Lurianic Kabbalah.

SCIENCE & TECHNOLOGY

1542 The Portuguese introduce **firearms** to Japan.

1543 **Nicolaus Copernicus** proposes a heliocentric universe in *On the Revolutions of the Celestial Spheres*.

ARTS & ARCHITECTURE

1533 Birth of **Michel de Montaigne**, French writer who established the essay as a new literary form (d. 1592).

1532 Niccolò Machiavelli publishes **The Prince**, written in 1513.

1537–42 **Suleiman the Magnificent** rebuilds the walls of Jerusalem.

1550–57 Sinan, the **Suleimaniye mosque**, Istanbul.

*Approximate date

1555 **Peace of Augsburg**: princes of the Holy Roman empire are allowed to decide the faith of their subjects.

Defeat of the **Spanish Armada**, sent by **1588** Philip II to invade England.

1559 Treaty of Cateau-Cambrésis ends the **Habsburg-Valois wars**: France gives up territorial claims in Italy.

Beginning of **Dutch rebellion** against Spanish **1568** rule (independence recognized 1648).

1572 The Mughals conquer the **Gujarat** region of western India.

1581–82 Conquest of the khanate of Sibir begins Russian expansion into **Siberia**.

1562–89 **French Wars of Religion**.

Suleiman the Magnificent dies on campaign in Hungary. **1566**

1571 **Cyprus** falls to the Ottomans.

1580 **Philip II of Spain** becomes king of Portugal.

▲ *Artist's imagining of English ships battling wih the Spanish Armada.*

1556 The **Mughals** under Akbar destroy the Suri army at Panipat.

1565 **Vijayanagara** sacked after defeat by Bijapur at Talikota.

1576 The Mughals conquer **Bengal**.

Ottoman sultan **Mehmet III** murders **1595** 27 brothers to win power.

1557 The **Portuguese** establish a permanent colony at Macao.

1568–82 Warlord **Oda Nobunaga** begins the reunification of Japan.

Hideyoshi completes the **1590** **reunification of Japan**.

1592–93 **Japanese invasion of Korea** is defeated by the Chinese.

Akbar defeats the Rajputs at Chittaurgarh and Rathambor. **1568–69**

1571 The Holy League defeats the Ottomans at the **naval battle of Lepanto**, Greece.

Tokugawa Ieyasu founds the **Tokugawa dynasty of shoguns** which rules Japan until 1868. **1600**

Spanish settlers found the first European settlement in **1565** **North America**, at St Augustine, Florida.

1570* China begins to import **silver** from America.

Second Japanese invasion of Korea defeated; death of **Hideyoshi**. **1597–98**

Toyotomi Hideyoshi succeeds Oda Nobunaga as dominant warlord in Japan. **1582**

Akbar makes **Agra** the capital of the Mughal empire. **1598**

Portuguese found **Rio de Janeiro**, Brazil. **1565–67**

1571 The Spanish found **Manila** as capital of the Philippines.

The first Dutch trading fleet arrives at **Java**. **1596**

Foundation of the **Iroquois Confederacy**. **1570**

1575 Brazil becomes the world's largest **sugar producer**.

1584–90 Raleigh's **English Roanoke colony** in Virginia fails.

Bornu becomes the major Islamic power between the **1570** Nile and the Niger under Idris III Aloma.

1578–79 **Francis Drake** plunders Spanish settlements on the Pacific coast during his circumnavigation of the world (1577–80).

The Ottomans capture **Tunis** from the Spanish. **1574**

1578 Moroccans defeat and kill Portugal's king Sebastian I at **Alcazarquivir**.

The Portuguese capture **Mombasa**. **1598**

Portuguese colonization of **Angola** begins at Luanda. **1574**

1591 A Moroccan invasion destroys **Songhay** as a major power.

◄ *Painting of the battle of Lepanto by Andrea Micheli 'Vicentino'.*

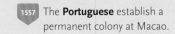

1555 Portuguese Jesuit mission to **Ethiopia**.

1559 Elizabeth I establishes the **Church of England** (Anglican Church).

The **Edict of Nantes** grants toleration to **1598** Huguenots (French Protestants).

Toyotomi Hideyoshi executes 26 Christians to **1597** discourage other Japanese from converting.

◄ *Miniature showing Akbar riding an elephant, c. 1610.*

1577 Altan Khan makes reformed **Tibetan Buddhism** the official religion of the Mongols.

Flemish cartographer **1569** Gerardus Mercator publishes his **world map**.

1578 **Li Shizhen**, *Compendium of Materia Medica*, describes 1,800 drugs and 11,000 prescriptions.

1593 **Galileo Galilei** invents the first thermometer.

1570 Andrea Palladio popularizes the Palladian style of classical architecture across Europe in *Four Books of Architecture*.

1564–1616 Life of the English dramatist **William Shakespeare**.

1555–60 Postnik, the **cathedral of St Basil**, Moscow.

1570* Wu Cheng'en writes the novel *Journey to the West* (better known in the West as *Monkey*).

Meenakshi Sundareswarar temple, dedicated **1600*** to Shiva and Parvati, Madurai, India.

1569–75 Sinan, the **Selimiye mosque**, Edirne.

1576–79 Oda Nobunaga builds **Azuchi Castle**, revolutionizing Japanese castle architecture.

1588 Construction of the Sikhs' **Golden Temple at Amritsar** begins (ends 1608).

1600

THE SPREAD OF WORLD RELIGIONS TO 1600 –
CHRISTIANITY IS THE FIRST GLOBAL RELIGION

In the wake of the 7th-century Arab conquests, Islam became the fastest growing and most widespread of the world religions. The adoption of Islam by the Turks *c.* AD 1000 spread the religion into Central Asia. Much of India came under Muslim rule but Islam failed to displace Hinduism as the majority religion. Arab merchants spread Islam to West and East Africa, and to the East Indies, where it replaced Hinduism and Buddhism as the dominant faith. Islam suffered one major schism, following a disputed succession to the caliphate in the 7th century, splitting into Sunni and Shi'ite branches. The minority Shi'a tradition's main strongholds in 1600 were Persia and Mesopotamia: this was a recent development promoted by the Persian Safavid dynasty. The mystical Sufi tradition of Islam, which developed in the 8th century, was particularly influential in the Ottoman world.

By 1600 Christianity had divided into three main branches: Orthodoxy, Roman Catholicism and Protestantism. After losing ground to Islam in the early Middle Ages, Christianity was again expanding. The Spanish and Portuguese had introduced Catholicism to Central and South America, Central Africa, and Southeast Asia. The intellectual Jesuit order played a leading role in Catholic missionary enterprise and in combating Protestantism in Europe. Orthodoxy was spreading into Siberia with Russian settlers. At the start of the 17th century, Protestantism was introduced to North America by English settlers. Expulsions and forced conversions had eradicated Judaism from much of Christian Europe by 1600. Except for Poland and Italy, the main centres of Jewish settlement were all in the relatively more tolerant Muslim world.

Buddhism spread to Tibet in the 7th century, where it partly assimilated the native shamanistic Bön religion. This distinctive form of Buddhism was later adopted by the Mongols, largely replacing Tengriism, their traditional shamanistic religion. Elsewhere, Buddhism lost ground to Hinduism and Islam, becoming effectively extinct in Indonesia and its original homeland of India.

The ancient Persian Zoroastrian religion also became almost extinct in its homeland, after the Arab conquests. Persian refugees took the religion to India, where it survived among their descendants, the Parsis and Iranis. The new religion of Sikhism became established in Punjab. Founded by Guru Nanak (1469–1539), it attempted to reconcile Hindus and Muslims.

VICEROYALTY OF
NEW SPAIN

VICEROYALTY
OF PERU

BRAZIL
(Portuguese)

Christian in 1600:

Predominantly
Roman Catholic

Predominantly
Protestant

Predominantly
Orthodox

Predominantly
Muslim in 1600

Shi'a Muslim
majority in 1600

Confucian in
1600

Predominantly
Hindu in 1600

Sikh area in 1600

Predominantly
Buddhist in 1600

Major area of
Jewish settlement

Jesuit missionary
areas *c.* 1600

Other area of
Jewish settlement

NETHERLANDS 1
SWISS 2
CONFEDERACY
PAPAL STATES 3
HUNGARY 4

DENMARK-
NORWAY
SWEDEN

SCOTLAND

ENGLAND

FRANCE

HOLY ROMAN
EMPIRE

POLAND

1

4

2

RUSSIAN
EMPIRE

Kazakhs

Kazan
Tatars

Nogai
Tatars

Kyrgyz

Kalmyks

Mongols

PORTUGAL
(in union with Spain)

SPAIN

3

GEORGIA

Turkmen

11

KHANATE
OF BUKHARA

CHAGATAI
KHANATE

KOREA

JAPAN

MOROCCO

OTTOMAN
EMPIRE

SAFAVID
EMPIRE

TIBET

MING
EMPIRE

FEZZAN

MUGHAL
EMPIRE

NEPAL

BHUTAN

12

Macao
(Portuguese)

Tropic of Cancer

Touaregs

Bedouin
Arabs

13

GREAT
FULO

ÄIR

OMAN
GHARRA

ARAKAN
BURMA

14

SIAM

DAI VIET

PHILIPPINES
(Spanish)

SONGHAY

DARFUR

FUNJ

MAHRA

SMALL
STATES

MALI

5

BORNU

6

WADAI

HADRAMAUT

Goa

INDIAN
STATES

CHAMPA

OYO

NUPE

ETHIOPIA

ADAL

9

15

SULTANATE
OF ACEH

MALAY
SULTANATES

TIMOR
(Portuguese)

7

IGBO

10

8

SINHALESE
KINGDOMS

AKAN
STATES

KONGO

SWAHILI CITY
STATES

11 KHANATE OF KHIVA

12 ASSAM

MATARAM

NDONGO

Mozambique
(Portuguese)

13 SHAN STATES

ANGOLA
(Portuguese)

14 LAOS

15 CAMBODIA

MOSSI KINGDOMS 5

MUTAPA

HAUSA CITY STATES 6

BENIN 7

OROMO STATES 8

BUTUA

AUSSA 9

HARAR 10

Equator

Tropic of Capricorn

Arctic Circle

75°

45°

45°

0° 30° 60° 90° 120° 150° 180°

1650

FRANCE BECOMES THE DOMINANT EUROPEAN POWER; THE MANCHU CONQUEST OF CHINA

The post-Reformation religious conflicts in Europe became entwined with a constitutional crisis in the Holy Roman empire's ruling Habsburg dynasty, precipitating the Thirty Years War (1618–48). The war began as a Protestant revolt against the Catholic Habsburg emperor Ferdinand II, but other powers could not ignore the troubles of the empire and gradually most of Europe was drawn into the conflict.

The war entered its decisive phase when France declared war on the Habsburgs. Germany was devastated and the Holy Roman empire was effectively destroyed as a meaningful political entity (it was finally abolished by Napoleon in 1806). The main beneficiaries of the war were France, which became Europe's strongest power, the Netherlands, whose independence was finally recognized by Spain, and Sweden, which emerged as the great power of the Baltic. England, which avoided the Thirty Years War, suffered its own civil war, leading to the execution of its king Charles I by a victorious Parliament in 1649.

The first decades of the 17th century saw France, the Netherlands and England join Spain and Portugal as colonial powers. Portugal's colonial interests were neglected after it entered a dynastic union with Spain in 1580, giving the Dutch an opportunity to break its monopoly of trade with the East Indies. England and France both founded colonies in North America and the West Indies, and trading posts in West Africa and India.

The costs of defending the Ming empire bore heavily on the Chinese peasantry. Widespread peasant rebellions broke out in 1628, and in 1641 rebel regimes began to seize power in the provinces. Exploiting the chaos, the Manchus invaded China in 1644, destroyed the rebel forces and seized power, installing their own Qing dynasty on the throne. From the outset, the Qing began to assimilate themselves to Chinese culture while retaining their own distinctive ethnicity.

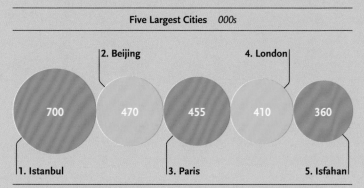

Five Largest Cities *000s*

2. Beijing
4. London

700 | 470 | 455 | 410 | 360

1. Istanbul
3. Paris
5. Isfahan

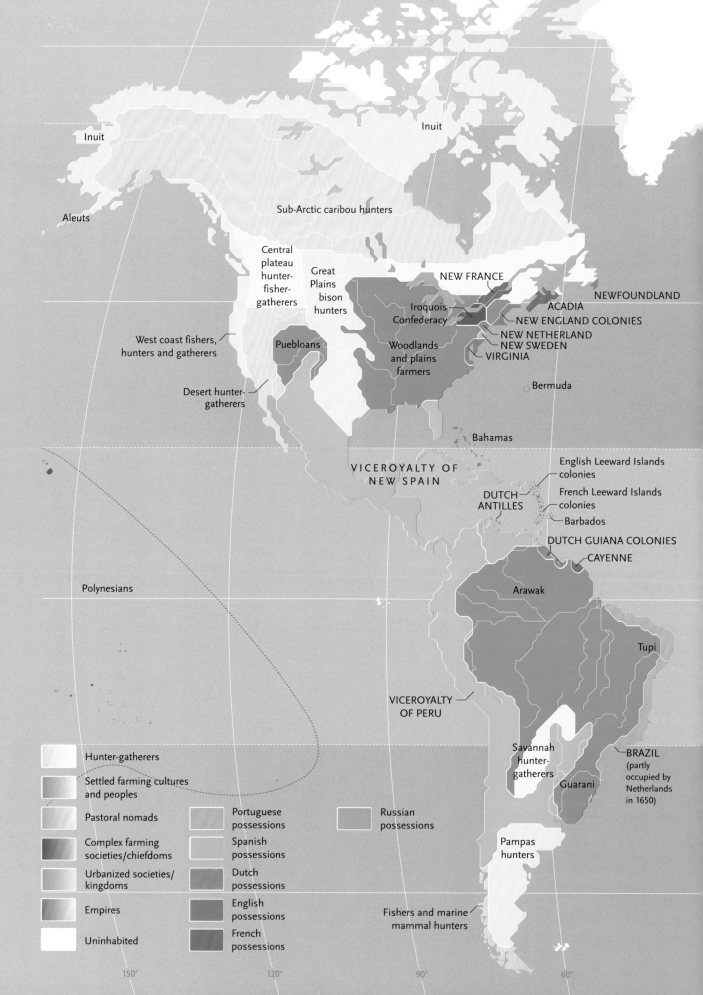

Inuit

Inuit

Aleuts

Sub-Arctic caribou hunters

Central plateau hunter-fisher-gatherers

Great Plains bison hunters

NEW FRANCE

NEWFOUNDLAND

Iroquois Confederacy

ACADIA

NEW ENGLAND COLONIES

West coast fishers, hunters and gatherers

Puebloans

Woodlands and plains farmers

NEW NETHERLAND

NEW SWEDEN

VIRGINIA

Bermuda

Desert hunter-gatherers

Bahamas

VICEROYALTY OF NEW SPAIN

English Leeward Islands colonies

French Leeward Islands colonies

DUTCH ANTILLES

Barbados

DUTCH GUIANA COLONIES

CAYENNE

Polynesians

Arawak

Tupi

VICEROYALTY OF PERU

Savannah hunter-gatherers

BRAZIL (partly occupied by Netherlands in 1650)

Guarani

Pampas hunters

Fishers and marine mammal hunters

Hunter-gatherers

Settled farming cultures and peoples

Pastoral nomads

Portuguese possessions

Russian possessions

Complex farming societies/chiefdoms

Spanish possessions

Urbanized societies/kingdoms

Dutch possessions

Empires

English possessions

Uninhabited

French possessions

150°   120°   90°   60°

NETHERLANDS 1
BRANDENBURG- 2
PRUSSIA
SWISS 3
CONFEDERACY
ITALIAN STATES 4
PAPAL STATES 5
VENICE 6
to VENICE 7
ICELAND
(to Denmark)

SCOTLAND
ENGLAND
London 4
Paris 3
FRANCE
PORTUGAL
SPAIN

DENMARK-
NORWAY
SWEDEN
POLAND
GERMAN
STATES
AUSTRIA

RUSSIAN
EMPIRE

Yakuts
Tungus
Palaeo-Siberians

Buryats

Kazakhs

Mongols

Ainu

Nogai
Tatars
Kyrgyz
Kalmyks

Turkmen 17
KHANATE
OF BUKHARA

CHAGATAI
KHANATE

2
Beijing
QING
(Manchu)
EMPIRE

KOREA
JAPAN

Istanbul 1
OTTOMAN
EMPIRE

MALTA 7

5
Isfahan
SAFAVID
EMPIRE

TIBET
NEPALESE
STATES
BHUTAN

22 23
MING
WARLORDS

MOROCCO
FEZZAN

Touaregs
ÄIR
St
Louis MASINA
GREAT
FULO
Fort
James
MALI
SONGHAY
BORNU
DARFUR

Bedouin
Arabs

FUNJ

MAHRA
YEMEN HADRAMAUT

MUGHAL
EMPIRE

Diu Surat
Bombay
Goa
18
ARAKAN

BURMA

24
Macao Zeelandia
TONGKING

SMALL
STATES

BORGU 8 10
NUPE
9 IGBO
11
12
Elmina

WADAI
ETHIOPIA
13
15 14

19
20
Madras
Pondicherry
21
CEYLON

SIAM

PHILIPPINES
COCHIN
CHINA
CAMBODIA
BRUNEI

MOSSI KINGDOMS 8
AKAN STATES 9
HAUSA CITY STATES 10
OYO 11
BENIN 12
AUSSA 13
HARAR 14
OROMO STATES 15
SMALL STATES 16

Bantu farmers
and pastoralists
KONGO 16
LUNDA LUBA
ANGOLA NDONGO
16
MUTAPA
BUTUA 16

Mombasa
SWAHILI CITY
STATES

Mozambique

Malagasy

Mauritius

SULTANATE
OF ACEH
Malacca
DUTCH EAST
INDIA COLONIES
BANTAM
MATARAM

Batavia
SMALL MALAY
SULTANATES

MACASSAR

Tidore

Amboina Papuans

PORTUGUESE TIMOR
DUTCH TIMOR

Micronesians

Melanesians

Equator

St Helena

San

Quelimane
Delagoa Bay

Khoikhoi
pastoralists

17 KHANATE OF
KHIVA
18 GONDWANA
19 GOLCONDA
20 BIJAPUR

21 HINDU
KINGDOMS
22 ASSAM
23 SHAN STATES
24 LAOS

Australian Aborigines

Polynesians

Tasmanians

Maoris

Arctic Circle
75°
45°
Tropic of Cancer
Tropic of Capricorn
45°
0° 30° 60° 90° 120° 150° 180°

1650

Early 17th-century Europeans still held a primarily religious world view. God was seen as the ultimate source of political legitimacy and most monarchs claimed to rule by divine right. Religion was never far from the surface in the English Civil War fought between the absolutist king Charles I and Parliament, in which the Anglican establishment supported the king and the more extreme Protestant Puritans supported Parliament. The desire to create a godly society was the main aim of the English Puritans who settled in New England in the 1620s.

The Italian scientist Galileo, one of the pioneers of the use of telescopes for astronomy, was prosecuted for heresy by the papal Inquisition: he had advocated Copernicus' heliocentric universe which conflicted with the biblical doctrine that the Earth did not move. However, Kepler's discovery of the laws of planetary motion made the ancient belief that the Earth was at the centre of the universe increasingly untenable, while the works of Descartes and Bacon show the beginnings of a rationalistic and scientific approach to understanding the world.

During the 16th century, the Portuguese had introduced firearms and Christianity to Japan. Firearms played a decisive role in the wars of reunification, but once the wars were over the shoguns abolished them. Foreigners and foreign influences were deliberately kept at arm's length: the Portuguese were expelled for promoting Christianity and Japanese Christians were ruthlessly persecuted; Dutch traders were permitted to remain but were confined to a single small island near Nagasaki; and the Japanese were banned from travelling abroad.

The first half of the 17th century saw the development of the ornate Baroque architectural style in Italy and some of the finest achievements of Islamic architecture in the Ottoman empire, the Safavid empire and Mughal India.

World Population

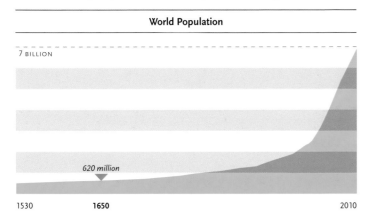

7 BILLION

620 million

1530   1650   2010

128

1601   1605   1610   1615

POLITICS & ECONOMY

1603 Union of the crowns of England and Scotland: James VI of Scotland becomes **James I of England**.

1601 **Dutch East India Company** founded.

Bohemian Protestant revolt against the Catholic Habsburg emperor begins the **Thirty Years War**: most of continental Europe is dragged into the conflict. **1618**

1604–13 The **Time of Troubles**: Sweden and Poland intervene in a Russian civil war.

1615 **Nurhachi** (d. 1626) becomes ruler of the Jürchen (Manchu).

1603–23 **Shah Abbas**, Safavid emperor of Persia, seizes Mesopotamia from the Ottoman empire.

1603 Shogun **Tokugawa Ieyasu** establishes his capital at Edo (Tokyo).

1608 The **English East India Company** is given its first trading concessions in India.

The Dutch East India Company takes **Batavia** (Jakarta) on Java. **1619**

1606 Dutch navigator **Willem Jansz** is the first European to sight Australia.

1608–37 Aceh becomes a major trading power under sultan **Iskander Muda**.

Champa absorbed by Dai Viet. **1611**

1613–46 **Mataram** dominates Java under sultan Agung.

1607 **Jamestown**, Virginia, the first permanent English colony in the Americas, is founded.

1608 Champlain founds the French colony of **Quebec**.

The English establish the **Fort James** trading post at the mouth of the Gambia river. **1618**

1609 Spanish found **Santa Fe**, New Mexico, as a fortified mission station.

1616 **Dutch Guiana** colony founded.

The **first African slaves** are imported into the English Virginia colony. **1619**

◄ *The Italian Matteo Ricci in traditional Chinese clothing.*

► *The richly decorated interior of the Blue Mosque.*

RELIGION & PHILOSOPHY

1601 **Matteo Ricci** leads a Jesuit mission to Beijing.

1603 The sultanate of Macassar officially adopts **Islam**.

Ieyasu prohibits Christianity in Japan. **1609**

1611 Publication of the **Authorized King James Version** of the Bible translated into English.

1606 Execution of Sikh guru **Arjan Dev** by Mughal emperor Jahangir.

1612 Ieyasu begins systematic **persecution of Japanese Christians**.

SCIENCE & TECHNOLOGY

1608 Hans Lippershey patents the **telescope**, Netherlands.

1609 German astronomer Johannes Kepler defines the **Laws of Planetary Motion**.

► *Telescope from the early 17th century.*

1609–10 Galileo discovers the **moons of Jupiter** using a telescope.

1614 **Logarithmic tables** devised by Scottish mathematician John Napier.

ARTS & ARCHITECTURE

1600–25* Development of the **Baroque architectural style** in Italy.

Miguel de Cervantes, **1605** **Don Quixote**, Spanish picaresque novel.

1606–69 Life of **Rembrandt**, Dutch painter and printmaker.

1609–18 **Blue Mosque** of Ahmed I, Istanbul.

1603 Dancer Izumo Okuni popularizes **Kabuki** in Japan.

1611–30 **Shah Mosque**, Isfahan, major achievement of Safavid architecture.

1601–9 **Himeji Castle**, Japan.

Mughal emperor **Jahangir** awards the outstanding painter Abu'l Hasan the title 'Wonder of the Age'. **1618**

1600–15 Guaman Poma, **The First New Chronicle and Good Government**, an indigenous Peruvian's history of the Incas and critique of Spanish colonial government.

1601   1605   1610   1615

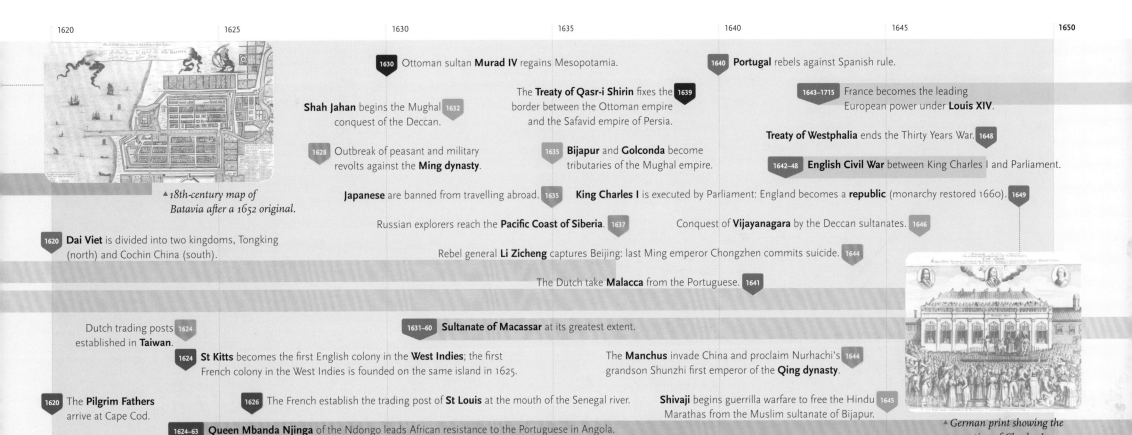

18th-century map of Batavia after a 1652 original.

1630 Ottoman sultan **Murad IV** regains Mesopotamia.

1640 **Portugal** rebels against Spanish rule.

The **Treaty of Qasr-i Shirin** fixes the **1639** border between the Ottoman empire and the Safavid empire of Persia.

1643–1715 France becomes the leading European power under **Louis XIV**.

Shah Jahan begins the Mughal **1632** conquest of the Deccan.

Treaty of Westphalia ends the Thirty Years War. **1648**

1628 Outbreak of peasant and military revolts against the **Ming dynasty**.

1635 **Bijapur** and **Golconda** become tributaries of the Mughal empire.

1642–48 **English Civil War** between King Charles I and Parliament.

Japanese are banned from travelling abroad. **1635**   **King Charles I** is executed by Parliament: England becomes a **republic** (monarchy restored 1660). **1649**

Russian explorers reach the **Pacific Coast of Siberia**. **1637**   Conquest of **Vijayanagara** by the Deccan sultanates. **1646**

1620 **Dai Viet** is divided into two kingdoms, Tongking (north) and Cochin China (south).

Rebel general **Li Zicheng** captures Beijing: last Ming emperor Chongzhen commits suicide. **1644**

The Dutch take **Malacca** from the Portuguese. **1641**

Dutch trading posts **1624** established in **Taiwan**.

1631–60 **Sultanate of Macassar** at its greatest extent.

1624 **St Kitts** becomes the first English colony in the **West Indies**; the first French colony in the West Indies is founded on the same island in 1625.

The **Manchus** invade China and proclaim Nurhachi's **1644** grandson Shunzhi first emperor of the **Qing dynasty**.

1620 The **Pilgrim Fathers** arrive at Cape Cod.

1626 The French establish the trading post of **St Louis** at the mouth of the Senegal river.

Shivaji begins guerrilla warfare to free the Hindu **1645** Marathas from the Muslim sultanate of Bijapur.

▲ *German print showing the execution of Charles I.*

1624–63 **Queen Mbanda Njinga** of the Ndongo leads African resistance to the Portuguese in Angola.

The Dutch settle **New Amsterdam** (New York), **1626** founding the New Netherland colony.

1629 The **Mutapa kingdom** in Southern Africa cedes control of its gold mines to the Portuguese.

1638 Swedish North American colony of **New Sweden** founded.

1642 **Abel Tasman** is the first European to visit Tasmania, New Zealand, Tonga and Fiji.

▼ *Figure from William Harvey's* Exercitatio *showing the veins in a human arm.*

1632 **Galileo** tried for heresy by the papal Inquisition for supporting Copernicus's heliocentric universe theory.

George Fox founds the **Society of Friends** (Quakers) in England. **1648**

1641 **Catholic uprising** against Protestant settlers in Ulster, Ireland.

Death of **Mulla Sadr**, Persian Shi'a Islamic philosopher and theologian. **1641**

First Catholic church opened in **Beijing**. **1650**

René Descartes, *Discourse on Method*. **1637**

Maryland assembly passes the **Toleration Act**, granting **1649** freedom of worship to all Trinitarian Christians.

William Harvey establishes the circulation of the blood. **1628**

▶ *Painting of a Portuguese youth by Reza Abbasi, c. 1634.*

1620 *Novum Organon*, on inductive scientific reasoning, by Francis Bacon.

1622 **Jesuits** introduce the telescope to Chinese astronomy.

1638–41 Church of **S. Carlo alle Quattro Fontane**, Rome: iconic Baroque design by Franceso Borromini (1599–1667).

Bernini, *Ecstasy of St Theresa*, Cornaro Chapel, Rome: high-Baroque sculpture. **1647–52**

1635 Death of **Reza Abassi**, founder of the Isfahan school of Persian painting.

◀ *Woodcut illustration from Guaman Poma's work showing Atawallpa being beheaded.*

1632–54 The **Taj Mahal** built by Shah Jahan.

Birth of Japanese poet Matsuo Basho, who would popularize **haiku verse** (d. 1694). **1644**

*Approximate date

1715

THE TREATY OF UTRECHT: BRITAIN EMERGES AS A MAJOR EUROPEAN POWER; DECLINE OF THE OTTOMAN AND MUGHAL EMPIRES

The Qing empire's conquest of Mongolia in 1697 marked the beginning of the end of the long nomad domination of the Eurasian steppes. From now on, the nomads would be inexorably squeezed between the Qing and the swiftly expanding Russian empire. Russia, previously isolated from the European mainstream, was rapidly modernizing under Tsar Peter the Great (r. 1682–1725). His victory over Sweden in the Great Northern War demonstrated his success in turning Russia into a major European power.

In Western Europe two great wars were fought in this period for dynastic advantage and to contain the power of Louis XIV's France: the War of the League of Augsburg, in which France defeated an alliance of the Netherlands, Austria, England and Spain, and the War of the Spanish Succession, which was caused by the extinction of the Habsburg line in Spain. The Treaty of Utrecht, which ended the second of these in 1713, confirmed France's position as the leading European power, but it was forced to make important concessions to Austria and Great Britain (formed by the union of England and Scotland in 1707). Britain was now Europe's leading financial and naval power and had become a serious colonial rival to France in North America, the Caribbean and India.

The two greatest Muslim powers of the 17th century were both in decline by 1715. The Ottoman empire's last invasion of Christian Europe was crushingly defeated at Vienna in 1683. Hungary and Transylvania were lost to the Habsburgs in 1699 and the empire's North African provinces drifted into semi-independence by 1715. Under Aurangzeb (r. 1658–1707) the Mughals came close to conquering all of India, but increasing religious intolerance caused frequent Hindu and Sikh revolts. By the time of Aurangzeb's death, the Hindu Marathas had broken away and founded their own kingdom in western India.

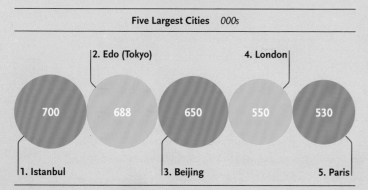

Five Largest Cities *000s*

2. Edo (Tokyo)			4. London	
700	688	650	550	530
1. Istanbul		3. Beijing		5. Paris

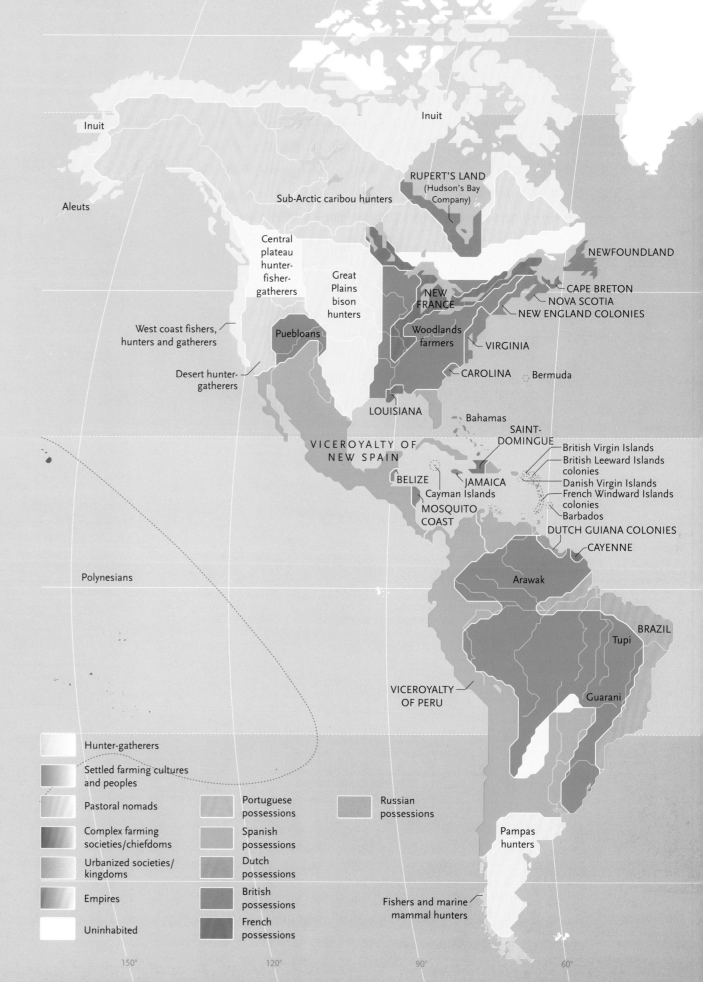

Inuit

Inuit

Aleuts

Sub-Arctic caribou hunters

RUPERT'S LAND (Hudson's Bay Company)

NEWFOUNDLAND

Central plateau hunter-fisher-gatherers

Great Plains bison hunters

NEW FRANCE

CAPE BRETON
NOVA SCOTIA
NEW ENGLAND COLONIES

West coast fishers, hunters and gatherers

Puebloans

Woodlands farmers

VIRGINIA

Desert hunter-gatherers

CAROLINA

Bermuda

LOUISIANA

Bahamas

SAINT-DOMINGUE

VICEROYALTY OF NEW SPAIN

British Virgin Islands
British Leeward Islands colonies
Danish Virgin Islands
French Windward Islands colonies
Barbados

BELIZE

JAMAICA

Cayman Islands

MOSQUITO COAST

DUTCH GUIANA COLONIES

CAYENNE

Polynesians

Arawak

BRAZIL

Tupi

VICEROYALTY OF PERU

Guarani

Pampas hunters

Fishers and marine mammal hunters

Legend

- Hunter-gatherers
- Settled farming cultures and peoples
- Pastoral nomads
- Complex farming societies/chiefdoms
- Urbanized societies/kingdoms
- Empires
- Uninhabited
- Portuguese possessions
- Spanish possessions
- Dutch possessions
- British possessions
- French possessions
- Russian possessions

150°   120°   90°   60°

NETHERLANDS 1
PRUSSIA 2
SWISS
CONFEDERACY 3
ITALIAN STATES 4
PAPAL STATES 5
VENICE 6

ICELAND
(to Denmark)

DENMARK-
NORWAY

SWEDEN

RUSSIAN EMPIRE

Chukchi
(Palaeo-Siberians)

Arctic Circle

GREAT
BRITAIN

London 4
5
Paris
FRANCE

GERMAN
1
2
POLAND
AUSTRIAN
EMPIRE
3
6
4 5

1 Istanbul

OTTOMAN
EMPIRE

Kazakhs

Nogai
Tatars

Kyrgyz

Turkmen 16
KHANATE
OF BUKHARA

Dzungar
Khanate
(Mongols)

Koryaks
(Palaeo-Siberians)

Ainu

3
Beijing

KOREA
JAPAN 2
Edo (Tokyo)

PORTUGAL

SPAIN

Gibraltar
MOROCCO
ALGIERS
(Ottoman)
TUNIS
(Ottoman)
MALTA
TRIPOLI
(Ottoman)
FEZZAN

SAFAVID
EMPIRE

TIBET
NEPALESE
STATES
BHUTAN
19 20

QING
EMPIRE

Macao

Tropic of Cancer

Touaregs

St
Louis
GREAT
FULO

SEGU
9
BORGU
7 8
11
PORTUGUESE
GUINEA 10
KONG
BORNU
14
NUPE
12
13

DARFUR

FUNJ

WADAI
ETHIOPIA
OROMO
STATES
15
HARAR

Bedouin
Arabs

YEMEN

OMAN

Bombay
MARATHAS
Goa
MYSORE
Madras
Pondicherry
17 CEYLON
18

MUGHAL
EMPIRE

Calcutta

ARAKAN
BURMA

SIAM 21
TONGKING
COCHIN
CHINA
CAMBODIA
BRUNEI

PHILIPPINES

Mariana
Islands

Micronesians

Bunce
Island
Cape Coast
Castle
Accra

KONGO
LUNDA
LUBA
15
ANGOLA
LOZI
15

Bantu farmers
and pastoralists

15

Mombasa

ZANJ
(to Oman)

Mozambique

16 KHANATE OF KHIVA
17 PALAIYAKKARAR
STATES
18 KANDY
19 ASSAM
20 SHAN STATES
21 LAOS

SULTANATE
OF ACEH
Malacca

DUTCH EAST INDIES

MATARAM
DUTCH TIMOR

PORTUGUESE TIMOR

Papuans

Melanesians

Equator

KAABU 7
SMALL STATES 8
MOSSI KINGDOMS 9
AKAN STATES 10
ASANTE (Akan) 11
OYO 12
BENIN 13
HAUSA CITY STATES 14
SMALL STATES 15

San

Khoikhoi
CAPE
COLONY

ROZWI
LOZI
15

Delagoa Bay

Malagasy

Mauritius

Réunion

Australian Aborigines

Tropic of Capricorn

Tasmanians

Polynesians

Maoris

0°   30°   60°   90°   120°   150°   180°

1715

The late 17th century saw the beginning of the Enlightenment, an intellectual and artistic reaction against the religious wars of the post-Reformation period. Enlightenment thinkers emphasized rationalism, empiricism and secularism, openly questioned the nature of society and the sources of political legitimacy, and stressed the freedom of the individual. An important aspect of the Enlightenment was the spread of scientific societies and astronomical observatories, promoting the study of 'natural philosophy' (science).

The most important scientific figure of the age was Isaac Newton, whose laws of universal gravity and motion dominated physics until the early 20th century. The reflecting telescope, Newton's invention, revealed the clearest views yet of the universe, while the development of the microscope expanded human knowledge in the other direction, revealing organisms too small for the naked eye to see. Another major technological development of the age was the first commercially viable steam engine, which could be used to operate pumps in mines.

The establishment of strong centralized government under the Tokugawa shogunate in the early 17th century ushered in a long period of peace, prosperity and stability in Japan. Kabuki theatre, poetry and printmaking flourished, and the Genroku era of 1688–1703 (named for the Japanese calendar then in use) in particular came to be regarded as a cultural golden age. The educated and literate samurai class played an important role in policing and administering Tokugawa Japan. Samurai wrote extensively during the period on bushido, the samurai code of ethics but at the same time their actual military role declined.

The period saw a new stage in the Jewish diaspora when in 1654 the first Jewish community in the New World was established at the Dutch colony of New Amsterdam.

World Population

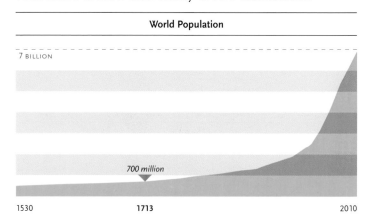

7 BILLION

700 million

1530   1713   2010

132

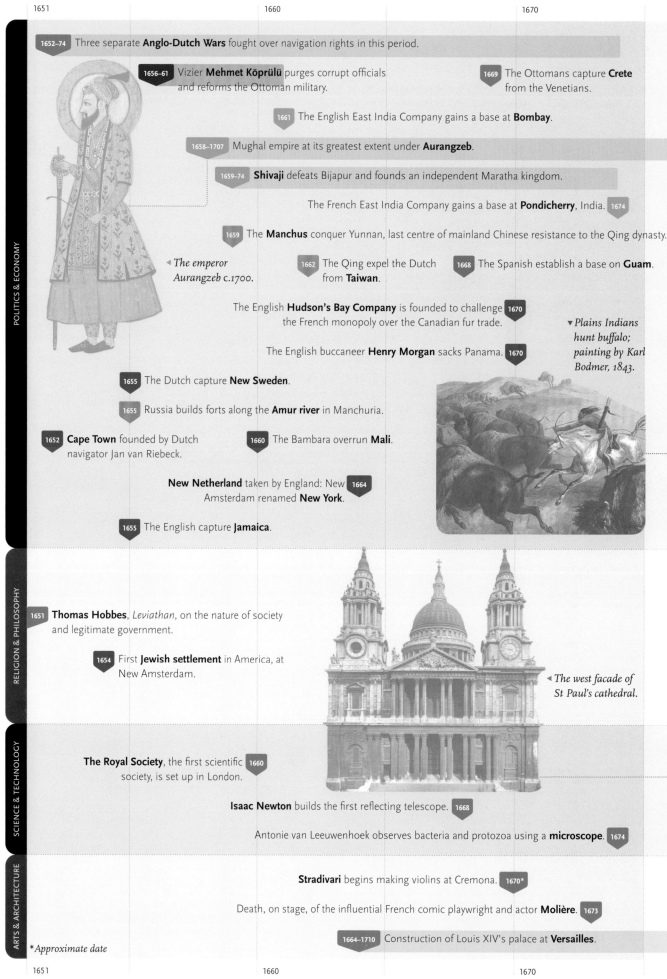

1651   1660   1670

POLITICS & ECONOMY

1652–74 Three separate **Anglo-Dutch Wars** fought over navigation rights in this period.

1656–61 Vizier **Mehmet Köprülü** purges corrupt officials and reforms the Ottoman military.

1669 The Ottomans capture **Crete** from the Venetians.

1661 The English East India Company gains a base at **Bombay**.

1658–1707 Mughal empire at its greatest extent under **Aurangzeb**.

1659–74 **Shivaji** defeats Bijapur and founds an independent Maratha kingdom.

The French East India Company gains a base at **Pondicherry**, India. **1674**

1659 The **Manchus** conquer Yunnan, last centre of mainland Chinese resistance to the Qing dynasty.

◀ *The emperor Aurangzeb c.1700.*

1662 The Qing expel the Dutch from **Taiwan**.

1668 The Spanish establish a base on **Guam**.

The English **Hudson's Bay Company** is founded to challenge the French monopoly over the Canadian fur trade. **1670**

▼ *Plains Indians hunt buffalo; painting by Karl Bodmer, 1843.*

The English buccaneer **Henry Morgan** sacks Panama. **1670**

1655 The Dutch capture **New Sweden**.

1655 Russia builds forts along the **Amur river** in Manchuria.

1652 **Cape Town** founded by Dutch navigator Jan van Riebeck.

1660 The Bambara overrun **Mali**.

New Netherland taken by England: New Amsterdam renamed **New York**. **1664**

1655 The English capture **Jamaica**.

RELIGION & PHILOSOPHY

1651 **Thomas Hobbes**, *Leviathan*, on the nature of society and legitimate government.

1654 First **Jewish settlement** in America, at New Amsterdam.

◀ *The west facade of St Paul's cathedral.*

SCIENCE & TECHNOLOGY

The Royal Society, the first scientific society, is set up in London. **1660**

Isaac Newton builds the first reflecting telescope. **1668**

Antonie van Leeuwenhoek observes bacteria and protozoa using a **microscope**. **1674**

ARTS & ARCHITECTURE

Stradivari begins making violins at Cremona. **1670***

Death, on stage, of the influential French comic playwright and actor **Molière**. **1673**

1664–1710 Construction of Louis XIV's palace at **Versailles**.

*Approximate date

1651   1660   1670

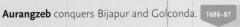

▼ *View of the city of Bantam in 1724.*

1682–1725 Russia is modernized during the reign of tsar **Peter the Great**.

1683 The second Ottoman siege of **Vienna** is defeated by the Austrians, Germans and Poles.

1701–13 **War of the Spanish Succession**.

England's **Glorious Revolution 1688** leads to the development of constitutional monarchy.

Treaty of Karlowitz: the **Ottomans** cede Hungary **1699** and Transylvania to the Austrian Habsburgs.

1703 **Tsar Peter the Great** founds St Petersburg as a new capital for Russia.

1688–97 **War of the League of Augsburg**.

1700–21 **Great Northern War** between Sweden and Russia.

Foundation of the **Bank of England** marks England's **1694** emergence as Europe's leading financial power.

Charles XII of Sweden defeated by Russia at **Poltava**: Russia **1709** occupies Swedish possessions east of the Baltic.

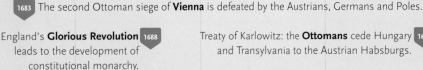

▲ *Peter the Great in full military regalia, painted by Jean-Marc Nattier.*

The **Qing dynasty** conquers Taiwan. **1683**

1679–1709 **Hindu Rajput uprising** against the Mughals.

Aurangzeb conquers Bijapur and Golconda. **1686–87**

1690 The British East India Company founds **Calcutta** (Kolkata).

Treaty of Utrecht ends the **War of the Spanish Succession**. **1713**

1678 The **Chagatai khanate** at Kashgar is overthrown by the Uzbeks and Oirats.

1689 **Treaty of Nerchinsk**: Russia withdraws from the Amur in return for trading concessions in China.

1707 **Act of Union** unites England and Scotland as Great Britain.

Dutch conquer the **sultanate of Bantam**. **1684**

1696 The **Mongols** under Galdan are defeated by the Qing near the Kerulen River.

1709 The Afghans of **Kandahar** rebel against the Safavids.

A popular rebellion against European influence in **Ayutthaya** leads to **1688** the overthrow of **King Narai** and a realignment of trade towards China.

1697 **Mongolia** becomes a province of the Qing empire.

1698 The **sultanate of Oman** conquers the Swahili cities of East Africa.

1707 Death of **Aurangzeb**: Mughal power goes into rapid decline.

1680* **Plains Indians** begin to use horses for bison hunting.

Osei Tutu founds the **1701** **Asante kingdom**, Africa.

1705–14 Tunis, Tripoli, and Cyrenaica become autonomous within the **Ottoman empire**.

The **Code Noir** defines the conditions **1685** of slavery in the French Caribbean.

▶ *King Narai in a French drawing.*

Britain wins a 30-year monopoly on the **slave trade** to the Spanish Americas. **1713**

La Salle explores the length of **1681–82** the **Mississippi River**.

1684–95 Rozwi under **Changamire Dombo** supplants the Mutapa kingdom.

British colonial troops take Acadia: it is renamed **Nova Scotia**. **1710**

1675–1775* **The Enlightenment**: intellectual movement emphasizing rationalism, empiricism and secularism.

1678 John Bunyan, ***Pilgrim's Progress***, the most characteristic expression of Puritan beliefs.

1690 John Locke's *Treatise on Government* asserts that all people have the right to liberty and ownership of property.

1694 Birth of **Voltaire**, French writer and philosopher (*d.* 1778).

▶ *Guru Gobind Singh holds a bird of prey in this 18th-century painting.*

Louis XIV revokes the Edict of Nantes, ending **1685** toleration for Huguenots in France.

1692–93 **Witch trials** at Salem, Massachusetts: 19 people are hanged for witchcraft.

Death of **Yamaga Soko**, Japanese Confucian philosopher **1685** and writer on samurai ethics (bushido).

1699 Guru Gobind Singh founds the **Khalsa order**, infusing the Sikh faith with military values.

Abraham Darby begins iron production **1712** using coke-fueled blast furnaces, England.

◀ *Witch trial at Salem: illustration from 1896.*

Isaac Newton, *Principia*, **1687** which defines the laws of gravity and motion.

Thomas Newcomen develops a **low- 1712 pressure steam pump** for mines, England.

1698 Thomas Savery patents the **first steam engine**, England.

Mercury thermometer invented by **1714** Gabriel Fahrenheit, in Germany.

Miyazaki Yasusada, *Cyclopaedia of Agriculture*, which **1696** disseminates good farming practices in Japan.

1688–1703 **Genroku era** in Japan: flourishing of Kabuki and puppet theatre, poetry, and printmaking.

1707 Beginning of construction of the **Old Summer Palace**, Beijing.

1675–1710 Christopher Wren, **St Paul's cathedral**, London.

1763

BRITAIN BECOMES EUROPE'S LEADING COLONIAL POWER; QING EMPIRE AT ITS PEAK

Anglo-French colonial rivalry came to a head in 1754 with the outbreak of the French and Indian War (1754–63) in North America, over rival claims to the Ohio river valley. Britain enjoyed the advantages of naval dominance, greater financial resources and a colonial population of around 1.5 million, compared with France's colonial population of barely 60,000. By 1759 Britain had conquered French North America.

The war was also fought in the French and British colonies in the Caribbean and India. In 1756 the war became subsumed into the Seven Years War, a European conflict that broke out when Austria, backed by France, Spain and Russia, attacked Prussia, which was backed by Britain. The end of the war in 1763 confirmed Prussia as a great European power. It also ensured Britain's position as the leading colonial power and the dominant foreign power in India.

The Qing empire of China reached its peak during this period, following its conquest of Tibet and the Dzungar khanate, which was the last Mongol state. The Safavid dynasty of Persia was overthrown in 1736 by Nader Shah, a brilliant general whose constant campaigning greatly enlarged the Persian empire but ruined its economy. Following his assassination in 1747, Persian power went into rapid decline.

Nader Shah's sack of Delhi in 1739 was the most dramatic sign of the decline of the Mughal empire. Mughal control of India looked set to be replaced by Hindu Maratha domination, but their rapid territorial expansion was ended by the Afghans at Panipat in 1761, leaving India divided among many rival powers.

The Atlantic slave trade began to have a serious destabilizing impact on West Africa in the mid-18th century, as stronger states, such as Dahomey and Asante, raided their weaker neighbours for captives.

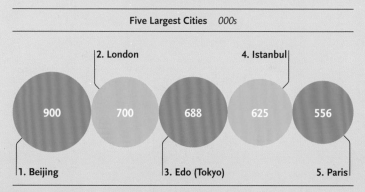

Five Largest Cities *000s*

2. London		4. Istanbul
900	700	688	625	556
1. Beijing		3. Edo (Tokyo)		5. Paris

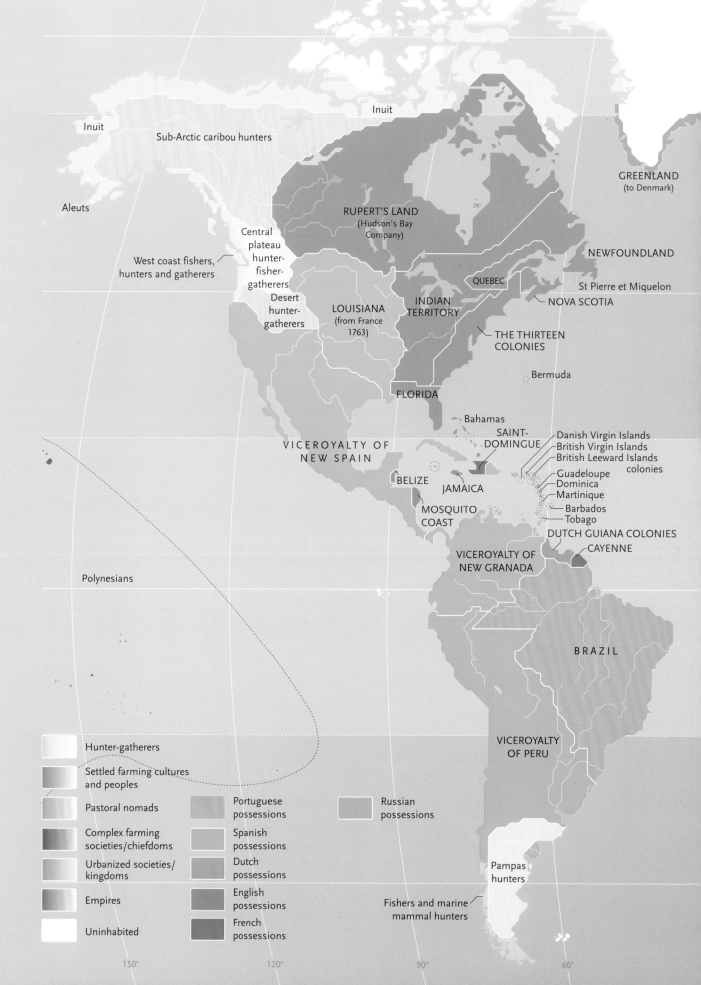

Inuit

Inuit

Sub-Arctic caribou hunters

GREENLAND
(to Denmark)

Aleuts

RUPERT'S LAND
(Hudson's Bay Company)

NEWFOUNDLAND

Central plateau hunter-fisher-gatherers

West coast fishers, hunters and gatherers

QUEBEC

St Pierre et Miquelon

NOVA SCOTIA

Desert hunter-gatherers

LOUISIANA
(from France 1763)

INDIAN TERRITORY

THE THIRTEEN COLONIES

FLORIDA

Bermuda

Bahamas

SAINT-DOMINGUE

Danish Virgin Islands
British Virgin Islands
British Leeward Islands colonies

VICEROYALTY OF NEW SPAIN

BELIZE

JAMAICA

Guadeloupe
Dominica
Martinique
Barbados
Tobago

MOSQUITO COAST

DUTCH GUIANA COLONIES
CAYENNE

VICEROYALTY OF NEW GRANADA

Polynesians

BRAZIL

VICEROYALTY OF PERU

Pampas hunters

Fishers and marine mammal hunters

Hunter-gatherers

Settled farming cultures and peoples

Pastoral nomads

Complex farming societies/chiefdoms

Urbanized societies/ kingdoms

Empires

Uninhabited

Portuguese possessions

Spanish possessions

Dutch possessions

English possessions

French possessions

Russian possessions

150°   120°   90°   60°

134

NETHERLANDS 1
PRUSSIA 2
SWISS 3
CONFEDERACY
VENICE 4
PAPAL STATES 5
KINGDOM OF 6
NAPLES

ICELAND
(to Denmark)

DENMARK-
NORWAY

SWEDEN

GREAT
BRITAIN 1

London 2

5
GERMAN
Paris STATES
FRANCE 3 AUSTRIAN
EMPIRE
4

5

PORTUGAL
SPAIN 6

Gibraltar
MOROCCO ALGIERS MALTA
TUNIS
(Ottoman)
TRIPOLI
(Ottoman)
FEZZAN

Touaregs

GREAT
FULO KAARTA
St
Louis SEGU
Fort
James
PORTUGUESE
GUINEA 7
KONG
Bunce Island

Cape Coast
Castle

8
13
9
10
12

14
NUPE
11
15
WADAI
BORNU

DARFUR

NEJD

Bedouin
Arabs

OMAN

YEMEN
ETHIOPIA AUSSA
OROMO HARAR
STATES

Bantu farmers
and pastoralists

KONGO
LUNDA
ANGOLA LUBA
15

15
15

ZANJ
(to Oman)

FUNJ

RUSSIAN EMPIRE

Chukchi   Arctic Circle

Kazakhs

Kyrgyz

KHANATE 16
OF
BUKHARA

GEORGIA

PERSIA

AFGHANISTAN

Ainu

QING EMPIRE 1
Beijing

KOREA
JAPAN 3
Edo (Tokyo)

NEPALESE
STATES
BHUTAN

18 19
20 26 27
17
21
Calcutta
22
Bombay
23
Goa
Madras
Pondicherry
24 CEYLON
25

BURMA
28
ARAKAN

SIAM

Macao

TONGKING

COCHIN
CHINA
CAMBODIA

SULTANATE
OF ACEH Malacca

SMALL MALAY
STATES
DUTCH EAST INDIES

PHILIPPINES

BRUNEI

PORTUGUESE TIMOR

Micronesians

Melanesians

75°

45°

Tropic of Cancer

Equator

MOZAMBIQUE
LOZI
ROZWI

San

Delagoa Bay

Khoikhoi

CAPE
COLONY

Malagasy

Mauritius

Réunion

FUTA JALON 7
MOSSI KINGDOMS 8
ASANTE 9
DAHOMEY 10
OYO 11
BENIN 12
BORGU 13
HAUSA CITY STATES 14
SMALL STATES 15

16 KHANATE OF
KOKAND
17 MUGHAL
EMPIRE
18 RAJPUTANA
19 SMALL INDIAN
STATES
20 OUDH
21 MARATHA
CONFEDERACY

22 HYDERABAD
23 MYSORE
24 NORTHERN
CIRCARS
25 KANDY
26 BENGAL
27 ASSAM
28 LAOS

OTTOMAN
EMPIRE

Istanbul 4

Tasmanians

Australian Aborigines

Maoris

Polynesians

Tropic of Capricorn

45°

0°   30°   60°   90°   120°   150°   180°

1763

The early 18th century saw the beginning in Britain of the Industrial Revolution, which was one of the major turning points of human history. It transformed the society and economy of Great Britain, followed by Europe and North America, and then the rest of the world. Mechanization of production, which was the central characteristic of the Industrial Revolution, enabled a huge increase in production and, eventually, began to deliver greatly improved living standards for the mass of ordinary working people. The revolution began with the gradual mechanization of the British textile industry, which even at the end of this period was still mainly a cottage industry reliant on manually operated machines.

Britain's industrial development was aided by the control of the Atlantic slave trade it had gained in the 1713 Treaty of Utrecht. British manufactured goods had little appeal in India or China, but could be sold in West Africa for slaves, who in turn were exchanged in the Caribbean and North America for industrial raw materials such as sugar, cotton, dyes and tobacco. This became known as the 'slave trade triangle'. The British paid close attention to the science of navigation, developing the marine chronometer in the mid-18th century, which allowed a ship's longitude to be calculated accurately for the first time.

Around 1740 the Muslim scholar Muhammad ibn Abd al-Wahhab founded the Wahhabi (or Salafi) Islamic fundamentalist movement. In 1744 he allied with Muhammad ibn Saud to whom he offered spiritual backing in return for the imposition of Wahhabism by force in the Saudi lands. In West Africa, the Muslim state of Futa Jalon used the doctrine of jihad to justify its conquests of non-Muslim neighbours. Another significant development around this time was the foundation of the mystical Hasidic branch of Judaism.

World Population

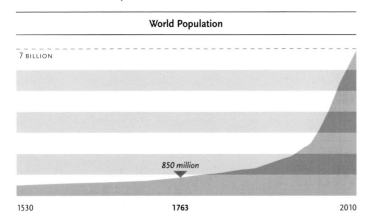

7 BILLION

850 million

1530   **1763**   2010

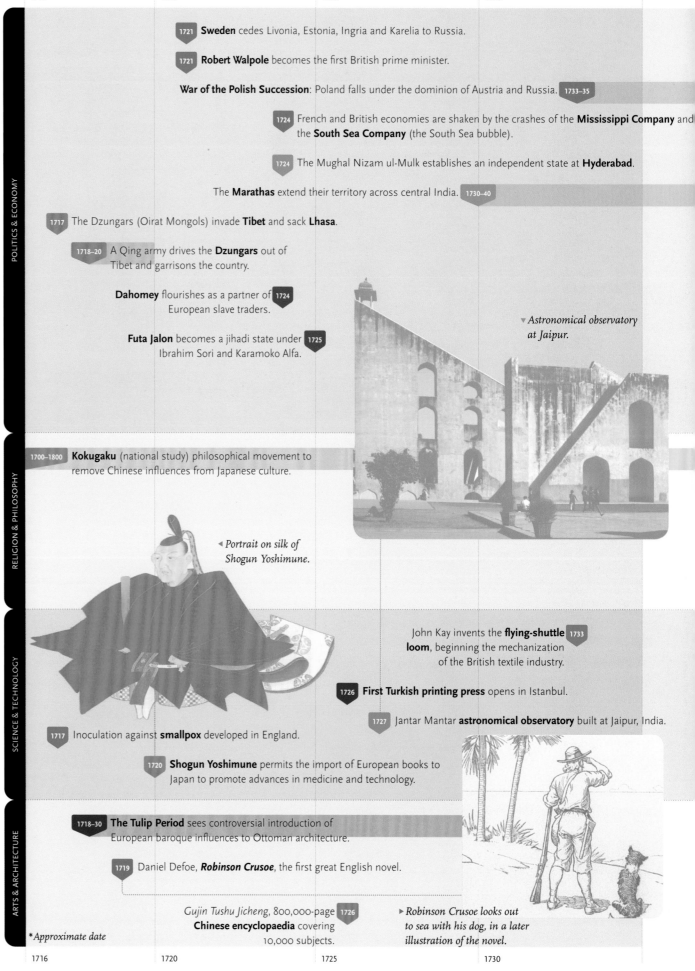

1716   1720   1725   1730

POLITICS & ECONOMY

1721 **Sweden** cedes Livonia, Estonia, Ingria and Karelia to Russia.

1721 **Robert Walpole** becomes the first British prime minister.

War of the Polish Succession: Poland falls under the dominion of Austria and Russia. **1733–35**

1724 French and British economies are shaken by the crashes of the **Mississippi Company** and the **South Sea Company** (the South Sea bubble).

1724 The Mughal Nizam ul-Mulk establishes an independent state at **Hyderabad**.

The **Marathas** extend their territory across central India. **1730–40**

1717 The Dzungars (Oirat Mongols) invade **Tibet** and sack **Lhasa**.

1718–20 A Qing army drives the **Dzungars** out of Tibet and garrisons the country.

Dahomey flourishes as a partner of European slave traders. **1724**

Futa Jalon becomes a jihadi state under Ibrahim Sori and Karamoko Alfa. **1725**

▼ *Astronomical observatory at Jaipur.*

RELIGION & PHILOSOPHY

1700–1800 **Kokugaku** (national study) philosophical movement to remove Chinese influences from Japanese culture.

◄ *Portrait on silk of Shogun Yoshimune.*

SCIENCE & TECHNOLOGY

John Kay invents the **flying-shuttle loom**, beginning the mechanization of the British textile industry. **1733**

1726 **First Turkish printing press** opens in Istanbul.

1727 Jantar Mantar **astronomical observatory** built at Jaipur, India.

1717 Inoculation against **smallpox** developed in England.

1720 **Shogun Yoshimune** permits the import of European books to Japan to promote advances in medicine and technology.

ARTS & ARCHITECTURE

1718–30 **The Tulip Period** sees controversial introduction of European baroque influences to Ottoman architecture.

1719 Daniel Defoe, ***Robinson Crusoe***, the first great English novel.

Gujin Tushu Jicheng, 800,000-page **1726** **Chinese encyclopaedia** covering 10,000 subjects.

▶ *Robinson Crusoe looks out to sea with his dog, in a later illustration of the novel.*

*Approximate date

1716   1720   1725   1730

1740–86 **Prussia** becomes a major European power under Frederick II 'the Great'.

1736 **Nader Shah** overthrows the Safavid dynasty in Persia.

1740 The **Mons** rebel against Burmese rule.

1744 Prince Muhammad ibn Saud founds the first **Saudi state** in Nejd, Arabia, with Wahhabi support.

1756–63 The **Seven Years War** pits Austria, Russia and France against Britain and Prussia.

1739 Nader Shah sacks **Delhi** and removes the Mughals' Peacock Throne to Persia.

1750* **Derebeys** (valley lords) become semi-autonomous local rulers in Ottoman Anatolia.

Assassination of **Nader Shah** leads to **1747** decades of political conflict in Persia.

1757 The British under **Robert Clive** defeat Siraj ud-Daulah, nawab of Bengal, at **Plassey**.

1761 The **Afghans** defeat the Marathas at Panipat.

The **British East India Company** allies with Mysore and the **1751** Marathas against Nizam Chanda Sahib and the French.

The British capture the French base at **Pondicherry** (returned by **1761** treaty in 1763), ending French power in India.

Ahmed Shah Durrani founds the Afghan state. **1747** The Qing conquer **Tibet**. **1751**

Burmese king **Alaungpaya** **1757** reconquers the Mons.

1759 The Qing conquer the **Dzungar khanate**.

1741 **Vitus Bering** discovers that the Bering Straits separate Siberia from North America.

Qing empire reaches its territorial peak at 11.5 million km² (4.4 million square miles). **1759**

1743–48 **King George's War**: the British capture Louisbourg on Cape Breton.

Census records that the population of China is over **200 million**. **1762**

1754–63 **The French and Indian War**.

▸ *Benjamin Franklin in a contemporary engraving.*

Treaty of Paris: France cedes Canada to Britain; Spain cedes **1763** Florida to Britain, but gains Louisiana from France.

1759 The **British** conquer France's North American territories.

▲ *Nader Shah on horseback in battle.*

1739 **David Hume**, *A Treatise of Human Nature*, examination of the psychological basis of human behaviour.

Jean-Jacques Rousseau, *The Social* **1762** *Contract*, on political legitimacy.

1739 **John Wesley** founds the Methodist movement.

1740* Israel ben Eliezer founds **Hasidic Judaism** in Ukraine.

◂ *Allan Ramsay's portrait of Rousseau, 1766.*

1740* Muhammad ibn Abd al-Wahhab founds the **Wahhabi Islamic fundamentalist movement**.

Benjamin Franklin, *Experiments and Observations on Electricity*. **1751**

◂ *A marine chronometer, 1770.*

1735–62 John Harrison perfects the **marine chronometer**, greatly improving the accuracy of navigation.

▸ *Portrait on silk of the Qianlong emperor.*

▸ *The young Mozart directs an ensemble from the keyboard.*

Knobelsdorf, the **1745–47** **Sanssouci palace**, Potsdam.

1750 Death of the German Baroque composer **Johann Sebastian Bach** (b. 1685).

1742 First performance of Handel's oratorio, **The Messiah**, in Dublin.

1747 Qing emperor Qianlong rebuilds part of his **summer palace** in Western style using Jesuit architects.

Musical child prodigy **Wolfgang** **1762–73** **Amadeus Mozart** tours Europe giving keyboard concerts.

Cao Xueqin, **The Dream of the Red Chamber** (or *The* **1750*** *Story of the Stone*), classical Chinese novel.

1763

WORLD TRADE ON THE EVE OF THE INDUSTRIAL REVOLUTION: BRITISH DOMINANCE OF THE GLOBAL TRADE NETWORK; ATLANTIC SLAVE TRADE AT ITS PEAK

The European maritime discoveries of the late 15th and early 16th centuries had completely transformed the patterns of global trade by 1763. Europe's geographical position, so disadvantageous in 1492, now placed it at the centre of a global trade network. The new routes freed European traders from reliance on Islamic middlemen and overland trade routes for access to Asian goods. The Islamic world suffered serious economic, political and military decline as a result.

A second transformation resulted from the huge amount of silver released into the European economy following the Spanish conquests in the Americas. This greatly increased the credit available for financing European mercantile ventures. There was little demand for European products in India, China and the East Indies, but there was considerable demand for silver as a means of everyday exchange. American silver gave Europeans the means to purchase eastern luxuries at prices they considered to be cheap and also enabled them to put less well-financed native traders out of business.

By the later 18th century, the Dutch had achieved complete commercial dominance of the East Indies trade area and the British were on the brink of doing the same in India. The Americas were completely incorporated into the European trading system. Large areas in the New World were given over to plantations worked by imported African slave labour, supplying raw materials like sugar and cotton to European industries. European states, following the economic doctrine of mercantilism, tried to monopolize all trade with their own colonies, though piracy and smuggling subverted this ideal.

The new trade routes also led to major biological migration. Cattle, horses, sheep, pigs, chickens and other Old World domestic animals were introduced to the Americas (which had very few domestic animals), along with crops such as wheat, barley, rice, coffee, olives and vines. The Old World benefited from the introduction of New World crops such as maize (which became a staple in Africa), potatoes, sweet potatoes, sunflowers, tomatoes, cocoa and chillies. The agriculture and diets of both hemispheres were transformed in this way.

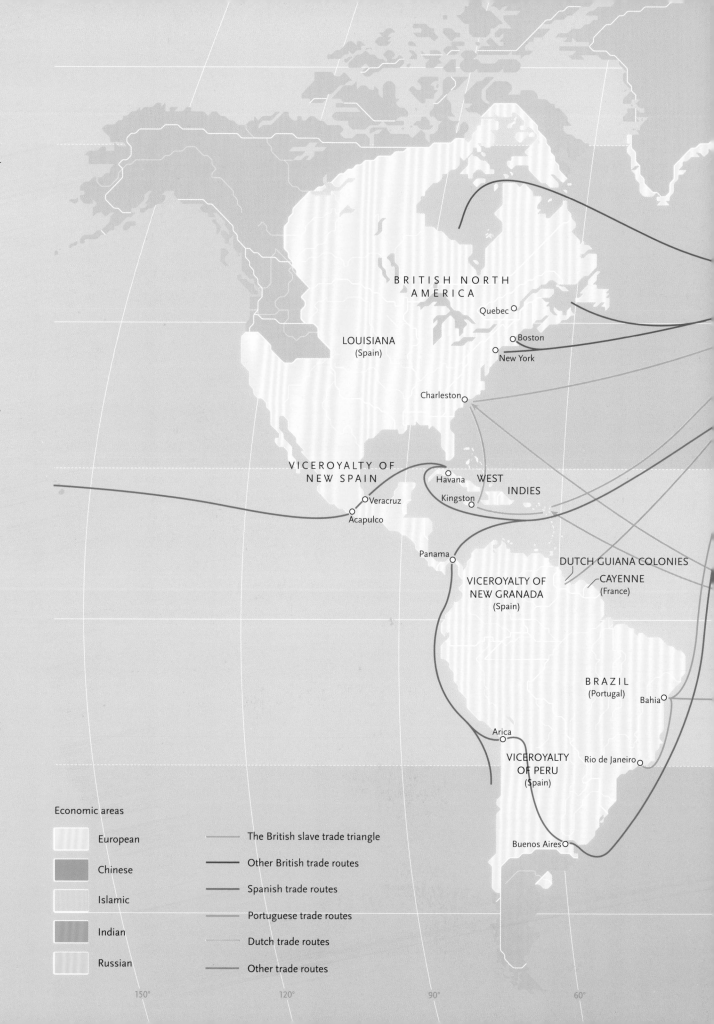

Economic areas

European

Chinese

Islamic

Indian

Russian

——— The British slave trade triangle

——— Other British trade routes

——— Spanish trade routes

——— Portuguese trade routes

——— Dutch trade routes

——— Other trade routes

DENMARK-
NORWAY
SWEDEN
Archangel
St Petersburg
RUSSIAN EMPIRE
NETHERLANDS
Moscow
Tobolsk
GREAT
BRITAIN
Hamburg
Irkutsk
Liverpool
Amsterdam
Bristol
London
POLAND
St Malo
Paris
FRANCE
AUSTRIAN
Venice
EMPIRE
PORTUGAL
Marseille
Genoa
Astrakhan
QING EMPIRE
Beijing
SPAIN
Istanbul
KOREA
Lisbon
Bukhara
Xi'an
JAPAN
Cadiz
Aleppo
Nanjing
Nagasaki
Algiers
Tunis
OTTOMAN
AFGHANISTAN
MUGHAL
Hangzhou
MOROCCO
Tripoli
EMPIRE
Baghdad
EMPIRE
Cairo
PERSIA
Delhi
GREAT
Muscat
BENGAL
Guangzhou
FULO
KAARTA
RAJPUTANA
MARATHAS
Calcutta
Macao
Timbuktu
OMAN
Bombay
BURMA
FUNJ
SEGU
BORGU
DARFUR
Goa
LAOS
TONGKING
WADAI
BORNU
YEMEN
MYSORE
SIAM
ASANTE
HAUSA CITY
Madras
COCHIN
FUTA
STATES
CHINA
Manila
JALON
OYO
ETHIOPIA
CAMBODIA
PHILIPPINES
GUINEA COAST
NUPE
CEYLON
(Spain)
BENIN
(Netherlands)
DAHOMEY
SWAHILI CITY
STATES
Malacca
(Oman)
MALAY
KONGO
STATES
LUNDA
DUTCH EAST INDIES
Zanzibar
LUBA
Batavia
Luanda
ANGOLA
MOZAMBIQUE
(Portugal)
(Portugal)
LOZI
ROZWI

CAPE
COLONY
(Netherlands)
Cape Town

1783
BRITAIN RECOGNIZES THE INDEPENDENCE OF THE USA

Britain's domination of North America proved short-lived. The British government generally left its American colonies to run their own affairs, omitting to define their exact status, rights and responsibilities. When the British government tried to recoup some of the costs of the Seven Years War by taxing its American colonial subjects, the relationship between the two quickly broke down. In 1776 the Thirteen Colonies declared independence as the United States of America.

When the British failed to act quickly to suppress the rebellion, first France, then Spain and the Netherlands saw the opportunity to regain colonies lost in 1763, and joined the war on the side of the Americans. In 1783 Britain recognized American independence, but it had successfully defended the rest of its empire and made only minor territorial concessions to its European rivals.

The Qing empire remained the world's richest and most populous state in 1783. However, its expansion had ground to a halt after an attempt to conquer Burma had ended with a face-saving tributary agreement in 1769. As the long-reigning emperor Qianlong (r. 1736–95) aged, the government became increasingly corrupt and dysfunctional. High European demand for Chinese products kept the economy strong, but around this time the British began to redress the balance of trade by smuggling Indian opium into China.

In India, Muslim and Hindu rulers continued to struggle to fill the vacuum left by the decline of Mughal power. The British East India Company, which commanded its own army and navy, exploited these divisions to establish itself as a major territorial power, conquering Bengal, Bihar and the Northern Circars in the 1760s. During his voyages of exploration in the Pacific, James Cook landed in Australia in 1770 and claimed it for Britain: the Aborigines' long isolation was coming to an end.

Five Largest Cities   000s

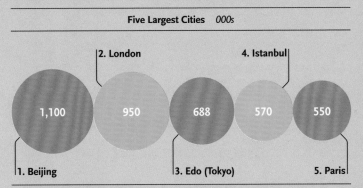

2. London		4. Istanbul	
1,100	950	688	570	550
1. Beijing		3. Edo (Tokyo)		5. Paris

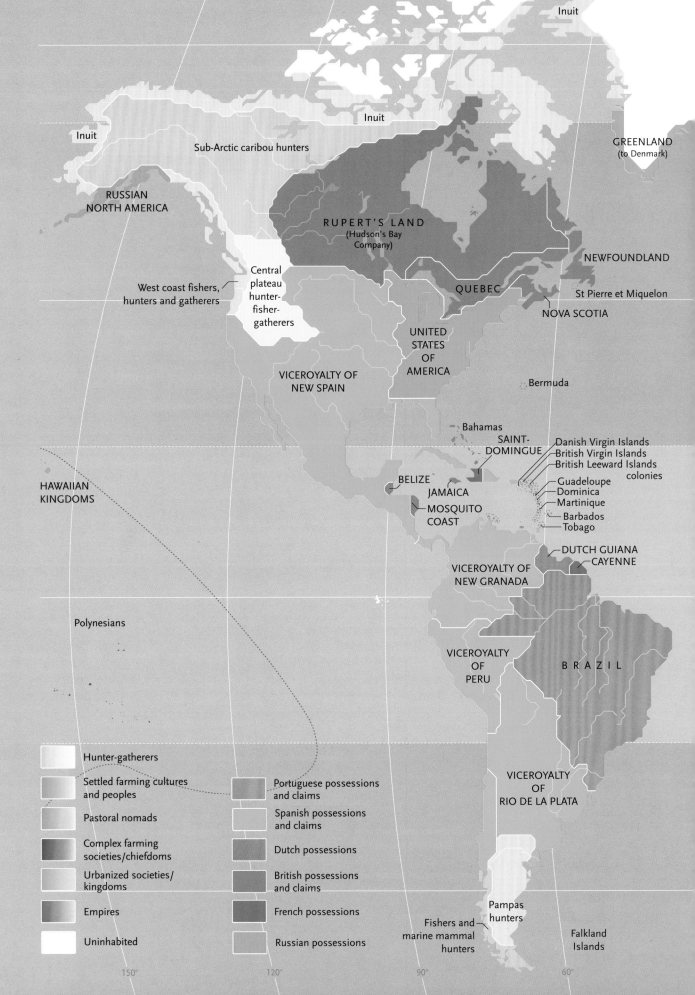

Inuit

Inuit

GREENLAND
(to Denmark)

Inuit

Sub-Arctic caribou hunters

RUSSIAN
NORTH AMERICA

RUPERT'S LAND
(Hudson's Bay Company)

NEWFOUNDLAND

West coast fishers, hunters and gatherers

Central plateau hunter-fisher-gatherers

QUEBEC

St Pierre et Miquelon

NOVA SCOTIA

UNITED STATES OF AMERICA

VICEROYALTY OF NEW SPAIN

Bermuda

Bahamas

SAINT-DOMINGUE

Danish Virgin Islands
British Virgin Islands
British Leeward Islands colonies

HAWAIIAN KINGDOMS

BELIZE

JAMAICA

MOSQUITO COAST

Guadeloupe
Dominica
Martinique
Barbados
Tobago

DUTCH GUIANA
CAYENNE

VICEROYALTY OF NEW GRANADA

Polynesians

VICEROYALTY OF PERU

B R A Z I L

VICEROYALTY OF RIO DE LA PLATA

Pampas hunters

Fishers and marine mammal hunters

Falkland Islands

Legend

- Hunter-gatherers
- Settled farming cultures and peoples
- Pastoral nomads
- Complex farming societies/chiefdoms
- Urbanized societies/kingdoms
- Empires
- Uninhabited
- Portuguese possessions and claims
- Spanish possessions and claims
- Dutch possessions
- British possessions and claims
- French possessions
- Russian possessions

150°   120°   90°   60°

NETHERLANDS [1]
SWISS
CONFEDERACY [2]
ITALIAN STATES [3]

ICELAND
(to Denmark)

Chukchi

Arctic Circle

DENMARK-
NORWAY

SWEDEN

RUSSIAN EMPIRE

75°

GREAT
BRITAIN

PRUSSIA

POLAND

Kazakhs

Ainu

2
London [1]
5
Paris
FRANCE

GERMAN
STATES [2]
[3]
[4]
[5]

AUSTRIA

Kyrgyz

SMALL
UZBEK
KHANATES

Beijing [1]

KOREA

Edo (Tokyo) [3]

45°

VENICE [4]
PAPAL STATES [5]

Istanbul [4]

GEORGIA

[13]

QING EMPIRE

JAPAN

PORTUGAL
Azores

SPAIN

NAPLES

PERSIA

AFGHANISTAN

[15]

Madeira
MOROCCO

Gibraltar

ALGIERS

MALTA
O T T O M A N   E M P I R E

[16]

NEPAL
BHUTAN

ASSAM

Macau

Tropic of Cancer

TUNIS
(Ottoman)

TRIPOLI
(Ottoman)

[11]
[17]

BENGAL

BURMA

Touaregs

FEZZAN

NEJD

[12] [19] [18]

MARATHA
CONFEDERACY

LAOS

TONGKING

St
Louis
FUTA
TORO

KAARTA

MOSSI
STATES

WADAI

FUNJ

OMAN
Bombay

ARAKAN

SIAM

COCHIN
CHINA

PHILIPPINES

SEGU

HAUSA
STATES

BORNU

YEMEN

[14]
[10]

Goa

[19] [15]

Madras
Pondicherry

[21]

BRUNEI

GAMBIA

BORGU
KONG [6]
OYO

DARFUR
BAGIRMI

AUSSA
HARAR

Micronesians

PORTUGUESE
GUINEA

[7]
[8]

ETHIOPIA

[20]

CEYLON

Malacca

SULTANATE
OF ACEH

SMALL
MALAY
STATES

FUTA
JALON

Cape Coast
Castle

Madagascar

Réunion

ASANTE [6]
DAHOMEY [7]
BENIN [8]
SMALL KINGDOMS [9]

[9]

KONGO

LUBA

[9]

ANGOLA

LUNDA

KAZEMBE

ZANJ
(to Oman)

Seychelles

[10] NORTHERN CIRCARS
[11] MUGHAL EMPIRE
[12] BALUCHISTAN
[13] KHANATE OF BUKHARA
[14] HYDERABAD
[15] SMALL INDIAN STATES
[16] SIKH STATES
[17] OUDH
[18] RAJPUTS
[19] MYSORE
[20] KANDY
[21] CAMBODIA

DUTCH EAST INDIES

Papuans

SMALL MALAY
STATES

PORTUGUESE
TIMOR

Melanesians

LOZI

Malagasy

Mauritius

St Helena

ROZWI

MOZAMBIQUE

Réunion

Tropic of Capricorn

San

Australian Aborigines

Polynesians

CAPE
COLONY

Khoikhoi

Tasmanians

Maoris

0°
30°
60°
90°
120°
150°
180°

Equator

45°

1783

In terms of absolute industrial production, in 1783 China remained the biggest workshop of the world, but this was not a status it would keep for much longer. In Britain, the Industrial Revolution was in full swing by the 1760s, as a succession of technological innovations, the most famous being the Spinning Jenny, made mechanized mass production of textiles possible. In its earlier stages, the Industrial Revolution depended on renewable power sources, such as watermills. James Watt's improvements to the design of steam engines turned them into a viable source of power for industrial processes. Britain's growing network of canals, begun in the 1750s, allowed coal (and other bulk commodities) to be transported easily and cheaply around the country. By the end of the century, British industry was becoming rapidly dependent on fossil fuels. Abundant and cheap coal fuelled a rapid increase in the production of iron, which was used not only for weapons and tools but also now for construction.

The period saw continuing advances in European science, with important new discoveries in astronomy and chemistry, such as the isolation of the gases hydrogen and oxygen. European geographical knowledge was greatly expanded by the voyages of James Cook, which produced the first accurate charts of the Pacific Ocean. The growing sense of mastery of the natural world was a major factor in the birth of the Romantic movement, a cultural rebellion against rationalism and materialism that exalted imagination, individualism and the love of wild nature. Romanticism began as a literary movement and was particularly influential in Germany. Among its first great works were Goethe's novel *The Sorrows of Young Werther* (1774) and Schiller's play *The Robbers* (1781). Romanticism subsequently exercised a profound influence on European art and music, as well as literature.

World Population

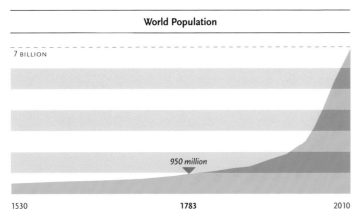

7 BILLION

950 million

1530   1783   2010

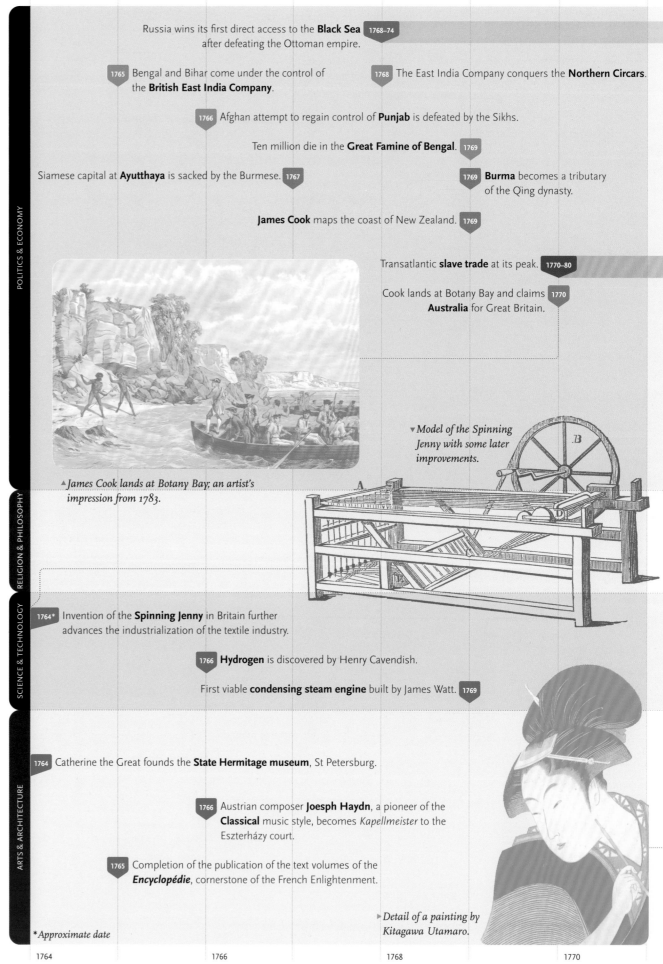

1764   1766   1768   1770

POLITICS & ECONOMY

Russia wins its first direct access to the **Black Sea** `1768–74` after defeating the Ottoman empire.

`1765` Bengal and Bihar come under the control of the **British East India Company**.

`1768` The East India Company conquers the **Northern Circars**.

`1766` Afghan attempt to regain control of **Punjab** is defeated by the Sikhs.

Ten million die in the **Great Famine of Bengal**. `1769`

Siamese capital at **Ayutthaya** is sacked by the Burmese. `1767`

`1769` **Burma** becomes a tributary of the Qing dynasty.

James Cook maps the coast of New Zealand. `1769`

Transatlantic **slave trade** at its peak. `1770–80`

Cook lands at Botany Bay and claims `1770` **Australia** for Great Britain.

▲ *James Cook lands at Botany Bay; an artist's impression from 1783.*

▼ *Model of the Spinning Jenny with some later improvements.*

RELIGION & PHILOSOPHY

SCIENCE & TECHNOLOGY

`1764*` Invention of the **Spinning Jenny** in Britain further advances the industrialization of the textile industry.

`1766` **Hydrogen** is discovered by Henry Cavendish.

First viable **condensing steam engine** built by James Watt. `1769`

ARTS & ARCHITECTURE

`1764` Catherine the Great founds the **State Hermitage museum**, St Petersburg.

`1766` Austrian composer **Joesph Haydn**, a pioneer of the **Classical** music style, becomes *Kapellmeister* to the Eszterházy court.

`1765` Completion of the publication of the text volumes of the *Encyclopédie*, cornerstone of the French Enlightenment.

▶ *Detail of a painting by Kitagawa Utamaro.*

*Approximate date

1764   1766   1768   1770

1776 Adam Smith, *The Wealth of Nations*, lays the foundations of modern economics.

1779–83 **Spain** unsuccessfully lays siege to Gibraltar.

1771 Marathas capture **Delhi** and install a puppet Mughal ruler.

1774 The Saudis capture **Riyadh**.

1774 Accession of **Louis XVI**, the last pre-Revolution king of France.

1778 France enters the **American War of Independence** against Britain, followed by Spain (in 1779) and the Netherlands (in 1780).

1772 **Edo**, capital of the Japanese shogunate, is destroyed by fire.

1775 **Oudh** cedes the Hindu holy city of Benares (Varanasi) to the East India Company.

1780 The British defeat a Maratha siege of **Madras**.

1772 **Tay Son peasant rebellion** breaks out in Tongking and Cochin China.

Qing suppress revolt by the Muslim Hui of **Gansu province**. 1781–84

1772 First partition of **Poland** between Russia, Austria and Prussia.

Temmei famine in Japan causes peasant uprisings and urban riots. 1781–88

British conquer the **Dutch East Indies** (later to exchange them for trading concessions). 1781

Tibet brought under indirect Chinese administration. 1783

Russia annexes the khanate of the **Crimea**. 1783

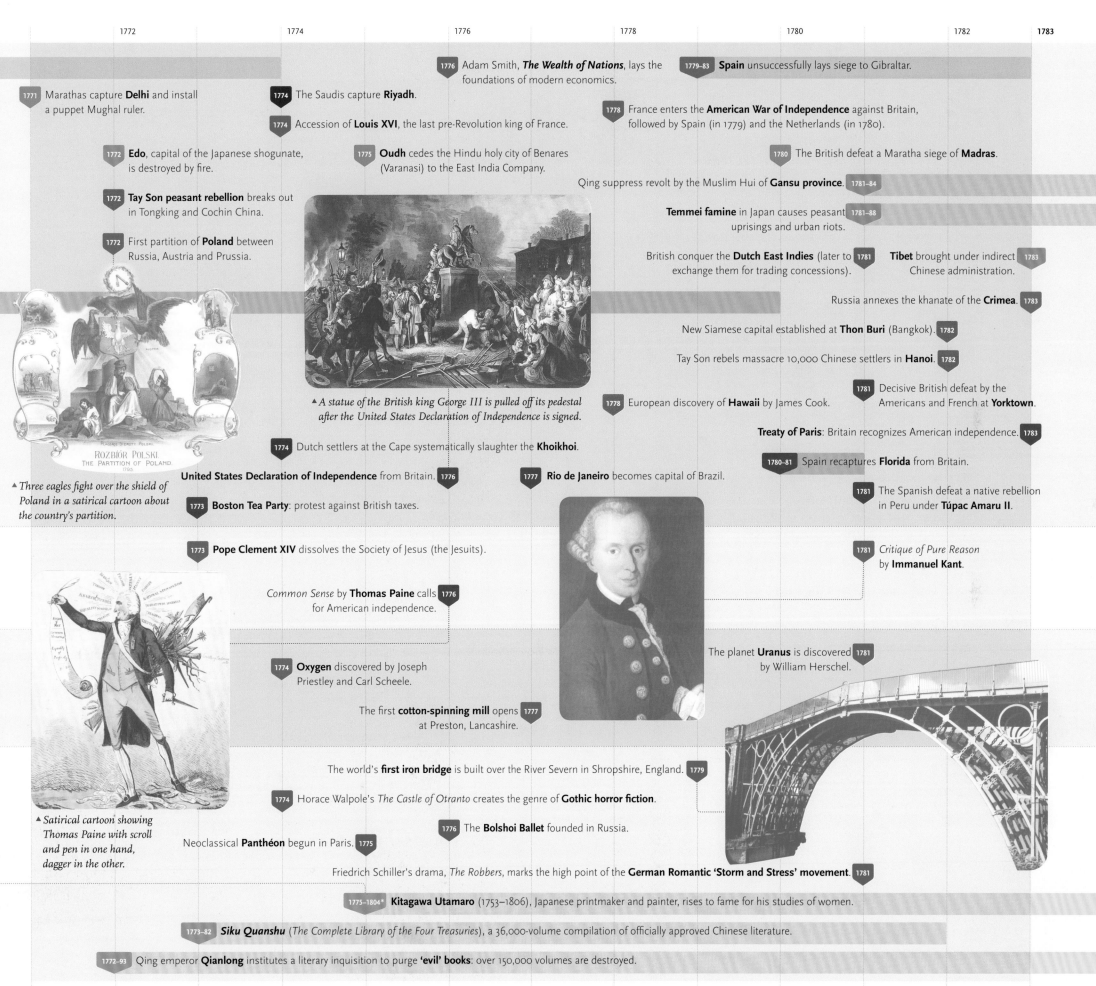

ROZBIÓR POLSKI.
THE PARTITION OF POLAND.
1795.

▲ *Three eagles fight over the shield of Poland in a satirical cartoon about the country's partition.*

New Siamese capital established at **Thon Buri** (Bangkok). 1782

Tay Son rebels massacre 10,000 Chinese settlers in **Hanoi**. 1782

▲ *A statue of the British king George III is pulled off its pedestal after the United States Declaration of Independence is signed.*

1778 European discovery of **Hawaii** by James Cook.

1781 Decisive British defeat by the Americans and French at **Yorktown**.

Treaty of Paris: Britain recognizes American independence. 1783

1774 Dutch settlers at the Cape systematically slaughter the **Khoikhoi**.

1777 **Rio de Janeiro** becomes capital of Brazil.

1780–81 Spain recaptures **Florida** from Britain.

United States Declaration of Independence from Britain. 1776

1781 The Spanish defeat a native rebellion in Peru under **Túpac Amaru II**.

1773 **Boston Tea Party**: protest against British taxes.

1773 **Pope Clement XIV** dissolves the Society of Jesus (the Jesuits).

1781 *Critique of Pure Reason* by **Immanuel Kant**.

Common Sense by **Thomas Paine** calls for American independence. 1776

▲ *Satirical cartoon showing Thomas Paine with scroll and pen in one hand, dagger in the other.*

The planet **Uranus** is discovered 1781 by William Herschel.

1774 **Oxygen** discovered by Joseph Priestley and Carl Scheele.

The first **cotton-spinning mill** opens 1777 at Preston, Lancashire.

The world's **first iron bridge** is built over the River Severn in Shropshire, England. 1779

1774 Horace Walpole's *The Castle of Otranto* creates the genre of **Gothic horror fiction**.

1776 The **Bolshoi Ballet** founded in Russia.

Neoclassical **Panthéon** begun in Paris. 1775

Friedrich Schiller's drama, *The Robbers*, marks the high point of the **German Romantic 'Storm and Stress' movement**. 1781

1775–1804* **Kitagawa Utamaro** (1753–1806), Japanese printmaker and painter, rises to fame for his studies of women.

1773–82 *Siku Quanshu* (*The Complete Library of the Four Treasuries*), a 36,000-volume compilation of officially approved Chinese literature.

1772–93 Qing emperor **Qianlong** institutes a literary inquisition to purge **'evil' books**: over 150,000 volumes are destroyed.

1812

FRANCE BIDS FOR EUROPEAN DOMINANCE; THE ESTABLISHMENT OF BRITISH COLONIES IN AUSTRALIA

France's support of the American Revolution left its economy ruined. Inflation, food shortages and high taxes, not to mention the example of the successful revolution of the American colonists, led to a republican revolution in 1789. While Austria and Prussia considered intervening, France acted first and declared war on Austria in 1792, beginning over 20 years of near continuous conflict which affected almost all of Europe. Britain, secure in its control of the seas, supported a succession of continental coalitions raised against France. France defeated them one after another and by 1812 dominated continental Europe.

French success was due in large part to the brilliant generalship of Napoleon Bonaparte, who seized power in 1799 and, in 1804, crowned himself emperor of France. Napoleon overreached himself, however, when he invaded Russia in 1812 to enforce his Continental System, which sought to block Britain's trade with Europe. The invasion was a disaster. Napoleon found that his strongest supporters outside France were the Poles, who hoped he would restore their country, which had been carved up between Prussia, Austria and Russia in 1795.

Independence rebellions broke out in the Spanish Americas after Napoleon occupied Spain in 1808: Paraguay became the first independent Latin American state in 1811. To raise cash for his wars, Napoleon sold Louisiana to the USA, which doubled in size as a result. Thanks to its naval power, Britain was able to pursue its colonial ambitions unhindered during the war years, occupying French and Dutch colonies and expanding its territories in India. Shortly before the war, Britain had established its first convict settlement in Australia. The British and Ottomans expelled a French army from Egypt in 1798–1801, but the Ottoman government was unable to regain full control and the country became effectively independent.

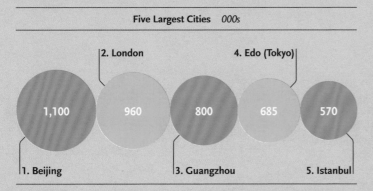

Five Largest Cities   000s

1,100	960	800	685	570
1. Beijing	2. London	3. Guangzhou	4. Edo (Tokyo)	5. Istanbul

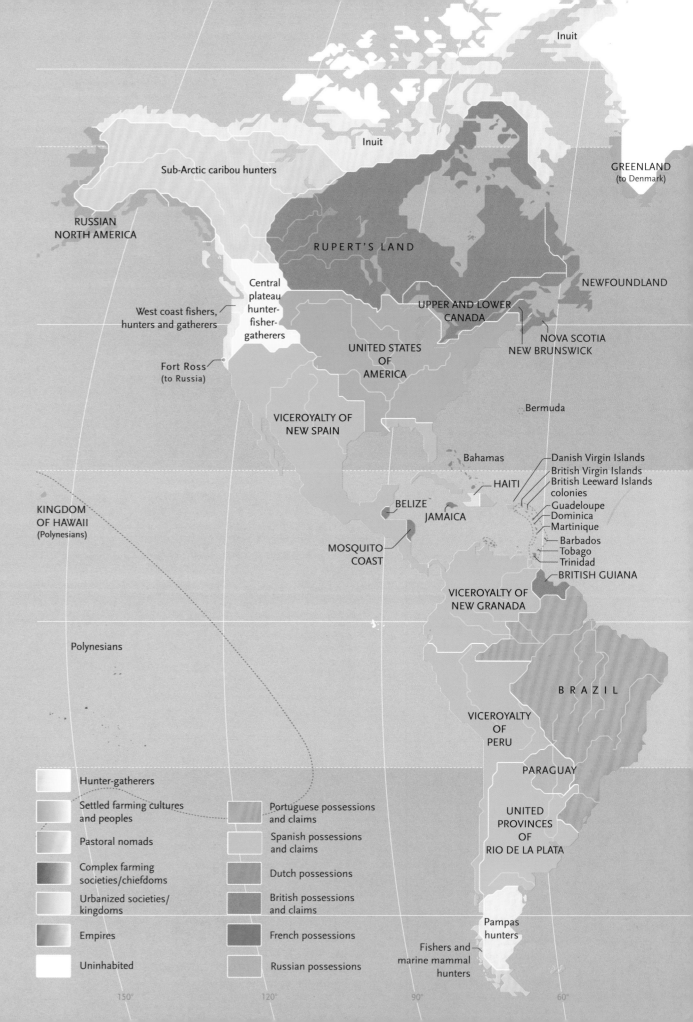

Inuit

Sub-Arctic caribou hunters

Inuit

GREENLAND
(to Denmark)

RUSSIAN
NORTH AMERICA

RUPERT'S LAND

NEWFOUNDLAND

West coast fishers,
hunters and gatherers

Central
plateau
hunter-
fisher-
gatherers

UPPER AND LOWER
CANADA

UNITED STATES
OF
AMERICA

NOVA SCOTIA
NEW BRUNSWICK

Fort Ross
(to Russia)

VICEROYALTY OF
NEW SPAIN

Bermuda

Bahamas

Danish Virgin Islands
British Virgin Islands
British Leeward Islands
colonies
Guadeloupe
Dominica
Martinique
Barbados
Tobago
Trinidad

HAITI

KINGDOM
OF HAWAII
(Polynesians)

BELIZE
JAMAICA

MOSQUITO
COAST

BRITISH GUIANA

VICEROYALTY OF
NEW GRANADA

Polynesians

BRAZIL

VICEROYALTY
OF
PERU

PARAGUAY

Hunter-gatherers

Settled farming cultures
and peoples

Portuguese possessions
and claims

UNITED
PROVINCES
OF
RIO DE LA PLATA

Pastoral nomads

Spanish possessions
and claims

Complex farming
societies/chiefdoms

Dutch possessions

Urbanized societies/
kingdoms

British possessions
and claims

Pampas
hunters

Empires

French possessions

Fishers and
marine mammal
hunters

Uninhabited

Russian possessions

NETHERLANDS ①
CONFEDERATION ②
OF THE RHINE
GRAND DUCHY ③
OF WARSAW
SWISS ④
CONFEDERACY
KINGDOM OF ⑤
ITALY
KINGDOM OF ⑥
NAPLES
ICELAND
(to Denmark)
DENMARK-
NORWAY
SWEDEN
GREAT
BRITAIN
2
London ①
PRUSSIA ③
KINGDOM OF SICILY ⑦
FRANCE ②
AUSTRIAN
EMPIRE
④
⑤
5
KINGDOM OF ⑧
SARDINIA
PORTUGAL
SPAIN
⑧
⑥
Istanbul
Gibraltar
⑦
MOROCCO
ALGIERS
Malta
TUNIS
(Ottoman)
OTTOMAN
EMPIRE
Touaregs
TRIPOLI
(Ottoman)
EGYPT
(nominally
Ottoman)

RUSSIAN EMPIRE

Arctic Circle

75°

Kazakhs

Kyrgyz
Turkmen
⑯
⑰
PERSIA
⑱

SMALL
UZBEK
KHANATES
KASHMIR

45°

Ainu

QING EMPIRE
Beijing ①
KOREA
JAPAN
Edo (Tokyo) ④

NEPAL
⑳ BHUTAN ASSAM
⑲ ⑳
RAJPUTANA ㉑
NEJD
OMAN
Bombay
Goa
MYSORE
TRAVANCORE
㉔
Maldive
Islands
SENEGAL
FUTA
TORO
KAARTA
MOSSI
STATES
HAUSA
STATES
SEGU
WADAI
BORNU
FUNJ
GAMBIA
⑨
KONG
⑩
⑪
⑫
⑭
⑮
DARFUR
YEMEN
AUSSA
PORTUGUESE
GUINEA
Cape Coast
Castle
ETHIOPIA HARAR
SIERRA LEONE
BUNYORO
ANKOLE
RWANDA
BURUNDI
LUBA
BUGANDA
KONGO
ANGOLA
LUNDA
KAZEMBE
LOZI
ROZWI
⑮
San
CAPE
COLONY
MOZAMBIQUE
ZANJ
(to Oman)
Seychelles
Mauritius
Réunion
MERINA
(Malagasy)

LAOS ③ **Guangzhou**
Macau
BURMA
ARAKAN ㉓
SIAM VIETNAM PHILIPPINES
㉕
CEYLON
SULTANATE
OF ACEH
Malacca
MALAY STATES

Tropic of Cancer

DUTCH EAST INDIES
JAVA
PORTUGUESE
TIMOR

Micronesians

Papuans

Melanesians

Equator

FUTA JALON ⑨
ASANTE ⑩
DAHOMEY ⑪
OYO ⑫
BENIN ⑬
SOKOTO CALIPHATE ⑭
SMALL KINGDOMS ⑮

⑯ KHANATE OF KHIVA
⑰ KHANATE OF BUKHARA
⑱ AFGHANISTAN
⑲ BALUCHISTAN
⑳ SMALL INDIAN STATES
㉑ OUDH
㉒ HYDERABAD
㉓ BRITISH INDIA
㉔ KANDY
㉕ CAMBODIA

Australian Aborigines

Tropic of Capricorn

Polynesians

NEW
SOUTH
WALES

VAN DIEMEN'S
LAND

Maoris

45°

0°   30°   60°   90°   120°   150°   180°

1812

Enlightenment thinkers were critical of Europe's absolute monarchies, often advocating individual liberty, representative institutions and the separation of powers. These ideals became all the more potent after they were enshrined in the Constitution of the United States in 1787. French revolutionaries sought a much more thoroughgoing transformation of society to accord with Enlightenment ideals of reason and secularism: Christianity was abolished and replaced with a Cult of Reason, and a revolutionary calendar was introduced to signal the start of a new era.

Because of the use of systematic mass terror against both counter-revolutionaries and ideological dissidents within the revolutionaries' own ranks, the French Revolution has often been seen as the prototype of 20th-century communist revolutions. Napoleon ended the revolution, but his *Code Napoléon* enshrined its principles of liberty and equality as the basis of French civil law.

During the 18th century, a strong anti-slavery movement began to develop in Britain and the USA. In 1802 Denmark became the first European country to ban the slave trade, a move followed by Britain in 1807. Slavery was left unresolved by the US constitution. Many abolitionists hoped slavery would gradually die out. However, Eli Whitney's invention of the cotton gin in 1793 enabled a great increase in American cotton production, revitalizing slavery in the southern states.

The French revolutionary principles of liberty and equality were not applied to African slaves, but they inspired a successful slave rebellion in the French colony of Saint-Domingue, which became independent as Haiti. Nor did women benefit: some of the earliest feminist literature began to appear in Britain and France. Important technological developments of this period included hot air balloon flights, steam locomotives and steamboats.

World Population

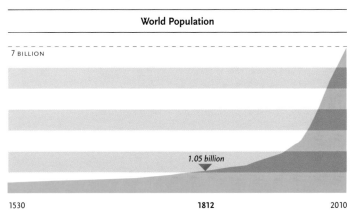

7 BILLION

1.05 billion

1530   **1812**   2010

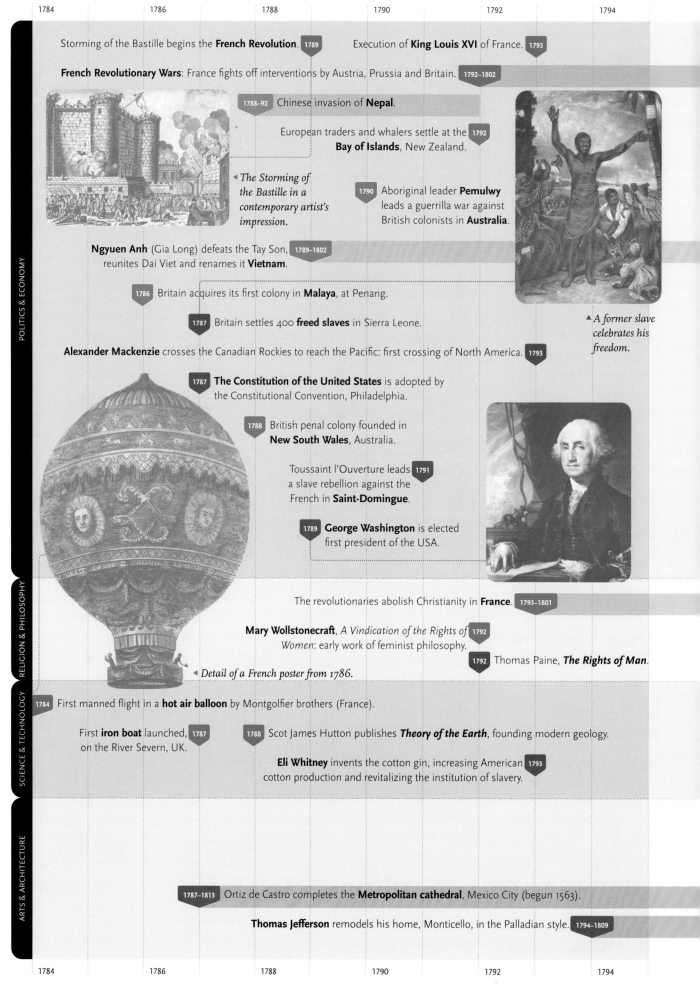

POLITICS & ECONOMY

Storming of the Bastille begins the **French Revolution**. `1789`   Execution of **King Louis XVI** of France. `1793`

French Revolutionary Wars: France fights off interventions by Austria, Prussia and Britain. `1792–1802`

`1788–92` Chinese invasion of **Nepal**.

European traders and whalers settle at the `1792` **Bay of Islands**, New Zealand.

◀ *The Storming of the Bastille in a contemporary artist's impression.*

`1790` Aboriginal leader **Pemulwy** leads a guerrilla war against British colonists in **Australia**.

Ngyuen Anh (Gia Long) defeats the Tay Son, `1789–1802` reunites Dai Viet and renames it **Vietnam**.

`1786` Britain acquires its first colony in **Malaya**, at Penang.

`1787` Britain settles 400 **freed slaves** in Sierra Leone.

▲ *A former slave celebrates his freedom.*

Alexander Mackenzie crosses the Canadian Rockies to reach the Pacific: first crossing of North America. `1793`

`1787` **The Constitution of the United States** is adopted by the Constitutional Convention, Philadelphia.

`1788` British penal colony founded in **New South Wales**, Australia.

Toussaint l'Ouverture leads `1791` a slave rebellion against the French in **Saint-Domingue**.

`1789` **George Washington** is elected first president of the USA.

RELIGION & PHILOSOPHY

The revolutionaries abolish Christianity in **France**. `1793–1801`

Mary Wollstonecraft, *A Vindication of the Rights of* `1792` *Women*: early work of feminist philosophy.

`1792` Thomas Paine, **The Rights of Man**.

◀ *Detail of a French poster from 1786.*

SCIENCE & TECHNOLOGY

`1784` First manned flight in a **hot air balloon** by Montgolfier brothers (France).

First **iron boat** launched, `1787` on the River Severn, UK.

`1788` Scot James Hutton publishes **Theory of the Earth**, founding modern geology.

Eli Whitney invents the cotton gin, increasing American `1793` cotton production and revitalizing the institution of slavery.

ARTS & ARCHITECTURE

`1787–1813` Ortiz de Castro completes the **Metropolitan cathedral**, Mexico City (begun 1563).

Thomas Jefferson remodels his home, Monticello, in the Palladian style. `1794–1809`

1795 **Poland** is partitioned for a second time between Russia, Austria and Prussia.

1802 **Denmark** becomes the first European country to ban its citizens from participating in the **slave trade**.

1807 **Britain** abolishes the slave trade.

Napoleon's invasion of **Russia** ends in retreat. **1812**

1798 **United Irishmen's rebellion** against British rule.

1803 Outbreak of the **Napoleonic Wars** (to 1815).

1808 Napoleon appoints his brother **Joseph** king of Spain.

Napoleon Bonaparte becomes dictator of France. **1799**

1804 **Napoleon** crowns himself emperor of the French.

The **USA declares war** on Britain and invades Canada. **1812**

1795 **Qajar Shah** makes Tehran the capital of Persia.

1800 Act of Union of Great Britain and Ireland creates the **United Kingdom**.

1805 Nelson's victory over the French and Spanish at **Trafalgar** confirms British naval supremacy; Napoleon routs the Russians and Austrians at **Austerlitz**.

1795 Britain takes **Malacca** from the Dutch.

1801 **Georgia** becomes part of the Russian empire.

1807 French invasion of **Portugal**.

Tipu Sultan of Mysore defeated and killed by the British at **Seringapatam**. **1799**

1802 **Wahhabis** sack the Shi'ite holy city of Karbala.

1806 Napoleon abolishes the **Holy Roman empire** and reorganizes Germany as the Confederation of the Rhine.

1803–11 Wahhabi occupation of **Mecca**.

Britain occupies Dutch colonies in **Ceylon**. **1798**

1801 The Ottomans and British defeat the French army in Egypt at the battle of **Aboukir**.

1803 The British capture the Mughal capital at **Delhi**.

King Kamehameha I unites the **1810** **Hawaiian Islands**.

1795 Retirement of emperor **Qianlong** marks the beginning of the decline of the Qing empire.

1803–5 War breaks out between Britain and the **Marathas**.

The British occupy **Java** (until 1814). **1811**

1796–1804 The **White Lotus peasant rebellion** devastates much of central China.

1805 **Muhammad Ali** becomes viceroy of Egypt under nominal Ottoman authority.

1797 Andrianampoinimerina founds the **Merina kingdom** in Madagascar.

1804–11 **Usman dan Fodio** leads a jihad against the Hausa, incorporating them into the Sokoto caliphate.

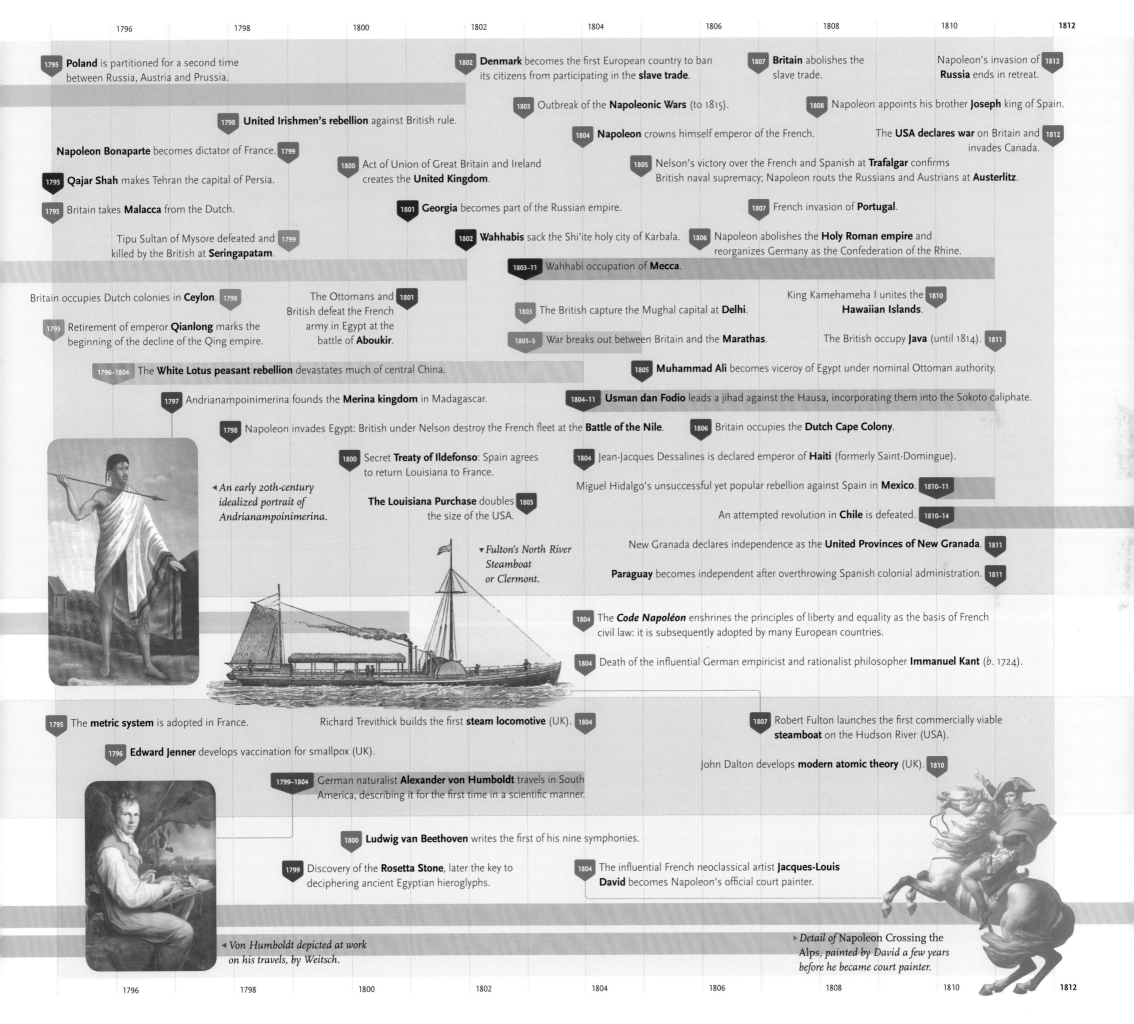

◄ *An early 20th-century idealized portrait of Andrianampoinimerina.*

1798 Napoleon invades Egypt: British under Nelson destroy the French fleet at the **Battle of the Nile**.

1806 Britain occupies the **Dutch Cape Colony**.

1800 Secret **Treaty of Ildefonso**: Spain agrees to return Louisiana to France.

1804 Jean-Jacques Dessalines is declared emperor of **Haiti** (formerly Saint-Domingue).

The Louisiana Purchase doubles **1803** the size of the USA.

Miguel Hidalgo's unsuccessful yet popular rebellion against Spain in **Mexico**. **1810–11**

An attempted revolution in **Chile** is defeated. **1810–14**

▼*Fulton's North River Steamboat or Clermont.*

New Granada declares independence as the **United Provinces of New Granada**. **1811**

Paraguay becomes independent after overthrowing Spanish colonial administration. **1811**

1804 The **Code Napoléon** enshrines the principles of liberty and equality as the basis of French civil law: it is subsequently adopted by many European countries.

1804 Death of the influential German empiricist and rationalist philosopher **Immanuel Kant** (*b*. 1724).

1795 The **metric system** is adopted in France.

Richard Trevithick builds the first **steam locomotive** (UK). **1804**

1807 Robert Fulton launches the first commercially viable **steamboat** on the Hudson River (USA).

1796 **Edward Jenner** develops vaccination for smallpox (UK).

1799–1804 German naturalist **Alexander von Humboldt** travels in South America, describing it for the first time in a scientific manner.

John Dalton develops **modern atomic theory** (UK). **1810**

1800 **Ludwig van Beethoven** writes the first of his nine symphonies.

1799 Discovery of the **Rosetta Stone**, later the key to deciphering ancient Egyptian hieroglyphs.

1804 The influential French neoclassical artist **Jacques-Louis David** becomes Napoleon's official court painter.

◄ *Von Humboldt depicted at work on his travels, by Weitsch.*

► *Detail of Napoleon Crossing the Alps, painted by David a few years before he became court painter.*

1824

THE FALL OF THE SPANISH–AMERICAN EMPIRE

The failure of Napoleon's invasion of Russia was the turning point of the Napoleonic Wars. In 1813 Prussia, Austria, Russia, Britain and Sweden allied against an increasingly war-weary France. As the allies closed in on Paris in spring 1814, Napoleon abdicated and went into exile. He returned to power in 1815, but his defeat by Britain and Prussia at Waterloo in that year was final: he was exiled again, this time for life, to the remote island of St Helena in the South Atlantic.

The Congress of Vienna in 1814–15, which was called to decide on the shape of post-Napoleonic Europe, reinstated conservative monarchies and tried to establish a stable balance of power. The German states were organized into a loose German Confederation under Prussian and Austrian leadership. The former Austrian Netherlands were united with the kingdom of the Netherlands and Austria was compensated with Venice, Milan and other north Italian city states. Sweden, which had lost Finland to Russia during the war, was compensated with Norway, at the expense of Denmark, which had consistently backed the losing side.

The Ottoman empire continued its slow decline when it was forced to grant local autonomy to the Serbs in 1817, following a rebellion. When the Greeks rebelled against Ottoman rule in 1821, their cause was taken up by wealthy Western Europeans and Americans who, influenced by the Romantic movement and their Classical education, saw the struggle as an extension of the ancient Greek wars against Persia. Egypt, one of the Ottomans' nominal dependencies, expanded, conquering Sudan and restoring Ottoman rule in Arabia.

Western Africa was destabilized by the rise of the Masina jihadi state; Southern Africa by the rise of the Zulu kingdom under Shaka, whose savage campaigns forced entire peoples to flee in the Mfecane (the 'crushing'). Britain continued its empire building in India and Southeast Asia.

Five Largest Cities *000s*

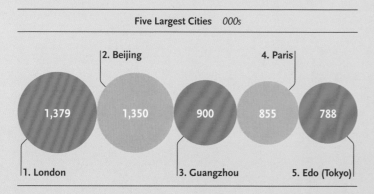

2. Beijing		4. Paris	
1,379	1,350	900	855	788
1. London		3. Guangzhou		5. Edo (Tokyo)

Hunter-gatherers

Settled farming cultures and peoples

Pastoral nomads

Complex farming societies/chiefdoms

Urbanized societies/ kingdoms

Empires

Uninhabited

Portuguese possessions and claims

Spanish possessions and claims

Dutch possessions

British possessions and claims

French possessions

Russian possessions

NETHERLANDS 1
GERMAN STATES 2
SWISS
CONFEDERACY 3
PIEDMONT-
SARDINIA 4
PAPAL STATES 5
KINGDOM OF 6
THE TWO SICILIES

ICELAND
(to Denmark)

NORWAY
(in union
with
Sweden)

SWEDEN

RUSSIAN EMPIRE

GREAT
BRITAIN 1
London
DENMARK
PRUSSIA 1
2
4
Paris
FRANCE 3
AUSTRIAN
EMPIRE
5
6

PORTUGAL
SPAIN

Gibraltar
Malta

ALGIERS

MOROCCO
TUNIS
(Ottoman)

OTTOMAN
EMPIRE

TRIPOLI
(Ottoman)

Kazakhs

Kyrgyz

SMALL
UZBEK
KHANATES

KASHMIR

QING EMPIRE

Ainu

Beijing 2

KOREA

JAPAN 5
Edo (Tokyo)

Turkmen

PERSIA

15

16

17

18

19

NEPAL
BHUTAN
ASSAM

OUDH

LAOS

Guangzhou 3
Macau

Touareg

SENEGAL
FUTA
TORO KAARTA
MOSSI
STATES

GAMBIA

PORTUGUESE
GUINEA

SIERRA
LEONE LIBERIA GOLD
COAST

WADAI

BORNU

SOKOTO
CALIPHATE DARFUR

ETHIOPIA HARAR

10

7

8
12

9

11

13

EGYPT
(nominally
Ottoman)

Bedouin
Arabs

OMAN

Goa
MYSORE
Pondicherry

TRAVANCORE
CEYLON

Maldive
Islands

BRITISH
INDIA

19

20

BURMA

ARAKAN

SIAM
VIETNAM

PHILIPPINES

Micronesians

AUSSA

BUNYORO
ANKOLE
RWANDA
BURUNDI
LUBA

KONGO

BUGANDA

ZANJ
(to Oman)

Seychelles

SULTANATE
OF ACEH

Malacca
MALAY STATES

22

DUTCH EAST INDIES

Papuans

Melanesians

SEGU 7
FUTA JALON 8
ASANTE 9
MASINA 10
DAHOMEY 11
OYO 12
BENIN 13
SMALL
KINGDOMS 14

ANGOLA

St Helena

LUNDA

LOZI

ROZWI

San

KAZEMBE

MERINA

Mauritius

Réunion

15 KHANATE OF KHIVA
16 KHANATE OF BUKHARA
17 AFGHANISTAN
18 BALUCHISTAN
19 SMALL INDIAN STATES
20 HYDERABAD
21 CAMBODIA
22 Singapore (British)

PORTUGUESE
TIMOR

Australian Aborigines

Polynesians

Tristan da
Cunha

MOZAMBIQUE
ZULU KINGDOM
Port Natal
BASUTOLAND

CAPE
COLONY

NEW
SOUTH
WALES

VAN DIEMEN'S
LAND

Maoris

1824

The end of the Napoleonic Wars allowed Spain to send troops to suppress the South American independence movements. Vast distances, difficult conditions, and charismatic and skilful rebel leaders ultimately defeated the Spanish and by 1824 all that was left of their American empire were Cuba and Puerto Rico. Inspired by the American Revolution, the leading rebel leader Simón Bolívar hoped to create a United States of Latin America, but regional interests were too strong to be overcome. The new states were divided by race and conflicting sectional interests and frequently fell under the control of military dictatorships. Brazil declared independence from Portugal in 1822, as a monarchy under a Portuguese prince.

The United States benefited from the decline of Spanish power, gaining Florida in 1819. However, the Americans feared that other European powers might use the break-up of the Spanish empire to establish their own influence or control over the newly independent states. This led to the proclamation in 1823 of the Monroe Doctrine of opposition to further European colonialism in the Americas. This could not be enforced (and it was mainly British opposition that deterred other European powers from intervening in Latin America), but as American power grew later in the century it became a major principle of US foreign policy.

Another sign of American assertiveness was its declaration of war against Britain in 1812 over border tensions with Canada and Britain's interference in neutral shipping. Peace was agreed in 1814 but, because of slow transatlantic communications, fighting continued into 1815. Only minor concessions were made by both sides, but agreement to settle future disputes by arbitration allowed the USA and Canada to expand west without coming into violent conflict. Success in repelling American invaders during the war began a sense of Canadian national identity.

World Population

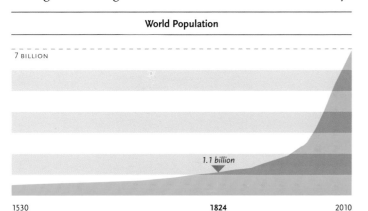

7 BILLION

1.1 billion

1530   **1824**   2010

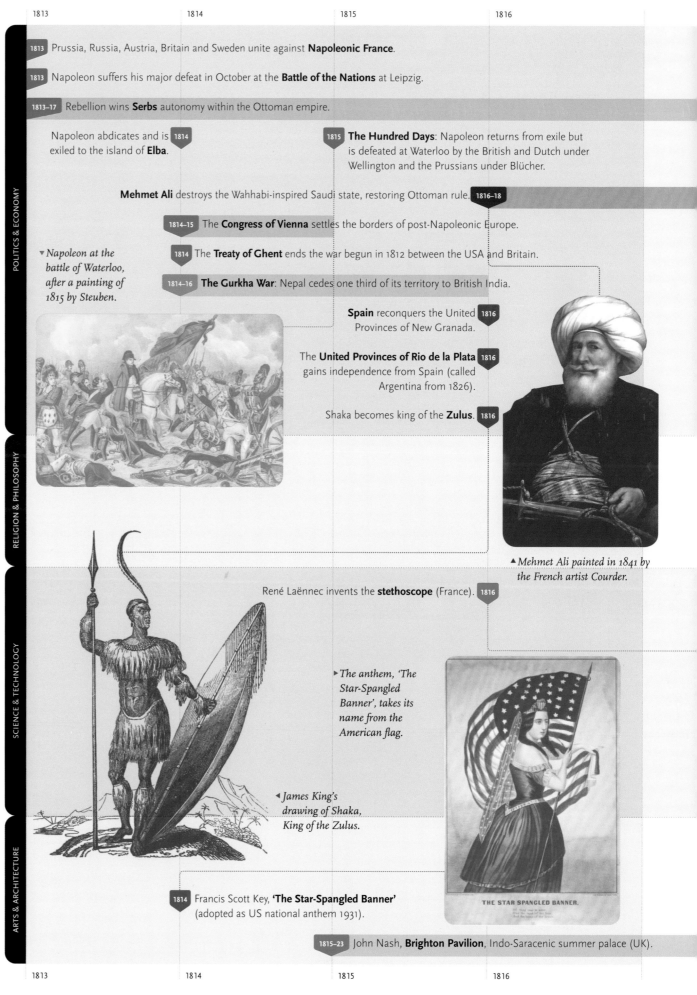

1813 | 1814 | 1815 | 1816

POLITICS & ECONOMY

1813 Prussia, Russia, Austria, Britain and Sweden unite against **Napoleonic France**.

1813 Napoleon suffers his major defeat in October at the **Battle of the Nations** at Leipzig.

1813–17 Rebellion wins **Serbs** autonomy within the Ottoman empire.

Napoleon abdicates and is **1814** exiled to the island of **Elba**.

1815 **The Hundred Days**: Napoleon returns from exile but is defeated at Waterloo by the British and Dutch under Wellington and the Prussians under Blücher.

Mehmet Ali destroys the Wahhabi-inspired Saudi state, restoring Ottoman rule. **1816–18**

1814–15 The **Congress of Vienna** settles the borders of post-Napoleonic Europe.

▼ *Napoleon at the battle of Waterloo, after a painting of 1815 by Steuben.*

1814 The **Treaty of Ghent** ends the war begun in 1812 between the USA and Britain.

1814–16 The **Gurkha War**: Nepal cedes one third of its territory to British India.

Spain reconquers the United **1816** Provinces of New Granada.

The **United Provinces of Rio de la Plata** **1816** gains independence from Spain (called Argentina from 1826).

Shaka becomes king of the **Zulus**. **1816**

▲ *Mehmet Ali painted in 1841 by the French artist Courder.*

RELIGION & PHILOSOPHY

SCIENCE & TECHNOLOGY

René Laënnec invents the **stethoscope** (France). **1816**

▶ *The anthem, 'The Star-Spangled Banner', takes its name from the American flag.*

◀ *James King's drawing of Shaka, King of the Zulus.*

THE STAR SPANGLED BANNER.

ARTS & ARCHITECTURE

1814 Francis Scott Key, **'The Star-Spangled Banner'** (adopted as US national anthem 1931).

1815–23 John Nash, **Brighton Pavilion**, Indo-Saracenic summer palace (UK).

1813   1814   1815   1816

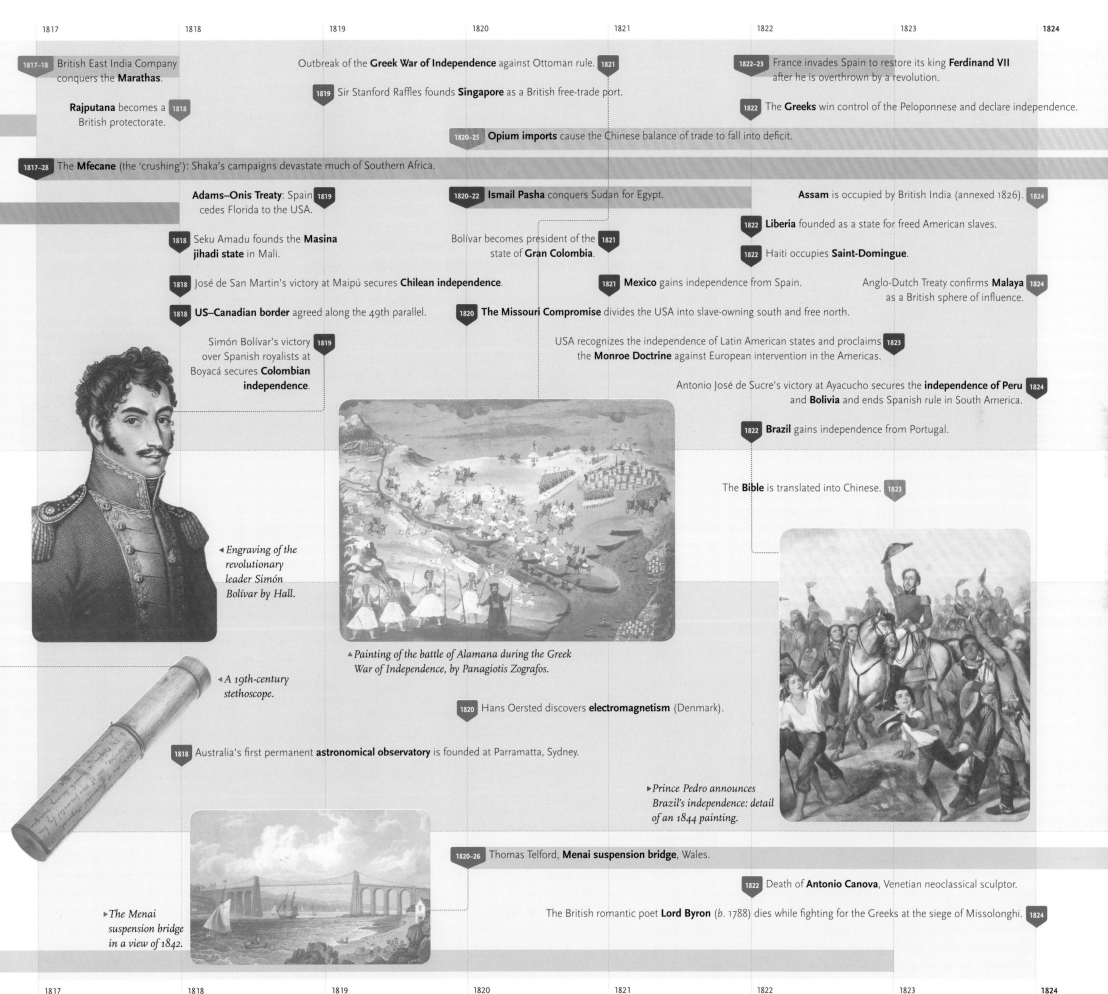

1817–18 British East India Company conquers the **Marathas**.

Rajputana becomes a British protectorate. **1818**

1817–28 The **Mfecane** (the 'crushing'): Shaka's campaigns devastate much of Southern Africa.

Adams–Onis Treaty: Spain cedes Florida to the USA. **1819**

1818 Seku Amadu founds the **Masina jihadi state** in Mali.

1818 José de San Martin's victory at Maipú secures **Chilean independence**.

1818 **US–Canadian border** agreed along the 49th parallel.

Simón Bolívar's victory over Spanish royalists at Boyacá secures **Colombian independence**. **1819**

◀ *Engraving of the revolutionary leader Simón Bolívar by Hall.*

◀ *A 19th-century stethoscope.*

1818 Australia's first permanent **astronomical observatory** is founded at Parramatta, Sydney.

▶ *The Menai suspension bridge in a view of 1842.*

Outbreak of the **Greek War of Independence** against Ottoman rule. **1821**

1819 Sir Stanford Raffles founds **Singapore** as a British free-trade port.

1820–25 **Opium imports** cause the Chinese balance of trade to fall into deficit.

1820–22 **Ismail Pasha** conquers Sudan for Egypt.

Bolívar becomes president of the state of **Gran Colombia**. **1821**

1821 **Mexico** gains independence from Spain.

1820 **The Missouri Compromise** divides the USA into slave-owning south and free north.

USA recognizes the independence of Latin American states and proclaims the **Monroe Doctrine** against European intervention in the Americas. **1823**

Antonio José de Sucre's victory at Ayacucho secures the **independence of Peru** and **Bolivia** and ends Spanish rule in South America. **1824**

1822 **Brazil** gains independence from Portugal.

The **Bible** is translated into Chinese. **1823**

▲ *Painting of the battle of Alamana during the Greek War of Independence, by Panagiotis Zografos.*

1820 Hans Oersted discovers **electromagnetism** (Denmark).

▶ *Prince Pedro announces Brazil's independence: detail of an 1844 painting.*

1820–26 Thomas Telford, **Menai suspension bridge**, Wales.

1822–23 France invades Spain to restore its king **Ferdinand VII** after he is overthrown by a revolution.

1822 The **Greeks** win control of the Peloponnese and declare independence.

Assam is occupied by British India (annexed 1826). **1824**

1822 **Liberia** founded as a state for freed American slaves.

1822 Haiti occupies **Saint-Domingue**.

Anglo-Dutch Treaty confirms **Malaya** as a British sphere of influence. **1824**

1822 Death of **Antonio Canova**, Venetian neoclassical sculptor.

The British romantic poet **Lord Byron** (b. 1788) dies while fighting for the Greeks at the siege of Missolonghi. **1824**

1848

NATIONALISM AND THE RISE OF THE NATION STATES; REVOLUTIONS BREAK OUT IN EUROPE

The major political development of the early 19th century was the growth and spread of nationalism: the ideal that each nation should have its own state and that every member of a nation should live in the same state. For most of history a person's political allegiance had been given to a dynastic or city state, or to a feudal overlord. The implications of nationalism in a world dominated by multi-ethnic dynastic states were profound and they were not confined to politics. Nationalism demanded a cultural expression, too, in art, literature and music.

Nationalism developed from the Enlightenment ideas of popular sovereignty and the rights of man. These displaced the ruler as the embodiment of the state in favour of the people. Nationalism first became a major political force in the American and French revolutions: their success inspired nationalist movements among many other European peoples. The Congress of Vienna made few concessions to nationalism but the influence of nationalist sentiment steadily grew. In 1831 Giuseppe Mazzini founded a movement for the unification of Italy; in 1832 the Greeks achieved statehood; and in 1839 Belgium became independent of the Netherlands.

In 1848 suppressed nationalist and republican sentiments burst out in a wave of revolutions across Europe: nationalists installed democratic governments in Hungary, Bohemia, Moravia and Croatia; Poles rose against Prussia and Russia; Irish nationalists rose against British rule; anti-Austrian rebellions broke out across northern Italy; a parliament met in Frankfurt aiming to unite Germany. The only successful challenge, however, took place in France, where a republican revolution overthrew the restored monarchy. The *Communist Manifesto*, published in 1848 by Karl Marx and Friedrich Engels, looked beyond nationalism to class struggles and international communism.

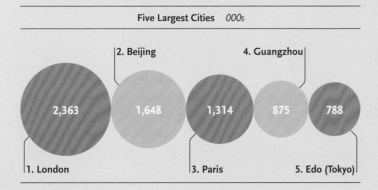

Five Largest Cities *000s*

2. Beijing		4. Guangzhou		
2,363	1,648	1,314	875	788
1. London		3. Paris		5. Edo (Tokyo)

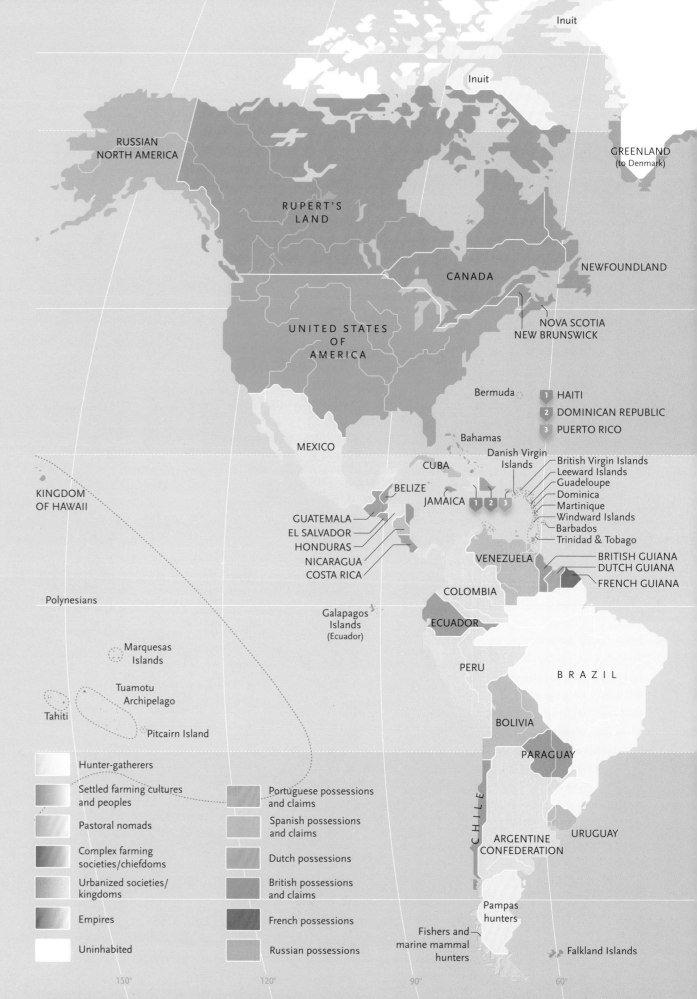

NETHERLANDS 4
GERMAN STATES 5
BELGIUM 6
SWITZERLAND 7
KINGDOM OF
PIEDMONT-SARDINIA 8
PAPAL STATES 9
KINGDOM OF
THE TWO SICILIES 10

ICELAND
(to Denmark)

NORWAY
(in union
with
Sweden)

SWEDEN

RUSSIAN EMPIRE

Arctic Circle

GREAT
BRITAIN 1
London
3
Paris
FRANCE

DENMARK
4
6
PRUSSIA
5
7
AUSTRIAN
EMPIRE
8
9
10

Kyrgyz

SMALL
UZBEK
KHANATES

QING EMPIRE

Beijing 2

KOREA

Ainu

5 Edo (Tokyo)

JAPAN

45°

75°

PORTUGAL

SPAIN

Gibraltar

MOROCCO

ALGERIA

GREECE
Malta

TUNIS
(Ottoman)

OTTOMAN EMPIRE

23 KHANATE OF KHIVA

24 KHANATE OF BUKHARA

Turkmen

PERSIA

25

26

NEPAL
BHUTAN

OUDH

INDIA

4 Guangzhou
Hong Kong
Macau

BURMA 27

ARAKAN

Tropic of Cancer

Touareg

SENEGAL
FUTA
TORO KAARTA
GAMBIA
13
12
LIBERIA

PORTUGUESE
GUINEA

SIERRA
LEONE

MOSSI
STATES
14
18
SOKOTO
CALIPHATE
15 16
17 19
11

IVORY GOLD
COAST COAST

WADAI
BORNU

DARFUR

EGYPT

Bedouin
Arabs

OMAN

Aden
AUSSA

ETHIOPIA HARAR

BUGANDA

BUNYORO
ANKOLE
RWANDA
BURUNDI
LUBA

TEKE

GABON

ZANJ
(to Oman)

Goa

Pondicherry

CEYLON

Maldive
Islands

SIAM

TENASSERIM

VIETNAM

PHILIPPINES

28

29

SULTANATE
OF ACEH

MALAY STATES

30

Micronesians

Equator

Seychelles

Chagos
Islands

DUTCH EAST INDIES

Papuans

Rio Muni 11
FUTA JALON 12
SEGU 13
MASINA 14
ASANTE 15
DAHOMEY 16

ANGOLA

LUNDA

KAZEMBE

20

LOZI

NDEBELE

MERINA

Nossi Bé
Island

Amirante
Islands

Ste Marie Island

Mauritius

PORTUGUESE
TIMOR

Melanesians

KINGDOM
OF TONGA
(Polynesians)

New
Caledonia

Tropic of Capricorn

IBADAN 17
BORGU 18
BENIN 19
SMALL
KINGDOMS 20

San

22

CAPE
COLONY

21

MOZAMBIQUE

ZULU KINGDOM

NATAL

Réunion

21 BASUTOLAND

22 BOER REPUBLICS

23 KHANATE OF KHIVA

24 KHANATE OF BUKHARA

25 AFGHANISTAN

26 BALUCHISTAN

27 LAOS

28 CAMBODIA

29 Malacca

30 Singapore

WESTERN
AUSTRALIA

Australian Aborigines

SOUTH
AUSTRALIA

VAN DIEMEN'S
LAND

NEW
SOUTH
WALES

Polynesians

NEW
ZEALAND

0° 30° 60° 90° 120° 150° 180°

1848

Europe's global influence grew rapidly up to 1848. By 1846 Britain had won control of almost the entire Indian subcontinent, begun the conquest of Burma and annexed New Zealand. Britain's easy victory in the First Opium War (1839–42) forced China to open its ports to foreign trade, gave Britain the island of Hong Kong and exposed the technological backwardness of China's armed forces. A British invasion of Afghanistan in 1839–42 ended in disaster, however, and in Southern Africa the Boers of Cape Colony escaped British rule by migrating into the interior to found their own republics. In 1846 Britain and the USA agreed to extend the US–Canadian border along the 49th parallel to the Pacific.

Between 1830 and 1848, France began the conquest of Algeria and annexed Tahiti and other Polynesian islands. The Dutch began to tighten their control of the East Indies. Texas joined the USA in 1845 after a successful rebellion by American settlers against Mexican rule in 1836. This precipitated the Mexican–American War (1846–48) during which the USA gained vast territories, including California. The arrival of large numbers of Catholic Irish immigrants, fleeing the Great Famine in Ireland, was the first challenge to the 'Anglo-Saxon' Protestant dominance of the USA.

Britain was the world's leading industrial and mercantile nation at this period, accounting in 1830 for c. 45 per cent of international trade. By 1848 other European countries and the USA were industrializing quickly and experiencing rapid urban growth. The development of railways in Britain revolutionized transport, providing for the first time fast, comfortable overland travel, as well as economically viable long-distance land transport for bulky raw materials like coal and iron ore. However, railways turned out to be of greater advantage to large continental countries like the USA and Russia than to a compact island like Britain.

World Population

7 BILLION

1.23 billion

154

1530   1848   2010

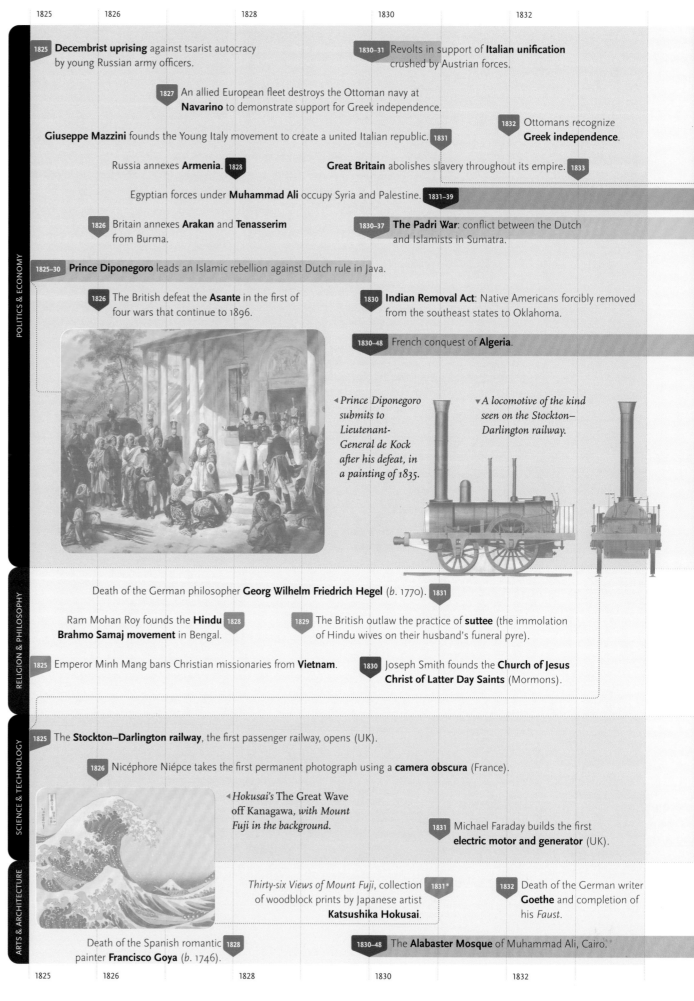

POLITICS & ECONOMY

1825 **Decembrist uprising** against tsarist autocracy by young Russian army officers.

1830–31 Revolts in support of **Italian unification** crushed by Austrian forces.

1827 An allied European fleet destroys the Ottoman navy at **Navarino** to demonstrate support for Greek independence.

Giuseppe Mazzini founds the Young Italy movement to create a united Italian republic. **1831**

1832 Ottomans recognize **Greek independence**.

Russia annexes **Armenia**. **1828**

Great Britain abolishes slavery throughout its empire. **1833**

Egyptian forces under **Muhammad Ali** occupy Syria and Palestine. **1831–39**

1826 Britain annexes **Arakan** and **Tenasserim** from Burma.

1830–37 **The Padri War**: conflict between the Dutch and Islamists in Sumatra.

1825–30 **Prince Diponegoro** leads an Islamic rebellion against Dutch rule in Java.

1826 The British defeat the **Asante** in the first of four wars that continue to 1896.

1830 **Indian Removal Act**: Native Americans forcibly removed from the southeast states to Oklahoma.

1830–48 French conquest of **Algeria**.

◄ *Prince Diponegoro submits to Lieutenant-General de Kock after his defeat, in a painting of 1835.*

▼ *A locomotive of the kind seen on the Stockton–Darlington railway.*

RELIGION & PHILOSOPHY

Death of the German philosopher **Georg Wilhelm Friedrich Hegel** (b. 1770). **1831**

Ram Mohan Roy founds the **Hindu Brahmo Samaj movement** in Bengal. **1828**

1829 The British outlaw the practice of **suttee** (the immolation of Hindu wives on their husband's funeral pyre).

1825 Emperor Minh Mang bans Christian missionaries from **Vietnam**.

1830 Joseph Smith founds the **Church of Jesus Christ of Latter Day Saints** (Mormons).

SCIENCE & TECHNOLOGY

1825 The **Stockton–Darlington railway**, the first passenger railway, opens (UK).

1826 Nicéphore Niépce takes the first permanent photograph using a **camera obscura** (France).

◄ *Hokusai's The Great Wave off Kanagawa, with Mount Fuji in the background.*

1831 Michael Faraday builds the first **electric motor and generator** (UK).

ARTS & ARCHITECTURE

Thirty-six Views of Mount Fuji, collection **1831*** of woodblock prints by Japanese artist **Katsushika Hokusai**.

1832 Death of the German writer **Goethe** and completion of his *Faust*.

Death of the Spanish romantic painter **Francisco Goya** (b. 1746). **1828**

1830–48 The **Alabaster Mosque** of Muhammad Ali, Cairo.

1825   1826   1828   1830   1832

1825   1826   1828   1830   1832

Belgium gains independence from the Netherlands. `1839`

The **Ottomans** recognize Muhammad Ali as hereditary ruler of `1840` **Egypt** in return for his withdrawal from Syria and Palestine.

`1836` English becomes the official language of government in **India**.

`1837` **Oshio Heihachiro** leads an unsuccessful revolt against the *bakufu* (military government) in Osaka.

◄ Engraving of Mazzini, based on a photograph.

`1834` The **Zollverein**, a German customs union, is established under Prussian leadership.

Mzilikaze founds the `1840` **Ndebele kingdom**.

`1835–36` **The Great Trek**: Boers (Dutch South Africans) leave Cape Colony to escape British rule.

The **Great Famine in Ireland**: mass migration to the USA and Britain. `1845–47`

Repeal of the British Corn Law begins the **free-trade era**. `1846`

The **Year of Revolutions**: widespread liberal and nationalist revolutions in Europe. `1848`

Kashmir becomes a British protectorate. `1846`   **France** abolishes slavery `1848` in its colonies.

`1839–42` British invasion of **Afghanistan** to counter perceived Russian influence is disastrously defeated.

During two **Anglo-Sikh Wars**, Britain conquers Punjab. `1845–49`

`1840` **Treaty of Waitangi**: the Maoris of New Zealand accept British sovereignty.

`1839–42` Britain defeats China in the **First Opium War**: China cedes Hong Kong to Britain and opens five ports to foreign trade.

The **USA** and **France** sign trade agreements with China. `1844`   **Russia** completes its conquest `1847` of the Kazakhs.

`1842` **France** annexes Tahiti, the Tuamotu Archipelago and the Marquesas Islands.

`1843–48` **Maori rising** against British rule.

`1836` **Texas** wins independence from Mexico at the battle of San Jacinto (joins the USA in 1845).

Zanzibar becomes capital of the sultanate of Oman. `1840`

`1837–38` Failed republican rebellions in **Canada**.

▼ The Houses of Parliament.

Mexican–American War: Mexico loses New Mexico, California, Nevada, Utah and Arizona. `1846–48`

The Dominican Republic (formerly Saint-Domingue) `1844` gains independence from Haiti.

`1845` Aided by British missionaries, Taufa'ahau becomes the first king of **Tonga**, ruling as George Tupou.

`1840–50` Beginning of mass immigration of non-British Europeans to the **USA**.

The Oregon Treaty: Britain and the USA divide the Oregon country along the 49th parallel. `1846`

◄ Engraving of the SS Great Britain showing her original six masts.

`1837` Sayyid Muhammad ibn Ali as-Senussi founds the **Sufi Senussi movement**.

`1836` Transcendentalist American philosopher **Ralph Waldo Emerson**, *Nature*.

Karl Marx and Friedrich Engels, ***The Communist Manifesto***. `1848`

Brigham Young leads the **Mormon Great Migration** to the Great Salt Lake in Utah. `1847`

`1837` Charles Wheatstone patents the **electric telegraph** (UK).

German astronomer Johann Galle discovers the planet **Neptune**. `1846`

`1837` The British paddle steamer *Sirius* makes the **first crossing of the Atlantic under steam**.

`1843` Brunel's *Great Britain*: the first **screw-propellor-driven passenger liner**.

First **underwater** `1838` **telegraph cable** laid, beneath the Hooghly River, Calcutta (Kolkata).

`1839` Charles Goodyear invents **vulcanized rubber**, revolutionizing the use of rubber (USA).

Samuel Morse and Alfred Vail develop **Morse Code** for their telegraph system (USA). `1844`

► Diagram of Samuel Morse's original telegraph.

Edgar Allan Poe, *The Murders in the Rue Morgue*: first modern detective story. `1841`

`1835` Completion of the **Arc de Triomphe**, Paris, a memorial to Napoleon's victories.

`1840–60` Charles Barry, neo-Gothic **Palace of Westminster** (Houses of Parliament), London.

*Approximate date

1861

THE US CIVIL WAR; REBELLIONS AND SOCIAL CHANGE IN JAPAN AND CHINA

The USA's westward expansion raised the possibility of new slave-owning states being admitted into the union, sharply polarizing opinions on the issue. The issue came to a head following the election in 1860 of Abraham Lincoln to the presidency, largely on the votes of the northern free states. Lincoln's refusal to extend slavery to any new states led 11 southern slave-owning states to secede from the union and, in 1861, form the Confederate States of America. A Confederate attack on the Union garrison at Fort Sumter in South Carolina in April 1861 led to the outbreak of civil war.

In 1853 the Tokugawa shogunate was forced to end its policy of maintaining Japan as a closed society by the arrival of a squadron of US warships under Commodore Perry. The following year Japan opened two ports to foreign ships; more trade concessions followed in 1858. In China, the Qing faced a succession of rebellions, by far the most serious of which was the radical egalitarian religious and political Taiping (Heavenly Kingdom) rebellion, which broke out in 1850. The Qing finally suppressed the rebellion in 1864, at the cost of around 20 million lives, but the dynasty's authority never recovered.

In the midst of the rebellion, the British and French fought together against China in the Second Opium War (1856–60), forcing more trade concessions from the Qing, and Russia annexed the Amur region of Manchuria. Russian ambitions to seize the ailing Ottoman empire's Danubian provinces were thwarted by Britain and France in the Crimean War (1854–56). France began to create a Southeast Asian empire with the occupation of Saigon in 1859. King Mongkut successfully staved off European intervention in Siam by taking the initiative to open his country to foreign trade. In East Africa, the emperor Tewodros II began to create a centralized government, effectively founding the modern Ethiopian state.

Five Largest Cities *000's*

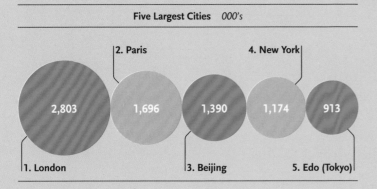

2. Paris	4. New York

2,803	1,696	1,390	1,174	913

1. London	3. Beijing	5. Edo (Tokyo)

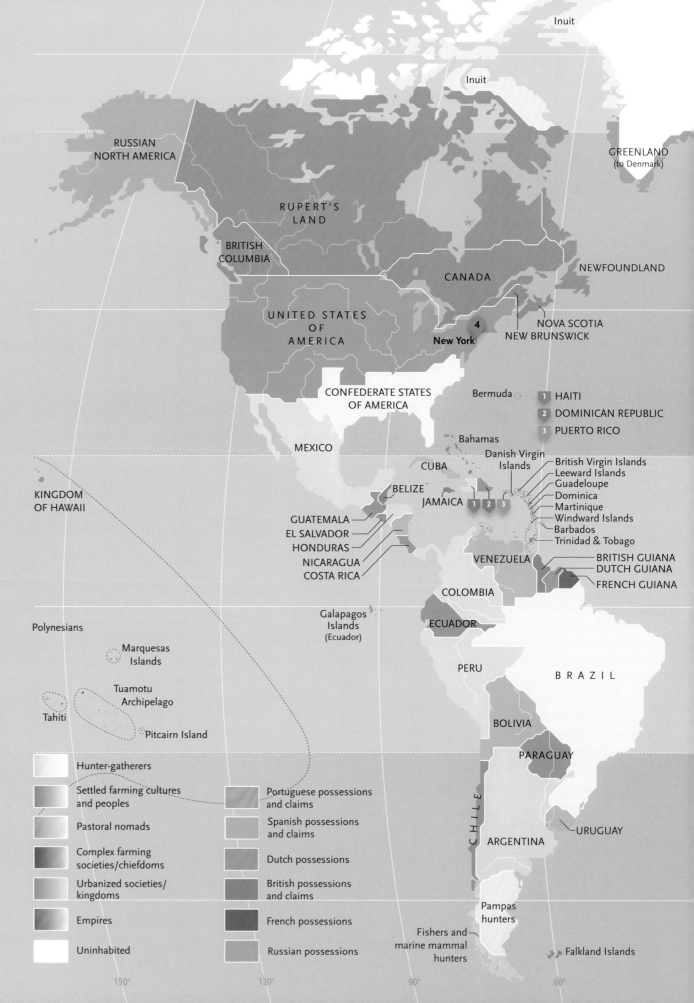

Inuit

RUSSIAN
NORTH AMERICA

Inuit

GREENLAND
(to Denmark)

RUPERT'S
LAND

BRITISH
COLUMBIA

NEWFOUNDLAND

CANADA

UNITED STATES
OF
AMERICA

4
New York

NOVA SCOTIA
NEW BRUNSWICK

CONFEDERATE STATES
OF AMERICA

Bermuda

1 HAITI
2 DOMINICAN REPUBLIC
3 PUERTO RICO

MEXICO

Bahamas

Danish Virgin
Islands

CUBA

British Virgin Islands
Leeward Islands
Guadeloupe
Dominica
Martinique
Windward Islands
Barbados
Trinidad & Tobago

KINGDOM
OF HAWAII

BELIZE
JAMAICA 1 2 3

GUATEMALA
EL SALVADOR
HONDURAS
NICARAGUA
COSTA RICA

VENEZUELA

BRITISH GUIANA
DUTCH GUIANA
FRENCH GUIANA

COLOMBIA

Galapagos
Islands
(Ecuador)

ECUADOR

Polynesians

Marquesas
Islands

PERU

BRAZIL

Tuamotu
Archipelago

Tahiti

BOLIVIA

Pitcairn Island

PARAGUAY

C H I L E

Hunter-gatherers

Settled farming cultures
and peoples

Portuguese possessions
and claims

ARGENTINA

URUGUAY

Pastoral nomads

Spanish possessions
and claims

Complex farming
societies/chiefdoms

Dutch possessions

Urbanized societies/
kingdoms

British possessions
and claims

Pampas
hunters

Empires

French possessions

Fishers and
marine mammal
hunters

Uninhabited

Russian possessions

Falkland Islands

NETHERLANDS **4**
GERMAN STATES **5**
BELGIUM **6**
SWITZERLAND **7**
PAPAL STATES **8**

ICELAND
(to Denmark)

NORWAY
(in union
with
Sweden)

SWEDEN

RUSSIAN EMPIRE

Arctic Circle

75°

45°

GREAT
BRITAIN
1
London
2
Paris
FRANCE

DENMARK
4
6
PRUSSIA
5
AUSTRIAN
EMPIRE
7
ITALY
8

QING EMPIRE

Beijing **3**

KOREA

JAPAN

Edo (Tokyo) **5**

PORTUGAL
SPAIN

Gibraltar
MOROCCO

GREECE
Malta

OTTOMAN EMPIRE

Turkmen

23

24

Uzbeks

PERSIA

25

26

Shanghai (Anglo-French concessions)

BHUTAN

NEPAL

Hong Kong
Macau

ALGERIA

TUNIS
(Ottoman)

TRUCIAL
OMAN

BAHRAIN

Touareg

EGYPT

SENEGAL
FUTA
TORO

MASINA

WADAI

BORNU

GAMBIA

13

14

18

SOKOTO
CALIPHATE

DARFUR

12

LIBERIA

15

16

17

ETHIOPIA

AUSSA

HARAR

Bedouin
Arabs

Aden

OMAN

INDIA

Goa
Pondicherry

Maldive
Islands

CEYLON

SULTANATE
OF ACEH

BURMA

27

PEGU
TENASSERIM

Andaman
Islands

SIAM

VIETNAM

PHILIPPINES

28

Saigon

29

MALAY STATES

30

Micronesians

PORTUGUESE
GUINEA

SIERRA
LEONE

IVORY
COAST
GOLD
COAST

19

9 **10**

11

GABON

TEKE

BUNYORO
ANKOLE
RWANDA
BURUNDI
LUBA

BUGANDA

SULTANATE
OF ZANZIBAR

Comoro
Islands

DUTCH EAST INDIES

PORTUGUESE
TIMOR

Papuans

Equator

Melanesians

KINGDOM
OF TONGA

Cotonou **9**
LAGOS **10**
Rio Muni **11**
FUTA JALON **12**
TUKULOR EMPIRE **13**
MOSSI STATES **14**
ASANTE **15**
DAHOMEY **16**
IBADAN **17**
BORGU **18**
BENIN **19**

ANGOLA

LUNDA

KAZEMBE

20

LOZI

NDEBELE

TRANSVAAL

San

MERINA

Mauritius

Réunion

20 SMALL
KINGDOMS
21 SWAZILAND
22 ORANGE FREE STATE

23 KHANATE OF KHIVA
24 KHANATE OF BUKHARA
25 AFGHANISTAN
26 BALUCHISTAN
27 LAOS
28 CAMBODIA
29 Malacca
30 Singapore

New
Caledonia

Tropic of Capricorn

Polynesians

WESTERN
AUSTRALIA

SOUTH
AUSTRALIA

QUEENSLAND

NEW
SOUTH
WALES

MOZAMBIQUE

ZULU KINGDOM

NATAL

BASUTOLAND

21

22

CAPE
COLONY

VICTORIA

TASMANIA

NEW
ZEALAND

45°

0°   30°   60°   90°   120°   150°   180°

Tropic of Cancer

1861

Despite the failure of the 1848 revolutions, nationalism continued its rise in Europe. The movement for Italian national unification, often called the Risorgimento (resurgence), began in earnest in 1859, when Piedmont–Sardinia expelled the Austrians from Italy with French support. The following year, a small revolutionary army led by Garibaldi invaded and conquered the Kingdom of the Two Sicilies. Garibaldi handed his conquest over to King Victor Emmanuel II of Piedmont–Sardinia, who was proclaimed king of Italy in 1861.

British colonization of Australia expanded rapidly after the end of the Napoleonic Wars, and by 1859 free settlers far outnumbered convicts. The Aboriginal population declined sharply, mainly because of epidemics of introduced European diseases. Britain had formally annexed New Zealand in 1840, but the land hunger of British settlers caused many conflicts with the indigenous Maori. The commercialism and cultural insensitivity of the British East India Company created growing resentment of British rule in India. In 1857 the company's Indian troops mutinied and seized Delhi. The rebellion was defeated in 1858, destroying hopes of preserving traditional Indian society free of Western influences.

The most important scientific development in this period was the publication of Charles Darwin's *On the Origin of Species* in 1859, which presented his theory of evolution by natural selection. Although the implications of his theory outraged the religious establishment, it quickly gained acceptance in the scientific community and revolutionized the study of biology. The laying of the first transatlantic telegraph cable in 1858 brought the age of instantaneous global communication a step nearer. The mid-19th century also saw the birth of the petroleum industry.

World Population

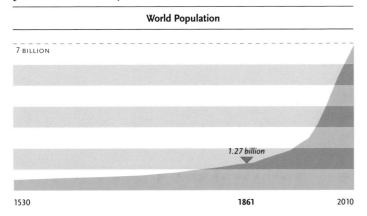

7 BILLION

1.27 billion

1530   1861   2010

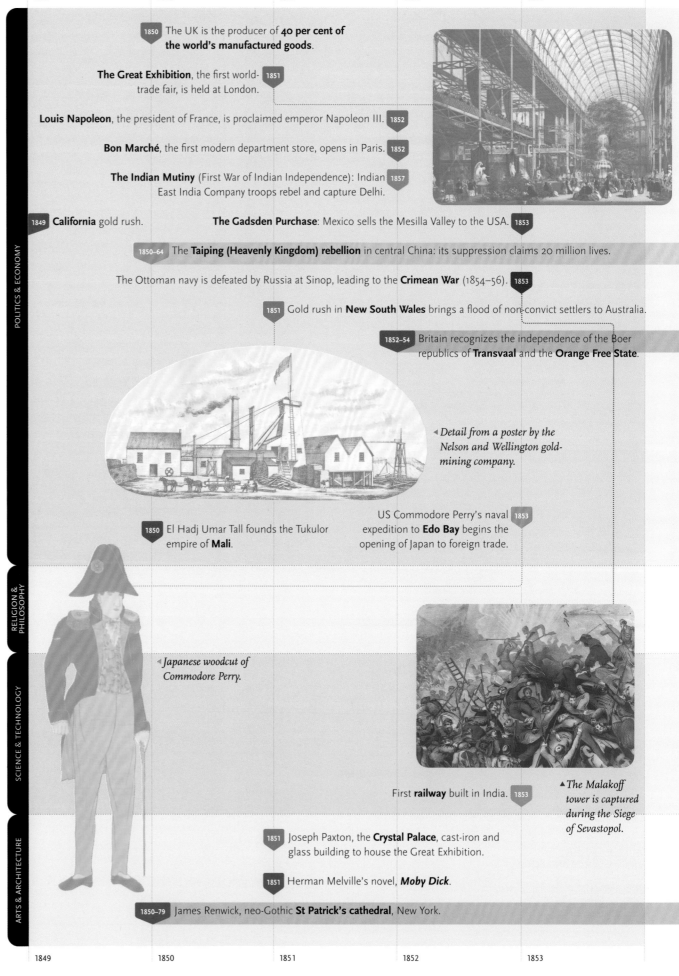

1849   1850   1851   1852   1853

1850 The UK is the producer of **40 per cent of the world's manufactured goods**.

The Great Exhibition, the first world-trade fair, is held at London. **1851**

Louis Napoleon, the president of France, is proclaimed emperor Napoleon III. **1852**

Bon Marché, the first modern department store, opens in Paris. **1852**

The Indian Mutiny (First War of Indian Independence): Indian East India Company troops rebel and capture Delhi. **1857**

1849 **California** gold rush.

The Gadsden Purchase: Mexico sells the Mesilla Valley to the USA. **1853**

1850–64 The **Taiping (Heavenly Kingdom) rebellion** in central China: its suppression claims 20 million lives.

The Ottoman navy is defeated by Russia at Sinop, leading to the **Crimean War** (1854–56). **1853**

1851 Gold rush in **New South Wales** brings a flood of non-convict settlers to Australia.

1852–54 Britain recognizes the independence of the Boer republics of **Transvaal** and the **Orange Free State**.

◀ *Detail from a poster by the Nelson and Wellington gold-mining company.*

1850 El Hadj Umar Tall founds the Tukulor empire of **Mali**.

US Commodore Perry's naval expedition to **Edo Bay** begins the opening of Japan to foreign trade. **1853**

◀ *Japanese woodcut of Commodore Perry.*

First **railway** built in India. **1853**

▲ *The Malakoff tower is captured during the Siege of Sevastopol.*

1851 Joseph Paxton, the **Crystal Palace**, cast-iron and glass building to house the Great Exhibition.

1851 Herman Melville's novel, ***Moby Dick***.

1850–79 James Renwick, neo-Gothic **St Patrick's cathedral**, New York.

POLITICS & ECONOMY

RELIGION & PHILOSOPHY

SCIENCE & TECHNOLOGY

ARTS & ARCHITECTURE

1849   1850   1851   1852   1853

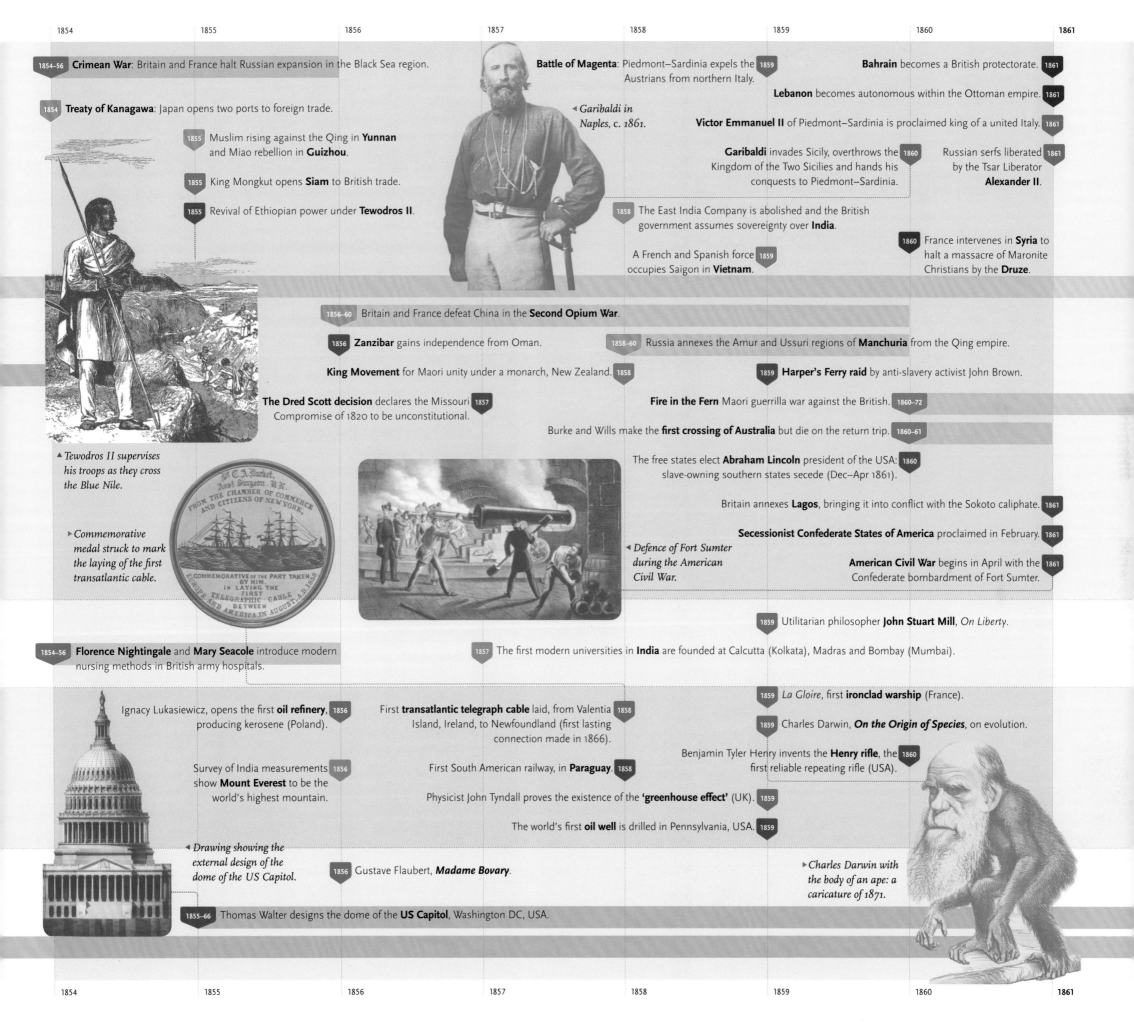

1854–56 **Crimean War**: Britain and France halt Russian expansion in the Black Sea region.

1854 **Treaty of Kanagawa**: Japan opens two ports to foreign trade.

1855 Muslim rising against the Qing in **Yunnan** and Miao rebellion in **Guizhou**.

1855 King Mongkut opens **Siam** to British trade.

1855 Revival of Ethiopian power under **Tewodros II**.

◄ Garibaldi in Naples, c. 1861.

Battle of Magenta: Piedmont–Sardinia expels the **1859** Austrians from northern Italy.

Bahrain becomes a British protectorate. **1861**

Lebanon becomes autonomous within the Ottoman empire. **1861**

Victor Emmanuel II of Piedmont–Sardinia is proclaimed king of a united Italy. **1861**

Garibaldi invades Sicily, overthrows the **1860** Kingdom of the Two Sicilies and hands his conquests to Piedmont–Sardinia.

Russian serfs liberated **1861** by the Tsar Liberator **Alexander II**.

1858 The East India Company is abolished and the British government assumes sovereignty over **India**.

A French and Spanish force **1859** occupies Saigon in **Vietnam**.

1860 France intervenes in **Syria** to halt a massacre of Maronite Christians by the **Druze**.

1856–60 Britain and France defeat China in the **Second Opium War**.

1856 **Zanzibar** gains independence from Oman.

1858–60 Russia annexes the Amur and Ussuri regions of **Manchuria** from the Qing empire.

King Movement for Maori unity under a monarch, New Zealand. **1858**

1859 **Harper's Ferry raid** by anti-slavery activist John Brown.

The Dred Scott decision declares the Missouri **1857** Compromise of 1820 to be unconstitutional.

Fire in the Fern Maori guerrilla war against the British. **1860–72**

Burke and Wills make the **first crossing of Australia** but die on the return trip. **1860–61**

▲ Tewodros II supervises his troops as they cross the Blue Nile.

The free states elect **Abraham Lincoln** president of the USA; **1860** slave-owning southern states secede (Dec–Apr 1861).

► Commemorative medal struck to mark the laying of the first transatlantic cable.

Britain annexes **Lagos**, bringing it into conflict with the Sokoto caliphate. **1861**

Secessionist Confederate States of America proclaimed in February. **1861**

◄ Defence of Fort Sumter during the American Civil War.

American Civil War begins in April with the **1861** Confederate bombardment of Fort Sumter.

1859 Utilitarian philosopher **John Stuart Mill**, *On Liberty*.

1854–56 **Florence Nightingale** and **Mary Seacole** introduce modern nursing methods in British army hospitals.

1857 The first modern universities in **India** are founded at Calcutta (Kolkata), Madras and Bombay (Mumbai).

1859 *La Gloire*, first **ironclad warship** (France).

Ignacy Lukasiewicz, opens the first **oil refinery**, **1856** producing kerosene (Poland).

First **transatlantic telegraph cable** laid, from Valentia **1858** Island, Ireland, to Newfoundland (first lasting connection made in 1866).

1859 Charles Darwin, **On the Origin of Species**, on evolution.

Survey of India measurements **1856** show **Mount Everest** to be the world's highest mountain.

First South American railway, in **Paraguay**. **1858**

Benjamin Tyler Henry invents the **Henry rifle**, the **1860** first reliable repeating rifle (USA).

Physicist John Tyndall proves the existence of the **'greenhouse effect'** (UK). **1859**

The world's first **oil well** is drilled in Pennsylvania, USA. **1859**

◄ Drawing showing the external design of the dome of the US Capitol.

1856 Gustave Flaubert, **Madame Bovary**.

► Charles Darwin with the body of an ape: a caricature of 1871.

1855–66 Thomas Walter designs the dome of the **US Capitol**, Washington DC, USA.

1871

NEW BORDERS DRAWN IN AMERICA AND EUROPE

The American Civil War initially went the Confederacy's way but by 1863 the Union's superior resources began to tell. Following the Union's decisive victory at Gettysburg in July 1863, the Confederacy was slowly ground down, and it finally surrendered in April 1865. The important part played by railways, industrialized armaments production, and ironclad warships has led to it being seen as the first modern war.

An immediate consequence of the Union victory was the abolition of slavery. The postwar reconstruction programme's aim of introducing multiracial democracy in the former slave states produced a violent white backlash, and by the early 1870s white supremacy had been restored. In 1867 the continental USA achieved its present extent with the purchase of Alaska from Russia. Also in 1867, the British North American colonies (except Newfoundland) were federated and granted self-government as the Dominion of Canada. Unresolved border disputes led to the War of the Triple Alliance (Brazil, Uruguay and Argentina) against Paraguay. The worst war in South American history, it cost Paraguay 70 per cent of its population. The failure of the French-sponsored Habsburg empire in Mexico (1864–67) ended European imperialist ambitions in the Americas.

Nationalism continued to rearrange the political map of Europe, bringing about Germany's unification in 1871. The creation of the *Zollverein* (customs union) under Prussian leadership in 1834 had begun to integrate the economies of the German states. Prussia consolidated its leadership of Germany with wars against Denmark (1864) and Austria (1866). When Bismarck manoeuvred France into declaring war in 1870, so reviving memories of the Napoleonic occupation of Germany, the smaller German states united with Prussia: its king Wilhelm I was proclaimed German emperor following France's defeat, which cost it the provinces of Alsace and Lorraine. During the war, Italy annexed Rome, completing national unification.

Five Largest Cities *millions*

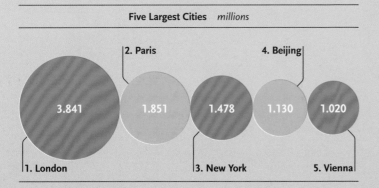

1. London — 3.841
2. Paris — 1.851
3. New York — 1.478
4. Beijing — 1.130
5. Vienna — 1.020

Legend:
- Hunter-gatherers
- Settled farming cultures and peoples
- Pastoral nomads
- Complex farming societies/chiefdoms
- Urbanized societies/ kingdoms
- Empires
- Uninhabited
- Portuguese possessions and claims
- Spanish possessions and claims
- Dutch possessions
- British possessions and claims
- French possessions
- Russian possessions

Map labels:
Inuit, ALASKA (to USA), GREENLAND (to Denmark), CANADA (autonomous), NEWFOUNDLAND, UNITED STATES OF AMERICA, New York, 3, Bermuda, 1 HAITI, 2 DOMINICAN REPUBLIC, 3 PUERTO RICO, MEXICO, BRITISH HONDURAS, Bahamas, CUBA, Danish Virgin Islands, British Virgin Islands, Leeward Islands, Guadeloupe, Dominica, Martinique, Windward Islands, Barbados, Trinidad & Tobago, JAMAICA, GUATEMALA, EL SALVADOR, HONDURAS, NICARAGUA, COSTA RICA, VENEZUELA, BRITISH GUIANA, DUTCH GUIANA, FRENCH GUIANA, COLOMBIA, KINGDOM OF HAWAII, Galapagos Islands (Ecuador), ECUADOR, Polynesians, Marquesas Islands, PERU, BRAZIL, Tuamotu Archipelago, Tahiti, Pitcairn Island, BOLIVIA, PARAGUAY, CHILE, ARGENTINA, URUGUAY, Pampas hunters, Fishers and marine mammal hunters, Falkland Islands

150° 120° 90° 60°

NETHERLANDS **4**
BELGIUM **5**
LUXEMBOURG **6**
SWITZERLAND **7**

ICELAND
(to Denmark)

NORWAY
(in union
with
Sweden)

SWEDEN

RUSSIAN EMPIRE

GREAT
BRITAIN **1**
London

DENMARK

GERMANY **4** **5**
6
7

AUSTRO-
HUNGARIAN
EMPIRE **5**
Vienna

2
Paris
FRANCE

ITALY

PORTUGAL
SPAIN

GREECE

Gibraltar

Malta

OTTOMAN EMPIRE

MOROCCO

ALGERIA **8**

Touareg

Turkmen **25**

Uzbeks

26

27

PERSIA

BAHRAIN

TRUCIAL
OMAN

QING EMPIRE

Beijing **4**

KOREA

JAPAN

Shanghai

BHUTAN

NEPAL

INDIA

BURMA **28**

Hong Kong
Macau

SENEGAL
FUTA
TORO

TUKULOR
EMPIRE

WADAI

13

BORNU

12

SOKOTO
CALIPHATE

15

16

DARFUR

EGYPT

Aden

AUSSA

Bedouin
Arabs

OMAN

Goa
Pondicherry

LOWER
BURMA

SIAM

Andaman
Islands

VIETNAM

PHILIPPINES

29

COCHIN
CHINA

GAMBIA

LIBERIA

14

PORTUGUESE
GUINEA

SIERRA
LEONE

IVORY
COAST

9

GOLD
COAST

10

17

11

ETHIOPIA

HARAR

BUNYORO

BUGANDA

TEKE

19

18

20

Maldive
Islands

CEYLON

Nicobar
Islands

Malacca **30**

MALAY STATES

31

SULTANATE
OF ACEH

Micronesians

DUTCH EAST INDIES

GABON

LUBA

21

SULTANATE
OF ZANZIBAR

Comoro
Islands

Papuans

PORTUGUESE
TIMOR

Melanesians

KINGDOM
OF TONGA

FIJI

BEYLIK OF TUNIS **8**
(Ottoman)

Cotonou **9**

LAGOS **10**

Rio Muni **11**

FUTA JALON **12**

MOSSI STATES **13**

ASANTE **14**

DAHOMEY **15**

IBADAN **16**

BENIN **17**

ANGOLA

LUNDA

KAZEMBE

22

LOZI

NDEBELE

TRANSVAAL

San

MERINA

Mauritius

Réunion

23

24

MOZAMBIQUE

ZULU KINGDOM

NATAL

BASUTOLAND

CAPE
COLONY

25 KHANATE OF KHIVA
26 AFGHANISTAN
27 BALUCHISTAN
28 LAOS
29 CAMBODIA
30 Malacca
31 Singapore

WESTERN
AUSTRALIA

SOUTH
AUSTRALIA

QUEENSLAND

NEW
SOUTH
WALES

New
Caledonia

Polynesians

KINGDOM
OF TONGA

FIJI

18 Tippu Tib's
trading empire

19 ANKOLE

20 RWANDA

21 BURUNDI

22 SMALL
KINGDOMS

23 SWAZILAND

24 ORANGE FREE STATE

TASMANIA

VICTORIA

NEW
ZEALAND

Arctic Circle

Tropic of Cancer

Equator

Tropic of Capricorn

1871

The increasing Western influence on Japan that followed Perry's missions in 1853–54 was resisted by young samurai warriors, who organized attacks on foreigners and foreign shipping. After British, US, French and Dutch naval forces retaliated by bombarding Japanese ports, popular discontent became focused on the shogunate. A brief civil war in 1867–68 overthrew the shogunate and restored the emperor to power. The emperor took up residence in Edo, the capital of the Tokugawa shoguns, which was renamed Tokyo. The Meiji (enlightened rule) restoration, as this development was called, began a period of rapid modernization in Japan.

The opening of the Suez Canal in 1869 linked the Mediterranean directly with the Red Sea and created a new, and much shorter, route between Europe and India than sailing around Africa. This saved not only time but also fuel for the steamships that, by the 1870s, were becoming more and more important for both commercial and naval use. Because India was its most important colonial possession, control of the canal immediately became a crucial strategic issue for Britain, which purchased it in 1875. Steamships could hold a course independent of the wind direction, but they were much less self-sufficient than sailing ships. As a result small oceanic islands assumed a new strategic significance as coaling stations. Another world-shrinking development of the period was the completion, also in 1869, of the first transcontinental railway, in the USA.

In 1866 Gregor Mendel founded the science of genetics. He published his results in an obscure journal and it was many years before they became widely known. The mid-19th century also saw the birth in Britain of the world's most popular spectator sport, Association Football or soccer. It was just one of many popular sports that was spread globally through the influence of the British empire.

World Population

7 BILLION

1.31 billion

1530   **1871**   2010

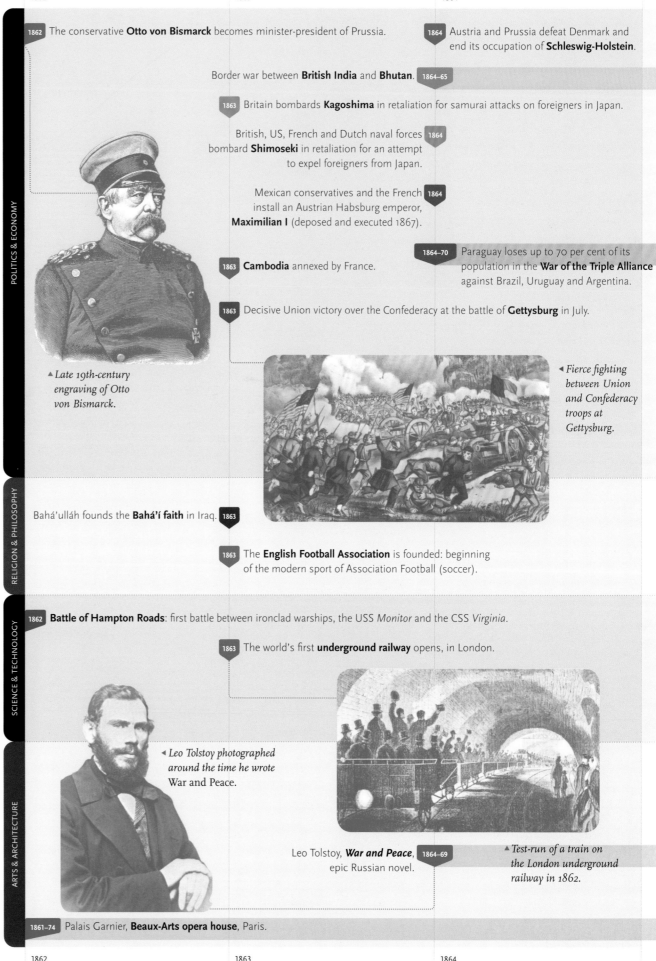

POLITICS & ECONOMY

1862 The conservative **Otto von Bismarck** becomes minister-president of Prussia.

1864 Austria and Prussia defeat Denmark and end its occupation of **Schleswig-Holstein**.

Border war between **British India** and **Bhutan**. **1864–65**

1863 Britain bombards **Kagoshima** in retaliation for samurai attacks on foreigners in Japan.

British, US, French and Dutch naval forces bombard **Shimoseki** in retaliation for an attempt to expel foreigners from Japan. **1864**

Mexican conservatives and the French install an Austrian Habsburg emperor, **Maximilian I** (deposed and executed 1867). **1864**

1863 **Cambodia** annexed by France.

1864–70 Paraguay loses up to 70 per cent of its population in the **War of the Triple Alliance** against Brazil, Uruguay and Argentina.

1863 Decisive Union victory over the Confederacy at the battle of **Gettysburg** in July.

▲ *Late 19th-century engraving of Otto von Bismarck.*

◀ *Fierce fighting between Union and Confederacy troops at Gettysburg.*

RELIGION & PHILOSOPHY

Bahá'u'lláh founds the **Bahá'í faith** in Iraq. **1863**

1863 The **English Football Association** is founded: beginning of the modern sport of Association Football (soccer).

SCIENCE & TECHNOLOGY

1862 **Battle of Hampton Roads**: first battle between ironclad warships, the USS *Monitor* and the CSS *Virginia*.

1863 The world's first **underground railway** opens, in London.

◀ *Leo Tolstoy photographed around the time he wrote* War and Peace.

ARTS & ARCHITECTURE

Leo Tolstoy, **War and Peace**, epic Russian novel. **1864–69**

▲ *Test-run of a train on the London underground railway in 1862.*

1861–74 Palais Garnier, **Beaux-Arts opera house**, Paris.

1866 **Prussia** asserts leadership of Germany after defeating Austria in the Seven Weeks War.

Prussia enrols the northern German states into the **North German Confederation**. **1867**

Cochin China (southern Vietnam) is annexed by France. **1867**

Transportation of convicts to **Australia** ends. **1867**

Diamonds are discovered in Cape Colony. **1867**

1865 **Morant Bay rebellion** in Jamaica brings constitutional change to British colonies.

▶ *The modernization of Japan included widespread adoption of Western carriages as pictured here.*

Franco-Prussian War ends in French defeat and abdication of Napoleon III. **1870–71**

1868 **Qatar** becomes a British protectorate.

1868 **Meiji restoration**: rebel samurai overthrow the shogunate and restore the emperor to power, beginning the modernization of Japan.

Swahili merchant **Tippu Tib** starts to build a slave- and ivory-trading empire in Central Africa. **1870**

1869 The Hudson's Bay Company's lands are sold to **Canada**.

1870 **Italy** annexes Rome, completing national unification.

Wilhelm I of Prussia is **1871** proclaimed emperor of Germany at Versailles.

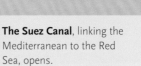

1865 The **Thirteenth Amendment** to the US Constitution abolishes slavery in December.

1865 Chinese 'coolie' labourers brought to the USA to work on **railway construction**.

1865 The Confederacy surrenders in April ending the **American Civil War**; President Lincoln is assassinated.

1867 **Canada** is granted self-government as a Dominion of the British Empire.

1867 The USA buys **Alaska** from Russia for US $7.2 million.

British invasion of **Ethiopia**: emperor **1868** Tewodros II commits suicide.

1869 **The Suez Canal**, linking the Mediterranean to the Red Sea, opens.

▲ *Portrait of Tippu Tib.*

◀ *The grand opening of the Suez Canal.*

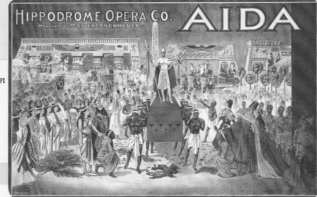

▲ *Assassination of Lincoln in a contemporary engraving.*

1867–94 **Karl Marx**, *Das Kapital (Capital)*, critique of capitalism.

Dogma of papal infallibility proclaimed by the **Vatican Council**. **1870**

Shinto becomes the state religion of Japan. **1871–72**

1865 Rasmus Malling-Hansen invents the **Hansen Writing Ball**, the first commercially produced typewriter (Denmark).

1866 Austrian monk **Gregor Mendel** establishes the principles of heredity.

1867 Joseph Lister introduces **antiseptic surgery** (UK).

Dmitri Mendeleev formulates the **periodic table of 1869 chemical elements** (Russia).

1869 Completion of the **Pacific Railroad**, the first transcontinental railway (USA).

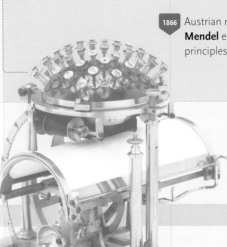

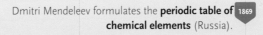

▶ *Poster from the 1908 production of Verdi's Aida.*

▶ *Painting by Kobayashi Eitaku showing the Shinto deities Izanagi and Izanami.*

1867–68 English writer **Charles Dickens** tours the USA giving readings from his works.

Giuseppe Verdi's opera **Aida**, set in ancient **1871** Egypt, premieres in Cairo.

1900

THE EUROPEAN COLONIAL EMPIRES DOMINATE THE WORLD

In 1900 European global dominance was at its peak, with approximately half the world's land mass directly controlled by European colonial empires. While the Americas were largely independent of Europe, the general population of the USA and the ruling elite of Latin America were mainly of European descent. The end of Native American resistance in 1890 and the government declaration, in the same year, that the western frontier no longer existed, marked the final consolidation of the continental USA.

The European takeover of Africa in this period was astonishingly rapid. Except in Algeria and the Cape, European power was still confined to disease-ridden coastal enclaves in 1872, but in 1884 the European powers agreed to partition Africa between themselves at the Congress of Berlin and within the next 15 years they brought almost the entire continent under their control. Germany, Italy and Belgium became colonial powers as a result of the carve-up. Such rapid colonization was made possible by the Europeans' vastly superior military technology and by advances, earlier in the century, in medicine, which improved their life expectancy in tropical Africa. In 1900 the British empire was, however, struggling to conquer the white South African Boer republics, which were newly equipped with modern German weapons.

The remaining non-European powers reacted to European dominance in different ways: Japan adopted European science and technology wholesale; the nationalist Young Turk movement campaigned to turn the crumbling Ottoman empire into a scientific secular state; Ethiopia bought modern weapons and defeated an attempted conquest by Italy. The Qing dynasty's failures to modernize China effectively or to defend the empire culminated in a humiliating eight-power invasion after Boxer sectarian rebels attacked foreign missionaries and diplomats in the summer of 1900.

Five Largest Cities *millions*

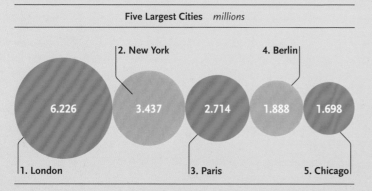

6.226	3.437	2.714	1.888	1.698
1. London	2. New York	3. Paris	4. Berlin	5. Chicago

GREENLAND
(Denmark)

CANADA
(autonomous)

NEWFOUNDLAND

St Pierre et Miquelon

5 Chicago

2 New York

UNITED STATES OF AMERICA

Bermuda

1 Cayman Islands
2 Jamaica
3 BRITISH HONDURAS
4 Netherlands Antilles
5 Puerto Rico
6 HAITI
7 DOMINICAN REPUBLIC

Hawaii

MEXICO

Bahamas

CUBA

Danish Virgin Islands

British Virgin Islands
Leeward Islands
Guadeloupe
Dominica
Martinique
Windward Islands

GUATEMALA
EL SALVADOR
HONDURAS
NICARAGUA
COSTA RICA

Barbados

Trinidad & Tobago

VENEZUELA

BRITISH GUIANA
DUTCH GUIANA
FRENCH GUIANA

COLOMBIA

Galapagos Islands
(Ecuador)

ECUADOR

Marquesas Islands

BRAZIL

PERU

Tuamotu Archipelago

Tahiti

BOLIVIA

Pitcairn Island

PARAGUAY

Easter Island
(Chile)

CHILE

ARGENTINA

URUGUAY

Falkland Islands

Portuguese possessions

Spanish possessions

Dutch possessions

British possessions

French possessions

German possessions

Italian possessions

Russian possessions

Japanese possessions

USA and possessions

Pastoral nomads

Other states and territories

Other empires

150°   120°   90°   60°

1900

European global dominance was as clear in science and technology as it was in the political sphere. Even global time would be calculated in reference to a meridian which ran through London. Major inventions of the period included the internal combustion engine, the automobile, the submarine, cinema, the telephone and the electric light. In medicine, Sigmund Freud pioneered psychoanalysis. It was in Germany and the USA that most of the technological and scientific breakthroughs of the period were made. This was a clear sign that Britain had lost the technological and industrial dominance that had sustained its global power during the previous century.

In sharp contrast to such dazzling scientific progress, the period saw a strong resurgence in Central and Eastern Europe of the violent popular anti-Semitism of medieval times. Jews reacted by founding the Zionist movement to establish a homeland in Palestine. Thanks to the relatively tolerant Ottoman authorities, the first modern Jewish settlements were founded in Palestine in the 1880s.

During this period, the first skyscrapers heralded architectural modernism in the USA. European neoclassical and neo-Gothic styles of architecture, however, remained dominant and were vigorously exported to the colonies, often with little regard to their suitability for the local climate. European architecture was even adopted in Japan as part of its modernization programme.

Japan's adoption of European culture was a selective process and it did not undermine Japan's cultural identity. Nevertheless, it did result in major social change as the introduction of modern military technology made the old samurai military aristocracy obsolete. A samurai rebellion in 1877 was easily crushed by the new government army and its modern weapons, but their values and culture remained influential in Japanese society.

World Population

7 BILLION

1.65 billion

1530   1900   2010

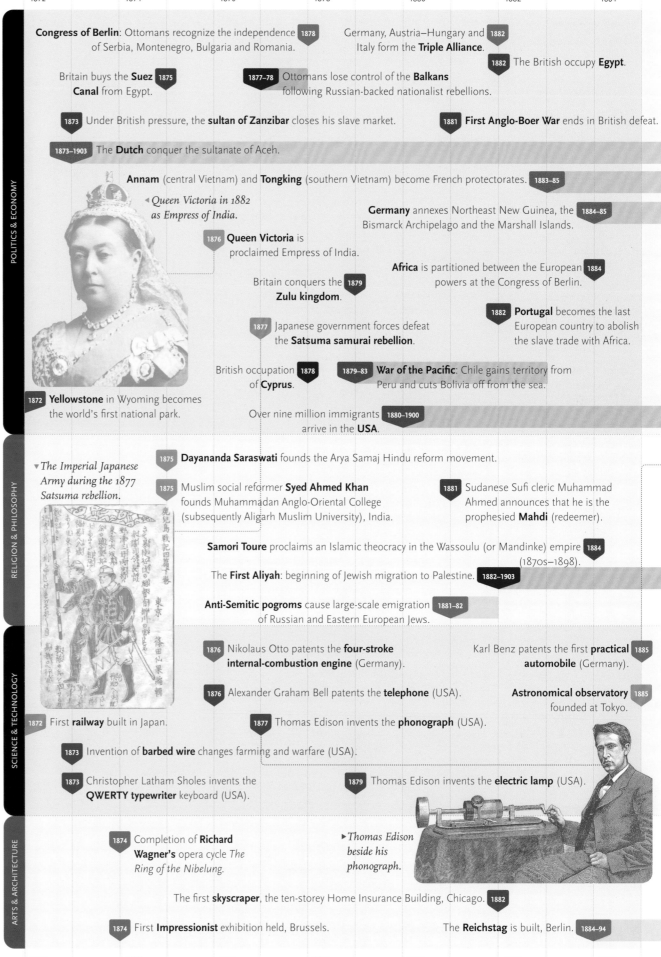

1872   1874   1876   1878   1880   1882   1884

POLITICS & ECONOMY

Congress of Berlin: Ottomans recognize the independence 1878 of Serbia, Montenegro, Bulgaria and Romania.

1882 Germany, Austria–Hungary and Italy form the **Triple Alliance**.

1882 The British occupy **Egypt**.

Britain buys the **Suez** 1875 **Canal** from Egypt.

1877–78 Ottomans lose control of the **Balkans** following Russian-backed nationalist rebellions.

1873 Under British pressure, the **sultan of Zanzibar** closes his slave market.

1881 **First Anglo-Boer War** ends in British defeat.

1873–1903 The **Dutch** conquer the sultanate of Aceh.

Annam (central Vietnam) and **Tongking** (southern Vietnam) become French protectorates. 1883–85

◀ *Queen Victoria in 1882 as Empress of India.*

Germany annexes Northeast New Guinea, the 1884–85 Bismarck Archipelago and the Marshall Islands.

1876 **Queen Victoria** is proclaimed Empress of India.

Africa is partitioned between the European 1884 powers at the Congress of Berlin.

Britain conquers the 1879 **Zulu kingdom**.

1882 **Portugal** becomes the last European country to abolish the slave trade with Africa.

1877 Japanese government forces defeat the **Satsuma samurai rebellion**.

British occupation 1878 of **Cyprus**.

1879–83 **War of the Pacific**: Chile gains territory from Peru and cuts Bolivia off from the sea.

1872 **Yellowstone** in Wyoming becomes the world's first national park.

Over nine million immigrants 1880–1900 arrive in the **USA**.

RELIGION & PHILOSOPHY

▼ *The Imperial Japanese Army during the 1877 Satsuma rebellion.*

1875 **Dayananda Saraswati** founds the Arya Samaj Hindu reform movement.

1875 Muslim social reformer **Syed Ahmed Khan** founds Muhammadan Anglo-Oriental College (subsequently Aligarh Muslim University), India.

1881 Sudanese Sufi cleric Muhammad Ahmed announces that he is the prophesied **Mahdi** (redeemer).

Samori Toure proclaims an Islamic theocracy in the Wassoulu (or Mandinke) empire 1884 (1870s–1898).

The **First Aliyah**: beginning of Jewish migration to Palestine. 1882–1903

Anti-Semitic pogroms cause large-scale emigration 1881–82 of Russian and Eastern European Jews.

SCIENCE & TECHNOLOGY

1876 Nikolaus Otto patents the **four-stroke internal-combustion engine** (Germany).

Karl Benz patents the first **practical automobile** (Germany). 1885

1876 Alexander Graham Bell patents the **telephone** (USA).

Astronomical observatory 1885 founded at Tokyo.

1872 First **railway** built in Japan.

1877 Thomas Edison invents the **phonograph** (USA).

1873 Invention of **barbed wire** changes farming and warfare (USA).

1873 Christopher Latham Sholes invents the **QWERTY typewriter** keyboard (USA).

1879 Thomas Edison invents the **electric lamp** (USA).

ARTS & ARCHITECTURE

1874 Completion of **Richard Wagner's** opera cycle *The Ring of the Nibelung*.

▶ *Thomas Edison beside his phonograph.*

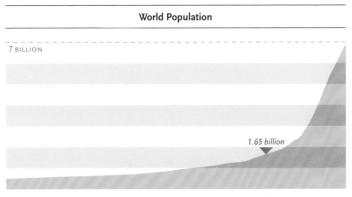

The first **skyscraper**, the ten-storey Home Insurance Building, Chicago. 1882

1874 First **Impressionist** exhibition held, Brussels.

The **Reichstag** is built, Berlin. 1884–94

1872   1874   1876   1878   1880   1882   1884

1891 Construction of the **Trans-Siberian railway** begins.

1894 **Franco-Russian Alliance** formed to counter the Triple Alliance.

1885 The nationalist **Indian National Congress party** founded in Bombay (Mumbai).

The **Young Turk nationalist movement** founded: it aims to modernize the Ottoman empire. **1895**

Kuwait becomes a British protectorate. **1899**

1885 **Muhammad Ahmed** captures Khartoum and founds a Mahdist state in Sudan.

New Zealand becomes the **1893** first country to grant women equal voting rights.

1894–95 **Sino-Japanese War**: China is forced to cede Taiwan to Japan.

Boxer uprising 1900 against foreign influence in China.

Japan's **Meiji Constitution**: political parties formed and **1890** general elections to a House of Representatives held.

The **Hundred Days' Reform**, a Chinese national reform **1898** programme, is ended by the conservative empress Cixi.

Easter Island is annexed by Chile. **1888**

Sun Yat-sen leads a failed republican **1895** nationalist revolution in China.

Samoa is divided between Germany and the USA. **1899**

1886 **Upper Burma** is annexed to British India.

American settlers overthrow the **1893** kingdom of **Hawaii**.

Germany annexes **Qingdao** in northern China. **1897**

Outbreak of the **Second 1899 Anglo-Boer War.**

1885 Completion of the **Canadian–Pacific transcontinental railway.**

The **Ethiopians** defeat an Italian **1896** invasion at the battle of Adowa.

1898 **Hawaii** is annexed by the USA.

Brazil becomes the last American **1888** country to ban slavery.

◄ *Afrikaner officers photographed during the Second Boer War.*

The USA takes the **Philippines** during the Spanish–American War. **1898–99**

▼ *Benz's Motorwagen no.3 from 1888.*

The **Fashoda Incident**, a clash between French and British expeditions in Sudan, creates Anglo-French tension. **1898**

Massacre of the Sioux at **Wounded Knee** marks the **1890** end of Native American resistance in the USA.

France conquers the **1892** **Tukolor empire**, Mali.

Battle of Omdurman: the British destroy the Mahdist state of Sudan. **1898**

1889 **Brazil** becomes a republic.

France annexes **Laos**. **1896**

1898 **Spanish–American War**: Spain loses the last of its American possessions.

▶ *Contemporary lithograph of the 1898 naval battle of Manila Bay during the Spanish–American War.*

First **Zionist Congress** held at **1897** Basle, Switzerland.

1885 German philosopher Friedrich Nietzsche writes **Thus Spoke Zarathustra**.

Muhammad Abduh, founder of Islamic Modernism, **1899** becomes mufti of Egypt.

1895 Wilhelm Konrad Röntgen discovers **X-rays** (Germany).

1895 Sigmund Freud founds **psychoanalysis** (Austria).

Rudolf Diesel demonstrates the **1900** **diesel engine** (Germany).

Marie and Pierre Curie discover **radium** (France). **1898**

▲ *Poster of can-can dancer Jane Avril by Art Nouveau painter Henri de Toulouse-Lautrec.*

1894 Charles Parsons invents the **steam turbine** (UK).

1897 John P. Holland launches the first **modern submarine** (USA).

Ronald Ross identifies the Plasmodium parasite as the cause of **malaria** (UK). **1898**

Tower Bridge completed, London. **1894**

1895 Lumière brothers open the first **public cinema**, in Paris.

1886 Frédéric Bartholdi, **The Statue of Liberty**, New York.

1889 The **Eiffel Tower**, Paris.

1893 Czech composer **Antonín Dvořák** composes the 'New World Symphony' during his time in the USA.

1887 Gothic–Saracenic style **Victoria Terminus railway station**, Calcutta (Kolkata).

1890–1910 **Art Nouveau movement.**

Yan Fu translates Adam Smith's *Wealth of Nations* into Chinese. **1900**

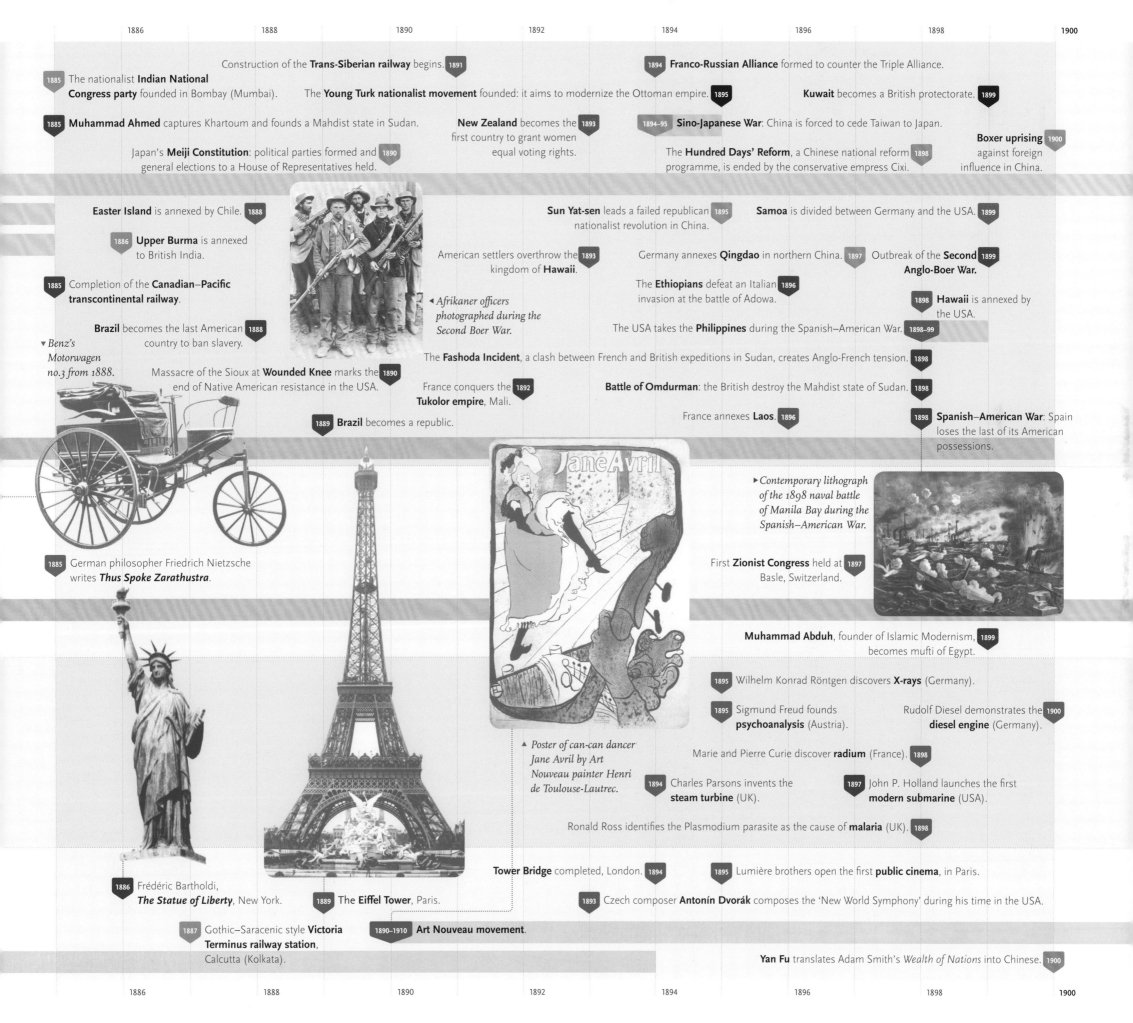

1900

MIGRATIONS IN THE 19TH CENTURY: EUROPE A GREAT EXPORTER OF POPULATION

The 19th century witnessed the largest migrations yet undertaken. The main source of migrants was Europe, which was experiencing a population boom as a result of industrialization and agricultural improvements. An estimated 40 million people emigrated from Europe during the century, yet the continent's population still increased by over 75 per cent.

The most popular destination throughout the 19th century was the USA. Up to around 1890, most immigrants came from Germany, Britain, Ireland and Scandinavia. After that the majority were Italians, Greeks and Eastern Europeans, many of them Jews escaping pogroms. In 1900, 13.6 per cent of the population of the USA had been born abroad.

There was also considerable movement of people within empires: British and Irish migrants settled in other territories belonging to Britain, mainly Canada, Australia, New Zealand and South Africa; many European Russians moved east into Siberia; French residents travelled to France's colonies in North Africa; Spanish and Portuguese settlers looked to Latin America. Many Italians settled in Argentina. Because of the uncomfortable climate and diseases, and the environmental unsuitability for European farming methods, few Europeans settled in their tropical African colonies.

Britain's abolition of the slave trade in 1807 ended forced emigration from West Africa, but slaves continued to be shipped from Portuguese colonies to Brazil until 1882 (illegally after 1831). The establishment of European colonial rule ended the Arab-controlled East African slave trade. The decline of slavery left a huge demand for cheap labour. This was satisfied by indentured labour, a system where labourers engaged to work for a fixed period in return for free passage to the location of the work.

The main sources of indentured labourers were India and China. Indian labourers sought work mainly in other countries in the British empire. Chinese also emigrated as labourers and traders to Southeast Asia, the British empire, Latin America and the USA to work on construction projects. Japanese labourers emigrated to plantations in Hawaii and construction projects in the USA and Canada. Many Pacific islands were depopulated by 'blackbirders' who kidnapped islanders and transported them to work as indentured labourers in South America and Australia. Easter Island lost 90 per cent of its population in this way.

GREENLAND (Denmark)

CANADA

NEWFOUNDLAND

UNITED STATES OF AMERICA

MEXICO

CUBA

Hawaii (USA)

Jamaica (GB)

GUATEMALA
EL SALVADOR
HONDURAS
NICARAGUA
COSTA RICA

VENEZUELA

COLOMBIA

ECUADOR

BRAZIL

PERU

BOLIVIA

PARAGUAY

CHILE

URUGUAY

ARGENTINA

Easter Island (Chile)

BRITISH HONDURAS 1
Netherlands 2
Antilles
HAITI 3
DOMINICAN REPUBLIC 4
Trinidad & Tobago (GB) 5
BRITISH GUIANA 6
DUTCH GUIANA 7
FRENCH GUIANA 8

Major importers of population 1815–1914

Major exporters of population 1815–1914

Slave exporting regions 1815–1882

European emigration

Indian indentured labourers

Chinese indentured labourers

Japanese emigration

African slaves (until c. 1882)

Other emigration

150°   120°   90°   60°

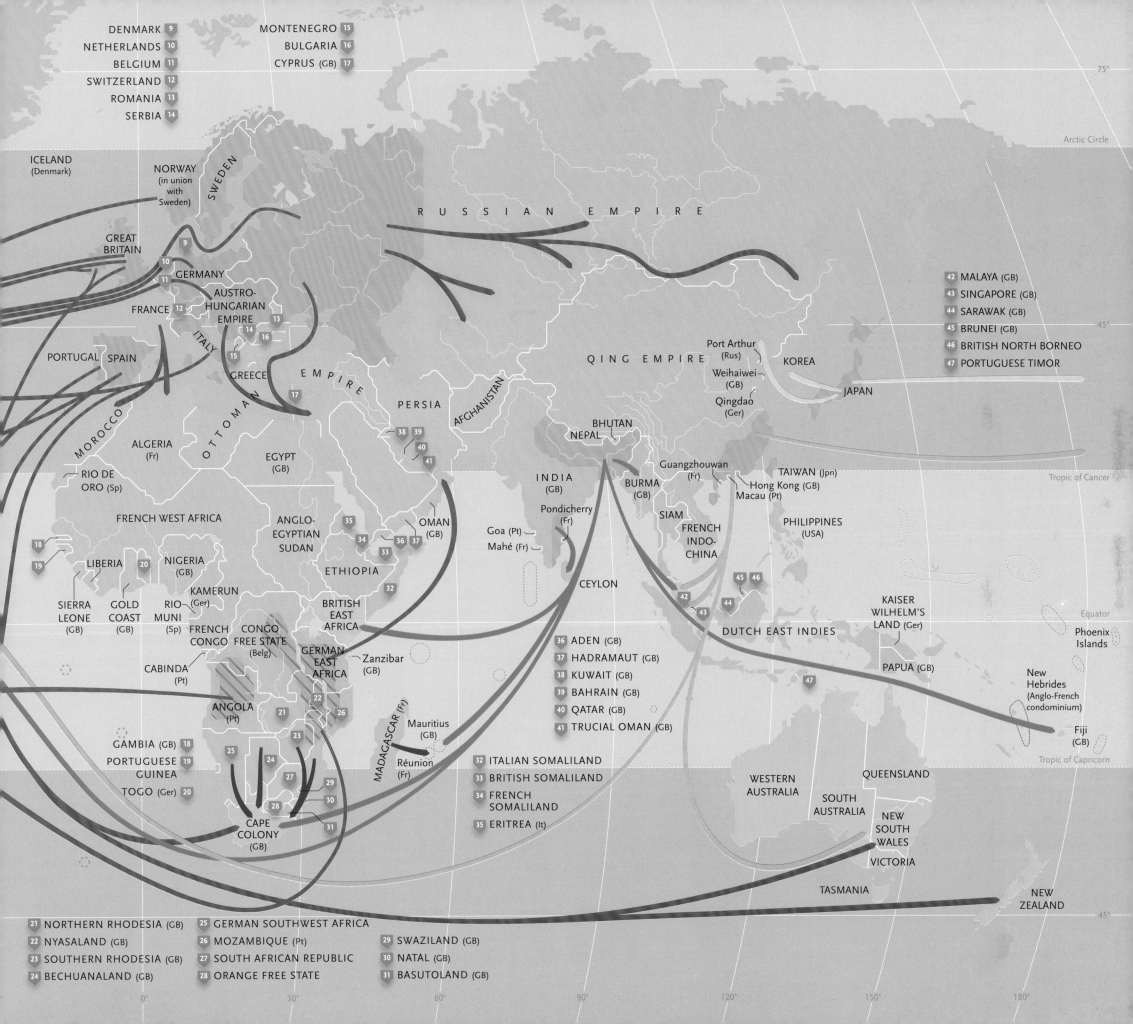

DENMARK **9**
NETHERLANDS **10**
BELGIUM **11**
SWITZERLAND **12**
ROMANIA **13**
SERBIA **14**

MONTENEGRO **15**
BULGARIA **16**
CYPRUS (GB) **17**

ICELAND
(Denmark)

NORWAY
(in union
with
Sweden)

SWEDEN

GREAT
BRITAIN

9
10
11
GERMANY
FRANCE **12**
AUSTRO-
HUNGARIAN
EMPIRE
13
14
16
ITALY
PORTUGAL SPAIN
15
GREECE
EMPIRE
17
OTTOMAN
MOROCCO
ALGERIA
(Fr)
EGYPT
(GB)

RUSSIAN EMPIRE

PERSIA
AFGHANISTAN

QING EMPIRE

Port Arthur
(Rus)
Weihaiwei
(GB)
Qingdao
(Ger)

KOREA

JAPAN

42 MALAYA (GB)
43 SINGAPORE (GB)
44 SARAWAK (GB)
45 BRUNEI (GB)
46 BRITISH NORTH BORNEO
47 PORTUGUESE TIMOR

BHUTAN
NEPAL

Guangzhouwan
(Fr)

TAIWAN (Jpn)
Hong Kong (GB)
Macau (Pt)

Tropic of Cancer

RIO DE
ORO (Sp)

FRENCH WEST AFRICA

ANGLO-
EGYPTIAN
SUDAN

35
34
36 **37**
33
OMAN
(GB)

Goa (Pt)
Mahé (Fr)

Pondicherry
(Fr)

INDIA
(GB)

BURMA
(GB)

SIAM

FRENCH
INDO-
CHINA

PHILIPPINES
(USA)

45 **46**

18
19
LIBERIA
20
NIGERIA
(GB)

ETHIOPIA

32

CEYLON

42

KAISER
WILHELM'S
LAND (Ger)

Equator
Phoenix
Islands

SIERRA
LEONE
(GB)
GOLD
COAST
(GB)
KAMERUN
(Ger)
RIO
MUNI
(Sp)
FRENCH
CONGO
CONGO
FREE STATE
(Belg)

BRITISH
EAST
AFRICA

43 **44**

DUTCH EAST INDIES

PAPUA (GB)

CABINDA
(Pt)
GERMAN
EAST
AFRICA
Zanzibar
(GB)

36 ADEN (GB)
37 HADRAMAUT (GB)
38 KUWAIT (GB)
39 BAHRAIN (GB)
40 QATAR (GB)
41 TRUCIAL OMAN (GB)

47

New
Hebrides
(Anglo-French
condominium)

ANGOLA
(Pt)
21
22
26

Madagascar (Fr)
Mauritius
(GB)

Fiji
(GB)

GAMBIA (GB) **18**
PORTUGUESE
GUINEA **19**
TOGO (Ger) **20**

23
25
24
27 **29**
30
28
31
CAPE
COLONY
(GB)

MADAGASCAR (Fr)

Réunion
(Fr)

32 ITALIAN SOMALILAND
33 BRITISH SOMALILAND
34 FRENCH
SOMALILAND
35 ERITREA (It)

WESTERN
AUSTRALIA

QUEENSLAND

SOUTH
AUSTRALIA

NEW
SOUTH
WALES

VICTORIA

TASMANIA

NEW
ZEALAND

Tropic of Capricorn

21 NORTHERN RHODESIA (GB)
22 NYASALAND (GB)
23 SOUTHERN RHODESIA (GB)
24 BECHUANALAND (GB)

25 GERMAN SOUTHWEST AFRICA
26 MOZAMBIQUE (Pt)
27 SOUTH AFRICAN REPUBLIC
28 ORANGE FREE STATE

29 SWAZILAND (GB)
30 NATAL (GB)
31 BASUTOLAND (GB)

Arctic Circle

75°

45°

45°

1912

EUROPEAN COLONIAL EXPANSION; THE END OF
IMPERIAL CHINA; THE RISE OF JAPAN

Although it had lost its industrial dominance, Britain
entered the 20th century as the leading colonial, financial
and naval power. The British empire continued to expand,
with the conquest of the Boer republics in Africa and
the annexation of Malaya, and it also evolved: Australia,
New Zealand and South Africa all became self-governing
dominions in this period.

   Britain's pre-eminence was challenged by the rising
power of Germany and the USA. Britain saw the USA as
a potential ally as well as a rival, but feared a militaristic
Germany's ambitions in Europe and overseas. When
Germany began to construct a large battlefleet, the
British responded with the revolutionary battleship HMS
Dreadnought, triggering an international naval arms-race.
Britain also agreed 'ententes' with its colonial rivals France
and Russia, which also felt threatened by Germany.

   European expansion in Africa continued: France
annexed Morocco and Italy conquered Libya; only Ethiopia
and Liberia remained independent. The balance of power
in East Asia shifted dramatically after Japan humiliated
Russia in a war over spheres of influence in Manchuria in
1904–5. In 1910 Japan invaded and annexed Korea (it had
already taken Taiwan from China in 1895). Russia's defeat
created discontent with the tsarist regime and led to the
introduction of an elected national assembly (the *duma*)
with limited powers.

   In China, the discredited Qing dynasty was overthrown
by Sun Yat-sen's Tongmenghui revolutionary alliance
following popular uprisings in 1911 and the country
was declared a republic. From the outset, the republican
government struggled to assert its authority: the Tibetans
and Mongolians expelled Chinese garrisons and became
independent. The new president, Yuan Shikai, banned his
rivals, leading Sun Yat-sen to lead an unsuccessful rebellion
against him in 1913.

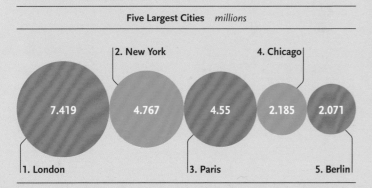

Five Largest Cities *millions*

2. New York		4. Chicago		
7.419	4.767	4.55	2.185	2.071
1. London	3. Paris			5. Berlin

GREENLAND
(Denmark)

C A N A D A
(autonomous)

NEWFOUNDLAND
(autonomous)

St Pierre et Miquelon

4 Chicago   **2** New York

UNITED STATES OF AMERICA

1	Jamaica
2	BRITISH HONDURAS
3	Netherlands Antilles
4	Puerto Rico
5	HAITI
6	DOMINICAN REPUBLIC

Bermuda

Cayman Islands (GB)

Bahamas

MEXICO   CUBA   Danish Virgin Islands

British Virgin Islands
Leeward Islands
Guadeloupe
Dominica
Martinique
Windward Islands

Hawaii

GUATEMALA
EL SALVADOR
HONDURAS
NICARAGUA
COSTA RICA
PANAMA

Panama
Canal
Zone (US)

Barbados
Trinidad & Tobago

VENEZUELA

BRITISH GUIANA
DUTCH GUIANA
FRENCH GUIANA

COLOMBIA

Galapagos
Islands
(Ecuador)

ECUADOR

B R A Z I L

French
Polynesia

PERU

BOLIVIA

Pitcairn Island

Easter Island
(Chile)

PARAGUAY

C H I L E

Legend

Portuguese possessions	Russian possessions
Spanish possessions	Japanese possessions
Dutch possessions	USA and possessions
British possessions	Pastoral nomads
French possessions	Other states and territories
German possessions	Other empires
Italian possessions	

ARGENTINA   URUGUAY

Falkland Islands

150°   120°   90°   60°

NETHERLANDS 7
BELGIUM 8
LUXEMBOURG 9
SWITZERLAND 10
ROMANIA 11
SERBIA 12
MONTENEGRO 13

ICELAND
(Denmark)   Faroe Islands
             (Denmark)

NORWAY
SWEDEN

GREAT
BRITAIN   DENMARK   5
     1   7 Berlin
London 3 8 GERMANY
    Paris 9
FRANCE 10   AUSTRO-
                HUNGARIAN
BULGARIA 14   EMPIRE
Dodecanese 15   ITALY 13   12 14 11

PORTUGAL SPAIN
Azores   GREECE   OTTOMAN
                                  EMPIRE
Madeira   16   MALTA   CYPRUS 15
              MOROCCO TUNISIA
Canary   PERSIA   AFGHANISTAN
Islands   ALGERIA LIBYA   TIBET
SPANISH   32 33
SAHARA   EGYPT   34
Cape   Bedouin   35   NEPAL
Verde   Arabs   BHUTAN
Islands   FRENCH WEST AFRICA FRENCH   OMAN   INDIA   BURMA
GAMBIA   EQUATORIAL ANGLO-   HADRAMAUT
PORTUGUESE   AFRICA   EGYPTIAN 31 ADEN   SIAM
GUINEA   LIBERIA 17 NIGERIA   SUDAN 30 29 Socotra   Goa Pondicherry   FRENCH
SIERRA   GOLD   KAMERUN ETHIOPIA   Mahé Andaman   INDO-
LEONE   COAST 18   ITALIAN   Islands   CHINA
             20   19   BRITISH   SOMALILAND   Maldive   Nicobar
             21   EAST 22   Islands CEYLON   Islands   MALAYA
                        AFRICA   36
        CABINDA BELGIAN   GERMAN Zanzibar   Seychelles
Ascension   CONGO   EAST
Island   AFRICA Comoro   Chagos
                                  Islands Amirante Islands
                 ANGOLA   Islands   Cocos   Christmas
SPANISH 16   Islands   Island
MOROCCO   24   MADAGASCAR Mauritius
TOGO 17   23   25   28
Fernando Póo 18   27   26   Réunion   BRITISH SOMALILAND 29   KUWAIT 32
RIO MUNI 19   FRENCH   BAHRAIN 32
Príncipe 20 Walvis Bay   SWAZILAND   SOMALILAND 30   QATAR 34
São Tomé 21   ERITREA 31   TRUCIAL OMAN 35
                   SOUTH   BASUTOLAND
                   AFRICA
Tristan da   (autonomous)
Cunha

22 UGANDA   26 BECHUANALAND
23 NORTHERN RHODESIA 27 GERMAN SOUTHWEST AFRICA
24 NYASALAND   28 MOZAMBIQUE
25 SOUTHERN RHODESIA

Kerguelen
Island

RUSSIAN EMPIRE

URJANCHAI

MONGOLIA

REPUBLIC
OF
CHINA
Tianjin (Int.)   Dalian
Weihaiwei   KOREA
Qingdao   JAPAN

Shanghai (Int.)

Guangzhouwan   TAIWAN
Hong Kong
Macau

36 SINGAPORE
37 SARAWAK
38 BRUNEI
39 BRITISH NORTH BORNEO
40 PORTUGUESE TIMOR

PHILIPPINES   Mariana
                   Islands
          Guam   Caroline
       Palau   Islands   Marshall
                                    Islands

DUTCH EAST INDIES   Gilbert
                            Islands
                   KAISER
   38 39   WILHELM'S   Nauru
37   LAND
   36   Bismarck Archipelago   Phoenix
                                                      Islands
40   PAPUA   Solomon
                                      Islands   Ellice
                                                     Islands
                              New
                              Hebrides
                              (Anglo-French
                              condominium)   Tonga
                       New   Fiji
                       Caledonia

AUSTRALIA
(autonomous)

NEW
ZEALAND
(autonomous)

1914

THE OUTBREAK OF THE FIRST WORLD WAR IN EUROPE

Tensions between the European powers grew steadily through 1913 and 1914, leading to the outbreak of the First World War in August of that year. The flashpoint was the Balkans, where both Russia and the Austro-Hungarian empire were competing for influence over the new states that had emerged from the collapse of Ottoman power in the region following the Balkan War of 1912–13.

The Austro-Hungarian emperors feared that nationalism would tear apart their multi-ethnic state. The empire's annexation of Bosnia and Herzegovina brought under its control a large Serbian population, which aspired to unity with the Serbian state. The assassination of the Austrian archduke Franz Ferdinand in Sarajevo by a Serbian nationalist on 28 June 1914 began a chain of events that drew almost all of Europe into a war which would destroy the German, Austro-Hungarian, Russian and Ottoman empires.

Austria–Hungary blamed Serbia for the assassination and declared war on 28 July after being assured of unconditional German support. Determined not to allow Austria–Hungary to destroy Serbia, Russia mobilized for war. When it refused to demobilize, Germany declared war on Russia and its ally France. Wishing to avoid a long war on two fronts, Germany planned to defeat France quickly, by outflanking its defences by invading through Belgium, then transfer troops east to deal with Russia.

Britain's ententes with France and Russia were not binding military alliances. Nevertheless, Germany's declaration of war against Belgium drew Britain into the war too, as it had guaranteed Belgian independence. The German war plan failed: slowed by Belgian and British resistance, its invading armies were stopped by the French short of Paris, thus committing Germany to the two-front war it had wished to avoid.

The progress and prosperity of the early 20th century fed strong nationalist passions and the outbreak of war was greeted with wild popular enthusiasm almost everywhere. Most people, including politicians and generals, expected a short war, vastly underestimating the capacity of the industrial state to mobilize its population and economy. The widespread practice of conscription and national service enabled the continental European powers to field armies of millions within weeks of the outbreak of war. Of the major powers, only Britain relied on a volunteer professional army, but it too introduced conscription in 1916.

Central Powers 5 August 1914

Allied Powers 5 August 1914

Unaligned states

NETHERLANDS 7
BELGIUM 8
LUXEMBOURG 9
SWITZERLAND 10
ROMANIA 11
SERBIA 12
MONTENEGRO 13

75°

Arctic Circle

ICELAND
(Denmark)   Faroe Islands
(Denmark)

NORWAY   SWEDEN

RUSSIAN EMPIRE

URJANCHAI

DENMARK
GREAT
BRITAIN   GERMANY   MONGOLIA   Dalian
(Jpn)

ALBANIA 14   AUSTRO-
HUNGARIAN
EMPIRE   Tianjin (Int.)   KOREA
(Jpn)

BULGARIA 15   FRANCE   Weihaiwei (GB)   JAPAN
Dodecanese 16   OTTOMAN
EMPIRE   REPUBLIC
OF
CHINA   Qingdao
(Ger)   34 SINGAPORE (GB)
35 SARAWAK (GB)
36 BRUNEI (GB)
37 BRITISH NORTH BORNEO
38 PORTUGUESE TIMOR

45°

ITALY   GREECE   Shanghai (Int.)

PORTUGAL   SPAIN

Azores   GREECE   16   CYPRUS
(GB)   PERSIA   AFGHANISTAN   TIBET
Gibraltar   MALTA   Guangzhouwan
(Fr)
Madeira   17   TUNISIA
(Fr)   NEPAL
BHUTAN   TAIWAN (Jpn)   Tropic of Cancer
MOROCCO
(Fr)   ALGERIA
(Fr)   LIBYA
(It)   EGYPT
(GB)   30 31   BURMA
(GB)   Hong Kong (GB)
Canary
Islands   32   INDIA
(GB)   Macau
(Pt)
SPANISH
SAHARA   33   Bedouin
Arabs   OMAN (GB)   SIAM   PHILIPPINES
(USA)   Mariana
Islands
(Ger)
Cape
Verde
Islands   FRENCH WEST AFRICA   FRENCH   ANGLO-
EGYPTIAN
SUDAN   29   HADRAMAUT (GB)   Goa
(Pt)   Pondicherry
(Fr)   FRENCH
INDO-
CHINA   Guam (USA)   Caroline
Islands
(Ger)   Marshall
Islands
(Ger)
GAMBIA
(GB)   EQUATORIAL   28   ADEN (GB)
Socotra
(GB)   Mahé   Andaman
Islands
(GB)   Palau
(Ger)   Gilbert
Islands
(GB)   Equator
PORTUGUESE
GUINEA
(Pt)   LIBERIA   18   NIGERIA
(GB)   AFRICA   27   Maldive
Islands
(GB)   CEYLON
(GB)   Nicobar
Islands
(GB)   MALAYA (GB)   36 37   Nauru
(Ger)   Phoenix
Islands
(GB)
SIERRA
LEONE
(GB)   GOLD
COAST
(GB)   19   KAMERUN
(Ger)   ETHIOPIA   ITALIAN
SOMALILAND   35   KAISER
WILHELM'S
LAND
(Ger)   Ellice
Islands
(GB)
BELGIAN
CONGO   20   BRITISH
EAST
AFRICA   34   DUTCH EAST INDIES   Bismarck Archipelago
(Ger)
CABINDA
(Pt)   Zanzibar
(GB)   Seychelles
(GB)   Chagos
Islands
(GB)   Cocos
Islands
(GB)   PAPUA
(GB)   Solomon
Islands (GB)
Ascension
Island
(GB)   GERMAN
EAST
AFRICA   Comoro
Islands
(Fr)   Amirante
Islands
(GB)   Christmas
Island
(GB)   New
Hebrides
(Anglo-French
condominium)
ANGOLA
(Pt)   21   22   26   MADAGASCAR
(Fr)   Mauritius
(GB)   Tonga
(GB)
St Helena
(GB)   23   Réunion
(Fr)   27 BRITISH SOMALILAND   30 KUWAIT (GB)   New
Caledonia
(Fr)   Fiji (GB)
25   24   28 FRENCH
SOMALILAND   31 BAHRAIN (GB)   AUSTRALIA
SPANISH
MOROCCO   17   Walvis Bay
(GB)   29 ERITREA (It)   32 QATAR (GB)   Tropic of Capricorn
TOGO (Ger)   18   SWAZILAND (GB)   33 TRUCIAL OMAN (GB)
RIO MUNI (Sp)   19   SOUTH
AFRICA   BASUTOLAND (GB)

Tristan da
Cunha
(GB)   20 UGANDA (GB)   24 BECHUANALAND (GB)
21 NORTHERN RHODESIA (GB)   25 GERMAN SOUTHWEST AFRICA
22 NYASALAND (GB)   26 MOZAMBIQUE (Pt)   NEW
ZEALAND   45°
23 SOUTHERN RHODESIA (GB)

Kerguelen
Island

0°   30°   60°   90°   120°   150°   180°

1914

The First World War broke out at a time of unprecedented economic prosperity and technological progress in Europe and North America. Industrialization and the exploitation of overseas colonies were delivering improved living standards at all levels of society. With radio, long-distance communications were freed from dependence on expensive telegraph cables. The Wright brothers' first powered aeroplane flight in 1903 began the development of the aircraft industry, and Henry Ford's mass-produced and relatively inexpensive Model T car heralded the beginning of an era when everyday personal mobility was no longer the exclusive privilege of the wealthy.

Arguably even more important than all of these inventions was the development of the Haber–Bosch nitrogen fixation process, which led to the development of artificial fertilizers. These made possible the enormous increase in agricultural productivity in the 20th century, without which the rapidly increasing human population could not have been supported. Einstein's *Theory of Relativity* and Bohr's work on the structure of atoms revolutionized physics and provided new ways of understanding the universe.

Some of the last blank areas on world maps were filled in following successful expeditions to the North and South Poles. The greatest engineering achievement of the period was the construction of the Panama Canal, linking the Caribbean directly with the Pacific Ocean. The canal was of great strategic benefit to the USA, which could now transfer warships between the Atlantic and Pacific without the long passage around South America. The completion of the Trans-Siberian railway made it possible to travel by train across the whole breadth of the Eurasian continent. Huge passenger liners, powered by steam turbines, reduced transatlantic crossings to only five days.

World Population

7 BILLION

1.8 billion

1530   1914   2010

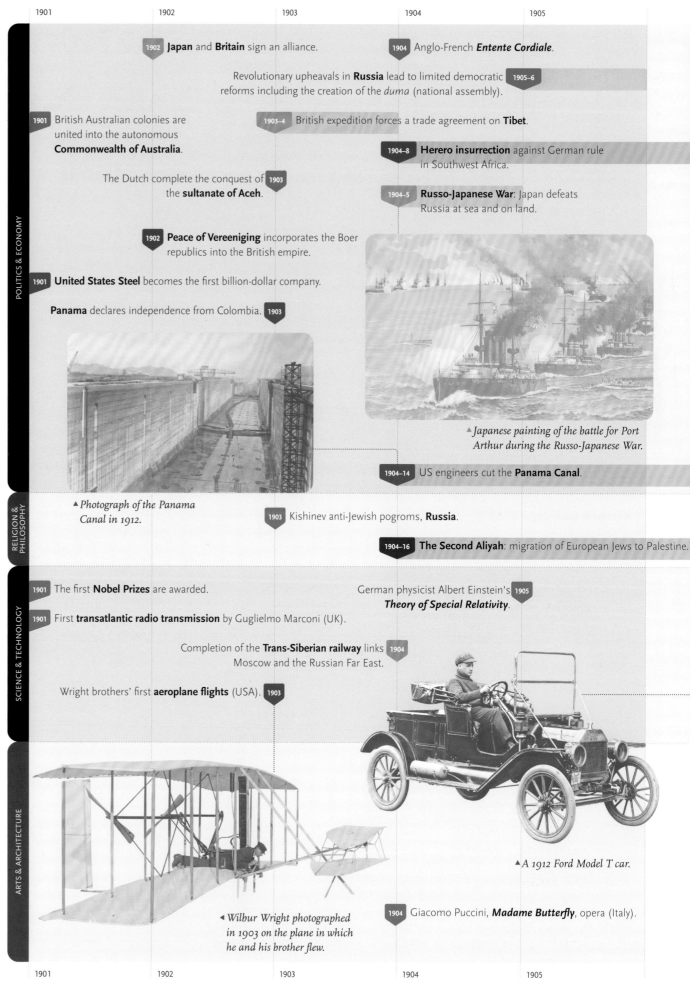

POLITICS & ECONOMY

1902 Japan and Britain sign an alliance.

1904 Anglo-French *Entente Cordiale*.

Revolutionary upheavals in **Russia** lead to limited democratic reforms including the creation of the *duma* (national assembly). **1905–6**

1901 British Australian colonies are united into the autonomous **Commonwealth of Australia**.

1903–4 British expedition forces a trade agreement on **Tibet**.

1904–8 **Herero insurrection** against German rule in Southwest Africa.

The Dutch complete the conquest of **1903** the **sultanate of Aceh**.

1904–5 **Russo-Japanese War**: Japan defeats Russia at sea and on land.

1902 **Peace of Vereeniging** incorporates the Boer republics into the British empire.

1901 **United States Steel** becomes the first billion-dollar company.

Panama declares independence from Colombia. **1903**

▲ *Japanese painting of the battle for Port Arthur during the Russo-Japanese War.*

1904–14 US engineers cut the **Panama Canal**.

▲ *Photograph of the Panama Canal in 1912.*

RELIGION & PHILOSOPHY

1903 Kishinev anti-Jewish pogroms, **Russia**.

1904–16 **The Second Aliyah**: migration of European Jews to Palestine.

SCIENCE & TECHNOLOGY

1901 The first **Nobel Prizes** are awarded.

German physicist Albert Einstein's **1905** *Theory of Special Relativity*.

1901 First **transatlantic radio transmission** by Guglielmo Marconi (UK).

Completion of the **Trans-Siberian railway** links **1904** Moscow and the Russian Far East.

Wright brothers' first **aeroplane flights** (USA). **1903**

▲ *A 1912 Ford Model T car.*

ARTS & ARCHITECTURE

◄ *Wilbur Wright photographed in 1903 on the plane in which he and his brother flew.*

1904 Giacomo Puccini, **Madame Butterfly**, opera (Italy).

1907 The **Triple Entente** formed by France, Russia and Britain.

1910 **Portuguese revolution**: the monarchy is abolished and Portugal becomes a republic.

The **Young Turk Revolution**, leading to the deposition of the conservative Ottoman sultan Abdülhamid. **1908–9**

Norwegian **Roald Amundsen** reaches the South Pole. **1911**

1912–13 **The Balkan Wars**: collapse of the Ottoman empire in the Balkans.

Austria–Hungary annexes Bosnia and Herzegovina. **1908**

Japan annexes **Korea**. **1910**

The Austrian archduke **Franz Ferdinand** is assassinated by a Serb nationalist at Sarajevo on 28 June. **1914**

Backed by Germany, **Austria–Hungary** declares war on **Serbia** on 28 July. **1914**

1906 **Persia's constitutional revolution** establishes a parliament and constitutional monarchy.

Between 1 and 5 August, **Germany** declares war on Russia and France; **France**, **Russia**, **Britain** and Britain's dependencies declare war on Germany and Austria–Hungary, beginning the **First World War**. **1914**

1907 **Persia** is divided into Russian and British spheres of influence.

1907 **New Zealand** is granted autonomy in the British empire.

American explorer Robert Peary reaches the **North Pole** (disputed). **1909**

◀ *Roald Amundsen dressed for polar exploration in 1912.*

1912 Chinese republic proclaimed: general **Yuan Shikai** becomes president.

1912 **Mongolia** and **Tibet** declare independence from China.

Anglo-Siamese Treaty gives Britain control of Malaya. **1909**

1912 **African National Congress Party** (ANC) is founded in South Africa.

The self-governing **Union of South Africa** is formed. **1910**

1911–12 **Italian–Turkish War** over Libya: first use of aircraft in warfare.

1909 **Morley–Minto reforms** introduce limited representative government to India.

1911 Chinese revolution: Sun Yat-sen's Tongmenghui overthrows the **Qing dynasty**.

1911 The **Agadir Incident**, an attempted German intervention in Morocco, causes tension in Europe.

Mexican revolution begins: supporters of the jailed reformer Francisco Madero overthrow the dictatorship of Porfirio Diaz. **1910–11**

1912 **Morocco** is partitioned between France and Spain.

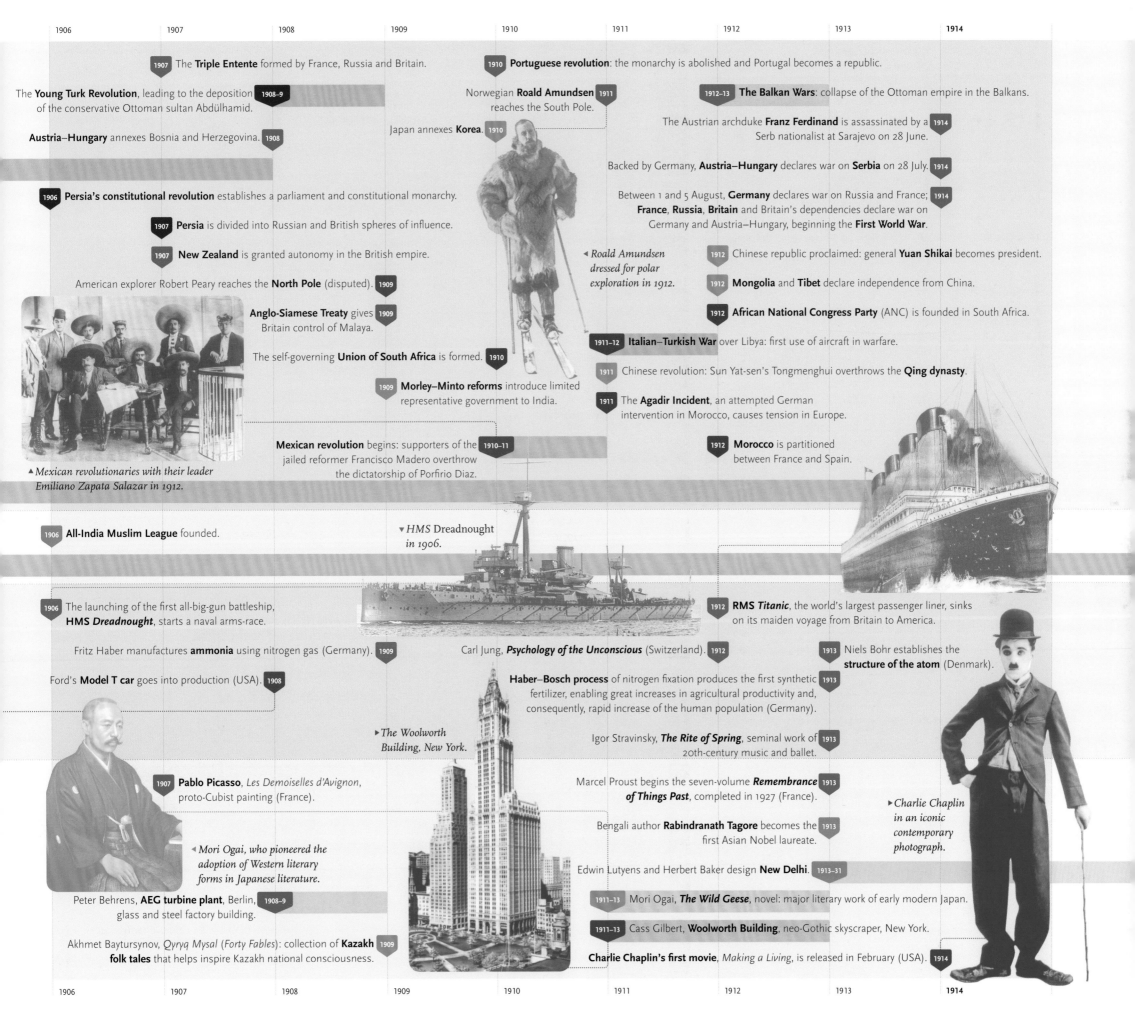

▲ *Mexican revolutionaries with their leader Emiliano Zapata Salazar in 1912.*

1906 **All-India Muslim League** founded.

▼ *HMS Dreadnought in 1906.*

1906 The launching of the first all-big-gun battleship, **HMS *Dreadnought***, starts a naval arms-race.

1912 RMS ***Titanic***, the world's largest passenger liner, sinks on its maiden voyage from Britain to America.

Fritz Haber manufactures **ammonia** using nitrogen gas (Germany). **1909**

Carl Jung, ***Psychology of the Unconscious*** (Switzerland). **1912**

1913 Niels Bohr establishes the **structure of the atom** (Denmark).

Ford's **Model T car** goes into production (USA). **1908**

Haber–Bosch process of nitrogen fixation produces the first synthetic fertilizer, enabling great increases in agricultural productivity and, consequently, rapid increase of the human population (Germany). **1913**

▶ *The Woolworth Building, New York.*

Igor Stravinsky, ***The Rite of Spring***, seminal work of 20th-century music and ballet. **1913**

1907 **Pablo Picasso**, *Les Demoiselles d'Avignon*, proto-Cubist painting (France).

Marcel Proust begins the seven-volume ***Remembrance of Things Past***, completed in 1927 (France). **1913**

▶ *Charlie Chaplin in an iconic contemporary photograph.*

Bengali author **Rabindranath Tagore** becomes the first Asian Nobel laureate. **1913**

◀ *Mori Ogai, who pioneered the adoption of Western literary forms in Japanese literature.*

Edwin Lutyens and Herbert Baker design **New Delhi**. **1913–31**

Peter Behrens, **AEG turbine plant**, Berlin, glass and steel factory building. **1908–9**

1911–13 Mori Ogai, ***The Wild Geese***, novel: major literary work of early modern Japan.

1911–13 Cass Gilbert, **Woolworth Building**, neo-Gothic skyscraper, New York.

Akhmet Baytursynov, *Qyryq Mysal* (*Forty Fables*): collection of **Kazakh folk tales** that helps inspire Kazakh national consciousness. **1909**

Charlie Chaplin's first movie, *Making a Living*, is released in February (USA). **1914**

1917

THE FIRST WORLD WAR CONTINUES; THE RUSSIAN REVOLUTION

Once the initial German offensive had been halted, the war on the Western Front quickly stagnated as each side dug a continuous line of trenches from the Swiss border to the North Sea. Offensives achieved tiny gains for enormous casualties as the war became one of attrition. The battle of the Somme in 1916, for example, cost the lives of 146,000 British and French soldiers, but achieved an Allied advance of less than ten km (just over six miles) in four months. The toll among the defending Germans was almost as high. On the Eastern Front, which was too long for either side to man a continuous trench line, the war remained mobile, but casualties were just as heavy and the strategic stalemate was just as real.

The war of attrition favoured the Allies. They had superior manpower and command of the sea, allowing them to import food and war materials from their colonies and the USA, whereas Germany, cut off by a British naval blockade, was already suffering food and other shortages by early 1915. Germany's only serious challenge to the blockade was defeated at the battle of Jutland in 1916, though at heavy cost to the British navy. Germany instead turned to unrestricted submarine warfare to try to cut Britain's supply lines, but attacks on neutral shipping alienated the USA, leading it to join the Allies in April 1917.

Before this point, Japan, Italy, Portugal and Romania had joined the Allies, and the Ottoman empire and Bulgaria had joined the Central Powers. Serbia surrendered to Austria–Hungary in the autumn of 1915. Because of the naval blockade, Germany was unable to defend its colonies, most of which were quickly occupied by the Allies. After it seized Germany's possessions in China, Japan forced concessions from the weak Chinese government.

Russia's economy was the least developed of any of the major combatants. Although Tsar Nicholas II hoped the war might unite his people, incompetent handling of the war effort and food shortages discredited his government. Faced with strikes and mutinies, Nicholas abdicated in March 1917. The provisional government which took power continued the war, but in November it too was overthrown in a coup by the Communist Bolshevik party under Lenin, which promised peace. The Bolsheviks signed an armistice with Germany in December, ending Russia's active participation in the war while peace terms were negotiated.

GREENLAND
(Denmark)

CANADA

UNITED STATES OF AMERICA

NEWFOUNDLAND

St Pierre et Miquelon

1 Jamaica (GB)
2 BRITISH HONDURAS
3 Netherlands Antilles
4 Puerto Rico (USA)
5 HAITI
6 DOMINICAN REPUBLIC

Bermuda

Hawaii
(USA)

MEXICO

Cayman
Islands
(GB)

Bahamas

CUBA

US Virgin
Islands

British Virgin Islands
Leeward Islands (GB)
Guadeloupe (Fr)
Dominica (GB)
Martinique (Fr)
Windward Islands (GB)
Barbados (GB)
Trinidad & Tobago (GB)
BRITISH GUIANA
DUTCH GUIANA
FRENCH GUIANA

GUATEMALA
EL SALVADOR
HONDURAS
NICARAGUA
COSTA RICA
PANAMA

VENEZUELA

COLOMBIA

Galapagos
Islands
(Ecuador)

ECUADOR

French
Polynesia

PERU

BRAZIL

Pitcairn Island (GB)

BOLIVIA

PARAGUAY

Easter Island
(Chile)

CHILE

ARGENTINA

URUGUAY

Central Powers and territory occupied by the Central Powers December 1917

Allied Powers and territory occupied by the Allied Powers December 1917

Unaligned states

Falkland Islands (GB)

150°   120°   90°   60°

NETHERLANDS 7
BELGIUM 8
LUXEMBOURG 9
SWITZERLAND 10
ROMANIA 11
SERBIA 12
MONTENEGRO 13

ICELAND
(Denmark)   Faroe Islands
              (Denmark)

NORWAY   SWEDEN   FINLAND

RUSSIA

Arctic Circle

75°

GREAT
BRITAIN   DENMARK   GERMANY

ALBANIA 14   7
BULGARIA 15   8
Dodecanese 16   9   AUSTRO-
(It)   FRANCE   HUNGARIAN
              EMPIRE

URJANCHAI

Dalian
(Jpn)

45°

PORTUGAL   SPAIN
Azores
Gibraltar
Madeira   17   TUNISIA
MOROCCO   (Fr)   MALTA
(Fr)

10   ITALY   12   11
13   OTTOMAN
14   EMPIRE
GREECE   15
CYPRUS   16
(GB)   PERSIA   AFGHANISTAN

MONGOLIA

Tianjin (Int.)
Weihaiwei (GB)   KOREA   JAPAN
(Jpn)
REPUBLIC   Qingdao
OF   (Ger)
CHINA   Shanghai (Int.)

34   SINGAPORE (GB)
35   SARAWAK (GB)
36   BRUNEI (GB)
37   BRITISH NORTH BORNEO
38   PORTUGUESE TIMOR

Canary
Islands
SPANISH-
SAHARA   ALGERIA   LIBYA   EGYPT
(Fr)   (It)   (GB)

30   31
32
33

TIBET
NEPAL
BHUTAN   Guangzhouwan
(Fr)   TAIWAN (Jpn)

Tropic of Cancer

Cape
Verde
Islands   FRENCH WEST AFRICA   FRENCH   ANGLO-
EQUATORIAL   EGYPTIAN
GAMBIA   AFRICA   SUDAN
(GB)
PORTUGUESE   LIBERIA   18   NIGERIA
GUINEA   (GB)
(Pt)
SIERRA   GOLD
LEONE   COAST   KAMERUN
(GB)   (GB)   (Ger)   19

Bedouin
Arabs   OMAN (GB)

HADRAMAUT (GB)
29   ADEN
(GB)
28   Socotra
27   (GB)

INDIA
(GB)   BURMA
(GB)

Goa
(Pt)   Pondicherry
(Fr)
Mahé   Andaman
Islands
(GB)   SIAM

FRENCH
INDO-
CHINA

Macau
(Pt)   Hong Kong (GB)

PHILIPPINES
(USA)

Mariana
Islands
(Ger)
Guam (USA)
Palau   Caroline Islands
(Ger)   (Ger)   Marshall
Islands
(Ger)

ETHIOPIA   ITALIAN
SOMALILAND

Maldive
Islands
(GB)   CEYLON
(GB)   Nicobar
Islands
(GB)

MALAYA (GB)   36   37
35
34

KAISER
WILHELM'S
LAND   Nauru
(Ger)   (Ger)   Gilbert
Islands
(GB)   Equator

Ascension
Island
(GB)
CABINDA
(Pt)   BELGIAN
CONGO   20
GERMAN
EAST
AFRICA   Zanzibar
(GB)   Seychelles
(GB)

BRITISH
EAST
AFRICA

DUTCH EAST INDIES   PAPUA
(GB)   Bismarck Archipelago
(Ger)   Solomon
Islands (GB)
Phoenix
Islands
(GB)
Ellice
Islands
(GB)

ANGOLA
(PT)   21   22
26
23
St Helena
(GB)
SPANISH
MOROCCO   17   24
25
Walvis Bay
(GB)
TOGO (Ger)   18
RIO MUNI (Sp)   19   SOUTH
AFRICA   SWAZILAND (GB)
BASUTOLAND (GB)

Comoro
Islands
(Fr)   Amirante
Islands
(GB)   Chagos
Islands
(GB)   Cocos
Islands
(GB)   Christmas
Island
(GB)

MADAGASCAR
(Fr)   Mauritius
(GB)
Réunion
(Fr)

27   BRITISH SOMALILAND
28   FRENCH
SOMALILAND
29   ERITREA (It)

30   KUWAIT (GB)
31   BAHRAIN (GB)
32   QATAR (GB)
33   TRUCIAL OMAN (GB)

38

New
Hebrides
(Anglo-French
condominium)
New
Caledonia
(Fr)   Tonga
(GB)
Fiji (GB)   Tropic of Capricorn

AUSTRALIA

Tristan da
Cunha
(GB)

20   UGANDA (GB)
21   NORTHERN RHODESIA (GB)
22   NYASALAND (GB)
23   SOUTHERN RHODESIA (GB)

24   BECHUANALAND (GB)
25   GERMAN SOUTHWEST AFRICA
26   MOZAMBIQUE (Pt)

NEW
ZEALAND

45°

🏴 Kerguelen
Island

0°   30°   60°   90°   120°   150°   180°

1917

The First World War was the first industrial war. National economies were mobilized to produce munitions on an unprecedented scale. Women took over many traditionally male industrial occupations to replace men who had been conscripted into the armed forces.

At the outbreak of war, few generals fully understood the potential of the new military technology developed in the late 19th and early 20th centuries. Machine guns, barbed wire and quick-firing breech-loading artillery and high-explosive shells gave a clear advantage to the defence. Cavalry, for centuries the elite offensive arm of most armies, was especially vulnerable to the new weapons and its obsolescence quickly became apparent. Both sides turned to technology to break the strategic stalemate. Lighter machine guns and heavier artillery were developed. Poison gas was deployed and quickly countered with gas masks. Flame throwers were used against bunkers. Tanks were developed by the British as a potential means of breaking through heavily fortified trench lines, but their low speed and mechanical unreliability limited their usefulness.

Submarines emerged as a potent naval weapon, stimulating the development of a range of countermeasures such as ASDIC (SONAR) and depth charges. The war was also a great stimulus to the new aircraft industry. In 1914 no power possessed purpose-built combat aircraft, yet within two years all were producing specialized fighter and bomber aircraft. Airships were used for naval reconnaissance and bombing raids. Though casualties were light, airship raids on London demonstrated that civilian populations living far from combat zones were highly vulnerable to aerial attack. The war also saw the first genocide of the 20th century, perpetrated against the Armenians by the Ottoman government in retaliation for their support of Russia.

The shocking scale of the war provoked a powerful cultural response in art and literature which emphasized not martial glory, as had been the case through so much of history, but the human suffering and destruction of war. An important factor in this was the mass participation in the war, especially for the British who had not experienced war in their own land since the 17th century. The conscript armies of the First World War were made up mainly of civilians, not professional soldiers, and many of them had the ability to express their horror at what they experienced.

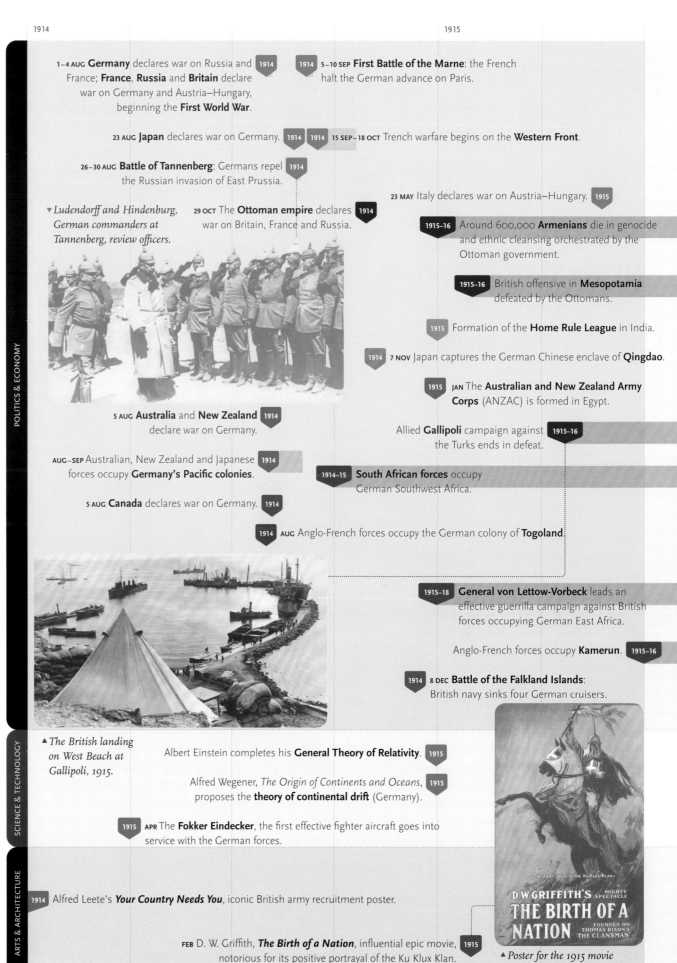

1914

1–4 AUG Germany declares war on Russia and France; **France**, **Russia** and **Britain** declare war on Germany and Austria–Hungary, beginning the **First World War**. `1914`

`1914` **5–10 SEP First Battle of the Marne**: the French halt the German advance on Paris.

23 AUG Japan declares war on Germany. `1914`   `1914` **15 SEP–18 OCT** Trench warfare begins on the **Western Front**.

26–30 AUG Battle of Tannenberg: Germans repel the Russian invasion of East Prussia. `1914`

23 MAY Italy declares war on Austria–Hungary. `1915`

▼ *Ludendorff and Hindenburg, German commanders at Tannenberg, review officers.*

29 OCT The **Ottoman empire** declares war on Britain, France and Russia. `1914`

`1915–16` Around 600,000 **Armenians** die in genocide and ethnic cleansing orchestrated by the Ottoman government.

`1915–16` British offensive in **Mesopotamia** defeated by the Ottomans.

`1915` Formation of the **Home Rule League** in India.

`1914` **7 NOV** Japan captures the German Chinese enclave of **Qingdao**.

`1915` **JAN** The **Australian and New Zealand Army Corps** (ANZAC) is formed in Egypt.

5 AUG Australia and **New Zealand** declare war on Germany. `1914`

Allied **Gallipoli** campaign against the Turks ends in defeat. `1915–16`

AUG–SEP Australian, New Zealand and Japanese forces occupy **Germany's Pacific colonies**. `1914`

`1914–15` **South African forces** occupy German Southwest Africa.

5 AUG Canada declares war on Germany. `1914`

`1914` **AUG** Anglo-French forces occupy the German colony of **Togoland**

`1915–18` **General von Lettow-Vorbeck** leads an effective guerrilla campaign against British forces occupying German East Africa.

Anglo-French forces occupy **Kamerun**. `1915–16`

`1914` **8 DEC Battle of the Falkland Islands**: British navy sinks four German cruisers.

▲ *The British landing on West Beach at Gallipoli, 1915.*

Albert Einstein completes his **General Theory of Relativity**. `1915`

Alfred Wegener, *The Origin of Continents and Oceans*, proposes the **theory of continental drift** (Germany). `1915`

`1915` **APR** The **Fokker Eindecker**, the first effective fighter aircraft goes into service with the German forces.

`1914` Alfred Leete's **Your Country Needs You**, iconic British army recruitment poster.

D. W. GRIFFITH'S MIGHTY SPECTACLE
THE BIRTH OF A NATION
FOUNDED ON THOMAS DIXON'S THE CLANSMAN

FEB D. W. Griffith, **The Birth of a Nation**, influential epic movie, notorious for its positive portrayal of the Ku Klux Klan. `1915`

▲ *Poster for the 1915 movie The Birth of a Nation.*

POLITICS & ECONOMY

SCIENCE & TECHNOLOGY

ARTS & ARCHITECTURE

1914   1915

Jan Feb Mar Apr May Jun Jul Aug Sep Oct Nov Dec Jan Feb Mar Apr May Jun

31 MAY–1 JUN **Battle of Jutland** in the North Sea between the British and German fleets: only major fleet action of the First World War. `1916`

`1917` 15 MAR Faced with strikes and mutinies, **Tsar Nicholas II** abdicates: a provisional government is formed in Russia.

1915 OCT–NOV **Serbia** surrenders to the Central Powers.

◄ *HMS* Birmingham *in the battle of Jutland, 1916.*

`1917` 15 JUN **Greece** formally joins the Allied Powers.

`1917` 31 JUL–10 NOV **Battle of Passchendaele** (Third Battle of Ypres).

1915 14 OCT **Bulgaria** joins the Central Powers.

APR Most successful month of the **German U-boat campaign**: 155 British merchant ships sunk. `1917`

20 NOV–8 DEC First large-scale use of **tanks** in battle, by the British at Cambrai. `1917`

`1916` 21 FEB–18 DEC Costly German offensive against the French at **Verdun**.

`1916` 24–29 APR **Easter Rising** in Dublin against British rule in Ireland.

▲ *Soldiers carry away a wounded comrade during the battle of Passchendaele, 1917.*

3 DEC The **Bolsheviks** sign an armistice with Germany. `1917`

NOV Ukraine, Finland and Estonia declare independence from **Russia**. `1917`

`1916` 9 MAR Germany declares war on **Portugal** for interning German shipping.

27 AUG **Romania** joins the Allied Powers. `1916`

7 NOV The **Bolsheviks** under **Lenin** seize power in Russia: civil war breaks out between 'Reds' (pro-Bolsheviks) and 'Whites' (anti-Bolsheviks). `1917`

▲ *Ruins of the city of Verdun after the 1916 bombardment.*

1915 12 DEC President **Yuan Shikai** declares his intention to become the new emperor of China, causing widespread rebellions under local warlords.

9 DEC Romania signs an armistice with the **Central Powers**. `1917`

`1916` 5 JUN **Yuan Shikei** dies: warlords control much of China.

`1917` 11 MAR British capture **Baghdad**.

`1916` JAN Britain introduces **conscription**.

2 NOV **Balfour Declaration** of British support for a Jewish homeland in Palestine. `1917`

`1916` 1 JUL–19 NOV Costly British offensive on the **Somme**.

11 DEC The British capture **Jerusalem**. `1917`

`1916` 6 JUN Beginning of Arab revolt against the Ottomans in **Hejaz**.

13 AUG **China** declares war on Germany. `1917`

▲ *British troops emerge from the trenches in an offensive at the Somme, 1916.*

`1916` 4 AUG The USA buys the **Danish Virgin Islands** for $25 million.

16 JAN The **Zimmermann Telegram**: Germany urges Mexico to invade the USA. `1917`

5 FEB Mexican **president Venustiano Carranza** introduces a reformed constitution. `1917`

6 APR The USA enters the war against the Central Powers. `1917`

JUN The British **Sopwith Camel**, the most successful fighter aircraft of the war, goes into action, helping the **Allies** gain air superiority over the western front. `1916`

FEB The British begin production of the first **tanks**. `1916`

`1916` **Henri Barbusse**, *Le Feu* (*Under Fire*): first novel about the experience of trench warfare.

`1916` The British government appoints offical **war artists** to record the war.

`1917` Completion of the **Trans-Australian railway**.

`1916` The German Gotha G. III is the first aircraft designed as a **bomber**.

►*Advertisement for the Trans-Australian railway from the 1930s.*

Travel by— TRANS-AUSTRALIAN RAILWAY

—in Comfort———— save Days—

ACROSS AUSTRALIA

Wilfred Owen's **'Anthem for Doomed Youth'** makes him the most influential of the war poets of the First World War. `1917`

The avant-garde **Dada** cultural movement starts in Zurich, Switzerland, as a protest against the First World War. `1916`

`1916` FEB Death of the Nicaraguan poet **Rubén Darío**, founder of the Latin American *modernismo* literary movement.

`1917` The **first jazz record**, *Dixieland Jazz Band One-Step*, is released (USA).

`1917` **Ubudiah Mosque**, Kuala Kangsar, Malaysia: Indo-Saracenic design by Arthur Benison Hubback.

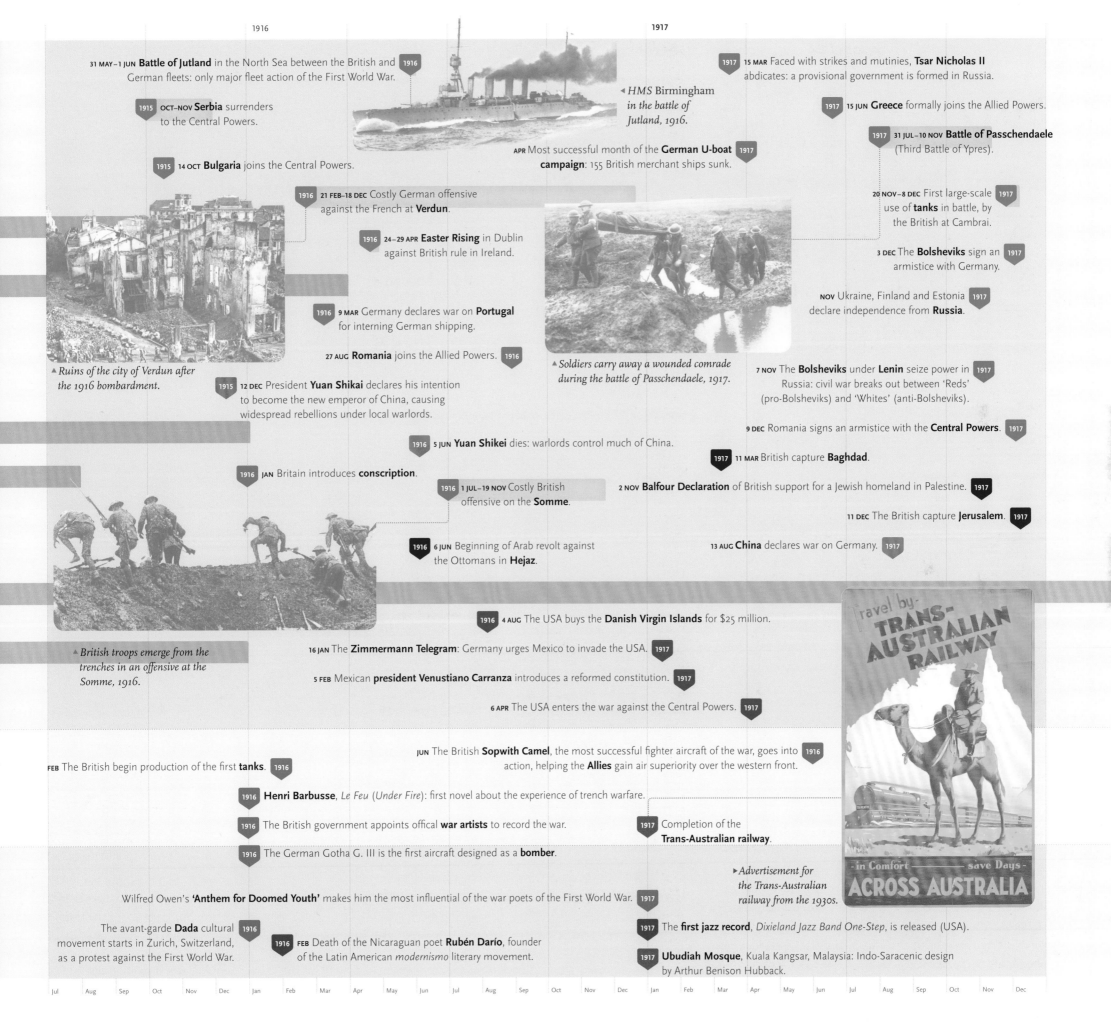

1923

THE END OF THE FIRST WORLD WAR AND ITS AFTERMATH

Russia paid a high price for peace with Germany, losing control of Ukraine, Transcaucasia, Poland, the Baltic states and Finland in the Treaty of Brest-Litovsk in March 1918. Russia's withdrawal allowed Germany to transfer troops to the Western Front, launching a series of offensives to try to break the British and French armies before the USA could fully mobilize its economy for war. The offensives failed and, by August 1918, the German armies were in steady retreat. Germany's allies Bulgaria and the Ottoman empire agreed armistices in September and October, and the Austro-Hungarian empire broke up as its constituent nationalities declared independence. Mutinies, strikes and protests over food shortages forced the German Kaiser from power and Germany signed an armistice on 11 November 1918, bringing the First World War to an end. It had cost around 20 million lives.

Formal peace was agreed by the Treaty of Versailles in 1919, which imposed heavy penalties on Germany for its role in starting the war. Germany lost its colonial empire and some of its home territory to Denmark, France and newly independent Poland. The Ottoman empire was reduced to present-day Turkey, which became a republic in 1923 under the leadership of Kemal Ataturk, who oversaw a radical programme of modernization and secularization.

Germany's defeat nullified the treaty of Brest-Litovsk, but Russia's Bolshevik government had to fight separatists and the Poles to regain control of Ukraine. It also had to recognize the independence of the Baltic states and Finland in order to concentrate on fighting a civil war against the White counter-revolutionaries, which broke out in 1918. With the Whites' defeat in October 1922, the Bolsheviks regained control of most of the Russian empire, restructuring it as the Union of Soviet Socialist Republics (USSR), a group of nominally autonomous, ethnically based republics.

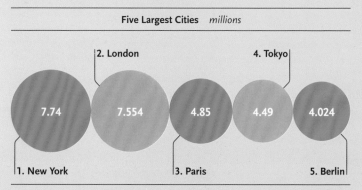

Five Largest Cities *millions*

2. London
4. Tokyo

7.74 | 7.554 | 4.85 | 4.49 | 4.024

1. New York
3. Paris
5. Berlin

GREENLAND
(Denmark)

CANADA

NEWFOUNDLAND

St Pierre et Miquelon

1 New York

UNITED STATES OF AMERICA

Bermuda

1 Jamaica
2 BRITISH HONDURAS
3 Netherlands Antilles
4 Puerto Rico
5 HAITI
6 DOMINICAN REPUBLIC

Hawaii

MEXICO

Cayman Islands (GB)

Bahamas

CUBA

US Virgin Islands

British Virgin Islands
Leeward Islands
Guadeloupe
Dominica
Martinique
Windward Islands
Barbados

GUATEMALA
EL SALVADOR
HONDURAS
NICARAGUA
COSTA RICA
PANAMA

Panama Canal Zone (US)

VENEZUELA

Trinidad & Tobago

BRITISH GUIANA
DUTCH GUIANA
FRENCH GUIANA

COLOMBIA

Galapagos Islands (Ecuador)

ECUADOR

BRAZIL

French Polynesia

PERU

BOLIVIA

Pitcairn Island

Easter Island (Chile)

PARAGUAY

CHILE

Portuguese possessions
Spanish possessions
Dutch possessions
British possessions
French possessions
Italian possessions

USSR
Japanese possessions
USA and possessions
Other states and territories

GREAT BRITAIN Member of the League of Nations in 1923

ARGENTINA
URUGUAY

Falkland Islands

150°   120°   90°   60°

1923

The mass slaughter of the First World War inspired strong pacifist sentiments. To prevent further wars, the victors set up the League of Nations to promote peace through collective security, disarmament and international arbitration of disputes. The League oversaw the division of Germany's former colonies among the victors as mandated territories, a form of trusteeship, the intention being that the territory would eventually become independent.

Britain and its dominions received the lion's share of the mandates, bringing the British empire to its greatest territorial extent. However, the war had helped consolidate emerging national identities in Canada, Australia, New Zealand and South Africa and strengthened nationalist resentment against British rule in Ireland. After a short war, most of Ireland achieved autonomy as the Irish Free State in 1922. India had contributed greatly to Britain's war effort and expected to be rewarded with autonomous-dominion status. When this did not happen, support for national independence grew rapidly.

President Woodrow Wilson was the major architect of the League of Nations, but he failed to overcome isolationist sentiment in the USA, which never joined. This, and the exclusion of Soviet Russia (because of its communist ideology) and of Germany left the League lacking in credibility. The USA was the main beneficiary of the First World War: Britain and France had become deeply indebted to it during the war and American industry had profited by supplying munitions to the Allies. By the war's end, the USA had supplanted Britain as the world's dominant financial power, as well as its leading industrial power. By the 1922 Washington Naval Treaty, Britain had accepted the USA as an equal naval power. In China, regional warlords backed by foreign governments fought for territory while revolutionary nationalism grew in the cities.

World Population

7 BILLION

1.9 billion

1530   1923   2010

1918   1919   1920

POLITICS & ECONOMY

1918 3 MAR **Treaty of Brest-Litovsk** formally ends the war on the Eastern Front: Russia gives up Finland, Poland, the Baltic states, Ukraine and Transcaucasia.

1919 26 NOV Outbreak of the **Irish War of Independence**.

1918 21 MAR–18 JUL German spring offensives on the **Western Front** fail to achieve a decisive breakthrough.

1918 8 AUG The Black Day of the German Army: British breakthrough begins the collapse of the German army.

12–18 SEP Meuse–Argonne **1918** offensive: first American offensive of the war.

1918 3 NOV The Allies sign an armistice with **Austria–Hungary**: Austro-Hungarian empire breaks up.

1918 9 NOV **Kaiser Wilhelm II** abdicates: Germany becomes a republic.

1920–21 Poland defeats an invasion by the **Red Army**.

11 NOV The Allies sign an **1918** **armistice** with Germany.

1919 18 JUN **Treaty of Versailles** assigns 'war guilt' to Germany.

13 APR **Amritsar Massacre** of 379 people at **1919** an Indian independence rally.

1920 JAN **League of Nations** inaugurated.

Former Ottoman territory in the **Middle East** is partitioned and mandated to Britain and France (Palestine, Transjordan and Iraq to Britain; Syria and Lebanon to France). **1920**

War between **Greece** and **Turkey**: ethnic Turks expelled from Greece, Greeks expelled from Turkey. **1920–22**

6 MAY–8 AUG **Third Anglo-Afghan War** ends inconclusively. **1919**

1918–20 Japanese occupation of **Manchuria** and part of **Siberia**.

1918 4 MAR First observed outbreak of the **Spanish influenza** pandemic at Fort Riley, Kansas: it kills over 50 million people worldwide by July 1919.

Former German colonies in **New Guinea** and the **Pacific** are **1920** mandated to Australia, Britain and Japan by the League of Nations.

16 JAN Implementation of the **18th Amendment** of the US Constitution **1920** bans the sale of alcohol, beginning the **Prohibition era** (to 1933).

1919 10 APR Mexican peasant-revolution leader **Emiliano Zapata** assassinated by government forces.

Former German colonies in **Africa** are **1920** mandated by the League of Nations to Britain, France, Belgium and South Africa.

RELIGION & PHILOSOPHY

1918–23 **Oswald Spengler**, *The Decline of the West*, philosophy of history and politics.

1918 21 JAN To promote atheism, Russia's **Bolshevik government** confiscates all property held by the church and other religious organizations.

SCIENCE & TECHNOLOGY

1918 **ASDIC** (or **SONAR**) **active sound detection apparatus** for detecting enemy submarines is developed (UK).

1919 14–15 JUN British aviators Alcock and Brown make the first **non-stop transatlantic flight**, from Newfoundland to Ireland.

1918 HMS *Argus* is the first aircraft carrier to have a purpose-built flight deck.

ARTS & ARCHITECTURE

Foundation of the **Bauhaus** school of **1919** contemporary arts and crafts at Weimar, Germany, by the architect **Walter Gropius**.

▸ *Alcock and Brown pose for a photograph in a plane.*

Jan Feb Mar Apr May Jun Jul Aug Sep Oct Nov Dec Jan Feb Mar Apr May Jun Jul Aug Sep Oct Nov Dec Jan Feb Mar Apr May Jun

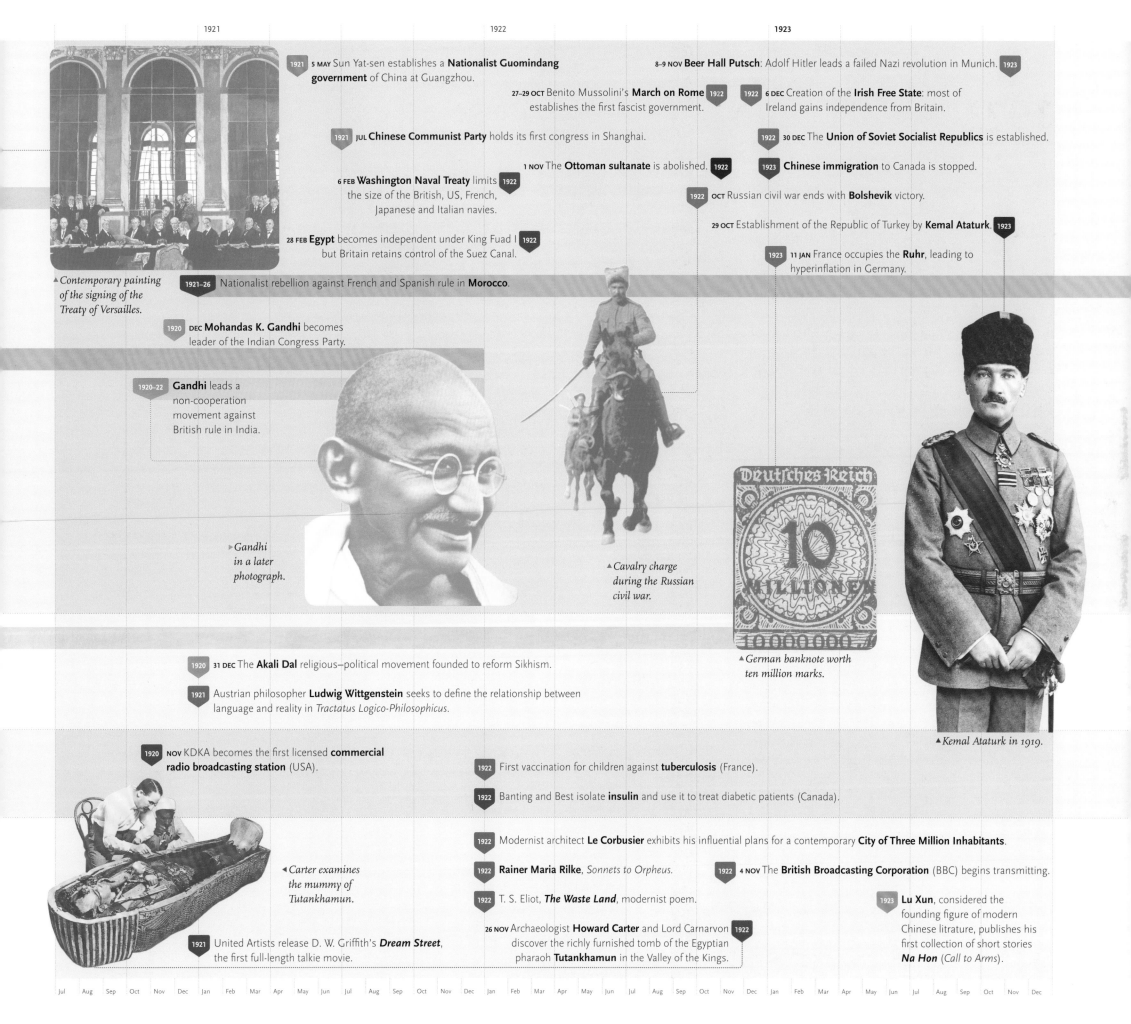

1921 5 MAY Sun Yat-sen establishes a **Nationalist Guomindang government** of China at Guangzhou.

8–9 NOV **Beer Hall Putsch**: Adolf Hitler leads a failed Nazi revolution in Munich. **1923**

27–29 OCT Benito Mussolini's **March on Rome** **1922** establishes the first fascist government.

1922 6 DEC Creation of the **Irish Free State**: most of Ireland gains independence from Britain.

1921 JUL **Chinese Communist Party** holds its first congress in Shanghai.

1922 30 DEC The **Union of Soviet Socialist Republics** is established.

1 NOV The **Ottoman sultanate** is abolished. **1922**

1923 **Chinese immigration** to Canada is stopped.

6 FEB **Washington Naval Treaty** limits **1922** the size of the British, US, French, Japanese and Italian navies.

1922 OCT Russian civil war ends with **Bolshevik** victory.

28 FEB **Egypt** becomes independent under King Fuad I but Britain retains control of the Suez Canal. **1922**

29 OCT Establishment of the Republic of Turkey by **Kemal Ataturk**. **1923**

1923 11 JAN France occupies the **Ruhr**, leading to hyperinflation in Germany.

▲ *Contemporary painting of the signing of the Treaty of Versailles.*

1921–26 Nationalist rebellion against French and Spanish rule in **Morocco**.

1920 DEC **Mohandas K. Gandhi** becomes leader of the Indian Congress Party.

1920–22 **Gandhi** leads a non-cooperation movement against British rule in India.

▶ *Gandhi in a later photograph.*

▲ *Cavalry charge during the Russian civil war.*

▲ *German banknote worth ten million marks.*

1920 31 DEC The **Akali Dal** religious–political movement founded to reform Sikhism.

1921 Austrian philosopher **Ludwig Wittgenstein** seeks to define the relationship between language and reality in *Tractatus Logico-Philosophicus*.

▲ *Kemal Ataturk in 1919.*

1920 NOV KDKA becomes the first licensed **commercial radio broadcasting station** (USA).

1922 First vaccination for children against **tuberculosis** (France).

1922 Banting and Best isolate **insulin** and use it to treat diabetic patients (Canada).

1922 Modernist architect **Le Corbusier** exhibits his influential plans for a contemporary **City of Three Million Inhabitants**.

◀ *Carter examines the mummy of Tutankhamun.*

1922 **Rainer Maria Rilke**, *Sonnets to Orpheus*.

1922 4 NOV The **British Broadcasting Corporation** (BBC) begins transmitting.

1922 T. S. Eliot, **The Waste Land**, modernist poem.

1923 **Lu Xun**, considered the founding figure of modern Chinese litrature, publishes his first collection of short stories *Na Hon* (*Call to Arms*).

26 NOV Archaeologist **Howard Carter** and Lord Carnarvon **1922** discover the richly furnished tomb of the Egyptian pharaoh **Tutankhamun** in the Valley of the Kings.

1921 United Artists release D. W. Griffith's **Dream Street**, the first full-length talkie movie.

1938

THE WORLD IN THE SHADOW OF THE GREAT DICTATORS; NEW GOVERNMENT IN CHINA

Most European economies struggled to recover from the First World War. In Central Europe, new national borders and customs regimes broke up what had been a highly integrated free-trade area under the Austro-Hungarian empire. In Germany, the liberal, democratic Weimar Republic was burdened with the consequences of defeat. High unemployment and inflation undermined its economic credibility.

Economic hardship and fear of Soviet communism fostered the rise of right-wing dictatorships, many of them inspired by the fascist dictator Benito Mussolini, who had seized power in Italy in 1922. In Germany the Nazi party leader Adolf Hitler was elected to power in 1933. Hitler repudiated the Versailles treaty, rebuilt Germany's armed forces, reoccupied the demilitarized Rhineland, pushed through a union with Austria and demanded – and got – British agreement to his annexation of the ethnically German Sudetenland in Czechoslovakia. The ideological battle between fascism and communism was fought out in the Spanish Civil War, which erupted in 1936.

China partially recovered from the political chaos into which it had descended in 1913, when the Guomindang party and its army under Jiang Jieshi launched its Northern Expedition against the warlords in 1926. The Communists in the south were defeated, but they retreated and re-established themselves in the north. The Japanese invasion of China in 1937 drove the Guomindang government and the Communists to unite in resistance. The Communists spread their power widely behind Japanese lines and benefited from being seen as patriotic.

The League of Nations was shown to be impotent after Japan's annexation of Manchuria in 1931 and the Italian conquest of Ethiopia in 1935. Japan's invasion of China led to tension with the USA, which increasingly saw it as a threat to its interests in the Pacific.

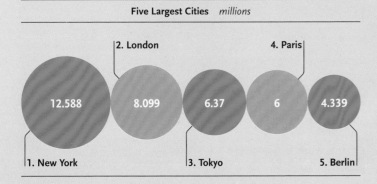

Five Largest Cities *millions*

12.588	8.099	6.37	6	4.339
1. New York	2. London	3. Tokyo	4. Paris	5. Berlin

GREENLAND (Denmark)

CANADA

NEWFOUNDLAND

St Pierre et Miquelon

1 New York

UNITED STATES OF AMERICA

Bermuda

1 Jamaica
2 BRITISH HONDURAS
3 Netherlands Antilles
4 Puerto Rico
5 HAITI
6 DOMINICAN REPUBLIC

Hawaii

Cayman Islands (GB)

MEXICO

CUBA

Bahamas

US Virgin Islands

British Virgin Islands
Leeward Islands
Guadeloupe
Dominica
Martinique
Windward Islands

GUATEMALA
EL SALVADOR
HONDURAS
NICARAGUA
COSTA RICA
PANAMA

Panama Canal Zone (US)

Barbados
Trinidad & Tobago

VENEZUELA

BRITISH GUIANA
DUTCH GUIANA
FRENCH GUIANA

COLOMBIA

Galapagos Islands (Ecuador)

ECUADOR

French Polynesia

BRAZIL

PERU

BOLIVIA

Pitcairn Island

PARAGUAY

Easter Island (Chile)

CHILE

URUGUAY

ARGENTINA

Portuguese possessions	Soviet possessions
Spanish possessions	Japanese possessions
Dutch possessions	USA and possessions
British possessions	Italian possessions
French possessions	Other states and territories

Falkland Islands

150° 120° 90° 60°

NETHERLANDS 7
BELGIUM 8
LUXEMBOURG 9
SWITZERLAND 10
CZECHOSLOVAKIA 11
HUNGARY 12
YUGOSLAVIA 13
ICELAND
(Denmark)

SVALBARD
(Norway)

75°

Arctic Circle

NORWAY
SWEDEN
FINLAND

UNION OF SOVIET SOCIALIST REPUBLICS

ESTONIA
LATVIA
LITHUANIA

GREAT
BRITAIN
IRELAND
2
London
BULGARIA 14
ALBANIA 15
Dodecanese 16

DENMARK
5
Berlin 7
GERMANY
9
4
Paris
8
FRANCE
10

POLAND
11
12
ROMANIA
13
14
ITALY
15
GREECE
16
MALTA

TUVA

MANZHOUGUO

MONGOLIA

KOREA

3
JAPAN Tokyo

42 Japanese-occupied China

PORTUGAL SPAIN

Azores

Madeira

Gibraltar

17

Canary
Islands

SPANISH
SAHARA

Cape
Verde
Islands

GAMBIA

PORTUGUESE
GUINEA

SIERRA
LEONE
LIBERIA

Ascension
Island

SPANISH 17
MOROCCO
CAMEROON 18
Fernando Póo 19
RIO MUNI 20
Príncipe 21
São Tomé 22

Tristan da
Cunha

MOROCCO TUNISIA

ALGERIA LIBYA

FRENCH WEST AFRICA

FRENCH
EQUATORIAL
AFRICA

GOLD
COAST
NIGERIA

19
21
22

18
20

CABINDA

St Helena

TURKEY
CYPRUS
31
33
32
IRAQ
34

38 39
40
41

IRAN

EGYPT

YEMEN
37
ADEN
36
35
Socotra

SAUDI
ARABIA

OMAN

ITALIAN
SOMALILAND

ANGLO-
EGYPTIAN
SUDAN

ETHIOPIA

BRITISH
EAST
AFRICA

23
UGANDA

BELGIAN
CONGO

RUANDA-
URUNDI

24
Zanzibar

Comoro
Islands

Seychelles

Amirante
Islands

AFGHANISTAN

TIBET

NEPAL
BHUTAN

INDIA

REPUBLIC OF
CHINA

42

42

42

BURMA

SIAM

FRENCH
INDO-
CHINA

Goa
Mahé
Pondicherry
Andaman
Islands

Maldive
Islands
CEYLON
Nicobar
Islands

Guangzhouwan
Hong Kong
Macau

TAIWAN

PHILIPPINES

MALAYA
45 46
44
43

43 SINGAPORE
44 SARAWAK
45 BRUNEI
46 BRITISH NORTH BORNEO
47 PORTUGUESE TIMOR

Mariana
Islands

Guam

Caroline Islands

Palau

Marshall
Islands

Gilbert
Islands

Nauru
(Australian
manadate)

Phoenix
Islands

Tropic of Cancer

Equator

ANGOLA

25
26

27

28

29

Walvis Bay
(to South Africa)

SOUTH
AFRICA

SWAZILAND

BASUTOLAND

30
MOZAMBIQUE

MADAGASCAR

Chagos
Islands

Cocos
Islands

Christmas
Island

DUTCH EAST INDIES

47

PAPUA
(to Australia)

NORTHEAST
NEW GUINEA
(to Australia)

Solomon
Islands

Ellice
Islands

New
Hebrides
(Anglo-French
condominium)

New
Caledonia

Fiji

Tonga

Tropic of Capricorn

Mauritius

Réunion

Comoro
Islands

31 LEBANON
32 SYRIA
33 PALESTINE
34 TRANSJORDAN
35 BRITISH SOMALILAND

36 FRENCH
SOMALILAND
37 ERITREA
38 KUWAIT
39 BAHRAIN
40 QATAR
41 TRUCIAL OMAN

AUSTRALIA

23 UGANDA
24 TANGANYIKA
25 NORTHERN RHODESIA
26 NYASALAND
27 SOUTHERN RHODESIA

28 BECHUANALAND
29 SOUTHWEST AFRICA
(to South Africa)
30 MOZAMBIQUE

Kerguelen
Island

NEW
ZEALAND

45°

0° 30° 60° 90° 120° 150° 180°

1938

The American economy grew quickly in the immediate postwar period, supported by rising wages and buoyant demand for consumer goods. American popular culture, such as jazz music and movies, was exported worldwide, creating a self-confident, glamorous image for the USA, which was not tarnished even by the crime wave of bootlegging and gangsterism that followed the prohibition of alcohol in 1920.

In October 1929, however, the overheated US stock market crashed. Millions of people from all walks of life who had poured their savings, and borrowings, into the stock market were bankrupted. The US economy began a sharp decline that continued unbroken until 1933: American GDP shrank by 30 per cent; unemployment exceeded 20 per cent. The USA's economic dominance ensured that the effects of the Great Depression were felt globally: they were especially severe in Europe.

The USSR had the double legacy of world war and civil war to overcome and in 1924 its productivity was still only two-thirds its prewar level. The power struggle that followed Lenin's death in that year revealed Josef Stalin as leader. Stalin's first Five Year Plan increased Soviet industrial production but at a terrible cost in human suffering, due to the widespread use of forced labour. His ideologically driven collectivization of agriculture led to mass starvation in Ukraine and Central Asia.

The totalitarianism of the European dictators extended to all aspects of culture. Stalin imposed Socialist Realism as the official art style to promote positive images of life in the USSR. The Nazis made skilful use of movies for propaganda while attacking the 'degenerate' modernist art of the Weimar period, burning 'un-German' books and banning performances of works by Jewish composers, as part of their wider attack on German Jews.

World Population

7 BILLION

2.25 billion

186

1923 **1938** 2010

POLITICS & ECONOMY

1924 21 JAN Death of **Lenin** begins power struggle between Lev Trotsky, Lev Kamenev, Grigory Zinoviev and **Josef Stalin**.

1924 OCT **Abd al-Aziz ibn Saud** of Nejd conquers Hejaz and takes control of Mecca.

First **Five Year Plan** of industrialization in the USSR. **1928–33**

1926–27 **Joseph Stalin** consolidates his dictatorship over the USSR.

1926–1928 General Jiang Jieshi's **Northern Expedition** superficially suppresses Chinese warlords.

9 MAY **Canberra** becomes **1927** capital of Australia.

▶ *Photograph of Jiang Jieshi in the* Illustrated London News, *1941.*

NOV **Stalin** announces the collectivization **1929** of agriculture in the USSR.

1927 APR **Jiang Jieshi** becomes leader of China's Nationalist government and purges suspected Communists.

1928 27 AUG **Kellogg–Briand Pact** prohibits war as an instrument of national policy.

1928 **Guomindang** government moves the capital of China from Beijing to Nanjing.

1927 4 JUL Ahmed Sukarno founds the **Indonesian National Party** to campaign for independence from the Netherlands.

28–29 OCT The Wall Street Crash is followed by the **Great** **1929** **Depression** and a global trading collapse.

RELIGION & PHILOSOPHY

▶ *American eight-cent stamp commemorating Goddard's rocket.*

4 OCT Islamic courts abolished in **Turkey**. **1926**

MAR The international Islamist party, the **Muslim** **1928** **Brotherhood**, is founded in Egypt by Hassan al-Banna.

ROBERT H. GODDARD — U.S. AIR MAIL — 8c

▶ *Poster from 1931 promoting the USSR's first Five Year Plan.*

SCIENCE & TECHNOLOGY

Robert Goddard builds and launches the **1926** **first liquid-fuelled rocket** (USA).

1925 John Logie Baird demonstrates the first **television** (UK).

1928 Alexander Fleming discovers the **antibiotic penicillin** (UK).

1928 William Park develops the **poliomyelitis vaccine** (USA).

ARTS & ARCHITECTURE

The **Afsluitdijk** (Enclosure Dam) turns the Zuiderzee into **1927–32** the Ijsselmeer lake (Netherlands).

D. H. Lawrence's sexually explicit novel **Lady Chatterley's Lover** is **1928** published in Italy to avoid British obscenity laws.

1926 Fritz Lang, **Metropolis**, expressionist futuristic movie.

Mies van der Rohe, **Villa Tugendhat**, modernist house, Brno, Czechoslovakia. **1928–30**

1924–32 Ralph Freeman, steel-arch **Sydney Harbour Bridge** (Australia).

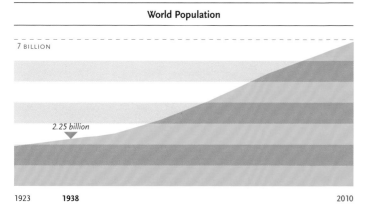

▶ *Poster for the 1926 movie* Metropolis.

1924 1925 1926 1927 1928 1929

Jan Apr Jul Oct Jan Apr Jul Oct Jan Apr Jul Oct Jan Apr Jul Oct Jan Apr Jul Oct Jan Apr Jul Oct

1934 1 DEC Assassination of Leningrad party secretary Sergei Kirov leads to Stalin's **Great Purge** (1936–40).

1930 25 APR System of **forced-labour camps** (Gulags) officially set up in USSR.

14 APR **Spain** becomes a republic. **1931**

1932–33 **Famine** in Ukraine and Soviet Central Asia.

MAR German army reoccupies the **Rhineland** **1936** (demilitarized after the First World War).

1936 17 JUL **Spanish Civil War** after an attempted fascist coup against the Republican government (to 1939).

MAR–JUN **President F. D. Roosevelt** introduces the New **1933** Deal to lift the USA out of the Depression.

FEB **John Maynard Keynes**, in *The Theory of Employment, Interest and Money*, defines Keynesian economics (UK). **1936**

29 SEP **Munich Agreement**: Britain acquiesces to German annexation of the Czech Sudentenland. **1938**

23 SEP Kingdom of **Saudi Arabia** proclaimed by ibn Saud. **1932**

21 MAR Persia changes its name to **Iran**. **1935**

12 MAR German **Anschluss** (link-up) with Austria. **1938**

1930 12 MAR Gandhi's **salt satyagraha march** against the British salt tax begins a campaign of civil disobedience that lasts until 1934.

1933 **Standard Oil** discovers oil in Saudi Arabia.

1935 AUG **British Government of India Act** allows free elections for Indian provincial governments.

▼ *A woman weeps with joy, giving the Nazi salute, during the Sudetenland occupation in 1938.*

1932 16 SEP Japan sets up puppet state of **Manzhouguo** in Manchuria.

1936–37 The **Indian National Congress Party** wins control of seven provincial governments in elections.

18 SEP **Mukden Incident** gives Japan the **1931** pretext to occupy Manchuria.

3 OCT **Iraq** becomes **1932** independent.

1933 27 MAR Japan withdraws from the **League of Nations**, beginning its decline.

1934–1936 Chinese Communists' **Long March** to escape Nationalist campaigns: **Mao Zedong** emerges as party leader.

1930 OCT-NOV Getúlio Vargas leads a revolution in **Brazil**.

1931 11 DEC **Australia** and **New Zealand** become fully independent of the UK.

JUL **Japan** invades China: Communists and Nationalists form a common **1937** front against the invasion; USA threatens Japan with an **oil embargo**.

1931 11 DEC **South Africa** becomes fully independent of the UK.

1932–1935 **Chaco War** between Bolivia and Paraguay.

1935–1936 **Mussolini** invades Ethiopia to create a new 'Roman empire'.

1931 11 DEC **Canada** becomes fully independent of the UK.

Enormous copper reserves discovered **1935** in **Northern Rhodesia** (Zambia).

13 DEC **Japanese** capture Nanjing and massacre civilians. **1937**

30 JAN **Adolf Hitler** becomes **1933** Chancellor of Germany.

1934 DEC Mexican dictator **Lázaro Cárdenas** institutes a land reform policy to help peasant farmers, bringing a final end to revolutionary activity.

1935 **University of Tehran** founded as part of a policy of secularization of Iranian society.

◄ *Dorothea Lange's iconic photo of the Great Depression.*

1935 15 SEP **Nuremberg Laws** deprive German Jews of civil rights.

10 NOV *Kristallnacht*: Nazi-orchestrated attacks on German Jews. **1938**

▶ *Hitler in the 1935 propaganda movie* Triumph of the Will.

1930 Clyde Tombaugh discovers the dwarf-planet **Pluto** (USA).

Otto Hahn and Fritz Strassman discover **nuclear** **1938** **fission**, the basis of atomic energy (Germany).

1933 Louis Breguet designs the Gyroplane Laboratoire, the first **practicable helicopter** – its first flight is in 1935 (France).

1935 Robert Watson-Watt develops **radar** (UK).

1937 Frank Whittle invents the **jet engine** (UK).

1935 Wallace Carothers invents **nylon** (USA).

Leni Riefenstahl, ***Triumph of the Will***, **1934** Nazi propaganda movie.

Dmitri Shostakovich's 1934 opera, **1936** ***Lady Macbeth of the Mtsensk District***, is denounced by Stalin.

1933–36 **The Hoover Dam**, Nevada, USA.

1933–37 **Golden Gate Bridge**, San Francisco.

▲ *Frank Whittle's W2B jet engine.*

Munshi Premchand, *Godaan (The Gift of a Cow)*, Urdu/Hindi **1936** novel of peasant life under colonialism.

1937 Pablo Picasso, ***Guernica***, painting inspired by the German bombing in the **Spanish Civil War**.

1932 Stalin makes **Socialist Realism** the official art style of the USSR.

1931 Paul Landowski, ***Christ the Redeemer***, monumental Art Deco statue, Rio de Janeiro, Brazil.

1935–37 Frank Lloyd Wright, **Fallingwater**, modernist house, Pennsylvania.

1930–31 William F. Lamb, the **Empire State Building**, New York.

Walt Disney's first full-length animated movie, ***Snow White***, is released. **1938**

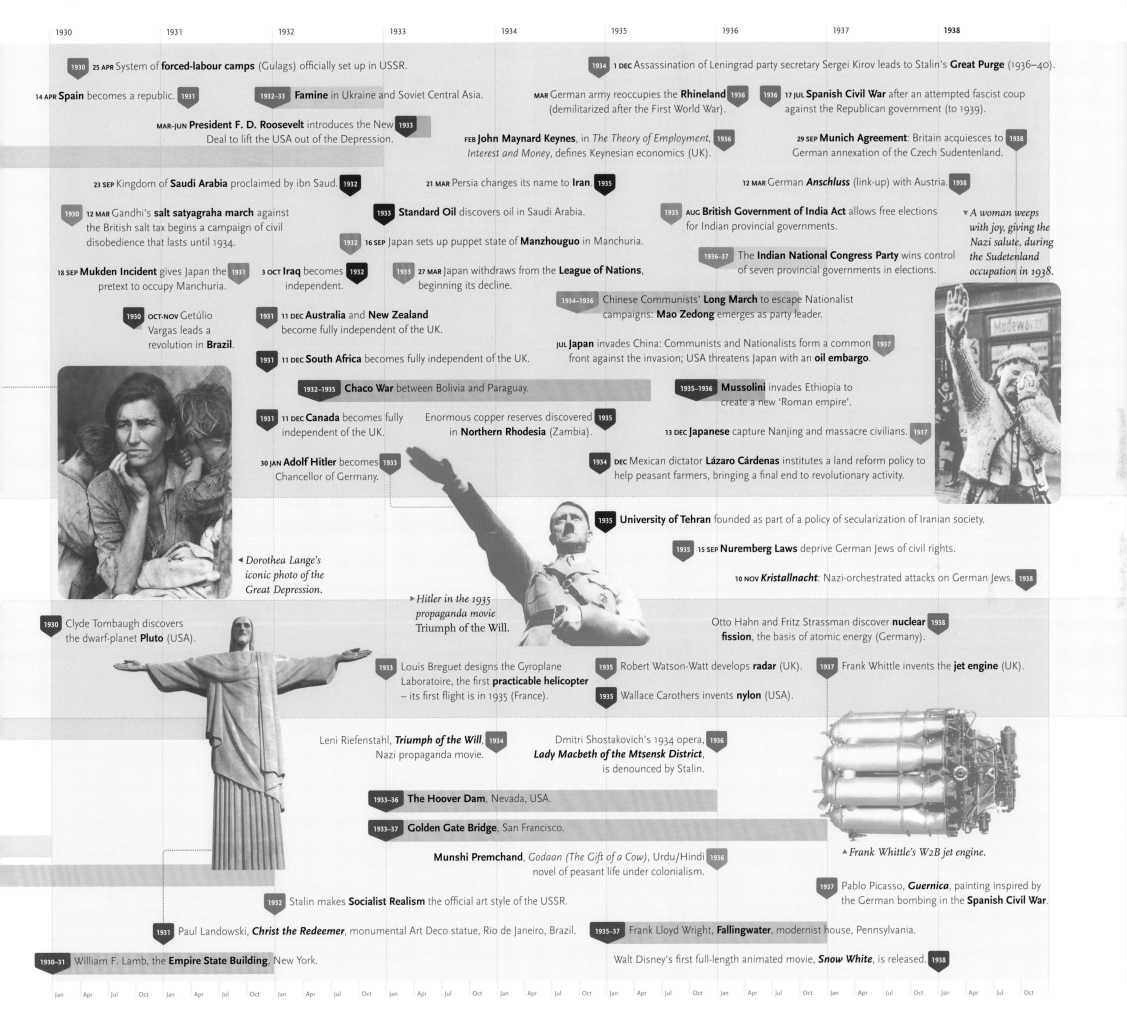

1942

THE MAXIMUM EXTENT OF AXIS ADVANCE IN THE SECOND WORLD WAR

Up until 1939, Hitler's territorial demands had concerned only areas of German ethnic settlement. Britain and France had acquiesced, hoping that German unity represented the limit of his ambitions. After Hitler's annexation of what remained of Czechoslovakia in March 1939, it was all too clear that this was not the case. When Germany invaded Poland in September 1939, Britain, France, Australia, New Zealand, South Africa and Canada declared war, beginning the Second World War.

To ensure Germany would not be faced with a two-front war, Hitler agreed with Stalin to divide Poland between them. Polish resistance was quickly crushed by the German combination of fast-moving armoured divisions and close air support, known as blitzkrieg (lightning war). In 1940 Germany conquered Denmark, Norway, the Netherlands, Belgium and France in just three months. France was partitioned, with German occupation of the north and a collaborationist government in the south at Vichy. France's colonies were divided between those loyal to Vichy and those loyal to the Free French government in exile.

Following France's surrender and the expulsion of British forces from the Continent, Hitler expected Britain to seek peace. However, the British government, led by Winston Churchill, resolved to continue the war. Hitler's hastily made plans to invade Britain were abandoned after the German air force was defeated in the Battle of Britain. The war widened to the Balkans and Africa after Italy joined Germany in June, forming the Axis Powers. However, the poorly equipped Italians needed to be rescued by the Germans in 1941 after suffering defeats by the Greeks and by the British in Libya and East Africa. Hitler's attempt to woo Spain's new fascist dictator Francisco Franco failed: Spain had not yet recovered from its devastating civil war.

With Britain still undefeated, Hitler turned on his former ally and invaded the USSR in June 1941, taking Stalin completely by surprise. The Germans advanced rapidly through the summer but were unprepared for the onset of the bitter Russian winter and they were fought to a halt outside Moscow in December. Despite the speed of the German advance, the USSR successfully removed much of its industrial capacity to safety beyond the Ural Mountains. Officially neutral, the USA under President Franklin D. Roosevelt gave Britain considerable material support through the Lend-Lease scheme begun in March 1941.

GREENLAND (Denmark)

CANADA

NEWFOUNDLAND (GB)

St Pierre et Miquelon

UNITED STATES OF AMERICA

1 Jamaica (GB)
2 BRITISH HONDURAS
3 Netherlands Antilles
4 Puerto Rico (USA)
5 HAITI
6 DOMINICAN REPUBLIC

Bermuda (GB)

MEXICO

Cayman Islands (GB)

Bahamas (GB)

CUBA

US Virgin Islands

British Virgin Islands
Leeward Islands (GB)
Guadeloupe (Vichy)
Dominica (GB)
Martinique (Vichy)
Windward Islands (GB)
Barbados (GB)
Trinidad & Tobago (GB)

Hawaii (USA)

GUATEMALA
EL SALVADOR
HONDURAS
NICARAGUA
COSTA RICA
PANAMA

Panama Canal Zone (US)

VENEZUELA

BRITISH GUIANA
DUTCH GUIANA
FRENCH GUIANA (Vichy)

COLOMBIA

Galapagos Islands (Ecuador)

ECUADOR

BRAZIL

French Polynesia

PERU

BOLIVIA

Pitcairn Island (GB)

PARAGUAY

C H I L E

Easter Island (Chile)

ARGENTINA

URUGUAY

Axis power or dependency mid-1942

Axis occupation mid-1942

Allied state at war with the European Axis powers

Occupied by Allied powers

Allied state at war with Japan

Maximum limit of Axis advance mid-1942

Other states and territories

Falkland Islands (GB)

150°   120°   90°   60°

NETHERLANDS **7**
(occupied)

BELGIUM **8**
(occupied)

LUXEMBOURG **9**
(occupied)

SWITZERLAND **10**

VICHY FRANCE **11**

SLOVAKIA **12**

SVALBARD
(Norway)

HUNGARY **13**

OSTLAND (Ger) **14**

UKRAINE (Ger) **15**

CROATIA **16**

SERBIA **17**

MONTENEGRO **18**

ICELAND
(Denmark)

Faroe Islands
(Denmark)

GREAT
BRITAIN

IRELAND

ALBANIA **19**

BULGARIA **20**

Dodecanese **21**
(It)

PORTUGAL

Azores

Gibraltar (GB)

Madeira

Canary
Islands

SPANISH
SAHARA

Cape
Verde
Islands

GAMBIA
(GB)

PORTUGUESE
GUINEA
(Pt)

SIERRA
LEONE
(GB)

GOLD
COAST
(GB)

LIBERIA

SPAIN

FRANCE

ITALY

MALTA
(GB)

GREECE

TUNISIA
(Vichy)

MOROCCO
(Fr)

ALGERIA
(Vichy)

LIBYA
(It)

FRENCH WEST AFRICA
(Vichy)

FRENCH
EQUATORIAL
AFRICA
(Fr)

NIGERIA
(GB)

FRENCH
CONGO (Fr)

CABINDA
(Pt)

BELGIAN
CONGO

RUANDA-
URUNDI
(Belgium)

ANGOLA
(Pt)

NORWAY

SWEDEN

FINLAND

DENMARK

GERMANY

ROMANIA

CYPRUS
(GB)

EGYPT

ANGLO-
EGYPTIAN
SUDAN

TURKEY

IRAQ

SAUDI
ARABIA

YEMEN

ADEN (GB)

Socotra
(GB)

ETHIOPIA

ITALIAN
SOMALILAND

BRITISH
EAST
AFRICA

UNION OF SOVIET SOCIALIST REPUBLICS

IRAN

AFGHANISTAN

OMAN
(GB)

TUVA

MONGOLIA

MANZHOUGUO
(Jpn)

CHINA

TIBET

NEPAL

BHUTAN

INDIA
(GB)

BURMA
(GB)

KOREA
(Jpn)

JAPAN

TAIWAN (Jpn)

Hong Kong (GB)

Macau
(Pt)

Goa (Pt)

Pondicherry
(Fr)

Mahé (Fr)

Andaman
Islands
(GB)

Maldive
Islands
(GB)

CEYLON
(GB)

Nicobar
Islands
(GB)

FRENCH
INDO-
CHINA
(Vichy)

MALAYA

PHILIPPINES
(USA)

Guam (USA)

Palau
(Jpn)

Mariana
Islands
(Jpn)

Caroline Islands
(Jpn)

Marshall
Islands
(Jpn)

Gilbert
Islands
(GB)

Nauru
(Australia)

Phoenix
Islands
(GB)

Ellice
Islands
(GB)

THAILAND **47**

SINGAPORE (GB) **48**

SARAWAK **49**

BRUNEI **50**

BRITISH NORTH BORNEO **51**

PORTUGUESE TIMOR **52**

DUTCH EAST INDIES

NORTH EAST
NEW GUINEA
(Australia)

Solomon
Islands (GB)

PAPUA
(Australia)

New
Hebrides
(Anglo-French
condominium)

New
Caledonia
(Fr)

Tonga
(GB)

Fiji (GB)

AUSTRALIA

NEW
ZEALAND

Ascension
Island
(GB)

SPANISH **22**
MOROCCO

CAMEROON (Fr) **23**

Fernando Póo (Sp) **24**

RIO MUNI (Sp) **25**

Príncipe (Pt) **26**

São Tomé (Pt) **27**

Tristan da
Cunha
(GB)

St Helena
(GB)

Walvis Bay
(South Africa)

SOUTH
AFRICA

SWAZILAND (GB)

BASUTOLAND (GB)

Seychelles
(GB)

Comoro
Islands
(Vichy)

Amirante
Islands
(GB)

Chagos
Islands
(GB)

Cocos
Islands
(GB)

Christmas
Island
(GB)

MADAGASCAR
(Vichy)
(Allied occupation
in progress)

Mauritius
(GB)

Réunion
(Vichy)

Kerguelen
Island

LEBANON (Fr) **36**

SYRIA (Fr) **37**

PALESTINE (GB) **38**

TRANSJORDAN (GB) **39**

BRITISH **40**
SOMALILAND

FRENCH **41**
SOMALILAND (Vichy)

ERITREA (It) **42**

KUWAIT (GB) **43**

BAHRAIN (GB) **44**

QATAR (GB) **45**

TRUCIAL OMAN (GB) **46**

UGANDA (GB) **28**

TANGANYIKA (GB) **29**

NORTHERN RHODESIA (GB) **30**

NYASALAND (GB) **31**

SOUTHERN RHODESIA (GB) **32**

BECHUANALAND (GB) **33**

SOUTHWEST AFRICA **34**
(South Africa)

MOZAMBIQUE (Pt) **35**

Arctic Circle

Tropic of Cancer

Equator

Tropic of Capricorn

75°

45°

45°

0° 30° 60° 90° 120° 150° 180°

1942

China received substantial American and Soviet aid and diplomatic support in its war with Japan. Fearing the consequences of a threatened US oil embargo, the Japanese planned to secure access to strategic raw materials by seizing British, French and Dutch colonial territories in Southeast Asia. To prevent American interference, the Japanese launched a surprise attack on the US Pacific Fleet at Pearl Harbor on 7 December 1941, bringing the USA into the Second World War. Germany and Italy declared war on the USA four days later.

For six months the Japanese enjoyed a spectacular run of victories, seizing the Philippines from the USA and humiliating the British by capturing their main Southeast Asian naval base at Singapore and routing them in Burma. Sensing British weakness, Indian nationalists increased their agitation for independence. Most important, the Japanese occupied the Dutch East Indies with their oilfields. In spring 1942 the Germans regained the initiative in the USSR, advancing rapidly towards the Caucasus oilfields. A German–Italian offensive in North Africa threatened British control of the Suez Canal. Earlier in 1942, Germany's Nazi leaders began to plan the war's greatest crime, the extermination of European Jews.

By the end of 1942 the Allies had begun to turn the tide of war. The British victory at El Alamein in October drove the Germans and Italians out of Egypt. Days later Anglo-American forces invaded Vichy-held Morocco and Algeria. The German army's offensive in the USSR was halted at Stalingrad in July amid bitter street fighting. A Soviet counter-offensive in November trapped nearly 300,000 Axis troops in the now ruined city: the survivors finally surrendered in February 1943.

The Japanese run of victories was halted by the USA at the naval battle of Midway, which established that the aircraft carrier, rather than the battleship, was the most important fighting unit of a battle fleet. By the end of the year, the Australians had pushed the Japanese back in New Guinea and the Americans were driving them out of the Solomon Islands.

Both sides in the Second World War put considerable resources into propaganda, using posters, the press and the popular mediums of movies and radio. Large audiences listened to Britain's BBC illegally in Nazi-dominated Europe because of its reputation for truthful reporting of events.

POLITICS & ECONOMY

1939 **1 APR** Surrender of Republican forces in Madrid ends **Spanish Civil War**: fascist dictatorship begins under Francisco Franco (to 1975).

10 JUN **Italy** declares war 1940 on France and Britain.

1939 **1 SEP** German invasion of **Poland**.

1939 **3 SEP** The UK and France declare war on Germany, beginning the **Second World War**.

1939–40 **Winter War**: Finland loses border territories after Soviet invasion.

9 APR–10 JUN German invasion of **Denmark** and **Norway**. 1940

1939 **23 AUG Molotov–Ribbentrop Pact**: Nazi–Soviet non-aggression treaty secretly agrees the partition of Poland and Soviet annexation of the Baltic states.

▲ *Finnish troops on skis in 1939 during the Winter War.*

1939 **27 MAY–3 JUN Dunkirk** evacuation of British forces from France.

10 MAY–25 JUN German invasion of **Netherlands**, **Belgium** and **France**. 1940

1939 Siam is renamed **Thailand** to celebrate its avoidance of colonial rule.

25 JUN French surrender: France divided between German 1940 military occupation and collaborationist **government at Vichy**.

23 MAR Muslim League demands the creation of **Pakistan**, a separate state for Indian Muslims. 1940

20–31 AUG Battle of **Khalkhin Gol**, Mongolia: Red 1939 Army defeats the Japanese in a border war.

1939 **17 SEP USSR** invades Poland.

1939 **3 SEPT Australia** and **New Zealand** declare war on Germany.

1939 **4 SEP South Africa** declares war on Germany.

◀ *Red Army soldiers and tank in an attack during the battle of Khalkhin Gol, 1939.*

1939 **10 SEP Canada** declares war on Germany.

RELIGION & PHILOSOPHY

SCIENCE & TECHNOLOGY

▲ *A T-34 tank from the Second World War.*

1939 Paul Müller develops the **insecticide DDT** (Switzerland).

1939 **27 AUG** First flight by a **jet-powered aircraft** (Germany).

MAR The Frisch–Peierls memorandum sets out the calculations 1940 necessary to produce an **atomic bomb** (UK).

ARTS & ARCHITECTURE

Arthur Koestler, **Darkness at Noon**, novel about Stalin's purges (UK). 1940

Ahmed Ali, *Twilight in Delhi*, Urdu novel. 1940

1939 John Steinbeck, **The Grapes of Wrath**, great novel of Depression-era America.

Viet Harlon, **The Jew Süss**, anti-Semitic movie comissioned by 1940 Nazi propaganda minister Josef Goebbels.

Jan Feb Mar Apr May Jun Jul Aug Sep Oct Nov Dec Jan Feb Mar Apr May Jun

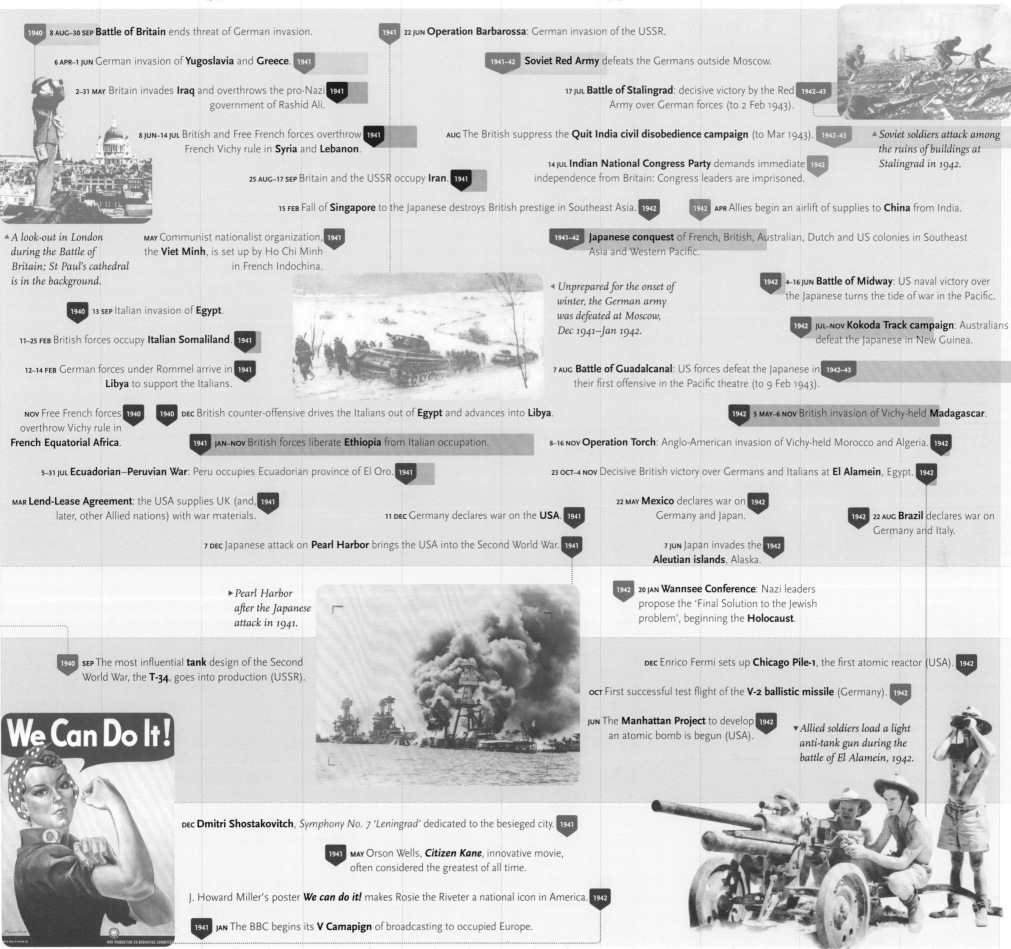

1940 8 AUG–30 SEP **Battle of Britain** ends threat of German invasion.

6 APR–1 JUN German invasion of **Yugoslavia** and **Greece**. **1941**

2–31 MAY Britain invades **Iraq** and overthrows the pro-Nazi **1941** government of Rashid Ali.

8 JUN–14 JUL British and Free French forces overthrow **1941** French Vichy rule in **Syria** and **Lebanon**.

25 AUG–17 SEP Britain and the USSR occupy **Iran**. **1941**

15 FEB Fall of **Singapore** to the Japanese destroys British prestige in Southeast Asia. **1942**

▲ *A look-out in London during the Battle of Britain; St Paul's cathedral is in the background.*

MAY Communist nationalist organization, **1941** the **Viet Minh**, is set up by Ho Chi Minh in French Indochina.

1940 13 SEP Italian invasion of **Egypt**.

11–25 FEB British forces occupy **Italian Somaliland**. **1941**

12–14 FEB German forces under Rommel arrive in **1941** **Libya** to support the Italians.

NOV Free French forces **1940** **1940** DEC British counter-offensive drives the Italians out of **Egypt** and advances into **Libya**. overthrow Vichy rule in **French Equatorial Africa**.

1941 JAN–NOV British forces liberate **Ethiopia** from Italian occupation.

5–31 JUL **Ecuadorian–Peruvian War**: Peru occupies Ecuadorian province of El Oro. **1941**

MAR **Lend-Lease Agreement**: the USA supplies UK (and, **1941** later, other Allied nations) with war materials.

11 DEC Germany declares war on the **USA**. **1941**

7 DEC Japanese attack on **Pearl Harbor** brings the USA into the Second World War. **1941**

▶ *Pearl Harbor after the Japanese attack in 1941.*

1940 SEP The most influential **tank** design of the Second World War, the **T-34**, goes into production (USSR).

We Can Do It!

DEC **Dmitri Shostakovitch**, *Symphony No. 7 'Leningrad'* dedicated to the besieged city. **1941**

1941 MAY Orson Wells, ***Citizen Kane***, innovative movie, often considered the greatest of all time.

J. Howard Miller's poster **We can do it!** makes Rosie the Riveter a national icon in America. **1942**

1941 JAN The BBC begins its **V Camapign** of broadcasting to occupied Europe.

1941 22 JUN **Operation Barbarossa**: German invasion of the USSR.

1941–42 **Soviet Red Army** defeats the Germans outside Moscow.

17 JUL **Battle of Stalingrad**: decisive victory by the Red **1942–43** Army over German forces (to 2 Feb 1943).

AUG The British suppress the **Quit India civil disobedience campaign** (to Mar 1943). **1942–43**

14 JUL **Indian National Congress Party** demands immediate **1942** independence from Britain: Congress leaders are imprisoned.

1942 APR Allies begin an airlift of supplies to **China** from India.

1941–42 **Japanese conquest** of French, British, Australian, Dutch and US colonies in Southeast Asia and Western Pacific.

◀ *Unprepared for the onset of winter, the German army was defeated at Moscow, Dec 1941–Jan 1942.*

▲ *Soviet soldiers attack among the ruins of buildings at Stalingrad in 1942.*

1942 4–16 JUN **Battle of Midway**: US naval victory over the Japanese turns the tide of war in the Pacific.

1942 JUL–NOV **Kokoda Track campaign**: Australians defeat the Japanese in New Guinea.

7 AUG **Battle of Guadalcanal**: US forces defeat the Japanese in **1942–43** their first offensive in the Pacific theatre (to 9 Feb 1943).

1942 5 MAY–6 NOV British invasion of Vichy-held **Madagascar**.

8–16 NOV **Operation Torch**: Anglo-American invasion of Vichy-held Morocco and Algeria. **1942**

23 OCT–4 NOV Decisive British victory over Germans and Italians at **El Alamein**, Egypt. **1942**

22 MAY **Mexico** declares war on **1942** Germany and Japan.

1942 22 AUG **Brazil** declares war on Germany and Italy.

7 JUN Japan invades the **1942** **Aleutian islands**, Alaska.

1942 20 JAN **Wannsee Conference**: Nazi leaders propose the 'Final Solution to the Jewish problem', beginning the **Holocaust**.

DEC Enrico Fermi sets up **Chicago Pile-1**, the first atomic reactor (USA). **1942**

OCT First successful test flight of the **V-2 ballistic missile** (Germany). **1942**

JUN The **Manhattan Project** to develop **1942** an atomic bomb is begun (USA).

▼ *Allied soldiers load a light anti-tank gun during the battle of El Alamein, 1942.*

1945

THE END OF THE SECOND WORLD WAR IN EUROPE AND THE ASIA—PACIFIC REGION

Following their defeat by the USSR at Stalingrad in the winter of 1942–43, the Germans managed to stabilize the Eastern Front. In an attempt to regain the initiative, they launched a new offensive at Kursk in July. The Soviet Red Army was prepared for the attack and defeated it in the largest tank battles of the war before launching a massive counter-offensive which forced the Germans into a steady retreat. This was only the worst of many setbacks Germany suffered in 1943, which also saw its ally Italy surrender after an Allied invasion.

In June 1944, the D-Day landings by US, British and Canadian forces in Normandy opened a full second front in Europe and began the liberation of France. In the same month, the Red Army launched its summer offensive, Operation Bagration, costing the Germans over 700,000 casualties and clearing them from Soviet soil. Finally, in 1945, Allied armies invaded Germany from east and west. Hitler committed suicide when the Red Army entered Berlin in April and, on 7 May, Germany surrendered, bringing the war in Europe to an end.

In the Pacific theatre, the US 'island-hopping' campaign took their forces ever closer to Japan, often in the face of suicidal resistance. In 1944, the British and Indian armies repulsed a Japanese invasion of India and then began to drive them out of Burma.

In June 1944, US bombers began raiding Japanese cities from China. A Japanese offensive to seize the American bases achieved big gains against the inefficient Guomindang army, which nevertheless tied down large numbers of Japanese troops. A planned Allied invasion of Japan proved unnecessary: Japan surrendered on 14 August 1945, shortly after the USA dropped the terrifyingly destructive new atomic bombs on Hiroshima and Nagasaki, and the USSR invaded Manchuria. By this time the war had cost some 60 million lives.

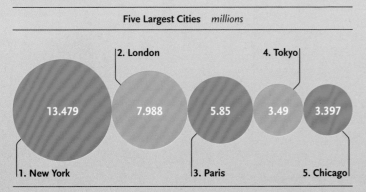

Five Largest Cities *millions*

1. New York	2. London	3. Paris	4. Tokyo	5. Chicago
13.479	7.988	5.85	3.49	3.397

GREENLAND
(Denmark)

CANADA

NEWFOUNDLAND

St Pierre et Miquelon

Chicago **5**

1 New York

UNITED STATES OF AMERICA

Bermuda

1 Jamaica
2 BRITISH HONDURAS
3 Netherlands Antilles
4 Puerto Rico
5 HAITI
6 DOMINICAN REPUBLIC

Hawaii

Cayman Islands (GB)

MEXICO

CUBA

Bahamas

US Virgin Islands

British Virgin Islands
Leeward Islands
Guadeloupe
Dominica
Martinique
Windward Islands

GUATEMALA
EL SALVADOR
HONDURAS
NICARAGUA
COSTA RICA
PANAMA

Panama Canal Zone

Barbados
Trinidad & Tobago

VENEZUELA

BRITISH GUIANA
DUTCH GUIANA
FRENCH GUIANA

COLOMBIA

ECUADOR

Galapagos Islands (Ecuador)

French Polynesia

BRAZIL

PERU

BOLIVIA

Pitcairn Island

PARAGUAY

Easter Island (Chile)

CHILE

ARGENTINA

URUGUAY

Falkland Islands

Portuguese possessions	USSR
Spanish possessions	USA and possessions
Dutch possessions	Other states and territories
British possessions	Allied occupation
French possessions	**GREAT BRITAIN** Founder member of the United Nations

NETHERLANDS 7
BELGIUM 8
LUXEMBOURG 9
SWITZERLAND 10
GERMANY 11
(Allied occupation)
AUSTRIA 12
(Allied occupation)
ICELAND
CZECHOSLOVAKIA 13

SVALBARD
(Norway)

HUNGARY 14
YUGOSLAVIA 15
ALBANIA 16
BULGARIA 17

Faroe Islands
(Denmark)

NORWAY   SWEDEN   FINLAND

UNION OF SOVIET SOCIALIST REPUBLICS

Arctic Circle

75°

GREAT
BRITAIN
IRELAND   2
London   7   11
Paris   8   3
FRANCE   9   10   12   14

DENMARK

POLAND

13

ROMANIA

ITALY   15   17

45°

PORTUGAL   SPAIN
Azores
Gibraltar
Madeira   18
MOROCCO
Canary
Islands
SPANISH
SAHARA

TUNISIA
MALTA
GREECE   TURKEY
CYPRUS   32   33
LIBYA   34   IRAQ   35
(Anglo-French   administration)
EGYPT

IRAN

MONGOLIA

EAST
TURKESTAN
REPUBLIC

COMMUNIST
CHINA

JAPAN
(US occupation)
4   Tokyo

KOREA
(US/USSR
occupation)

45°

43   THAILAND
44   SINGAPORE
45   SARAWAK
46   BRUNEI
47   BRITISH NORTH BORNEO
48   PORTUGUESE TIMOR

AFGHANISTAN

REPUBLIC OF
CHINA

TIBET

NEPAL
BHUTAN

Tropic of Cancer

ALGERIA

FRENCH WEST AFRICA

FRENCH

SAUDI
ARABIA
YEMEN

OMAN

ANGLO-
EGYPTIAN   38
SUDAN

ADEN   37
36

INDIA

BURMA

Hong Kong
Macau

PHILIPPINES

Guam
(USA)

Trust Territories
of the Pacific Islands
(USA)

Cape
Verde
Islands

EQUATORIAL

Socotra

Goa
Mahé   Pondicherry
Andaman
Islands

FRENCH
INDO-
CHINA   43

GAMBIA
PORTUGUESE
GUINEA   LIBERIA
NIGERIA
SIERRA
LEONE   GOLD
COAST
19
20
21
22
23

AFRICA
ETHIOPIA
SOMALIA
(UN Trust territory)

Maldive
Islands   CEYLON   Nicobar
Islands

MALAYA   46   47
44   45

Gilbert
Islands

Equator

BELGIAN
CONGO   24   BRITISH
EAST
AFRICA

Nauru
(Australia)

Phoenix
Islands

Ascension
Island   CABINDA

RUANDA-
URUNDI
(Belgium)

Seychelles

Chagos
Islands

DUTCH EAST INDIES   PAPUA AND
NEW GUINEA
(Australia)   Solomon
Islands

Ellice
Islands

25

ANGOLA   26

Comoro
Islands   Amirante
Islands

Cocos
Islands   Christmas
Island

48

New
Hebrides
(Anglo-French
condominium)   Tonga

SPANISH   18
MOROCCO
CAMEROON   19
Fernando Póo   20
RIO MUNI   21
Príncipe   22
São Tomé   23

St Helena
27

MADAGASCAR   Mauritius
31   Réunion

Fiji
New
Caledonia   Tropic of Capricorn

28

AUSTRALIA

29

Walvis Bay
(to South Africa)   30
SWAZILAND
SOUTH
AFRICA   BASUTOLAND

32   LEBANON
33   SYRIA
34   PALESTINE
35   TRANSJORDAN
36   BRITISH
SOMALILAND

37   FRENCH
SOMALILAND
38   ERITREA
(temporary UK administration)
39   KUWAIT
40   BAHRAIN
41   QATAR
42   TRUCIAL OMAN

Tristan da
Cunha

24   UGANDA
25   TANGANYIKA
26   NORTHERN RHODESIA
27   NYASALAND
28   SOUTHERN RHODESIA

29   BECHUANALAND
30   SOUTHWEST AFRICA
(to South Africa)
31   MOZAMBIQUE

NEW
ZEALAND

45°

Kerguelen
Island

0°   30°   60°   90°   120°   150°   180°

1945

There were many factors behind the Allied victory in the Second World War, but the most important was that the USA, Britain and the USSR possessed a far greater combined industrial capacity and were all far more effective at mobilizing their economies for war than any of the Axis Powers. Both sides made major technological advances during the war, such as the first operational jet fighter aircraft by Britain and Germany; the first cruise missiles and long-range ballistic missiles by Germany; and the first electronic computers, used by Allied code breakers. The development of atomic weapons by the USA left it the world's unchallenged military superpower.

Allied planning for the post-war period included the setting up of the United Nations Organization in June 1945 as a more effective replacement for the League of Nations to promote international cooperation and prevent wars. The International Monetary Fund and the World Bank were created in 1944 to promote international economic cooperation.

Summit meetings of the 'Big Three' – Roosevelt, Churchill and Stalin – decided the borders of postwar Europe. The USSR kept the Baltic States and the Polish territory it had gained through its pact with Hitler, and Poland was compensated with German territory. Germany and Austria were divided into US, Soviet, British and French occupation zones. The former Italian colonies in Africa were occupied by Britain and France. Japan was occupied by the USA and its former dependency of Korea was divided into US and Soviet occupation zones. Japan's half of Sakhalin, as well as the Kuril islands, were seized by the USSR. The Soviet forces which had driven the Japanese out of Manchuria remained in occupation to allow the Chinese Communist People's Liberation Army to move into the area.

World Population

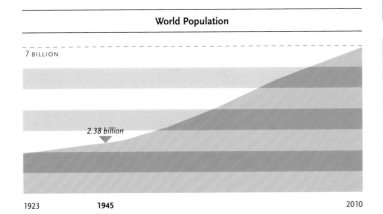

7 BILLION

2.38 billion

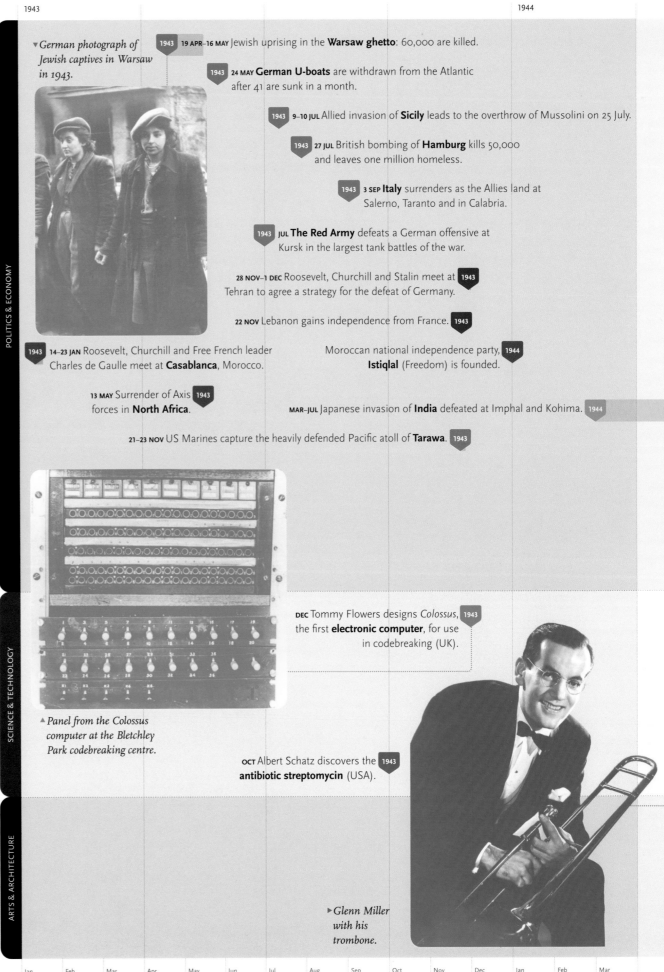

POLITICS & ECONOMY

▼ German photograph of Jewish captives in Warsaw in 1943.

1943 19 APR–16 MAY Jewish uprising in the **Warsaw ghetto**: 60,000 are killed.

1943 24 MAY **German U-boats** are withdrawn from the Atlantic after 41 are sunk in a month.

1943 9–10 JUL Allied invasion of **Sicily** leads to the overthrow of Mussolini on 25 July.

1943 27 JUL British bombing of **Hamburg** kills 50,000 and leaves one million homeless.

1943 3 SEP **Italy** surrenders as the Allies land at Salerno, Taranto and in Calabria.

1943 JUL **The Red Army** defeats a German offensive at Kursk in the largest tank battles of the war.

28 NOV–1 DEC Roosevelt, Churchill and Stalin meet at **1943** Tehran to agree a strategy for the defeat of Germany.

22 NOV Lebanon gains independence from France. **1943**

1943 14–23 JAN Roosevelt, Churchill and Free French leader Charles de Gaulle meet at **Casablanca**, Morocco.

Moroccan national independence party, **1944** **Istiqlal** (Freedom) is founded.

13 MAY Surrender of Axis **1943** forces in **North Africa**.

MAR–JUL Japanese invasion of **India** defeated at Imphal and Kohima. **1944**

21–23 NOV US Marines capture the heavily defended Pacific atoll of **Tarawa**. **1943**

SCIENCE & TECHNOLOGY

DEC Tommy Flowers designs *Colossus*, **1943** the first **electronic computer**, for use in codebreaking (UK).

▲ Panel from the Colossus computer at the Bletchley Park codebreaking centre.

OCT Albert Schatz discovers the **1943** **antibiotic streptomycin** (USA).

ARTS & ARCHITECTURE

▶ Glenn Miller with his trombone.

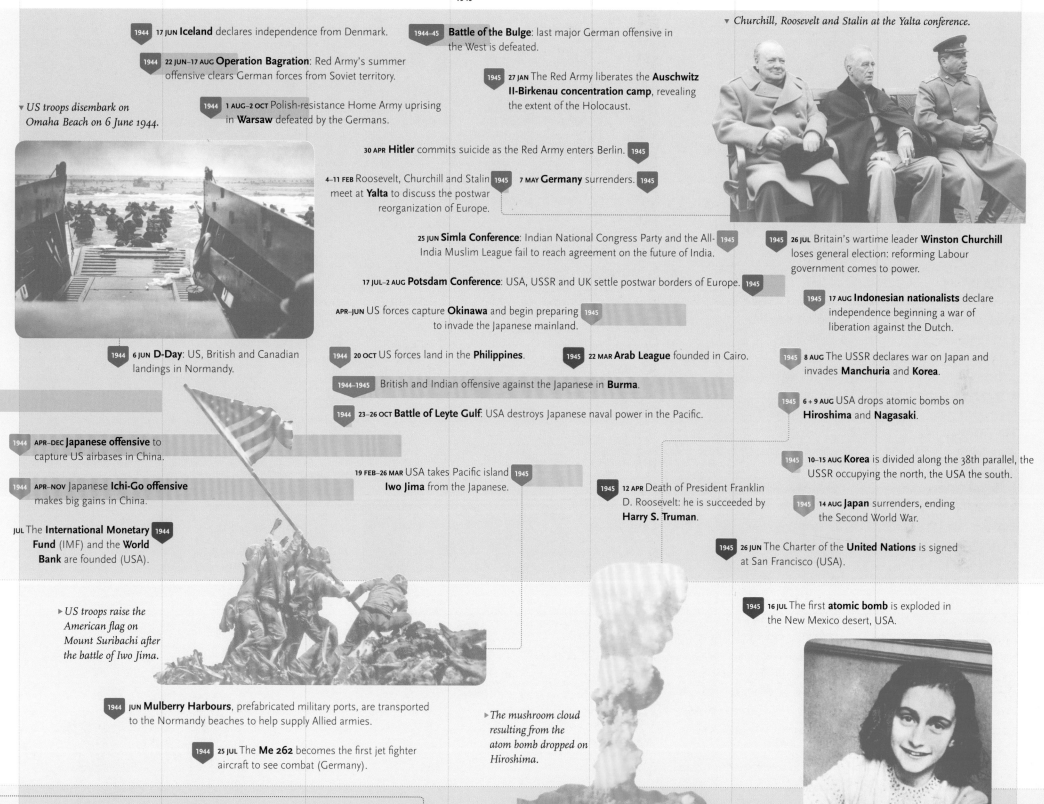

1944 17 JUN **Iceland** declares independence from Denmark.

1944 22 JUN–17 AUG **Operation Bagration**: Red Army's summer offensive clears German forces from Soviet territory.

1944 1 AUG–2 OCT Polish-resistance Home Army uprising in **Warsaw** defeated by the Germans.

1944–45 **Battle of the Bulge**: last major German offensive in the West is defeated.

1945 27 JAN The Red Army liberates the **Auschwitz II-Birkenau concentration camp**, revealing the extent of the Holocaust.

▼ *Churchill, Roosevelt and Stalin at the Yalta conference.*

▼ *US troops disembark on Omaha Beach on 6 June 1944.*

30 APR **Hitler** commits suicide as the Red Army enters Berlin. **1945**

4–11 FEB Roosevelt, Churchill and Stalin **1945** meet at **Yalta** to discuss the postwar reorganization of Europe.

7 MAY **Germany** surrenders. **1945**

25 JUN **Simla Conference**: Indian National Congress Party and the All-India Muslim League fail to reach agreement on the future of India. **1945**

1945 26 JUL Britain's wartime leader **Winston Churchill** loses general election: reforming Labour government comes to power.

17 JUL–2 AUG **Potsdam Conference**: USA, USSR and UK settle postwar borders of Europe. **1945**

APR–JUN US forces capture **Okinawa** and begin preparing **1945** to invade the Japanese mainland.

1945 17 AUG **Indonesian nationalists** declare independence beginning a war of liberation against the Dutch.

1944 6 JUN **D-Day**: US, British and Canadian landings in Normandy.

1944 20 OCT US forces land in the **Philippines**.

1945 22 MAR **Arab League** founded in Cairo.

1945 8 AUG The USSR declares war on Japan and invades **Manchuria** and **Korea**.

1944–1945 British and Indian offensive against the Japanese in **Burma**.

1944 23–26 OCT **Battle of Leyte Gulf**: USA destroys Japanese naval power in the Pacific.

1945 6 + 9 AUG USA drops atomic bombs on **Hiroshima** and **Nagasaki**.

1944 APR–DEC **Japanese offensive** to capture US airbases in China.

19 FEB–26 MAR USA takes Pacific island **1945** **Iwo Jima** from the Japanese.

1945 12 APR Death of President Franklin D. Roosevelt: he is succeeded by **Harry S. Truman**.

1945 10–15 AUG **Korea** is divided along the 38th parallel, the USSR occupying the north, the USA the south.

1944 APR–NOV Japanese **Ichi-Go offensive** makes big gains in China.

1945 14 AUG **Japan** surrenders, ending the Second World War.

JUL The **International Monetary Fund** (IMF) and the **World Bank** are founded (USA). **1944**

1945 26 JUN The Charter of the **United Nations** is signed at San Francisco (USA).

▶ *US troops raise the American flag on Mount Suribachi after the battle of Iwo Jima.*

1945 16 JUL The first **atomic bomb** is exploded in the New Mexico desert, USA.

1944 JUN **Mulberry Harbours**, prefabricated military ports, are transported to the Normandy beaches to help supply Allied armies.

▶ *The mushroom cloud resulting from the atom bomb dropped on Hiroshima.*

1944 25 JUL The **Me 262** becomes the first jet fighter aircraft to see combat (Germany).

15 DEC American swing bandleader **Glenn Miller** **1944** disappears on a flight across the English Channel.

MAR Death in Bergen-Belsen concentration camp of **Anne Frank** **1945** (b. 1929): her secret diary published as *Diary of a Young Girl* (1947).

AUG George Orwell, ***Animal Farm***, allegorical novel about the rise of Stalin. **1945**

▲ *Anne Frank in 1941.*

Apr   May   Jun   Jul   Aug   Sep   Oct   Nov   Dec   Jan   Feb   Mar   Apr   May   Jun   Jul   Aug   Sep   Oct   Nov   Dec

1950

THE COLD WAR AND THE RISE OF ANTI-COLONIALISM AND COMMUNISM IN ASIA

The immediate postwar period saw the beginning of the Cold War, a political, ideological, economic and military confrontation between the USA (with its allies) and the USSR (with its allies) that dominated global politics until 1991. The USA and USSR avoided direct conflict, but the Cold War was often waged through proxy wars fought out across Latin America, Africa and Southeast Asia.

The Second World War ended with Soviet forces in occupation of most of Eastern Europe. Suspicious of the Western allies, Stalin was not prepared to give up this advantageous position. Communist dictatorships were imposed on Czechoslovakia, Poland, Hungary, Romania, Bulgaria and East Germany, thus bringing down a so-called Iron Curtain between East and West. Communist regimes also seized power in Yugoslavia and Albania. The USA responded with a policy of containing Soviet influence and giving financial aid to rebuild the economies of Western Europe. Collective security against possible Soviet invasion was provided by the US-led alliance, set up in 1949 under the North Atlantic Treaty Organization (NATO). Later the same year the USSR exploded an atom bomb, thus achieving apparent military parity with the USA.

The USSR supported the Communist People's Liberation Army (PLA) against the Guomindang government in the Chinese civil war. In October 1949 the victorious Communist leader Mao Zedong proclaimed the foundation of the People's Republic of China. The Guomindang fled to Taiwan, followed by around two million refugees. Mao set about restoring the borders of the Qing empire by conquering Tibet in 1950, but the USSR refused to sanction Chinese reoccupation of Mongolia, which remained a Soviet satellite state. When the Soviet-backed Communist government of North Korea invaded South Korea in 1950, the UN authorized a US-led military intervention, beginning the Korean War.

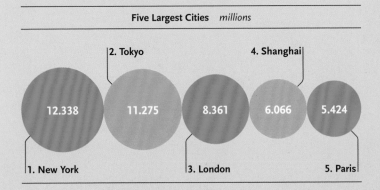

Five Largest Cities *millions*

2. Tokyo — 11.275
4. Shanghai — 8.361
1. New York — 12.338
3. London — 6.066
5. Paris — 5.424

GREENLAND
(Denmark)

CANADA

UNITED STATES OF AMERICA

St Pierre et Miquelon

1 New York

Bermuda

1 Jamaica
2 BRITISH HONDURAS
3 Netherlands Antilles
4 Puerto Rico
5 HAITI
6 DOMINICAN REPUBLIC

Cayman Islands (UK)

MEXICO

Bahamas

CUBA

US Virgin Islands

British Virgin Islands
Leeward Islands
Guadeloupe
Dominica
Martinique
Windward Islands

Hawaii

GUATEMALA
EL SALVADOR
HONDURAS
NICARAGUA
COSTA RICA
PANAMA

Panama Canal Zone

Barbados
Trinidad & Tobago

VENEZUELA

BRITISH GUIANA
DUTCH GUIANA
FRENCH GUIANA

COLOMBIA

Galapagos Islands (Ecuador)

ECUADOR

French Polynesia

BRAZIL

PERU

Pitcairn Island

BOLIVIA

PARAGUAY

CHILE

Easter Island (Chile)

ARGENTINA

URUGUAY

Legend

- Portuguese possessions
- Spanish possessions
- Dutch possessions
- British (UK) possessions
- French possessions
- USSR and client states
- Other communist states
- USA and possessions
- Other states and territories
- Member of NATO

Falkland Islands

150°   120°   90°   60°

NETHERLANDS 7
BELGIUM 8
LUXEMBOURG 9
SWITZERLAND 10
WEST GERMANY 11
AUSTRIA 12
EAST GERMANY 13
CZECHOSLOVAKIA 14

SVALBARD
(Norway)

HUNGARY 15
YUGOSLAVIA 16
ALBANIA 17
BULGARIA 18

75°

Arctic Circle

ICELAND

Faroe Islands
(Denmark)

NORWAY
SWEDEN
FINLAND

UNION OF SOVIET SOCIALIST REPUBLICS

UNITED
KINGDOM
DENMARK

IRELAND   3   7
London   8   13   POLAND
              9
5   11
Paris
10   12   14
FRANCE   15   ROMANIA
            16
            18
         17   GREECE
PORTUGAL   SPAIN
Azores
Gibraltar
Madeira   MALTA   CYPRUS
                              33   34
                                 36
                         35

MONGOLIA

NORTH
KOREA
SOUTH
KOREA

JAPAN
2   Tokyo

44   THAILAND
45   SINGAPORE
46   SARAWAK
47   BRUNEI
48   BRITISH NORTH BORNEO
49   PORTUGUESE TIMOR

TURKEY
19   TUNISIA
MOROCCO
Canary
Islands
SPANISH
SAHARA
ALGERIA
LIBYA
(Anglo-French
administration)
EGYPT
IRAQ
IRAN
AFGHANISTAN
PAKISTAN
40   41
42
43
SAUDI
ARABIA
OMAN
YEMEN
NEPAL
BHUTAN
PAKISTAN
INDIA
BURMA
PEOPLE'S
REPUBLIC OF
CHINA
Shanghai
4
REPUBLIC OF
CHINA
Macau   Hong Kong

Tropic of Cancer

Cape
Verde
Islands
GAMBIA
PORTUGUESE
GUINEA
FRENCH WEST AFRICA
FRENCH
EQUATORIAL
AFRICA
ANGLO-
EGYPTIAN
SUDAN
39
ADEN
38
37
Socotra
Goa
Mahé
Pondicherry
Andaman
Islands
(India)
Maldive
Islands
CEYLON
Nicobar
Islands
(India)
44
FRENCH
INDO-
CHINA
PHILIPPINES
Guam
(USA)
Trust Territories of
the Pacific Islands
(USA)

LIBERIA
SIERRA
LEONE
GOLD
COAST
NIGERIA
20
21
23
24
22
CABINDA
BELGIAN
CONGO
RUANDA-
URUNDI
(Belgium)
ETHIOPIA
25
BRITISH
EAST
AFRICA
SOMALIA
(UN Trust territory)
MALAYA
47   48
45
46
Gilbert
Islands
Nauru
(Australia)
Phoenix
Islands

Ascension
Island
26
DUTCH
NEW
GUINEA
PAPUA AND
NEW GUINEA
(Australia)
Solomon
Islands
Ellice
Islands

Equator

SPANISH
MOROCCO 19
CAMEROON 20
Fernando Póo 21
RIO MUNI 21
Príncipe 23
São Tomé 24

St Helena
ANGOLA
27
28
29
30
Comoro
Islands
MADAGASCAR
Seychelles
Amirante
Islands
Chagos
Islands
Cocos
Islands
Christmas
Island
49
INDONESIA
New
Hebrides
(Anglo-French
condominium)
New
Caledonia
Fiji
Tonga

Mauritius
AUSTRALIA
Tropic of Capricorn

Walvis Bay
(to South Africa)
31
SWAZILAND
32
Réunion

Tristan da
Cunha
SOUTH
AFRICA
BASUTOLAND

33   LEBANON
34   SYRIA
35   ISRAEL
36   JORDAN
37   BRITISH
      SOMALILAND

38   FRENCH
      SOMALILAND
39   ERITREA
      (temporary UK administration)
40   KUWAIT
41   BAHRAIN
42   QATAR
43   TRUCIAL OMAN

NEW
ZEALAND
45°

25   UGANDA
26   TANGANYIKA
27   NORTHERN RHODESIA
28   NYASALAND
29   SOUTHERN RHODESIA

30   BECHUANALAND
31   SOUTHWEST AFRICA
      (to South Africa)
32   MOZAMBIQUE

Kerguelen
Island

0°   30°   60°   90°   120°   150°   180°

1950

The Second World War left the main European colonial powers severely weakened and facing a rising tide of nationalism across Asia and Africa. France, desperate to restore its prestige after the humiliation of German occupation, committed to a long war against the communist Viet Minh insurgents in Indochina, while trying to bind its African colonies more tightly in a French Union. The Netherlands fought to regain control of the East Indies from an Indonesian nationalist movement that had declared independence after Japan's defeat, only to recognize Indonesia's independence in 1949.

Britain, bankrupted by the war, accepted that its position in India was untenable: unable to count on the loyalty of the Indian army and civil service, and facing escalating violence between Hindus and Muslims, it decided on a quick withdrawal. India became independent in 1947, having been partitioned to create the separate Muslim state of Pakistan. Partition was marked by communal violence as Hindus fled Pakistan and Muslims fled India. Less than three months later, India and Pakistan fought an inconclusive war over the northern territory of Kashmir. Ceylon and Burma gained their independence from Britain in 1948. The USA gave its only significant colonial possession, the Philippines, its independence in 1946.

Decolonization also proceeded apace in the Middle East: Lebanon had become independent from France during the war and Syria followed in 1946; Britain recognized Jordan's independence in the same year. Britain struggled to carry out a UN plan to partition Palestine into separate Jewish and Arab states. Unable to control immigration of Jewish Holocaust survivors from Europe, and attacked by both Jewish and Arab terrorists, Britain withdrew in 1948. Jewish settlers proclaimed the state of Israel, immediately defeating an attempt by the Arab states to expel them.

World Population

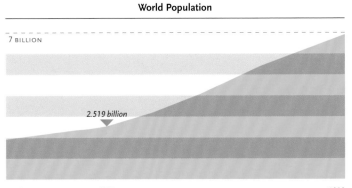

7 BILLION

2.519 billion

1923   1950   2010

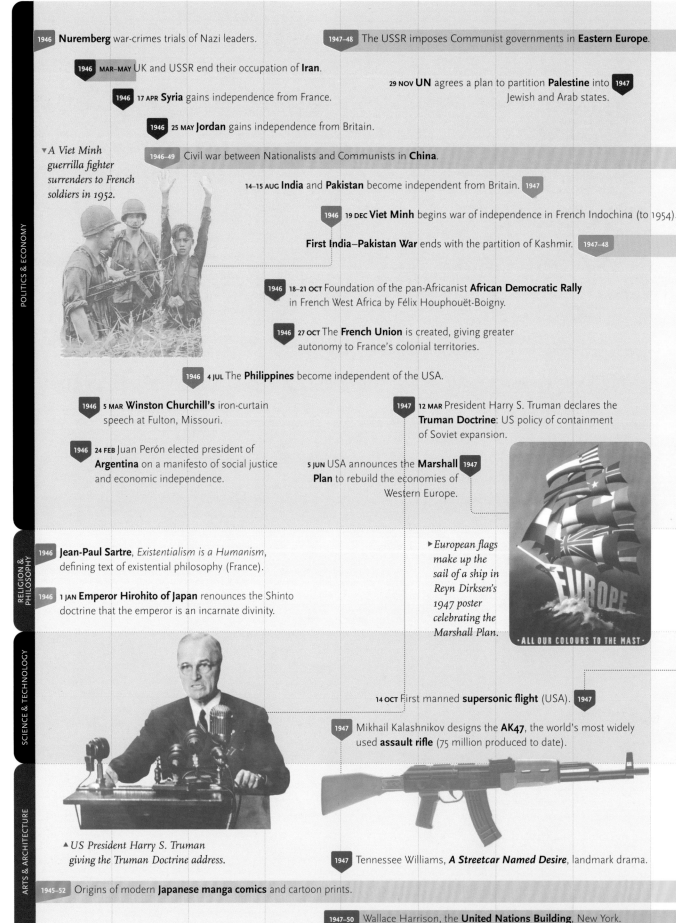

1946   1947

POLITICS & ECONOMY

1946 **Nuremberg** war-crimes trials of Nazi leaders.

1947–48 The USSR imposes Communist governments in **Eastern Europe**.

1946 **MAR–MAY** UK and USSR end their occupation of **Iran**.

29 NOV **UN** agrees a plan to partition **Palestine** into Jewish and Arab states. **1947**

1946 **17 APR** **Syria** gains independence from France.

1946 **25 MAY** **Jordan** gains independence from Britain.

1946–49 Civil war between Nationalists and Communists in **China**.

▼ *A Viet Minh guerrilla fighter surrenders to French soldiers in 1952.*

14–15 AUG **India** and **Pakistan** become independent from Britain. **1947**

1946 **19 DEC** **Viet Minh** begins war of independence in French Indochina (to 1954).

First India–Pakistan War ends with the partition of Kashmir. **1947–48**

1946 **18–21 OCT** Foundation of the pan-Africanist **African Democratic Rally** in French West Africa by Félix Houphouët-Boigny.

1946 **27 OCT** The **French Union** is created, giving greater autonomy to France's colonial territories.

1946 **4 JUL** The **Philippines** become independent of the USA.

1946 **5 MAR** **Winston Churchill's** iron-curtain speech at Fulton, Missouri.

1947 **12 MAR** President Harry S. Truman declares the **Truman Doctrine**: US policy of containment of Soviet expansion.

1946 **24 FEB** Juan Perón elected president of **Argentina** on a manifesto of social justice and economic independence.

5 JUN USA announces the **Marshall Plan** to rebuild the economies of Western Europe. **1947**

RELIGION & PHILOSOPHY

1946 **Jean-Paul Sartre**, *Existentialism is a Humanism*, defining text of existential philosophy (France).

1946 **1 JAN** **Emperor Hirohito of Japan** renounces the Shinto doctrine that the emperor is an incarnate divinity.

▶ *European flags make up the sail of a ship in Reyn Dirksen's 1947 poster celebrating the Marshall Plan.*

SCIENCE & TECHNOLOGY

14 OCT First manned **supersonic flight** (USA). **1947**

1947 Mikhail Kalashnikov designs the **AK47**, the world's most widely used **assault rifle** (75 million produced to date).

ARTS & ARCHITECTURE

▲ *US President Harry S. Truman giving the Truman Doctrine address.*

1947 Tennessee Williams, ***A Streetcar Named Desire***, landmark drama.

1945–52 Origins of modern **Japanese manga comics** and cartoon prints.

1947–50 Wallace Harrison, the **United Nations Building**, New York.

Jan   Feb   Mar   Apr   May   Jun   Jul   Aug   Sep   Oct   Nov   Dec   Jan   Feb   Mar   Apr   May   Jun   Jul   Aug   Sep   Oct   Nov   Dec

1948–49 Berlin Airlift breaks a Soviet blockade of **West Berlin**.

1949 OCT The **German Democratic Republic** (GDR) is created in the Soviet zone of occupation.

1949 4 APR The Treaty of Brussels sets up the **North Atlantic Treaty Organization** (NATO).

1949 JAN USSR creates **Comecon** to integrate the economies of Eastern Europe.

1949 SEP The **USSR** explodes its **first atomic bomb**, in Central Asia.

1949 1 OCT The victorious Communists under **Mao Zedong** proclaim the People's Republic of China.

1949 10 DEC Chinese Nationalists under **Jiang Jieshi** withdraw to Taiwan.

25 JUN Communist troops from North Korea invade **1950** South Korea, beginning the **Korean War** (to 1953).

▲ *Berliners celebrate the arrival of supplies in Allied aircraft.*

1948 14 MAY Proclamation of the state of **Israel**.

1950 The **Population Registration Act** begins the imposition of apartheid in South Africa.

1948–49 **First Arab–Israeli War** (War of Israeli Independence).

▶ *Joe One, the first Soviet test of an atomic bomb.*

1949 27 DEC **Indonesia** gains independence from the Netherlands under Sukarno.

OCT China invades and conquers **Tibet**. **1950**

1948 4 FEB **Ceylon** gains independence from the UK.

1948 30 JAN **Gandhi** is assassinated by a Hindu nationalist (India).

◀ *Mao Zedong proclaims the Peocple's Republic of China in 1949.*

1948 4 JAN **Burma** gains independence from the UK.

1948 SEP–NOV **Liaoning-Shenyang campaign**: Communists win control of Manchuria.

1949 31 JAN The **People's Liberation Army** (PLA) captures Beijing.

1948 4 JUN Afrikaner (Boer) dominated National Party wins power in **South Africa**.

1948 30 APR **Organization of American States** (OAS) founded to oppose communism in the Americas.

1948 12 MAR–24 APR Civil war in **Costa Rica** results in the abolition of the army.

1949 31 MAR **Newfoundland** joins Canada.

▲ *President Sukarno gives a speech in 1946.*

6062

1949 Gilbert Ryle, **The Concept of Mind**, rejects body–mind dualism (UK).

12 AUG Papal encyclical *Humani generis*: **Pius XII** accepts that the **1950** theory of evolution explains the biological origins of humanity.

◀ *The Bell X1, first plane to break the sound barrier.*

1949 27 JUL First flight of the **De Havilland Comet**, the first passenger jet; in service from 1952 (UK).

1948 JUN The **transistor radio** is demonstrated at Bell Laboratories (USA).

1948 **Alfred Kinsey**, *Sexual Behaviour in the Human Male*, controversial study of human sexuality.

MR. TRUMAN TAKE Sim OFF the American dollar

◀ *A 1956 Regency TR-1 transistor radio.*

1949 **George Orwell**, *1984*, dystopian novel set in a totalitarian future.

1949 **Simone de Beauvoir**, *The Second Sex*, major work of feminist literature (France).

▶ *Paul Robeson pickets the White House in 1949 in protest over discrimination in employment.*

African-American singer and actor **Paul Robeson** has his passport cancelled and is **1950** isolated from the US media because of his socialist and anti-racist views.

1962

THE WINDS OF CHANGE: THE EUROPEAN RETREAT FROM AFRICA

The dissolution of the European colonial empires gathered pace after 1950 and, by 1962, they were reduced mostly to small island territories. France's Indochinese empire was dissolved in 1954 after the decisive Viet Minh victory at Dien Bien Phu. France fought hard to retain control of Algeria, which had a large French population, but conceded defeat there also in 1962.

Britain began to give its African colonies independence in 1957. Portugal, Europe's oldest colonial power, showed no willingness to part from its colonies, but wars of independence broke out in Angola and Mozambique in 1961; India seized Goa in the same year. Nothing symbolized the decline of the European colonial powers so much as the failed Anglo-French intervention in Egypt after it nationalized the Suez Canal in 1956.

The Korean War, the first proxy war of the Cold War, ground to a stalemate in 1951 after the People's Republic of China intervened on behalf of North Korea. A ceasefire was finally agreed in 1953. The war led the USA to increase support for anti-communist regimes in Asia, such as the Guomindang in Taiwan and the government of South Vietnam which opposed the Communist Viet Minh in North Vietnam.

The USA gave uncritical support to repressive right-wing regimes in Latin America, but nevertheless failed to prevent a Communist government under Fidel Castro winning power in Cuba. When the USSR attempted to site armed nuclear missiles in Cuba in 1962 the USA threatened military retaliation. The world seemed to be on the brink of a nuclear war until the USSR backed down. In 1955 the USSR had created its own equivalent to NATO by enrolling its European satellites in the Warsaw Pact military alliance. Its first military action was the crushing of an anti-Soviet uprising in Hungary in 1956.

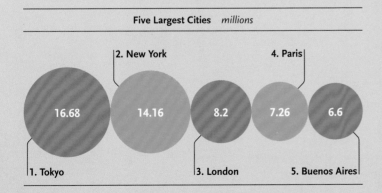

Five Largest Cities *millions*

16.68	14.16	8.2	7.26	6.6
1. Tokyo	2. New York / 1. Tokyo	3. London	4. Paris / 3. London	5. Buenos Aires

GREENLAND (Denmark)

CANADA

UNITED STATES OF AMERICA

New York

2

St Pierre et Miquelon

1 JAMAICA
2 Cayman Islands
3 BRITISH HONDURAS
4 Netherlands Antilles
5 Puerto Rico
6 HAITI
7 DOMINICAN REPUBLIC

Bermuda

Bahamas

MEXICO

Hawaii

CUBA

US Virgin Islands

British Virgin Islands
Leeward Islands
Guadeloupe
Dominica
Martinique
Windward Islands
Barbados

GUATEMALA
EL SALVADOR
HONDURAS
NICARAGUA
COSTA RICA
PANAMA

Panama Canal Zone

VENEZUELA

TRINIDAD & TOBAGO
BRITISH GUIANA
DUTCH GUIANA
FRENCH GUIANA

COLOMBIA

Galapagos Islands (Ecuador)

ECUADOR

BRAZIL

PERU

French Polynesia

BOLIVIA

Pitcairn Island

PARAGUAY

Easter Island (Chile)

CHILE

Buenos Aires
ARGENTINA

5

URUGUAY

Falkland Islands

Portuguese possessions

Spanish possessions

Dutch possessions

British (UK) possessions

French possessions

USSR and client states

Other communist states

USA and possessions

Other states and territories

Member of NATO

150°   120°   90°   60°

NETHERLANDS 8
BELGIUM 9
LUXEMBOURG 10
SWITZERLAND 11
WEST GERMANY 12
AUSTRIA 13
EAST GERMANY 14
CZECHOSLOVAKIA 15

SVALBARD
(Norway)

HUNGARY 16
YUGOSLAVIA 17
ALBANIA 18
BULGARIA 19

ICELAND

Faroe Islands
(Denmark)

NORWAY
SWEDEN
FINLAND

UNION OF SOVIET SOCIALIST REPUBLICS

Arctic Circle

UNITED
KINGDOM
IRELAND

DENMARK

London 3
Paris 4

FRANCE

PORTUGAL SPAIN

Azores

Madeira

Gibraltar
Ceuta
Melilla

Canary
Islands

SPANISH
SAHARA

Cape
Verde
Islands

SENEGAL
GAMBIA
PORTUGUESE
GUINEA

SIERRA LIBERIA
LEONE

Ascension
Island

UPPER VOLTA 20
GUINEA 21
IVORY COAST 22
TOGO 23
DAHOMEY 24

Fernando Póo 25
RIO MUNI 26
Príncipe 27
São Tomé 28

Tristan da
Cunha

8
9
10
11
12
14
15
13
16

POLAND

ROMANIA

ITALY
17
18
19

GREECE TURKEY

MALTA

TUNISIA

MOROCCO

ALGERIA LIBYA

MAURITANIA

MALI NIGER

GHANA

20

21

22

24

23

25
27
28

26

31

GABON
CABINDA

KATANGA

ANGOLA

Walvis Bay
(to South Africa)

29

30

CHAD

NIGERIA

REPUBLIC
OF
CONGO

RWANDA
BURUNDI

32

33

34

35

37

36

SOUTH
AFRICA

38

CYPRUS

40

42

41

43

44 46

47

48

SAUDI
ARABIA

YEMEN

EGYPT

SUDAN

45

ADEN

ETHIOPIA

SOMALIA

BRITISH
EAST
AFRICA

IRAQ

IRAN AFGHANISTAN

PAKISTAN

OMAN

Socotra

Seychelles

Comoro
Islands

Amirante
Islands

MADAGASCAR

Mauritius

Réunion

BHUTAN
NEPAL

PAKISTAN

INDIA

BURMA

Maldive
Islands

CEYLON

Andaman
Islands
(India)

Nicobar
Islands
(India)

Chagos
Islands

Cocos
Islands
(Australia)

MONGOLIA

PEOPLE'S
REPUBLIC OF
CHINA

NORTH
KOREA
SOUTH
KOREA

JAPAN
1
Tokyo

THAILAND 49
LAOS 50
NORTH VIETNAM 51
SINGAPORE 52
SARAWAK 53
BRUNEI 54
NORTH BORNEO 55
PORTUGUESE TIMOR 56

REPUBLIC OF
CHINA
Hong Kong
Macau

Tropic of Cancer

50 51

49

SOUTH
VIETNAM

CAMBODIA

54 55

MALAYA

52 53

PHILIPPINES

Guam
(USA)

INDONESIA

Christmas
Island
(Australia)

DUTCH
NEW
GUINEA

Trust Territories of
the Pacific Islands
(USA)

Gilbert
Islands

Nauru
(Australia)

Equator

Phoenix
Islands

PAPUA AND
NEW GUINEA
(Australia)

Solomon
Islands

Ellice
Islands

56

New
Hebrides
(Anglo-French
condominium)

New
Caledonia

Tonga

Fiji

Tropic of Capricorn

AUSTRALIA

NEW
ZEALAND

45°

St Helena

40 LEBANON
41 SYRIA
42 ISRAEL
43 JORDAN
44 KUWAIT

45 FRENCH
SOMALILAND
46 BAHRAIN
47 QATAR
48 TRUCIAL OMAN

29 CAMEROON
30 CENTRAL AFRICAN
REPUBLIC
31 CONGO
32 UGANDA
33 TANGANYIKA

34 NORTHERN RHODESIA
35 NYASALAND
36 SOUTHERN RHODESIA
37 BECHUANALAND
38 SOUTHWEST AFRICA
(to South Africa)
39 MOZAMBIQUE

SWAZILAND

BASUTOLAND

Kerguelen
Island

75°

45°

1962

The 1950s was a time of unparalleled affluence for ordinary Americans. US industry emerged from the Second World War completely undamaged by enemy bombing and was quickly turned from armaments to production of consumer goods. Car ownership became widespread and a television became the focus of every living room. America remained a conservative and racially segregated society, but established values were challenged by a rebellious youth culture, whose music and fashions were adopted worldwide.

Western Europeans experienced rising affluence in this decade too, as their economies recovered from the effects of war. In 1957, France, West Germany, Italy, the Netherlands, Belgium and Luxembourg began to integrate their economies in a single market area by founding the European Economic Community (EEC), the forerunner of today's European Union. The economies of communist Eastern Europe and the USSR grew more slowly, yet there was limited easing of political repression after Stalin's death in 1953. The USSR's achievements in putting the first artificial satellite in orbit in 1957 and the first man in orbit in 1961 challenged American technological leadership. Japan also recovered from the war and by 1960 had begun a period of rapid industrial expansion. The Chinese economy, however, went backwards as a result of Mao's disastrous communalization of industry and agriculture in his Great Leap Forward programme, begun in 1958.

While breakthroughs in nuclear and space technology grabbed the headlines, the most far-reaching scientific development of the period was the introduction of the oral contraceptive pill in 1960, which gave women effective control over their fertility. The social and economic consequences of this included a revolution in sexual behaviour and a great increase in women's participation in higher education and the labour market.

World Population

7 BILLION

3.155 billion

1923   **1962**   2010

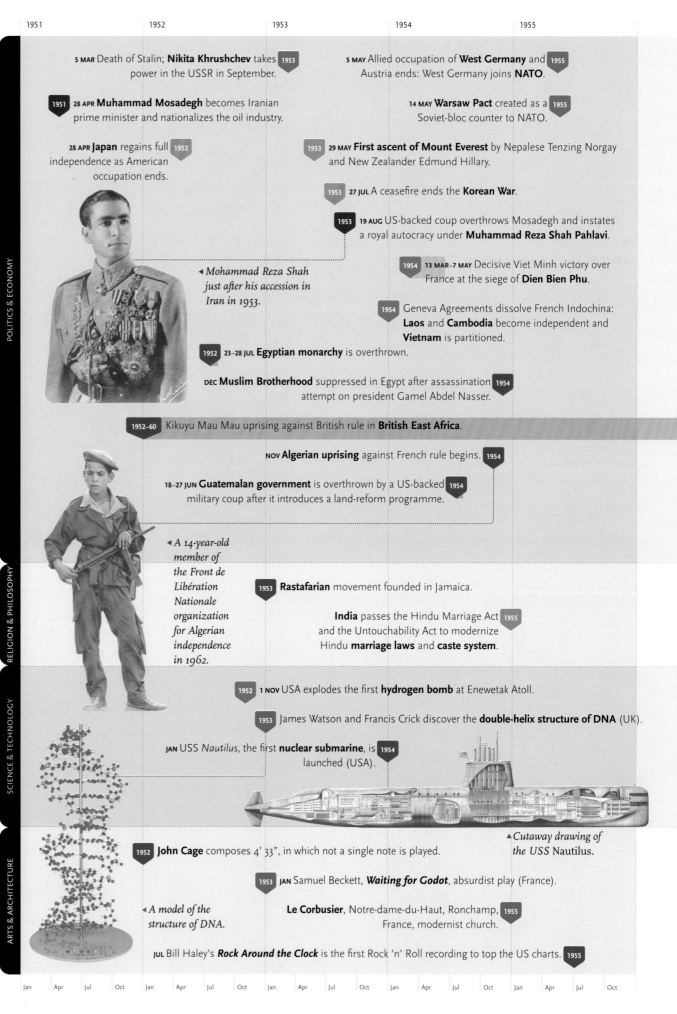

1951   1952   1953   1954   1955

5 MAR Death of Stalin; **Nikita Khrushchev** takes power in the USSR in September. `1953`

5 MAY Allied occupation of **West Germany** and Austria ends: West Germany joins **NATO**. `1955`

`1951` **28 APR** **Muhammad Mosadegh** becomes Iranian prime minister and nationalizes the oil industry.

14 MAY **Warsaw Pact** created as a Soviet-bloc counter to NATO. `1955`

28 APR **Japan** regains full independence as American occupation ends. `1952`

`1953` **29 MAY** **First ascent of Mount Everest** by Nepalese Tenzing Norgay and New Zealander Edmund Hillary.

`1953` **27 JUL** A ceasefire ends the **Korean War**.

`1953` **19 AUG** US-backed coup overthrows Mosadegh and instates a royal autocracy under **Muhammad Reza Shah Pahlavi**.

◄ *Mohammad Reza Shah just after his accession in Iran in 1953.*

`1954` **13 MAR–7 MAY** Decisive Viet Minh victory over France at the siege of **Dien Bien Phu**.

`1954` Geneva Agreements dissolve French Indochina: **Laos** and **Cambodia** become independent and **Vietnam** is partitioned.

`1952` **23–28 JUL** **Egyptian monarchy** is overthrown.

DEC **Muslim Brotherhood** suppressed in Egypt after assassination attempt on president Gamel Abdel Nasser. `1954`

`1952–60` Kikuyu Mau Mau uprising against British rule in **British East Africa**.

NOV **Algerian uprising** against French rule begins. `1954`

18–27 JUN **Guatemalan government** is overthrown by a US-backed `1954` military coup after it introduces a land-reform programme.

◄ *A 14-year-old member of the Front de Libération Nationale organization for Algerian independence in 1962.*

`1953` **Rastafarian** movement founded in Jamaica.

India passes the Hindu Marriage Act `1955` and the Untouchability Act to modernize Hindu **marriage laws** and **caste system**.

`1952` **1 NOV** USA explodes the first **hydrogen bomb** at Enewetak Atoll.

`1953` James Watson and Francis Crick discover the **double-helix structure of DNA** (UK).

JAN USS *Nautilus*, the first **nuclear submarine**, is `1954` launched (USA).

◄ *Cutaway drawing of the USS Nautilus.*

`1952` **John Cage** composes 4' 33", in which not a single note is played.

`1953` **JAN** Samuel Beckett, ***Waiting for Godot***, absurdist play (France).

◄ *A model of the structure of DNA.*

Le Corbusier, Notre-dame-du-Haut, Ronchamp, `1955` France, modernist church.

JUL Bill Haley's ***Rock Around the Clock*** is the first Rock 'n' Roll recording to top the US charts. `1955`

POLITICS & ECONOMY

RELIGION & PHILOSOPHY

SCIENCE & TECHNOLOGY

ARTS & ARCHITECTURE

Jan Apr Jul Oct Jan Apr Jul Oct Jan Apr Jul Oct Jan Apr Jul Oct Jan Apr Jul Oct

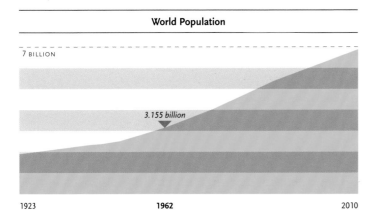

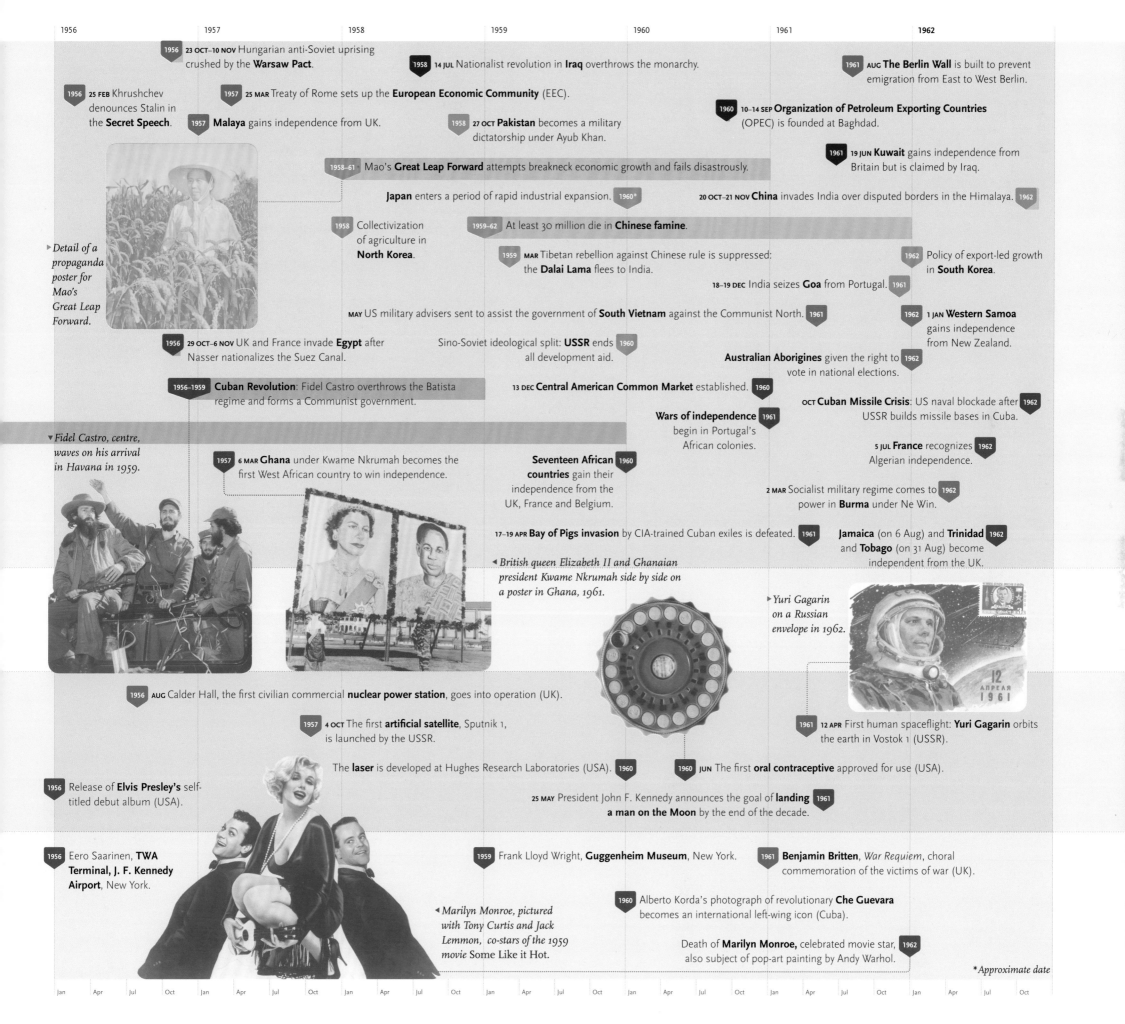

1956   **1957**   **1958**   **1959**   **1960**   **1961**   **1962**

1956 23 OCT–10 NOV Hungarian anti-Soviet uprising crushed by the **Warsaw Pact**.

1958 14 JUL Nationalist revolution in **Iraq** overthrows the monarchy.

1961 AUG **The Berlin Wall** is built to prevent emigration from East to West Berlin.

1956 25 FEB Khrushchev denounces Stalin in the **Secret Speech**.

1957 25 MAR Treaty of Rome sets up the **European Economic Community** (EEC).

1957 **Malaya** gains independence from UK.

1958 27 OCT **Pakistan** becomes a military dictatorship under Ayub Khan.

1960 10–14 SEP **Organization of Petroleum Exporting Countries** (OPEC) is founded at Baghdad.

1961 19 JUN **Kuwait** gains independence from Britain but is claimed by Iraq.

1958–61 Mao's **Great Leap Forward** attempts breakneck economic growth and fails disastrously.

Japan enters a period of rapid industrial expansion. **1960***

20 OCT–21 NOV **China** invades India over disputed borders in the Himalaya. **1962**

▶ *Detail of a propaganda poster for Mao's Great Leap Forward.*

1958 Collectivization of agriculture in **North Korea**.

1959–62 At least 30 million die in **Chinese famine**.

1959 MAR Tibetan rebellion against Chinese rule is suppressed: the **Dalai Lama** flees to India.

1962 Policy of export-led growth in **South Korea**.

18–19 DEC India seizes **Goa** from Portugal. **1961**

MAY US military advisers sent to assist the government of **South Vietnam** against the Communist North. **1961**

1962 1 JAN **Western Samoa** gains independence from New Zealand.

1956 29 OCT–6 NOV UK and France invade **Egypt** after Nasser nationalizes the Suez Canal.

Sino-Soviet ideological split: **USSR** ends all development aid. **1960**

Australian Aborigines given the right to vote in national elections. **1962**

1956–1959 **Cuban Revolution**: Fidel Castro overthrows the Batista regime and forms a Communist government.

13 DEC **Central American Common Market** established. **1960**

OCT **Cuban Missile Crisis**: US naval blockade after USSR builds missile bases in Cuba. **1962**

▼ *Fidel Castro, centre, waves on his arrival in Havana in 1959.*

Wars of independence begin in Portugal's African colonies. **1961**

5 JUL **France** recognizes Algerian independence. **1962**

1957 6 MAR **Ghana** under Kwame Nkrumah becomes the first West African country to win independence.

Seventeen African countries gain their independence from the UK, France and Belgium. **1960**

2 MAR Socialist military regime comes to power in **Burma** under Ne Win. **1962**

17–19 APR **Bay of Pigs invasion** by CIA-trained Cuban exiles is defeated. **1961**

Jamaica (on 6 Aug) and **Trinidad and Tobago** (on 31 Aug) become independent from the UK. **1962**

◀ *British queen Elizabeth II and Ghanaian president Kwame Nkrumah side by side on a poster in Ghana, 1961.*

▶ *Yuri Gagarin on a Russian envelope in 1962.*

1956 AUG Calder Hall, the first civilian commercial **nuclear power station**, goes into operation (UK).

1957 4 OCT The first **artificial satellite**, Sputnik 1, is launched by the USSR.

The **laser** is developed at Hughes Research Laboratories (USA). **1960**

1960 JUN The first **oral contraceptive** approved for use (USA).

1961 12 APR First human spaceflight: **Yuri Gagarin** orbits the earth in Vostok 1 (USSR).

12 АПРЕЛЯ 1961

1956 Release of **Elvis Presley's** self-titled debut album (USA).

25 MAY President John F. Kennedy announces the goal of **landing a man on the Moon** by the end of the decade. **1961**

1956 Eero Saarinen, **TWA Terminal, J. F. Kennedy Airport**, New York.

1959 Frank Lloyd Wright, **Guggenheim Museum**, New York.

1961 Benjamin Britten, *War Requiem*, choral commemoration of the victims of war (UK).

1960 Alberto Korda's photograph of revolutionary **Che Guevara** becomes an international left-wing icon (Cuba).

◀ *Marilyn Monroe, pictured with Tony Curtis and Jack Lemmon, co-stars of the 1959 movie* Some Like it Hot.

Death of **Marilyn Monroe**, celebrated movie star, also subject of pop-art painting by Andy Warhol. **1962**

*Approximate date

Jan Apr Jul Oct Jan Apr Jul Oct Jan Apr Jul Oct Jan Apr Jul Oct Jan Apr Jul Oct Jan Apr Jul Oct Jan Apr Jul Oct

1975

THE WORLD AT THE HEIGHT OF THE COLD WAR

In 1965 the USA committed combat troops to the war between South Vietnam and Viet Cong irregulars backed by Communist North Vietnam. Against US material superiority, the Communists resorted to guerrilla warfare, which spread into neighbouring Laos and Cambodia. The US withdrew after a face-saving peace deal with North Vietnam in 1973, but the Communist insurgency continued. Vietnam was reunited under a Communist government in 1975. Communist governments were established in Cambodia and Laos in the same year. In Latin America, the USA opposed even democratic communism, engineering a military coup against the elected Marxist government of Chile in 1973.

The USSR had shown equal intolerance of liberalization in its own back yard when it sent Warsaw Pact forces to occupy Czechoslovakia and crush the Prague Spring movement in 1968. A new element in the Cold War was the split between the USSR and the People's Republic of China (PRC). This began with ideological differences in 1960 and by 1969 had escalated to armed clashes along the Sino-Soviet border. The PRC's admission to the UN in 1971 (China's place at the UN had been occupied by the Guomindang government in Taiwan) and the opening of trade and diplomatic relations with the USA in 1972 marked a de facto Sino-US alliance against the USSR.

The independence in 1975 of Angola and Mozambique heralded the end of European colonialism in Africa: its last vestiges were the Spanish enclaves of Ceuta and Melilla in North Africa, the white apartheid regime in South Africa and a white-settler regime in Rhodesia, which had declared independence from Britain rather than accept black majority rule. Newly independent African states inherited a destabilizing legacy of suppressed ethnic tensions, which have often since led to civil war and humanitarian crises. India and Pakistan fought two wars in this period, in 1965 and 1971, the latter ending with the creation of Bangladesh.

Five Largest Cities *millions*

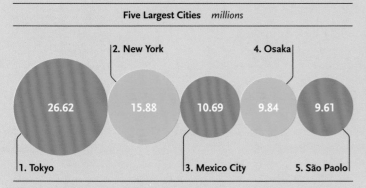

	2. New York		4. Osaka	
26.62	15.88	10.69	9.84	9.61
1. Tokyo		3. Mexico City		5. São Paolo

GREENLAND
(Denmark)

C A N A D A

UNITED STATES OF AMERICA

New York

St Pierre et Miquelon (Fr)

1 JAMAICA
2 BRITISH HONDURAS
3 Netherlands Antilles
4 Puerto Rico (USA)
5 HAITI
6 DOMINICAN REPUBLIC
7 GRENADA

Bermuda
(UK)

MEXICO

Cayman
Islands
(UK)

BAHAMAS
Turks and Caicos Islands (UK)

Mexico City

CUBA

US Virgin
Islands

British Virgin Islands
Leeward Islands (UK)
Guadeloupe (Fr)
Dominica (UK)
Martinique (Fr)
Windward Islands (UK)

Hawaii
(USA)

GUATEMALA
EL SALVADOR
HONDURAS
NICARAGUA
COSTA RICA
PANAMA

Panama
Canal
Zone (USA)

BARBADOS
TRINIDAD & TOBAGO
GUYANA
SURINAME
FRENCH GUIANA

VENEZUELA

COLOMBIA

Galapagos
Islands
(Ecuador)

ECUADOR

French
Polynesia

B R A Z I L

PERU

Pitcairn Island
(UK)

BOLIVIA

São Paolo

Easter Island
(Chile)

PARAGUAY

C H I L E

URUGUAY

ARGENTINA

Falkland Islands
(UK)

USSR and client states

Other communist states

Other states and territories

Member of NATO

IRAQ Member of OPEC (Organization
of Petroleum Exporting Countries)

150°   120°   90°   60°

NETHERLANDS 8
BELGIUM 9
LUXEMBOURG 10
SWITZERLAND 11
WEST GERMANY 12
AUSTRIA 13
EAST GERMANY 14
CZECHOSLOVAKIA 15

SVALBARD (Norway)

HUNGARY 16
YUGOSLAVIA 17
ALBANIA 18
BULGARIA 19

ICELAND

Faroe Islands (Denmark)

NORWAY
SWEDEN
FINLAND

UNION OF SOVIET SOCIALIST REPUBLICS

UNITED KINGDOM
IRELAND
DENMARK
POLAND
8
12   14
9
10
15
FRANCE
11   13
16
ROMANIA
ITALY
17
19
18
GREECE
TURKEY

MONGOLIA

NORTH KOREA

JAPAN
1
Tokyo
4
Osaka

PORTUGAL
SPAIN

Azores (Pt)

Gibraltar (UK)
Ceuta (Sp)
Madeira (Pt)
Melilla (Sp)

Canary Islands (Sp)

TUNISIA
MALTA
CYPRUS
39
40
41
42
IRAQ
IRAN
AFGHANISTAN
PAKISTAN

43   46
47
48

PEOPLE'S REPUBLIC OF CHINA

BHUTAN
NEPAL

THAILAND 49
LAOS 50
SINGAPORE 51
BRUNEI (UK) 52

WESTERN SAHARA (Morocco)

MOROCCO
ALGERIA
LIBYA
EGYPT
SAUDI ARABIA
YEMEN

OMAN

BANGLADESH
INDIA
BURMA

Hong Kong (UK)
Macau (Pt)

REPUBLIC OF CHINA

MAURITANIA
MALI
NIGER
CHAD
SUDAN
20
SENEGAL
GAMBIA
21
GUINEA BISSAU
22
23
25
NIGERIA
24
26
SIERRA LEONE
LIBERIA
GHANA
27
GABON
CABINDA (Angola)
28
29
ETHIOPIA
SOMALIA
44
45
30
31
KENYA
ZAIRE
RWANDA
BURUNDI

50
49
VIETNAM
CAMBODIA

PHILIPPINES

MALAYSIA
52
51

Guam (USA)

Trust Territories of the Pacific Islands (USA)

Gilbert Islands (UK)

NAURU

Andaman Islands (India)
Nicobar Islands (India)

MALDIVE ISLANDS
SRI LANKA

Seychelles (UK)
Chagos Islands (UK)

Cocos Islands (Australia)
Christmas Island (Australia)

INDONESIA

PAPUA NEW GUINEA

Solomon Islands (UK)

Phoenix Islands (UK)

Ellice Islands (UK)

CAPE VERDE 20
UPPER VOLTA 21
GUINEA 22
IVORY COAST 23
TOGO 24
BENIN 25
EQUATORIAL GUINEA 26
SÃO TOMÉ AND PRÍNCIPE 27

Ascension Island (UK)

St Helena (UK)

32
COMOROS
Amirante Islands (UK)

34
ANGOLA
33
38
35
36

MAURITIUS

Mayotte (Fr)

MADAGASCAR
Réunion (Fr)

TONGA
FIJI

New Hebrides (Anglo-French condominium)

New Caledonia (Fr)

Tristan da Cunha (UK)

Walvis Bay (to South Africa)
37
SWAZILAND
SOUTH AFRICA
LESOTHO

AUSTRALIA

CAMEROON 28
CENTRAL AFRICAN REPUBLIC 29
CONGO 30
UGANDA 31
TANZANIA 32

ZAMBIA 33
MALAWI 34
RHODESIA 35
BOTSWANA 36
SOUTHWEST AFRICA (to South Africa) 37
MOZAMBIQUE 38

LEBANON 39
SYRIA 40
ISRAEL 41
JORDAN 42
KUWAIT 43
PEOPLE'S DEMOCRATIC REPUBLIC OF YEMEN 44

FRENCH SOMALILAND 45
BAHRAIN 46
QATAR 47
UNITED ARAB EMIRATES 48

Kerguelen Island (Fr)

NEW ZEALAND

Arctic Circle
75°
45°
Tropic of Cancer
Equator
Tropic of Capricorn
45°
0°   30°   60°   90°   120°   150°   180°

1975

By 1975, the impact of the unresolved conflict between Israel and its Arab neighbours had spread far beyond the Middle East. In 1948–49, during its war of independence, Israel occupied all of Palestine except for the small territories of Gaza and the West Bank (not shown on the map for reasons of scale). Millions of Palestinian Arabs became stateless refugees. In the Six Day War in 1967, Israel defeated an alliance of Egypt, Syria, Jordan and Iraq, and occupied Gaza and the West Bank, as well as Egypt's Sinai Peninsula and Syria's Golan Heights. After Israel defeated a second Arab attack in 1973, Arab oil-exporting countries imposed an oil embargo on the USA and Europe in retaliation for their support of Israel, causing a worldwide recession. Attacks on Israeli targets abroad by the Palestine Liberation Organization (PLO) made international terrorism an issue of global concern.

The period 1962–75 was one of major cultural upheaval. In Western Europe and the USA society became more liberal as an affluent youth rebelled against traditional conservative and religious values. Opposition to institutionalized racism and the Vietnam War led to mass protest movements in the USA. Pop culture flourished, particularly in music and art. Mao's Cultural Revolution threw China into turmoil as young Red Guards attacked 'bourgeois' culture, persecuting intellectuals and destroying antiquities and historical sites. In Cambodia, the Khmer Rouge also targeted bourgeois culture, aiming to eradicate it with a genocidal campaign.

The most impressive technological achievement of the period was the US Apollo programme's successful manned landing on the Moon in 1969, which, however, owed more to Cold War rivalry than the search for scientific knowledge. The Boeing 747 'jumbo jet' airliner, which first flew in 1969, began the era of affordable long-distance air travel.

World Population

7 BILLION

4.061 billion

1923   1975   2010

POLITICS & ECONOMY

14 OCT Khrushchev ousted from power in [1964] the USSR: **Leonid Brezhnev** succeeds.

[1966–69] Mao's **Great Proletarian Cultural Revolution** causes social, political and economic chaos in China.

[1964] **28 MAY** The **Palestine Liberation Organization** (PLO) is founded in Jerusalem.

5 AUG–23 SEP Second India–Pakistan War breaks out [1965] over the border in the Rann of Kutch marshland.

[1963] **MAY Indonesia** annexes Dutch New Guinea (Irian Jaya).

5–10 JUN Six Day War: Israel defeats Egypt, Jordan, Syria and Iraq and [1967] occupies the West Bank, Gaza, the Golan Heights and Sinai.

[1963] **16 SEPT** Malaya, Sabah (North Borneo), Sarawak, Labuan and Singapore unite as the **Federation of Malaysia**.

31 MAR Coup establishes military [1964] dictatorship in **Brazil** (to 1985).

[1965] **8 MAR** USA dispatches the first combat troops to **South Vietnam**.

[1965–73] Australian and New Zealand combat troops support the USA in **Vietnam**.

[1963] **12 DEC Kenya** gains independence from Britain.

[1965] **9 AUG Singapore** leaves the Malaysian Confederation and becomes an independent city state.

[1963] **22 NOV President J. F. Kennedy** assassinated in Dallas, Texas.

Biafran War brings famine to southeast Nigeria. [1967–1970]

[1965] **11 NOV** White settlers in **Southern Rhodesia** declare unilateral independence from Britain.

[1965] **6 AUG** US **Voting Rights Act** outlaws discriminatory voting practices.

9 OCT The Marxist revolutionary **Che** [1967] **Guevara** is killed in Bolivia.

RELIGION & PHILOSOPHY

▲ *The Fab Four: the Beatles shown on merchandise at the height of their fame.*

[1964] Publication of **Quotations from Chairman Mao** (*The Little Red Book*) marks the intensification of the Mao cult in China.

[1966–69] Most Buddhist monasteries in **Tibet** are destroyed by Chinese Red Guards.

JUL Swami Prabhupada founds the **International Society for** [1966] **Krishna Consciousness** in New York.

SCIENCE & TECHNOLOGY

[1963] **Measles vaccine** introduced (USA).

[1964] **16 OCT** First Chinese **nuclear test**.

3 DEC The first **human-heart transplant** [1967] **operation** is carried out (South Africa).

[1964] *Shinkansen*, **high-speed bullet trains**, begin operating in Japan.

[1965] **6 APR** Intelsat 1, the first **commercial-communications satellite** is launched (USA).

ARTS & ARCHITECTURE

[1963–64] **Beatlemania**: intense hysteria shown by fans of the UK pop group the Beatles in UK and USA.

[1966] Tom Stoppard, **Rosencrantz and Guildenstern are Dead**, existentialist tragicomic drama (UK).

The **Cultural Revolution** in China is marked by persecution of intellectuals [1966–69] and destruction of art treasures by the **Red Guards**.

[1966] **5 MAR** Death of **Anna Akhmatova** (*b.* 1889), Russian modernist poet.

Jiang Qing imposes 'revolutionary' opera on Chinese theatre. [1966–69]

The **Summer of Love**, hippie [1967] counterculture rebellion in the USA.

British fashion designer Mary Quant [1965] creates the **miniskirt**.

Gabriel García Márquez, **One Hundred Years of Solitude**, magical-realist novel (Colombia). [1967]

Viljo Revell, City Hall, Toronto, modernist [1965] offices (Canada).

Minoru Yamasaki, [1967–72] **World Trade Center**, New York.

Jan Apr Jul Oct Jan Apr Jul Oct Jan Apr Jul Oct Jan Apr Jul Oct Jan Apr Jul Oct

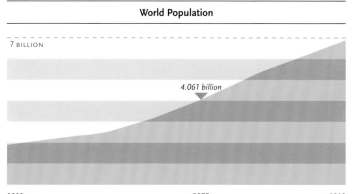

1969 25 MAR **Ayub Khan** overthrown: democracy restored in Pakistan.

1971 3–16 DEC **Third India–Pakistan War** ends with East Pakistan becoming independent as Bangladesh.

1974 25 APR Portuguese dictatorship overthrown in the **Carnation Revolution**.

1968 MAY Student riots in **Paris** lead to a liberalization of French social values.

1971 22 FEB **General Hafez al-Assad** seizes power in Syria.

JUL–AUG **Helsinki Agreement** establishes détente between NATO and the Warsaw Pact. **1975**

1969 MAR–SEP Military clashes on the **Sino-Soviet border**.

20 NOV Death of **Francisco Franco**, fascist dictator of Spain. **1975**

APR–JUL US campaign against Communist bases **1970** in **Cambodia**.

15 JAN **Paris Peace Accords** ends direct US intervention in Vietnam. **1973**

1973 6–26 OCT **Yom Kippur War**: Israel defeats a surprise attack by Egypt and Syria.

1968 JAN–SEP **Communist Tet Offensive** defeated by US and South Vietnamese forces.

1971 25 OCT The **People's Republic of China** takes the China seat in the UN.

21–28 FEB US president **Nixon** visits Beijing, opening trade and diplomatic relations between the PRC and the USA. **1972**

1973–74 Arab members of OPEC impose an **oil embargo** on the West.

1968 **Japan** becomes the world's second largest economy.

26 MAY Strategic Arms Limitation Talks between USA and **1972** USSR result in **Anti-Ballistic Missile Treaty**.

APR Civil war in **Lebanon** between Christians and Muslims (to 1977). **1975**

1974–75 Communist **North Vietnam** conquers South Vietnam.

14–18 JUL The **Football War** between Honduras **1969** and El Salvador.

MAY–OCT **Operation Linebacker**: US bombing campaign **1972** halts North Vietnamese Easter offensive.

17 APR Communist **Khmer Rouge** take over Cambodia, killing **1975** approximately 25 per cent of the population in forced-labour camps.

1968 21 AUG **Czechoslovak Prague Spring** liberalization movement is ended by the Warsaw Pact invasion.

25 JUN **Mozambique** gains independence from Portugal. **1975**

11 SEP US-backed military coup overthrows the elected Marxist government of **Chile**. **1973**

1974 9 AUG US president Nixon resigns after the **Watergate scandal**.

JUL–AUG Turkey invades **Cyprus** following a Greek-backed military coup. **1974**

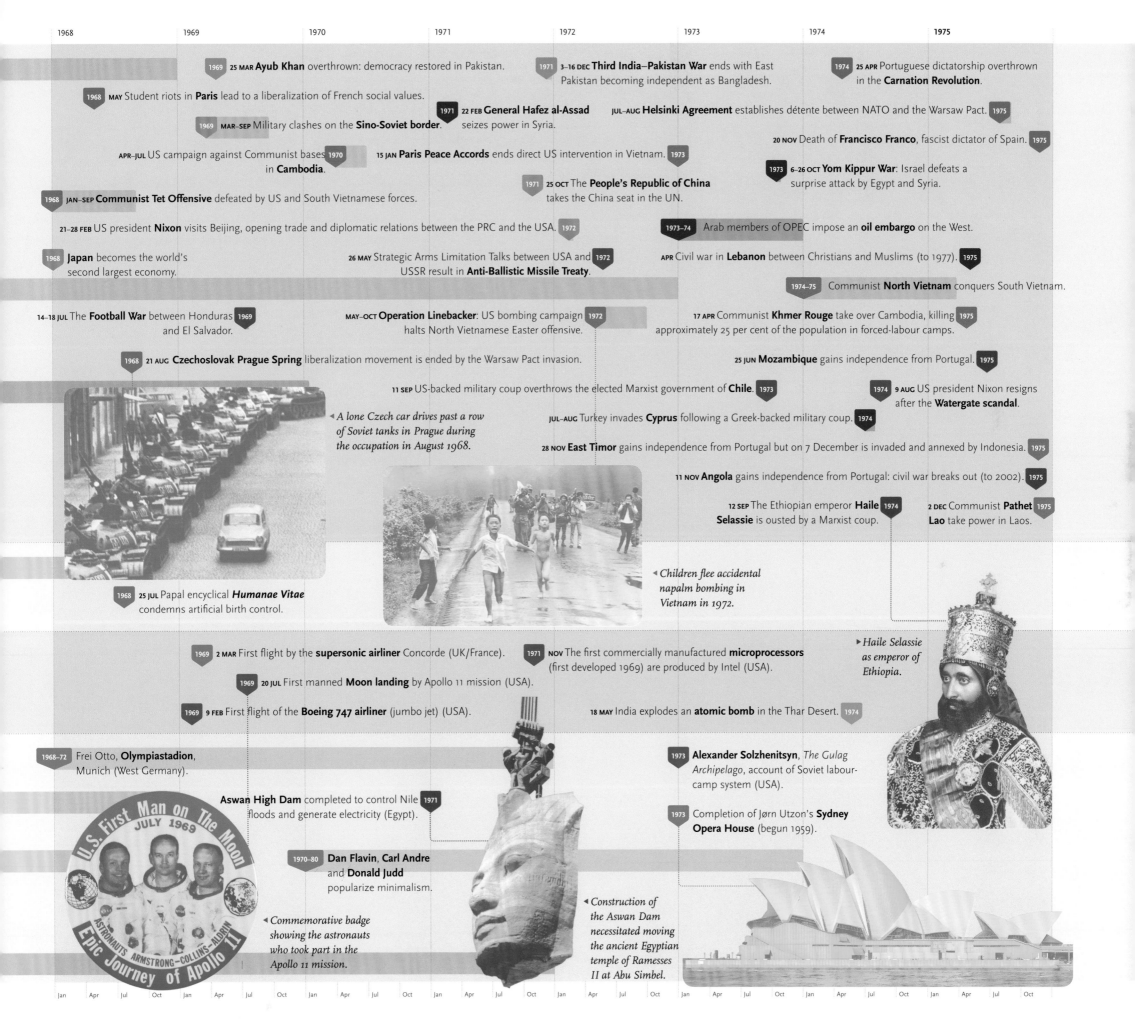

◄ *A lone Czech car drives past a row of Soviet tanks in Prague during the occupation in August 1968.*

28 NOV **East Timor** gains independence from Portugal but on 7 December is invaded and annexed by Indonesia. **1975**

11 NOV **Angola** gains independence from Portugal: civil war breaks out (to 2002). **1975**

12 SEP The Ethiopian emperor **Haile** **1974** **Selassie** is ousted by a Marxist coup.

2 DEC Communist **Pathet** **1975** **Lao** take power in Laos.

◄ *Children flee accidental napalm bombing in Vietnam in 1972.*

1968 25 JUL Papal encyclical **Humanae Vitae** condemns artificial birth control.

► *Haile Selassie as emperor of Ethiopia.*

1969 2 MAR First flight by the **supersonic airliner** Concorde (UK/France).

1971 NOV The first commercially manufactured **microprocessors** (first developed 1969) are produced by Intel (USA).

1969 20 JUL First manned **Moon landing** by Apollo 11 mission (USA).

1969 9 FEB First flight of the **Boeing 747 airliner** (jumbo jet) (USA).

18 MAY India explodes an **atomic bomb** in the Thar Desert. **1974**

1968–72 Frei Otto, **Olympiastadion**, Munich (West Germany).

1973 **Alexander Solzhenitsyn**, *The Gulag Archipelago*, account of Soviet labour-camp system (USA).

Aswan High Dam completed to control Nile **1971** floods and generate electricity (Egypt).

1973 Completion of Jørn Utzon's **Sydney Opera House** (begun 1959).

U.S. First Man on The Moon — JULY 1969 — ASTRONAUTS ARMSTRONG·COLLINS·ALDRIN — Epic Journey of Apollo 11

1970–80 **Dan Flavin**, **Carl Andre** and **Donald Judd** popularize minimalism.

◄ *Commemorative badge showing the astronauts who took part in the Apollo 11 mission.*

◄ *Construction of the Aswan Dam necessitated moving the ancient Egyptian temple of Ramesses II at Abu Simbel.*

1991

THE FALL OF THE IRON CURTAIN AND THE BREAK-UP OF THE USSR

The last great crisis of the Cold War began in 1979 when the USSR invaded Afghanistan to support its Communist government against an Islamic *mujahideen* insurgency. The Soviet forces in Afghanistan never managed to win full control of the country and soon became bogged down in a guerrilla war with the *mujahideen*, who received anti-aircraft missiles and other aid from the US Central Intelligence Agency (CIA). The USSR finally withdrew in 1989, its prestige damaged, leaving Afghanistan to be fought over by rival warlords.

The Soviet economy stagnated in the 1970s and failed to keep pace with US technological development, especially in military technology. Recognizing the need to revitalize the USSR, Mikhail Gorbachev, who became Soviet leader in 1985, introduced reforming policies of *glasnost* (openness) and *perestroika* (restructuring). The relaxation of state repression that followed encouraged popular demands for liberalization in the USSR's Warsaw Pact satellites, culminating in the overthrow of their Communist governments and the fall of the Berlin Wall in 1989 and the reunification of Germany in 1990.

Emboldened by this, the Estonians, Latvians and Lithuanians demanded independence from the USSR. Disaffected Soviet generals, dismayed by the loss of the USSR's influence in Eastern Europe, deposed Gorbachev and attempted a military coup. This precipitated the complete break-up of the USSR in 1991 as its constituent republics declared independence.

Events in Eastern Europe inspired a student democracy movement in China in 1989, but this was brutally crushed by the army. After Mao's death in 1976, the Chinese government had gradually abandoned Marxist economic policies while maintaining the party dictatorship. Thanks to healthy industrial growth and improving living standards, the Chinese Communist Party still stayed in power.

Five Largest Cities *millions*

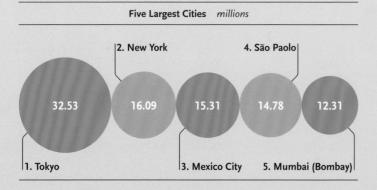

2. New York — 16.09
4. São Paolo — 14.78
1. Tokyo — 32.53
3. Mexico City — 15.31
5. Mumbai (Bombay) — 12.31

GREENLAND (Denmark)

CANADA

UNITED STATES OF AMERICA

Hawaii (USA)

MEXICO

Mexico City

Cayman Islands (UK)

BELIZE

GUATEMALA
EL SALVADOR
HONDURAS
NICARAGUA
COSTA RICA
PANAMA

Panama Canal Zone (USA)

COLOMBIA

Galapagos Islands (Ecuador)

ECUADOR

French Polynesia

Pitcairn Island (UK)

Easter Island (Chile)

CUBA

BAHAMAS

US Virgin Islands

VENEZUELA

New York

Bermuda (UK)

St Pierre et Miquelon (Fr)

1 JAMAICA
2 Netherlands Antilles
3 Puerto Rico (USA)
4 HAITI
5 DOMINICAN REPUBLIC
6 Turks and Caicos Islands (UK)
7 ST KITTS AND NEVIS
8 GRENADA

British Virgin Islands
Anguilla (UK)
ANTIGUA AND BARBUDA
Guadeloupe (Fr)
DOMINICA
Martinique (Fr)
ST LUCIA
BARBADOS
ST VINCENT AND THE GRENADINES
TRINIDAD & TOBAGO
FRENCH GUIANA

GUYANA
SURINAME

BRAZIL

PERU

BOLIVIA

PARAGUAY

São Paolo

CHILE

URUGUAY

ARGENTINA

Falkland Islands (UK)

Communist states

Member of NATO

Other states and territories

150°   120°   90°   60°

NETHERLANDS 8
BELGIUM 9
LUXEMBOURG 10
SWITZERLAND 11
Kaliningrad (RUS) 12
LITHUANIA 13
CZECHOSLOVAKIA 14
AUSTRIA 15
HUNGARY 16

SVALBARD
(Norway)

MOLDOVA 17
SLOVENIA 18
CROATIA 19
YUGOSLAVIA 20
ALBANIA 21
MACEDONIA 22

ICELAND

Faroe Islands
(Denmark)

NORWAY
SWEDEN
FINLAND

75°

Arctic Circle

RUSSIA

UNITED
KINGDOM
IRELAND

DENMARK
12
13
POLAND
8
GERMANY
9
10
14
FRANCE 11
15
18
16
17
19
20
ROMANIA
21
22
BULGARIA
GREECE
ITALY

BELARUS

ESTONIA
LATVIA

UKRAINE

GEORGIA
ARMENIA 42
TURKEY

KAZAKHSTAN

MONGOLIA

45°

NORTH
KOREA
SOUTH
KOREA
JAPAN

1 Tokyo

PORTUGAL
SPAIN

Azores
(Pt)

Gibraltar (UK)
Madeira
(Pt)
Canary Islands
(Sp)

WESTERN
SAHARA
(Morocco)

Ceuta (Sp)
Melilla
(Sp)

MOROCCO

TUNISIA

MALTA

CYPRUS
43
45
44
46

IRAQ

IRAN

UZBEKISTAN

TURKMENISTAN

KYRGYZSTAN

TAJIKISTAN

AFGHANISTAN

PAKISTAN

PEOPLE'S
REPUBLIC OF
CHINA

THAILAND 52
LAOS 53
SINGAPORE 54
BRUNEI 55

Tropic of Cancer

ALGERIA
LIBYA
EGYPT

SAUDI
ARABIA

OMAN

47 48
49
50

NEPAL

BHUTAN

BANGLADESH
MYANMAR

Hong Kong (UK)
Macau
(Pt)

REPUBLIC OF CHINA

PHILIPPINES

Mariana
Islands
(USA)

Guam
(USA)

MARSHALL
ISLANDS

MAURITANIA

MALI

NIGER

CHAD

SUDAN

YEMEN

SENEGAL 23
GAMBIA
GUINEA
BISSAU

NIGERIA

ETHIOPIA

SOMALIA

5
Mumbai
(Bombay)

INDIA

Andaman
Islands
(India)

Nicobar
Islands
(India)

53
52
VIETNAM

CAMBODIA

Palau
(USA)

FEDERATED STATES
OF MICRONESIA

Equator

24
25
26
27
28
51

31
32

MALDIVE
ISLANDS

SRI
LANKA

MALAYSIA
54
55

NAURU

KIRIBATI

SIERRA
LEONE
LIBERIA
GHANA

29
29
34
ZAIRE

KENYA

INDONESIA

PAPUA
NEW GUINEA

SOLOMON
ISLANDS

TUVALU

Ascension
Island
(UK)

30
33

GABON
CABINDA
(Angola)

RWANDA
BURUNDI

35

COMOROS

SEYCHELLES

British Indian
Ocean Territory

CAPE VERDE 23
BURKINA FASO 24
GUINEA 25
IVORY COAST 26
TOGO 27
BENIN 28
EQUATORIAL
GUINEA 29
SÃO TOMÉ AND
PRÍNCIPE 30

ANGOLA

36

37
41

Mayotte
(Fr)

Amirante
Islands
(Seychelles)

Cocos
Islands
(Australia)

Christmas
Island
(Australia)

VANUATU TONGA

FIJI

St Helena
(UK)

MADAGASCAR

38

MAURITIUS

Réunion
(Fr)

AUSTRALIA

New
Caledonia
(Fr)

Tropic of Capricorn

Tristan da
Cunha
(UK)

Walvis Bay
(to South Africa)

39

40
SOUTH
AFRICA

SWAZILAND

LESOTHO

AZERBAIJAN 42
LEBANON 43
SYRIA 44
ISRAEL 45
JORDAN 46
KUWAIT 47

BAHRAIN 48
QATAR 49
UNITED ARAB
EMIRATES 50
DJIBOUTI 51

SOMALILAND

CAMEROON 31
CENTRAL AFRICAN
REPUBLIC 32
CONGO 33
UGANDA 34
TANZANIA 35

ZAMBIA 36
MALAWI 37
ZIMBABWE 38
BOTSWANA 39
NAMIBIA 40
MOZAMBIQUE 41

Kerguelen Island
(Fr)

NEW
ZEALAND

45°

0°   30°   60°   90°   120°   150°   180°

1991

The USA was successful in containing communism in Latin America, supporting repressive right-wing dictatorships in Guatemala and El Salvador against left-wing peasant insurgencies and funding the right-wing Contra insurgency against the Communist Sandinista government in Nicaragua, which was defeated in elections in 1990. An attempted Marxist coup on the tiny island of Grenada in 1983 was stopped by a US invasion.

Continuing instability in the Middle East contributed to the rise of Islamic fundamentalism as a major political and cultural force in this period. Its first major manifestation was the Shi'ite Islamic revolution, led by the Ayatollah Khomeini, which overthrew the repressive regime of the US-backed shah of Iran in 1979. Fears that the Islamic revolution might spread to Iraq led its dictator Saddam Hussein to wage a bloody, but ultimately indecisive, eight-year war against Iran. Deeply indebted by the war, Iraq invaded neighbouring Kuwait to seize its oilfields in 1990, but was expelled by a US-led coalition the next year.

The Iranian revolution inspired the foundation of the Shi'ite Hezbollah movement in Lebanon in 1982, which pioneered the use of suicide bombers in its attacks on Israeli and US targets. The Sunni *mujahideen* fighting the Soviets in Afghanistan were inspired by the ideology of jihad or holy war. Their example in turn encouraged the foundation of the Palestinian Hamas jihadi movement in 1987 and the Muslim separatist insurgency that broke out in Indian-administered Kashmir in 1989.

The introduction of affordable personal computers and the development of the World Wide Web were probably the most important technological developments of this period. Although their full potential was scarcely evident in 1991, they would revolutionize the way people worked, spent their leisure time and communicated.

World Population

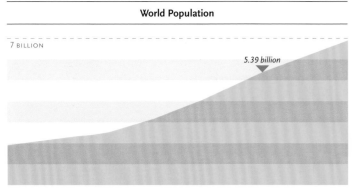

7 BILLION

5.39 billion

210

1923   **1991**   2010

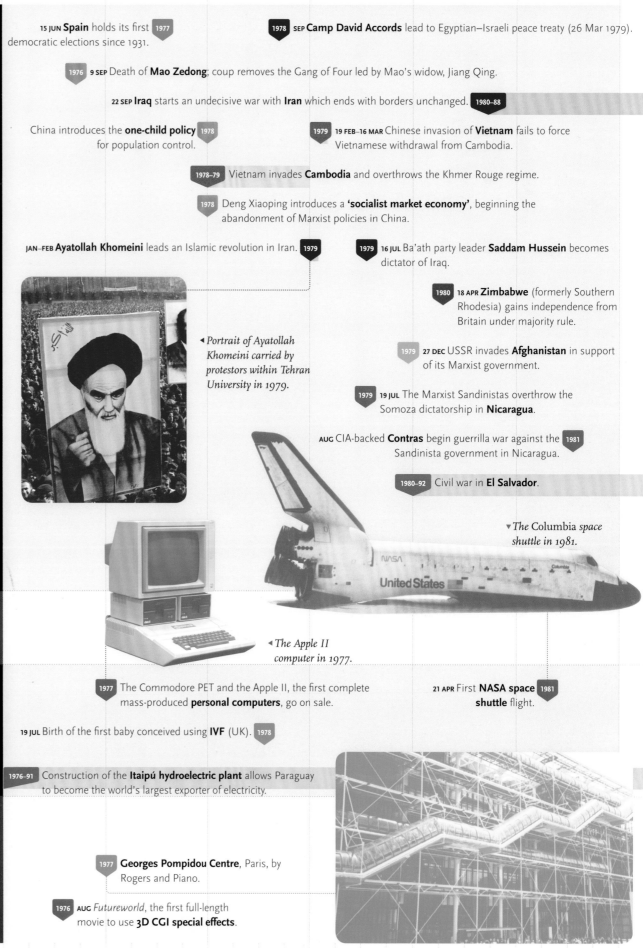

1976   1977   1978   1979   1980   1981

POLITICS & ECONOMY

15 JUN Spain holds its first `1977` democratic elections since 1931.

`1978` **SEP** Camp David Accords lead to Egyptian–Israeli peace treaty (26 Mar 1979).

`1976` **9 SEP** Death of **Mao Zedong**; coup removes the Gang of Four led by Mao's widow, Jiang Qing.

22 SEP Iraq starts an undecisive war with **Iran** which ends with borders unchanged. `1980–88`

China introduces the **one-child policy** `1978` for population control.

`1979` **19 FEB–16 MAR** Chinese invasion of **Vietnam** fails to force Vietnamese withdrawal from Cambodia.

`1978–79` Vietnam invades **Cambodia** and overthrows the Khmer Rouge regime.

`1978` Deng Xiaoping introduces a **'socialist market economy'**, beginning the abandonment of Marxist policies in China.

JAN–FEB Ayatollah Khomeini leads an Islamic revolution in Iran. `1979`

`1979` **16 JUL** Ba'ath party leader **Saddam Hussein** becomes dictator of Iraq.

`1980` **18 APR Zimbabwe** (formerly Southern Rhodesia) gains independence from Britain under majority rule.

◄ *Portrait of Ayatollah Khomeini carried by protestors within Tehran University in 1979.*

`1979` **27 DEC** USSR invades **Afghanistan** in support of its Marxist government.

`1979` **19 JUL** The Marxist Sandinistas overthrow the Somoza dictatorship in **Nicaragua**.

AUG CIA-backed **Contras** begin guerrilla war against the Sandinista government in Nicaragua. `1981`

`1980–92` Civil war in **El Salvador**.

▼ *The Columbia space shuttle in 1981.*

RELIGION & PHILOSOPHY

◄ *The Apple II computer in 1977.*

SCIENCE & TECHNOLOGY

`1977` The Commodore PET and the Apple II, the first complete mass-produced **personal computers**, go on sale.

21 APR First **NASA space** `1981` **shuttle** flight.

19 JUL Birth of the first baby conceived using **IVF** (UK). `1978`

`1976–91` Construction of the **Itaipú hydroelectric plant** allows Paraguay to become the world's largest exporter of electricity.

ARTS & ARCHITECTURE

`1977` **Georges Pompidou Centre**, Paris, by Rogers and Piano.

`1976` **AUG** *Futureworld*, the first full-length movie to use **3D CGI special effects**.

Jan Apr Jul Oct   Jan Apr Jul Oct Jan Apr Jul Oct Jan Apr Jul Oct   Jan Apr Jul   Oct Jan Apr Jul   Oct

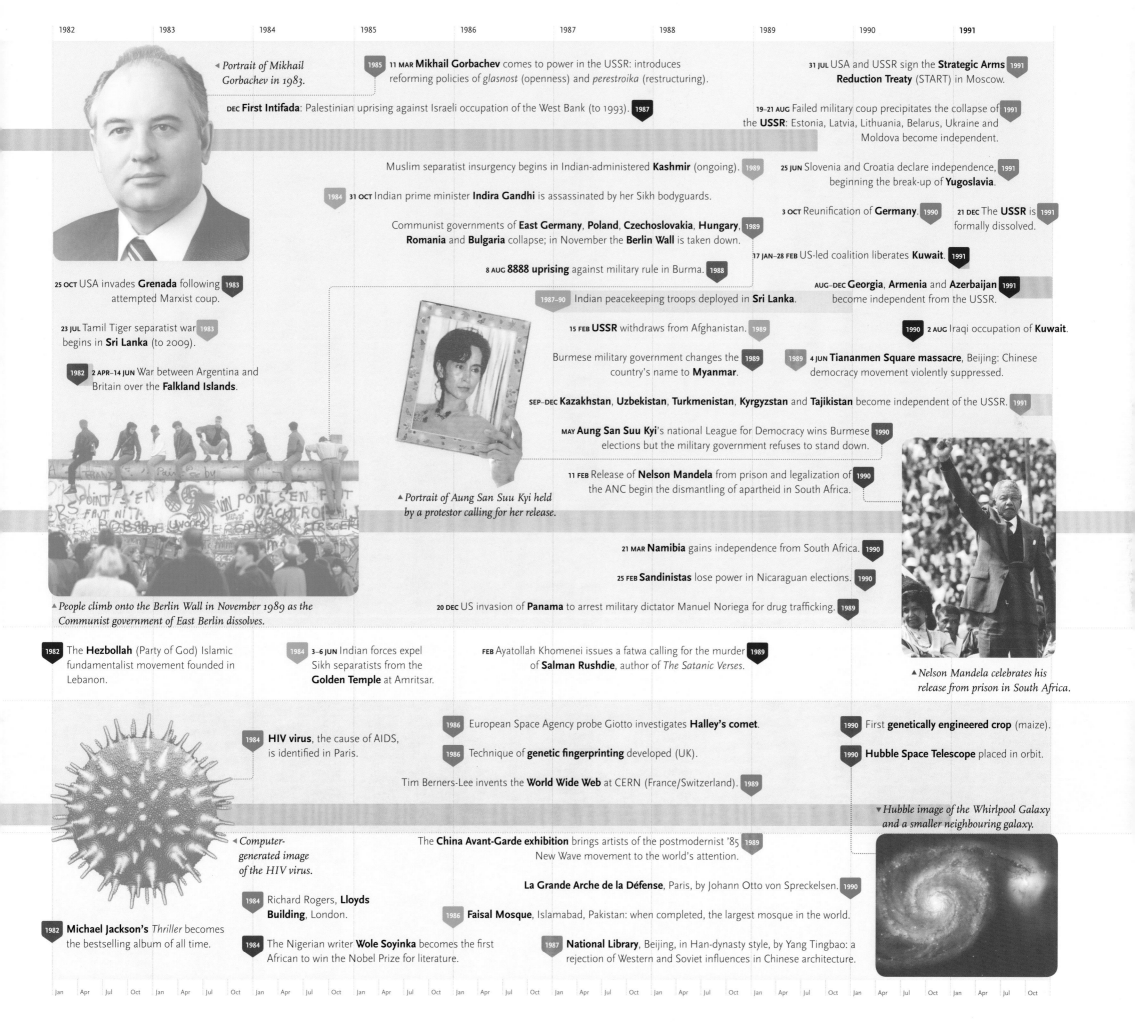

1982   1983   1984   1985   1986   1987   1988   1989   1990   **1991**

◄ *Portrait of Mikhail Gorbachev in 1983.*

1985 11 MAR **Mikhail Gorbachev** comes to power in the USSR: introduces reforming policies of *glasnost* (openness) and *perestroika* (restructuring).

31 JUL USA and USSR sign the **Strategic Arms Reduction Treaty** (START) in Moscow. **1991**

DEC **First Intifada**: Palestinian uprising against Israeli occupation of the West Bank (to 1993). **1987**

19–21 AUG Failed military coup precipitates the collapse of **1991** the **USSR**: Estonia, Latvia, Lithuania, Belarus, Ukraine and Moldova become independent.

Muslim separatist insurgency begins in Indian-administered **Kashmir** (ongoing). **1989**

25 JUN Slovenia and Croatia declare independence, **1991** beginning the break-up of **Yugoslavia**.

1984 31 OCT Indian prime minister **Indira Gandhi** is assassinated by her Sikh bodyguards.

3 OCT Reunification of **Germany**. **1990**

21 DEC The **USSR** is **1991** formally dissolved.

Communist governments of **East Germany**, **Poland**, **Czechoslovakia**, **Hungary**, **Romania** and **Bulgaria** collapse; in November the **Berlin Wall** is taken down. **1989**

17 JAN–28 FEB US-led coalition liberates **Kuwait**. **1991**

8 AUG **8888 uprising** against military rule in Burma. **1988**

25 OCT USA invades **Grenada** following **1983** attempted Marxist coup.

AUG–DEC **Georgia**, **Armenia** and **Azerbaijan** **1991** become independent from the USSR.

1987–90 Indian peacekeeping troops deployed in **Sri Lanka**.

23 JUL Tamil Tiger separatist war **1983** begins in **Sri Lanka** (to 2009).

15 FEB **USSR** withdraws from Afghanistan. **1989**

1990 2 AUG Iraqi occupation of **Kuwait**.

1982 2 APR–14 JUN War between Argentina and Britain over the **Falkland Islands**.

Burmese military government changes the **1989** country's name to **Myanmar**.

1989 4 JUN **Tiananmen Square massacre**, Beijing: Chinese democracy movement violently suppressed.

SEP–DEC **Kazakhstan**, **Uzbekistan**, **Turkmenistan**, **Kyrgyzstan** and **Tajikistan** become independent of the USSR. **1991**

MAY **Aung San Suu Kyi**'s national League for Democracy wins Burmese **1990** elections but the military government refuses to stand down.

11 FEB Release of **Nelson Mandela** from prison and legalization of **1990** the ANC begin the dismantling of apartheid in South Africa.

▲ *Portrait of Aung San Suu Kyi held by a protestor calling for her release.*

21 MAR **Namibia** gains independence from South Africa. **1990**

25 FEB **Sandinistas** lose power in Nicaraguan elections. **1990**

20 DEC US invasion of **Panama** to arrest military dictator Manuel Noriega for drug trafficking. **1989**

▲ *People climb onto the Berlin Wall in November 1989 as the Communist government of East Berlin dissolves.*

1982 The **Hezbollah** (Party of God) Islamic fundamentalist movement founded in Lebanon.

1984 3–6 JUN Indian forces expel Sikh separatists from the **Golden Temple** at Amritsar.

FEB Ayatollah Khomenei issues a fatwa calling for the murder **1989** of **Salman Rushdie**, author of *The Satanic Verses*.

▲ *Nelson Mandela celebrates his release from prison in South Africa.*

1986 European Space Agency probe Giotto investigates **Halley's comet**.

1990 First **genetically engineered crop** (maize).

1984 **HIV virus**, the cause of AIDS, is identified in Paris.

1986 Technique of **genetic fingerprinting** developed (UK).

1990 **Hubble Space Telescope** placed in orbit.

Tim Berners-Lee invents the **World Wide Web** at CERN (France/Switzerland). **1989**

▼ *Hubble image of the Whirlpool Galaxy and a smaller neighbouring galaxy.*

◄ *Computer-generated image of the HIV virus.*

The **China Avant-Garde exhibition** brings artists of the postmodernist '85 **1989** New Wave movement to the world's attention.

La Grande Arche de la Défense, Paris, by Johann Otto von Spreckelsen. **1990**

1984 Richard Rogers, **Lloyds Building**, London.

1986 **Faisal Mosque**, Islamabad, Pakistan: when completed, the largest mosque in the world.

1982 **Michael Jackson's** *Thriller* becomes the bestselling album of all time.

1984 The Nigerian writer **Wole Soyinka** becomes the first African to win the Nobel Prize for literature.

1987 **National Library**, Beijing, in Han-dynasty style, by Yang Tingbao: a rejection of Western and Soviet influences in Chinese architecture.

Jan Apr Jul Oct Jan Apr Jul Oct Jan Apr Jul Oct Jan Apr Jul Oct Jan Apr Jul Oct Jan Apr Jul Oct Jan Apr Jul Oct Jan Apr Jul Oct Jan Apr Jul Oct Jan Apr Jul Oct

2010

THE SHIFTING BALANCE OF GLOBAL POWER

The fall of the USSR in 1991 left the USA as the sole superpower, its economic, military and ideological dominance apparently unchallenged. Yet by 2010 the USA was faced with the reality of relative decline compared with emerging world economies such as Brazil, India and, especially, China, which became the world's second largest economy in 2010.

The end of the Cold War created new problems of its own. Soviet hegemony had suppressed ethnic tensions in the Balkans and the Caucasus: these now flared up in terrorism, war, ethnic cleansing and genocide. Worst affected was Yugoslavia, a federation of over half a dozen ethnic and religious groups. Only its independent-minded Communist government and fear of Soviet intervention had kept the country together. After the fall of the USSR, Yugoslavia quickly dissolved in a complex series of bloody civil wars. Czechoslovakia's two ethnic groups peacefully split the country into Czech and Slovak republics. Eastern European countries queued up to join NATO and the European Union, seeing this as the best guarantee of their independence and future prosperity.

The Russian economy struggled to make the transition to free-market capitalism. State assets fell into the hands of a small class of super-rich 'oligarchs' while most people's living standards fell. Democracy failed to take root and the Russian government became increasingly authoritarian. Exports of gas to Europe and China increased Russian government income in the early 21st century, underpinning a more assertive foreign policy. Threats to Ukraine's gas supply were used to discourage it from pursuing pro-Western policies. Russia's invasion of Georgia, which had applied to join NATO in 2008, was a warning to NATO not to expand into what Russia considered its own sphere of influence. Africa's last white regime fell in 1994 following the repeal of apartheid in South Africa and the introduction of majority rule under the recently freed Nelson Mandela.

Five Largest Cities *millions*

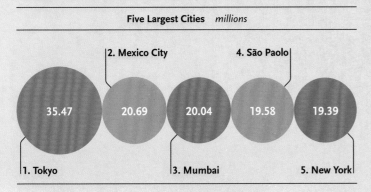

1. Tokyo	2. Mexico City	3. Mumbai	4. São Paolo	5. New York
35.47	20.69	20.04	19.58	19.39

GREENLAND (Denmark)

CANADA

UNITED STATES OF AMERICA

Bermuda (UK)

MEXICO

Mexico City

Hawaii (USA)

Cayman Islands (UK)

CUBA

BAHAMAS

New York

St Pierre et Miquelon (Fr)

1 JAMAICA
2 Netherlands Antilles
3 Puerto Rico (USA)
4 HAITI
5 DOMINICAN REPUBLIC
6 Turks and Caicos Islands (UK)
7 ST KITTS AND NEVIS
8 GRENADA

US Virgin Islands

British Virgin Islands
Anguilla (UK)
ANTIGUA AND BARBUDA
Guadeloupe (Fr)
DOMINICA
Martinique (Fr)
ST LUCIA
BARBADOS
ST VINCENT AND THE GRENADINES
TRINIDAD & TOBAGO
FRENCH GUIANA

BELIZE
GUATEMALA
EL SALVADOR
HONDURAS
NICARAGUA
COSTA RICA
PANAMA

VENEZUELA

COLOMBIA

GUYANA
SURINAME

Galapagos Islands (Ecuador)

ECUADOR

BRAZIL

French Polynesia

PERU

BOLIVIA

Pitcairn Island (UK)

São Paolo

PARAGUAY

Easter Island (Chile)

CHILE

URUGUAY

ARGENTINA

Falkland Islands (UK)

European Union

Member of NATO

Other states and territories

Communist or nominally communist states

NETHERLANDS 9
SVALBARD (Norway)
HUNGARY 18
BELGIUM 10
MOLDOVA 19
LUXEMBOURG 11
SLOVENIA 20
SWITZERLAND 12
CROATIA 21
Kaliningrad (RUS) 13
BOSNIA- HERZEGOVINA 22
LITHUANIA 14
SERBIA 23
CZECH REPUBLIC 15
SLOVAKIA 16
AUSTRIA 17

75°
Arctic Circle
45°
Tropic of Cancer
Equator
Tropic of Capricorn
45°

ICELAND
Faroe Islands (Denmark)
NORWAY
SWEDEN
FINLAND
ESTONIA
LATVIA
UNITED KINGDOM
DENMARK
9
10
11
GERMANY
POLAND
BELARUS
IRELAND
13
14
12
15 16
17
18
19
UKRAINE
FRANCE
ROMANIA
20
21 23 27
22
BULGARIA
24
26
MONTENEGRO 24
ALBANIA 25
MACEDONIA 26
KOSOVO 27
ITALY
25
GREECE
ARMENIA
TURKEY
47 48
49
PORTUGAL
SPAIN
Azores (Pt)
Gibraltar (UK)
Ceuta (Sp)
TUNISIA
MALTA
CYPRUS
51
50
IRAQ
IRAN
Madeira (Pt)
Melilla (Sp)
MOROCCO
52
53
Canary Islands (Sp)
WESTERN SAHARA (Morocco)
ALGERIA
LIBYA
EGYPT
SAUDI ARABIA
54 55
56
57
OMAN

RUSSIA

KAZAKHSTAN
UZBEKISTAN
TURKMENISTAN
49
KYRGYZSTAN
TAJIKISTAN
MONGOLIA
PEOPLE'S REPUBLIC OF CHINA
NORTH KOREA
SOUTH KOREA
JAPAN
1 Tokyo

AFGHANISTAN
PAKISTAN
NEPAL
BHUTAN
BANGLADESH
MYANMAR
60 THAILAND
61 LAOS
62 SINGAPORE
63 BRUNEI
REPUBLIC OF CHINA

3 Mumbai
INDIA
61
60
VIETNAM
PHILIPPINES
Mariana Islands (USA)
Guam (USA)
MARSHALL ISLANDS

28
SENEGAL
GAMBIA
GUINEA BISSAU
29
MAURITANIA
MALI
NIGER
CHAD
30
31
33
NIGERIA
32
37
SIERRA LEONE
LIBERIA
GHANA
34
36
34
DEMOCRATIC REPUBLIC OF CONGO
39
KENYA
35
38
Ascension Island (UK)
GABON
CABINDA (Angola)
RWANDA
BURUNDI
40
COMOROS
ERITREA
YEMEN
58
59 PUNTLAND
ETHIOPIA
SOMALIA (no effective central government)
MALDIVE ISLANDS
SRI LANKA
Andaman Islands (India)
Nicobar Islands (India)
CAMBODIA
PALAU
MALAYSIA
62
63
INDONESIA
FEDERATED STATES OF MICRONESIA
NAURU
KIRIBATI
PAPUA NEW GUINEA
SOLOMON ISLANDS
TUVALU
EAST TIMOR

SEYCHELLES
British Indian Ocean Territory
Amirante Islands (Seychelles)
Cocos Islands (Australia)
Christmas Island (Australia)

CAPE VERDE 28
BURKINA FASO 29
GUINEA 30
IVORY COAST 31
TOGO 32
BENIN 33
EQUATORIAL GUINEA 34
SÃO TOMÉ AND PRÍNCIPE 35
St Helena (UK)
ANGOLA
41
42
46
Mayotte (Fr)
MADAGASCAR
MAURITIUS
Réunion (Fr)
AUSTRALIA
VANUATU
TONGA
FIJI
New Caledonia (Fr)

Tristan da Cunha (UK)
43
44
45
SWAZILAND
SOUTH AFRICA
LESOTHO

47 ABKHAZIA
48 GEORGIA
49 AZERBAIJAN
50 LEBANON
51 SYRIA
52 ISRAEL
53 JORDAN

54 KUWAIT
55 BAHRAIN
56 QATAR
57 UNITED ARAB EMIRATES
58 DJIBOUTI
59 SOMALILAND

36 CAMEROON
37 CENTRAL AFRICAN REPUBLIC
38 CONGO
39 UGANDA
40 TANZANIA

41 ZAMBIA
42 MALAWI
43 ZIMBABWE
44 BOTSWANA
45 NAMIBIA
46 MOZAMBIQUE

Kerguelen Island (Fr)

NEW ZEALAND

0°
30°
60°
90°
120°
150°
180°

2010

Any sense of American invulnerability was abruptly shattered on 11 September 2001 when Islamist terrorists of the Al-Qaeda movement crashed hijacked airliners into the World Trade Center, New York, and the Pentagon, in Washington DC. After the Soviet withdrawal in 1989, most of Afghanistan had come under the control of the Islamic fundamentalist Taliban, which allowed Islamist groups like Al-Qaeda to set up terrorist training camps there. The USA responded by invading Afghanistan with its NATO allies. Fighting between NATO and the Taliban was still continuing in 2010 with no end in sight.

A US-led invasion of Iraq was scarcely more successful. The regime of Saddam Hussein was quickly overthrown, but the country subsequently suffered years of violence between Sunni and Shi'ite militias. The establishment, and survival, of popular left-wing governments in Venezuela and Bolivia was a sign that Latin America was emerging from the USA's shadow.

The great success story of the early 21st century was the spectacular growth of the Chinese economy. Thanks to a huge pool of cheap labour and a deliberately undervalued currency, China gained a great competitive advantage over other manufacturing economies, building huge trade surpluses and foreign currency reserves. China's growth was helped by buoyant consumer demand in the USA, funded by easy credit and an unsustainable real estate bubble. Levels of private debt soared. In 2008, the collapse of the overheated US real-estate market created a financial crisis in the US banking system that soon spread to Europe, triggering a serious recession in most Western economies. Growth in the emerging economies of Brazil, India and China remained strong, however, creating a growing sense that the balance of global economic power was shifting.

World Population

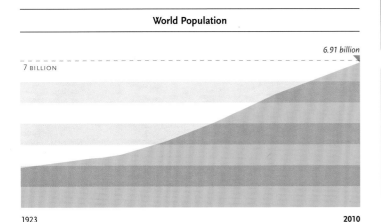

6.91 billion

7 BILLION

214

1923 — 2010

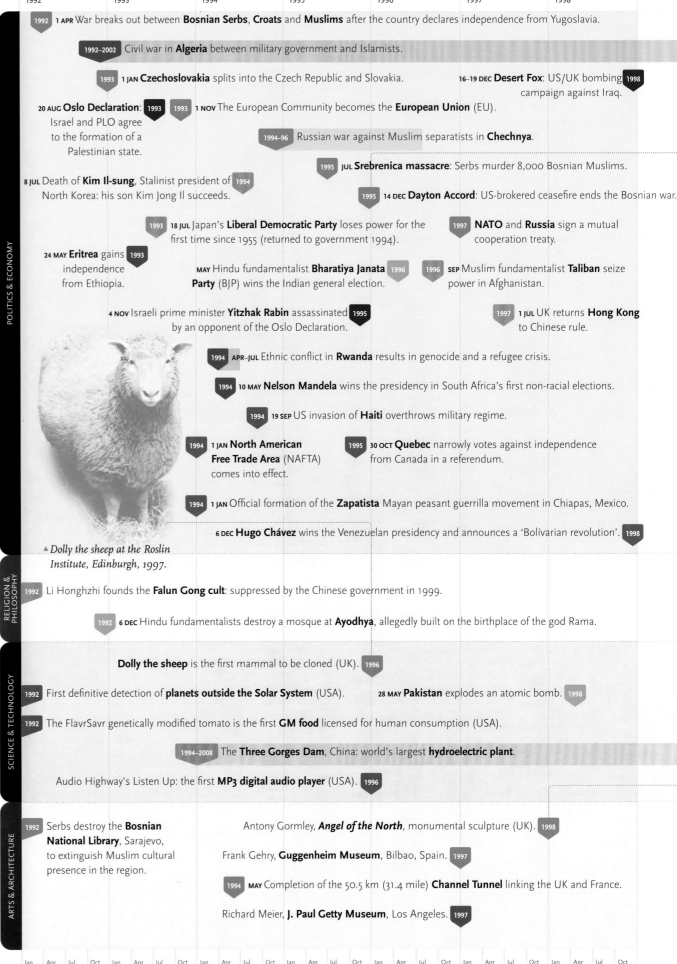

1992 | 1993 | 1994 | 1995 | 1996 | 1997 | 1998

POLITICS & ECONOMY

1992 1 APR War breaks out between **Bosnian Serbs**, **Croats** and **Muslims** after the country declares independence from Yugoslavia.

1992–2002 Civil war in **Algeria** between military government and Islamists.

1993 1 JAN **Czechoslovakia** splits into the Czech Republic and Slovakia.

16–19 DEC **Desert Fox**: US/UK bombing **1998** campaign against Iraq.

20 AUG **Oslo Declaration**: **1993** Israel and PLO agree to the formation of a Palestinian state.

1993 1 NOV The European Community becomes the **European Union** (EU).

1994–96 Russian war against Muslim separatists in **Chechnya**.

1995 JUL **Srebrenica massacre**: Serbs murder 8,000 Bosnian Muslims.

8 JUL Death of **Kim Il-sung**, Stalinist president of **1994** North Korea: his son Kim Jong Il succeeds.

1995 14 DEC **Dayton Accord**: US-brokered ceasefire ends the Bosnian war.

1993 18 JUL Japan's **Liberal Democratic Party** loses power for the first time since 1955 (returned to government 1994).

1997 **NATO** and **Russia** sign a mutual cooperation treaty.

24 MAY **Eritrea** gains **1993** independence from Ethiopia.

MAY Hindu fundamentalist **Bharatiya Janata Party** (BJP) wins the Indian general election. **1996**

1996 SEP Muslim fundamentalist **Taliban** seize power in Afghanistan.

4 NOV Israeli prime minister **Yitzhak Rabin** assassinated **1995** by an opponent of the Oslo Declaration.

1997 1 JUL UK returns **Hong Kong** to Chinese rule.

1994 APR–JUL Ethnic conflict in **Rwanda** results in genocide and a refugee crisis.

1994 10 MAY **Nelson Mandela** wins the presidency in South Africa's first non-racial elections.

1994 19 SEP US invasion of **Haiti** overthrows military regime.

1994 1 JAN **North American Free Trade Area** (NAFTA) comes into effect.

1995 30 OCT **Quebec** narrowly votes against independence from Canada in a referendum.

1994 1 JAN Official formation of the **Zapatista** Mayan peasant guerrilla movement in Chiapas, Mexico.

6 DEC **Hugo Chávez** wins the Venezuelan presidency and announces a 'Bolívarian revolution'. **1998**

▲ *Dolly the sheep at the Roslin Institute, Edinburgh, 1997.*

RELIGION & PHILOSOPHY

1992 Li Honghzhi founds the **Falun Gong cult**: suppressed by the Chinese government in 1999.

1992 6 DEC Hindu fundamentalists destroy a mosque at **Ayodhya**, allegedly built on the birthplace of the god Rama.

SCIENCE & TECHNOLOGY

Dolly the sheep is the first mammal to be cloned (UK). **1996**

1992 First definitive detection of **planets outside the Solar System** (USA).

28 MAY **Pakistan** explodes an atomic bomb. **1998**

1992 The FlavrSavr genetically modified tomato is the first **GM food** licensed for human consumption (USA).

1994–2008 The **Three Gorges Dam**, China: world's largest **hydroelectric plant**.

Audio Highway's Listen Up: the first **MP3 digital audio player** (USA). **1996**

ARTS & ARCHITECTURE

1992 Serbs destroy the **Bosnian National Library**, Sarajevo, to extinguish Muslim cultural presence in the region.

Antony Gormley, **Angel of the North**, monumental sculpture (UK). **1998**

Frank Gehry, **Guggenheim Museum**, Bilbao, Spain. **1997**

1994 MAY Completion of the 50.5 km (31.4 mile) **Channel Tunnel** linking the UK and France.

Richard Meier, **J. Paul Getty Museum**, Los Angeles. **1997**

Jan Apr Jul Oct Jan Apr Jul Oct Jan Apr Jul Oct Jan Apr Jul Oct Jan Apr Jul Oct Jan Apr Jul Oct Jan Apr Jul Oct

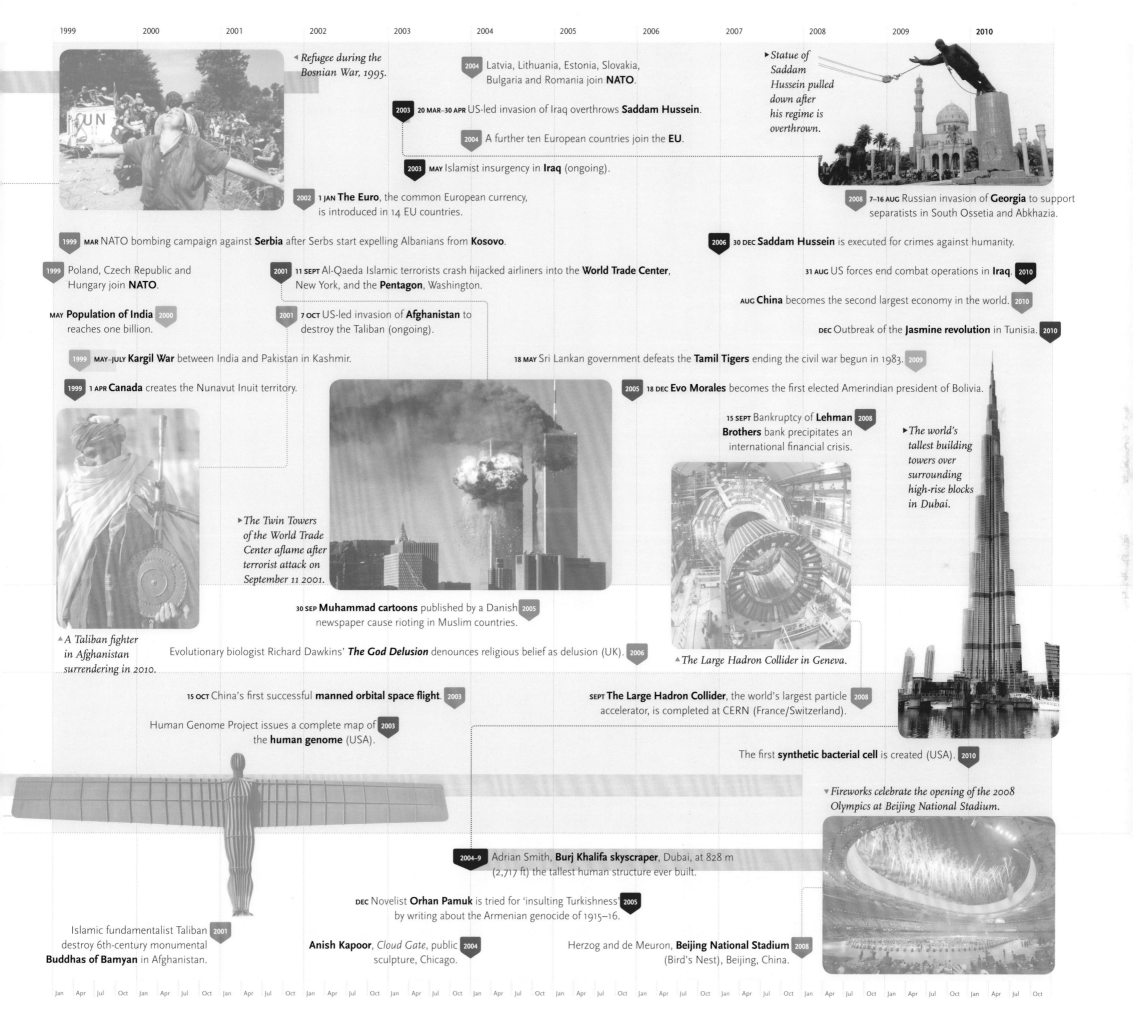

1999 2000 2001 2002 2003 2004 2005 2006 2007 2008 2009 **2010**

◀ *Refugee during the Bosnian War, 1995.*

`2004` Latvia, Lithuania, Estonia, Slovakia, Bulgaria and Romania join **NATO**.

`2003` **20 MAR–30 APR** US-led invasion of Iraq overthrows **Saddam Hussein**.

`2004` A further ten European countries join the **EU**.

`2003` **MAY** Islamist insurgency in **Iraq** (ongoing).

`2002` **1 JAN** **The Euro**, the common European currency, is introduced in 14 EU countries.

`1999` **MAR** NATO bombing campaign against **Serbia** after Serbs start expelling Albanians from **Kosovo**.

`1999` Poland, Czech Republic and Hungary join **NATO**.

MAY **Population of India** `2000` reaches one billion.

`2001` **11 SEPT** Al-Qaeda Islamic terrorists crash hijacked airliners into the **World Trade Center**, New York, and the **Pentagon**, Washington.

`2001` **7 OCT** US-led invasion of **Afghanistan** to destroy the Taliban (ongoing).

`1999` **MAY–JULY** **Kargil War** between India and Pakistan in Kashmir.

`1999` **1 APR** **Canada** creates the Nunavut Inuit territory.

▶ *Statue of Saddam Hussein pulled down after his regime is overthrown.*

`2008` **7–16 AUG** Russian invasion of **Georgia** to support separatists in South Ossetia and Abkhazia.

`2006` **30 DEC** **Saddam Hussein** is executed for crimes against humanity.

31 AUG US forces end combat operations in **Iraq**. `2010`

AUG **China** becomes the second largest economy in the world. `2010`

DEC Outbreak of the **Jasmine revolution** in Tunisia. `2010`

18 MAY Sri Lankan government defeats the **Tamil Tigers** ending the civil war begun in 1983. `2009`

`2005` **18 DEC** **Evo Morales** becomes the first elected Amerindian president of Bolivia.

15 SEPT Bankruptcy of **Lehman Brothers** bank precipitates an international financial crisis. `2008`

▶ *The world's tallest building towers over surrounding high-rise blocks in Dubai.*

▶ *The Twin Towers of the World Trade Center aflame after terrorist attack on September 11 2001.*

30 SEP **Muhammad cartoons** published by a Danish newspaper cause rioting in Muslim countries. `2005`

Evolutionary biologist Richard Dawkins' **The God Delusion** denounces religious belief as delusion (UK). `2006`

▲ *The Large Hadron Collider in Geneva.*

▲ *A Taliban fighter in Afghanistan surrendering in 2010.*

15 OCT China's first successful **manned orbital space flight**. `2003`

Human Genome Project issues a complete map of the **human genome** (USA). `2003`

SEPT **The Large Hadron Collider**, the world's largest particle accelerator, is completed at CERN (France/Switzerland). `2008`

The first **synthetic bacterial cell** is created (USA). `2010`

▼ *Fireworks celebrate the opening of the 2008 Olympics at Beijing National Stadium.*

`2004–9` Adrian Smith, **Burj Khalifa skyscraper**, Dubai, at 828 m (2,717 ft) the tallest human structure ever built.

DEC Novelist **Orhan Pamuk** is tried for 'insulting Turkishness' by writing about the Armenian genocide of 1915–16. `2005`

Islamic fundamentalist Taliban `2001` destroy 6th-century monumental **Buddhas of Bamyan** in Afghanistan.

Anish Kapoor, *Cloud Gate*, public `2004` sculpture, Chicago.

Herzog and de Meuron, **Beijing National Stadium** `2008` (Bird's Nest), Beijing, China.

Jan Apr Jul Oct Jan Apr Jul Oct Jan Apr Jul Oct Jan Apr Jul Oct Jan Apr Jul Oct Jan Apr Jul Oct Jan Apr Jul Oct Jan Apr Jul Oct Jan Apr Jul Oct Jan Apr Jul Oct Jan Apr Jul Oct Jan Apr Jul Oct

A–Z of Peoples, Nations and Cultures

This glossary provides fuller information about the places and peoples mentioned in the main text and on the maps and timelines. Cross-references are given in bold. Major world regions, language families and chronological periods are also defined.

Abasgia (Abkhazia) Early medieval kingdom of the Caucasus, absorbed by **Georgia** following a dynastic union in AD 978. See **Abkhazia**.

Abbasid caliphate The second major Islamic dynasty in the Middle East, the Abbasids seized power from the **Umayyads** in AD 750. The last Abbasid caliph was executed by the **Mongols** in 1258.

Abkhazia Unrecognized modern state in the Caucasus; became de facto independent from **Georgia** in 1992–93.

Aborigines The native peoples of **Australia**. The ancestors of the Aborigines arrived c. 60,000 years ago from Southeast Asia in what was one of the earliest seaborne migrations in human history. For most of their history, the Aborigines lived in near isolation from the rest of the world, following a hunter-gatherer way of life until the beginning of European colonization in the 18th century AD.

Acadia French North American colony founded in 1604; conquered by the British in 1710 and renamed **Nova Scotia**. Most French Acadian settlers were deported to **Louisiana**, becoming known as 'Cajuns'.

Aceh (Achin or Atjeh) Malay trading state of northern Sumatra. Through the influence of visiting **Arab** merchants, Aceh became, in the 13th century AD, the first state in **Indonesia** to accept Islam. Aceh was conquered by the Dutch between 1873 and 1903.

Adal Islamic state of Northeast Africa, flourished 15th–16th centuries AD.

Aden Strategically situated port in southern Arabia, now part of **Yemen**. A British colony 1838–1967.

Adena complex Ancient Indian culture of North America, centred on the Ohio river valley, c. 500 BC–AD 1. Hunters, fishers and gatherers, the Adena people also cultivated native food plants such as sunflowers.

Afanasievo culture The earliest **Neolithic** culture of the Central Asian steppes 4th–3rd millennia BC, possibly derived from the earlier **Yamnaya culture** of the western steppes. Often associated with the origins of the **Tocharian** steppe nomads.

Afghanistan Landlocked, ethnically diverse Asian country. Because of its strategic position at the crossroads of South Asia, Central Asia and the Middle East, a long succession of great empires have fought to control the region. The modern Afghan state was founded in 1747 by Ahmed Shah Durrani, who united

the region, which had become independent earlier in the century following rebellions against **Persian** rule.

Aghlabids Islamic dynasty in North Africa that ruled what is now **Tunisia** and eastern **Algeria** from AD 800 to 909.

Ahmadnagar Sultanate of northwest India, founded in 1494. Gradually conquered by the **Mughal** empire between 1600 and 1636.

Ainu Indigenous people of the Japanese archipelago, Sakhalin and the Kuril Islands. Probably descended from the prehistoric **Jomon** hunter-gatherers.

Aïr (Agadez) **Touareg** sultanate in the southern Sahara desert, now part of **Niger**, founded 1449. Part of the **Songhay** empire 1500–91, it declined into insignificance in the 17th century as trans-Saharan trade shifted to other routes.

Akan A group of peoples who settled on the Guinea coast of West Africa around the 11th century AD and had formed a number of small kingdoms by the 15th century. The Akan language belongs to the Niger–Congo language family.

Akkadian empire Mesopotamian empire, widely considered the world's earliest imperial state, founded by Sargon the Great (r. 2334–2279 BC), flourished c. 2334–c. 2193 BC.

Ak Koyunlu (White Sheep Turk) emirate Turkic tribal confederation from Central Asia that built a short-lived empire in **Iraq** and **Iran** in the later 15th century AD. The **Safavids** destroyed the emirate 1501–8.

Alans **Iranian**-speaking nomad people of the Caspian steppes. First recorded by the **Romans**, they are claimed as ancestors by the modern Ossetians of the Caucasus.

Alavids Shi'ite **Persian** dynasty of **Tabaristan** AD 864–928.

Albania Predominantly Muslim Southern European country, which became independent from the **Ottoman** empire in 1912. The Albanians are descended from the ancient **Illyrian** peoples.

Aleuts Native hunter-fisher-gatherer people of the Aleutian Islands, Alaska. Closely related to the **Inuit**, their ancestors migrated to the area from Northeast Asia c. 5400–4800 BC.

Algeria Muslim, mainly Arabic-speaking, North African state, most of whose population is of **Berber** descent. The modern state originated as a French colonial territory, conquered in 1830–48. Algeria became independent from **France** in 1962.

Algiers (Algeria) North African beylik of the **Ottoman** empire from 1529 until its conquest by **France** in 1830; increasingly autonomous after c. 1610.

Almohads **Berber** dynasty that supported Islamic reform and created an empire in North Africa and **Spain** (1125–1269).

Almoravids **Berber** dynasty that supported Islamic reform and created an empire in North and West Africa, and **Spain** (1056–1147). They were overthrown by the **Almohads**.

Alodia (Alwa) Christian **Nubian** kingdom in Africa, flourished from the 5th century AD to 1505 when it was conquered by the Islamic state of **Funj**.

Altaic Major language family of Central and Northeast Asia, which includes the Turkic, Mongol and Manchu–Tungus languages.

Amorites A nomadic Semitic people from Arabia of the 3rd–2nd millennia BC. They dominated Mesopotamia from 2000 to 1600 BC, founding important dynasties in **Babylon** and **Assyria**.

Ancestral Pueblo Early farming culture of the southwestern deserts of North America; flourished from c. AD 700 to c. 1300 when it collapsed, it is thought, due to prolonged drought.

Andaman Islands Indian Ocean archipelago first settled, in distant prehistoric times, by the ancestors of the modern-day Andamanese. The British East India Company established a base on the islands in 1789. Since 1947 the islands have been part of **India**.

Andronovo culture **Bronze Age** pastoralist culture of the western Eurasian steppes (2500–800 BC), often associated with the origins of the **Indo-Iranian** steppe nomads.

Anglo-Egyptian Sudan Anglo-Egyptian condominium over **Sudan** from 1899 until its independence in 1956.

Anglo-Saxons Early Germanic peoples, comprising the Angles, Saxons and Jutes, from northern **Germany** and **Denmark**, who migrated to Britain in the 5th century AD.

Angola Southern African country. Formerly a Portuguese colonial territory acquired between 1575 and the 1891, it became independent in 1975.

Anguilla Caribbean island in the Leeward Islands. Anguilla became an English colony in 1650 and remains a British dependent territory.

Ankole East African kingdom that became part of the British colony of **Uganda** in 1894.

Antigua and Barbuda Caribbean island state in the Leeward Islands. Antigua became an English colony in 1632, Barbuda in 1666. They became independent in 1967.

Anuradhapura **Sinhalese** kingdom of Ceylon (modern **Sri Lanka**), named for its capital city, founded around the 2nd century BC; collapsed c. 993 BC following an invasion by the **Cholas**.

Arabs A major Semitic people, originally from the Arabian peninsula, who became widespread across the Middle East and North Africa as a result of the Islamic conquests of the 7th century AD. The earliest record of the Arabs dates to 853 BC.

Aragon Christian Spanish kingdom founded in 1035. Aragon was united to **Castile** in 1469 by a dynastic marriage, leading to the creation of the kingdom of **Spain** in 1516.

Arakan Indianized Southeast Asian kingdom of the Rakhine people that emerged c. AD 818. Conquered by the **Burmese** in 1787.

Aramaeans A group of Semitic peoples of **Syria** first recorded in the 16th century BC. The Aramaeans disappeared as a distinct people around the 6th century BC, but Aramaic languages continued to be widely spoken in the Middle East until c. AD 650.

Araucanians A group of South American Indian peoples of central **Chile**. They fiercely resisted their Spanish conquerors, and later the Chileans, from 1541 until the 1880s.

Arawak Two groups of American Indian peoples: the Antillean Arawak or Taino, who lived in the Caribbean, and the South American Arawak, who lived in the northern Amazon basin. Small groups of Arawak survive in **Cuba** and **Puerto Rico**; in South America they number about three million.

Argentina Latin American republic. Argentina declared independence from **Spain** in 1816 as the **United Provinces of Rio de la Plata**. After **Bolivia** and **Uruguay** seceded from the United Provinces in 1825–28, the remaining provinces reorganized themselves as the Argentine Confederation: Argentina was constituted as a unitary state in 1853.

Armenia Kingdom of the Transcaucasus region that emerged from the break-up of the empire of Alexander the Great. Converted to Christianity c. AD 300, frequently under foreign rule since 428. Modern Armenia became independent of the **USSR** in 1991.

Asante A sub-group of the **Akan** peoples of the Guinea coast of West Africa. United by Osei Tutu c. 1701, the Asante formed a powerful kingdom, which was eventually conquered by the British in 1901.

Ascension Island in the South Atlantic Ocean discovered by the Portuguese in 1501. It became a British possession in 1815.

Aspero tradition Cultural tradition of the north coast of **Peru**, c. 3000–1800 BC. Fishing supported a complex society that built some of the earliest monumental buildings in the Americas.

Assam Region of northeast **India**, named for the Ahom people, originally from Yunnan (now part of eastern China), who founded a kingdom in the area in the 15th century AD. Assam was occupied by

British forces in 1824 and was formally annexed to British India in 1826.

Assyria Major power of northern Mesopotamia from *c.* 1800 BC until its conquest by the Babylonians and **Medes** in 612 BC. The Assyrians spoke Akkadian, a Semitic language also spoken by the Babylonians.

Astrakhan, khanate of Tatar state in Central Asia that emerged from the break-up of the **Golden Horde** in the 15th century AD. Conquered by **Russia** 1552–56.

Asturias Christian Spanish kingdom founded *c.* AD 712–22, known as the kingdom of **León** after 910.

Athens Major city state and leading cultural centre of **Greece**'s Classical Age (480–356 BC). Athens lost its independence in 338 BC, when it was conquered by Philip of **Macedon**. It became capital of the modern Greek state in 1832.

Atropatene Persian kingdom of the 4th to 1st centuries BC, approximating to modern **Azerbaijan**.

Aussa (Awsa) Islamic sultanate of the Afar people of modern-day **Eritrea** and Djibouti. Founded in 1577, Aussa came under Italian control in 1865.

Australia The modern country of Australia was formed when Britain united its Australian colonies to form the self-governing Commonwealth of Australia in 1901; became fully independent in 1931.

Austria German-speaking European state that originated as a duchy of the **Holy Roman empire** in 1156. Under the Habsburg emperors (1438–1918) Austria became the major Central European power; following the fall of the Habsburgs, Austria was reduced to a minor state. United to **Germany** 1938–45 by the *Anschluss*.

Austrian Netherlands The former **Spanish Netherlands**, ceded to Austria in 1713. The territory was annexed by **France** in 1795, and then united with the **Netherlands** in 1815. It declared independence as **Belgium** in 1831 (officially recognized in 1839).

Austro-Asiatics Group of peoples speaking Austro-Asiatic languages, native to Southeast Asia and eastern India, including the **Vietnamese**, **Khmer** and **Mon** peoples. Austro-Asiatic languages are thought originally to have been spoken throughout Southeast Asia, their range having been greatly reduced by later waves of immigration.

Austro-Hungarian empire State created by the introduction of the Dual Monarchy, a union of the crowns of the Austrian empire and **Hungary** in 1867 by which the Austrian Habsburg rulers agreed to share power with a separate Hungarian government. Officially known as Austria–Hungary because Hungarians refused to accept the implied unity of the Austro-Hungarian title. The Dual Monarchy collapsed in 1918 after Austria–Hungary's defeat in the First World War.

Austronesians A widespread group of peoples of Australasia, Southeast Asia and **Madagascar** speaking Austronesian languages, thought to have originated on Taiwan or mainland China in prehistoric times, including the **Malays**, **Chams**, **Polynesians** and **Malagasy**.

Avanti Early Hindu *mahajanapada* (great realm) of northern **India**, flourished 6th–4th centuries BC.

Avars A nomad people consisting of Turkic and other tribes who emerged from the break-up of the **Rouran** (or Juan-juan) nomad confederacy in the 6th century AD and migrated to Europe, founding a khanate on the Hungarian plain. Decisively defeated by the **Franks** in 796, the Avar khanate had disintegrated by *c.* 810.

Axum (Aksum) Early Ethiopian trading kingdom with links to southwestern Arabia, flourished *c.* 1 BC–AD 975.

Aymara Major ethnic/linguistic group of the Andes in southern Peru, Bolivia and northern **Chile**; they presently number around two million.

Ayyubids Sunni Muslim dynasty, founded by Saladin in 1174, that ruled **Egypt**, **Syria** and northern **Iraq** until 1250.

Azerbaijan Turkic-speaking, primarily Shi'ite Muslim, state of Transcaucasia. Formerly a republic of the **USSR**, Azerbaijan became independent in 1991.

Azores North Atlantic archipelago, first colonized by the Portuguese in 1436. Now an autonomous region of **Portugal**.

Aztecs Nahuatl-speaking peoples, originally from northwest **Mexico**, who migrated into the central Valley of Mexico around the 13th century AD. Between 1428 and 1519 they were the dominant power of **Mesoamerica**. Mexico gets its name from the most famous Aztec people, the Mexica.

Babylon Major Mesopotamian city state, founded mid-3rd millennium BC; conquered by the **Persians** in 539 BC and abandoned *c.* 140 BC.

Bactria Greek kingdom of Central Asia, **Afghanistan** and, from *c.* 180 BC, northern **India**; it became independent of the **Seleucid empire** *c.* 255 BC. The kingdom was destroyed by the **Kushans** in the 2nd century BC.

Bagan (Pagan) The earliest **Burmese** kingdom, named after its capital city Bagan, a major Buddhist centre. Flourished from the mid-9th century AD until its destruction by the **Mongols** in 1287.

Bagirmi Minor 18th-century Islamic state in present-day **Chad**.

Bahamas Group of islands in the Caribbean. Site of Columbus's first landfall in the Americas in 1492. British colony from 1650 until independence in 1973.

Bahmani sultanate Founded 1347, the major Muslim state of southern **India** in the 15th century AD; broke up into smaller states 1518–27.

Bahrain Arab state founded by the Khalifa dynasty in 1783. Bahrain was a British protectorate 1861–1971.

Balts Group of Northern European peoples, named for the Baltic Sea, though previously more widespread; their only modern representatives are the Lithuanians and Latvians. Baltic languages belong to the **Indo-European** language.

Baluchistan Mountainous region, now mostly in **Pakistan**, named for the majority ethnic group, the Balochi.

Bangladesh South Asian state, formerly East **Pakistan**. Bangladesh became independent in 1971 following a war of independence, aided by an Indian invasion.

Bantam (Banten) City and sultanate of west Java. Founded in 1527, it became a Dutch protectorate in 1684.

Bantu The major linguistic group of Central and Southern Africa, comprising 85 million people speaking around 500 distinct languages.

Barbados Caribbean island state, founded as an English colony in 1627; independent 1966.

Barcelona, county of Founded by Charlemagne in AD 801 following the conquest of the city from the Muslims; merged with **Aragon** in 1169.

Basketmaker cultures Preceding the **Ancestral Pueblo** culture in southwestern North America, Basketmaker cultures (*c.* 1200 BC–*c.* AD 700) were transitional between hunting and gathering, and maize farming, which was adopted around the end of the 1st millennium BC.

Basques People of northern **Spain** and southwest **France** whose lands became part of the kingdom of **Navarre** in the 10th century AD. The Basque language is unrelated to any other known European language.

Basutoland See **Lesotho**.

Bechuanaland British colonial territory in Southern Africa, annexed in 1885. It became independent as Botswana in 1966.

Bedouin Arab pastoral nomads of **Arabia**, **Iraq**, **Syria**, **Jordan**, **Israel**, **Egypt** and **Sudan**.

Belarus (White Russia) Eastern European state with **Slav** population. Formerly the Belorussian Soviet Socialist Republic, Belarus declared independence from the **USSR** in 1991.

Belgian Congo Belgian colony in Central Africa created after the Belgian government annexed the **Congo Free State** in 1908. It became independent as the **Democratic Republic of Congo** in 1960.

Belgium European kingdom with a French and Flemish (Dutch) speaking population. Belgium was originally the southern half of the **Spanish Netherlands** which remained under Spanish rule after the Dutch revolt in the 16th century. Transferred to Austrian control in 1713, the territory was formally annexed by **France** in 1795, and then united with the **Netherlands** in 1815. Following a rebellion against Dutch rule, Belgium became independent in 1839.

Belize 1. Former British Central American colony founded on the Belize river in the mid-17th century AD. 2. Modern independent nation of Belize. Also see **British Honduras**.

Bell Beaker cultures Widespread late **Neolithic**/early **Bronze Age** cultures of Western Europe, named

for the distinctive shape of their pottery drinking vessels. Flourished *c.* 2500–1800 BC.

Bengal Historic region of South Asia, now divided between India and **Bangladesh**.

Benin 1. Historical West African city and kingdom of the Edo people founded 1250; at its peak 15th–18th centuries. Conquered by the British in 1897, now part of **Nigeria**. 2. Modern West African republic, known until 1975 as **Dahomey**.

Berbers (Amazigh) Pre-Arab inhabitants of North Africa with scattered communities in **Morocco**, **Algeria**, **Tunisia**, **Libya**, **Egypt**, **Mauritania**, **Niger** and **Mali**. The Berbers of Mediterranean North Africa were often called Moors by Europeans after the Mauri, an ancient Berber people.

Bermuda British dependency in the North Atlantic Ocean. Discovered by the Spanish in 1505, it became an English colony in 1609.

Bhutan Small Tibetan-speaking, largely Buddhist, kingdom of the Himalaya that emerged in the 17th century AD.

Bijapur Muslim sultanate of southwest **India**, founded in 1527 following the fall of the **Bahmani sultanate**; conquered by the **Mughals** in 1686.

Bithynia Hellenized kingdom of northern Anatolia, founded 297 BC; bequeathed to the Roman empire by its last ruler in 74 BC.

Boers (Afrikaners) White South Africans of Dutch ancestry.

Bohemia Region of Central Europe and early medieval **Slav** kingdom absorbed into the **Holy Roman empire** in the 10th century AD, now part of the **Czech Republic**.

Bolivia South American republic, which became independent from **Spain** in 1824–25; its present-day borders were settled in 1938.

Borgu West African kingdom, flourished 15th–19th centuries AD. It came under the domination of the **Sokoto caliphate** in the 1870s, and in 1898 it was divided between the British and French empires.

Bornu West African kingdom, successor to the **Kanem** kingdom. Founded in 1396, it was annexed to the British colony of **Nigeria** in 1893.

Bosnia–Herzegovina Balkan state with a mixed Bosniak, Serb and Croat population. The country's declaration of independence from **Yugoslavia** in 1991 was followed by a civil war (1992–95) that left it divided into two autonomous entities, the Bosniak–Croat-dominated Federation of Bosnia and Herzegovina, and the Serb-dominated Republika Srpska.

Bosporos Hellenized kingdom of the Crimean peninsula, founded 480 BC; it became a Roman vassal state in 16 BC.

Botswana Southern African republic. Formerly the British colony of **Bechuanaland**, which became independent in 1966.

Brandenburg–Prussia German principality created by the union of the Electorate of Brandenburg and the Duchy of **Prussia** in 1618; it became the kingdom of Prussia in 1701.

Brazil South American republic. Brazil was claimed by **Portugal** in 1500 and colonization began in 1534. Brazil declared independence from Portugal in 1822.

British East Africa See **Kenya**.

British Guiana British South American colony. Originally part of **Dutch Guiana**, it was occupied by the British in 1803 and formally ceded to Britain in 1814. It became independent as **Guyana** in 1966.

British Honduras Name given to the British Central American colony of **Belize** from 1862 to 1981.

British Somaliland British East African colony, annexed in 1884. United with neighbouring **Italian Somaliland**, it became independent as **Somalia** in 1960.

British Virgin Islands British dependency in the Caribbean. The islands came under English control between 1672 and 1680.

Bronze Age Technological division of human prehistory defined by the use of bronze tools and weapons, but not iron. The term was first applied to European prehistory in the 19th century and subsequently applied to the rest of Eurasia and North Africa. The term is not applied to Sub-Saharan Africa, where bronze and iron technology were adopted at the same time. Bronze tools and weapons never became widely used in the pre-Columbian Americas.

Brunei Independent sultanate on the Southeast Asian island of Borneo. An important trade centre in the 16th–19th centuries AD, Brunei was a British protectorate from 1888 to 1984.

Buganda East African kingdom, at its peak in the early 19th century AD; it formed the core of the British colony of **Uganda**, created in 1894.

Bukhara Central Asian **Uzbek** khanate, centred on the caravan city of Bukhara, founded around 1500, annexed by the Russian empire in 1868–73.

Bulgaria East European republic, became independent of the **Ottoman** empire in 1878 and attained its modern borders in 1913. The Bulgarians are **Slav** in language and culture.

Bulgars Turkic nomad people who migrated to Eastern Europe in the 6th century AD and, dividing into two groups, settled on the Volga river in **Russia** and in the Balkans in present-day **Bulgaria**. The Volga Bulgars were conquered by the **Mongols** in 1237. The Balkan Bulgars were conquered by the **Byzantine empire** in 1018, regained their independence in the 12th century, but were conquered again by the **Ottomans** in 1393.

Bunce Island British slave-trading base on the coast of **Sierra Leone**, established in 1670 and destroyed by the French in 1779.

Bunyoro East African kingdom, became part of British colony of **Uganda** in 1894.

Burgundians Early **Germanic** people who invaded the **Roman empire** in AD 406–7.

Burgundy 1. The kingdom founded by the Burgundians in AD 443; conquered by the Franks in 532–34. 2. Frankish kingdom created in AD 887, absorbed by the **Holy Roman empire** in 1033.

Burkina Faso West African country, formerly the province of Upper Volta in **French West Africa**. Upper Volta became independent in 1960 and changed its name to Burkina Faso in 1984.

Burma Southeast Asian republic, known as Myanmar since 1989. The first Burmese state was founded at **Bagan** in the 9th century AD. Conquered piecemeal by the British in the 19th century, Burma regained its independence in 1948.

Burmese (Burmans or Bamar) The majority people of **Burma**, they probably originated in eastern China, migrating into Burma in the 1st millennium BC. The Burmese language is related to Tibetan and belongs to the Sino-Tibetan language family.

Burundi East African kingdom; at its peak c. 1790–1850, it became part of German East Africa in 1899. In 1923 it was united with **Rwanda** by the League of Nations as the Belgian mandate territory **of Ruanda–Urundi** until independence in 1962.

Buryats A Central Asian **Altaic** nomad people of southern Siberia, closely related to the **Mongols**. Conquered by the Russians 1689–1728.

Butua Kingdom of the Southern African Torwa dynasty, founded c. 1450, conquered by the **Rozwi** in 1683.

Buwayhid emirates (Buyid) **Persian** Shi'ite confederation that dominated an area approximating to present-day **Iran** and **Iraq** from c. AD 934 until its overthrow by the **Seljuk** Turks in 1055.

Byzantine empire Modern name given to the largely Greek-speaking eastern Roman empire following the fall of the western Roman empire in the 5th century AD. The name was never used by the Byzantine emperors themselves, who always regarded themselves as Roman emperors. There is no absolute agreement among historians as to the date that the eastern Roman empire became the Byzantine empire. In this atlas, it is taken as the reign of Heraclius (610–41), when Greek became the empire's official language. The empire ended with the conquest of its capital, Constantinople, by the **Ottomans** in 1453.

Cabinda Central African Portuguese colony north of the mouth of the Congo river annexed in 1885. Since 1975 it has been a detached province of **Angola**.

Cambodia Southeast Asian kingdom of the **Khmer** people, its development began with the kingdom Chenla (c. AD 550–802). French colony 1863–1953. Cambodia became a republic in 1970, but the monarchy was restored in 1993.

Cameroon Formerly the German colony of **Kamerun**, it became a French League of Nations mandated territory following the First World War and became independent in 1960.

Canaanites Middle Eastern Semitic-speaking peoples of the Levant 5th–2nd millennia BC; best known for devising the first alphabetic writing system.

Canada North American country. The name Canada was first applied to the area of **New France** north of the Great Lakes. Following the British conquest of New France, Canada became part of the colony of **Quebec**, which was later divided into the colonies of Upper and Lower Canada. In 1841 Upper and Lower Canada were reunited as the Province of Canada. Modern Canada was created by the confederation of the Province of Canada with the colonies of **Nova Scotia** and **New Brunswick** in 1867 as a self-governing Dominion of the British empire. Canada became fully independent of Britain in 1931 and attained its present territorial extent in 1949 when **Newfoundland** joined.

Canary Islands Spanish archipelago off the coast of Northwest Africa. Inhabited since prehistoric times, the islands were conquered by the Spanish kingdom of **Castile** between 1402 and 1495.

Cape Coast Castle Fortress in **Ghana**, built by the Swedes 1653. It became a major base for the Atlantic slave trade after its seizure by the English in 1664.

Cape Colony Dutch colony at the Cape of Good Hope, founded 1652. Annexed by Britain in 1806, it became a province of **South Africa** in 1910.

Cape Verde Islands Island group off West Africa, uninhabited before their discovery by the Portuguese in the 15th century AD. Since 1975, the independent republic of Cape Verde.

Cappadocia Hellenized kingdom in Anatolia c. 323 BC until 190 BC, when it became a Roman client state.

Caribs American Indian people of the Caribbean and adjacent areas of South America. Spanish slave raids and European diseases almost exterminated the Caribs in the 16th century AD.

Carolina English North American colony founded in 1663; divided into North and South Carolina in 1729.

Caroline Islands Archipelago in the western Pacific Ocean. **Spain** claimed the islands in 1875, but sold them to Germany in 1899. They were occupied by **Japan** in 1914 and in 1945 came under US administration as part of the **Trust Territories of the Pacific Islands**, from which they became independent as the **Federated States of Micronesia** in 1986.

Carolingian empire Empire founded by the Frankish ruler Charlemagne (r. AD 768–814). The name of the empire is derived from Charlemagne's name in Latin, *Karolus Magnus* (Charles the Great). The empire was partitioned between his grandsons in 843 and finally broke up in 889. Both **Germany** and **France** trace their origins to the break-up of the empire.

Carthage North African city state near modern Tunis. Founded by **Phoenician** settlers in, according to tradition, 814 BC, Carthage became a major mercantile power with a loose-knit empire in the western Mediterranean. In the 3rd century Carthage came into conflict with the **Romans**, who conquered and destroyed the city in 146 BC.

Castile Christian Spanish kingdom, originally part of **León**, but separated from it in 1065; temporarily reunited 1072–1137 as the kingdom of León and Castile. Castile in turn absorbed León in 1230. The union of the crowns of Castile and **Aragon**, which resulted from the marriage of Ferdinand of Aragon to Isabella of Castile in 1469, led to the creation of the kingdom of **Spain** in 1516.

Catacomb Grave cultures Bronze Age *kurgan* (burial mound) cultures of the western Eurasian steppes, flourished c. 2500–1800 BC.

Cayenne French South American colony founded in 1643, named after the island of Cayenne off the Guiana coast. It changed hands many times before it was permanently returned to French control in 1814. Now **French Guiana**.

Cayman Islands British Caribbean dependency, they became an English colony in 1670.

Celtiberians Celtic peoples of the Spanish Iberian peninsula, conquered by Rome 2nd–1st centuries BC.

Celts Major group of peoples speaking related **Indo-European** languages; they dominated Western and Central Europe during the European **Iron Age** of the 1st millennium BC. Linguistically their modern representatives include the Gaelic, Welsh and Breton languages.

Central African Republic Former territory of Ubangi-Shari in **French Equatorial Africa**; annexed 1889, independent 1960. Briefly (1976–79) known as the Central African empire.

Ceylon See **Sri Lanka**.

Chad Former territory of **French Equatorial Africa**; annexed 1900, independent 1960.

Chagatai khanate **Mongol** khanate in Central Asia created for Chagatai, second son of Chinggis Khan, in 1225. Effectively independent after 1260, its western territories were conquered by Timur the Lame in the later 14th century. The khanate survived in an increasingly decentralized form, divided into several sub-khanates, until it was overthrown by the **Uzbeks** and **Oirats** in 1678.

Chagos Islands Indian Ocean archipelago, claimed by **France** in the 18th century, ceded to Britain in 1814. The archipelago has been administered as the British Indian Ocean Territory since 1965.

Chalcolithic cultures Prehistoric societies in the Middle East and Europe that had begun to adopt copper metallurgy and were more complex socially and technologically than earlier farming societies, but did not use bronze.

Chaldaeans Semitic nomad people of northern Arabia who settled in Mesopotamia between 1000 and 900 BC, founding dynasties in many cities, including **Babylon**. They spoke a form of Aramaic.

Chalukyas Powerful dynasty that dominated central and southern **India** from the mid-6th century AD until 753 when they were overthrown by the **Rashtrakuta** dynasty. The dynasty revived in the mid-10th century, but declined again during the 12th century.

Champa Kingdom of the **Chams** in Southeast Asia, an important mercantile and naval power; founded *c.* AD 192, conquered by **Dai Viet** in 1611 after centuries of decline.

Chams An **Austronesian** people indigenous to the area that is now **Vietnam** and **Cambodia**.

Chavín culture The first regionally important culture and art style of **Peru**, named after the ritual complex at Chavín; flourished *c.* 850–300 BC.

Chenla Southeast Asian Indianized kingdom of **Cambodia**, the earliest **Khmer** state, founded *c.* AD 500, known as the **Khmer empire** after 802.

Chernigov Russian principality 11th–15th centuries AD.

Chile South American republic; became independent from **Spain** in 1818.

Chimú (Chimor) South American people and kingdom of **Peru**, founded *c.* AD 900, expanded to control the coastal lowlands *c.* 1200. Conquered by the **Incas** in 1470.

China, People's Republic of Chinese communist state proclaimed in 1949 by Mao Zedong. Since 1979 Marxist economics have been gradually abandoned but the Communist Party has maintained its monopoly on power. The People's Republic was admitted to China's seat at the United Nations in 1975.

China, Republic of Chinese republic founded in 1911 following the fall of the **Qing** dynasty. Since the Communist victory in the Chinese civil war in 1949 the Republic of China has consisted of Taiwan and two small offshore islands. The Republic of China held China's seat at the United Nations until 1975 when it was transferred to the **People's Republic of China**. Commonly known today as Taiwan, the Republic of China officially maintains that it is part of China, not an independent state.

Chinchorro tradition South American fishing culture of northern **Chile**, 7th century–late 1st century BC; the earliest in the world to practise mummification of the dead.

Chiripa culture Advanced farming culture of the Bolivian Andes in South America *c.* 1000–1 BC; developed an influential tradition of monumental architecture *c.* 600 BC.

Chola Hindu Tamil dynasty of southern **India** (3rd century BC–AD 1279), which was the major maritime power of the Indian Ocean from *c.* 850 to 1126.

Chorrera culture Farming and shellfish-gathering South American culture of **Ecuador**, flourished *c.* 18th–3rd centuries BC.

Chu 1. **Bronze Age** state of the middle Yangtze region, subdued by the Chinese **Zhou** kingdom after 1000 BC. Re-emerged as an independent state in the 7th century BC, conquered by **Qin** 225–223 BC. 2. Kingdom of southern China AD 907–51.

Chukchi Indigenous people of far-eastern Siberia who live as marine-mammal hunters on the coast and as reindeer herders inland. They speak a **Palaeo-Siberian** language.

Cimmerians The earliest of the **Iranian** horse-mounted nomad people of the western Eurasian steppes, absorbed by the **Scythians** in the 6th century BC.

Cochin China The southern third of **Vietnam**, independent under the Nguyen dynasty from 1620 to 1802, when it was absorbed into a unified Vietnam. French colony from 1864 to 1949.

Colchis Early Georgian kingdom, which emerged by the 6th century BC; it became known as **Lazica** after *c.* AD 250.

Colombia South American republic that became independent from **Spain** as **Gran Colombia** in 1819.

Comoro Islands Islands off West Africa. First inhabited 6th century AD, annexed by **France** 1841–86. Except Mayotte, which remains under French administration, became independent as the Union of the Comoros in 1975.

Confederate States of America Eleven southern slave-owning states, which seceded from the USA 1861–65: Alabama, Arkansas, North Carolina, South Carolina, Florida, Georgia, **Louisiana**, Mississippi, Texas, Tennessee and **Virginia**.

Confederation of the Rhine A French-dominated confederation of 16 German states formed by Napoleon after the abolition of the **Holy Roman empire** in 1806. The confederation was dissolved in 1813.

Congo African republic. Formerly part of **French Equatorial Africa** (annexed 1880s); independent in 1960.

Congo, Democratic Republic of Central African republic, formerly the **Belgian Congo**, it became independent in 1960 as the Republic of Congo. To avoid confusion with the former French colony of **Congo**, the name was changed to the Democratic Republic of Congo in 1964 and then, in 1965, to **Zaire**. In 1997 the name Democratic Republic of Congo was adopted again.

Congo Free State Colonial state created in 1885 as a private empire by Leopold II, king of the Belgians. Its infamous treatment of the native peoples led to its abolition and annexation by the Belgian government as the **Belgian Congo** in 1908.

Corded Ware cultures Northern and Eastern European late **Neolithic** farming cultures of the 3rd millennium BC, named for their characteristic cord-marked pottery.

Costa Rica Republic that became independent of the **Federal Republic of Central America** in 1838.

Croatia Historic region of the Balkans, named after the **Croats**, and former Yugoslav republic, independent 1991.

Croats Slav people of the Balkans in Eastern Europe, emerged 7th–8th centuries AD.

Crusader states Christian states in **Palestine** and **Syria** founded after the First Crusade (1095–99): the Kingdom of Jerusalem (1099–1291), County of Tripoli (1109–1289), Principality of Antioch (1098–1268), County of Edessa (1098–1150).

Cuba Caribbean republic. Claimed for **Spain** by Columbus in 1492. Spain relinquished sovereignty after its defeat in the Spanish–American War of 1898 and Cuba became formally independent in 1902.

Cumans Turkic nomad people who formed a confederation with the **Kipchaks** in the 11th–13th centuries AD.

Cushite A branch of the Afro-Asiatic language family, which also includes the Semitic, Berber and Chadic languages. Cushitic languages are spoken mainly in **Ethiopia**, **Somalia** and **Kenya**.

Cushitic pastoralists East African peoples who spoke Cushite languages.

Cyprus Mediterranean island state. Cyprus first became a state in its own right when it became a crusader kingdom in 1191; control passed to **Venice** in 1473 (formal annexation in 1489); conquered by the **Ottoman** Turks 1570; ceded to Britain in 1878; independent in 1960; divided into Greek and Turkish states since 1974.

Czechoslovakia Central European state of the Czech and Slovak peoples. It became independent on the collapse of the **Austro-Hungarian empire** in 1918; partially integrated into Germany 1939–45; divided into separate Czech and Slovak republics in 1993.

Czech Republic Central European country comprising the historic regions of **Bohemia** and Moravia created on the dissolution of **Czechoslovakia** in 1993.

Dacians Indo-European-speaking people of the Eastern European Carpathian region; conquered by the **Romans** AD 101–6.

Dahomey West African kingdom that prospered in the 18th century as a major participant in the transatlantic slave trade. Conquered by **France** 1892–94; independent in 1960. Known as **Benin** since 1975.

Dai Viet Vietnamese state that emerged following the fall of the Chinese Tang dynasty empire in 907; formally constituted as a kingdom in 939. Divided into **Tongking** and **Cochin China** after 1620; reunited and renamed **Vietnam** in 1802.

Dali Kingdom of Yunnan, now part of eastern China, the successor of **Nanzhao**; conquered by the **Mongols** in 1253.

Damot (D'mt) Early Ethiopian state known only from a few inscriptions.

Danishmend emirate Turkic state of eastern Anatolia 1071–1178.

Danish Virgin Islands The Caribbean islands of St John, St Thomas and St Croix acquired by **Denmark** between 1672 and 1733. Sold to the **USA** in 1916.

Darfur Islamic sultanate of the eastern Sahara, founded in the 14th century AD; incorporated into **Anglo-Egyptian Sudan** from 1899.

Dawenkou Neolithic culture of northeastern China *c.* 5000–2600 BC.

Delhi, sultanate of Major Islamic power of northern India under several Turkic and Afghan dynasties. Founded 1206, conquered by the **Mughals** in 1526.

Demak Southeast Asian Muslim sultanate on Java from 1475 to 1548, which overthrew the kingdom of **Majapahit** in 1527.

Denmark Scandinavian kingdom, emerged in the 9th–10th centuries AD.

Diafunu Mandinke kingdom in West Africa 12th–13th centuries AD.

Djibouti Former colony of **French Somaliland**, created 1894–96; it became independent in 1977.

Dodecanese Group of 12 islands in the Aegean Sea seized by **Italy** in 1912 informally united to **Greece** in 1945, formally ceded in 1947.

Dominica Caribbean island state. Possession was disputed between Britain and **France** in the 17th and 18th centuries. France recognized British title in 1763: independent 1978.

Dominican Republic Caribbean state in eastern Hispaniola, declared independence from **Spain** in 1821, but was immediately occupied by **Haiti**. Independence was regained in 1838.

Dong Son culture Late **Bronze Age**/early **Iron Age** culture of northern **Vietnam** *c.* 700–200 BC.

Dorset Inuit (Eskimo) culture Prehistoric Inuit culture of the North American Arctic, based on the hunting of marine mammals and caribou, which developed *c.* 1000 BC. It was replaced by the **Thule Inuit culture** after *c.* AD 1000.

Dravidian Major language family of South Asia, now mainly confined to southern **India**. The most important Dravidian languages today are Telugu, Tamil, Kannada and Malayalam.

Dutch East Indies The Dutch East Indian empire. The empire was founded when the Dutch East India Company founded a base at Bantam in Java in 1603. Over the next 300 years the Dutch gradually extended their control over most of the East Indian archipelago. The Dutch East Indies declared independence as **Indonesia** in 1945, which was recognized by the Dutch in 1949.

Dutch Guiana Dutch South American colony founded in 1600; it became independent as **Suriname** in 1975.

Dutch Timor See **Timor**.

Dvaravati Indianized kingdom of Southeast Asia, probably inhabited by the **Mons**, founded in the 6th century AD; gradually absorbed by the **Khmer empire** between the 10th and 12th centuries.

Dzungar khanate Oirat Mongol state, the last great independent nomad power of the Eurasian steppes, which developed in the 17th century AD; conquered by the Manchu **Qing** empire in 1759.

Easter Island Island in the South Pacific Ocean first settled by Polynesians c. AD 700, annexed by **Chile** in 1888. The island is famous for the giant *moai* (carved stone heads) erected by its inhabitants c. 1250–1500.

East Germany (German Democratic Republic) Communist state created in the Soviet occupation zone of **Germany** in 1949; united with **West Germany** in 1990.

East Turkestan republic Soviet-backed Turkic (mainly **Uighur**) republic in the present-day Xinjiang province of China 1944–49.

Ecuador South American republic. Ecuador became independent from **Spain** in 1822, becoming part of **Gran Colombia**, from which it seceded in 1830.

Egypt Egypt was home to the world's earliest territorial kingdom, founded c. 3000 BC. After the 8th century BC Egypt was, except for brief periods, subject to foreign rule until the 20th century. The history of the modern Egyptian state conventionally begins in 1882 with the establishment of a British protectorate over Egypt, intended to secure control over the Suez Canal. Nationalist agitation led Britain to grant Egyptian independence in 1922, although it maintained a military presence until 1954.

Elam The kingdom of the Elamites, in present-day southeast **Iran**; emerged c. 2700 BC, destroyed by the Assyrians in 644 BC. The ethnic origin of the Elamites is uncertain because their language was unrelated to any other known language.

Ellice Islands See **Tuvalu**.

Elmina Chief Portuguese trading post on the West African coast, founded 1482. Captured by the Dutch in 1637; sold to Britain in 1872; now part of **Ghana**.

El Paraiso culture Fishing, gathering and farming culture of coastal **Peru** c.1800–850 BC, named for a large U-shaped ceremonial site.

El Salvador Central American republic which became independent in 1841 following the break-up of the **Federal Republic of Central America**.

Empire of Harsha See **Kannauj**.

Empire of Timur the Lame See **Timurids**.

England Kingdom of the English, created AD 927; united with **Scotland** to form the Kingdom of Great Britain in 1707.

Ephthalites (White Huns or, in India, Hunas) Central Asian nomad confederation of the 5th–6th centuries AD; founded a kingdom in **Afghanistan** and northwest India c. 475, which broke up in the later 6th century. Their exact relationship to the **Huns** of Europe is uncertain.

Epirus, despotate of Greek successor state to the **Byzantine empire** created following the capture of

Constantinople by crusaders in 1204. It was annexed by the re-established Byzantine empire in 1337.

Equatorial Guinea West-Central African country comprising two parts: the continental region of **Rio Muni** and the islands of Bioko (formerly **Fernando Póo**) and Annobón. It became independent of **Spain** in 1968.

Eritrea Country in the Horn of Africa. Eritrea was annexed by **Italy** in 1890 and occupied by the British in 1941. In 1951 Eritrea was federated with **Ethiopia**. Discontent with Ethiopian rule led Eritrea to declare independence in 1991, recognized internationally in 1993.

Estonia Baltic republic. Estonia became independent of the Russian empire in 1918. It was occupied by Soviet forces in 1939, becoming a republic of the **USSR**. Estonia regained its independence in 1991.

Ethiopia Christian East African kingdom (republic since 1974), successor to **Axum**; emerged around the late 10th–early 12th centuries AD. Ethiopia successfully resisted European colonization in the 19th century, but was conquered by **Italy** in 1935; liberated by British forces in 1941.

Etruscans Major people of pre-Roman Italy, in the 6th century BC they formed a loose league of city states that was conquered by the **Romans** in the 4th century BC. The Etruscans' origins are unknown: their language is unrelated to any other.

Falkland Islands (Islas Malvinas) British dependency in the South Atlantic Ocean. Sovereignty was disputed by Britain and **Spain** in the 18th century. A settlement was founded by the **United Provinces of Rio de La Plata** in 1832, but the British reasserted their claim to sovereignty and occupied the islands in 1833.

Faroe Islands North Atlantic archipelago first settled permanently by **Norse** c. AD 825; currently an autonomous province of **Denmark**.

Fatimid caliphate Shi'ite **Berber** state, AD 909–1171, founded in **Tunisia**. At its height in the late 10th century, the caliphate controlled all of North Africa. The capital was moved to Cairo in 969.

Federal Republic of Central America Latin American state formed in 1823 by former provinces of the Spanish American empire. In its first year it was called the United Provinces of Central America. The union broke up in civil wars between 1838 and 1841 into the independent countries of **Costa Rica**, **El Salvador**, **Guatemala**, **Honduras** and **Nicaragua**.

Federated States of Micronesia Island nation in the western Pacific Ocean centred on the Caroline Islands. It became independent in 1986, having formed part of the US-administered **Trust Territories of the Pacific Islands**.

Fernando Póo Island off the coast of equatorial Africa. The island was claimed by **Portugal** in 1472 and was ceded to **Spain** in 1778. It became independent of Spain in 1968 as part of **Equatorial Guinea**.

Fezzan **Touareg** state in present-day Libya, 16th–18th centuries AD. Absorbed into the **Ottoman** empire in the 19th century.

Fiji Pacific archipelago first settled by the Austronesian **Lapita culture** c. 1500 BC and, a millennium later, by **Melanesians**. British colony 1874–1970.

Finland North European country. Finland came under Swedish rule in the **Middle Ages** and was conquered by **Russia** in 1809. Finland declared independence from Russia in 1917, recognized 1918.

Finno-Ugrian (Finno-Ugric) The major branch of the Uralic language family. The main modern Finno-Ugrian languages are Hungarian, Finnish, Estonian, Mordvin (spoken in western **Russia**) and Sami.

Finns 1. A formerly widespread group of Finnic-speaking peoples of Northeast Europe. 2. Inhabitants of modern Finland.

Five Dynasties A succession of five short-lived dynasties, which ruled various parts of the Yellow river region of China between the fall of the **Tang** dynasty in AD 907 and the accession in 960 of the **Song** dynasty, which reunified China in 979.

France Western European country, named for the **Franks**, which emerged from the break-up of the Frankish **Carolingian empire** in AD 889.

Franks Early German tribal confederation, originating in the 3rd century AD. Following the fall of the western Roman empire they won control of Gaul (the region comprising modern **France**, **Belgium** and part of western **Germany**) forming a powerful kingdom under the Merovingian dynasty (511–751). Under the Carolingian dynasty, which came to power in 751, the Frankish kingdom (an empire from 800) dominated Western Europe. The modern nations of France and Germany emerged from the break-up of this empire in 889.

French Congo See **French Equatorial Africa**.

French Equatorial Africa French African colony comprising the territory of the modern countries of **Chad**, **Central African Republic**, **Congo** and **Gabon**. Its borders were defined in 1910. In 1958 it became the Union of Central African Republics until its territories became fully independent in 1960.

French Guiana Former French South American colony, originally known as **Cayenne**; it became an overseas department of **France** in 1946.

French Indochina French Southeast Asian colony comprising the countries of **Laos**, **Vietnam** and **Cambodia**, which **France** conquered between 1859 and 1900.

French Polynesia French Pacific territory comprising the Society Islands (including **Tahiti**), Bass Islands, Gambier Islands, **Marquesas Islands** and the Tuamotu Archipelago. French rule established between 1842 and 1889.

French Somaliland See **Djibouti**.

French West Africa Federation of French

colonial territories in West Africa comprising the territories of the modern countries of **Mauritania**, **Senegal**, **Mali**, **Guinea**, **Ivory Coast**, **Burkina Faso**, **Benin** and **Niger**. The federation was formed in 1895 from colonial territories acquired by **France** since the 17th century.

Funan Indianized Southeast Asian kingdom founded 1st century AD; at its peak in the 3rd century; absorbed by **Chenla** in the 6th century.

Funj (Sultanate of Sennar) Muslim Sudanese state of the Funj people founded in the 15th century AD; conquered by Ottoman **Egypt** in 1821.

Futa Jalon (Fouta Djallon) West African kingdom of the Fulani people founded in the 17th century AD; from 1725 a Muslim jihadi state; conquered by **France** 1896.

Futa Toro (Fouta Tooro) West African kingdom of the **Fulani** people founded in the 18th century AD; from 1776 a Muslim jihadi state; became tributary to the **Tukulor empire** in 1861 and was annexed to the French colony of **Senegal** in 1877.

Gabon Former territory of **French Equatorial Africa**, it became independent in 1960.

Galatia Anatolian kingdom of the Galatians, a Celtic people who migrated from Central Europe in 277 BC; Roman client state 64 BC, fully annexed in 25 BC.

Gambia West African country, named for the Gambia river. The English, Dutch, Germans and French vied for control of the Gambia river in the 17th century. British possession was formally recognized in 1783. Gambia became independent in 1965.

Gandhara Grave culture Archaeological culture of northern **Pakistan** of the late 2nd millennium BC, notable for horse-riding gear as grave goods and horse burials.

Gangas Indian Hindu dynasty of **Orissa** and western **Bengal** from the 13th to mid-15th centuries AD.

Gao Trading city on the Niger river in West Africa. An independent kingdom in the 9th century AD, it became capital of the **Songhay** empire in the 15th century and was largely abandoned after **Morocco**'s conquest of the empire in 1591.

Garamantes A Saharan **Berber** people who founded a kingdom in what is now **Libya** based on a sophisticated underground irrigation system. The kingdom was at its height from the 1st to 5th centuries AD. Depletion of the underground aquifers caused the kingdom's collapse.

Genoa Italian mercantile republic; effectively autonomous from c. AD 1100, it acquired several colonies around the Mediterranean and the Black Sea. The city lost most of its colonies in the 15th century and its independence was ended by **France** in 1797.

Georgia Christian kingdom of the Caucasus region, founded in AD 978. It was divided between the **Ottoman** and **Safavid** empires in 1555. Recovered independence in the 18th century, but was annexed by **Russia** in 1801. Constituted a republic of the **USSR** in 1936, Georgia became independent in 1991.

Gepids An early Eastern European Germanic people. Founded a kingdom on the middle Danube in the 5th century AD; conquered and absorbed by the **Avars** in 567.

German East Africa German East African colony, annexed in 1885. Occupied by the Allies in the First World War, the colony was divided into **Tanganyika**, which was administered by Britain, and **Ruanda-Urundi**, which was administered by Belgium.

Germans 1. Group of peoples originating in **Bronze Age** Europe, speaking Germanic languages, a branch of the **Indo-European** language family. Modern Germanic languages include German, Danish, Norwegian, Swedish, Icelandic, Dutch, Flemish and English. 2. The inhabitants of modern **Germany**.

German Southwest Africa German colony in Southern Africa, annexed in 1884. Occupied in 1915 by **South Africa**, which ruled the territory until its independence as **Namibia** in 1990.

Germany 1. Medieval European kingdom that developed from the break-up of the **Carolingian empire** in the 9th century AD. From 962 the kingdom of Germany was the dominant part of the **Holy Roman empire**. 2. Modern European nation state created in 1871 following the unification of Germany under Prussian leadership. Between 1949 and 1990 Germany was divided into two states, **West Germany** and **East Germany**.

Ghana 1. Early West African trading kingdom in present-day **Mali** and **Mauritania**, flourished 7th–11th centuries AD; conquered by the **Almoravids** in 1076. 2. The former British West African colonial territory of **Gold Coast**, which became independent in 1957.

Ghaznavid emirate State founded by Mahmud of Ghazni (r. 997–1030), which controlled **Afghanistan**, **Iran**, the Indus valley and parts of Central Asia. The emirate survived until 1151.

Gibraltar Strategically situated peninsula commanding the entrance to the Mediterranean Sea. First fortified by the Arabs after they took it from the **Visigoths** in AD 711, it was captured by the Spanish in 1462. An Anglo-Dutch force seized it in 1704, but it was ceded to Britain by **Spain** by the Treaty of Utrecht in 1713.

Gilbert Islands See **Kiribati**.

Goa Indian city-port captured by the Portuguese in 1510, annexed by **India** in 1961.

Golconda Central Indian kingdom, 14th–17th centuries AD. Under the Qutb Shahi dynasty (1507–1687), it was a major centre of Shi'a Islam in **India**.

Gold Coast British West African colony. British presence on the Gold Coast was established with the acquisition of **Cape Coast Castle** in 1664. The Gold Coast colony was formally created in 1821 and reached its maximum extent in 1902 following four wars with **Asante**. It became independent as **Ghana** in 1957.

Golden Horde (Ulus of Jochi) Mongol khanate of the western Eurasian steppes founded in 1241 by Chinggis Khan's grandson Batu. Although Mongol-led, the Horde was made up mainly of Turkic **Tatars**.

The khanate broke up in 1502 after a century of decline.

Gondwana Historic region of India; in the 15th–17th centuries AD it was divided into several small Hindu kingdoms.

Goths Early German people first recorded in the 3rd century AD. In the 5th century they became divided into two groups: the **Visigoths**, who founded a kingdom in Aquitaine and **Spain** (417–711), and the **Ostrogoths**, who founded a kingdom in **Italy** (493–562).

Granada, emirate of The last Muslim state in **Spain**, founded in 1228, conquered by **Castile** and **Aragon** in 1482–92.

Gran Colombia South American state comprising approximately the viceroyalty of **New Granada** which became independent from **Spain** in 1819–23. **Ecuador** and **Venezuela** seceded from Gran Colombia in 1830, the remainder of which adopted the name **Colombia**.

Great Britain See **United Kingdom**.

Great Fulo Kingdom of the Fula (Fulani) people in West Africa (1490–1776); at its peak in the early 17th century.

Great khanate Mongol empire, founded by Chinggis Khan in 1206, which survived until 1370. From 1260 to 1368 the Great Khans also used the Chinese dynastic title Yuan.

Great Zimbabwe Southern African city and kingdom, probably of the Shona people; flourished 13th to mid-15th centuries AD.

Greece European country. In ancient times Greece was divided into hundreds of city states. In the 4th century BC, Greece was conquered by **Macedon** and subsequently came under the control of the **Roman**, **Byzantine** and **Ottoman** empires. The modern Greek state declared independence from the Ottoman empire in 1822, officially recognized in 1832.

Greeks Influential Greek-speaking people of Southeast Europe whose language was first recorded in the 2nd millennium BC. Greek is a branch of the **Indo-European** language family.

Greenland The world's largest island. Greenland was first inhabited by ancestral **Inuit** peoples over 4,000 years ago. In AD 986 a **Norse** colony was founded in southwest Greenland, which accepted Norwegian sovereignty in 1261. After the union of the Norwegian and Danish crowns in 1376 the Norse sovereignty passed to Denmark–Norway. The Norse colony died out in the 15th century but Denmark–Norway reasserted sovereignty in 1721. When **Norway** was united with **Sweden** in 1814, Greenland came under Danish sovereignty. Since 2009 Greenland has been an autonomous country of the kingdom of **Denmark**.

Grenada Caribbean Island nation. Claimed, but not colonized, by **England** in 1609 and sold to **France** in 1650. Captured by the British in 1762, briefly reoccupied by France 1779–83; independent in 1974.

Guadeloupe French overseas department in the Caribbean. It was first settled by the French in 1635 and formally annexed by **France** in 1674.

Guam US dependency in the western Pacific Ocean. First settled from **Indonesia** c. 2000 BC, the island was claimed by **Spain** in 1565, though not colonized until 1668, and was ceded to the USA in 1898.

Guarani Group of American Indian peoples indigenous to Brazil, Paraguay, **Argentina**, **Uruguay** and **Bolivia**. At the time of first contact with Europeans in the 16th century, they subsisted by maize and manioc (cassava) farming, supplemented by hunting.

Guatemala Central American republic that became independent of the **Federal Republic of Central America** in 1838.

Guinea West African republic. Colonized by France in the 1890s, it became independent in 1958.

Guinea Bissau West African republic, formerly **Portuguese Guinea**, which became independent in 1974.

Gujarat Historic region of South Asia, now divided between **India** and **Pakistan**; an independent Muslim sultanate 1411–1572.

Guptas Major Hindu dynasty of **Magadha** that dominated northern **India** c. AD 320–c. 550.

Gurjara–Pratiharas Hindu dynasty of northern India (6th–11th centuries AD); at their peak c. 836–910 they were a major barrier to the expansion of Muslim control in **India**.

Guyana South American republic, formerly **British Guiana**, which became independent in 1966.

Hadramaut (Hadramawt) Historic, frequently autonomous, region of southern Arabia; a British protectorate 1886–1967; now part of Yemen.

Hafsid emirate North African **Berber** dynasty of **Tunisia** 1229–1574.

Haiti Caribbean state comprising western Hispaniola. Formerly the French colony of **Saint-Domingue**, it became independent in 1804 following a slave rebellion.

Hammadid emirate North African **Berber** dynasty of **Algeria** 1014–1152.

Han The second dynasty of imperial China 206 BC–AD 220, which has given its name to the ethnic Chinese. The dynasty is conventionally divided into Western Han (206 BC–AD 9) and Eastern Han (AD 25–220) separated by the short-lived Xin dynasty of the usurper Wang Mang.

Harar Muslim state of the Horn of Africa, a successor to **Adal**, mid-16th century AD to 1875, when it was conquered by **Egypt**. Now part of **Ethiopia**.

Haripunjaya Mon kingdom of Southeast Asia, probably emerged in the 8th century AD, at its peak in the 11th, and conquered by the Thais in 1292.

Hausa People of the West African Sahel who formed a number of city states by the 12th century AD, around which time they also converted to Islam; conquered by the Fulani **Sokoto caliphate** in the early 19th century.

Hawaii, kingdom of **Polynesian** kingdom created in 1810, annexed by the USA in 1898.

Hebrews Semitic-speaking people of the Levant, probably of **Canaanite** origin, whose religious beliefs formed the basis of Judaism. Their kingdom, founded c. 1020 BC, split into the rival kingdoms of **Israel** and **Judah** c. 928 BC.

Hejaz Historic region of Arabia, including Mecca and Medina. Independent kingdom 1916–24; merged with **Nejd** to create **Saudi Arabia**.

Hemudu culture Early rice-farming **Neolithic** culture of the lower Yangtze region, China, c. 5000–3000 BC.

Himyarite kingdom Mercantile Semitic kingdom of southern Arabia c. 110 BC–AD 520.

Hittites **Indo-European**-speaking people of Anatolia, first recorded 19th century BC. A major imperial power from c. 1600 until c.1200 BC when most of their territory was conquered by the **Phrygians**. The Hittites finally disappeared in the early 1st millennium BC.

Hohokam culture Early farming culture of southwest North America, ancestral to the modern Pima and Papago nations; at its peak c. AD 500–c. 1375.

Holy Roman empire German-dominated European empire, founded when the German king Otto I was crowned Roman emperor in AD 962, with pretensions to be the successor to both the **Carolingian empire** and the **Roman empire**. Conflicts with the papacy in the 11th–12th centuries undermined the authority of the emperors and the empire gradually developed into a loose confederation of autonomous principalities. The title of Holy Roman emperor, held by the Austrian Habsburg dynasty from the mid-15th century, continued to be prestigious, however. The empire was abolished by Napoleon in 1806.

Honduras Central American republic that became independent of the **Federal Republic of Central America** in 1838.

Hong Kong Island off southern China ceded to Britain in 1842 following the First Opium War. Adjacent territories on the mainland were added in 1860 following the Second Opium War. Returned to Chinese sovereignty in 1997.

Hopewell culture Cultural complex with distinctive burial traditions centred on the Ohio valley in eastern North America, flourished c. 100 BC–AD 500. Although Hopewell people cultivated maize and other crops, they were primarily hunter-gatherers.

Hoysalas Hindu dynasty of southern **India**, founded 1026. Initially vassals of the **Chalukyas**, they became a major territorial power in the 12th century. Attacks by Muslim states in the early 14th century weakened the Hoysala kingdom and its remaining territory became part of the **Vijayanagara** kingdom in 1343.

Hunas See **Ephthalites**.

Hungary Central European state founded in AD 1000. In 1541 most of Hungary came under **Ottoman** control. The remainder was annexed by the Austrian Habsburg emperors and was fully incorporated into the Austrian empire in the 17th century. By 1718, the Habsburgs had driven the Ottomans out of Hungary. Following a Hungarian revolt, Hungary became an equal partner with Austria in the **Austro-Hungarian empire** in 1867. Hungary became independent on the collapse of the empire in 1918.

Huns Confederation of pastoral nomad peoples from Central Asia who migrated to Eastern Europe in the late 4th century AD: they possibly spoke a Turkic language. The Huns broke up after the death of their greatest leader, Attila, in 453 and disappeared in the 6th century.

Hurrians People of northern Mesopotamia and Anatolia, known mid-3rd millennium–early 1st millennium BC, who spoke a language unrelated to other known languages. Their most important kingdoms were **Mitanni** and **Urartu**.

Hyderabad Muslim principality of southern **India**, which became independent of the Mughal empire in 1724; under British domination from 1798.

Ibadan West African kingdom of the **Yoruba** people founded in 1829. It became a British protectorate in 1893, now part of **Nigeria**.

Iberia, kingdom of Early Georgian kingdom of the Caucasus region, emerged in the 4th century BC. Frequently tributary to Rome or Persia, Iberia came under **Arab** rule in AD 653.

Iberians Early peoples of the south and east of the Iberian peninsula (modern **Spain**) who spoke a non-**Indo-European** language unrelated to any modern languages. They were in the early stages of state formation when conquered by the Carthaginians and **Romans** in the 3rd century BC.

Iceland North Atlantic country, it became autonomous under the Danish crown in 1918 and became an independent republic in 1944.

Icelandic Commonwealth Aristocratic state founded by **Norse** settlers in **Iceland** in the 10th century AD; came under the control of Norway in 1263.

Idrisids Muslim dynasty of **Arab** origin that ruled **Morocco** AD 780–985.

Ifat Muslim sultanate in the Horn of Africa, founded c. 1285, conquered by **Ethiopia** c. 1415.

Ife City and kingdom of the **Yoruba** people in present-day southwest **Nigeria**, at its peak between AD 1200 and 1400.

Igbo (Ibo) A major ethnic group of southeast **Nigeria**, the Igbo were organized on a tribal basis and never formed any significant kingdoms. They were one of the major sources of slaves for the Atlantic slave trade.

Ilkhanate Mongol khanate of Persia and **Iraq**, founded by Chinggis Khan's grandson Hülegü in 1256. The khanate broke up in 1335.

Illyrians Group of **Indo-European**-speaking peoples of the western Balkans, ancestral to the modern Albanians. Their recorded history begins in the 6th century BC. The Illyrians were conquered by the **Romans** between 228 and 11 BC.

Incas A Quechua-speaking people of the Peruvian Andes, present by at least c. AD 1200, who take their name from the title of their ruler, the Inca. In the late 15th and early 16th centuries they controlled the largest empire known to have existed in the pre-Columbian Americas. They were conquered by the Spanish in 1531–35.

India Republic comprising the greater part of the Indian subcontinent. The modern state of India became independent in 1947 following the partition of the British Indian empire into the Hindu-majority state of India and the Muslim state of **Pakistan**.

Indo-European The world's most widespread language family, believed to have originated in western Eurasia in the 4th millennium BC. Excluding extinct branches, such as Anatolian (Hittite) and Tocharian, the family is divided into nine branches: **Indo-Iranian**, Greek, Celtic, Armenian, Baltic, Slavic, Albanian, Romance (including Latin, French, Italian and Spanish) and Germanic (including English).

Indo-Iranian A major branch of the **Indo-European** language family, consisting of the Indo-Aryan (Sanskrit and the modern languages of northern India such as Hindi and Urdu), Iranian, Dardic and Nuristani languages. Its origins are sometimes associated with the **Andronovo** steppe culture.

Indonesia Country of Southeast Asia and Australasia. Indonesia was founded when the **Dutch East Indies** declared independence in 1945 (recognized in 1949). In 1962 Indonesia annexed Dutch New Guinea, achieving its present-day borders.

Inuit (Eskimo) Hunting peoples of the North American Arctic, **Greenland** and far northeastern Siberia, from where their ancestors migrated to North America c. 5400–4800 BC.

Iran Major Middle Eastern country with a largely Shi'ite Muslim population. Although its inhabitants have used the name since the 3rd century AD, Iran was known internationally as Persia until 1935. The modern Iranian state was founded by the **Safavid** dynasty, which ruled 1501–1736.

Iranians 1. Major group of peoples speaking Iranian languages, a branch of the **Indo-European** language family. The most important modern Iranian languages are Persian, Pashto, Kurdish and Baluchi. 2. The people of modern **Iran**.

Iraq Middle Eastern country, created as a British League of Nations mandated territory in 1920 from territory formerly ruled by the **Ottoman** empire: it became independent in 1932.

Ireland European country comprising most of the island of Ireland. The modern state of Ireland was founded in 1922 with the creation of the Irish Free State, a self-governing dominion of the British empire. It became fully independent as Ireland (or Éire) in 1937, although the British monarch

remained legally head of state. This final link with Britain was broken by the adoption of a republican constitution in 1949.

Irish The people of Ireland. When first recorded in the early 1st millennium AD, the Irish were a Celtic-speaking people divided into many small kingdoms and chiefdoms. One of the many cultural consequences of the English conquest of Ireland in the **Middle Ages** is that the Irish are now largely English-speaking.

Irish Free State See **Ireland**.

Iron Age Technological division of human prehistory in which iron tools and weapons came into widespread use. It is a largely Eurasian concept, but is also applied to sub-Saharan Africa where it is associated with **Bantu** expansion. The dating of the Iron Age is variable because iron technology was adopted at different times in different parts of the world. Iron technology was not adopted in the Americas before the arrival of Europeans.

Iroquois Confederacy (Iroquois League) An expansionist association of Iroquoian-speaking North American Indian peoples formed c. 1570, broke up in the 18th century.

Israel 1. Biblical Hebrew kingdom founded c. 928 BC, conquered by Assyria in 721 BC. 2. Modern Jewish state founded in Palestine in 1948.

Italian Somaliland Italian East African colony, annexed 1889. Occupied by British forces in 1941, it was united with **British Somaliland** to create the independent republic of **Somalia** in 1960.

Italics Peoples of Iron Age Italy who spoke Italic languages, including the Oscans, Umbrians, Veneti and Latins. All were conquered by the Romans (a Latin tribe) in the 4th century BC.

Italy 1. Medieval kingdom comprising the northern half of present-day Italy which emerged from the final break-up of the Frankish **Carolingian empire** in AD 889. It became part of the **Holy Roman empire** in the mid-10th century. 2. French puppet state in northern Italy created by Napoleon in 1805; dissolved 1814. 3. The modern state of Italy was created in 1861 following the annexation of the kingdom of the **Two Sicilies** by the kingdom of Piedmont–Sardinia. Rome became the capital of Italy after its annexation from the papacy in 1871.

Ivory Coast (Côte d'Ivoire) West African republic that became independent from **France** in 1960. France established a base on the Ivory Coast as early as 1637, but effective French control of the interior was established only between 1878 and 1898.

Jamaica Caribbean nation. Jamaica became a Spanish colony around 1524; it was captured by **England** in 1655; independent in 1962.

Japan Island nation in East Asia. The first Japanese kingdom emerged c. AD 300 and by c. 600 it had developed centralized institutions and an imperial constitution based on Chinese models. After 1192 the emperors were sidelined by powerful military

governors called shoguns who ruled in their name. The origins of the modern Japanese state date to the overthrow of the shogunate in 1868 and the restoration of imperial government.

Jin 1. State in northern China 8th–5th centuries BC. 2. Chinese dynasty, ruled AD 265–420, divided into Western Jin (265–316) and Eastern Jin (317–420). Western Jin briefly unified China in 280 after a period of division. Eastern Jin controlled only south China. 3. Short-lived kingdom in northern China c. 900–23. 4. **Jürchen** dynasty which ruled northern China from 1125 until 1234 when their state was destroyed by the **Mongols**.

Jizan Port city-state of southern Arabia of the 15th century AD.

Johor Malay sultanate 1528–1857, at its peak in the early 17th century, but gradually declined in importance after c. 1640.

Jomon Hunter-fisher-gatherer culture of Japan 10,000–300 BC, probably representing the ancestors of the modern **Ainu** people. It was one of the earliest cultures in the world to make extensive use of pottery vessels. In the culture's later stages, metalworking and other technology were introduced from mainland Asia, and rice cultivation increasingly supplemented hunting, fishing and gathering wild plants.

Jordan (officially the Hashemite Kingdom of Jordan) Middle Eastern country, known as **Transjordan** before its independence from Britain in 1946.

Judah Biblical Hebrew kingdom founded c. 928 BC, conquered by **Babylon** in 586 BC.

Jürchen A Tungusic people of Manchuria who adopted the name Manchu in the 17th century AD.

Kaabu Minor Mandinke kingdom of **Senegal** 16th–19th centuries AD.

Kaarta West African kingdom of the Bambara people founded 1753, destroyed 1853 by the **Tukulor empire**.

Kadambas Dynasty of southern India, founded in AD 345; became a significant territorial power in the 5th century, but became subject to the **Chalukya** kingdom in the mid-6th century.

Kaiser Wilhelm's Land German protectorate in **Northeast New Guinea** established in 1884. It was occupied by Australian forces in 1914.

Kakatiyas Hindu dynasty of southeastern **India**, founded in 1083. It had become a major territorial power by c. 1162, but was conquered by the **Delhi sultanate** in 1323.

Kalinga Ancient kingdom of eastern **India**. Conquered by the Mauryan emperor Asoka c. 265 BC, but re-emerged in the 2nd century BC; finally collapsed c. AD 10.

Kaliningrad The formerly German city of Königsberg, which was annexed by the **USSR** in 1945. Since the fall of the USSR in 1991 it has been an isolated Russian enclave surrounded by Polish and Lithuanian territory.

Kalmyks A branch of the **Oirats**, a Mongol people. Pastoral nomads, they ranged over a vast area of modern **Kazakhstan**, **Russia**, China and **Mongolia**.

Kamerun German Central African colony, annexed 1884. Occupied by the Allies in 1915 and subsequently French-administered as the League of Nations mandated territory of **Cameroon** (UN mandate after 1945) until independence in 1960.

Kandy Sinhalese kingdom of Ceylon (**Sri Lanka**), probably founded in the later 14th century AD. It remained the last independent **Sinhalese** kingdom after the Dutch won control of the coast of Ceylon in the 17th century; finally conquered by the British in 1815.

Kanem Kingdom of present-day **Nigeria** and **Chad**, probably founded in the 9th century AD. A major participant in trans-Saharan trade, the kingdom collapsed in the 14th century as a result of civil war and invasions, but was re-established as **Bornu** in 1396.

Kannauj Historic region of northern **India**. Under King Harsha (r. AD 606–47) it was the centre of an empire that controlled most of northern India.

Karakhanid khanate Confederation of **Karluk** Turk tribes in Central Asia that overthrew the **Samanid** emirate in AD 999; came under the domination of the **Karakhitai khanate** in 1140.

Karakhitai khanate **Khitan** state in Central Asia, founded 1124, destroyed by the **Mongols** in 1218.

Kara-Khoja khanates Uighur khanates in Central Asia, founded mid-9th century AD, conquered by the **Khitans** in the early 13th century.

Karasuk culture Late **Bronze Age** pastoralist culture of the Central Asian steppes, a development of the **Andronovo** culture.

Karluks A Turkic nomad people of Central Asia known from the 7th century AD. They lost their identity after their conquest by the **Mongols** in the 13th century.

Kashmir Strategically important region in the northwest corner of South Asia, frequently disputed by neighbouring great powers. Currently divided between **India** and **Pakistan**.

Kassites A people of the Middle East, late 3rd–late 1st millennium BC. They conquered **Babylon** in the early 16th century BC, ruling it until c. 1158 BC.

Katanga Central African state which seceded from the Republic of Congo (see **Democratic Republic of Congo**) in 1960. It was brought back under the control of the Congolese government in January 1963.

Kazakhs Nomadic Turkic people of Central Asia who emerged in the 15th century AD.

Kazakhstan The former Kazakh Soviet Socialist Republic which became independent on the break-up of the **USSR** in 1991. Ethnic **Kazakhs** form the majority of the population.

Kazan, khanate of Tatar state on the middle Volga river, **Russia**; broke away from the **Golden Horde** in 1438; conquered by Russia in 1552.

Kazembe Luba kingdom of Central Africa founded in the 18th century AD, divided between Britain and **Belgium** in 1894.

Kenya East African country, formerly the colonial territory of British East Africa, annexed 1895–1902; independent in 1963.

Kerguelen Island French territory in the southern Indian Ocean. Formally annexed by **France** in 1893, it has no permanent inhabitants.

Khazar khanate State founded by a semi-nomadic Turkic people on the lower Volga river, **Russia**, in the 7th century AD. The khanate declined as a result of attacks by the **Rus** and **Pechenegs** in the late 10th century, but probably survived until c. 1030.

Khitans East Asian nomadic Mongol people 4th–13th centuries AD.

Khiva, khanate of **Uzbek** khanate south of the Aral Sea in Central Asia, founded in 1511; became a Russian protectorate in 1873.

Khmer empire Indianized state AD 802–1431, the direct precursor of **Cambodia**. At its peak in the 11th–13th centuries, the empire was the major power of Southeast Asia; its decline was probably a result of environmental problems leading to a failure of agriculture. The removal of the Khmer capital from Angkor to the region of Phnom Penh conventionally marks the end of the empire.

Khmers Austro-Asiatic-speaking people who form the majority population of **Cambodia**.

Khoikhoi (Khoekhoe) **Khoisan** pastoralist peoples of Southern Africa, known to white settlers as Hottentots.

Khoisan Group of African peoples speaking Khoisan languages, characterized by the use of 'click' consonants. In prehistoric times Khoisan peoples were widespread in Eastern and Southern Africa. Encroachment by **Bantu** and, from the 18th century AD, European settlers, has since restricted their range to parts of **South Africa**, **Botswana** and **Namibia**.

Khwarezm shahdom Turk-ruled state, formerly a province of the **Seljuk** sultanate, which became independent c. 1157. At its peak c. 1200 it controlled **Iran** and much of Central Asia; destroyed by the **Mongols** in 1231.

Kiev, principality of Early Russian state founded by the Scandinavian **Rus** c. AD 882, but with a largely **Slav** population. By 1000 the state had become Slav in language and culture, and Orthodox Christian in religion. From the mid-11th century Kiev began to break up into separate principalities.

Kimeks Confederation of nomadic Turkic tribes 8th–12th centuries AD.

Kingdom of the Serbs, Croats and Slovenes Balkan state founded in 1918 by merging Serbia and territories of the former **Austro-Hungarian empire**.

Commonly known as **Yugoslavia**, it was known officially by that name from 1929.

Kipchaks (Qipchaqs) Central Asian Turkic nomad people, possibly of **Kimek** origin, who formed a confederation with the **Cumans** in the 11th–13th centuries AD.

Kiribati Island nation consisting of the Gilbert Islands archipelago and other smaller archipelagos in the western Pacific Ocean, settled by **Micronesians**. The Gilbert Islands became a British protectorate in 1892, becoming independent as Kiribati in 1979.

Knights Hospitaller Crusading order established on the island of **Malta** in 1530. The order was expelled by the French in 1798.

Koguryo Early Korean kingdom founded, according to tradition, in 37 BC (but possibly over a century later); destroyed by the Chinese **Tang** empire in AD 668.

Kokand, khanate of Uzbek khanate in Central Asia which became independent of **Bukhara** in the early 18th century.

Kong West African Muslim kingdom founded 1710, at its peak c. 1730–1800, but thereafter declined rapidly to insignificance.

Kongo Central African kingdom of the **Bantu**-speaking Bakongo people, founded in the 15th century AD. From the 17th century onwards Kongo gradually lost its territory to the Portuguese, becoming part of **Angola** in the 19th century.

Korea East Asian country unified by, and named for, the Koryo dynasty (founded AD 918) in 936. Korea was annexed by **Japan** in 1910. Following Japan's defeat in 1945, Korea was divided along the 38th parallel, with the **USA** administering the south and the **USSR** the north. Two separate governments, North Korea and South Korea, were established in 1948; they have been officially at war since 1950.

Koreans East Asian people probably originally of mainly Tungusic or other **Altaic** origin.

Koryaks Hunter-gatherer and reindeer-herding people of the Kamchatka peninsula in eastern Siberia.

Kosala Early Hindu *mahajanapada* (great realm) of northern India; originated 6th century BC, conquered by **Magadha** in the 4th century BC.

Kosovo Partially recognized Balkan state with primarily Muslim Albanian population; became de facto independent from Serbia in 1999.

Kush Egyptian-influenced **Nubian** kingdom of the middle Nile, emerged c. 900 BC. Known as the kingdom of **Meroë** after 590 BC.

Kushans Central Asian Indo-European-speaking nomad people. They originated as a tribe of the **Yuezhi** confederation, which they took over in the 1st century BC. Invaded **India** c. AD 46–50 and established an empire that survived until the 4th century.

Kuwait Country in northern Arabia. Kuwait developed in the 17th century as a trading centre

under nominal **Ottoman** control. It became a British protectorate in 1899 and became independent in 1961.

Kyrgyz Traditionally nomadic Turkic people of Central Asia.

Kyrgyzstan Central Asian country, with a mainly **Kyrgyz** population. The former Kirghiz Soviet Socialist Republic, it became independent on the fall of the **USSR** in 1991.

Lagos West African port city; its seizure by the British in 1861 was the prelude to their colonization of **Nigeria**.

Lannathai Tai kingdom of Southeast Asia, founded in 1292, conquered by the **Burmese** in 1558.

Laos Southeast Asian country, founded in 1354 though not securely united until the 16th century. The country is named for its main ethnic group, the Lao, a **Tai** people. Laos became part of **French Indochina** in 1893, becoming independent again in 1954.

Lapita culture (c. 1600–500 BC) Archaeological culture associated with the spread of **Austronesian** farming peoples from Southeast Asia to the archipelagos of the western Pacific Ocean.

Later Liang Chinese dynasty which ruled the Yellow river region AD 907–923.

Latin empire Crusader state based on Constantinople, the Byzantine capital captured by the Fourth Crusade in 1204. Recaptured by the Byzantines in 1261.

Latins Ancient Latin-speaking **Italic** peoples of present-day Lazio in central Italy.

Latvia Baltic country. Latvia became independent of **Russia** in 1918. It was annexed by the **USSR** in 1939, but regained independence in 1991.

Lazica Early Georgian state, successor to **Colchis**. Frequently occupied by neighbouring empires, it was the nucleus around which the kingdom of Georgia developed in the 10th century AD.

Lebanon Middle Eastern country with a mainly **Arab** population. Lebanon was created as a French-administered League of Nations mandated territory in 1920 from former territory of the **Ottoman** empire. It declared independence in 1941, recognized in 1943.

León Christian Spanish kingdom, known as **Asturias** until AD 910. Absorbed by **Castile** in 1230.

León and Castile See **Castile**.

Lesotho Southern African kingdom of the Sotho (or Basotho), a **Bantu**-speaking people, founded in 1821–23. It became the British protectorate of Basutoland in 1868, which became independent as Lesotho in 1966.

Lesser Armenia Armenian kingdom in Cilicia in southern Anatolia 12th–13th centuries AD.

Liao Khitan dynasty, established AD 915, which ruled much of **Mongolia** and northern China; overthrown by the **Jürchen Jin** dynasty in 1125.

Liberia West African country founded as a homeland for freed slaves by the American Colonization Society in 1821–22. It was the only African country never to come under European rule.

Libu The name used by the ancient Egyptians to describe the **Libyans**.

Libya In ancient times Libya was used in a general sense to describe all of Africa. The modern state of Libya originated when **Italy** conquered the **Ottoman** province of **Tripoli** in 1911–12. It was occupied by British forces in 1943 and after the Second World War came under joint British and French administration until independence in 1951.

Libyans 1. An ancient **Berber** people. 2. The inhabitants of modern **Libya**.

Lithuania Baltic country. Lithuania became a unified state in 1253. In 1386 it entered a dynastic union with **Poland** in return for accepting Christianity (the last European country to do so), becoming a full political union in 1569. Following the partition of Poland in the 18th century, Lithuania became part of the Russian empire. Lithuania became independent of **Russia** in 1918 but was annexed by the **USSR** in 1939. It became independent again on the fall of the USSR in 1991.

Livonia State roughly equivalent to Estonia and Latvia, founded by the crusading Livonian Order in the 13th century AD. Subordinate to the **Teutonic Knights** until the dissolution of the order in 1525. Divided between **Sweden** and **Poland** in 1561.

Lombards An early German people, first recorded in the 1st century AD. Invaded **Italy** in 568 and founded a number of states, the last of which fell to the **Normans** in the 11th century.

Longshan culture Later **Neolithic** culture of the Yellow river region, China, with walled proto-urban settlements, 3200–1800 BC.

Louisiana French-claimed territory in North America comprising the entire Mississippi river basin, established 1682. Ceded to **Spain** in 1763. Returned to **France** in 1800 and sold to the **USA** in 1803.

Lozi Southern African kingdom of the **Bantu**-speaking Barotse people, founded in the 17th century AD. It became a British protectorate in 1890, now part of **Zambia**.

Luba Central African kingdom of the Luba peoples founded late 16th or early 17th century AD. Incorporated into the **Congo Free State** in the 1890s.

Lukka (Lycia) Late **Bronze Age** kingdom or people of southwest Anatolia.

Lunda Central African kingdom of the Lunda people, founded in the 17th century AD. The kingdom collapsed in the later 19th century and was divided between Portuguese **Angola** and the **Congo Free State**.

Luxembourg European Grand Duchy, which was recognized as an independent state in 1815.

Maan (Ma'in) Kingdom of the Minaean **Arabs** 4th–1st centuries BC.

Macassar (Makassar) Port city on Sulawesi, **Indonesia**, and independent sultanate from late 16th century AD until its conquest by the Dutch in 1667.

Macau Port city in the Pearl river delta, southern China, leased to the Portuguese in 1557, returned to Chinese sovereignty in 1999.

Macedon Hellenized kingdom of the Balkans, founded c. 640 BC, with a mixed population of **Greeks**, **Illyrians**, and **Thracians**. Briefly a great power under Alexander the Great (r. 336–323 BC), it was conquered by Rome in 168 BC.

Madagascar Island nation in the Indian Ocean, settled by **Austronesians** in the 1st century AD. Most of the island came under the control of the **Malagasy** kingdom of **Merina** in the 19th century until its conquest by **France** in 1895; it became independent in 1960.

Madeira Archipelago in the North Atlantic Ocean, settled by the Portuguese in 1420 and now an autonomous region of **Portugal**.

Magadha The most powerful of the early Hindu *mahajanapadas* (great realms) of northern **India**. Emerged in the 7th century BC; under the Mauryan dynasty (321–185 BC) and again under the Gupta dynasty (AD 320–550) it dominated India.

Magyars (Hungarians) A **Finno-Ugrian**-speaking nomad people probably originating in northeast **Russia** or Siberia who invaded Central Europe in AD 896, founding the kingdom of **Hungary** in 1000.

Mahra (Mahrah) **Arab** sultanate in Hadramaut; became part of the British **Aden** protectorate in 1886.

Majapahit Javanese kingdom 1293–1527, the last major Hindu state in the East Indies; at its peak in the 14th century it created a maritime hegemony over much of Sumatra, Borneo and **Malaya**. It was overthrown by the Muslim state of **Demak**.

Makuria (Makkura) Christian **Nubian** kingdom, a successor to the kingdom of **Meroë**, established c. AD 350. Civil war caused the kingdom to collapse in 1317.

Malacca City and sultanate commanding the Straits of Malacca between **Malaya** and Sumatra founded c.1400. After the Portuguese captured Malacca in 1511 the sultanate was re-established at **Johor**.

Malagasy People of **Madagascar**, of **Austronesian** and East African origin.

Malawi Southern African country. Formerly the British colony of **Nyasaland**, annexed in 1891, it became independent in 1964.

Malaya British colony on the Malayan peninsula. The British presence in Malaya began with its acquisition of Penang in 1786. Britain had brought all the Malay states on the peninsula under its control by 1909. Britain federated the Malay states in 1948; the federation became independent as Malaya in 1957, and a part of **Malaysia** in 1963.

Malays An ethnic group of the Malayan peninsula, but also, more generally, the **Austronesian** peoples inhabiting **Malaysia**, **Indonesia** and the **Philippines**.

Malaysia Southeast Asian country created in 1963 by the federation of **Malaya** with the former British colonies of **Sarawak**, North Borneo (Sabah and **Singapore**. Singapore left Malaysia in 1965.

Maldive Islands Indian Ocean archipelago and nation. The islands, which have a long history of settlement, became an informal British protectorate in 1796 and a formal protectorate in 1887. They became independent in 1965.

Mali 1. West African trading kingdom of the Mandinke (or Malinke) people; founded some time in the late 1st millennium AD according to oral traditions, it was the dominant power in West Africa in the 13th–14th centuries, but was supplanted by **Songhay** in the 15th century. The kingdom finally collapsed in 1670. 2. Former French West African colony comprising much of the territory of the historical Mali state; became independent in 1960.

Malta Mediterranean island state. Malta was the state of the **Knights Hospitaller** from 1530 until their expulsion by the French in 1798. Malta became a British protectorate in 1800 and became independent in 1964.

Mamluk sultanate Turkic slave (mamluk) dynasty, which ruled Egypt 1250–1517. The Mamluks inflicted the first serious defeat on the **Mongols** in 1260 and expelled the crusaders from **Palestine** in 1291.

Manchu See **Jürchen**.

Manzhouguo Japanese puppet state of Manchuria (northeast China) under the nominal rule of the deposed Chinese **Qing** dynasty emperor Puyi 1932–45.

Maoris Polynesian people of **New Zealand**, descended from the first settlers of the islands who arrived c. 1200.

Mapungubwe Early **Bantu** kingdom of Southern Africa c. 1075–1220. Its stone architecture and social structures are precursors of those of the later **Great Zimbabwe** kingdom.

Marathas Hindu warrior clans of **India** united by Shivaji who founded an independent kingdom in 1674 that came to dominate central India in the 18th century. Broke up into a confederacy of allied states in 1761, most of which had been absorbed into British India by 1820.

Mariana Islands US dependency in the western Pacific Ocean. The archipelago was formally claimed by **Spain** in 1667. **Guam**, the largest island of the archipelago, was ceded to the **USA** in 1898 while the remainder of the islands were bought by **Germany** in 1899. These islands were occupied by **Japan** in 1914 and in 1944 by the USA, which continues to administer them separately from Guam.

Marinids **Berber** dynasty who won control of **Morocco** from the **Almohads** in 1244. They were overthrown by the **Wattasids** in 1465.

Marquesas Islands See **French Polynesia**.

Marshall Islands Island nation in the western Pacific Ocean. The islands came under German rule in 1884 but were occupied by **Japan** in 1914 and in 1944 by the USA, which administered the islands as part of the UN **Trust Territories of the Pacific Islands**. The islands became independent in 1986.

Martinique French overseas department in the Caribbean, claimed by **France** in 1635.

Masina (Macina) Much-disputed fertile inland delta of the Niger river, West Africa and centre of a Fulani jihadi state founded c. 1818; conquered by **Tukulor** in 1862.

Mataram 1. Hindu Javanese kingdom 9th–11th centuries AD. 2 Muslim Javanese sultanate from the late 16th century to 1746.

Mauretania **Berber** kingdom in North Africa 3rd–1st centuries BC; Roman client kingdom in 46 BC, fully annexed by Rome AD 40–42.

Mauritania West African country; formerly part of **French West Africa**, it became independent in 1960.

Mauritius Island nation in the Indian Ocean. First settled by the Dutch in 1638, the island became a French colony in 1715. Mauritius was captured by the British in 1810 and became independent in 1968.

Mauryan empire Ancient Indian empire founded by the Mauryan dynasty of **Magadha** (321–185 BC).

Maya Mayan-speaking native American peoples of southern **Mexico**, **Belize**, **Guatemala**, **El Salvador** and **Honduras**.

Medes Ancient **Iranian** people who entered present-day **Iran** in the early 1st millennium BC from the Eurasian steppes. They built a considerable empire in the late 7th century, but were conquered by the **Persians** in 546 BC.

Megalithic tomb cultures **Neolithic** cultures of Atlantic Europe characterized by the construction of tombs and ritual structures using megaliths (large stones) c. 4500–1500 BC. Megalithic construction was also a feature of many other prehistoric cultures across the world.

Melanesians An ethnic and cultural group of the western Pacific islands and New Guinea who speak mainly **Austronesian** languages.

Merina **Malagasy** kingdom, first unified in the late 18th century AD. Merina dominated **Madascagar** in the 19th century until its conquest by **France** in 1895.

Meroë Nubian kingdom on the middle Nile, 590 BC–c. AD 350, the successor to **Kush**. The kingdom fragmented after an invasion from **Axum**.

Mesoamerica Prehispanic cultural region of Central America, extending south from central **Mexico** to northern **Honduras** and **El Salvador**, the ancient civilizations of which (including the **Aztecs** and **Maya**) shared many cultural characteristics.

Mesolithic (Middle Stone Age) Term used to describe the period between the end of the **Palaeolithic** and the beginning of the **Neolithic** during which hunter-gatherers adapted to post-glacial conditions and began the transition to a farming way of life. The term is most commonly used with regard to European prehistory.

Mexico Central American country. The modern state of Mexico was founded when the Spanish viceroyalty of **New Spain** declared independence in 1821. Mexico was unable to hold on to all the territory of the viceroyalty. In 1823 the **Federal Republic of Central America** seceded, Texas seceded in 1836 and vast territories, including California, were lost to the **USA** in 1848. In 1853 further territories were sold to the USA (the Gadsden Purchase), establishing the country's modern borders. Mexico is named for the Mexica, the most prominent **Aztec** tribe.

Micronesians A diverse ethnic and cultural group of the northwest Pacific islands; the western islands were settled by peoples from the **Philippines** and **Indonesia**, those in the east by peoples from Melanesia.

Middle Ages The period of European history between the fall of the western Roman empire in the 5th century AD and the Renaissance (roughly the 15th century).

Min Chinese kingdom of the Ten Kingdoms and Five Dynasties period in what is now Fujian in southeastern China (AD 907–965).

Ming Chinese imperial dynasty 1368–1644.

Minoans Ancient people of Crete, probably of Anatolian origin. Though they were literate, their language has not been deciphered. Disappeared after their conquest by the **Mycenaean** Greeks *c.* 1450 BC.

Minyue (Min Yue) Viet people and state in present-day Fujian, southeast China, founded in the later 4th century BC. Conquered by the Han dynasty *c.* 110 BC.

Mississippians Advanced maize-farming cultures of the Mississippi basin characterized by temple-mound construction, long-distance exchange and shared religious beliefs 8th–16th centuries AD.

Mitanni Hurrian kingdom of **Syria** *c.* 1500–1300 BC.

Mixtecs Native American people of southwest **Mexico**, formed a kingdom by the 12th century AD. They conquered the **Zapotecs** in the 14th–15th centuries, resisted the **Aztecs**, but were conquered by the Spanish in the 1520s.

Moche Kingdom, or group of kingdoms, of **Peru** that dominated the coastal lowlands *c.* 100 BC –*c.* AD 700.

Mogollon Early farming culture of the southwestern deserts of North America; it had merged into the **Ancestral Pueblo** cultures by the 14th century AD.

Moldavia Medieval Romanian principality. Independent 1359; **Ottoman** vassal 1504. Its territory is now divided between Moldova, **Ukraine** and **Romania**.

Moldova The former Moldovan Soviet Socialist Republic which became independent on the collapse of the **USSR** in 1991. That part of the country east of the Dneister river is controlled by the internationally unrecognized government of Transnistria (not shown on the maps for reasons of scale).

Mongolia Central Asian country, historically at the heart of many nomad empires, including that of the **Mongols**. Following the **Qing** conquest of the Mongols in the 17th century AD, the area became the autonomous Chinese province of Outer Mongolia. The modern Mongolian state was created when Outer Mongolia declared independence from China on the fall of the Qing dynasty in 1911.

Mongols A group of nomadic **Altaic** peoples of Central Asia. The term is also used in a general sense to describe the many Mongolic and Turkic peoples united under the rule of Chinggis Khan in the 13th century AD.

Mons An **Austro-Asiatic** people of Southeast Asia, now largely assimilated by the Thais and **Burmese**.

Montenegro Balkan country. Montenegro became formally independent of the **Ottoman** empire in 1878. It united with Serbia and subsequently became part of the **Kingdom of the Serbs, Croats and Slovenes** (later **Yugoslavia**). Montenegro's declaration of independence in 2006 marked the final break-up of Yugoslavia.

Morocco North African kingdom with an **Arab** and **Berber** population. A Moroccan state has existed in some form since the country was first unified by the **Idrisid** dynasty in AD 789, but it was only permanently unified in the 17th century. Between 1912 and 1956 the country was divided into French and Spanish protectorates.

Moscow (Grand Duchy of Moscow) Russian state founded 1283, a tributary of the **Golden Horde** until 1480. By 1521 Moscow had conquered all the other Russian principalities and formally became a unitary state when Ivan IV adopted the title Tsar of **Russia** in 1547.

Mosquito Coast Part of the Caribbean coast of Central America, named after the Miskito Indians. Colonized by the English in 1655, it was ceded to **Nicaragua** in 1894.

Mossi kingdoms Three West African kingdoms of the Mossi people, formed between the 12th and 15th centuries AD; conquered by **France** 1894–97.

Mozambique Southeast African country. Formerly a Portuguese colonial territory built up from 1508, it became independent in 1975.

Mughals Turkic Muslim dynasty of **Timurid** descent 1526–1857, which ruled most of northern **India** from the mid-16th to mid-18th centuries. The last ruler was deposed by the British in 1857.

Multan City and district in **Pakistan** and early centre of Islam in South Asia.

Mutapa (Mwenemutapa) Shona successor kingdom to **Great Zimbabwe**, founded mid-15th century AD; conquered by **Rozwi** in 1695.

Myanmar See **Burma**.

Mycenaeans Modern name given to the Late **Bronze Age** Greeks (*c.* 1650–1100 BC), named after the site of Mycenae.

Mysore Hindu kingdom of southern **India**; gained independence following the collapse of the **Vijayanagara** kingdom in the 16th century AD. Came under direct British rule in 1831.

Nabataea Trading kingdom of the Nabataean **Arabs** in northern Arabia, formed by *c.* 300 BC, Roman vassal by *c.* 60 BC, fully annexed in AD 106. The date of the end of Roman rule is uncertain.

Namibia Southern African country. Originally the German colony of **German Southwest Africa**, it was named Southwest Africa and awarded to **South Africa** as a League of Nations mandated territory in 1919. Administered by South Africa until its independence in 1990. **South Africa** ceded its enclave at **Walvis Bay** to Namibia in 1994.

Nanyue (Nam Viet) Kingdom in southern China and northern **Vietnam** with a primarily **Vietnamese** population founded by rebel Chinese general Zhao Tuo in 204 BC. Conquered by the **Han** in 111 BC.

Nanzhao Kingdom of Yunnan in southern China, with a Tibeto-Burman-speaking ruling class, founded in AD 729; it was succeeded by the kingdom of **Dali** after 902.

Naples, kingdom of Kingdom of southern **Italy**, split from the kingdom of **Sicily** in 1282. Under the rule of **Aragon** (and, later, **Spain**) from 1442 until 1714 when it was ceded to **Austria**. Recaptured by Spain in 1734. Reunited with Sicily in 1816 to form the kingdom of the **Two Sicilies**.

Natal British South African colony created in 1843, it became a province of **South Africa** in 1910.

Nauru Island nation in the western Pacific Ocean. Settled by **Micronesians**, it was annexed by **Germany** in 1888. Occupied by Australian forces in 1914, it became an Australian-administered League of Nations mandated territory in 1923. It became independent in 1968.

Navarre Basque kingdom of northern **Spain** and southwest **France**, known as the Kingdom of **Pamplona** before AD 987. Southern Navarre was conquered by **Castile** in 1513; northern Navarre became part of France in 1589.

Nazca (Nasca) Culture of the southern coast of **Peru** *c.* 100 BC–AD 750, a successor to the **Paracas** culture. Famous for its geoglyphs, the culture was at its peak *c.* 1 BC–AD 400.

Ndebele (Matabele) A branch of the **Zulus** who migrated north and founded their own kingdom on the **Zimbabwe** plateau in 1840.

Ndongo Kingdom of the Mbundu people in present-day **Angola** founded in the 16th century AD. Destroyed by the Portuguese in 1671.

Nejd Region of central Arabia controlled since the 15th century AD by the house of Saud. United with Hejaz in 1925 to create the kingdom of **Saudi Arabia**.

Neolithic (New Stone Age) Technological division of human prehistory covering the period in which people first began to practise agriculture, but were still reliant on stone tools. The dating of the Neolithic is variable because agriculture was developed at different times in different parts of the world. Originally defined on the basis of polished stone technology; pottery and agriculture were added later. The term is not used in **New World** archaeology.

Nepal South Asian country in the Himalaya mountains. The modern state of Nepal began with the unification of three rival Nepalese kingdoms in 1768. The country's modern borders were established following the Anglo-Nepalese War of 1814–16.

Netherlands The Netherlands was formed from the seven northern provinces of the **Spanish Netherlands** which formed a union as the Republic of the Seven United Netherlands in 1579 to fight their war of independence against **Spain**, which had broken out in 1568. The provinces formally declared independence from Spain in 1581. Spain formally recognized the independence of the Netherlands in 1648 after several attempts at reconquest had failed.

New Brunswick Province of **Canada**. The area became part of **New France** in the 17th century, but was captured by the British in 1759 and administered as part of **Nova Scotia** until 1784 when it became a separate province. It became part of Canada in 1867.

New Caledonia French dependency in the southwest Pacific Ocean, claimed by **France** in 1843 and formally annexed in 1853.

New England The modern US states of Maine, New Hampshire, Vermont, Massachusetts, Rhode Island and Connecticut. The name was first given to the region in 1614 and the first successful English colony in the area was founded at Plymouth, Massachusetts, by the Pilgrim Fathers in 1620.

Newfoundland English North American colony claimed in 1497, but not colonized until 1610. Newfoundland was a self-governing Dominion of the British empire from 1907 until 1949 when it became part of **Canada**.

New France The area of North America colonized or claimed by **France** in the 17th and 18th centuries. New France was ceded to Britain and Spain in 1763.

New Granada Spanish viceroyalty in South America, comprising approximately the territories of modern **Colombia**, **Panama**, **Venezuela** and **Ecuador**, created in 1717; effectively dissolved in 1819.

New Hebrides See **Vanuatu**.

New Netherland Dutch North American colony founded in 1614. Captured by the English in 1664 (formally ceded by the **Netherlands** in 1667), its capital, New Amsterdam, was renamed New York.

New South Wales Britain's first Australian colony founded in 1788. It became a state of the Commonwealth of **Australia** in 1901.

New Spain Spanish viceroyalty covering at its greatest extent Central America, much of the Caribbean and southwest North America, and Florida. The Philippines were also considered part of New Spain. The viceroyalty was created following the conquest of the **Aztec** empire in 1521 and was dissolved in 1821.

New Sweden Swedish North American colony founded in 1638; it was conquered by the Dutch and incorporated into the **New Netherland** colony in 1655.

New World The continents of North and South America and the associated islands.

New Zealand Island nation in the South Pacific Ocean. New Zealand was first settled by the Polynesian **Maoris** c. AD 1200. It was annexed by Britain in 1840, becoming a self-governing dominion in 1907 and fully independent in 1931.

Nicaea, empire of Byzantine successor state created after the capture of Constantinople by the Fourth Crusade in 1204; it recaptured Constantinople in 1261, re-establishing a much diminished **Byzantine empire**.

Nicaragua Central American republic that became independent after seceding from the **Federal Republic of Central America** in 1838.

Nicobar Islands Archipelago in the Indian Ocean. Several European powers attempted to colonize the islands before Britain took possession in 1869. They are now an Indian dependency.

Niger West African nation, a former territory of **French West Africa**, which became independent in 1960.

Nigeria West African country, formerly a British colony created from territories annexed between 1861 and 1900. It became independent in 1960.

Nilotes Large group of peoples of **Sudan**, **Uganda**, **Kenya** and **Tanzania** who speak Nilo-Saharan languages.

Nobatia **Nubian** successor kingdom to **Meroë**, founded c. AD 350, conquered by **Makuria** c. 600.

Nogai Tatars A nomad people of the western steppes who split from the **Golden Horde** c. 1500; mostly under Russian control by the 1760s.

Nok culture Early **Iron Age** culture of central **Nigeria** known almost entirely from its terracotta figurines of animals and stylized humans, c. 600 BC–c. AD 400.

Normans French-speaking people descended from **Scandinavians** (Northmen) who settled in the area of northern **France** known after them as Normandy c. AD 900 and went on to conquer **England**, southern **Italy** and **Sicily** in the 11th century.

Norse Early medieval **Scandinavians**.

Northeast New Guinea Australian-administered League of Nations mandated territory comprising the former German colonies of **Kaiser Wilhelm's Land** and the Bismarck Archipelago (1920–45).

Northern Circars Historic peoples of eastern **India**, now part of **Orissa** state, conquered by the British 1768.

Northern Wei Dynasty founded by the Tuoba clan of the **Altaic** Xianbei people, originally nomads, which ruled northern China AD 386–535. Divided following civil wars into Eastern Wei (534–50) and Western Wei (535–56).

North Korea See **Korea**.

Northumbria Anglo-Saxon kingdom of northern **England** and southern **Scotland**, founded in AD 653. It was fully absorbed into the kingdom of England between 927 and 954.

North Vietnam See **Vietnam**.

Norway European kingdom, formed in the late 9th century AD. Norway was in union with **Denmark** from 1388 to 1814 when it was united with **Sweden**. It became independent of Sweden in 1905.

Nova Scotia British North American colony, the former French colony of **Acadia**, which was captured by the British in 1710. Nova Scotia became a province of **Canada** in 1867.

Novgorod (Lord Novgorod the Great) Russian principality founded late 11th century AD. From 1136 it was governed by an aristocratic and priestly oligarchy, and an elective prince, and is often described as a republic. Novgorod avoided conquest by the **Mongols** but became a vassal state; it was conquered by **Moscow** in 1478.

Nubians African peoples of southern **Egypt** and **Sudan** who speak Nobiin, a Nilo-Saharan language. A distinct Nubian culture emerged as early as 5000 BC.

Numidia Berber kingdom of North Africa, founded in 200 BC; annexed by the **Roman empire** in 46 BC.

Nupe Decentralized kingdom of the Nupe people 15th–18th century AD, now part of **Nigeria**.

Nyasaland See **Malawi**.

Ochre-coloured pottery culture North Indian culture of the 2nd millennium BC, characterized by distinctive ceramics showing the influence of the earlier Indus Valley civilization.

Oguz (Oghuz) Turkic nomad confederation of Central Asia related to the **Pechenegs** and **Kimeks** 8th–early 13th century AD.

Oirats Confederation of nomadic Mongol peoples that dominated the eastern Eurasian steppes after the end of Mongol rule in China in 1368.

Old World The continents of Europe, Asia and Africa.

Olmecs Modern name for the people of Mexico's southern Gulf coast who founded the first Mesoamerican civilization c. 1200 BC.

Oman Country in southeast Arabia; emerged as a fully independent state in the 12th century AD. Its capital Muscat was occupied by the Portuguese from 1508 to 1648. It became a major naval and commercial power in the Indian Ocean, bringing the **Swahili** coast of East Africa under its control in

1690. Oman was a British protectorate from 1891 to 1971.

Orange Free State Boer republic of Southern Africa, founded 1854. Conquered by the British in 1899–1902, it became a province of **South Africa**.

Oregon Region of western North America between California and 54° 40' north. Disputed between Britain and the **USA**, it was divided along the 49th parallel in 1846.

Orissa (Odisha) Region of eastern **India**, heartland of the ancient kingdom of **Kalinga**, but generally divided into several small kingdoms. Briefly, a powerful Hindu kingdom under Pratuprudradeva (r. 1497–1541).

Orkney, earldom of **Norse** principality of the Orkney and Shetland Isles, founded c. AD 870, brought under the control of **Norway** c. 1100.

Oromo Cushitic-speaking people of the Horn of Africa, the largest ethnic group in **Ethiopia**.

Ostland Administrative region of German-occupied Eastern Europe, 1941–45, intended for German settlement after the elimination of its indigenous population.

Ostrogothic kingdom The Italian kingdom of the Ostrogothic branch of the **Goths** who invaded and conquered **Italy** in AD 489–-93. The kingdom was conquered by the eastern Roman empire in 535–54.

Ottomans Turkish dynasty 1299–1923. At their peak in the 16th–17th centuries, the Ottomans ruled an empire which controlled most of the Middle East, North Africa and Southeast Europe. The empire declined steadily through the 18th and 19th centuries, and by 1918 it was reduced to Anatolia and part of Thrace in Southeast Europe. The last Ottoman sultan was effectively deposed in 1922, and in 1923 the sultanate was legally abolished and what remained of the empire was proclaimed the Republic of **Turkey**.

Oudh (Awadh) Fertile region of northern **India** and an independent Muslim state founded 1722; annexed to British India 1856.

Oyo Kingdom of the **Yoruba** people in present-day **Nigeria**, founded 15th century AD; destroyed by the **Sokoto caliphate** in 1836.

Paekche (Baekje) Early Korean kingdom, according to tradition founded in 18 BC, but more likely in the mid-3rd century AD. Destroyed in 660 by an alliance of **Silla** and **Tang** China.

Pakistan South Asian country that became independent in 1947. Pakistan was created as a Muslim homeland by the partitioning of British India and originally consisted of two geographically widely separated and ethnically distinct parts. The larger, West Pakistan, was centred on the Indus river valley, while East Pakistan comprised the eastern half of **Bengal**. East Pakistan became independent as **Bangladesh** in 1971.

Palaeo-Asiatic A term used to describe a group of mostly unrelated languages believed to have been

spoken widely in Northeast Asia in prehistoric times before they were largely displaced by **Altaic** languages.

Palaeolithic (Old Stone Age) Technological division of human prehistory extending from the first appearance of tool-using human ancestors c. 2.6 million years ago to the end of the last glaciation c. 11,500 years ago.

Palaeo-Siberian A term used to describe a group of largely unrelated language families believed to have been spoken more widely in Siberia prior to the spread of **Altaic** languages.

Palas Buddhist dynasty of **Bengal** AD 756–1174, at its peak c. 770–850 and c. 1100.

Palau Island nation in the western Pacific Ocean. It became independent from the US-administered **Trust Territories of the Pacific Islands** in 1994.

Palestine 1. Historic much-contested territory in the Middle East, often also known as the 'Holy Land'. 2. British-administered League of Nations mandated territory 1922–48.

Pallavas Tamil dynasty of southern **India** 4th–9th centuries AD.

Pamplona Basque kingdom of northern **Spain** and southwest **France** founded in AD 824, known as **Navarre** from 987.

Panama Central American country; became independent of **Colombia** in 1903.

Panama Canal Zone A ten-mile-wide zone ceded by **Panama** to the **USA** in 1903 for the purpose of building the Panama Canal. The zone came under joint US–Panamanian control in 1979 and full Panamanian control was restored in 1999.

Pandyas Tamil dynasty of southern **India** 6th–14th centuries AD; subject to **Chola** rule in the 10th–11th centuries.

Papal states Territories in central **Italy** ruled by the papacy, annexed to Italy 1861–71.

Papua and New Guinea See **Papua New Guinea**.

Papua New Guinea Country in Australasia comprising the eastern half of the island of New Guinea and the islands of the Bismarck Archipelago. The country was created by uniting the Australian colony of Papua with the territory of **Northeast New Guinea** to create the territory of **Papua and New Guinea** in 1945 (formally recognized internationally in 1949); it became independent in 1975.

Papuans Culturally and linguistically diverse peoples who have inhabited New Guinea for at least 40,000 years. The Papuan language group is made up of a dozen different language families, comprising a total of around 800 different languages, many of them spoken by fewer than 100 people.

Paracas Culture of the south coast of **Peru**, c. 800–100 BC, showing the influence of the religious centre at **Chavín**. The culture is notable for its fine textiles.

Paraguay South American country that became independent of **Spain** in 1811. The country's present borders were established in 1935.

Parhae (Balhae or Bohai) Korean kingdom founded AD 698, a successor to the kingdom of **Koguryo**. Parhae was destroyed by the **Khitans** in 926.

Parthia Middle Eastern kingdom founded by the Parni, an **Iranian** nomad people, in 238 BC, which at its peak comprised most of modern **Iran** and **Iraq**. The kingdom was overthrown by the **Sasanians** in AD 224–26.

Pechenegs (Patzinaks) Semi-nomadic Turkic people of the western Eurasian steppes 9th–12th centuries AD. As the Pechenegs' lifestyle became more sedentary, they were assimilated by the neighbouring Hungarians and Bulgarians.

Pegu (Bago) **Mon** kingdom of the lower Irrawaddy region, **Burma**. Conquered by the **Burmese** kingdom of **Bagan** in AD 1056, regained its independence after that kingdom was destroyed by the **Mongols** in 1287. Reconquered by the Burmese in 1539.

Pereyaslavl Russian principality 11th century AD–1302.

Pergamon Ancient Greek city state in Anatolia, became independent in 281 BC, bequeathed to Rome by its last ruler Attalus III in 133 BC.

Persia See **Iran**.

Persian empire Major imperial state, also known as the Achaemenid empire after its ruling dynasty, created in the mid-6th century BC and conquered by Alexander the Great of Macedon in 334–330 BC. At its height in the 5th century BC, it controlled almost all of the Middle East as well as **Egypt** and parts of Southeast Europe, Central Asia and northern **India**.

Persians An **Iranian** people who settled in Fars (Parsa) in southwest **Iran** around the 9th century BC. The Persians have called themselves Iranians since around the 3rd century AD, but the name Persians remained in use by their neighbours into the 20th century.

Peru South American country that declared independence from **Spain** in 1821, secured following the defeat of Spanish loyalist forces at Ayacucho in 1824.

Peru, Viceroyalty of Spanish viceroyalty founded in 1542 to govern Spain's South American empire. Its northern territories were separated to form the viceroyalty of **New Granada** in 1717, and its southern territories to form the Viceroyalty of **Rio de la Plata** in 1776. The viceroyalty was dissolved in 1824.

Philippines Southeast Asian country. The Philippines were conquered by **Spain** between 1521 and 1565. The Philippines were ceded to the **USA** in 1898 and became independent in 1946.

Phoenicians A seafaring Semitic people of the Levant, closely related to the **Canaanites**, late 2nd–late 1st millennium BC. The Phoenicians gradually lost their identity after their conquest by Alexander the Great in 332 BC.

Phrygians **Indo-European**-speaking people of Anatolia, 13th century BC–4th century AD. The Phrygian kingdom dominated Anatolia in the early 1st millennium BC; it was destroyed by the **Cimmerians** in 690 BC.

Piedmont–Sardinia See **Sardinia**.

Pitcairn Island British island dependency in the South Pacific Ocean which became a British colony in 1838.

Poland–Lithuania East European kingdom created by the union of crowns of Poland and **Lithuania** in 1386. Full political union under the name Poland came in 1568.

Polonnaruwa Sinhalese kingdom founded in **Sri Lanka** 1070 following the expulsion of the **Cholas** from Ceylon. By 1200 the kingdom had lost control of most of the island and was conquered by the **Pandyas** in 1284.

Polotsk Russian principality founded late 11th century AD; conquered by **Lithuania** 1307.

Polynesians **Austronesian** people of the central Pacific islands, including **Tonga**, **Tahiti**, **Hawaii**, **Easter Island** and New Zealand.

Pontus Anatolian kingdom founded by a **Persian** dynasty in 302 BC; conquered by Rome in 65 BC.

Portugal European country. Portugal originated as a county of the Spanish kingdom of León and Castile that achieved de facto independence in 1128 and was proclaimed a kingdom in 1139. It achieved its present-day borders in 1249.

Portuguese Guinea Portuguese West African colony, established from 1446; became independent as **Guinea Bissau** in 1974.

Portuguese Timor See **Timor**.

Poverty Point culture Complex hunter-gatherer culture of southeastern North America, 2nd–early 1st millennium BC, centred on a massive semi-circular earthwork ritual site.

Príncipe See **São Tomé and Príncipe**.

Provence Region of southern **France** and medieval Frankish kingdom founded AD 879; united with the kingdom of **Burgundy** in 933.

Prussia Militaristic German kingdom created in 1701 when the Elector of **Brandenburg–Prussia** was elevated to kingship. The kingdom was the leader of German unification in the 19th century.

Pskov Russian principality that became formally independent of **Novgorod** in 1348; annexed by **Moscow** in 1510.

Ptolemaic kingdom Greek-ruled kingdom of **Egypt** founded in 304 BC by Ptolemy I, one of Alexander the Great's generals. Annexed by Rome in 30 BC.

Pucara culture Advanced farming culture of the Peruvian Andes 500 BC–AD 100 whose traditions of monumental architecture and elaborate painted ceramics influenced the later **Tiwanaku** and **Wari** civilizations.

Puebloans (Pueblo peoples) Native American peoples of the desert in the southwest of North America believed to be descended from the **Ancestral Pueblo**, **Hohokam** and **Mogollon** cultures.

Puerto Rico US dependency in the Caribbean. Puerto Rico became a Spanish colony in 1508 and was ceded to the **USA** in 1898.

Puntland Unrecognized African state that declared independence from **Somalia** in 1998.

Pygmies Term used to describe several ethnic groups worldwide whose adult males grow to less than 150 cm (59 inches) average height. The best known Pygmy peoples live in the forests of Central Africa.

Pyu Tibeto-Burmese-speaking people of Southeast Asia c. 100 BC–c. AD 850; assimilated by the **Burmese**.

Qarmatians **Arab** Shi'ite movement that rebelled against the **Abbasid caliphate** and founded a utopian state in Arabia in AD 899. The state broke up c. 1050.

Qataban Yemeni kingdom of the late 1st millennium BC.

Qatar Middle Eastern state. Although formally part of the **Ottoman** empire, the Qatari state was founded under British protection in 1878. Ottoman rule officially ended in 1913, when Qatar became a formal British protectorate until full independence in 1971.

Qi 1. Chinese state of the Spring and Autumn, and the Warring States periods (770–221 BC). It was conquered by **Qin** in 221. 2. Short-lived Chinese imperial dynasty AD 479–502.

Qin Chinese state of the Spring and Autumn, and the Warring States periods (770–221 BC), which conquered China between 230 and 221 BC under King Zheng. 2. The first Chinese imperial dynasty 221–207 BC, founded by King Zheng of Qin who took the title Shi Huangdi.

Qing Manchu imperial dynasty of China, founded 1644. Overthrown in 1911, the last Qing emperor formally abdicated in 1912.

Quebec Province of British North America founded in 1763, formerly part of **New France**. Quebec was divided into separate provinces of Upper and Lower **Canada** in 1791. The present-day Canadian province of Quebec, created in 1867, was originally roughly equivalent to Lower Canada, but other territories have been added subsequently.

Queensland British Australian colony separated from **New South Wales** in 1859. It became a state of the Commonwealth of **Australia** in 1901.

Rajputs Aristocratic Hindu warrior clans of northern **India**, originating in the early **Middle Ages**.

Rashtrakutas Major dynasty of southern **India** AD 753–982; overthrown by the West **Chalukya** dynasty.

Réunion Overseas department of **France** in the Indian Ocean. Claimed by France in 1642, but colonization began only in 1665.

Rhodes Greek state formed when the cities of Rhodes united in 408 BC. Under a succession of foreign rulers 357–304 BC; became a Roman client state in 164 BC.

Rhodesia, Northern British colony in Southern Africa formed from territories annexed in the 1890s. It became independent as **Zambia** in 1964.

Rhodesia, Southern British colony in Southern Africa, created in 1895. To prevent the introduction of majority rule, its white minority unilaterally declared independence as Rhodesia in 1965. British rule restored in 1979 to oversee the transition to majority rule and official independence as **Zimbabwe** in 1980.

Rio de la Plata, Viceroyalty of Spanish viceroyalty in South America founded in 1776, comprising roughly the modern countries of **Argentina**, Uruguay, Paraguay and **Bolivia** (until 1811 when it became part of the **Viceroyalty of Peru**): effectively dissolved in 1814.

Rio de Oro See **Spanish Sahara**.

Rio Muni Spanish colony in Equatorial Africa, founded in 1843. Since 1968 it has been part of **Equatorial Guinea**.

Roman empire Roman state founded by Augustus in 27 BC following the collapse of the **Roman republic** into civil war in the mid-1st century BC; characterized by a monarchical form of government under emperors. The Roman empire was divided into western and eastern parts in the 4th century AD, each with its own emperor. The western Roman empire fell in 476; the eastern Roman empire, commonly known as the **Byzantine empire**, survived until 1453.

Romania Eastern European country which became independent from the **Ottoman** empire in 1878.

Roman republic The Roman state, governed by elected magistrates, from the abolition of the monarchy in 509 BC to the establishment of imperial government by Augustus in 27 BC.

Romans Originally, the Latin-speaking inhabitants of the city of Rome. As Rome developed as an imperial power from the 4th century BC, Roman citizenship was gradually extended to conquered peoples as a reward for loyalty, assimilating them to Roman identity. In AD 312 citizenship was granted to all free inhabitants of the **Roman empire**.

Rostov–Suzdal Russian principality founded in 1093; conquered by **Ryazan** in 1146.

Rouran (Juan-juan) A powerful confederation of nomadic tribes, led by the **Altaic** Xianbei, which dominated the eastern Eurasian steppes c. AD 330–552. The confederation collapsed when its Turk vassals rebelled.

Rozwi Southern African kingdom of the Rozwi people, founded c. 1660; conquered by the **Ndebele** in 1838.

Ruanda-Urundi Belgian-administered Central African territory comprising the kingdoms of

Rwanda and **Burundi**, which, until 1916, had been part of **German East Africa**. The territory became a League of Nations mandate in 1923. **Rwanda** and **Burundi** became independent in 1962.

Rupert's Land North American land-claim of the English Hudson's Bay Company comprising the entire catchment of Hudson Bay; sold to **Canada** in 1869.

Rus Swedish Vikings active in Eastern Europe in the 9th–10th centuries AD who imposed their rule on the indigenous **Slav** peoples and who were ultimately assimilated by them. They have given their name to **Russia**.

Russia Transcontinental country in Europe and Asia, by area the world's largest. The first Russian state was founded at **Kiev** in c. AD 882. This state broke up into independent principalities in the later 11th century. The modern Russian state originated in the 16th century when the Grand Duchy of **Moscow** conquered the other Russian principalities. The adoption of the title Tsar of Russia by Ivan IV in 1547 marks the formal emergence of Russia as a unitary state. After it began to expand into Asia in 1581–82, Russia developed into a major imperial power. Following the 1917 revolution, the Russian empire was divided into nominally autonomous ethnically based Soviet Socialist Republics, by far the largest of which was the Russian Soviet Federative Socialist Republic (RSFSR). This was the dominant republic of the **USSR**, which was formally declared in 1922. On the break-up of the USSR in 1991 the RSFSR became independent as the Russian Federation or Russia.

Rwanda Central African kingdom formed by the 17th century AD. Annexed by Germany in 1884. In 1923 it was united with **Burundi** by the League of Nations as the Belgian mandate territory of **Ruanda–Urundi** until independence in 1962.

Ryazan Russian principality founded c. 1155; annexed by **Moscow** in 1521.

Saba Ancient kingdom of **Yemen**, often identified as the homeland of the Biblical queen of Sheba; conquered by the **Himyarites** in 25 BC.

Safavids Enormously influential Shi'ite Iranian dynasty, ruled **Iran** 1501–1736.

Saffarids Persian dynasty AD 861–1003 that ruled eastern **Iran**, **Afghanistan**, the Indus valley and parts of Central Asia under its founder Ya'qub bin Laith as-Saffar (r. 861–79); it quickly declined under his successors.

Saint-Domingue French Caribbean colony in western Hispaniola. **France** seized the territory from **Spain** in 1659; it became independent as **Haiti** in 1804.

St Helena British island dependency in the South Atlantic Ocean. The island was claimed by the **Netherlands** in 1633, but was never occupied by them; the English took possession of the island in 1659.

St Kitts and Nevis St Kitts was the earliest English colony in the Caribbean, founded in 1624. Nevis became an English colony in 1628. St Kitts and Nevis became independent in 1983.

St Lucia Caribbean island nation. The island became a French colony in 1660 but possession of the island changed hands between Britain and **France** 14 times before British sovereignty was conclusively recognized in 1814. The island became independent in 1979.

St Pierre and Miquelon French overseas territory off the coast of **Newfoundland**. The islands changed hands several times between Britain and **France** before French sovereignty was conclusively recognized in 1815.

St Vincent and the Grenadines Caribbean island nation. The islands became a French colony in 1719 and were ceded to Britain in 1763. They became independent in 1979.

Sakas Old Iranian name for the **Scythians**.

Samanids Persian Sunni dynasty of Central Asia AD 819–999; conquered by the **Karakhanids**.

Sami (Saami or Lapps) Semi-nomadic reindeer-herding people of far-Northern Europe who speak **Finno-Ugrian** languages. The Sami have inhabited the area for at least 5,000 years.

Samoyeds Siberian reindeer-herding peoples, including the Nenets, Enets, Nganasan and Selkup, who speak Uralic languages.

San (Bushmen) Hunter-gatherer peoples of Southern Africa, a branch of the **Khoisan** peoples.

São Tomé See **São Tomé and Príncipe**.

São Tomé and Príncipe Island nation off the west coast of Central Africa. São Tomé and Príncipe were uninhabited when discovered and claimed by the Portuguese c. 1471. The islands became independent in 1975.

Sarawak British protectorate on Borneo established in 1888. Previously, from 1841, Sarawak was an independent kingdom under the British Brooke dynasty. Sarawak became a state of **Malaysia** in 1963.

Sardinia Kingdom of Sardinia and Piedmont in northwest **Italy** 1720–1861, generally known as Piedmont–Sardinia after 1815. The kingdom was the leader of Italian unification.

Sarmatians The last major Iranian nomad people of the Eurasian steppes, originated c. 6th century BC. They lost much of their lands to the **Goths** in the 3rd century AD; the remainder was conquered by the **Huns** in the 4th century.

Sasanians Major **Persian** dynasty that overthrew the **Parthians** in AD 224–26; conquered by the **Arabs** in 637–51.

Satavahana Southern Indian dynasty founded c. 230 BC. It became a major kingdom in the 2nd century BC, but declined rapidly after c. AD 200, disappearing around the mid-3rd century.

Saudi Arabia Kingdom of the Saudi dynasty comprising the greater part of the Arabian peninsula; founded in 1924 after the Saudi state of **Nejd** annexed **Hejaz**.

Scandinavians North European peoples speaking Scandinavian languages (a sub-group of the Germanic languages): the Danes, Swedes, Norwegians, Icelanders and Faroese. They were often referred to collectively as the **Norse** in the early **Middle Ages**.

Scotland Kingdom of northern Britain founded c. AD 843 with a mixed Celtic and, from the late 10th century, Anglo-Saxon population. United with **England** in 1707 to create the Kingdom of **Great Britain**.

Scythians Iranian nomad people who dominated the Eurasian steppes 8th–1st centuries BC. They were absorbed by the **Sarmatians** and other nomad peoples.

Segu West African kingdom of the Bambara people founded c. 1712, destroyed in 1861 by the **Tukulor empire**.

Seleucid empire Greek empire of the Middle East founded by Seleucos, one of Alexander the Great's generals, in 312 BC. The empire's history was one of steady decline, finally collapsing in 83 BC.

Seljuks (Seljuqs) A branch of the **Oguz** Turks who conquered most of the Middle East 1037–87 and established Turkish dominance in Anatolia. Their sultanate broke up into separate states in 1092.

Semites Ancient and modern peoples speaking Semitic languages, including the **Arabs**, **Hebrews**, **Canaanites**, **Phoenicians**, Assyrians, Babylonians, **Aramaeans**, **Chaldaeans** and Ethiopians.

Senegal West African country, formerly a territory of **French West Africa**, which became independent in 1960. The French established a trading base at the mouth of the Senegal river in the 17th century AD, but only began to extend their rule to inland territories of Senegal from the 1850s.

Serbs Slav people of the Balkans, emerged in the early 7th century AD.

Shan People of Southeast Asia who speak a Tai language who migrated from Yunnan, China, to **Burma** around the 10th century AD. Following the destruction of the Burmese **Bagan** kingdom by the **Mongols** in 1287, the Shan formed several independent states. These were gradually brought under **Burmese** rule between the 1550s and 1760s.

Shang Bronze Age dynasty in northern China c. 1600–1046 BC.

Shijiahe culture Late Neolithic rice-farming culture of the middle Yangtze region 2500–2000 BC with large proto-urban settlements.

Shirvan Historic region of the eastern Caucasus, now mostly in **Azerbaijan**. From the 9th century AD to 1607 it was ruled by the Shirvanshahs, who were usually vassals of neighbouring great powers, but occasionally asserted their independence.

Shu 1. **Bronze Age** kingdom of the Sichuan region of eastern China, with a non-Chinese culture. 2. Chinese kingdom of the Five Dynasties and Ten Kingdoms period AD 907–65.

Siam Tai kingdom founded at Ayutthaya in 1351 (often called the Kingdom of Ayutthaya until 1767), renamed **Thailand** in 1939.

Sibir Tatar khanate, split from the **Golden Horde** in 1490; conquered by **Russia** in 1581–98.

Sicily Norman kingdom of Sicily and southern **Italy** founded in 1130. The kingdom's southern Italian possessions became independent in 1282 as the kingdom of **Naples** after Sicily itself came under the rule of **Aragon**. Sicily was reunited with Naples in 1816 to form the **Kingdom of the Two Sicilies**.

Sierra Leone West African country, founded by the British as a colony for freed slaves in 1792. It became independent in 1961.

Silla Early Korean kingdom, founded c. 57 BC. In the 9th century AD the kingdom suffered civil wars and peasant rebellions and in 935 it was overthrown by the Koryo dynasty, which unified **Korea**.

Sindh Fertile region of the Indus river delta, now in **Pakistan**. Conquered by the **Arabs** in AD 711–13, independent Muslim state 10th–12th centuries.

Singapore Southeast Asian island state, founded as a British colony in 1819. It became independent in 1965.

Sinhalese Indigenous people of **Sri Lanka** whose ancestors are traditionally held to have migrated from **India** in the 5th century BC.

Slavs Major group of Eastern European peoples, including the Russians, Belorussians, Ukrainians, Poles, Czechs, Slovaks, Slovenes, **Serbs**, Croats and Bulgarians, who speak Slavonic languages, a branch of the **Indo-European** language family.

Slovakia Central European country. Part of **Czechoslovakia** from 1918, it was a German puppet-state 1939–45 and became independent in 1993.

Slovenia Former Yugoslav republic that became independent in 1991.

Smolensk Russian principality, founded later 11th century AD; conquered by Lithuania in 1404.

Socotra Island off the Horn of Africa. It became a British protectorate in 1876 and in 1967 became part of the **People's Democratic Republic of Yemen**.

Sokoto caliphate Fulani jihadi state, founded 1804–11, which controlled much of **Nigeria** and **Niger**. The caliphate was broken up between the British and French empires in the 1890s.

Solomon Islands Island nation in the western Pacific Ocean. Settled by **Melanesians**, the islands became a British protectorate in 1893. They became independent in 1978.

Somalia African state created by uniting the former colonies of **British** and **Italian Somaliland** in 1960. The country has had no effective central government since 1991.

Somaliland 1. Territory in the Horn of Africa, inhabited by Somali peoples, divided into British,

Italian and French colonies in the late 19th century AD. **British** and **Italian Somaliland** were united to create the independent republic of **Somalia** in 1960. French Somaliland became independent as **Djibouti** in 1977. 2. Unrecognized state, controlling most of the territory of **British Somaliland**, which declared independence from Somalia in 1991.

Song Chinese imperial dynasty that unified most of China in AD 979. Northern Song, 960–1126, had its capital at Kaifeng. Southern Song 1127–1279, following the loss of the north to the **Jin**, had its capital at Hangzhou. The dynasty was ended by the Mongol conquest.

Songhay (Songhai) Muslim kingdom of the Songhay people, which became independent of **Mali** in 1340 and expanded to control much of the West African Sahel. Its power was broken by the Moroccans in 1591.

Sosso Kingdom of the Sosso people in West Africa, a successor to the **Ghana** empire, 12th–13th centuries AD. Conquered by **Mali** c. 1240.

South Africa Southern African country created by the union of the British colonies of **Cape Colony**, **Natal**, the **Orange Free State** and **Transvaal** (the last two former **Boer** republics) as a self-governing dominion in 1910. It became independent under white rule in 1931; majority rule was achieved in 1994.

South Australia British Australian colony, separated from **New South Wales** in 1834. It became a state of the Commonwealth of Australia in 1901.

Southern Han Independent dynasty that ruled the Guangdong region of southern China AD 917–71.

South Korea See **Korea**.

South Semites Ancient Semitic-speaking peoples of southern Arabia.

South Vietnam See **Vietnam**.

Southwest Africa See **Namibia**.

Spain Western European country created in 1516 by the union of the kingdoms of **Aragon** and **Castile**.

Spanish Morocco Spanish protectorate over northern **Morocco** and Ifni 1912–56.

Spanish Netherlands Wealthy territory approximating to the modern **Netherlands** and **Belgium**, which came under the Spanish crown in 1519. The northern provinces rebelled in 1568, becoming independent as the Republic of the Seven United Netherlands. The southern provinces were ceded to **Austria** in 1713.

Spanish Sahara Spanish protectorate in the western Sahara consisting of **Rio de Oro**, annexed in 1884, and part of southern **Morocco**, annexed in 1912. Now **Western Sahara**; the Spanish withdrew in 1975.

Sri Lanka Island nation in South Asia, known as **Ceylon** until 1972. The first states in Sri Lanka formed in the 5th century BC. The Portuguese gained control of coastal areas in the 16th century AD, but were driven out by the Dutch in the mid-17th century. The Dutch were, in turn, driven out in 1796 by the British, who conquered the whole island in 1815; became independent in 1948.

Srivijaya Indianized Malay kingdom of Sumatra, which dominated **Malaya** and Java from the 7th to 13th centuries AD. It was conquered by the short-lived Singhasari kingdom of Java in c. 1280 and was under the control of its successor state **Majapahit** by 1300.

Srubnaya (Srubna) Late **Bronze Age** pastoralist culture of the Eurasian steppes 16th–9th centuries BC, sometimes associated with the origins of the **Cimmerians**.

Sudan North African country, formerly **Anglo-Egyptian Sudan**, which became independent in 1956. By a referendum in January 2011 the country's southern provinces voted to become independent as South Sudan.

Sueves (Suebi) Early German people first recorded in the 1st century BC. Invaded the **Roman empire** in the 5th century AD and founded a kingdom in northwest **Spain**; conquered by the Visigoths in 585.

Sukhothai Tai kingdom founded in northern **Thailand** in c. 1238. It became a tributary of **Siam** in 1378 and was fully absorbed into Siam in 1448.

Sumerians Ancient people of southern Mesopotamia who founded the first urban civilization in the 4th millennium BC. They spoke a language unrelated to other known languages. In the 2nd millennium BC they were gradually assimilated by neighbouring **Semitic** peoples.

Surabaya Sultanate of eastern Java founded in the 16th century AD; conquered by **Mataram** in 1625.

Suren Kingdom of southwest **Afghanistan** ruled by the **Parthian** Suren family c. 1st century BC.

Suriname South American country, formerly the colony of **Dutch Guiana**; it became independent in 1975.

Svalbard (Spitzbergen) Arctic archipelago. Norwegian sovereignty was recognized by a treaty in 1920 that also established Svalbard as a demilitarized zone.

Swahili **Bantu**-speaking people of the East African coast whose culture and language have been greatly influenced by trading contacts with the Arab and **Persian** worlds.

Swaziland Southern African kingdom founded in the 1840s. It became a British protectorate in 1894, becoming independent in 1968.

Sweden Scandinavian country that was formed by the union of the Svear and Götar peoples in c. AD 995. Joined in a union of crowns with **Denmark** in 1397, Sweden regained full independence again in 1523.

Swiss Confederacy See **Switzerland**.

Switzerland European federal state formed in 1848 by the Swiss Confederacy, a loose confederation of Swiss states formed in 1291 that gained independence from the **Holy Roman empire** in 1499.

Syria Middle Eastern, mainly Arab, country, created in 1922 as a French-administered League of Nations mandated territory from territory formerly ruled by the **Ottoman** empire; became independent in 1946.

Tabaristan (Tapuria) Territory on the south coast of the Caspian Sea, the last centre of **Persian** resistance to the Arabs in the 7th century AD.

Tahiti Archipelago in the South Pacific Ocean, settled by **Polynesians** c. 200 BC. The islands were annexed by **France** in 1842, along with the **Marquesas Islands** and the Tuamotu Archipelago. In 1946 the islands collectively became the French overseas department of **French Polynesia**.

Tais Peoples of southern China and Southeast Asia who speak Tai languages, including the modern Thais (i.e. the people of **Thailand**) and Laotians.

Taiwan See **Republic of China**.

Tajikistan Central Asian country, formerly the Tajik Soviet Socialist Republic, which became independent on the fall of the **USSR** in 1991. The Tajiks are a Persian-speaking people.

Takrur West African kingdom on the Senegal river, formed c. 9th century AD; conquered by **Mali** in 1285. It was one of the earliest West African states to accept Islam, converting c. 1030.

Tang Chinese imperial dynasty AD 618–907.

Tanganyika British League of Nations mandated territory created 1922 comprising most of the territory of the former **German East Africa** colony. It became independent in 1962.

Tanguts A pastoralist people of Tibetan origin 9th–13th centuries AD; founded the kingdom of **Xixia** c. 1038.

Tanzania East African country formed from the union of **Tanganyika** with the island of **Zanzibar** in 1964.

Tasmanians Aboriginal people of Tasmania, sharing a common origin with the Australian **Aborigines**, but isolated from them, and from all other outside contacts from c. 6000 BC until AD 1772.

Tatars Turkic nomad people who originated in **Mongolia** c. 7th century AD. Conquered by the **Mongols** in the 13th century, they migrated west and settled on the Eastern European steppes as part of the **Golden Horde**.

Teke Central African Bantu-speaking people of the middle Congo river basin.

Tenasserim Part of southern **Burma** ceded to the British in 1826.

Teotihuacán Ancient city state of the Valley of Mexico, founded c. 200 BC. In the early 1st millennium AD it became a major power whose influence spread throughout **Mesoamerica**. It was destroyed and abandoned c. 650.

Ternate Muslim Malay sultanate of the Maluku islands (Moluccas). Founded in the mid-13th century AD, it rose to prominence in the 16th century through its participation in the spice trade. Conquered by the Dutch in 1683.

Teutonic Knights German crusading order that campaigned against the Baltic pagans. Founded 1198, it ceased to be a territorial power in 1525.

Thailand Southeast Asian country, known as **Siam** until 1939.

Thirteen Colonies The British North American colonies of Connecticut, Delaware, Georgia, Maryland, Massachusetts, New Hampshire, New Jersey, New York, North Carolina, Pennsylvania, Rhode Island, South Carolina and **Virginia**, which became the founding states of the **United States of America**.

Thracians Indo-European-speaking peoples of Southeast Europe, noted for their fine metalwork. They were usually under foreign rule from the 4th century BC and had lost their identity by the 6th century AD.

Thule Inuit culture The most sophisticated **Inuit** marine-mammal hunting culture, superbly adapted to Arctic conditions, it originated around the Bering Sea c. AD 1000 and spread west to Greenland, displacing the early **Dorset** Inuit culture.

Tibet High plateau in Central Asia and kingdom founded in the early 7th century AD. Briefly a major expansionist power in the 8th–9th centuries, Tibet was under Mongol rule from 1251 to 1346–54. In 1751 Tibet was conquered by the Chinese **Qing** empire, regaining de facto independence on the fall of the Qing dynasty in 1911; reconquered by China in 1950.

Tibetans People of the Tibetan plateau and the Himalaya mountains.

Tibeto-Burman Asian language family related to the Chinese languages, including Tibetan and **Burmese**.

Timbuktu West African city on the northern bend of the Niger river, a terminus for major trans-Saharan caravan routes, founded by the **Touareg** c. AD 1000.

Timor East Indian island. Under Portuguese influence from around 1515 until the Dutch occupied western Timor in 1613. Dutch western Timor became part of **Indonesia** in 1949. Portuguese East Timor became legally independent in 1975 but was immediately occupied by Indonesia; East Timor finally achieved independence in 1999.

Timurids Turkic dynasty of Central Asia 1370–1506, founded by Timur (Tamberlaine) (r. 1370–1405) who conquered an empire that stretched from the Indus to the Black Sea.

Tippu Tib's trading empire A loosely organised trading empire in Central Africa built in the 1870s by the **Swahili** slave trader Tippu Tib, which was incorporated into the **Congo Free State** in 1887.

Tiwanaku (Tiahuanaco) Ancient city on Lake Titicaca in the Bolivian Andes, developed into a locally important cult centre by the early 1st millennium AD, beginning a period of imperial expansion c. 375. The empire fell c. 1000, possibly because of climate change.

Tocharians The most easterly of the **Indo-European** pastoralist people of Central Asia, probably related to the **Yuezhi** and the **Kushans**. Their language is first recorded c. AD 300 and they had disappeared by 800.

Togo West African country that originated as a German protectorate in 1884. It was occupied by the Allies in 1914–16. In 1920 the colony was divided into two League of Nations mandated territories administered by Britain and **France**. British Togo was administered as part of the **Gold Coast** and became part of independent **Ghana** in 1956. French Togo was administered as part of **French West Africa**, becoming an independent republic in 1960.

Toltecs Nahuatl-speaking people of central **Mexico** who emerged around the 8th century AD. They dominated **Mesoamerica** during the 11th century, but their state collapsed abruptly in 1168.

Tonga Island nation in the South Pacific Ocean. The archipelago was united into a single kingdom in 1845. Tonga was never formally colonized, but was a British protected state from 1900 to 1970.

Tongking Kingdom of northern **Vietnam** 1620–1802.

Touareg Nomadic pastoralist **Berber** people of the Sahara desert.

Transjordan British-administered League of Nations mandated territory in the Middle East created in 1922 from territory formerly ruled by the **Ottoman** empire. It became independent as **Jordan** in 1946.

Transvaal Boer republic in Southern Africa, established 1852, conquered by the British in 1899–1902. It became a province of **South Africa** in 1910.

Trebizond, empire of Byzantine successor state, independent 1204, conquered by the **Ottoman** Turks in 1461.

Trinidad and Tobago Caribbean republic. The islands were claimed by **Spain** in 1498. Tobago was ceded to Britain in 1763, Trinidad in 1802. The two colonies were united in 1889 and became independent in 1962.

Tripoli Pashalik (province) of the **Ottoman** Turk empire formed in 1551, which became effectively autonomous after 1714. Direct Ottoman rule was restored in 1835.

Tristan da Cunha British dependency in the South Atlantic Ocean, discovered by the Portuguese in 1506. Britain annexed the islands in 1816.

Trucial Oman See **UAE**.

Trust Territories of the Pacific Islands The former Japanese possessions of the **Caroline** and **Marshall Islands** in the Pacific, which were placed under US administration after the Second World War by the UN. The Caroline Islands (except **Palau**) became independent in 1986 as the **Federated States of Micronesia**. The Marshall Islands became an independent republic in the same year.

Tukulor empire West African jihadi state of the Tukulor, a Fulani people. Established in 1850, it became a major territorial power after its conquest of **Segu** in 1861. It was conquered by **France** in 1890.

Tungus Group of peoples of Siberia and Northeast Asia who speak Tungusic languages. The most numerous of the Tungusic peoples are the Manchus (or **Jürchen**) of Manchuria.

Tunis, beylik of North African province of the **Ottoman** empire, effectively autonomous by 1705; became a French protectorate in 1881.

Tunisia North African country with an **Arab** and **Berber** population. The modern country of Tunisia roughly corresponds to the former Ottoman beylik of **Tunis**, which became a French protectorate in 1881. Tunis became independent of **France** in 1956.

Tupi Native American tribal peoples of **Brazil** who lived primarily by farming maize and manioc (cassava) at the time of their first contacts with Europeans in the 16th century AD.

Turkey Middle Eastern and European country, the successor state to the **Ottoman** empire; founded in 1923.

Turkmen Traditionally nomadic Turkic people of western Central Asia descended from the **Oguz** Turks.

Turkmenistan Central Asian country, formerly the Turkmen Soviet Socialist Republic, which became independent on the fall of the **USSR** in 1991.

Turks A major group of peoples of Western, Central and Northern Asia who speak Turkic languages, including the **Kazakhs**, **Kyrgyz**, **Tatars**, Turkish (the people of modern Turkey), **Turkmen**, **Uighurs**, **Uzbeks** and **Yakuts**. Historical Turkic peoples included the **Cumans**, **Huns**, **Oguz**, **Ottomans**, **Seljuks**, Khazars and **Xiongnu**.

Turks and Caicos Islands British Caribbean dependency. The islands were annexed by Britain in 1799 and governed as part of the **Bahamas** until 1973.

Tuva Republic of the Tuvans, a Turkic-speaking people, in southern Siberia. It became independent of China as Urjanchai following the fall of the **Qing** dynasty in 1911 and became the People's Tuvan Republic in 1921. It was effectively under Soviet control by 1926 and was formally annexed by the **USSR** in 1944.

Tuvalu Island nation in the western Pacific Ocean formerly known as the Ellice Islands. The islands became a British protectorate in 1892, becoming independent in 1978.

Tuyuhun A coalition of pastoralist peoples centred on the highlands of present-day Qinghai, eastern China, probably under **Altaic** leadership, but whose subjects were mainly Qiang, a Tibeto-Burmese people. Caught between the expanding Chinese **Tang** empire and **Tibet**, they disappeared in the 7th century AD.

Tver Russian principality, founded 1247; conquered by **Moscow** in 1485.

Two Sicilies, kingdom of the Kingdom of southern **Italy** and **Sicily** formed by the union of Naples and Sicily in 1816. Annexed by **Piedmont–Sardinia** in 1860, which led to the creation of the kingdom of Italy in 1861.

Ubaid culture Complex farming culture of Mesopotamia practising irrigation agriculture with proto-urban settlements 5900–4200 BC.

Uganda East African country. Uganda originated when the kingdoms of **Buganda**, **Bunyoro**, **Ankole** and other territories were brought together as a British protectorate in 1894. Uganda became independent in 1962.

Uighurs (Uyghur) Originally a Turkic nomad people who ruled a khanate centred in present-day **Mongolia** from the 740s until it was destroyed by the **Kyrgyz** in 840. Survivors migrated east to present day Xinjiang giving their name and language to the local settled population. In the 20th century the name came to be used for all Turkic-speaking settled peoples of Chinese-ruled Xinjiang.

Ukraine Eastern European country with a **Slav** population. Formerly the Ukrainian Soviet Socialist Republic, Ukraine became independent on the collapse of the **USSR** in 1991.

Umayyads 1. The first major Islamic dynasty; ruled the **Arab** caliphate AD 661–750. 2. After the dynasty's overthrow by the **Abbasids**, a survivor founded an independent Umayyad emirate in **Spain** in 756 (also called the emirate of Córdoba). The emir Abd al-Rahman III adopted the title caliph in 929. The caliphate broke up into petty kingdoms in 1031.

USSR (Union of Soviet Socialist Republics) Communist state comprising most of the territory of the Russian empire, founded in 1922. It was a Russian-dominated federation of nominally autonomous ethnically based Soviet Socialist Republics. The USSR broke up in 1991 when its constituent republics declared independence.

UAE (United Arab Emirates) A group of **Arab** sheikdoms on the Persian Gulf that became the British protectorate of **Trucial Oman** in 1853. They became independent as the United Arab Emirates in 1971.

United Kingdom The United Kingdom of Great Britain was created by the union of **England** and **Scotland** in 1707; it became the United Kingdom of Great Britain and **Ireland** in 1801, and the United Kingdom of Great Britain and Northern Ireland in 1921. Until the dissolution of the British empire, the UK was more commonly known simply as Great Britain.

United Provinces of Rio de la Plata Latin American state, declared independence from **Spain** in 1816; known as **Argentina** from 1826.

United States of America (USA) North American federal republic. Founded by the **Thirteen Colonies** that declared independence from Britain in 1776. Britain recognized the United States' independence in 1783. The United States' westward expansion across the North American continent began with the

Louisiana Purchase in 1803; it achieved its modern borders with the annexation of **Hawaii** in 1898.

United States Virgin Islands Formerly the **Danish Virgin Islands**, purchased by the USA in 1917.

Upper Volta See **Burkina Faso**.

Urartu Hurrian kingdom centred in **Armenia**, founded c. 860 BC; conquered by the **Medes** c. 585 BC.

Urjanchai See **Tuva**.

Urnfield cultures A complex of cultures of later **Bronze Age** and early **Iron Age** Europe, c. 1350–900 BC, characterized by cremation burials in urns in large open cemeteries. Originating in Central Europe, Urnfield practices had spread across much of Western Europe by 1000 BC.

Uruguay South American republic. Originally part of the Spanish viceroyalty of **Rio de la Plata**, Uruguay was occupied by Portuguese forces from **Brazil** in 1816. Uruguay declared independence from Brazil in 1825; recognized 1828.

Uzbeks Turkic-speaking people of Central Asia, emerged in the 15th century AD from the break-up of the **Golden Horde**. In recent centuries they have been predominantly settled farmers and town dwellers.

Vakatakas Dynasty of central **India**, 3rd–6th centuries AD.

Vandals Early Germanic people, first recorded in the 1st century AD. They invaded the Roman empire in 406 and, after an epic migration through **Spain** and North Africa, founded a kingdom in present-day **Tunisia** in 439; conquered by the eastern Roman empire in 533–34.

Van Diemen's Land The original European name for Tasmania. Van Diemen's land became part of the British Australian colony of **New South Wales** in 1803, becoming a colony in its own right in 1824. The name Tasmania was adopted in 1856. It became a state of the Commonwealth of **Australia** in 1901.

Vanuatu Pacific Island nation comprising the **New Hebrides** archipelago. Administered jointly by Britain and **France** from the 1880s, Vanuatu became independent in 1980.

Vatsa Early Hindu *mahajanapada* (great realm) of northern **India**, annexed c. 5th century AD by **Avanti**.

Venezuela South American republic. Following a war of independence against **Spain** (1811–23), Venezuela became part of **Gran Colombia**, from which it seceded in 1830.

Venice Italian mercantile republic, became independent of the **Byzantine empire** in the early 9th century AD, at its peak from the 11th to 16th centuries. Conquered by **France** in 1797.

Veracruz civilization Civilisation of northeast Vera Cruz on **Mexico**'s Gulf coast whose main centre was the city of El Tajín, at its peak c. 7th–8th centuries AD.

Vichy France Collaborationist French state, based at Vichy, formed after the German conquest of **France**

in 1940. It ceased to exist with the liberation of France in 1944.

Victoria British Australian colony, separated from **New South Wales** in 1850. Became a state of the Commonwealth of **Australia** in 1901.

Vietnam Southeast Asian country, known as **Dai Viet** until 1802. Conquered by **France** between 1859 and 1885, it became part of **French Indochina**. On independence in 1954, Vietnam was partitioned along the 17th parallel into Communist North Vietnam and US-backed South Vietnam. North Vietnam conquered the south in 1975, reuniting the country.

Vietnamese (Viets) Austro-Asiatic-speaking people of Southeast Asia whose origins can be traced back to the **Dong Son culture**. Now confined primarily to **Vietnam**, in early historic times they also inhabited southeast China.

Vijayanagara Major Hindu kingdom of southern India, founded 1336, named after its capital Vijayanagara (city of victory). The capital was captured and destroyed by **Bijapur** in 1565; a much-diminished kingdom survived until 1646.

Vikings Early medieval **Scandinavian** pirates, active late 8th–11th centuries AD; often used to describe early medieval Scandinavians in general.

Virginia England's first colony in North America. The first English attempts to settle Virginia, in the 1580s, failed; the first successful settlement was founded at Jamestown in 1607. The name Virginia was originally applied to all of the North American coast between the 34th and 39th parallels. The present-day borders of the US state of Virginia were defined in 1863.

Visigothic kingdom Kingdom founded by the Visigothic branch of the **Goths** in AD 418. At its peak the kingdom controlled what is now **Spain**, **Portugal** and southwest **France**. It was conquered by the **Arabs** and their **Berber** allies (Moors) in 711–13.

Vladimir–Suzdal Russian principality founded 1168; absorbed by Moscow in 1389.

Vrijji (Vajji) Early Hindu *mahajanapada* (great realm) of northeast **India** 7th–5th centuries BC.

Wadai (Ouaddai) African kingdom, broke away from **Darfur** in the 16th century AD, now part of **Chad**. Annexed by **France** in 1900, but not subdued until 1912.

Wales Country in western Britain named for the **Welsh**. Never a politically united state, Wales was conquered by **England** in the 13th century AD, but retained a separate identity.

Wallachia Medieval Romanian principality, formed *c.* 1330, **Ottoman** vassal 1415.

Walvis Bay The only deep-water harbour on the African coast between **Angola** and the Cape of Good Hope, annexed by Britain in 1879. Became part of **South Africa** in 1910, ceded to **Namibia** in 1994.

Wari (Huari) Expansionist state of the Peruvian Andes and rival of **Tiwanaku**, *c.* AD 500–*c.* 1000.

Warsaw, Grand Duchy of French-dominated Polish state created by Napoleon in 1807 from Polish lands ceded by **Prussia**. In 1815 it was partitioned between Prussia and **Russia**.

Wattasids **Berber** dynasty of **Morocco** 1472–1554.

Welsh The people of **Wales** in western Britain. They are of mainly Celtic origin and, although the majority are now English-speaking, they include the largest surviving community of Celtic-speakers.

Wessex Anglo-Saxon kingdom in southern Britain, founded in the early 6th century AD, that united all the **Anglo-Saxons** under its control by 927 to create the kingdom of **England**.

Western Australia British Australian colony established 1829; it became a state of the Commonwealth of **Australia** in 1901.

Western Sahara Former colonial territory of **Spanish Sahara** that was occupied by **Morocco** in 1975 following Spain's withdrawal.

West Germany (Federal Republic of Germany) Federal republic formed in the US, British and French occupation zones of **Germany** in 1949. In 1990 it was reunited with the former communist state of **East Germany**.

Wilusa Region or kingdom of **Bronze Age** Anatolia probably to be identified with Ilios, the alternative Greek name for Troy.

Wolof (Djolof) Kingdom of the Wolof people in present-day **Senegal** *c.* 1350–1549.

Wu 1. Major Chinese state of the Spring and Autumn period, founded late 6th century BC; conquered by **Yue** in 473 BC. 2. Kingdom of central and south China, AD 222–80, formed following the fall of the **Han** dynasty. 3. Chinese kingdom of the middle and lower Yangtze region, 892–937.

Wucheng culture Bronze Age urbanized culture of the lower Yangtze region, contemporary with the **Shang** dynasty.

Wusun Nomadic steppe people, probably **Indo-European**-speaking, in the Tianshan region of China 2nd century BC–5th century AD.

Wuyue Chinese state in the Zhejiang region, founded AD 893, conquered by the **Song** in 978.

Xiongnu A powerful confederation of **Altaic** nomad peoples, which dominated the eastern steppes from the 3rd to 1st centuries BC. Their appearance marked the beginning of the decline of the **Indo-Iranian** nomad peoples. Though often identified with the **Huns**, the evidence for this is inconclusive. The confederation broke up in the 1st century AD.

Xixia Kingdom of the **Tanguts**, in present-day Gansu, Shaanxi and Ningxia provinces, China, founded in AD 1038; conquered by the **Mongols** in 1227.

Yadavas Hindu dynasty of central **India**. Originally vassals of the **Chalukyas**, they came to dominate the Deccan around the end of the 12th century AD. Conquered by the sultanate of **Delhi** in 1317.

Yakuts Semi-nomadic Turkic pastoralist peoples of Siberia who originated in the region of Lake Baikal.

Yamnaya (Yamna) culture The earliest steppe pastoralist culture, characterized by burial under *kurgans* (burial mounds) and the use of wheeled vehicles. The Yamnaya culture developed on the European steppes between the Black Sea and the Ural Mountains *c.* 3600–2500 BC. The culture is associated by many archaeologists with the origins of the **Indo-European** languages.

Yan 1. Chinese state of the Spring and Autumn, and Warring States periods (770–221 BC); conquered by **Qin** in 222 BC. 2. A short-lived kingdom of northeast China at the beginning of the Five Dynasties and Ten Kingdoms period (AD 907–65).

Yangshao culture Early Neolithic culture of China's Yellow river region based on millet farming *c.* 5000–3200 BC.

Yayoi culture Japanese farming culture, flourished *c.* 300 BC–AD 300, which saw the introduction of intensive rice cultivation in paddy fields and of iron tools and weapons.

Yemen Arab country in southeast Arabia. The modern state of Yemen was founded in 1918; it was united with the **People's Democratic Republic of Yemen** in 1990.

Yemen, People's Democratic Republic of Arabian state, formerly the British **Aden** protectorate. Independent in 1967, merged with **Yemen** in 1990.

Yoruba Major ethnic group of **Nigeria** and neighbouring countries. Though sharing the same language and culture, they have never been politically united, but were divided into small kingdoms, the most important of which were **Ibadan**, **Ife** and **Oyo**.

Yue Sino-Viet state in eastern China contemporary with the **Zhou** kingdom; conquered by **Chu** in the 4th century BC.

Yuezhi Indo-Iranian pastoralist confederation of Central Asia 5th–1st centuries BC. The **Kushan** clan became dominant in the 1st century BC and their name was adopted for the whole confederation.

Yugoslavia Multi-ethnic Balkan federation founded in 1918 as the **Kingdom of the Serbs, Croats and Slovenes**; officially known as Yugoslavia since 1929. The federation broke up in a series of civil wars between 1991 and 1999. The last two members, Serbia and **Montenegro**, abandoned the name in 2003 and became independent of each other in 2006.

Zaghawa Semi-nomadic pastoralists of the eastern Sahara, at their most powerful in the 12th century AD.

Zaire The name by which the **Democratic Republic of the Congo** was known 1971–97.

Zambia Southern African country, formerly the British colony of **Northern Rhodesia**, which became independent in 1964.

Zanj The **Swahili** coast of East Africa under Omani rule from *c.* 1698 to 1856.

Zanzibar Island and **Swahili** city off the coast of **Tanzania** founded around the 12th century AD. Under Portuguese control from 1505 to 1698 when it was captured by **Oman**. It split from Oman in 1856 and became an independent sultanate until coming under British control in 1897.

Zapotecs Indigenous people of southern **Mexico** and major pre-Columbian civilization of **Mesoamerica**, flourished *c.* 600 BC–AD 1500. By the time of the Spanish conquest of Mexico, most Zapotec lands had been occupied by the **Mixtecs** and the **Aztecs**.

Zayyanids (Ziyyanids) **Berber** dynasty of **Algeria**, 1235–1556.

Zhao Chinese kingdom of the Warring States Period, founded 403 BC, conquered by **Qin** in 222 BC.

Zhou Chinese dynasty 1046–256 BC. The dynasty is conventionally divided into two periods, Western Zhou (1046–771 BC), when the capital was near present-day Xi'an and the Zhou king ruled China through vassals, and Eastern Zhou (770–256 BC), when Zhou controlled only the royal domain around Luoyang and great powers struggled for control of China.

Zimbabwe Southern African country, formerly the British colony of **Southern Rhodesia**, which became independent in 1980. Named for the ancient site of **Great Zimbabwe**.

Zirids Berber dynasty founded in AD 973 that, at its peak *c.* 1000, controlled most of present-day **Morocco**, **Algeria**, **Tunisia** and **Libya**. After 1057 the dynasty was reduced to parts of Tunisia; it was overthrown by the **Almohads** in 1152.

Zulu The largest ethnic group of **South Africa**; originated as a clan of the Nguni, a **Bantu**-speaking people, *c.* 1709.

Further Reading

General Atlases

Bahn, Paul (ed.), *Atlas of World Archaeology* (London and New York, 2000; new edn London, 2003)

Black, Jeremy (ed.), *Dorling Kindersley World History Atlas* (2nd edn, London and New York, 2005; 3rd edn, London, 2008)

Fernández-Armesto, Felipe, *Times Atlas of Exploration* (London and New York, 1991)

Haywood, John (et al.), *Cassell's Atlas of World History* (London, 2001)

Haywood, John, *The Penguin Historical Atlas of Ancient Civilizations* (London and New York, 2005)

Hemming, John, *Philip's Atlas of Exploration* (London and New York 1997; 2nd edn, London, 2006)

Kinder, Hermann and Werner Hilgemann, *The Penguin Atlas of World History* (2 vols, London, 2003)

Livesey, Anthony, *The Viking Atlas of World War I* (London, 1994) (published in New York as *The Historical Atlas of World War I*)

McEvedy, Colin, *The New Penguin Atlas of Ancient History* (2nd edn, London and New York, 2002)

Onians, John, *Atlas of World Art* (London and New York, 2004)

Overy, Richard, *Collins Atlas of 20th Century History* (London, 2005)

Overy, Richard (ed.), *The Times Complete History of the World* (8th edn, London, 2010)

Pimlott, John, *The Viking Atlas of World War II* (London, 1995) (published in New York as *The Historical Atlas of World War II*)

Scarre, Chris, *Past Worlds: The Times Atlas of Archaeology* (London and Maplewood, 1988; 2nd edn London, 1995)

Smart, Ninian (ed.), *Atlas of the World's Religions* (Oxford and New York, 1999)

Swift, John, *The Palgrave Concise Historical Atlas of the Cold War* (Basingstoke and New York, 2003)

General Books

Aldrich, Robert (ed.), *The Age of Empires* (London and New York, 2007)

Bayly, Christopher A., *The Birth of the Modern World 1780–1914: Global Connections and Comparisons* (Oxford and Malden, 2004)

Barker, Graeme, *The Agricultural Revolution in Prehistory* (Oxford and New York, 2007)

Bell, Julian, *Mirror of the World: A New History of Art* (London and New York, 2010)

Bellwood, P., *The First Farmers* (Oxford and Malden, 2005)

Black, Jeremy (ed.), *Great Military Leaders and their Campaigns* (London and New York, 2008)

Black, Jeremy, *Maps and History: Constructing Images of the Past* (New Haven and London, 1997)

Bowker, John (ed.), *Cambridge Illustrated History of Religions* (Cambridge and New York, 2002)

Brook, Timothy, *Vermeer's Hat: the Seventeenth Century and the Dawn of the Global World* (New York and London, 2008)

Chamberlain, Muriel E., *Decolonization: the Fall of the European Empires* (2nd edn, Oxford and Malden, 1999)

Dalziel, Nigel, *The Penguin Historical Atlas of the British Empire* (London, 2006)

Diamond, Jared, *Collapse: How Societies Choose to Fail or Collapse* (New York and London, 2005)

Diamond, Jared, *Guns, Germs and Steel* (New York and London, 2005)

Elliott, John H., *Empires of the Atlantic World: Britain and Spain in America (1492–1830)* (New Haven and London, 2007)

Fagan, Brian, *People of the Earth: An Introduction to World Prehistory* (13th edn, London 2009; Upper Saddle River, 2010)

Fagan, Brian (ed.), *The Seventy Great Inventions of the Ancient World* (London and New York, 2004)

Fernández-Armesto, Felipe, *Millennium: A History of Our Last Thousand Years* (London and New York, 1995)

Frampton, Kenneth, *Modern Architecture* (4th edn, London and New York, 2007)

Gamble, Clive, *Timewalkers: The Prehistory of Global Colonization* (London and Cambridge, Massachusetts, 1995)

Harrison, Thomas (ed.), *The Great Empires of the Ancient World* (London and New York, 2009)

Haywood, John, *Great Migrations: From the Earliest Humans to the Age of Globalization* (London, 2008)

Headrick, Daniel R., *Power over Peoples: Technology, Environments and Western Imperialism, 1400 to the Present* (Princeton and Woodstock, 2010)

Hoerder, Dirk, *Cultures in Contact: World Migrations in the Second Millennium* (Durham, North Carolina, and London, 2003)

Howe, Stephen, *Empire: A Very Short Introduction* (Oxford and New York, 2002)

Kennedy, Paul, *The Rise and Fall of the Great Powers* (New York and London, 1987)

Lewis-Williams, David, *The Mind in the Cave: Consciousness and the Origins of Art* (London and New York, 2004)

Livi-Bacci, Massimo, *A Concise History of World Population* (4th edn, Oxford and Malden, 2007)

MacGregor, Neil, *A History of the World in 100 Objects* (London, 2010)

Manning, Patrick, *Migration in World History* (New York and London, 2005)

Mithen, Steven, *After the Ice: A Global Human History, 20,000–5000 BC* (London and Cambridge, Massachusetts, 2004)

Morris, Ian, *Why the West Rules – For Now* (New York and London, 2010)

Ostler, Nicholas, *Empires of the Word: A Language History of the World* (London and New York, 2005)

Prina, Francesca and Elena Demartini, *1000 Years of World Architecture* (London and New York, 2006)

Renfrew, Colin, *Prehistory: The Making of the Human Mind* (London and New York, 2008)

Roberts, Alice, *The Incredible Human Journey: The Story of How We Colonized the Planet* (London, 2009)

Roberts, John M., *The New Penguin History of the World* (5th edn, London, 2007)

Robinson, Andrew, *The Story of Writing* (new edn, London and New York, 2007)

Scammell, G. V., *The First Imperial Age: European Overseas Expansion 1400–1715* (London and Boston, 1989)

Scarre, Chris (ed.), *The Human Past: World Prehistory and the Development of Human Societies* (2nd edn, London and New York, 2009)

Strachan, Hew, *The First World War: A New Illustrated History* (London and New York, 2003)

Stringer, Chris and Peter Andrews, *The Complete World of Human Evolution* (rev. edn, London and New York, 2011)

Taylor, Timothy, *The Artificial Ape: How Technology Changed the Course of Human Evolution* (London and New York, 2010)

30,000 Years of Art: The Story of Human Creativity Across Time and Space (London and New York, 2007)

Weinberg, Gerhard L., *A World at Arms: A Global History of World War II* (2nd edn, Cambridge and New York, 2005)

Wesseling, Henk L., *The European Colonial Empires: 1815–1919* (London and New York, 2004)

North America

Atlases:

Coe, Michael D., Dean Snow and Elizabeth Benson, *Atlas of Ancient America* (Oxford and New York, 1986)

Gilbert, Martin, *The Routledge Atlas of American History* (6th edn, London and New York, 2009)

Goetzman, William H. and Glendwr Williams, *Atlas of North American Exploration: from the Norse Voyages to the Race to the Pole* (Norman, Oklahoma, 1998)

Homberger, Eric, *The Penguin Historical Atlas of North America* (London and New York, 1995)

Matthews, Geoffrey J., *Historical Atlas of Canada* (3 vols, Toronto and London, 1987–93)

Wexler, Alan, *Atlas of Westward Expansion* (New York, 1995)

Other works:

Anderson, Fred and Andrew Cayton, *The Dominion of War: Empire and Liberty in North America, 1500–2000* (New York and London, 2005)

Berlin, Ira, *The Making of African America: Four Great Migrations* (New York and London, 2010)

Bothwell, Robert, *The Penguin History of Canada* (Toronto and London, 2006)

Brogan, Hugh, *The Penguin History of the United States of America* (2nd edn, London and New York, 2001)

Davis, David Brion, *Inhuman Bondage: The Rise and Fall of Slavery in the New World* (Oxford and New York, 2006)

Fagan, Brian, *Ancient North America: the Archaeology of a Continent* (4th edn, London and New York, 2005)

Fagan, Brian, *The First North Americans: An Archaeological Journey* (London and New York, 2011)

Jones, Maldwyn A., *The Limits of Liberty: American History 1607–1992* (2nd edn, Oxford and New York, 1995)

Middleton, Richard, *Colonial America 1565–1776* (3rd edn, Oxford and Malden, 2002)

Oberg, Michael L., *Native America: A History* (Chichester and Malden, 2010)

South and Central America

Atlases:

Coe, Michael D., Dean Snow and Elizabeth Benson, *Atlas of Ancient America* (Oxford and New York, 1986)

LaRosa, Michael and Germán R. Mejía, *An Atlas and Survey of Latin American History* (New York and London, 2006)

Other works:

Chasteen, John C., *Born in Fire and Blood: A Concise History of Latin America* (3rd edn, New York and London, 2011)

Coe, Michael D., *The Maya* (8th edn, London and New York, 2011)

Coe, Michael D. and Rex Koontz, *Mexico: From the Olmecs to the Aztecs* (6th edn, London and New York, 2008)

Evans, Susan Toby, *Ancient Mexico and Central America* (2nd edn, London and New York, 2008)

Lynch, John, *The Spanish American Revolutions 1808–26* (2nd edn, New York, 1986)

Martin, Simon and Nikolai Grube, *Chronicle of the Maya Kings and Queens* (rev. edn, London and New York, 2008)

Meyer, Michael C. and William H. Beezley (eds.), *The Oxford History of Mexico* (Oxford and New York, 2000)

Morris, Craig and Adriana von Hagen, *The Incas* (London and New York, 2011)

Moseley, Michael E., *The Incas and their Ancestors: the Archaeology of Peru* (rev. edn, London and New York, 2001)

Thomas, Hugh, *The Conquest of Mexico* (London, 2004)

Townsend, Richard F., *The Aztecs* (3rd edn, London and New York, 2010)

Williamson, Edwin, The Penguin History of Latin America (rev. edn, London, 2009)

Wilson, Samuel M. *The Archaeology of the Caribbean* (Cambridge, 2007)

Europe

Atlases:

Almond, Mark, *The Times Atlas of European History* (2nd edn, London, 1998)

Black, Chris F., *Cultural Atlas of the Renaissance* (London and New York, 1993)

Cornell, Tim and John Matthews, *Atlas of the Roman World* (Oxford and New York, 1982)

Davies, John K., *Democracy and Classical Greece* (2nd edn, London and Cambridge, Massachusetts, 1993)

Haywood, John, *The Historical Atlas of the Celtic World* (London and New York, 2001)

Haywood, John, *The Penguin Historical Atlas of the Vikings* (London and New York, 1995)

Jotischky, Andrew and Caroline Hull, *The Penguin Atlas of the Medieval World* (London and New York, 2005)

Levi, Peter, *Atlas of the Greek World* (2nd edn, Oxford and New York, 1991)

Magocsi, Paul R., *Historical Atlas of Central Europe* (rev. edn, London and Seattle, 2002)

McEvedy, Colin, *The New Penguin Atlas of Recent History: Europe Since 1815* (London and New York, 2002)

Milner-Gulland, Robin and Nikolai Dejevsky, *Cultural Atlas of Russia and the Former Soviet Union* (Oxford and New York, 1998)

Other works:

Abulafia, David (ed.), *The Mediterranean in History* (London and Los Angeles, 2003)

Anthony, David W., *The Horse, the Wheel and Language: How Bronze Age Riders from the Eurasian Steppes Shaped the Modern World* (Princeton and Woodstock, 2010)

Bartlett, Robert, *The Making of Europe: Conquest, Colonization and Cultural Change 950–1350* (London and Princeton, 1993)

Bartlett, Robert, *Medieval Panorama* (London and Los Angeles, 2001)

Blanning, T. C. W., *The Oxford History of Modern Europe* (3rd edn, Oxford and New York, 2000)

Boardman, John, Jasper Griffin and Oswyn Murray (eds), *The Oxford History of Greece and the Hellenistic World* (Oxford and New York, 2001)

Boardman, John, Jasper Griffin and Oswyn Murray (eds), *The Oxford History of the Roman World* (Oxford and New York, 2001)

Camp, John, *The Archaeology of Athens* (New Haven and London, 2001)

Cunliffe, Barry, *The Ancient Celts* (Oxford and New York, 1997)

Cunliffe, Barry, *Europe between the Oceans: 9000 BC–AD 1000* (New Haven and London, 2008)

Hobsbawm, Eric, *Industry and Empire: From 1750 to the Present Day* (rev. edn, London and New York, 1999)

Lane Fox, Robin, *The Classical World: An Epic History from Homer to Hadrian* (London and New York, 2005)

MacCulloch, Diarmaid, *Reformation: Europe's House Divided 1490–1700* (London and New York, 2004)

Mazower, Mark, *Dark Continent: Europe's Twentieth Century* (London and New York, 1998; new edn, London, 2008)

Norwich, John Julius, *The Middle Sea: A History of the Mediterranean* (London and New York, 2006)

Osborne, Robin, *Greece in the Making* (2nd edn, London and New York, 2009)

Outram, Dorinda, *Panorama of the Enlightenment* (London and Los Angeles, 2006)

Potter, David, *Rome in the Ancient World* (London and New York, 2009)

Sawyer, Peter, *The Oxford Illustrated History of the Vikings* (Oxford and New York, 1997)

Service, Robert, *The Penguin History of Modern Russia: From Tsarism to the Twenty-first Century* (London, 2009)

Southern, Richard, *The Making of the Middle Ages* (new edn, New Haven, 1992, London, 1993)

Spivey, Nigel and Michael Squire, *Panorama of the Classical World* (London and Los Angeles, 2008)

Tuchman, Barbara W., *A Distant Mirror: The Calamitous 14th Century* (new edn, New York 1987; London, 1991)

Weisner-Hanks, Merry E., *Early Modern Europe 1450–1789* (Cambridge and New York, 2006)

Wickham, Chris, *The Inheritance of Rome: a History of Europe from 400 to 1000* (London and New York, 2010)

Wilson, Peter H., *Europe's Tragedy: A History of the Thirty Years War* (London, 2010) (published in New York as *The Thirty Years War: Europe's Tragedy*)

Middle East

Atlases:

De Lange, Nicholas, *Atlas of the Jewish World* (Oxford and New York, 1984)

Freeman-Grenville, Greville S. P., *Historical Atlas of the Middle East* (New York and London, 1993)

Hull, Caroline and Andrew Jotischky, *The Penguin Historical Atlas of the Bible Lands* (London and New York, 2009)

Riley-Smith, Jonathan (ed.), *The Atlas of the Crusades* (London and New York, 1991)

Roaf, Michael, *Cultural Atlas of Mesopotamia and the Ancient Near East* (Oxford and New York, 1990)

Robinson, Francis, *Atlas of the Islamic World since 1500* (Oxford and New York, 1982)

Other works:

Axelworthy, Michael, *A History of Iran: Empire of the Mind* (London and New York, 2008)

Briant, Pierre, *From Cyrus to Alexander: A History of the Persian Empire* (Winona Lake, 2002)

Gelvin, James L., *The Modern Middle East: A History* (2nd edn, New York and Oxford, 2005)

Hourani, Albert, *A History of the Arab Peoples* (London and Cambridge, Massachusetts, 1991; new edn, London, 2005)

Kennedy, Hugh, *The Great Arab Conquests: How the Spread of Islam Changed the World We Live in* (London and Philadelphia, 2007)

Leick, Gwendolyn, *Mesopotamia: the invention of the city* (London, 2001; New York, 2002)

Lewis, Bernard, *The Middle East* (London and New York, 1995)

Mansel, Philip, *Constantinople: City of the World's Desire 1492–1924* (London, 1995; New York, 1996)

McCarthy, Justin, *The Ottoman Turks: An Introductory History to 1923* (London, 1997)

Norwich, John Julius, *A Short History of Byzantium* (London and New York, 1997)

Riley-Smith, Jonathan, *The Oxford Illustrated History of the Crusades* (Oxford and New York, 2001)

Robinson, Francis, *Cambridge Illustrated History of the Islamic World* (Cambridge and New York, 1996)

Van de Mieroop, Marc, *A History of the Ancient Near East ca. 3000–323 BC* (2nd edn, Oxford and Malden, 2007)

Africa

Atlases:

Baines, John and Jaromír Málek, *Cultural Atlas of Ancient Egypt* (rev. edn, Oxford and New York, 2000)

McEvedy, Colin, *The Penguin Atlas of African History* (rev. edn, London and New York, 1995)

Murray, Jocelyn (ed.), *Cultural Atlas of Africa* (rev. edn, Oxford and New York, 1998)

Other works:

Brett, Michael and Elizabeth Fentress, *The Berbers* (Oxford and Cambridge, Massachusetts, 1996)

Connah, Graham, *African Civilizations: An Archaeological Perspective* (2nd edn, Cambridge and New York, 2001)

Davidson, Basil, *West Africa Before the Colonial Era: a History to 1850* (London, 1998)

Ehret, Christopher, *The Civilizations of Africa: A History to 1800* (Oxford and Charlottesville, 2002)

Fage, John D. and William Tordoff, *A History of Africa* (4th edn, London and New York, 2002)

Insoll, Timothy, *The Archaeology of Islam in Sub-Saharan Africa* (Cambridge and New York, 2003)

Kemp, Barry, *Ancient Egypt: Anatomy of a Civilization* (2nd edn, London and New York, 2006)

Lancel, Serge, *Carthage: A History* (Oxford and Cambridge, Massachusetts, 1995)

Naylor, Phillip C., *North Africa: A History from Antiquity to the Present* (Austin, 2009)

Pakenham, Thomas, *The Scramble for Africa 1876–1912* (London and New York, 1991)

Phillipson, David W., *African Archaeology* (3rd edn, Cambridge and New York, 2005)

Reid, Richard J., *A History of Modern Africa* (Oxford and Malden, 2009)

Ross, Robert, *A Concise History of South Africa* (2nd edn, Cambridge and New York, 2008)

Shaw, Ian, *The Oxford History of Ancient Egypt* (new edn, Oxford and New York, 2003)

Thomas, Hugh, *The Slave Trade: The History of the Atlantic Slave Trade 1440–1870* (London, 2006)

Welsby, Derek, *The Kingdom of Kush: The Napatan and Meroitic Empires* (London and Princeton, 1998)

Wilkinson, Toby, *The Rise and Fall of Ancient Egypt* (London, 2010; New York, 2011)

South Asia

Atlases:

Johnson, Gordon, *A Cultural Atlas of India* (Oxford and New York, 1996)

Schmidt, Karl J., *An Atlas and Survey of South Asian History* (New York and London, 1995)

Other works:

De Silva, K. M., *A History of Sri Lanka* (rev. edn, London and New York, 2005)

Judd, Denis, *The Lion and the Tiger: The Rise and Fall of the British Raj 1600–1947* (Oxford and New York, 2009)

Keay, John, *India: A History* (London and New York, 2000)

Kulke, Hermann and Dietmar Rothermund, *A History of India* (5th edn, London and New York, 2010)

Robinson, Francis, *The Mughal Emperors and the Islamic Dynasties of India, Iran and Central Asia 1206–1925* (London and New York, 2007)

Thapar, Romila, *Early India: From the Origins to AD 1300* (London and Berkeley, 2002)

Wright, Rita P., *The Ancient Indus: Urbanism, Economy and Society* (Cambridge and New York, 2010)

Wynbrandt, James, *A Brief History of Pakistan* (New York, 2008)

East and Central Asia

Atlases:

Abazov, Rafis, *The Palgrave Concise Historical Atlas of Central Asia* (Basingstoke and New York, 2008)

Blunden, Caroline and Mark Elvin, *Cultural Atlas of China* (rev. edn, Oxford, 1998)

Collcutt, Martin, Marius Jansen and Isao Kumakura, *Cultural Atlas of Japan* (Oxford and New York, 1988)

Other works:

Barnes, Gina L., *The Rise of Civilization in East Asia: The Archaeology of China, Korea and Japan* (London and New York, 1999)

Beckwith, Christopher I., *Empires of the Silk Road: A History of Central Eurasia from the Bronze Age to the Present* (Princeton and Woodstock, 2009)

Brook, Timothy, *Troubled Empire: China in the Yuan and Ming Dynasties* (Cambridge, Massachusetts, and London, 2010)

Cullen, Louis M., *A History of Japan 1582–1941: Internal and External Worlds* (Cambridge and New York, 2003)

Ebrey, Patricia B., *Cambridge Illustrated History of China* (2nd edn, Cambridge and New York, 2010)

Elliott, Mark, *Emperor Qianlong: Son of Heaven, Man of the World*, (New York, 2009)

Fenby, Jonathan, *The Penguin History of Modern China: The Fall and Rise of a Great Power 1850–2008* (London and New York, 2008)

Huffman, James L., *Japan in World History* (Oxford and New York, 2010)

Keay, John, *China: A History* (London and New York, 2009)

Lewis, Mark E., *The Early Chinese Empires: Qin and Han* (Cambridge, Massachusetts, and London, 2007)

Loewe, Michael and Edward L. Shaughnessy

(eds), *The Cambridge History of Ancient China: From the Origins of Civilization to 221 BC* (Cambridge and New York, 1999)

Morgan, David, *The Mongols* (2nd edn, Oxford and Malden, 2007)

Nelson, Sarah Milledge, *The Archaeology of Korea* (Cambridge and New York, 1993)

Paludan, Ann, *Chronicle of the Chinese Emperors* (London and New York, 2008)

Pratt, Keith L., *Everlasting Flower: A History of Korea* (London, 2006)

Rawson, Jessica (ed.), *Mysteries of Ancient China: New Discoveries from the Early Dynasties* (London, 1996)

Totman, Conrad, *A History of Japan*, (2nd edn, Oxford and Malden, 2005)

Van Schaik, Sam, *Tibet: A History* (New Haven, 2011)

Wood, Alan, *The History of Siberia: From Russian Conquest to Revolution* (London and New York, 1991)

Southeast Asia and Australasia

Atlases:

McEvedy, Colin, *The Penguin Historical Atlas of the Pacific* (London and New York, 1998)

Nile, Richard and Christian Clerk, *Cultural Atlas of Australia, New Zealand and the South Pacific* (New York and Oxford, 1996)

Pluvier, Jan M., *Historical Atlas of South-East Asia* (Leiden and New York, 1995)

Other works:

Coe, Michael D., *Angkor and the Khmer Civilization* (London and New York, 2004)

Denoon, Donald (ed.), *The Cambridge History*

of the Pacific Islanders (Cambridge and New York, 1997)

Denoon, Donald and Philippa Mein-Smith, *A History of Australia, New Zealand and the Pacific* (Oxford and Malden, 2000)

Hall, Daniel G. E., *A History of South-East Asia* (4th edn, London and New York, 1981)

Lockard, Craig A. *Southeast Asia in World History* (Oxford and New York, 2009)

Milner, Anthony, *The Malays* (Oxford and Malden, 2008)

Mulvaney, John and Johan Kamminga, *Prehistory of Australia* (Washington and London, 1999)

Ricklefs, M. C. (et al.), A *New History of Southeast Asia* (Basingstoke and New York, 2010)

Taylor, Jean G., *Indonesia, Peoples and Histories* (New Haven and London, 2003)

Sources of Data

Population Figures

This atlas includes figures for the global population through time and for the populations of what are thought to have been the world's five largest cities at approximately the date of the accompanying map in the atlas. Both global and urban population figures for the post-Second World War period are based on United Nations statistics.

Global population figures for all periods before 1945 are based on data from the HYDE History Database of the Global Environment (http://themasites.pbl.nl/en/themasites/hyde/index.html), a website maintained by the Netherlands Environmental Assessment Agency. This site presents estimated global population figures through time from a range of published sources: the figures used in this atlas are extrapolated from the median average of these sources as calculated by HYDE.

The urban population figures are drawn from a wide range of archaeological and historical publications. For periods before the 19th century the figures are subject to the (often considerable) limitations of the historical evidence available to researchers.

The Chronology of Ancient Egypt and Mesopotamia

Ancient Mesopotamia and ancient Egypt both have recorded histories extending back to around 3000 BC. However, neither the Mesopotamians nor the Egyptians had fixed points, like the birth of Christ in the Christian calendar, for dating events. This means that while the relative chronology of events is known (that is, the order in which they occurred), historians face great difficulties in determining their absolute chronology (that is, the exact year in which they occurred).

Because of these difficulties, historians have calculated several different chronologies for the histories of ancient Mesopotamia and ancient Egypt, and the dates given in this atlas for events in these areas may differ from those found in other sources. The chronology used here for ancient Mesopotamia is the one known as the Middle Chronology. The chronology used for ancient Egypt is the one used by John Baines and Jaromír Málek in their *Cultural Atlas of Ancient Egypt* (Oxford, 2000).

Acknowledgments

Writing even a concise history of the whole world is a daunting undertaking for a single author and I could not have completed this project without the advice and guidance of many other scholars. In particular I would like to thank Bill Jenner, Jim Mallory, Michael Prestwich, Chris Scarre, Dennis Showalter, Chris Stringer, John Swift, David Webster, Michael Whitby and Peter Wilson, all of whom gave generously of their time and saved me from many errors.

A work of this nature is necessarily a synthesis and I would also like to acknowledge, in a general way, my debt to the many archaeologists and historians upon whose primary research this book has been based. I also wish to thank the Department of History at Lancaster University for supporting my work with an honorary research fellowship.

An atlas would be nothing without good maps and I feel fortunate to have been able to work with such a fine cartographer as Tim Aspden, whose patience in dealing with endless revisions never seemed to wear thin.

At Thames & Hudson I would especially like to thank Colin Ridler for his enthusiastic support throughout; Ashley Olsson for devising the clear and attractive page designs; Vanessa Fay for designing the vivid timelines with illustrations picture researched by Louise Thomas; Philip Collyer for coordinating the book's production; and Alice Reid, the editor and project manager, whose consistent attention to detail has made an enormous contribution to the book.

Sources of Illustrations

The illustrations are identified by their page numbers in **bold**.

Key: a=above; b=below; c=centre; l=left; r=right

LoC - Library of Congress, Washington, D.C.; NARA - The U.S. National Archives and Records Administration, Maryland

8cl Musée des Antiquités, St Germain-en-Laye **8ar** Lucian Mortula/iStockphoto.com **8bc** Egyptian National Museum, Cairo **8br** LoC **9al** Ajay Bhaskar/iStockphoto.com **9ac** National Palace Museum, Taipei **9ar** National Gallery, London **9b** Courtesy Apple **12a** John Sibbick **12c** Liba Taylor/Alamy **12b, 13al, 13ar** John Sibbick **13cal** José-Manuel Benito Álvarez **13car** Bill Grove/iStockphoto.com **13cl** John Sibbick **13bc (axe)** Musée du Louvre, Paris **13bc (artwork)** Peter Bull Art Studio **13br** Cantonal Natural History and Zoological Museum, Lausanne **13br** Dr. Hartmut Thieme **16c** John Sibbick **16bc** South African Museum, Cape Town **17al, 17ac, 17ar** John Sibbick **17cl** French Ministry of Culture and Communications, Regional Direction for Cultural Affairs - Rhône-Alpes Region **17c** Naturhistorisches Museum, Vienna **17bc** Arizona State Museum, University of Arizona **20a** Nick Jakins **20c** Bible Land Pictures/Alamy **20bl** Deutsches Archäologisches Institut, Berlin **20br** Sam Noble Oklahoma Museum of Natural History **21a** Nick Jakins **21cl** Museum of Anatolian Civilizations, Ankara **21cr** Jericho Excavation Fund, University of London **21bl** Çatalhöyük Research Project, University College London **24c** Archäologie-Museum Oberfranken, Forchheim **24bc** Frank Willett **24br** K.F. Rowland **25ac** Musée du Louvre, Paris **25cl** National Museum of History, Sofia **25cr** Barnenez Tumulus, Breton **25br** National Transylvanian History Museum, Cluj-Napoca **28ac** after Shilov Yu, *Ostatki vozov*, 1975 **28ar** Shanghai Museum **28ca** Peruvian National Insitute/EPA/Corbis **28cb** Warwick Lister-Kaye/iStockphoto.com **28bc** Magyar Nemzeti Múzeum, Budapest **28br** Musée du Louvre, Paris **29al** Egyptian National Museum, Cairo **29ar** Iraq Museum, Baghdad **29bl** Museum of Pakistan, Karachi **29br** Boston Museum of Fine Arts **32c** Shanghai Museum **32cr** Musée du Louvre, Paris **32bc** Tracy Wellman **33al** Heraklion Archaeological Museum **33ar** National Archaeological Museum, Athens **33c** British Museum, London **33bl** State Museum of Prehistory, Halle **33br** Egyptian National Museum, Cairo **36c** Roger Wood **36cr** Metropolitan Museum of Art, New York **36bc, 36br** British Museum, London **37al** Ashmolean Museum, Oxford **37cr** Nationalmuseet, Copenhagen **37bl** Michael D. Coe **37br** David Lyons/Alamy **40a** LoC **40c** The Art Archive/Alamy **40b** Michael Everson **41al** Ashmolean Museum, Oxford **41cl** Yves Gellie/Corbis **41bc** British Museum, London **41br** Museo Nacional de Arqueología, Antropología e Historia del Perú, Lima **44c** Museo Nazionale Etrusco di Villa Giulia, Rome **44cr** Museum für Asiatische Kunst, Berlin **44bc** Oriental Institute, University of Chicago **44br** National Archaeological Museum, Athens **45al** State Hermitage Museum, St Petersburg **45cla** Photo Heidi Grassley © Thames & Hudson Ltd., London **45clb, 45c** British Museum, London **45cr** Burstein Collection/Corbis **45bl** Musée du Louvre, Paris **48c** Angelika Stern/iStockphoto.com **48b** British Museum, London **49l** Museo Nazionale della Magna Grecia, Reggio Calabria **49c** Museo Archeologico Nazionale, Naples **49cr** British Museum, London **49br** Private Collection **52c** Paolo Cipriani/iStockphoto.com **52cr** Duncan Walker/iStockphoto.com **52b** University of Pennsylvania, Philadelphia **53l** akg-images **53c** Archaeological Museum, Sarnath **53cr** David Kerkhoff/iStockphoto.com **53bl** Mark Weiss/iStockphoto.com **56a** Ashmolean Museum, Oxford **56b** British Museum, London **57al** Claire Venables **57ar** Museo della Civiltà Romana, Rome **57cl** after Michael E. Moseley **57c** National Museum of Korea, Seoul **57bl** Musée du Louvre, Paris **60c** Museum of London **60br** Hao Liang/iStockphoto.com **61al** Archaeological Museum, Ankara **61ac** Martyn Unsworth/iStockphoto.com **61cl** Tokyo National Museum **61c** Bible Land Pictures/Alamy **61cra** Gansu Provincial Museum, Lanzhou **61crb** iStockphoto.com **61br** Dmitry Rukhlenko/iStockphoto.com **64c** Museo Nacional de Arqueología, Antropología e Historia del Perú, Lima **64cr** Bibliothèque Nationale de France, Paris **64bc** iStockphoto.com **64br** Metropolitan Museum of Art, New York **65cl** National Museum of India, New Delhi **65ca** Tracy Wellman **65cb** The Art Archive/Alamy **65br** National Palace Museum, Taipei **68c** Cathedral of Christ the Light, Oakland, California **68br** British Museum, London **69al** after Jones & Satterthwaite, 1982 **69c** Chiesa di Ognissanti, Florence **69bl** Eye Ubiquitous/Alamy **69bc** Byron Aihara **69crb** Museo Nacional de Arqueología, Antropología e Historia del Perú, Lima **72c** National Gallery of Art, Washington, D.C. **72bc** Basilica of San Vitale, Ravenna **72br** Anat Bamrungwongse **73al** Philip Wilson after Simon Martin **73cl** Museum of the Imperial Collections, Tokyo **73bl** British Museum, London **73crb** Topkapi Sarayi Museum, Istanbul **78c** Freer Gallery of Art and Arthur M. Sackler Gallery, Smithsonian Institution, Washington, D.C. **78cr** British Museum, London **78bc** Whitby Abbey, North Yorkshire **79al** National Museum of Korea, Seoul **79cr** Anasazi Heritage Center, Colorado **79cb** LoC **79br** The Art Archive/Alamy **82ac** British Museum, London **82ar** Davide Benato/iStockphoto.com **82b** from Hartmann Schedel, *Nuremberg Chronicle*, 1483 **83al** Historiska Muséet, Stockholm **83ar** Imperial Cathedral Treasury, Aachen **83bl** iStockphoto.com **83bc** Peabody Museum of Archaeology and Ethnology, Harvard University, Massachusetts **83br** Trinity College Library, Dublin **86c** Dewitt Jones/Corbis **86bc** Dinesh Kannambadi **86br** iStockphoto.com **87al** Hamo Thornycroft, *Alfred the Great*, 1899 **87c** Jeremy Edwards/iStockphoto.com **87cr** from Gerardus Cremonensis, *Recueil del traités de médecine*, 1250–60 **87bl** British Library, London **90c** from Georg Dehio and Gustav von Bezold, *Kirchliche Baukunst des Abendlandes*, Stuttgart, 1887–1901 **90cr** LoC **90br** Mausoleum of the Samanids, Bukhara **91al** Jeremy Richards/iStockphoto.com **91ac** Bibliothèque Nationale de France, Paris **91bl** Graham Klotz/iStockphoto.com **91br** LoC **94c** Musée Guimet, Paris **94bc** Dmitry Rukhlenko/iStockphoto.com **94br** National Museum of Iran, Tehran **95al** Davids Samling, Copenhagen **95ac** Musée de la Tapisserie, Bayeux **95c** from Al-Biruni, *Kitab al-tafhim*, 973–1048 **95cra** from Charles Mackay, *Extraordinary Popular Delusions and the Madness of Crowds*, 1841–52 **95crb** Nick Webley/iStockphoto.com **95bl** Sakyamuni Pagoda, Fogong Temple, Shanxi Province **98tl** Musée Guimet, Paris **98c** Jeremy Edwards/iStockphoto.com **98cr** Museum of Islamic Art, Cairo **99al** Museo Nacional de Antropología, Mexico City **99ac** British Library, London **99c** Bibliothèque Nationale de France, Paris/Bridgeman Art Library **99bl** Jones Archaeological Museum, Moundville Archaeological Park, Alabama **99bc** Klaas Lingbeek van Kranen/iStockphoto.com **102cb** from Roger Bacon, *The cure of old age and preservation of youth*, 1683 **102br** iStockphoto.com **103a** Fornsalen Museum, Visby **103cl** Royal Armouries Museum, Leeds **103c** Hulton Archive/Getty Images **103bc** Rafat Cichawa/iStockphoto.com **103br** Bibliothèque Nationale de France, Paris **106c** Topkapi Sarayi Museum, Istanbul **106cr** Alan Ladadu/iStockphoto.com **106bc** Cappella degli Scrovegni, Padua **106br** Japan Society, London **107a** from Guy Marchant, *La Danse Macabre*, 1486 **107cla** National Palace Museum, Taipei **107cl** Bibliothèque Nationale de France, Paris **107clb** Henry E. Huntington Library, California **107cb** Bibliothèque Nationale de France, Paris **107br**

Reference Map

The maps on these pages give the locations of key geographical features and site locations that are mentioned throughout the book.

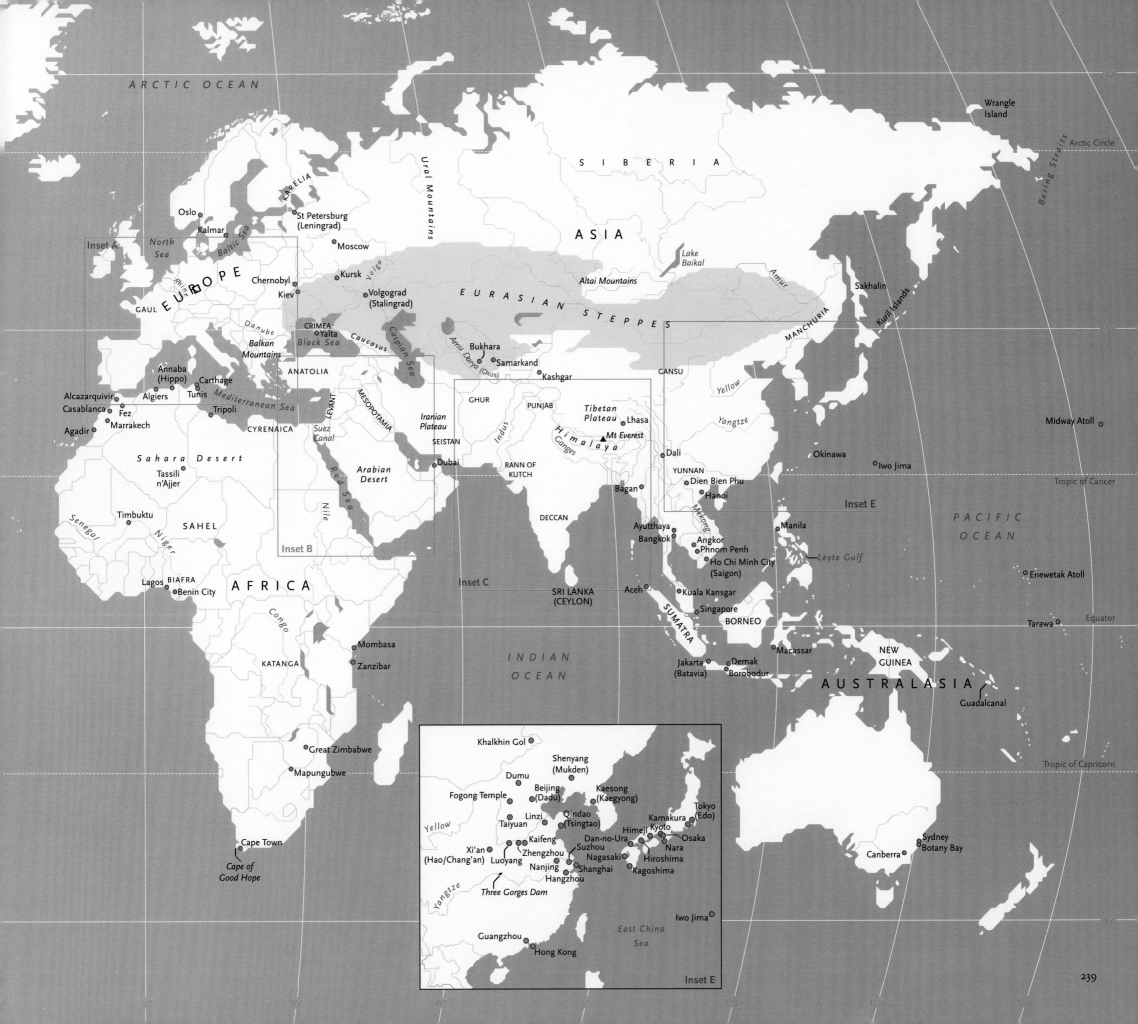

Index

Gold Coast **149**, **153**, **157**, **161**, **165**,

245

251

The Author and Publisher gratefully acknowledge the editorial advice and assistance of the following scholars:

Professor William J. Jenner, School of Oriental and African Studies, London, UK

Professor James Mallory, Queen's University, Belfast, Northern Ireland

Professor Michael Prestwich, Durham University, UK

Professor Chris Scarre, Durham University, UK

Professor Dennis Showalter, Colorado College, USA

Professor Chris Stringer, Natural History Museum, London, UK

Dr John Swift, University of Cumbria, UK

Professor David Webster, Pennsylvania State University, USA

Professor Michael Whitby, University of Warwick, UK

Professor Peter H. Wilson, University of Hull, UK

Any faults that remain are the responsibility of the Author and Publisher.

All maps by Tim Aspden, Latitude Mapping Ltd © Thames & Hudson Ltd, London.
Design concept and art direction by Ashley Olsson.
Jacket and interior page design by Vanessa Fay.

First published in the United Kingdom in 2011 by Thames & Hudson Ltd,
181A High Holborn, London WC1V 7QX

Reprinted 2016

A New Atlas of World History © 2011 Thames & Hudson Ltd, London

British Library Cataloguing-in-Publication Data

A catalogue record for this book is available from the British Library

ISBN 978-0-500-25185-0

Printed and bound in Thailand by Imago

To find out about all our publications, please visit **www.thamesandhudson.com**. There you can subscribe to our e-newsletter, browse or download our current catalogue, and buy any titles that are in print.